LIFE TOGETHER IN THE WAY
OF JESUS CHRIST

LIFE TOGETHER IN THE WAY OF JESUS CHRIST

An Introduction to Christian Theology

Dan R. Stiver

BAYLOR UNIVERSITY PRESS

Cover design by Daniel Huenergardt

Library of Congress Cataloging-in-Publication Data

Stiver, Dan R.
Life together in the way of Jesus Christ : an introduction to Christian
theology / Dan R. Stiver.
p. cm.
Includes bibliographical references and index.
ISBN 978-1-60258-061-9 (pbk. : alk. paper)
Printed Case ISBN: 978-1-4813-1475-6 1.
Theology, Doctrinal. I. Title.

BT65.S75 2008
230--dc22

2008011909

Dedicated to Dale Moody and Richard Cunningham

Master teachers, genuine humans,
passionate Christians

CONTENTS

Preface ix

1 Beginning the Journey 1

2 Mapping the Journey 11

3 Revelation 59
Lighting the Way

4 God 105
The Beginning and the End

5 Creation 163
The Beginning

6 Humanity and Sin 207
Rising and Falling

7 Christ 253
The Light of the Way

8 Salvation 307
The Way

9 Church 365
Walking Together

10 Last Things 427
The End

Notes 483
Bibliography 557
Scripture Index 593
Index of Names 601
Index of Subjects 609

Preface

My theological journey has itself been a circuitous one, perhaps fitting for one who envisages theology as a hermeneutical spiral. I began my higher education with passion for the study of Scripture. This carried all the way through my M.Div. studies, which is a three-year program past undergraduate studies. Along the way I became fascinated with philosophy and theology, but as more of a sideline or even hobby.

Toward the end of my Master of Divinity, I realized how much my preoccupation with Scripture was theological and philosophical in nature, so I began my doctoral studies with a rather major switch to concentrate on systematic theology with a side area of Christian philosophy. My major professor in theology was Dale Moody and in philosophy Richard Cunningham, to both of whom I am dedicating this book. If it is true that having the right teacher at the right time is crucial, it was certainly true in my case. Both were models in their own very distinctive ways of passion and rigor. They exemplified the kind of confessional, open, and yet critical approach that I describe in these pages, revealing not a science but a deft art of integrating conviction and critique. I took as much philosophy as I could, in many ways just for fun. In the middle of my dissertation, Dale, who was nearing retirement, fell into denominational conflict and was not permitted to continue teaching. Dick had the happy chore of supervising my dissertation the rest of the way. Ironically, when I began teaching, I was asked to concentrate on Christian philosophy, which I taught for fourteen years. Because that area is very much in dialogue with theology, I continued the study of theology, and even doctoral supervision of theological theses, but now with philosophy as the lead. These years were shared with Dick as my senior colleague in Christian philosophy, who was as able a mentor as a teacher. Some of the richest times of all were the colloquia every semester that involved both of us meeting with all of the Christian philosophy doctoral students once a week to discuss things philosophical and theological. I can never repay or calculate the debt I owe to these two master teachers.

When I traveled to Hardin-Simmons University, out of the convulsions of a denominational takeover, to be part of the new Logsdon Seminary in 1998, my path took a midcareer spiral back to theology as the lead area with philosophy as the accompaniment. I began teaching introductory theology to undergraduates and graduates for the first time on a regular basis. It was a strange path from a focus on higher-level study of theology back to introductory theology.

In the process of that shift, I felt that I had a fresh perspective on that introductory task, coming from a more philosophical orientation for many years. It took several years to bring those two together, but I felt in the end that it gave me at least a different perspective. In many ways, it involved thinking about that task for the first time, not as a beginner but with those resources of years of experience teaching and reflecting on theology and philosophy. Perhaps it was a handicap! The students and readers will be the best witnesses to that. It did lead to a growing interest in writing an introduction to systematic theology that would reflect these wide interests.

My practice in teaching undergraduate theology had been to use two one-volume texts. One was from a non-Baptist source such as the Reformed theologians Shirley Guthrie or Daniel Migliore or the Lutheran Ted Peters.[1] The other was preferably from a Baptist,

Free church tradition. Here was where I had difficulty finding the right level of difficulty and orientation that was also dealing with contemporary issues in theology. I was especially interested in my students having the benefit of the rich Baptist tradition that had so benefited me, which in contemporary Baptist parlance is often called a "moderate Baptist" perspective. Besides my aforementioned professors, I think here of the legacy of E. Y. Mullins, A. T. Robertson, W. O. Carver, W. T. Conner, Eric Rust, Russell Newport, Wayne Ward, Morris Ashcraft, Hugh Wamble, Bill Morton, Frank Stagg, J. J. Owens, Roy Honeycutt, John Watts, Marvin Tate, Pierce Matheney, Kenneth Wolfe, Gerald and Doris Borchert, Alan Culpepper, David and Diana Garland, Anne Davis, Raymond and Pat Bailey, Findley Edge, Glenn Hinson, Bill Leonard, Walter Shurden, T. B. Maston, Henlee Barnette, Paul Simmons, Glen Stassen, Bill Hendricks, Wayne Oates, Dan Aleshire, Andy Lester, and my other two doctoral professors of theology, Frank Tupper and David Mueller. The list could go on. Fortunately, Hardin-Simmons University is related to the strongest moderate Baptist state convention, the Baptist General Convention of Texas, which has made this a hospitable place to be in the midst of so many changes among Baptists in what Bill Leonard calls "permanent transition."[2]

So, in the summer of 2004, I embarked on a trip thanks to sabbatical funds from Hardin-Simmons University to consult with a number of people about the need for a theology book that would meet these various requirements. It would reflect this moderate Baptist tradition yet also bring in the paradigmatic changes in theology and philosophy that have occurred over the last century, yet it would not be any more obvious in being Baptist than Peters or Migliore have been about their tradition. They do not particularly advertise, but one can tell that they are Lutheran and Reformed, respectively. I consulted lay people, theologians, and nontheologians. Thanks are due to Dwight Moody (at an earlier stage), Lisa Cromer, Jim and Linda Bennett, Charles Hawkins, Michael Robinson, Phyllis Pleasants, Bill Tuck, Mike Harton, Graham Walker, and Susan Collins, among others, for helpful feedback. They felt the same need and gave great encouragement. The title *Life Together in the Way of*

Jesus Christ is inspired by two great books whose themes I wanted to emphasize. Jürgen Moltmann's Christology, *The Way of Jesus Christ*, stresses the messianic practice of following Jesus Christ. The Christian martyr Dietrich Bonhoeffer stresses that such practice is always *Life Together*.[3]

I owe a special thanks to Logsdon School of Theology of Hardin-Simmons University. The administration of the university; my two deans, Vernon Davis and Tommy Brisco; and my associate dean, Bob Ellis, have always supported and encouraged me in numerous ways. This work would not have been possible without them—or especially the students. They have suffered my ideas, dialogued, and inspired all along the way. I appreciate especially classes who used earlier versions of the manuscript: a class in eschatology in the fall of 2006, an introductory class (online, no less) in the summer of 2007, an ecclesiology class in the fall of 2007, and graduate systematic theology classes in the spring and fall of 2007. My graduate assistant for almost four years, David Tankersley, aided in immeasurable ways, through dialogue both in and outside of classes, as well as having the unenviable job of suggesting cuts of one hundred pages of the original, longer manuscript along with suggestions about the writing and content. He showed wisdom beyond his years in doing so well what I could never have done. Out of an impressive master's thesis on postconservative theology as a parallel to postliberal theology, he convinced me that I belong in the postconservative camp, which includes Stanley Grenz, John Franke, Jim McClendon, Nancey Murphy, Roger Olson, and Kevin Vanhoozer.[4] My current graduate student, Russell Almon, who has also field-tested the manuscript in class, is due much thanks for extensive work on the indices. Brian Layman, as an undergraduate student, volunteered to read several chapters and was extremely helpful in smoothing and clarifying my sometimes undulating sentences. I also should not fail to mention the stimulus that comes from the adult Sunday school class that I teach at First Baptist Church, Abilene. Mostly lay people, they remind me over and over how significant and fruitful theology is for all of us. My pastor, Phil Christopher, has been a dialogue partner far beyond what he knows as his thoughtful sermons have engaged my theological preoccupations with the life of the church Sunday after Sunday over several years.

Colleagues have also contributed more than they know. My continuing conversations with colleagues at Hardin-Simmons have refined ideas for which the reader should be grateful. I think especially of Travis Frampton, Ken Lyle Jr., Tim Maddox, Ronnie Prevost, Rob Sellers, Ron Smith, and Rod Taylor, who are good enough friends to push and prod but always with a sense of being constructive and affirming. The essence of such constructive friend-ship and colleagueship is Charlie Scalise, professor of historical the-ology at Fuller Seminary in Seattle. Over two decades now, he has provided lively conversation about theology and has perfected the fine art of providing criticism within the scope of the other person's project. I give acknowledgements to Fuller Seminary Northwest for the chance every few years to teach a class for them and to continue that conversation with Charlie face to face. He read the manuscript carefully and improved it considerably with his acute historical and theological sensibility. The book would have been better if I could have had more such response from Charlie and these others. I value them too much, however, to ascribe to them responsibility for the ideas in the book and their limitations.

Carey Newman, first colleague and now director of Baylor University Press, has encouraged me through two books. He always reminds me to remember the reader, for which all readers should give thanks. Appreciation is due to Baylor University Press and their staff, who shepherded this book through to completion.

This book was conceived about the time grandchildren came into my life, Iylan (three years) and Canyon (six months), who are a constant reminder that theology is reflection about life but not life itself. It is my joy to share them and also the life of faith with my wife, Beth, whose wonderful patience and conversation about theo-logical matters makes so many things possible.

Dan R. Stiver
New Year's Day
2008

1

BEGINNING THE JOURNEY

Jan sat on the other side of my desk, discussing her impending entry into a year-long class on systematic theology with some consternation. "But I am not a theologian," she said. I could hardly keep from smiling because I knew that she was a mature student, a practiced minister, a powerful preacher, and one who did not refrain from expressing her views with great vigor in class. "I am good at the practical part of leading a church but I just don't understand theology," she added.[1]

Jan's dismay at theology is not uncommon, especially if, God forbid, it is termed *dogmatics*. What she did not realize, however, is that as a dedicated Christian, especially as a pastor and a preacher, she was already a fairly well-developed theologian. Any Christian is a theologian as an aspect of becoming a Christian; every Christian has an implicit theology.[2] Some are simply more self-aware and self-critical than others. What I found was that Jan, far from being a blank slate in taking a new class, already had deeply held views on every theological topic, promoting them not only with a great deal of emotional support but also with biblical and argumentative support. Her tradition, which required an involved ordination process, had already instilled in her a strong theological perspective that would influence all that she did. The presence of presuppositions, or bias perhaps, did not single her out as different from anyone else, for all have such biases by the time a class in theology is taken as part of preparation for ministry. Our culture, however, has trained us to be suspicious of such presuppositions and perspectives, preferring us to be neutral and unbiased—often making us think that we are neutral when we are deeply enculturated. A part of studying theology is becoming aware not only of our theological tradition but also of our contemporary cultural tradition that shapes, often unconsciously, what we think and do—even if it is a cultural heritage that is antitradition.

What is crucial in understanding theology is to see that it is already a part of our life of faith and already shapes not only our explicit beliefs but our unconscious attitudes and even our emotions. Theology is a reflective process, to be sure, but it is reflection upon the meaning of our lives as Christians. It is reflection upon what makes us tick as Christians: what motivates us, what moves us, what guides us, what sustains us in life and in death. Studying theology, while a deeply intellectual discipline, should engage us in those things that touch us most deeply and that shape us most existentially. Unlike a discipline like, say, physics or even engineering, which may impinge upon our practical lives only tangentially and in highly selective ways, theology relates to everything in our lives because it has to do with the heart of who we are—that is, if we are believers. As Martin Luther expressed it, "Not understanding, reading, or speculation, but living, nay, rather dying and being damned make a theologian."[3]

Plato said that philosophy begins in wonder.[4] Theology, too, begins in wonder at the majestic and mysterious God who is interested in us here and now, no matter what that here and now is. One of the most unusual places that theology took me was to be a theological consultant for a supervised ministry of prison chaplains in a federal prison with several inmates on death row. The supervisory chaplain had an uncanny way of asking her students in the midst of their dramatic accounts of encounters with prisoners, at just the right moment, "Now, where is God in this?" Theology begins with the wonder of that question.

Theology, in the sense in which we are engaging it, is a task for Christian believers. While certainly people of other faiths or persuasions can study the Christian religion and Christian theology, Christian theology as understood here is an activity of the church, an ecclesial practice, if you will.[5] Theology often takes place in the "academy," but its primary audience is not the academy but the church, as Karl Barth, whom many see as the greatest theologian of the twentieth century, especially emphasized. To be even more specific, Barth could say "Its [dogmatics] primary object, therefore, is neither biblical theology nor church doctrine, nor faith, nor religious awareness, but Christian preaching as it is actually given."[6] Although he focused on preaching, one can easily extend his statement into all of the life of the church. Theology gets tested in the academy, but its truest test is whether it rings true and is helpful to the church. Students of theology, then, are not doing something that other Christians do not do, nor are they doing it for the first time. They are engaging in theology more consciously, more analytically, and more studiously than others. Their work is, however, not for them alone but is a part of their function as members of the body of Christ, reflecting theologically for the sake of the church.

In the end, however, theology must nevertheless be our theology, not someone else's. This is especially true in the free church movement that emphasizes the priesthood of all believers and believer's baptism.[7] These together mean that no one can answer to God for another or take away anyone's inherent responsibility before God to minister for the church and as the church. It means that all are fundamentally equal before God, equally loved by God and having equal access to God. In apparently the first affirmation of religious liberty in the English language, Thomas Helwys, the lay pastor of the first Baptist church on English soil, appealed to King James I in 1612.[8] In his work he desired, long before its time, religious liberty on the basis of liberty of conscience, which itself was based on a deep theological conviction. He argued that when we stand before God in the day of judgment, we will answer not only for our own actions but for our own beliefs. When God is addressing Thomas Helwys, he said, God will not ask about King Henry's beliefs. Such an insight, combining in a profound way freedom and responsibility, has borne immense religious and political fruit since that time. Theology is always my theology as a member of the body of Christ, my local church, and the church universal. This complicates matters due to the diversity that it engenders, but it cannot finally be avoided. It means that understanding the church today and its beliefs is much more complex than it was before the Protestant Reformation.

Systematic theology, while deeply personal, is focused on thinking critically, reflectively, and coherently about what the church believes about God. Every aspect of this definition is important. As we have said, it is my thinking that is involved and, in the end, my judgments about theology; but the thinking is directed toward God from within the church. It is thus not a "Lone Ranger" enterprise even though the individual element cannot be avoided. Critical thinking means that it is not only thinking about what others believe but what they should believe. Hence, while theology is for the church, it is not meant just to be an exercise in self-congratulation for the church that has everything already figured out. The theologian's purpose is to edify the church, but as the Old Testament prophets found, this process often follows a path of troubling God's people. For the Christian, the church is the body of Christ and serves its Lord. One cannot understand theology apart from the sense in which the church serves the Trinitarian mission of God the Father, through the Son, in the Spirit. Theology serves the church by being faithful to God—and is thus inherently critical. Remember that virtually all of the accepted theology that is a part of our tradition was at one time relatively new and challenging. Thomas Aquinas, perhaps the most influential and established theologian in the Western church, was declared to be a heretic before he was declared to be a saint— and the official theologian of the Roman Catholic Church.

Systematic theology is coherent, so it tries to be consistent, or systematic. This does not mean that there are not mysterious aspects of theology, such as the Trinity, any more than there are not mysterious aspects of the physical world, such as light acting both like a wave and a particle. Rather, these places are seen more as things that we do not understand than as outright logical contradictions. One of the great challenges for most of us is not that we have failed to think about theology but that we have failed to think systematically. For example, many of us in one situation may emphasize human free will and God's not being responsible for great evils in order to protect God's goodness; at other times, we may imply that God sovereignly directs everything that happens, despite free will, in order to affirm God's power. But we do not always see the tension between these beliefs or how they could fit together. Perhaps we avoid thinking through such issues because we realize at some level that they are contradictory, and we are uncomfortable with confronting the consequences of making them compatible. Theology is sometimes therefore avoided because it can be perplexing and strenuous. It can lead to changing at least some of our beliefs—and even more threatening, our actions. Systematic theology arose, however, because people at various places and times did the hard work of trying to think such things through. Most of our theology is the result of people seeing such tensions between one belief and another, whether they are divine power and goodness, God being one and three, Jesus Christ being divine and human, faith and works, and so on. We often think of theology, as we do the Bible, as just being dropped from heaven, fully formed in one fell swoop. In actuality, as we shall see, our theological beliefs have a long history behind them—of many people struggling, often in fits and starts, to put things together. When we wrestle with theological beliefs, such as the issue between eternal security and falling from grace, we are doing what theologians before us have done. The reason that we have such received beliefs, seemingly fully formed, is that people have already gone through the difficult process of working through such things when they were barely conceived.

It would be nice, as some think, if all the work were already done. We could breathe a sigh of relief, memorize a catechism or confession or two, and try not to think anymore about such things. It should be obvious, however, that our world does not work that way. Virtually every denomination is riven with theological strife. Much theological work has already been done, which greatly benefits us as we study historical theology. But much work remains to be done. If we understand the theological enterprise aright, much work will always need to be done; for theology is not something completely finished in a proposition or two but a living and dynamic activity that must be related to every new epoch and movement of God's Spirit in the world. This does not mean that the central confession of the Christian faith radically changes; the Nicene Creed, based on Paul in 1 Corinthians 15, who likely already was borrowing a confession that was in place, has been very durable. Life is complex enough, however, that we constantly are challenged in new ways to relate the gospel to the changing world around us. Moreover, if we understand that the depths of God and of Scripture are never fully plumbed, we will always have more to learn. The watchword of early sixteenth- and seventeenth-century Separatists and Baptists can guide us: "The Lord has yet more Light and Truth yet to break forth from His Holy Word."[9] This was reportedly said to the Pilgrims, the sister church to the first Baptist church that Helwys led when in Holland, as they set sail from Holland to the New World. It was, in retrospect, the influence of modernity perhaps more than faith itself that caused even evangelicals to see the Bible as a dry collection of propositions, particularly in the nineteenth century, that needed only to be strung together with little challenge to interpretation or integration into life. Bookstores are full of bestsellers reflecting the excitement and energy of scientists continually discovering new insights into physical reality; it seems to me that understanding more of the God in whom we are not just interested, as the physicists are of the world, but whom we love, should represent a quantum level of complexity and depth beyond the scientific world.

As we have said, theology is for the church, but we might ask the questions, Which church? Which denomination? In which century? In which part of the world? A tension with which we continue to struggle is the relationship between the local church and the church universal, or the denomination and the universal church, or the church of one region and the church of other regions. The "one, holy, catholic (universal) church" is commonly confessed, but particular churches vary immensely—not getting along, sometimes not wanting to get along. We can have particular groups claiming to be the only church, and that there is no salvation outside of that church. It is almost comical to see one group after another making such claims to being the one true church. The evangelical, Catholic, and Orthodox traditions—which certainly constitute a great segment of the church—have been particularly prone to excluding others altogether. The lines can be drawn rather narrowly, as when Bob Jones criticized fellow fundamentalist Jerry Falwell as being "the most dangerous man in America" and Billy Graham for "building the church of Antichrist."[10] A major challenge for us will be to do justice to particularity *and* to universality while avoiding such rancor. Sometimes, as in my situation, there is virtually as much difference between various Baptist churches as between Baptist denominations and other denominations. There can be enormous theological differences within a large church itself. So one of the factors that keeps us continually theologizing for every generation has to do with relating this particularity to the entire church. The church is now moving sharply away from its center in Europe and the United States and into the Southern Hemisphere, from the developed countries to the "two-thirds" world, from being white to being people of color, from being established and wealthy to being poor.[11] This surge is affecting every denomination and thus the whole church. It will certainly deeply shape theology.

Rather than lamenting this complicating situation, we may relate it to the fact that the Christian faith is deeply incarnational. Rooted in its center is the incarnation, the becoming flesh, of the Son of God (John 1:14). Being incarnational means that the church always exists in a particular time, place, and context, just as Jesus Christ did. The revelation of God came in its supreme sense, in Jesus Christ, in an incarnational way. So did the Scriptures, as we shall see. We have no reason to expect otherwise in the continuing understanding of that revelation in our theology. This should be something therefore to bless and appreciate, not to lament. It does mean, however, that every theology will be partial and perspectival, representing one part of the church. It points away from seeing systematic theology as a once-and-for-all, one-size-fits-all project to be finished and done with. Theology as incarnational is not out of this world but deeply in this world. It means that we need each other. It means that we learn from each other—that you and your perspective are both essential. This incarnational dynamic of theology, which will be a major emphasis of this text, points again to the corporate and ecclesial dimension of theology as well as to the individual and personal.

A final introductory point to make about doing systematic theology is to be aware of the levels of centrality in faith. Typically, as in the finger-pointing examples above, we have worked with only two levels—to the detriment of the church universal and likely to the witness of the church to the world—namely, us and them, those inside the church and those outside. Roger Olson has helpfully emphasized that we should think of at least three levels.[12] Given that so much of the time we are concerned with things that divide us, it is important over and over to remind ourselves that virtually every denomination agrees on very central things. In comparison with other beliefs and other religions, affirming the existence of a personal God who desires communion with people is highly significant. Virtually all Christian confessions affirm that this God created the world from nothing, that the world is not God (versus pantheism), that the world is thus not evil (versus dualism), that human beings are in the image of God and are the crown of creation, that salvation is by grace through faith, that atonement is through Jesus Christ, that God is Trinitarian, that the church is the body of Christ, that Christians are called to follow Christ and make disciples, that the church is not located in a geographical place or building, that Jesus Christ is coming again, that there will be a final judgment, that an eternal afterlife is the gift of God, and that there will be a new heaven and a new earth.

When one thinks about secular naturalism and the diversity of other world religions, this is an amazing set of particular beliefs that we hold in common. To be sure, when we move to more detail, differences crop up quickly. How crucial is baptism? The mode of baptism? What is the structure of the church? Do we practice infant or believer's baptism? Is there free will, or does God determine every-thing? Did Christ die for everyone or just for the elect? Can one fall from grace? What is the relationship of the clergy to the laity? What is the nature of God's creative activity to modern science? What is the nature of the millennium? Of the intermediate state? Of heaven? Of hell?

Olson thus points out that we should keep in mind the basic beliefs that we have in common, which represent the center of Christian belief, on one level, which he terms *dogmas* or *orthodox beliefs*.[13] At a second level, we may consider differences that divide us but should not keep us from being brothers and sisters in Christ, which he terms *doctrines*. I am a part of a believer's church, but I cannot regard the long history of the Roman Catholic Church and Orthodox Church, who practice infant baptism, as not being Christian. It is this middle category that we have neglected. If we had a more robust sense of the unity in diversity that can be seen as a natural, and not unnatural, aspect of the church, we might have avoided many of the damaging, "unnatural" divisions of the church. This is a failing in the doctrine of the church, ecclesiology, which we will have to explore further, but it is a key framework as we explore every doctrine.

Having a second level can help us in dealing with the third level that distinguishes Christian beliefs from non-Christian beliefs. The historical tendency has been to make every particular belief that "our" group has that "yours" does not into a criterion for being Christian at all. If we have the second level in mind, however, we can see that the crucial test is the first level. The issue of being outside of historic Christian faith would then concern basic and central beliefs, deny-ing the dogmas. It would relate to the denial of God's existence, for example, which would be extremely significant. Denial of salvation by grace through faith would be another. It would mean that many of the beliefs that have caused one group to consign other groups to hell could not be so regarded, such as the structure of the church, the nature of baptism, the number of sacraments, and so on.

This does not mean, however, that the second level of beliefs is not important. The beliefs of this level are so important that they probably determine the particular church and tradition in which one lives. They have been important enough for people to give their lives for them. One person might not in good conscience be able to defend believer's baptism, while another might reject infant baptism, limiting the traditions in which they could be ordained. One may not be able to affirm strong Calvinism with its view of predestination, while others cannot affirm Arminianism, which gives believers a say in their salvation (more on these traditions later), thus determining one's incarnational place of church life and ministry. What we need to develop more fully is the praxis of recognizing each other as brothers and sisters in Christ and in the church universal while still respecting our deep differences on second-level issues. This is an issue for ecclesial life, and it is a crucial dynamic in doing systematic theology.

I close these introductory remarks, even as we embark on our study of theology, with an expression of what the study of theology is. One of the most vivid images of what we are about was given with reference to reading Scripture, but I apply it to theology: it is like going off the high dive for the first time: you really do not want to do it—you are scared and exhilarated at the same time—but once you jump, you can't wait to go back and try again.[14] My hope is that this indeed characterizes your journey in theology.

2

MAPPING THE JOURNEY

Doing theology has been illuminatingly compared to mapmaking.[1] From the first hours after the cross of Christ to the years after the Reformation in the sixteenth century, Christians have sought to get their bearings. Despite the enigma at the outset, for example, of the resurrection and of Christ's relationship to God, now after centuries, Christians are tempted to see this reflection as a simple task, one that occurred rather quickly and is simply repeated thereafter. This obscures the fact that Christians have continually been mapmaking, not just repeating what was done a long time ago, every time the church entered a new situation.[2] They did it when moving from a Jewish sect to a Gentile one in the first century. They did it when moving from a small, persecuted movement to becoming the dominant religion of the Roman Empire in the fourth century. The split from the Eastern Orthodox Church, codified in 1051, that led to the primacy of Rome and the pope, was yet another transition. Protestants point to the Reformation in the sixteenth century as another such move. Free churches point to the rediscovery of believer's baptism in the Radical Reformation as another significant reformulation of faith. Pentecostals in the twentieth century represent another such shift, with the twenty-first century perhaps becoming the Pentecostal century worldwide. Realizing that almost all of the theological maps have been drawn by men, women worldwide have lamented, "The maps they gave us were out of date."[3] As the church is projected to become a Southern Hemisphere, two-thirds world, non-Caucasian phenomenon in the twenty-first century, it is safe to say that another major shift looms on the horizon.[4]

A map is not a picture; thus it is not complete in itself. It allows one to get around but does not take the place of getting around. It does not say everything, but it says enough to provide orientation. As C. S. Lewis similarly said at one point, "You will not get to Newfoundland by studying [the map]. . . . Neither will you get anywhere by looking at maps without going to sea. Nor will you be very safe if you go to sea without a map."[5] As the church moves from the modern to the postmodern world in the West, it provides yet another challenge for theology, especially for theology that came into its own in a modernity that is now rapidly falling by the wayside.

Methodology, or *prolegomena*, in theology is the map for the map, so to speak. It helps us read the map well. It especially points to the way theology in a certain time and place is to be done and understood. One of the shifts from modernity to postmodernity is to realize that theology is situated. At times, theologians have thought that they were writing the one and only theology. They were not doing European theology, or modern theology, liberal theology, or conservative theology—they were just doing theology. They thought that everyone else's theology was contextual—but not their own. A mark of our time is that such a claim is seen to be more pretension than accomplishment, more illusion than dream. It is not a sign of reverence before the truth so much as it is human pride to desire to transcend the human situation. Thus, a prolegomena is perhaps more crucial than ever in providing the lay of the land for anyone doing theology. It not only indicates where it wants people to go but also from where it is coming.

In myriad ways, in discipline after discipline, from one part of culture to another, dramatic, paradigmatic changes have occurred and are occurring. Since some of these strike at the heart of what has been understood to be the nature of faith and knowledge since before the time of Christ, going back to the origins of philosophy in Greece in the fifth century B.C.E., they have enormous implications for the task of theology. Numerous significant changes have occurred that impinge directly upon the theological task, much like earthquakes can alter geography. Major changes have occurred in the understanding of the Bible itself. While some of these shifts will be dealt with in their pertinent chapters, it will be the task of this chapter to orient us. It will indicate something of the scope of these changes, promontories so to speak, that provide new challenges for doing theology and point to what they might mean for the very nature of the theological task itself.

In each chapter, we will begin with a case study to provide a grounding for the contents of each chapter. In this case, we will begin with perhaps an odd choice, René Descartes (1596–1650). Some have compared our time to his time, the beginning of the sixteenth century. Descartes is usually seen as the father of modernity, the paradigmatic figure of the modern age. In many ways, we are in a similar transition, but a transition from the end of that age to a new one, usually termed *postmodernity*. The very name suggests that we do not yet know what to make of it, any more than Descartes knew that he was inaugurating a new age. Understanding Descartes provides insight into where we have been. It also aids us in considering what it might mean to move beyond modernity in some sort of "post" way. After looking at Descartes, we will consider some of the major shifts in the postmodern context that relate to theology. In light of these changes, we will reexamine the sources on which we draw to do theology. Then we will look at a viable model for doing postmodern theology that will guide us throughout.

Case Study: Descartes, the Founder of Modernity

The very word postmodern suggests that the current situation can hardly be understood apart from the modern. As the father of modernity, Descartes makes for an interesting comparison because, as we shall see, he stood with one leg still firmly planted in the premodern world even as he gingerly searched for a foothold in the modern world that was to come. We, too, find ourselves "between the worlds."[6]

When Descartes entered his famous and fateful room with a stove in 1619 to embark upon a skeptical voyage of doubting everything, he promised to leave the motherland behind, to chart a new path, and to light upon new lands.[7] He was a new Columbus of thought who discerned the "foundations of a marvelous science."[8] Such grandiose visions usually turn out to be as fleeting and insubstantial as the dreams they are; occasionally, however, they are as prophetic as the dreams of any Old Testament sage. The vision becomes reality. So it was with Descartes.

His journey into doubt, published in 1637 (*Discourse on Method*), is generally regarded as the beginning of the modern age. The same decade also saw the publication of Galileo's *Dialogues Concerning the Two Principal World Systems*, which marks the beginning of modern science. By the end of the century, their influence was followed and confirmed in many ways in the English-speaking world by John Locke in philosophy and Isaac Newton in science. The common threads that run between these works represent the form and matter of modernity. This was the womb out of which our own nation was later birthed and the milk which we imbibed. Our eyeteeth were cut on these ideas, so much so that we are hardly aware of them as our framework. They are rather like the air that we breathe, so close to us that we are unaware of our dependence upon it. This framework has lasted three centuries. Only now are we seeing its demise. Like houses in Florida or levees in New Orleans that withstood many other ravages of nature, the last fifty years have been a hurricane that has exposed modernity's weakness, and it is in the process of sweeping modernity away.

Consider Descartes again. He obviously realized his dream, but like Columbus, who landed in the Bahamas thinking it was Asia, Descartes' itinerary did not turn out exactly as he supposed. What seemed self-evident for so long now begins to appear riddled with contradictions.

First, a project that began with doubt ended with certainty. The only thing that can count as knowledge is what we know "clearly and distinctly," in other words, what is indubitable.[9] This radical doubt in pursuit of radical certainty has led to that curious oscillation in our attitude toward reason: between overweening confidence and despairing skepticism.

Second, it was a remarkable narrative that eschews narrative as a way to truth. Descartes expounds his ideas in the context of autobiography but advocates a methodology of logical analysis antagonistic to any such narrative approach.

Third, it was the result of rich experience that rejects experience as a source of truth. He studied medieval theology and philosophy. He then set out to read the book of the world. He traveled to many lands. He served in several armies. Then he claimed to shut the books of the world and of the past and to write his own afresh. Little did he realize that the new book was simply written upon the faint remains of the old. His method of doubt was a recapitulation of Augustine. His dualism of mind and body, his privileging of reason over experience, and his preference of certainty over probability, all were rooted in Plato.

Finally, a project that claimed to rise above the contingencies of time and place to a universal, disinterested standpoint functioned rather as a timely, politically expedient, desperate measure to save Europe from itself. It has been said that Descartes lived a life of pure thought, that his only connections to history were the dates of his birth and death.[10] To the contrary, Descartes lived out his entire adult life during the so-called Thirty Years' War—a war following a century of religious conflict that, along with the accompanying dislocation and plagues, decimated the population, the economy, and the policies of Europe. To many, fanatical religion had proven to be lethal. Moderate politics had failed. What was needed was a political blueprint by which issues could be settled on some common and dispassionate ground. Small wonder that Descartes' appeal to universal reason and objective certainty was a battle plan that caught on with astonishing rapidity. Within a few decades, the medieval and Renaissance appeal to religion, tradition, and prudence had been swept away in favor of an intellectual project that birthed and brought to maturity the modern world. Stephen Toulmin, whose book on modernity and postmodernity has been called the best of them all by Robert Bellah, expresses this point well:

> The 17th-century philosophers' "Quest for Certainty" was no mere proposal to construct abstract and timeless intellectual schemas, dreamed up as objects of pure, detached intellectual study. Instead, it was a timely response to a specific historical challenge—the political, social, and theological chaos embodied in the Thirty Years' War. Read in this way, the projects of Descartes and his successors are no longer arbitrary creations of lonely individuals in separate ivory towers, as the orthodox texts in the history of philosophy suggest. The standard picture of Descartes' philosophical development as the unfolding of a pure *esprit* untouched by the historical events of his time . . . gives way to what is surely a more lifelike and flattening alternative: that of a young intellectual whose reflections opened up for people in his generation a real hope of reasoning their way out of political and theological chaos, at a time when no one else saw anything to do but continue fighting an interminable war.[11]

And on the same night, November 10, 1619, of this new direction of thought that would function to place the calmness of reason over the unruly enthusiasm and fanaticism of religion, we discover that "having retired to rest full of this enthusiasm and entirely taken up with the thought of having discovered the foundations of a science so marvellous, he had in a single night three consecutive dreams which he imagined could only have come from on high."[12] The next day, he vowed that he would devote the rest of his life to this new science and promised, as thanks for the vision, to visit the shrine of Our Lady of Lareto.[13]

THE CONTEXT OF THEOLOGY

In this movement from the modern to a postmodern world, which is often lamented in nostalgia for modernity, some positive potentialities await to be realized. Many polarizing issues have been reframed in such a way that long-held and embittered problems have almost evaporated. Theological combatants who were deeply dug into trench warfare have had the armies, so to speak, slip away under cover of night because the real challenges have moved elsewhere.[14] We will look at some of these challenges in terms of the cultural and philosophical context and then in the biblical and theological context.

Cultural Context

The world that Descartes inaugurated persisted for about three hundred years and is widely regarded as waning. In fact, it is often put more strongly than that: The modern world has died. Some of us may pine longingly for that world, but increasingly young people can hardly make sense of it. What I want to do in this section is to identify some of the dramatic shifts that have occurred, in many ways just in the last half century, and their implications for theology. When one sees them not as piecemeal but as cumulative, they indicate that theology's context, at least in the West, has changed paradigms.

Experience. One of the first ways to understand this shift is in terms of three primary ways that people experience the world: experience, knowledge, and language. All of these have undergone a virtual revolution.[15] With regard to experience, rather than understanding the self in a dualistic fashion as mind and body or soul and body—as Descartes did, as Plato did long before, and as Christian theology largely has—the self is now understood more holistically. Rather than the rational dimension of the self being seen as quintessentially human, even as the essential meaning of the image of God, the self is seen as more than just a supreme computer. It is a social self rather than an individualistic, solitary self. Love characterizes the human as much as reason. Perhaps the development of the computer, which can perform some rational tasks far better than humans, has given pause to the simple identification of reason as the supreme essence of the human. In any case, many see this shift as in some ways a return to a more Hebraic—or biblical—view of the self. As we shall see in the chapter on the self, things are a little more complicated than that, but there is truth in this picture in several ways. Just as philosophy, psychology, and biology were seeing experience in a holistic way, biblical scholars in the last century, from an independent perspective, were rediscovering the holistic Hebraic sense of the self. They especially pointed out that although Paul, especially, used language that was easily understood in Platonic terms, it was a misunderstanding.

Theologians have often been suspicious of experience and have wanted rather to trust theological ideas, as revealed by Scripture of course. They have often been leery of the body and of the emotions, just as the philosophers were. All that has changed. Now it is realized that one cannot understand reason apart from a more holistic account of experience. Contra Descartes, reason itself is holistic and embodied. A major neurological researcher, in fact, entitled his book about this change *Descartes' Error*.[16] One cannot think theologically, therefore, without the emotions and the body.

In a major directional change from Descartes and modernity, a postmodern view understands experience as deeply interpersonal and social. Moving away from the isolated and self-sufficient self of the Enlightenment—and of the great heroes of the "wild West"— younger people even in the West crave community. The notion of the unencumbered self has been treated to withering critique. Humans do not start out on their own, as the great modern social theorists imagined, but vitally need others all along the way. The great question in modern philosophy was how one, beginning from being a full-blown self, could know that the external world and other people were truly real, a question epitomized by a movie like *The Matrix*. In this movie, people are living a virtual reality but in actuality are suspended in vats to provide energy for machines. The question of how one would know such a difference with certainty has plagued modern philosophers going back to Descartes, who expressed it in terms of how he could know whether he was dreaming or not. In the twentieth century, finally, this theoretical, skeptical question of whether there were other selves was seen as a nonsensical question because there could be no individual human with a language and thought to communicate apart from others. As the German philosopher Martin Heidegger, who raised this issue in an original way, put it, we live in a "with-world" (*Mitwelt*) and have always done so.[17]

Ludwig Wittgenstein was another philosopher who finally questioned the possibility of such radical doubt apart from living already in a tradition with other people and a common language and assumptions. He pointed out in a picturesque way that Cartesian doubt is an impossibility: "The questions that we raise and our doubts depend on the fact that some propositions are exempt from doubt, are as it were like hinges on which those turn. . . . If I want the door to turn, the hinges must stay put."[18]

Such a transition in consciousness certainly has import for the church since Christianity has suffered from understanding faith as primarily a transaction between oneself and God, with other believers and the church as optional add-ons. Distinguished Yale literary critic Harold Bloom, in a quixotic yet sometimes insightful look at Southern Baptists, judged that they are one of the best manifestations of what he called "the American Religion" due to their radical individualism. He claims, "Nothing that I have perceived of the American Religion is more persuasive than the image of the Southern Baptist alone in the garden with Jesus."[19] In actuality, this is a skewed picture of a movement heavily centered on congregational church life, but Bloom's critique certainly represents a tendency among both evangelicals and mainline denominations to match the radical individualism of the Enlightenment. The recent recovery of *The Gospel of Judas* and the emphasis on more lost gospels found in the twentieth century in *The DaVinci Code* has made many people aware of the variant understandings of Christianity in terms of Gnosticism. Gnosticism covered a broad range of movements, much like New Age does today, but a common emphasis was a Platonic one, namely, the denigration of the body and matter as inferior, even evil, as opposed to the mind and the spirit. While Gnosticism came to be seen as heretical, this Platonic thought world surrounded the early church and deeply affected it, leading to renunciation of the world and to ascetic practices for their own sake. The more one deprived oneself of pleasures such as food, drink, sleep, and warmth, the more spiritual one was considered to be. How many young people died before their time due to these practices? Lest we be too judgmental, it has been said that the contemporary church continues to be Gnostic in its own way, separating the spiritual life from the rest of life and disconnecting Sunday and spirituality from the rest of the week. In contrast, theologians more recently have focused on the way experience is inherently embodied and social and the resultant consequences for the church and its worship. Theology itself is seen not as a purely individual effort but as "ecclesial reflection" (Edward Farley) or "church dogmatics" (Karl Barth). Karl Barth, in fact, changed the name of his great theological effort from *Christian Dogmatics* in the first volume to *Church Dogmatics* thereafter to reflect this shift in understanding.[20]

Knowledge. In this light, knowledge and understanding have also been seriously reevaluated in light of the decline of modernity. The paradigm of unembodied reason enshrined in Descartes' great quest has been termed *foundationalism,* or better, *classical foundationalism.*[21] It assumes the metaphor of a building where knowledge has foundations that are "clear and distinct" so that everything can be built securely upon them—with the help of a rigorous method, of course, to guarantee further certainty. Descartes was primarily a mathematician, and it was the model of mathematics that has guided most of the Western approach to knowledge.

Long before Descartes, Plato, also obsessed with mathematics, sharply distinguished between knowledge and opinion (or faith).[22] In Plato's famous "Parable of the Cave," he pictures people who can only see shadows on a wall and mistake them for reality.[23] Finally, one person gets loose (the philosopher) and makes his way to the mouth of the cave, where he sees reality in the bright (Descartes would say "clear and distinct") light of the sun. At first, it takes awhile for his eyes to adjust; then he sees reality. When he returns to enlighten others, they become exasperated with him and finally kill him—an allusion to his mentor Socrates' fate.

Here we see the emphasis upon clarity and certainty along with the prominence of the visual metaphor that has characterized the West. In other words, knowledge is like clear sight, with its implications of objectivity and detachment as compared to touch or hearing (the latter being more prominent in Hebrew conceptuality). Later, because of this sharp demarcation between reason and faith, Thomas

Aquinas could say that if one believes something, one cannot know it; if one knows something, one cannot believe it.[24] This is based on his view that faith is somewhat like opinion (like Plato) and involves believing something based on an authority, not on knowledge proper or, as he would say, knowledge belonging to science.[25]

While mathematics guided classical thought, modern thought with the rising prestige of science has turned to empirical science for its model. While absolute certainty is less attainable than in mathematics, still a premium is placed upon objectivity, verification in terms of public evidence, and as much certainty as possible. Whereas Aquinas could still value faith, increasingly in the modern period faith has come off much the worse against this high standard for knowledge and reason. This charge has been raised only recently by Richard Dawkins, with the claim that religion is a dangerous virus, due to its not being "scientific."[26]

Once the two have been so sharply separated, the history of Christian thought reveals various attempts to put Humpty Dumpty back together again, such as reason preceding faith (Aquinas), faith preceding reason (Augustine), reason opposed to faith (Toland), or faith opposed to reason (Tertullian). Sometimes theologians have acknowledged that faith can never meet such high standards and so have retreated to fideism (faith apart from reason), appealing to a miracle of revelation or a leap of faith. Occasionally, theologians have attempted to depict faith as being as technically or instrumentally rational as science and thus have made it subject to the claims of public, scientific reason. Interestingly, this has sometimes been the direction of quite conservative thought as well as liberal. The Bible was claimed to be a book of science with objective facts that can be rationally assembled. Neither pole of the dilemma seems satisfactory. For centuries, these approaches have been seen as quite opposed to one another. With the benefit of hindsight, we can now see that in a sense they were all playing variations of the same game (or paradigm).

The significance of the postmodern paradigm shift is that it rejects the entire paradigm rather than representing another move within the same game. After several centuries, nothing was found that could quite measure up to the idealistic standards of the Cartesian paradigm. As a result, some turned to relativism, skepticism, and even nihilism, revealing that, contrary to a popularized negative image of postmodernity, relativism is a highly modern phenomenon more than a postmodern phenomenon. A sharp relativism is thus not so much postmodern, but, in the words of David Griffin, "most-modern."[27]

While reason was utilized as never before in the modern period, it took some time before the assumptions of reason were ever seriously questioned. In terms of the skeptical question, no one, not even the skeptics, thought to question the question—namely, the assumptions about reason behind the question. Finally, virtually all those who are considered postmodern rejected the Cartesian model, with its objectivism, detachment, craving for absolute certainty, reliance on rigorous methodology, classical foundationalism, and antipathy toward tradition.

In fact, from within the citadel of the standard of reason itself, science, came some of the sharpest criticisms of this model of knowledge as not doing justice even to the hard sciences, which is still news to some scientists like the aforementioned Dawkins. One of the most shocking realizations was not that religion should finally live up to the standards of science but that science was a lot more like religion than people had ever thought.[28] James K. A. Smith speaks of this in terms of an Augustinian understanding of faith and reason in saying, "There is no reason that is not grounded in at least *a* faith."[29]

The upshot is that one can, as some have done, give up on reason altogether, and even in a postmodern context, take the relativistic and even nihilistic road. What increasingly has happened, however, is that two trajectories of postmodernism have emerged.[30] One is relativistic or deconstructive, which some see as actually lingering within modernity, being "most-modern." Another is constructive. In theology, this is evidenced by a plethora of theological approaches across the spectrum from liberal to conservative that are considered postmodern. *The Cambridge Companion to Postmodern Theology*, for example, includes seven different thematic approaches, none of which are decidedly skeptical.[31] In the articles devoted to theological topics, still other constructive approaches are indicated. The editor himself later developed yet another postmodern model.[32]

The variety of approaches might be surprising, but if one reflects historically, it probably is not. As I have suggested, the modern paradigm in its broad features is not just modern, it is premodern as well, going back to the roots of Western thought in Plato and Aristotle. In this sense, Christianity has never really existed outside of this paradigm. The crumbling of the paradigm that has shaped the understanding of faith and reason has meant thinking it through in some ways for the first time in a different paradigm. Considering that the early church took several centuries to work out such basic issues as the formulation of the canon and the understanding of Christ, we are in some sense like the first-century church in this regard. Like the early church, it may also take us several centuries, and several models, to work through some of these issues.

This is part of the agony and ecstasy of theology. It is a thrilling time to be considering constructive theology. It is not an ivory tower exercise but a vitally important task for the church to deal with such basic issues as the relationship of faith and reason in the context of a pluralistic society, yet it can also be perplexing because the answers are no clearer to us than some of the questions faced by the early church. As mentioned, another comparison can be made between our time and the Reformation or the beginning of modernity per se with Descartes. [33] They were living in the choppy waters between the demise of one paradigm and the very beginning of another. It is clear that neither Luther nor Descartes was conscious of just how much change they were initiating, or what all of it meant. Neither are we.

One way that reason has been recast has been to turn Aristotle on his head, so to speak. Aristotle privileged certain, definite, and demonstrated truth, such as mathematics, but he also observed a kind of practical wisdom (*phronesis*) that enables one to make concrete judgments in the uncertain complexities of ethics and politics.[34] Hermeneutical philosophers such as Hans-Georg Gadamer and Paul Ricoeur have extended this "phronetic" thinking more widely, seeing in it the kind of judgment involved in the interpretation of texts—namely, in hermeneutics. In fact, Gadamer saw that the foundations of virtually any discipline are reached not by some rule-governed formula but by a holistic judgment like phronesis. In this sense, rather than practical wisdom being a lesser form of knowledge, it becomes the basis for the foundations even of math and the sciences. Aristotle is truly turned upside down.

The significance for theology is that its kind of thinking is dominated by this kind of discerning judgment.[35] It involves evidence and arguments, to be sure, but the conclusions are often underdetermined by them. As Gadamer pointed out, this practical wisdom is much like the kind of hermeneutical reasoning involved in interpreting literature or in legal judgments.[36] These areas involve situations where one might have literary experts, say on Shakespeare, who can provide a bevy of arguments for their interpretations—but they still disagree. As one might recognize, such dynamics occur in the interpretation of Scripture, which is why we have different views of creation, of free will, or of baptism. It is not just that people find themselves believing one thing rather than another (fideism); they usually subscribe strongly to arguments and evidence for their view. Obviously, however, their warrants do not coerce a conclusion but underdetermine it, at least for some others. Rather than this relegating theology to a kind of nonrational enterprise, recent paradigm changes in virtually every field reveal that such phronetic reasoning is crucial everywhere. Susan Hekman, an interpreter of Gadamer, expresses well the significance of this change: "Postmodernism does not espouse 'relativism' as its critics claim. Rather, it calls for a redefinition of knowledge that displaces the relative/absolute dichotomy and identifies all knowledge as hermeneutic."[37] Theology in this sense is a rational enterprise, even if major disagreements persist among Christians. In fact, the sharp distinction between faith and reason is undermined, so that faith can be said to involve the kind of reasoning appropriate to its object or its interest: namely, God and the spiritual dimension of life.[38] When one becomes uncomfortable with the insight that all the world is a text—that is, mediated through interpretation—it is a sign of modernity's insistence on pure objectivity. James K. A. Smith expresses this well:

If the interpretive status of the gospel rattles our confidence in its truth, this indicates that we remain haunted by the modern desire for objective certainty. But our confidence rests not on objectivity but rather on the conviction or power of the Holy Spirit (which isn't exactly objective); the loss of objectivity then, does not entail a loss of kerygmatic boldness about the truth of the Gospel.[39]

From yet another angle in the context of science, one of the striking features of the dramatic breakthroughs in science in the twentieth century, especially in physics, which is the epitome of a hard science, was how the world is so complex, mysterious, and difficult to grasp. In fact, Niels Bohr once commented, "Anyone who is not shocked by the quantum theory does not understand it."[40] Many are familiar with the physicists' challenges to understand light as both a wave and a particle and to deal with the enigma of the observer apparently affecting what is seen. Things become even more complex when one considers the likelihood of multiple dimensions.[41] As with Bohr, physicists themselves acknowledge how much they do not understand and even how counterintuitive "reality" appears. Michael Polanyi, a major philosopher of science, argues in a way similar to Aristotle on ethics that one cannot understand scientific practice without realizing a "tacit dimension" that feeds into these phronetic type of judgments based on long hours of training and apprenticeship.[42] Similarly, with theology, when it comes to faith and reason it is a remnant of modernity that makes us think that lack of precision and certainty automatically guarantee lack of rationality.

In yet another aspect of change, the modern paradigm sharply distinguished between knowledge and tradition. Even with Aquinas, faith was based on believing something on another's authority and therefore did not count as knowledge. In the modern period, there was often antipathy toward tradition as being what one must leave behind in order to find out for oneself. I am from Missouri, the "Show Me" state, which captures well this attitude of not believing anything on anybody else's authority. Jeffrey Stout summarizes the attitude:

> The unifying historical theme is this: that modern thought was
> born in a crisis of authority, took shape in flight from authority,

and aspired from the start to autonomy from all traditional influence whatsoever; that the quest for autonomy was also an attempt to deny the historical reality of having been influenced by tradition; and that this quest therefore could not but fail.[43]

It took several centuries, however, to realize its failure. The very tools with which we examine are a result of tradition; the questions we ask are shaped by tradition. Alasdair MacIntyre thus speaks of "tradition-constituted enquiry."[44] Gadamer likewise provocatively criticizes the Enlightenment "prejudice against prejudice."[45] What he argues is that all thought is shaped by tradition, long before we can consciously reflect on reality. It is true that tradition can be a prejudice in the negative sense and be harmful. The answer, however, is not to try to rise above time, history, and the human situation as the Enlightenment valiantly attempted to do but to see that tradition can be good as well as bad. It is to become more aware of one's tradition in order to criticize it and develop it, thus recognizing that human beings are incarnational beings rooted in time, history, and tradition.[46]

Historically, many have found it hard to accept that God's greatest revelation came as an incarnation—and thus turned and still turn in various degrees to a Gnosticism that rejects Jesus' humanity and his situatedness in a particular time and place. Jesus thus becomes a cipher for a modern business model or feel-good therapy. The change in paradigm actually may help us to appreciate better the incarnation at the center of Christian faith. Certainly the realization that every view is "traditioned," again, makes new room for Christian theology, which is so deeply shaped by dialogue with tradition, in the public square. The upshot of these changes is that the approach to faith and reason can be significantly reconceptualized, with many implications for theology and the church. Christian wisdom is not faith apart from reason; it is phronetic or practical wisdom that includes the whole embodied self in community in making discerning judgments.

Language. Another dramatic shift has occurred in the case of language. This may seem surprising since language is so close to us and is so much of who we are that it is difficult to imagine, for example, that modern North Americans approach language in a quite different way than the biblical writers or readers. I am not meaning here changes from one language to another, though the shift from Hebrew to modern English, for example, is significant. Nor am I thinking of the changes in English from the time of King James I to the present. Rather, I am talking about how our understanding of the way language relates to the world can bring about seismic shifts, virtually unnoticed, in our understanding of a written work as important as the Bible. For example, the modern West, with its privileging of science, has prized literal, descriptive language as the primary, if not only, medium for expressing truth. Just a moment's thought reminds one that this was a very unlikely assumption for premodern, prescientific cultures. The fact that Scripture is full of narrative and poetic language and has virtually no example of something like a modern systematic theology or technical treatise is evident upon reflection—but its significance is often unnoticed. A recent article announced that a Gallup poll shows that the percentage of people understanding the Bible as literal is down ten points over the last thirty years.[47] The tenor of the article is that the change is negative, revealing the loss of significance of Scripture in society. On the other hand, one could take these results as being positive if one realizes that it is a misunderstanding and distortion of Scripture to take it all literally. In that sense, the pattern might reflect that more people understand the nature of biblical language than before. Our approach to language, as we shall see, can be of enormous theological importance. Interestingly, in this case, the assumption is that very conservative Christians are the ones who take the Bible most literally—but then they ironically are also the ones who fit the modernist assumptions about language and perhaps *not* those of the biblical writers.

In fact, a sea change in the understanding of language has occurred over the last century. In general, modern philosophers saw literal, descriptive language as the best way to convey truth but did not even see language itself as philosophically significant. Reality was philosophically significant; concepts were philosophically significant; language, however, was just the medium through which to convey concepts.[48] As mentioned, the rise of modern science and its primary role in society exacerbated these tendencies. As we shall see in the next chapter, which will deal with Scripture more fully, the most conservative to the most liberal of Christians tended to fall in line with this approach to language.

What happened in the twentieth century is essentially two-fold, with major consequences for theology. First was the realization that one cannot understand concepts without understanding language, because thoughts are expressed in language. The second was the realization that literal language was not necessarily the only way to express truth, perhaps not even the best. It was certainly not the way ancient societies expressed their understanding of reality. In this light, one could say that the twentieth century became the century of the linguistic turn. Virtually every major philosophical movement turned eventually to a preoccupation with the philosophical significance of language.

Concerning the second, greater appreciation arose for the cognitive significance of figurative language such as metaphor and narrative, giving rise eventually in theology to movements of metaphorical theology and narrative theology. This recast dramatically, for example, the understanding of the parables of Jesus.[49] A major implication of this reflection on figurative language was that rich symbolic language cannot be fully replaced with literal language. Since such a substitutional approach has dominated all of Western thought, this is a rather major shift. The idea was that one could explain a metaphor, or a parable, or a story in literal language without remainder. The perhaps unintended implication was also that one could thereby leave behind the figurative language once one possessed its literal language meaning. The repercussions were that even conservative theologians could move quickly beyond the Bible to their systematic theologies and virtually need no return. A preacher could exposit the Bible and leave behind the story or parable once it was explained. Another implication was that illustrations, being figurative, were seen as decorative in preaching, concessions to human weakness but not cognitively significant.

All of this has changed. Symbol and story are now seen as irreplaceable in the sense that they cannot fully be "translated" into literal language, underscoring the irreplaceability of Scripture. Part of this realization is due to the recognition that "the medium is the message" and that changing the "genre," so to speak, transforms the message just as changing some of the words does. Another aspect of this change is due to the way figurative language is so fertile that it can become a virtually inexhaustible source of insight and commentary, much in the way that we say a picture (figurative language) is worth a thousand (literal) words. Symbolic language can focus much in a brief space. Think of the endless commentaries and sermons about Jesus' parable of the Prodigal Son. A surplus of meaning in such language continually gives rise to fresh understanding.[50] Paul Tillich pointed out, in one of the first gestures toward this new understanding, that some things can be said better in symbols than in any other way.[51] This fertile dynamic is perhaps the basis for a common experience of people returning to the same Scripture passage again and again throughout their lives and continually seeing new things. This does not mean that they are slow, but rather that the Scripture is rich. It can help us see that the literal explanation is often made possible by the new insights conveyed by a narrative or a parable, rather than the other way around. The "illustration" may actually be the key to the sermon more than the literal exposition, rather than just being an ancillary ornament. This rich surplus of meaning may be due in part to the way a text can have innumerable applications, such as the commandment to love one's enemies. It probably goes deeper than that, however, into understanding the actual meaning of a passage. What does it mean to love one's enemy? That God is like the father of the prodigal son? That we are saved "by grace through faith"? Understanding these images in part means to recognize the surplus of meaning and the mystery involved. A quick and easy answer is often what we want in our hurry-up society as well as in our churches, where we might expect one sermon, or at the most a weekend retreat, to answer everything. Answering these questions, conversely, may take a lifetime.

Even the nature of literal language has been probed from two directions. The philosopher John Austin developed the term *descriptive fallacy* for the assumption that language primarily describes in literal language.[52] Rather, he pointed out that we do many things with words, even literal words, that are much more complex than simply stating facts, such as commanding, promising, urging, and committing. From another direction, Wittgenstein indicated that we press words for more clarity and precision than is warranted, leading us to mistaken meaning. A common assumption in the West, going back to Plato and Aristotle, is that in order to understand something, we must have a thorough conception of its essence. Thus, as Wittgenstein pointed out in connection with a word like *game*, we should be able to pinpoint what all things we call games have in common, which is difficult if not impossible to do.[53] Rather, the similarity is more like a family resemblance, where there are overlapping similarities but perhaps not the same properties in every case.[54] Also, many words function well without being too precise. In Wittgenstein's example, when we ask a person to stand somewhere, we do not have to break it down in hundredths of inches.[55] He cautions, "Leave ragged what is ragged," which Western philosophy has been loathe to do.[56]

These reflections are especially significant in the modern period, when there was a tendency to see all truth as expressed in simple propositional language and to castigate theological language for lack of precision. In one approach, Scripture was combed just for the propositional statements that could occasionally be found, not realizing that they might be expressing, in a complex way, convictions that were embedded in larger narratives. In another, figurative language was reduced to literal and then left behind. In yet another, even the literal language about God was pressed for a precision that it could not stand.

Even though the twentieth century was the century of the linguistic turn, theologians have always wrestled with the fact that "God-talk is odd-talk."[57] In fact, the most dominant view of language about God, stemming from Thomas Aquinas, is that literal language can never express adequately the majesty and uniqueness of the Creator over against the creature, so the best we can do is to use analogical language. It may be surprising to realize that in Christianity there has even been a significant mystical tradition that, out of reverence for the wholly Other nature of God, thought that our language could not even analogically speak adequately of God.[58] The literal meaning must be denied in the so-called *via nega-tiva*, negative way, in order to open up a mystical experience of God that was so intense and real that it could not be expressed in words. This is perhaps the dominant approach to language about divine reality in Eastern religions, but it has had a role in Christianity as well. Under the pressure of modernity, many evangelicals, such as Carl F. H. Henry, thought that all expression of truth about God must be literal and expressed in propositions. Even Henry, however, expressed doubts that this could adequately work, and he was followed by more and more evangelicals who felt that such an approach puts the Bible and theology in an unnecessary straitjacket and called for a "post-propositionalist" theology.[59] Interestingly, this was expressed well in an interview by *Newsweek* with Billy Graham as he offered reflections in the midst of growing old (age eighty-seven):

> He is an evangelist still unequivocally committed to the Gospel, but increasingly thinks God's ways and means are veiled from human eyes and wrapped in mystery. "There are many things that I don't understand," he says. He does not believe that Christians need to take every verse of the Bible literally; "sincere Christians," he says, "can disagree about the details of Scripture and theology—absolutely."[60]

As one might imagine, C. S. Lewis is another impressive example of someone who saw that imaginative language, such as what he used in children's stories and even science fiction, could convey the gospel sometimes better than in his more systematic treatises.

These new developments in the philosophy of language ironically have opened up a way to appreciate the irreplaceability of Scripture and thus the rich, diverse language of Scripture. Prominent Old Testament scholar Walter Brueggemann indicates that such an understanding better fits the nature of Scripture—and the God to whom it bears witness: "There is in Israel's God-talk a remarkable restlessness and openness, as if each new voice in each new circumstance must undertake the entire process anew."[61] Theology has often, conversely, sought to flatten and stifle the biblical, theological conversation. These insights have provided a freedom to do theology with the recognition that one is not exhausting the mystery of God even as one penetrates it. They have also allowed for theology not to be so rigidly tied to systematic propositions, as important as they are, thus fostering various narrative and metaphorical theologies.

In light of these dramatic changes in understanding experience, thought, and language, we might appreciate a vivid statement of their significance by researchers George Lakoff and Mark Johnson from the perspective of cognitive science at the beginning of their book, *Philosophy in the Flesh*:

> The mind is inherently embodied.
> Thought is mostly unconscious.
> Abstract concepts are largely metaphorical.
> These are three major findings of cognitive science. More than two millennia of a priori philosophical speculation about these aspects of reason are over. Because of these discoveries, philosophy can never be the same again.[62]

Understanding these shifts and relating them to faith and theology may seem to be an overwhelming task, and a huge task it is. The upside, however, is that perhaps now we can draw on the full range of language, analogical and literal, metaphorical and propositional, as well as wider wells of wisdom from embodied reason and tacit understanding in addition to the West's rich development of clear and precise concepts and language. Unlike an orchestra limited to a few instruments, we have instruments with ranges and registers largely untapped, especially when harmoniously played together. Possibilities have increased rather than decreased.

Practice. The collapse of yet another dualism, very significant for theology, is that between theory and practice. Traditionally, the twain have not met. Moreover, theory has generally been prized over practice. A Greek philosopher in the time of Plato and Aristotle, for example, was not supposed to have to work, which was considered inferior, but to have time to think, especially, as we have seen, of eternal, immutable truths. Even in the modern period, theoretical scientists have often seen themselves as superior to applied scientists such as engineers. Pure science is played off against instrumental science. Even in connection with theology, systematic theology and biblical studies, the classical disciplines, have been seen as superior to the "practical" fields of pastoral care, preaching, evangelism, and so on. For example, in one seminary where I taught, the story was told that at the beginning of the pastoral care discipline, the professor of that field was not allowed to have an office in the preferred wing where dwelt the superior classical, theoretical disciplines.

Neither in science nor in theology is such a dichotomy any longer sustainable. An aspect of a more holistic view of experience and of epistemology sees theory as incarnate in life. The way this is expressed in the area of biblical interpretation is that, traditionally, a major distinction was made between understanding what the text meant (exegesis), what it means (interpretation proper, hermeneutics, systematic theology itself), and application (praxis or practice).[63] Gadamer and Ricoeur, for example, have argued cogently that the second, interpretation, already comes in at the first level. More dramatically, the third, application, is already involved in the first two. Gadamer expressed this in his striking image that any act of interpretation involves a "fusion of horizons."[64] This does not mean that understanding is always a compromise between past and present, where an interpreter can never understand a past insight or even adopt it as more true than one's contemporary view; it means, rather, that the past is always understood through the present and in light of what it may mean for the present.[65] "It is enough," Gadamer adds, "to say that we understand in a different way, if we understand at all."[66] In terms of learning, it is best understood as an active rather than a passive process, contrary to the way it is often understood as a teacher filling empty vessels with knowledge.[67] Learning does not occur when the material has been offered, nor when the student can repeat or mimic it back, but only when learners are able to relate it to their lives.[68] Just as the Christian faith is deeply incarnational, so is thus the study of theology.

Because we are always embodied and embedded beings in our worlds (or horizons), our actions or practices are a part of our understandings. Any act of interpretation, therefore, is a some-what creative act (of fusion and integration of differing horizons) that involves our practices. From yet another angle, Wittgenstein argued that our language is immersed "in the stream of life," in lan-guage games.[69] Meaning is rooted in these larger "forms of life," as he called them, that involve our complex activities.[70] He could therefore say, borrowing words from Goethe, "In the beginning was the act."[71] To draw again upon Polanyi in science, not everything is explicit, but rather judgments are underdetermined by external evidence. A holistic judgment is often involved that has significant tacit, even unconscious, elements drawn upon depths of practice and experience. Polanyi could say even of science, "We know more than we can tell"—which students have been fond of quoting back to me, especially after an exam![72]

Theologians have begun to appropriate these insights and to understand the way theology is inseparable from the faith practices that give it meaning. Christianity was not at first called "the Way" for nothing. In fact, Polanyi said this kind of background depth of training is even essential for scientists to know their field, which he called "indwelling."[73] If this is true of science, how much more "indwelling" of the Christian life would be crucial for understanding theology. It is a mistake, therefore, to think that one can pick up a book of theology and hope to understand it without already having been immersed in the life of faith. Martin Luther rightly implied that to have theological understanding, we must be on our knees.[74] For someone to attempt to do theology without a life of prayer, of faith, of worship, is like someone who is tone deaf playing music by ear.

This means that sometimes one has to become trained in certain practices to be in a position to understand. It does not mean that meaning is entirely produced by the knower, or the training, but it means that the knowledge or even perception of reality is impossible apart from training. While this kind of emphasis may have been seen at one point as a special pleading for the believer, whereas the secular, rational person looks at things without presuppositions, the cause is helped by realizing that science itself must say the same thing. In fact, a host of philosophers and psychologists argue that this is true of every field.[75]

With regard to Scripture's relation to theology, Kevin Vanhoozer has emphasized that the purpose of the full canon (authorized collection of the books that make up the Bible) of scriptural writings is to instill "canonical practices."[76] In other words, the emphasis is not so much on bare information but on "formation." In a complex interplay, therefore, one must have some formation in order to theologize about Scripture, but Scripture itself inculcates that formation. This provides a way of understanding the crucial role of Scripture in theology that goes beyond being a source of revelational data, as important as that is. More on that in the next chapter.

Thus, in every area of theology, one has to presuppose and point to the practices that give it life. Theology is first lived before it is thought. This insight also points to the fundamental nature of practice itself. In some circles, the word *praxis* is used to point to the essential integration of reflection and practice, with the emphasis upon practice. In this sense, one can think of God first as an active agent, even as some have said, a Verb, a Doer.[77] Theology becomes, in the words of Frederick Herzog, "theopraxis" and Christianity, first of all, a way of life that relates to all of life. It cannot be an enclave, separate from society and related only to the life of the mind. It is the life of the mind inseparable from life as a whole. As Herzog sharply reminds us in an article actually titled "The End of Systematic Theology," "if theopraxis, God acting in creation and God's struggling for justice, is left out, and if we move immediately from our doctrines to theological reflection, our social location is easily overlooked."[78] If our social location is omitted, then we, the church, and the world are left out.

Contextuality. This emphasis on the situated, living context of theology underscores another major revolution in the understanding of theology, that is, its ineradicably contextual nature. Systematic theology in Western Christianity has largely been done by European and American males. More recently, theology has been enlivened by a host of other perspectives under the rubrics of liberation and contextual theologies. Major influences have been black theology in the United States, including "womanist" theology (from African-American women); liberation and Pentecostal theology in Latin America, Africa, and Korea (including *mujerista* theology from Hispanic women); and feminist theology, first in the European and American settings but now from around the world. All of these have dramatized what should have been obvious from the beginning but was not, namely, that one's social location influences how one does theology, what one emphasizes, and how one interprets things. They have especially pointed out how more-affluent, economically comfortable theologians have downplayed the implications of the gospel for the poor, contrary to a central emphasis of the whole of Scripture, sometimes going so far as to make such an emphasis irrelevant for this life. A major characteristic of evangelical white theology in the United States in the twentieth century, for example, has been that the gospel is for "saving souls" but not for improving the physical lot of those souls. For instance, Randall Balmer reminds us that significant leaders of the Religious Right opposed the Civil Rights movement in the sixties. Jerry Falwell said in 1965, "Believing the Bible as I do, I would find it impossible to stop preaching the pure saving gospel," and become involved in civil rights.[79] Thus, there has been what one might call an unembodied, disincarnational, spiritualized gospel that is now seen, even by many evangelicals, as very distorted, as if one of a person's legs was crippled. In fact, one of the scandals in Caucasian theology in the United States is that conservative churches have often rejected an emphasis on social justice as being liberal, and liberal churches have often rejected an emphasis on evangelism and missions as being conservative, rather than the much more holistic emphasis in the Bible—and one found in many liberation theologies. White male theologians (of which I am one) have tended to claim that they were doing "universal" theology, that is, for everyone, but other interest groups were just writing theologies for their particular situation, such as Latin American liberation theology, feminist theology, *mujerista* theology, black theology, and so on. At this point, we can recognize that everyone does theology from their own situation, and it is a special pleading to maintain otherwise, hence so much attention to the current context for *this* theology!

Liberation theologians have especially emphasized "God's preferential option for the poor," which often comes across as a scandal to prosperous Northern Hemisphere Christians. Yet it is difficult to argue against this on a biblical basis. Again and again, for example, in the Prophets, a central measuring stick for Israel was how they treated the widow, the orphan, and the resident alien, in other words, the most vulnerable in their society. Jesus, who followed so closely the prophetic tradition, could say simply, "Blessed are you who are poor" (Luke 6:20). Theologians whose context is poverty, which will likely be the context for most Christians throughout the century, are no more partial in giving a special emphasis on God's concern for the needy than comfortable Caucasian theologians who have stressed inwardness. What we have learned, hopefully, is that no one theology can say everything but always represents a particular perspective in time and place. This is a way of repeating the earlier emphasis on all theology being embodied and incarnational. What it can mean is

- we can, without embarrassment, look to theologies that speak especially to our situation and note the special insights that we have from our own situation;
- we can thus all learn from each other and find blind spots in our perspectives that have limited our understanding and living before God;
- through this worldwide and churchwide dialogue, we can ultimately, even from our own perspectives, offer better, more rounded theologies.

The liberation emphasis is actually the more specific tinder for Herzog's deep questions about the future of systematic theology. He sees the centrality of theology in the midst of God's activity for liberation as so crucial that it challenges, from the ground up, the more traditionally Western intellectual approach to theology. He says,

> Yet if we first concentrate on theopraxis, that is on God's acting in history, we will not look for teaching formation in the library in the first place, as important as the library is. The Bible, which in a theology of liberation is our starting point, is, after all, not a book

which becomes meaningful only in the library. Being the eucharistic book of the church it is near God's justice struggle in the world. We will only understand it in its depth if we read it where God in Messiah Jesus is working in the world. God's standing up for the oppressed and the enslaved creation, which we celebrate in the Eucharist, is the social location of our Christian thinking.[80]

The challenge for us is not, in the end, to jettison systematic theological thinking, which Herzog does not finally advise, but to be able to reformulate it in light of these changing currents that help us to see what we need to see, that is, "where God in Messiah Jesus is working in the world."

Globalization. The emphasis on context and localization ironically points to another major shift, perhaps in the long run the most significant one, namely, the globalization of Christianity. The realization of particularity raises awareness of plurality and in the end broadens our vision to a global one. Specifically, this shift points to the center of Christianity moving away from Northern Hemisphere, white, male dominance. Whether we in the Northern Hemisphere like it or not, it is happening and appears to be accelerating. With trust in the providence of God that brings good out of everything (see the later section on providence), we can celebrate the benefits that came from Christianity's move to the Northern Hemisphere and the contributions that have flowed from that turn, just as we celebrate the contributions from the earlier dominance of the church in the East, in Antioch, in Alexandria, and in Constantinople (Istanbul). At this point, however, we are in the midst of one of those great shifts in the history of the world and of Christianity. As early as mid-century, for example, it is estimated that only one out of every five Christians will be white. At that time, Philip Jenkins suggests, "Soon, the phrase, 'a White Christian' may sound like a curious oxymoron, as mildly surprising as 'a Swedish Buddhist.'"[81]

If context and presuppositions do have influence, as we have argued now from a number of angles, then the move of the vast majority of Christians to Latin America, to Africa, and to Asia will spell changes as dramatic as the shift from the East to Rome, from Rome to Europe, and from Europe to North America. When most

Christians will be people of color, from the Southern Hemisphere, poor, and either Roman Catholic or Pentecostal, Protestant theology will be deeply affected, to say the least. It is projected that such influences will move in the direction of a more holistic view of the gospel, with an emphasis both on economic needs *and* evangelism; a conservative emphasis on the Bible; and more openness to the supernatural than is often prevalent in European theology.[82] While practical needs will predominate, it is obvious that theologizing will be more necessary than ever.

Along with greater awareness of the global presence of Christianity is the global pluralism of religion in general. A major difference due to increased population, travel, and communication is the "next-door" character of such pluralism. No longer for North Americans—shaped by the traditional Protestant-Catholic-Jew coalition—are the Muslims, the Hindus, and the Bahais overseas, but they are working and living alongside. With the differences in some of these religions as great as the differences within Christianity, it challenges us to grapple with much greater diversity. Even Billy Graham contemplated calling George W. Bush before the war with Iraq to help him distinguish between Shiite and Sunni Muslims![83] Beyond this, ours is an age also of syncretism, where older traditions mix and mingle in unprecedented ways with newcomer spiritualist and New Age movements. In North America, people are often drawn to spirituality but not always to religion, to transcendence but not always to tradition.[84] Contributing to the mixture in a dramatic way is the presence of the Internet and other communications that, in Thomas Friedman's words, have made the world "flat."[85] Jenkins says that even in regard to such secular changes, "I suggest that it is precisely religious changes that are the most significant, and even the most revolutionary, in the contemporary world. Before too long, the turn-of-the-millennium neglect of religious factors may come to be seen as comically myopic, on a par with a review of the eighteenth century that managed to miss the French Revolution."[86] Such a situation increases the challenge of relating traditional ways of understanding doctrines to a changing, global, diverse context. It calls for theologians to be nimbler on their feet.

In sum, these various aspects of what is usually referred to as the postmodern paradigm represent a dramatically new context for the church and for theology. In some ways, they represent an opportunity and a chance to move beyond several stultifying impasses. On the other hand, they may lead into new and heretofore unthought-of deadlocks.[87] A great temptation will be to try to sidestep the challenge and pine for previous days, even previous controversies. Harry Poe speaks alertly to this temptation:

> Part of the horror of postmodernity for many Protestant theologians is that the arsenal of weapons no longer work that Christianity developed over five hundred years for combating naturalism, materialism, nihilism, communism, and secularism. Postmodernity renders the old weapons obsolete because postmodernity changes the list of questions that the culture asks. Many yearn for the good old days when we were on such comfortable terms with our old enemy, Modernity, most of whose working assumptions about daily life we had adopted![88]

Theological Context

The following changes are specifically theological in nature and are indicated here to give something of an idea of the scope of changes in the last century that directly impinge upon theology. All of these will be followed up later, but these brief descriptions provide a portent of things to come.

Theology of Hope. A distinctly theological change is the recovery of eschatology, traditionally the study of issues such as heaven and hell, but in this case particularly an emphasis on future hope. Faith and love have always been central; hope, perhaps due to the shift to the two-thirds world just mentioned, is taking center stage. From gospel hymns of hope that sustained slaves in the American South to the current profusion of liberation theologies focused on hope for the downtrodden in the global South, eschatology is also one of those shifting theological tectonic plates that alters the landscape.

For much of the modern period, eschatology has been seen as a stepchild. More liberal theologians did not quite know what to do with it, while popular movements ran wild with end-of-the-world speculation. The former sometimes were so uncomfortable that they moved away from any affirmation of the afterlife altogether in favor of a "realized eschatology" that reinterpreted eternal life in terms of a quality of life in the present. The latter moved from one form of millennialism to another, finally camping on a brand new view in Christian history that posited two future comings of Christ rather than one, exemplified in Tim LaHaye's Left Behind series. Academic theology thus tended to shy away from the subject.

The situation changed dramatically after World War II when two major European Protestant theologians, Jürgen Moltmann and Wolfhart Pannenberg, both developed eschatological theologies with God seen as "the power of the future."[89] Moltmann's landmark book, *Theology of Hope*, also became a major spark for the rise of liberation theology (showing that European theology does not have to be antithetical but can be conducive to two-thirds world theology).[90] Other theologians were quick to see that eschatology is not just the final topic for systematic theology, it runs throughout all of theology. My doctoral supervisor, Dale Moody, who also in the early 1960s wrote a major work on eschatology, tended to begin the discussion of every theological topic with the future first, then the present, then the past.[91] Free church theologians James McClendon and Thomas Finger both begin their theologies with eschatology rather than placing it at the end.[92]

Moltmann, however, makes an important distinction between a secular view of linear time and the biblical categories of advent, where God brings the future, or perhaps better, comes from the future, to bring about transformation of the world. In other words, the future is not just an unfolding of the present and the past but is the *novum*, the genuinely new.[93] As Moltmann says, "God's future is not that he will be as he was and is, but that he is on the move and coming towards the world. God's Being is in his coming, not [even] in his becoming."[94]

While we will still deal with traditional categories of eschatology such as heaven and hell in the last section, eschatology will have an impact on all of the doctrines. In this sense, it reminds us of a basic characteristic of systematic theology in general, namely, that every doctrine presupposes all of the others. One could in fact begin with any of the doctrines. There is also a sense in which one is only prepared to deal with any one doctrine after treating all of them, thus the importance of reading the whole of a theology at least twice.

The Suffering of God. It is difficult for many contemporary Christians, with just a taste of biblical reading and hardly any knowledge of theology or church history, to realize that the orthodox view of God for almost the whole of Christian history was that God could neither change nor suffer (immutability and impassibility). The latter followed from the former since to suffer would be to change from a state of perpetual peacefulness. All of the biblical stories with a God of passion, change, and dynamism were seen as anthropomorphisms, that is, expressions in human terms for us to understand better. God was classically seen by a theologian as prominent as Thomas Aquinas as not even able to be affected by humans or anything in the mutable world. God affects the world, but the world cannot affect God.[95] In response to the question of how the cross of Jesus could be reconciled with this view, the main theological response was that Jesus Christ suffered only in his human nature but not in his divine nature. In another one of those sea changes, this conception fell out of favor, almost overnight it seems, in the last half of the twentieth century, "with very few theological shots ever having to be fired," as one commentator observed.[96]

The challenge is that we are just in the beginning of thinking through what a suffering God means. With almost two millennia to work out the previous view, we are in the very beginning of imagining how God might be a suffering God and yet "a steadfast anchor for our souls." This is one of those place where it is tremendously exciting to do theology and yet complicated and even frustrating.

Atonement without Scapegoating. Yet another change in consciousness concerning a major doctrine, the atonement—what God did through Jesus on the cross for human reconciliation—has become a major concern. As some liberation theologians have pointed out, the glorification of sacrifice can easily be abusive to those who are most vulnerable and weak in society. With fresh attention to language, especially the importance of figurative language, has come increased consciousness that our understanding of the atonement has been shaped by metaphorical images, not literal descriptions, and that there have been many such metaphors, not just one, in the history of the church. The tendency of many to think of just one model, usually called the "penal-substitutionary" model, neglects the fact that this was a model developed after the first millennium of the church and that it arose in a particular milieu, the medieval and premodern, that is no longer present. In fact, each of the four major models of atonement has arisen and corresponded to particular cultural contexts, all laying claim to being legitimate interpretations of the diverse images of the atonement in Scripture itself. While these observations by themselves do not mean that one model might not be the best way to express the atonement in a contemporary context, contemporary theologians have realized that the Cross is such a rich event that it probably cannot be fully captured in any one metaphor, any more than Jesus himself can be captured in one metaphor—or one Gospel.

After the Holocaust, Christian theologians have been more sensitive to issues of sacrificial scapegoating and have wondered how to understand what happened to Jesus in such a way that it does not promote or glorify scapegoating. Out of this has come the possibility that the scriptural narratives work within such a context actually to undermine the common (fallen) human tendency to scapegoat others, usually the weak and vulnerable. Just as other epochs have developed views of the atonement that spoke to them in their own terms, perhaps we face just such a challenge today. Again, more on this later when we treat the doctrine of salvation.

The Full Image of God. As mentioned, liberation theologians have raised questions about going too far in glorifying sacrifice. Feminist liberation theologians in particular have set such issues in relation to the way Christian history has virtually never done justice to what seems to be the biblical teaching of both males and females being fully in the image of God. Major Christian theologians in history have seen women as especially being the tool of the devil (over against innocent men!), as being inferior males (following Aristotle but not the Bible), and as not having the capacity to do what we see them doing in the pages of Scripture, such as speaking the word of God as prophets, leading men, and giving leadership to the church. Again, we have almost two millennia of a certain view of the subordination of women that is severely challenged today. How have these passages of Scripture been overlooked? How are they reconciled with other passages that seem to subordinate women? If one reconciles these views with the teaching in the first chapter of the Bible (and arguably the second) that men and women are created equally in the image of God, which was God's intention, what does this mean after teaching otherwise for so long? What are the implications for men and women for the practice of the church today? Again, we are virtually in the first generation of people who take these questions seriously, leaving us in a time of challenge and controversy.

The Social Trinity. On a topic that is not nearly so controversial among the laity but one that is of great concern for theologians, the past century has seen some of the greatest ferment since the church's early centuries about the doctrine of the Trinity.[97]

The idea of the Trinity in general in the modern period tended to be secondary and peripheral. With a heavily rationalistic and empirical approach to theology, it was difficult to make sense of a conception that made three equal to one, always regarded as a mystery in the church. Not only did it confuse fellow monotheists like the Jews and Muslims, it confused Christians. A classic example is Friedrich Schleiermacher, often called the father of modern theology, placing the doctrine of the Trinity in an appendix because it could not be rooted in direct religious experience, which was his criterion for all doctrines. About a century ago, Karl Barth, who specifically set himself over against Schleiermacher, *began* his theology with the Trinity. He thus marked a renaissance in the doctrine of the Trinity that shows no signs of abating.

An aspect of this renaissance has to do with the new influence of the Eastern church on the Western. Generally, the Western church has emphasized an individual model of the Trinity, where the three-in-oneness is seen as analogous to the way a person has, say, a mind, will, and emotions, yet is still one person. This dovetailed in the modern period with the emphasis on individualism. Some have pointed out that it reinforced medieval hierarchical ideas where God is the highest authority, the king or the pope is under him, and others are under them. Such hierarchical ideas, along with the domination of the one over the three, tended then to privilege power and domination as an attribute of God.

The Eastern church, on the other hand, has emphasized a more social model, where they begin with the three, as three persons, who are so united that they are one. This emphasis has always undergirded a social rather than an individualistic view of the self. While this model historically has not led to an emphasis on equality between persons, contemporary theologians argue that it can, based on the equality of the three persons in the Trinity. The idea is that our image of God deeply shapes the way we view reality. A "social Trinity" thus represents more the attributes of love and equality between persons, even on the human plane, rather than the isolated, solitary One of the Western model.

With the fall of the Berlin Wall and the Iron Curtain, this idea from the Eastern church has swept over Western theology within just the last half century. A number of theologians have made the social Trinity the centerpiece of their theologizing. Stanley Grenz, for example, made "community" his central rubric, which is based on the social Trinity. Consequently, the self is seen as a social self and the church as a community of love, all modeled on the social Trinity.

Rapprochement with Science. In what is an ongoing challenge that may not seem directly theological, theologians continue to grapple with the rise of the prestige of science and its understanding of reality. This began with Galileo in the seventeenth century, at about the same time as Descartes' influence, and has continued to convulse the church. Only in the 1990s did the Catholic Church apologize for its treatment of Galileo (about 350 years later). We hope that it will not take that long to deal with more-recent issues such as evolution, chance, and genetic engineering—but we should not hold our breath. Even at the time of Galileo, science raised critical issues with respect to the interpretation of Scripture and how one relates theology to scientific understanding. Ironically, Galileo, a faithful Roman Catholic, had already worked out a fruitful hermeneutic, but the church has hesitated to learn from this first fateful misstep. The church no longer worries about Galileo, but things are not so easy when it comes to other areas. How does the Big Bang relate to creation? How does evolution relate to the doctrine of humanity? How does the recently projected death of the universe by running out of energy trillions of years in the future relate to the Christian view of the end? How does the increasing acceptance of chance or randomness relate to Christian views of providence? Many theologians have hardly begun to deal with these questions, yet they are unavoidable.

The Greening of Theology. The connection to scientific issues points to another major change in theological consciousness, even from the 1960s and 1970s, namely, the development of ecological theology. Taking in the sobering news that science delivers about spaceship earth, consciousness has developed that the earth is not an infinite, but a finite, resource. Population cannot continue to explode forever, from about one billion a hundred years ago to almost seven billion today, and expected to reach ten billion by the end of the century. Students are quite aware that the world can be despoiled not just in one but in numerous ways. They realize, to take just one example, that the very oxygen we breathe is dependent upon the rain forest in South America, which is disappearing at an alarming rate. Not only can we use things up, we can make things unusable by the way we treat the earth.

Theologians across the board, from conservative to liberal, have realized that concern about the fate of individual human beings is not enough to do justice to the full range of Scripture.[98] Along with greater appreciation for the fully embodied nature of human beings, involving our complex relation to the entire world's ecosystem, the doctrine of creation has therefore come in for major overhaul. No longer is ecology just an issue for extremists, but it is now a concern for everyone. The dualistic tendency so deeply ingrained in Christian theology, which we have discussed, that denigrates the physical and material led to resistance to ecological concerns, seeing this world only as a temporary and transitory way station for souls to leave as soon as possible to get to heaven. No theology today is adequate that does not reflect a robust ecological dimension.

Every movement mentioned in this section, which does not include all the new theological developments, has had significant repercussions on our theologizing. All have crested virtually within the last fifty years. The cumulative effect is why many see the current situation as comparable to earlier paradigmatic shifts to the Roman church, the split between East and West, and the Reformation. This work is an effort to take these changes into consideration and to indicate how they might be integrated into theology. Since theology is, in the end, a collaborative task, the readers who continue the work of theology will have much to do with how the church finally works out these questions.

THE NATURE OF THEOLOGY

In light of the previous reflections on the changes marking our transition from a modern to a postmodern context, one particular resource that has arisen is very helpful for understanding the place of systematic theology in the Christian life—for putting it in its place, so to speak. Hermeneutical philosophy, especially based on Gadamer and Ricoeur, is a postmodern philosophical movement that takes as its root metaphor the interpretation of texts and applies it to understanding things in general, even to our very nature as "hermeneutical beings." It should not be surprising that a philosophy oriented toward the dynamics of interpreting powerful texts would have deep affinity with theology. Ricoeur suggested that our theory of interpretation, or hermeneutics, be understood as a hermeneutical arc with three "moments."[99]

The first moment involves our first encounter with a text. The first understanding of any text or, we might add today, of a movie or even an event, is a somewhat uncritical and naive one. How could it be otherwise? This is nevertheless opposed to the modern classical foundationalist model that stresses beginning with secure and certain knowledge. Ricoeur, rather, saw that we always start reflecting too late:

> In contrast to philosophies concerned with starting points, a meditation on symbols starts from the fullness of language and of

meaning already there; it begins from within language which has already taken place and in which everything in a certain sense has already been said; it wants to be thought, not presupposition-less [as in the Enlightenment], but in and with all its presuppositions. Its first problem is not how to get started but, from the midst of speech, to recollect itself.[100]

If one thinks of a movie, the first impression, so to speak, is more holistic, drawing upon one's mental understanding, to be sure, but also upon one's emotional responses, which are in turn related to one's past experiences, fears, and struggles. One's appraisal may end up being rather accurate after further reflection and analysis, but then again, it may not. To say that one should not have a view until one has given a detailed analysis is, one, unrealistic, and two, makes for a terrible movie partner who is analyzing everything all through the movie! The same, by the way, could be said for listening to sermons.

This first stage may well not be a single moment. The religious experience upon which one is reflecting theologically is not necessarily something that happened at one time but could represent years of nurture in a religious tradition. Rather than trying to set such experience aside and start over, the implications of Ricoeur's arc are that this is a resource, not an impediment. It is probably the motivation of interest in theology in the first place. Even one's interpretation of Scripture is likely the result of a tacit background of teaching and practices that convey the weightiness of Scripture. Ricoeur said in *The Symbolism of Evil* that "symbols give rise to thought."[101] Rather than being an obstacle to thought, which was a common view in modernity, symbols, with their wealth of linguistic and emotional connotations, fund thought. An example is the principal who said that what she looked for in hiring teachers was their passion for the job and their love for the kids. Other things can be taught, and can in fact be taught more easily when combined with passion. The conclusion: "If you can't feel the music, you'll never be able to play the music."[102] Similarly, these deeply felt experiences and interpretations that we bring to theology are its rich springs.

The second moment of the hermeneutical arc is what Ricoeur called the "explanatory" moment. This is where one turns on the analytical process. In relation to a movie, one may read about the movie, read movie reviews, and perhaps zoom in on key events to take them apart. Obviously, this is a less holistic and more of a "dissecting" mode of evaluation. It can be painful, especially when evaluating beliefs that are close to the core of our being.

In terms of larger cultural movements, Ricoeur has suggested that modernity represents this critical phase—with peril as well as promise. Criticism can help avoid egregious mistakes, such as thinking that the Bible dictates that the earth is flat or at the center of the universe—or damaging misinterpretation of something as powerful as the nature of God or of human beings. In any case, Ricoeur thinks that in this general sense we dare not go back before modernity to a precritical naivete.

The problem is, though, that we might get "stuck in the desert of criticism."[103] We might become paralyzed when we realize that there is no completely objective proof of anything: in other words, when we find no "clear and distinct" answer to the great modern philosophical question of whether or not we can know we are being deceived. This can, and has, led to an enervating skepticism or a cantankerous habit of poking holes in everyone else's views but having none of one's own. This is perhaps the philosophical counterpart to the person who never makes a commitment to a relationship. In my own experience with theological students, it can go either way. One can become so frightened or repelled by the challenge to one's beliefs that one tries to return to a precritical, childhood faith that never allows itself to grow. Worse, it can harden and become the source of bitter castigation of anyone who dares to change such traditional beliefs. On the other hand, one can become so enthralled with critique that one loses one's conviction, except perhaps the conviction that something is wrong with everyone else's convictions.

Ricoeur was particularly interested in the third stage of the hermeneutical arc, where one, in the words of the title of one of his books, can combine critique *and* conviction. This third moment in understanding he has called a "post-critical naivete."[104] It is a kind of "second understanding" as well, which reveals that it is more of a holistic judgment, drawing on all facets of the self, emotion as well as reason. It is like reading the Bible for the first time, yet with the benefit of all of one's critical study. To return to the movie analogy, one would never, I presume, want to replace a movie, a great movie at least, with a movie review. A great movie review of a great movie, however, functions best when it causes us to want to see the movie again. Seeing the movie again in this third stage is not the analytical, dissecting experience of criticism per se but an experience similar to seeing it the first time, yet with the criticism in mind. Perhaps this is something that is easier to experience than to describe, so I am trusting the reader's experience to understand the difference in the *type* of comprehension that is involved between the second and the third moments. This third kind of understanding can be called "phronetic" judgment in light of the earlier discussion, as compared to technical, explanatory judgment. To turn to a specific example, sometimes the study of preaching leads to one becoming quite critical of other preachers. It often takes a certain effort, even a certain discipline, to move to a postcritical receptivity where one can hear the word of God, as if for the first time, from another preacher and yet not be unaware of all that one has learned.[105]

Ricoeur has also called this third stage "appropriation" or "application." This is the place where one understands in such a holistic way that it is integrated into one's life. It is as much a *living* of one's judgment as *expressing* it. Ricoeur also points out that the arc virtually becomes a spiral because one can return again and again to one's earlier understanding, criticize it, and move to a new postcritical understanding.[106] Theological reappropriation in a continuing hermeneutical spiral underscores the richness of God, of faith, and of Scripture itself. It points to Ricoeur's notion of a "surplus of meaning," which refers to fertile language that can never be exhausted but must be taken up again and again.[107] It is also a reason why theology has to be redone, not because people simply have an itch for something new or that everyone before has gotten it wrong; it is because we can never fully get it in our grasp and are continually confronted with the fecundity of revelation.

The "appropriation" of Ricoeur's hermeneutical arc for theology is that it affirms this kind of mystery even as it applauds the effort of understanding. In addition, it is postmodern in moving beyond both premodern naivete *and* the modern desert of criticism. It does not require beginning with Cartesian "clarity and distinctness" but acknowledges the propriety even of naivete. For our purposes, it means that Scripture, as a source, is never left behind, and neither is our religious experience. Rather, we continually spiral back to them in fresh reflection and appropriation. It acknowledges that we usually begin our journey of faith with a conviction borne of tradition, religious experience, and Scripture—perhaps so deeply embedded that we are unconscious of their synergy. Then there is a place for examining them. In scriptural terms, this is moving from being babes in Christ to mature Christians, from milk to solid food (1 Cor 3:1-2; Heb 5:12). It is, as Paul enjoins, to "test everything" (1 Thess 5:21). The place of systematic theology, as well as of other critical disciplines, lies primarily in this critical stage. Along with various critical biblical methodologies, the study of church history, archaeology, and so on, systematic theology is what one might call a "second-order" practice for understanding the first-order experiences of reading Scripture, hearing the Word of God, praying to God, and giving a cup of cold water, among many other spiritual acts.

It is important to realize that theology does not supplant Scripture and the more immediate life of faith as in everyday religious experience and worship. Theology is crucial, however, in understanding them and in developing a more mature understanding—and life—of faith. As mentioned already, it is something that we all do in some nascent manner—systematic theology is but a more disciplined and focused way of such reflection. It is also important to realize that theology is not an end in itself. Theology points beyond itself to the life of faith—to the Way of Jesus Christ.[108] In this light, theology has an indispensable but subordinate role to play in the life of faith and in the church. The church would be poorer without it; the church would be destitute with it only. To return to Luther, theologians begin with prayer, in other words, with the life of faith. Correspondingly, theologians must end in prayer—or their theology has failed them.

The Sources of Theology

When doing theology, a major question has always concerned one's sources, at which we have just hinted. Another way of putting it is, what is our authority for doing theology? Once we as Christians recognize that God and the revelation of God in Jesus Christ are the supreme authority, what is our authority for knowing them? Where do we begin? With other systematic theologies? With the Bible? With a particular, unique religious experience? With the experience of the great crowd of faithful witnesses through the centuries? Or maybe with the experience of just one particular group? With impressive reasoned arguments, even proofs? To deal with these questions is already to engage the very nature of theology itself and to continue one of the great modern debates. This is an area where traditional battle lines especially have been redrawn so that the fears earlier engendered seem to be a part of the distant past. In some cases, they remain with us, treatises yet to be written.

A helpful rubric to approach this issue is what is called the Wesleyan Quadrilateral, rooted in the thought of John Wesley, the great Anglican (Episcopalian) in the seventeenth century who, like Martin Luther a couple of centuries before, ended up his attempts at reform with the formation of a new denomination.[109] Wesley at times pointed to four sources for theology: Scripture, reason, tradition, and experience.[110] He thought that each one was significant, but as with most, placed Scripture as having higher authority. As Roger Olson put it, "Wesley's quadrilateral of sources and tools for theological method was no equilateral."[111] One way that this has been expressed is that Scripture is a norm that is itself not normed by anything else (*norma non normata*), while the other three are norms that are normed by Scripture (*norma normata*).[112] This is obviously a Protestant way of putting things, since Roman Catholics, especially in reaction to the Protestant Reformation, place much higher value on tradition, at times having virtually an equal "two-source" theory of revelation.[113] In reaction to Roman Catholics, a Reformation watchword was *sola scriptura*, Scripture alone. While at best this meant the above conception—that Scripture was the highest authority—it sometimes has been taken to mean that Scripture is the only authority.

This has meant not only the rejection of tradition but at times the rejection of reason and experience in reaction to others who elevated them more highly. The early Enlightenment raised the authority of reason over faith. Deists, for example, who had great influence on early North American leaders such as Thomas Jefferson, explicitly made reason the criterion for judging what is true in Scripture. John Locke, probably the most influential philosopher in the early United States but not a full-fledged deist, still made reason the arbiter for revelation.[114] As reason seemed to edge out religion altogether in the later Enlightenment, even liberal theologians sometimes moved to experience as a source for theology beyond the reach of reason.[115] Experience became the virtual authority over Scripture as well as over reason and tradition. Karl Barth, as a young theology teacher trained in the liberal tradition, expressed his sense of a widespread move away from scriptural authority even as he exemplifies the way theologians always face a challenge of doing theology in a new context:

> I sat in my study in Göttingen, confronted with the task of giv-
> ing my first lectures on dogmatics. No one can have been more
> plagued than I was with the questions "Can I do it?" and "How
> shall I do it?" Alienated increasingly from the good society of con-
> temporary theology and, as I saw more and more clearly, from
> almost the whole of modern theology, by the biblical and histori-
> cal studies which I had hitherto undertaken, I found myself so to
> speak without a teacher, all alone in the vast field. I knew that the
> Bible had to be the master in Protestant dogmatics.[116]

Even among evangelicals, reason and experience could be evaluated so highly that they were virtually at the same level as Scripture
in practice. As outsiders would note, despite their Protestant pro-
testations, tradition continued to have great, if not superior, authority in many denominations and churches. Among many seminarians
with experience serving in the midst of such churches, a common
question is, what are the seven last words of the church? And
the answer is, "We've never done it that way before!" In reaction,
Scripture was highlighted again in the nineteenth and twentieth
centuries among some, while the turn to reason and experience in

late modernity continued apace. The charge, for example, against some liberation theologians is that they place the experience of their own interest group above everything else, whether it be women's experience, African-American experience, Latin-American experience, or Latin-American women's experience. As one can see, each point of the Quadrilateral has had its day. The legacy is that any theology has to grapple with this issue.

The good news is that developments represented by the postmodern turn make many of these debates passé. The value of the Quadrilateral is that it finds a place for each of the four, rather than choosing one or two or three. As Timothy George said in relation to Martin Luther's approach to Scripture, "*Sola scriptura* was not *nuda scriptura*."[117]

A new paradigm, however, throws the entire Quadrilateral into question—but not out the window. It is not difficult to see how this is so. When one examines what it means to understand Scripture, it is obvious that one cannot do away with reason altogether. The very process of understanding the words is a process of reasoning, especially when one is comparing passages. Translations themselves involve a reasoning process. Just to notice how one passage relates to another or is in tension with another is a reflective process that calls for an attempt at reconciliation, which is another way of saying "theologizing." Basic questions such as how the Old Testament relates to the New, how the two creation stories in Genesis 1 and 2 relate, how both of them relate to modern science, how faith relates to works—in Paul and in James—how free will relates to sovereignty, all of these call for the use of our reason, which involves all that we are: our training, our language, our experience, and our traditions. This last point reminds us that even the use of our reason does not occur in a vacuum but is itself shaped by experience and tradition. Alister McGrath expresses this interweaving in relation to the way that, in a modern paradigm, what we are talking about can only appear as "fideism":

> Fideism has become little more than a pejorative way of speaking about tradition-mediated rationality by those who hanker for the good old days of the Enlightenment. But that was then; this is now. A tradition-specific rationality which is capable of

accounting for the ideas of other traditions cannot be dismissed as "fideism," especially when there is no universal rationality or globally-valid vantage point from which to judge things. The best we can hope for after the demise of foundationalism is a tradition-specific rationality which reaches beyond that tradition in its explanatory potency.[118]

We have already discussed the rejection of the Cartesian, Enlightenment dream of a reason uninfluenced by anything. Our experience itself has been shaped by our tradition, which gives us a perspective and helps us interpret our experiences. We are engaged in ongoing processes of thinking about, reasoning about, our experiences and our traditions. When Wesley's heart was strangely warmed in a new religious experience that changed his life, it led through more reflection and further experiences to a new denomination(s).[119] Luther's reflection on his Bible studies led to new insights and new experiences—and eventually a new denomination(s).[120] The Western perspective is not for nothing seen as shaped by the Judeo-Christian tradition, which means that even secular people are deeply formed in unconscious ways by this tradition, for example, the linear sense of time discussed earlier. In short, it does not take very long to realize that one cannot even take the Scripture as one's highest authority without including all of the others. None of the sources comes "pure," as it were, uncontaminated by all the others. Obviously, in one fell swoop this undoes the traditional debates that fasten upon one or the other as authoritative.

Anytime one experiences a new paradigm in things that matter, which reframes at once everything, much like the familiar duck-rabbit pictures, a certain vertigo, a discomfort at the new way of seeing things, may occur. And at first, for those brought up in the tradition (and experience) of the modern paradigm, where these different sources could be neatly parceled out, a different perspective is complicated.[121] Well, then, which is the authority? one might ask. How can Scripture be an authority in this situation? For those not so influenced by the older paradigm, however, the old one can seem strange and even bizarre, a reaction I often get from younger students. The advantage of seeing the sources more holistically is not only that it seems more accurate and less distorting of reality, it allows one to draw upon more resources and to be more self-critical of various influences. And, as we shall see, one can still appeal to Scripture as the norming norm of authority.

How could one even begin to understand Scripture without some experience of the problems of life and of experiences of grace and peace? How could one understand the teachings of Scripture on prayer if one had never prayed, never experienced anyone praying, and never desired to pray? How could one appreciate Paul's admonition not to "worry about anything" without the experience of worry and, hopefully, some experience of prayer and the "peace of God, which surpasses all understanding" (Phil 4:6-7) that is supposed to deal with it? The Pentecostal traditions that put such a premium on experience and are growing so rapidly worldwide have no reason to shrink from their emphasis any more than liberation theologians and liberals who also value experience.

Those who see a significant place for reason and its corollary, learning from any source of truth about reality, whether it be Scripture, physics, biology, or psychology, have no reason to be embarrassed about their concern either. The early church struggled over this issue with its first push beyond Judaism into the Hellenistic world. While some claimed to stick with the Bible and Christian faith alone as a source of truth, probably the success of the Christian movement was due in part to its openness to truth from other sources. One striking image was from Augustine, highly trained in classical rhetoric, who thought that just as the Israelites took what they needed from the Egyptians as they fled, so Christians should take whatever truth that they find from any source.[122] He was concerned, for example, that Christians not make themselves look foolish in the eyes of the world by ignoring the findings of others about the nature of the world—a pertinent word of wisdom for our day. We will be developing the dynamics of such a holistic view more fully in later chapters, particularly the next one on revelation, but the point now is to see how the issue has been reframed.

The question thus is not the traditional one of whether we should use any of Wesley's four points of the Quadrilateral; the question is how we should use them. The Quadrilateral has value as long we do not seek to segregate each point too strictly from the others and neglect their holistic interpenetration. With this different vantage point, we can still consider how to use them. The view of most Christian confessions, even the Roman Catholic and Orthodox, who highly value tradition, is that Scripture has pride of place. Certainly, tradition, reason, and experience are involved in understanding Scripture, but distinctions, rough and ready as they are, can still be made between them. One can still ask, to take a contemporary issue, whether the current experience of speaking in tongues is the same as that of Acts 2 or 1 Corinthians 14. If we judge it to be the same, we can still place the experience within the guidelines given by Paul. Or to take another example, a not unfamiliar one, unfortunately, someone experiences a revelation that is in direct conflict with Scripture, such as to abuse someone or even murder someone. One can still place Scripture and, hopefully, tradition above such an experience. The latter example points to the fact that tradition itself is not all of one piece. There are many traditions in the church. The Protestant principle, as Paul Tillich called it, is always to examine tradition—but this does not mean that one must always reject it.[123] A critical approach to tradition can lead to prizing it, which often means esteeming one strand over another, such as free will over determinism (or divine sovereignty), or vice versa. Reason can be drawn upon but not uncritically. It was helpful, in light of new scientific findings, for the modern church to rethink its hermeneutic that saw Scripture as teaching a geocentric universe. The church, however, has reason to be critical of major scientists who, in the name of reason, claim that religious belief is irrational, that reason by itself will eradicate evil, or that reason shows that life is meaningless. All of these can be seen as the overreaching of reason, which has itself been undermined by postmodern critique of the Enlightenment pretensions of reason. It can also be seen as a critique of reason by Scripture, by experience, and by tradition.

In the end, we should be open to sources of insight and truth from any direction and not make the mistake of the Enlightenment of presuming that our particular perspective is the only one above the context of history and untouched by tradition. We should seek to be aware of all of the influences upon us and, in an ongoing process of spiritual discernment, bring out of our "treasure what is new and what is old" (Matt 13:51). In this process, the Wesleyan Quadrilateral, with primacy being given to Scripture, can still be the compass, so to speak, for our theological mapmaking.

CONCLUSION

As we embark on this common journey, all of us being theologians already of one sort or another, we hopefully now have a sense of the lay of the land and how to approach it. At this point of beginning in our venture, it is important to remind ourselves again of the place of theology, as we discussed, namely, to understand that we are engaged in theological mapmaking, in providing direction for living and not replacing the practice of faith itself. It is only in the living of faith, actually walking the terrain, that we provide material for our maps, require our maps, and, sometimes, correct our maps. In the end, it is only, as Paul would put it, in our walking in the Spirit that we test the worthiness of our theology.

3

REVELATION
Lighting the Way

Theology is sometimes depicted as the systematic treatment of the *revelation* of God, which points to the central significance of the idea of revelation. The Enlightenment period often emphasized that an adequate understanding of God was available through reason alone and that, in fact, this general revelation through reason should stand in judgment over any kind of special revelation. Such an outlook has faded with the dwindling optimism of the Enlightenment view of reason, where every mind works alike in reaching the same conclusions. The church has consequently reemphasized the premodern insight that God is too majestic and too mysterious and humans are too finite and too fallible to understand God without help. Thus the need for special revelation of God, especially given as Scripture, has again come to the fore—with new questions from the rise of biblical criticism and modern science that make this a postmodern and not premodern issue.

In the Protestant world, no more important topic appears in theology than the doctrine of Scripture. This is evidenced by the fact that confessions before the Protestant Reformation did not begin with the doctrine of Scripture but began with the doctrine of God.

Historically, it is quite noticeable that confessions after the Protestant Reformation begin with a statement about Scripture, notably the Westminster Confession of Faith of 1646 upon which several major Baptist confessions of faith are styled. As Protestant systematic theologies developed, they commonly started with a methodological introduction that often related to the place of Scripture and then to a section on revelation, which again focused on Scripture. Even before the Protestant Reformation, as Clark Pinnock has pointed out in *The Scripture Principle*, "For better or for worse, belief in the Scriptures as the canon and yardstick of Christian truth, the unique locus of the Word of God, is part of an almost universal Christian consensus going back to at least the second century."[1] The church's common affirmation of Scripture as the primary authority for revelation follows the authority of Scripture attested by Jesus and elsewhere in the writings of the fledgling Christian movement.

This is all the more remarkable when it is realized that Scripture as the word of God is derivative in a two-fold way. In the first sense, God is the Word of God as the origin and focus of our faith. In the second, Jesus Christ is the supreme revelation, or Word, of God. One might point out that the main place in which we learn both of these things is Scripture. Nevertheless, Scripture attests to both but is itself not divine, not a fourth member of the Trinity, not an end in itself. Much like John the Baptist says of himself in John 1, the purpose of the written Scripture is not to point to itself but to point beyond itself to Christ (v. 30). Coming to grips with this remarkable but complex feature of Christians as "people of the Book" is crucial for understanding Christian faith.

Another significant feature about the doctrine of Scripture in the Protestant era is the debate about the very nature of Scripture itself. An obvious reason for this debate in the aftermath of the Reformation is due to the authority for belief shifting to Scripture away from councils, magisteria, or popes. This shift put enormous weight on the capacity of appeals to the meaning of Scripture to settle differences. The split from the Roman Catholic Church into innumerable movements and denominations after the Protestant

Reformation in the sixteenth century underscores the gravity of this issue. For example, more than sixty Baptist denominations exist in the United States alone.[2] If Scripture, under the rubric of "Scripture alone" (*sola scriptura*), is to be the primary authority for access to God's revelation, and its meaning is not easily agreed upon by all, then the task of interpretation is crucial. As a result, perhaps an inordinate amount of attention has been paid to the nature of Scripture and how to interpret it.

With the rise of modern science, and greater appreciation for reason, arose a hope that the "Book of the world" might be a guide or even a replacement for the problems of interpreting the "Book of Scripture." Perhaps God provided access to necessary revelation quite apart from Scripture, in reason and in nature, so the thinking went. Hence the need arose to consider the fuller issue of revelation as God's communication through Scripture *and* through creation, called special and general revelation, respectively. We will consequently treat both in this chapter.

In the spirit of dealing with methodological issues at the beginning, not because they have to be first but because they are strategically important in a pluralistic world, there is a place for following the modern practice of treating revelation before other doctrines. In other words, this does not mean that the doctrine of Scripture is more important than the doctrine of God, but it reflects a conviction that Scripture is the premier source of revelation about God. Much can be said for beginning in many other places, remembering that systematic theology is quite circular. Nevertheless, dealing in more-specific ways than in the previous chapter with the nature of biblical interpretation and also with the issue of knowledge of God from other sources will be helpful in developing the doctrines that follow, such as the doctrines of God and of humanity.

Two Case Studies

The significance of the nature of revelation and Scripture may be seen in two pivotal events that have indelibly marked the outset of the Reformation and, subsequently, the modern period.

Luther's Revolution

After the young monk Martin Luther, who had developed into a skillful biblical teacher and a sensitive pastor, began to raise serious questions about corrupt practices of the church, he stirred great consternation among church authorities. Even they, however, could hardly have imagined the whirlwind that he was bringing forth upon the church.[3] As authorities attempted to silence him, he was supported by local political leaders in ways that would have been impossible in earlier times. The time was thus ripe for Luther to raise such questions and survive, when earlier he likely would have met the fate of martyrdom as did previous rebels like John Hus and John Wycliffe. Perhaps the famous words of the hymn he later wrote captured his feelings:

> Let goods and kindred go, This mortal life also;
> The body they may kill: God's truth abideth still,
> His kingdom is forever.[4]

Finally, he was brought before the authorities in Worms in 1521 and, as far as he was concerned, faced possible death if he did not recant. The famous words he is reputed to have said have stirred the Protestant world ever since: "Unless I can be convinced by the testimony of the Scriptures or by clear reason . . . , I am bound by the Scriptures I have quoted and my conscience is captive to the Word of God. I cannot and I will not retract anything since it is neither safe nor right to go against conscience. Here I stand, may God help me, Amen."[5] Luther's words are full of great moment. He was placing the church and the pope under the authority of Scripture, which implied his own understanding of Scripture. Thus fell by the wayside the medieval world.

Although Luther himself would not allow all others the same privilege of freedom, fomenting persecution of Roman Catholics and other Protestants, he had cracked the dike.[6] His appeal to reason also pointed ahead to the way some people would turn not to church authority to interpret Scripture but to rational examination of it—and later to reason itself above Scripture.

It is not that the Catholic Church did not see Scripture as the primary authority. They would not, however, allow an individual to challenge the authority of the church and church tradition in the interpretation of Scripture. To the contrary, Luther himself emphasized the priesthood of all believers even if he found it difficult to carry out. The slogan of *sola scriptura* captures the seismic shift that was occurring. By this, he did not mean that one need turn only to Scripture but that Scripture functions as the primary authority.

Luther's stance implies that Scripture can be understood well. This led to the common Protestant emphasis on the "perspicuity" of Scripture, meaning that the basic message of Scripture is accessible to all.[7] The turn to a clearly understood founding document was supported by the impending rise in the modern paradigm of the need for "clear and distinct" foundations, in Descartes' words about a century later, closely allied to a suspicion of tradition. With the puncturing of this dream of a transparent foundation in the realization of the modern "conflict of interpretations"[8] and its replacement by a postmodern paradigm a few centuries later, we are left again, much as in the time of Luther, with determining just what role Scripture should play. Where and how does one locate authority in the church?

Galileo's Revolution

Another major event occurred about one hundred years after Luther. Galileo Galilei was hauled before the Roman Catholic Inquisition in 1633 and forced to deny the claim that the earth moves around the sun, something he clearly had come to believe based on empirical evidence—which however appeared to clash with the clear teaching of Scripture, according to the pope.[9] In reality, it was also a clash with Aristotle's view of the world, which, in practice, carried virtually as much authority as Scripture. In addition, rather than this being a controversy between the church and secular science, Galileo himself appears to have been a devoted Catholic who was genuinely torn between allegiance to two authorities. The empirical evidence at the time was not as clear as we might think. Also, Pope Urban VIII, who had earlier been Galileo's champion and whose ascension to the papal office may even have given rise to misplaced optimism on the part of Galileo, was having to defend the Catholic Church against a bitter fight with the Protestants. In other words, it was no time for innovation and change. Galileo did not help his cause, moreover, in his defense of his views by picturing the obviously ignorant and foolish antagonist in his writing, tellingly named Simplicio, as suspiciously resembling the pope.[10]

In the end, the condemnation of Galileo did enormous damage to the image of the church in relation to science. Ironically, Galileo himself had already developed a viable hermeneutic that avoided clash with Scripture. Most simply put, in words that he remembered apparently from a Vatican librarian, "The Bible was a book about how one goes to Heaven—not how the heavens go."[11] More specifically, he argued that the Bible's main purpose was not to teach scientific truths but to teach about God and salvation. Thus, one should not look to the Bible for the law of gravity or the details of how God made the universe, only for the basis of the universe and perhaps the motivation to study the universe. Despite Galileo's condemnation at the time, even the most ardent inerrantist—whose ostensible claim is that the Bible is not false in anything—does not claim what many in the church took for granted at the time, namely, that the Bible taught that the sun moves around the earth, not to mention earlier beliefs in a flat earth based on Scripture. The effect of the scandal of the Galilean episode means that no hermeneutic can be a simple one, if there ever was one. Any understanding of Scripture must recognize Scripture's purpose and the distinction between cultural assumptions such as a flat earth and a geocentric universe, clearly expressed at times in the Bible, and the Bible's revelatory teaching, no matter what one's technical view of Scripture's inspiration might be.

This event also reminds us of how the view of Scripture relates to a context. Political, philosophical, and cultural assumptions shape us deeply. It is virtually impossible to examine the meaning of Scripture apart from a dialogue with the wider world and things believed to be true by other means. Cultural assumptions play a role that cannot simply be identified with Scripture, such as the Aristotelian worldview at the time of Galileo. Part of the shock wave that Galileo created was due to the Aristotelian idea that the heavens were perfect, even created from different material than the lesser earth. When Galileo saw craters on what was supposed to be a perfectly rounded moon, it was not a minor detail but the end of a worldview that had existed for almost two millennia. Even as Protestants laud Luther's appeal to Scripture, his own commitment and success was likewise shaped by cultural, political, and rational factors. Often Protestants have appealed to the Bible as if it stands apart from the rest of life and can be brought to bear in a pristine way upon everything else. It is now more widely recognized that our incarnational human situation makes this impossible. To accentuate this fact, at the center of the Bible is the incarnation of God's revelation in Christ. We cannot avoid taking the incarnational context seriously. How then do we understand the primary authority of Scripture as well as its nature as incarnational? How does its authority relate to other sources of truth?

PARADIGMS OF INSPIRATION

As the above cases show, Christians have not so much debated the value or authority of Scripture as they have struggled with how to understand its authority. There has not been just one approach, but many, in Christian history. It will be helpful to examine some of these traditional models, or paradigms, of how Scripture is seen as inspired because they deeply shape the way in which it is interpreted.[12]

Traditional Models

A debate occurring around the third and fourth centuries centered on approaches from what are called the Alexandrian and Antiochan schools of interpretation.[13] The Alexandrian school, nurtured by classical learning in Plato and Greek philosophy, prized allegory. This allowed them, with their Platonic tendency, to emphasize the spiritual over the material and thus to avoid what they saw as the cruder, literal parts of the biblical message. They especially were concerned about places that pictured God as appearing in embodied form, as in Genesis 2, or as being too human in being angry or repenting, much like the discredited Greek mythology, as in Genesis 6. They saw these as anthropomorphisms presenting spiritual truths in more understandable human terms. Often, they thought of all of Scripture as having four meanings: literal, historical; spiritual, allegorical; moral; and mystical or perhaps eschatological. A common example was the reference to Jerusalem as a literal city, as an allegory of the church, morally as the ideal city above, and eschatologically as the new Jerusalem. In practice, it was more common just to distinguish a literal and a spiritual meaning. If the literal was too crude to be believed, it was a sign that one should turn to the spiritual; thus, the literal meaning was often actually denied. Because this took place in the context of the church and in the tradition of the "rule of faith," the confessional beliefs that affirmed the basics of the gospel, it was kept under control and could be illuminating. At other times, it allowed for creative and uncontrolled excess, where one could find almost anything anywhere. One critic, upon hearing that the red color of the sacrificial cow stood for Christ's blood shed on the cross, remarks on this danger: "It would be all the same if the cow had been black; the allegory is worthless; whatever the color of the cow, some sort of allegory could be found for it."[14]

The Antioch school, more influenced by Jewish exegesis, was oriented toward the literal, straightforwardly historical meaning and rejected the excesses of allegory. They were open to what is often called typology, where a past event or thing could be symbolic of a future, as King David could be a type of the later messiah. Another would be Matthew's Gospel understanding Jesus as a new Moses, giving a new law and bringing about a new liberation from slavery. They argued, however, that there is actually a historical connection and appropriateness to typology that is not present in allegory. Ironically, the Protestant tradition has favored the Antioch school on hermeneutics but not their Christology, which tended not to see Jesus as fully divine, reminding us that even a good theory cannot guarantee good results.

More recently, it has been pointed out that we have to be careful in making this distinction too neatly. In fact, it seems that ancient exegetes and theologians, much like today, used various approaches to Scripture for polemical and rhetorical purposes, not always consistently. Margaret Mitchell, an expert in this area of early Christian studies, performed a similar study of the Christian Right in U.S. politics and noticed the same thing. This is significant, because it is a movement that is quite conservative and tends to insist, like the Antioch school, that it only takes the Bible literally. What she found was that references to the Bible were actually somewhat rare and typically vague.[15] She adds, "Along with a polemical intent similar to what we see in ancient commentators, *what most characterizes the Christian Right's biblical interpretation is no single method, but rather its selection of passages and topics.*"[16]

To be fair, as she points out, this has been common from all sides of the church through history. The challenge for us is not to follow suit in what is often called "Scripture-twisting" but to be consistent, fair, and honest. It does mean that code words such as *literal* or *inerrant* should not conceal the fact that almost all—including, if not especially, evangelicals—interpret the Bible in a variety of ways. This is not always a mistake; the Bible itself is not one "flat genre," for it contains many genres. What is important is not to be arbitrary or capricious but to do justice to the biblical genres themselves, on the one side, and on the other to recognize what we are doing. However, we often are inconsistent: for example, emphasizing the priority of Jesus' teaching in the New Testament (on putting people's needs before the Sabbath) in one case but relativizing them in another (on peacemaking); appealing to a flat Bible in one case (capital punishment) but not in another (polygamy); looking at context in one case (flat earth and wearing braids) but not in others (literal days in Genesis and subordination of women).

In the medieval period, a rough synthesis emerged, epitomized by Thomas Aquinas, who affirmed allegory but required that allegory must always be able to be found expressed literally somewhere else in Scripture: for instance, the Jerusalem example cited above.[17] The magisterial Reformers Luther and Calvin, however, turned to the Antioch tradition with a vengeance, identifying allegory with the Catholic Church that they were rejecting. For example, Luther said:

> No violence is to be done to the words of God, whether by man or angel; but they are to be retained in their simplest meaning wherever possible, and to be understood in their grammatical and literal sense unless the context plainly forbids, lest we give our adversaries occasion to make a mockery of all the Scriptures. Thus Origen was repudiated, in olden times, because he despised the grammatical sense and turned the trees, and all else written concerning Paradise, into allegories; for it might therefrom be concluded that God did not create trees.[18]

Such emphasis on the historical context was taken up by modern biblical criticism that stresses that passages should always be understood in their historical context. Nevertheless, a certain breadth was still allowed in how to understand inspiration. While at times the language might suggest mechanical dictation, that God simply wrote what God wanted through the instrumentality of the human writers with little human mediation at all, at other times there was recognition of the human role, as in Calvin's notion of accommodation and in Luther's stress on the hermeneutical key of Christ, namely, that the meaning of Scripture lies in what it preaches about Christ. On these grounds, Luther even notoriously questioned whether the Epistle of James should be in the canon.

Scripture was thus seen as reliable and trustworthy in light of its message, often expressed as its being "infallible."[19] With the rise of the modern period, this loose understanding was put to the test. The modern premium on clear and distinct truth, historical facts, chronology, and propositional, literal language deeply affected the understanding of Scripture's inspiration. On the one hand, liberal critics questioned the strict historicity of biblical accounts, noting that one could not verify much of the biblical story, such as the stories of Abraham and Moses, and pointed out the lack of strict chronology in the Gospel accounts, among many other cases. Thus, Scripture came to be seen as true insofar as it pointed to a moral way of life, a profound philosophy such as that of Kant or Hegel, an inexpressible experience, or as an indirect record of God's acts in history. As Pinnock put it, there was "a major and widespread shift in contemporary theology toward seeing the Bible as a fallible testament of human opinion and religious experience, not the reliable deposit and canon of normative instruction."[20]

On the other side of the ledger, conservatives unconsciously accepted the same premises of modernity in preoccupying themselves with the Bible's historicity, often developing elaborate and strained attempts at harmonization. Examples are obsession with how many times the cock crowed at Peter's denial or of how many times Jesus went to Jerusalem. As Hans Frei noted, the result of this focus upon the historical world "behind the text" was an actual eclipse of the biblical texts themselves, from both the liberal and conservative sides.[21] One can see how neither was sensitive to the actual nature of the texts in their historical context but were imposing modern assumptions about inspiration upon these ancient documents.

One of the most astonishing developments was the rise of the notion of "inerrancy" as a response to these pressures of modernity in the late nineteenth century. It is remarkable because it was virtually a wholesale adoption of a modern framework for inspiration from those who were champion antimodernists. They thus placed priority on factual truth that was clear, propositional, and certain.[22] Even as evangelicals were critical of modernity, they were obviously adopting a very modern, contemporary view of the prestige of science and philosophy for understanding Scripture. As Marsden sums up evangelical views of that time:

> Common Sense philosophy affirmed their ability to know "the facts" directly. With the Scriptures at hand as a compendium of facts, there was no need to go further. They needed only to classify the facts, and follow wherever they might lead.[23]

Evangelicals thus claimed to be scientific in their approach to Scripture. Scripture was an encyclopedia of facts corresponding to the natural world, which was itself a storehouse of natural facts. To be sure, this was the way most understood science at the time, and before the evolution controversy caused a rift between evangelicals and science, evangelicals wanted science to be on their side.

The effect of this modern paradigm upon conservatives implied that what was important about the Bible was the collection of propositional facts that could be identified, collated, and summarized.[24] The sharp distinction made between fact and theory meant that they saw their conclusions as certain without any admixture of theoretical interpretation. As Nancey Murphy and others have pointed out, the classical foundationalist metaphor that was so dominant in modernity pointed to the need to have an inerrant foundation in faith, just as philosophy and science were based on inerrant factual and rational foundations.[25] Since much of the theology of the movement came from those steeped in the Reformed tradition, which originally had been suspicious of the claims of reason, it is surprising that many at this time were almost unrestrained in their praise of how much their views were indubitable from a rational perspective. For example, B. B. Warfield, often seen as the father of the doctrine of inerrancy, claimed, "It is the distinction of Christianity that it has come into the world clothed with the mission to *reason* its way to dominion."[26]

At the same time, liberal theology was appealing to its own indubitable experiential foundation, perhaps more consistently accommodating the expectations of modernity.[27] Especially in the conservative approach to Scripture, the emphasis was placed on the literal propositions that were in Scripture or that could be derived directly from Scripture. The modern suspicion of figurative language from both sides left the dynamic sense and variety of Scripture far behind.[28] The message of Scripture as something that was mostly conveyed in symbol and story and more to be incarnated in life, even as it made important truth claims, was a conception hardly thinkable. As Thomas Kuhn later highlighted in his study of science, basic paradigms allow some things to be conceived and not others, which was true in this case.[29] It has taken more than one hundred years for it to be evident how much this conservative approach—on the surface quite anti-modern—as well as the liberal approach were so deeply influenced by the modern paradigm.

Pinnock called this paradigm "technical inerrancy," also known as "strict inerrancy."[30] It is the view that has tended toward a mechanical dictation theory. It is better called a "plenary-verbal" theory, where God so controlled all of the writing that Scripture is true in whatever it says about anything with little regard to historical context.[31] When questions about the absence of all of the original manuscripts were raised, the assumption was that any error could not have been in the originals (which have been lost to history) but was added later, making the view irrefutable since one could never verify the claim. Yet such an appeal to an indubitable foundation was necessary for the foundationalist assumptions of epistemology to be valid. This view had difficulty with basic questions such as, if God so controlled the writings, why do they reveal the differing personalities of the writers so much, even to the point of some exhibiting good Greek grammar and others not? Why are there deeply ambiguous passages because of not knowing the vowels in Hebrew? Even though few, why are there disputed manuscripts such as the presumably missing ending of Mark? Could not God have preserved the original manuscripts if they were so crucial and God exerted so much meticulous control?

At this point, with the benefit of hindsight we are in a better position to assess the strengths and weaknesses of both the conservative and liberal paradigms at that time. It is important in that they are still very influential and very much with us. These ways of approaching Scripture are still often the unconscious assumptions that are implicit in a church as plain or common sense. As noted in the previous chapter, Ludwig Wittgenstein pointed out that in philosophy "a picture held us captive." Similarly with regard to the Bible, a picture has held us transfixed. For Wittgenstein, the role of philosophy was to provide therapy for examining our pictures. Likewise, the therapeutic work of the theologian is to examine pictures like this that have shaped us, often unawares, especially after they come to light and seem to be so inconsistent with the nature of Scripture itself.

Contemporary Models

David Kelsey, identified with the Yale postliberal theology of Hans Frei and George Lindbeck, has helpfully pointed out that, despite the conflict over the Bible's authority, the strife is misplaced. It is difficult to find a major church group that does not ascribe to the Bible's primary authority.[32] As he puts it, biblical authority is virtually "analytic" for the church, that is, it is true by definition. Rather, what differs is the way people *construe* such authority in terms of varying paradigms. As we have seen, evangelicals have tended to construe Scripture as primarily conveying propositional facts that can be collated like an encyclopedia. George Lindbeck described this view as the "cognitive-propositional" paradigm and contrasted it with the liberal "experiential-expressive" paradigm that saw Scripture as primarily giving voice to a common, underlying religious experience had by all.[33] Lindbeck proposed his own "cultural-linguistic" approach that saw Scripture as providing the narrative basis for the church's social "form of life."[34] As this view developed, it emphasized the way various church communities (the readers) determine the plain meaning of the text, opening the door to relativism.[35] Kelsey indicated various ways that people have construed Scripture in terms of basic paradigms besides propositions and experience such as narrative meaning, existential meaning, or the Bible as a record of God's mighty acts. More recently, the Wisdom material has been emphasized, with Jesus as a sage or philosopher.[36]

Kevin Vanhoozer has pointed out a problem, in that these approaches tend to focus on one aspect of Scripture and make it determinative of the whole.[37] These approaches also suffer from an impoverished understanding of religious language, which tends to draw a line between propositional language on the one hand and the symbolic language of metaphor, parable, and narrative on the other, tending to see the former as cognitive (descriptive of reality) and the other as noncognitive or at least as less cognitive. One of the fresh changes is a reappraisal of language that tends to disarm these dilemmas. Vanhoozer draws on Paul Ricoeur's reminder that there are many genres in Scripture in which God communicates— cognitively—in a variety of ways.[38] A canonical view of inspiration, drawing on the whole of Scripture, will thus be complex and varied; it calls for "canonical competence" in giving due justice to the various genres. What is more significant, the content is in part mediated through the genre, or form, as much as the content. As Vanhoozer puts it:

> No one genre . . . is "foundational"; *all* are necessary in order adequately to render the gospel. A Christian theology without apocalyptic, or prophecy, or wisdom, not to mention narrative, would be unthinkable. It follows that the biblical interpreter must be competent in more than one literary form, for it is precisely the canonical forms that mediate to the reader the capacity to see, taste, and feel *biblically*.[39]

It also means that the growth of much of the material through oral stages, through multiple authors and editors, combined into a larger canon, and preserved in the context of the church indicates a much more complex view of inspiration than is common. Vanhoozer aptly understands biblical revelation therefore as "divine communicative action," or God "doing many things with words," in order to undergird the diverse ways in which Scripture is seen as "the Word of God."[40]

Giving due weight to this diversity, Ricoeur and the Yale theologians have nevertheless emphasized an important narrative background to the whole, just as legal maxims, which might be seen as freestanding, actually presupposed the story of God leading Israel out of Egypt to a land and making a covenant with them to which they are to be faithful.[41] One can argue that human identity as well as traditions of thought are inherently storied in that they presuppose a narrative movement through time. Alasdair MacIntyre, for example, argues that all three competing philosophical rivals for modern understanding are actually narratives. He points out that the Enlightenment scientific model prided itself on leaving behind tradition and story but ended up blinded to its own storied nature.[42] An aspect of reading each part of the Bible in terms of the whole Bible, therefore, is to develop narrative, canonical skill in applying the wider scriptural story, derived from various parts, back to each individual part. On the one hand, one has to develop a nuanced understanding of this wider narrative; on the other, one has to be able to let it be shaped by—and in turn shape—individual parts. This is the famed hermeneutical circle on a large scale.[43] One interprets the (canonical) whole in the light of the parts and the parts in light of the whole. An example is a passage such as John 15:7, which promises that "if you abide in me, and my words abide in you, ask for whatever you wish, and it will be done for you." This may suggest unlimited response to any request of God until one recalls that in the wider biblical story many desires went unfulfilled, and many saints suffered. Specifically, one can think of Paul's prayer to remove a "thorn in the flesh," but the response was no, "my grace is sufficient for you" (2 Cor 12:9). The canonical context (in addition to life experience) thus helps one put much more weight on the condition in John 15:7, "if you abide in me," and to consider that asking has something to do with desiring what God desires.

Vanhoozer himself has suggested an innovative way of doing justice to this unity in diversity through a paradigm of understanding Scripture as the script of a drama that the church is not just to understand but to perform.[44] In this way, the tendency to see the point of Scripture as just understanding propositions is overcome. Scripture is not complete, so to speak, until it is enacted. Vanhoozer has to turn to improvisatory theater as the model in order to make the transition from the biblical context to the contemporary context, but such an approach aids in showing how one can have a high view of Scripture yet be sensitive to all of the nuances, including all of the various genres. In his words, it is a "postpropositional," "postconservative," and "postmodern" model.[45]

As part of his approach, Vanhoozer emphasizes that Scripture also goes beyond, while including, the imparting of information by fostering canonical practices that we display as growth in Christlikeness, as an aspect of being canonically shaped. While his dramatic model sometimes seems forced, this latter emphasis fits naturally with Ricoeur's hermeneutical arc, mentioned in the previous chapter. Ricoeur points to the more natural way in which readers "appropriate" texts. Texts imply a "world in front of the text," an imaginative world in which the reader is invited to live. One is grasped initially by a text and its implications for living. In the final analysis, one moves from a text, say, of Peter denying Christ three times, not in terms of repeating that script, which we all too often do, but in terms of appropriating it in learning not to deny Christ in the face of opposition.

This appropriation or application can be understood in terms of living out the practices implied by a text. This is true whether one is speaking of modern history or fiction. The recent rash of books about George Washington, for example, depict him as a past figure, but even objective histories point to his story as one that might re-shape contemporary stories in terms of courage, perseverance, and a willingness to give up power.[46] A fictional work such as *Huckleberry Finn*, while the "world of the text" is firmly placed in a certain his-torical context, continues to inspire a "world in front of the text" that powerfully contests racism.

With this in mind, we can come to the scriptural text with all of its diversity and allow it, in Ricoeur's terms, to "project" a world in front of the text in which we might live—or practice. Both Ricoeur and Vanhoozer's models imply that one should let Scripture be Scripture and not allow a priori assumptions about what it must be like to dictate our understanding. Rather, we must more induc-tively let Scripture shape us canonically, with the help of the Holy Spirit. Ricoeur and Vanhoozer, of course, both understand the way in which the appropriation process is complex, involving not only all of the biblical genres and the Holy Spirit but also reason, experi-ence, and tradition.

One of the problems with the inerrantist approach was that it implied that objective, instrumental knowing was sufficient in itself. The goal of Scripture, rather, is understanding at an intui-tive, embodied level. This does not rule out factual knowledge and even propositional knowledge. It presupposes, in terms of Ricoeur's hermeneutical arc, a stage of criticism and examination. Theology indeed can be helpful in spelling out some of the propositional under-pinnings, but one might say that the factual and propositional is nec-essary but not sufficient. What the church has consistently affirmed is the sufficiency of the Spirit's working through the Scripture to foster canonical practices and a canonical life. The ability of the var-ied genres of Scripture to transform—the narratives, the legal, the proverbs, the parables, the sermons—is well attested by "training in righteousness" (2 Tim 3:16-17). This means that Scripture, in a sense, is not understood until it reaches the stage of appropriation, the postcritical naivete, the level of transformation of our way of living in the world. This, of course, involves creative, imaginative appropriation in different times and contexts. We might say, with Gadamer, "It is enough to say that we understand in a *different* way, *if we understand at all.*"[47] Again, it is the purpose of theology, of sermons, of church (the *ekklesia*) to help with that creative translation. In this sense, the postliberal Yale theology is correct to emphasize the role of the church. Understanding the Bible is ultimately ecclesial understanding and is impossible apart from tradition.

On the other hand, neither the church nor tradition in principle is as authoritative as Scripture. In a formal way, the Protestant churches, at least, have attested that tradition and the church are fallible but that the Scriptures are infallible. In reality, it is also true that *interpretations* of Scripture are fallible and subject to testing by returning to Scripture. Tradition and the contemporary ecclesial context are like theology in providing a context and aid for the understanding and appropriation of Scripture, but they are not deemed as authoritative as Scripture. While in practice these are difficult to disentangle, the "Scripture principle" provides a crucial basis for continuing prophetic critique and reformation of tradition and the church.

None of this is possible, finally, apart from the Holy Spirit. It is interesting that Paul says in Ephesians 6 to take up the "sword of the Spirit," which is "the Word of God" (v. 17). It is true that anyone with a good mind can study the Bible and learn factual aspects of it. To let it transform one into a living out of spiritual practices can only stem from an intimate walk with the Spirit and the Word. This was captured in the seal of a seminary where I taught, which was an open Bible with a dove, representing the Holy Spirit, hovering over it. One would never suppose that "walking in the Spirit" (Rom 8:4) is a mere matter of learning factual information; rather, it requires an in-depth, intuitive feel for the ways of the Spirit. The book of Hebrews suggests that this only comes through practice (5:11-14), which may be surprising given our penchant for the hope of a quick, supernatural change without much effort on our part. In other words, maturity only comes about over time, through a process, which applies even to learning to read and appropriate Scripture. This understanding will be significant when we treat the theology of the Christian life (sanctification). The point is also that this is not a purely subjective, individualistic matter any more than learning any scientific discipline is subjective. It does involve, however, indwelling the reality of God as conveyed through Scripture and the Spirit so much that one develops a tacit sense of the word of God. This is not an exact science, so there is room for dialogue and difference as Christians seek to plumb the direction of God in their lives.

The movement of the Enlightenment period was to begin to study the Scripture like other books were studied, almost as an exact science. In many ways, this was a gain. It allowed for genuine examination of the historical background and literary dimensions of Scripture. Yet it also fostered, with its objective assumptions, a way of reading that minimized commitment and accentuated detachment. This style of reading is now under heavy fire even in the academy because its assertion of detached, presuppositionless comprehension is so untenable.

Conversely, reading Scripture from a faith perspective just cannot be slotted into the neutral, detached Enlightenment ideal. Scripture demands to be read with openness, with expectancy, with passion, and with conviction. It calls for a reverential attitude, not to a book but to the God who speaks through it and to whom it attests. This means that a more genuinely Christian approach to Scripture is a practice involving its own virtues and excellences. It involves humility—not assuming that a problem lies in Scripture but with one's interpretation. It involves expectancy, which is why one might read and re-read Scripture, trusting that one will learn about God and life and be transformed by canonical practices. It involves diligence and studiousness. Meditative practices for the study of Scripture, such as the *lectio divina* (divine reading), teach that one must be able to "live into" the world of the text, which takes time, in order to understand it. Then one must be able imaginatively to "live out" to the world in front of the text, which takes even greater imagination. This is because such a "second understanding" involves drawing on all dimensions of the Wesleyan Quadrilateral and then, even more challenging, applying the meaning to one's particular life.

What may seem a naive, pietistic reading does not rule out criticism, because one's interpretations, and those of others, are themselves fallible and must always be brought before the test of Scripture. It is, in fact, a lack of piety to avoid applying prophetic critique to our own interpretations. Sometimes it is only one's passion and conviction about the reliability of Scripture that can move one to change a traditional belief that no longer stands up to the canonical test. This is a common experience—and should be. For example, I was nurtured in an environment that valued Scripture but also limited women's leadership roles. As I was confronted with different understandings of Scripture, I painfully had to acknowledge to myself that my view and that of my tradition could not be sustained. If Scripture was not at stake, the easy way at the time would have been not to change. It was because of Scripture that I could not walk away from the evidence, so to speak. The conviction about the authority of Scripture as God's word then implied a commitment to support women in ministry, eventually to leaving a much-loved teaching position and seeking one that supported women in ministry. Such self-criticism, repeated over and over in the history of the church, is also one of the virtues and excellences of the approach of faith to Scripture.

As Vanhoozer has suggested, the tables might be turned, and we might learn something about reading other books through the virtues involved in reading Scripture.[48] While one would not have the final trust in other books as with Scripture, one could do well to approach other books by reading with expectancy, giving the author the benefit of the doubt, and not reading with cynicism—approaches that any author would appreciate.

Vanhoozer's emphasis on canonical virtues underlines the recent emphasis by many theologians, as pointed out in the previous chapter, on understanding the Christian faith in terms of Christian practices.[49] The connection is that excellent practices rely upon virtues such as we have just mentioned. Reading Scripture well is a practice that involves virtues such as humility, discernment, and courage. Understanding Scripture is, moreover, not just learning new factual information; it is incomplete until its purpose of fostering canonical practices is evidenced in readers' lives.

Here is a place for a salutary reminder: few debates since the Reformation have been more bitter and divisive than debates about Scripture. From the bloodshed at the time of the Reformation to more recent firings and denominational splits in the twentieth century, conflict about the nature of Scripture has often had the dubious honor of being an example of what in philosophy is called a "performative contradiction." In other words, if I contradict with my actions what I am professing with my words, I am performatively undermining myself. (In biblical language, it was simply called hypocrisy.) It is a shame that so often Christians, professing sincerely to be defending biblical authority that teaches love of one's enemy, have done so in mean-spirited and bitter ways, often caricaturing and thus in essence bearing false witness concerning their opponent's positions. If one is defending biblical authority, the least one would expect would be that it is done in such a way that shows that one takes the Bible seriously and thus portrays canonical virtues such as honesty, fairness, and magnanimity (grace).

AN INCARNATIONAL VIEW OF SCRIPTURE

The Holy Spirit through Scripture thus inculcates canonical practices, one of which is the practice and virtue involved in reading Scripture well—the hermeneutical circle again. With our vantage point of being able to look behind us, we can perhaps re-envision in exciting, if not also challenging, ways a current paradigm for understanding the authority of Scripture. If we were treating the doctrine of Christ first in theology, we would have talked about the centrality of the incarnation, the fact that "the Word (*logos*) became flesh" (incarnate; John 1:14). This means that the greatest revelation of God to which Christians attest is one that is securely located in history and in a person. It would not be surprising then to suspect that the primary authority for understanding the incarnation of Christ, namely, Scripture, would itself be incarnational, rooted in history and in persons. This is not to equate the two, Christ and Scripture, but it is to recognize the distinctiveness of the Christian understanding of Scripture even as opposed to other religions of the Book. This means that we can appreciate the historical development of the canon, that is, the books that make up the Christian Bible, with an affirmation of this rootedness in history. This does not mean, however, that Christians have not often popularly thought of their Scripture as a kind of static entity, almost as if it dropped out of heaven, premade and prefab, as it were, written by a single divine author with little mediation. While virtually all theologians reject this nowadays, many have in practice veered close to a mechanical-diction view of Scripture, whereby the human agency is virtually null. This view of Scripture actually is more reflective of an Islamic or Mormon view that downplays the historical and personal mediation of the word of God. We are used to understanding a Christian view of God as being monotheistic yet different from other monotheistic religions. We are not so used to seeing a Christian view of Scripture as distinctive from other peoples of the Book. Nevertheless, there is a distinctively Christian approach to Scripture, which is modeled on the incarnation itself.

Canonization

This incarnational Christian approach to Scripture becomes more clear when one examines the development of the New Testament. The first writings were apparently Paul's letters, in the fifties, about two decades after Christ's death and resurrection. The Gospels are usually dated from the sixties through the nineties. Apparently, much oral tradition occurred in between, with different regions harboring different perspectives that coalesced into the various Gospels, for example, Mark from Rome, John from Ephesus, and Matthew from Antioch. The very fact that we have four different Gospels is significant in that various perspectives and personalities are reflected, not to mention independent perspectives on Christ from Paul and the book of Hebrews. Such a developmental process is a far cry from thinking that the Bible was written by God alone and dropped out of heaven. Even early on, this complexity bothered people enough that Tatian, a student of Justin the Martyr, in the second century made the four into one gospel. Wisely, the early church did not follow his lead. It apparently wanted to preserve the distinctive voices and perspectives reflected in the different sources, in other words, the incarnational nature of Scripture.

In addition, it took some time for the church to establish a New Testament canon. At first, it was not even obvious that more than the Old Testament was necessary. Ignatius of Antioch, writing around 113, simply affirmed the Old Testament but did not appeal to new authoritative writings. Justin the Martyr, however, around 153 in Rome did appeal to the Gospels and to the letters of Paul. In part, the church's move to a specific canon was prompted by controversy—not an unusual stimulus! Marcion had come to Rome around 139 rejecting the Old Testament altogether and accepted only parts of Luke and Paul's main letters. His reasoning was that the Old Testament God, as creator of the inferior material world, was a different God completely from the Christian God. Valentinus was a prominent gnostic with similar sentiments about the material world who also came to Rome around 140 and rejected the Old Testament.

In response, the church moved toward the canon that we now have. The famous Muratorian fragment, which some have thought to be written in the late second century, has a list of New Testament books that contain all of the current ones except for Hebrews, James, and 1 and 2 Peter—but it includes the *Apocalypse of Peter* and the Wisdom of Solomon. Even though the main core of the Gospels and the main letters of Paul were settled upon by mid-second century, the exact twenty-seven did not seem to be strongly accepted until the late fourth century, and even then some continued to be disputed for several centuries.[50] Several books were debated along the way, often representing different geographical regions. Revelation, for example, was for a time accepted in the West but not in the East. Other early second-century books such as the *Didache* and the *Shepherd of Hermas* were accepted as authoritative by some but not finally by all.

Such a history is bothersome to some who assume a nonincarnational understanding of Scripture. It appears too messy and unseemly to have so much involvement of people, history, geography, and politics in a matter so important—that is, until one thinks again of the incarnation of Jesus Christ, which was also rooted in a person, in history, in a specific locale, and certainly included politics. It is understandable that anyone who has seen up close the human—all too human—frailties and foibles involved in church politics might wonder how God could work in such an atmosphere. We would rather God go it alone, so to speak. The problem is that, speaking from a perspective of faith, that is not the way God did it—either in Christ or in the testimony to Christ found in Scripture. We may even have some questions for God in heaven along this line as to the wisdom of entrusting so much to human beings, but this seems to be God's way. The history of canonization is thus fraught with theological meaning itself.

Looked at from another angle, however, one can think of the incarnation as such a rich event that no one perspective could do it justice—especially when one is thinking of human attempts at communication in very human language, remembering that the Greek of the New Testament is called *koine*, or common, because it was the common spoken Greek, any attempt at understanding can be both revealing and limiting. Why would we expect that such a complex, marvelous event could be exhausted by any number of books? The last words of the Gospel of John get at this point well: "There are also many other things that Jesus did; if every one of them were written down, I suppose that the world itself could not contain the books that would be written" (21:25). The early church recognized that one book could not do justice to the events without the aid of other books—and even these books could not say everything.

So the Christian Scripture is understood as arising through history, expressed through the various and diverse human personalities who were involved, and reflecting the historical context of the various times in which it arose. When one is thinking of the whole Bible, that time frame is rather extensive. It is difficult to tell how far back the history of the oral tradition behind the written tradition goes. When it comes to the written tradition, we have a little better idea of the time frame, but even then, texts extend back for millennia. Especially in the Old Testament, written works developed over a period of perhaps a thousand years. When one thinks of English and how much it has changed since, for example, the King James version of the Bible, not to mention Chaucer's English in the Middle Ages, one can appreciate just what kind of changes are possible in a language over a millennium. We know that in the New Testament someone like Luke, for example, explicitly says that he was aware of and presumably drew upon other sources (Luke 1:1-4). A common understanding is that Luke and Matthew utilized Mark in the writing of their Gospels. The second Epistle of Peter seems to be cognizant of the writings of Paul and even regards them as Scripture (3:15-16). Thus, a great deal of development occurs—even in the telescoped period of the New Testament—from various oral traditions to various written documents.

Just accentuate this process when thinking about the Old Testament. In fact, the Old Testament canon was not settled until well into the Christian era. The focus upon the written word likely did not occur until after the exile, that is, in the sixth through fourth centuries B.C.E. The Old Testament itself gives evidence of drawing on previous documents that arose at different times in history. It reveals development even in the understanding of God, for example, when Jeremiah and Ezekiel around 600 B.C.E. indicated that, in the past, people had thought that the sins of the fathers were visited upon the children, but now it would no longer be so (Jer 31:29-30; Ezek 18:2-3). Especially when one is thinking of the difference between an old covenant and a new covenant, the developmental shifts from the Old Testament to the New Testament are rather marked. Jesus' Sermon on the Mount, for example, is the stellar example of how Jesus could interpret much of the Old Testament in a dramatically new framework, yet without disregarding the Old Testament (Matt 5–7). Some of Jesus' emphases were present in the Old Testament, too, but they were in tension with other emphases that had arisen over time. Like the prophets of old, he put much less emphasis on the sacrificial system and the technicalities of worship. Like the Pharisees, Jesus affirmed bodily resurrection and an afterlife against the more conservative Sadducees, who were following more closely the Old Testament Torah, which did not have a robust view of an afterlife. Jesus, however, was not the first to talk about hypocrisy and a worship that was full of outward form but vacuous in internal content. It is difficult to get more scathing than Amos, in the eighth century B.C.E., who said that God hated and despised their festivals and their singing (Amos 5:21-24). Jeremiah could even suggest that the sacrificial system was not something that God had commanded (Jer 7:22).

This means that when thinking of the inspiration of Scripture, we cannot only think of a single author being inspired at a given moment. Along with this picture in our minds, we often think of interpretation as figuring out what that one author intended to say. The problem is that we do not know the authors of many of the books of the Bible and that many of the books of the Bible draw on other sources and have been edited. For example, 1 and 2 Samuel specifically refer to drawing on several other sources, and most scholars see Genesis as composed from earlier, separate works as reflected in the two creation stories and differences in terminology. As mentioned, Luke and Matthew are usually seen as drawing on Mark, and many think that Matthew and Luke drew on another work, named Q (for *Quelle*, the German word for "source"). In short, the process of inspiration has to include all of this history—sometimes from oral tradition passed down until it comes to writing, which is perhaps then edited and included in other works. While issues of intention are still germane, the focus has to be kept on the canonical text rather than, as has sometimes been the case, on a hidden author's intention "behind the text." As one can see, a simple hermeneutic or theology of inspiration will not be adequate.

And then these documents must be preserved for history. Think of the historical works mentioned in the Old Testament that we do not possess and the many other Old Testament prophets whose words we do not have. The dramatic findings in the twentieth century of the Dead Sea Scrolls, the Gnostic Gospels, and other works remind us how precious it is for an ancient work to survive.[51] Preservation thus has to be a part of the providence of inspiration. Since we do not have any original manuscripts, the work of copyists, which is seen to be remarkably reliable though not infallible, is also crucial. Then we have to consider the judgment of numerous Jews and Christians who esteemed certain books as inspired more than others. Such acts of spiritual discernment and acknowledgment, which can be seen as *illumination* as a counterpart to *inspiration*, are as important as the works themselves; otherwise, we would likely not have the works at all—and even if we did, we might not value them. In fact, illuminative reading is a continuing process. Every generation of Christians must continue this valuation, or it will be lost. Part of the role of theology is to aid us in seeing how to value Scripture as "inspired by God" in light of all that we know in the twenty-first century.

Scripture, therefore, must be understood as a very human work through which the divine speaks, as "treasure in earthen vessels" (2 Cor 4:7, KJV). The incarnational nature of Scripture implies that we pay attention, which may require arduous study, to the various writers and perspectives in their various times and places. On the other side of this equation, it means that we actually have access to the word of God, for it involves human language, such as we speak, and human beings, such as we are. We can have insight into the authors' motives and purposes because we, too, have motives and purposes.

Another major realization in understanding Scripture stems from the easily overlooked fact that each work does not stand alone but now stands in a canonical context; thus, each work must be interpreted in light of the full canon and of the wider framework of revelation. An effect of the modern penchant for analysis is that much effort has been devoted to breaking Scripture down into component parts, trying to discern the earlier documents that have been edited (tradition and redaction criticism) and the even earlier smaller units of oral tradition that were likely passed along (form criticism). While this analysis has sometimes been helpful and is worthwhile, as we have seen it led to what Frei called "the eclipse of the biblical narrative" for both theological conservatives and liberals. Both were obsessed with finding out the true "world behind the text."

More recently, the tide has turned to look at the significance of each work in its place in the canon and how this affects meaning (canonical hermeneutics or even "theological interpretation of the

Bible").[52] For much of Christian history, this has meant that the earlier has to be interpreted in light of the later or, one might say, more complete and fuller revelation. Hebrews 1:1 is a striking example of what has been called "progressive revelation"[53]: "Long ago God spoke to our ancestors in many and various ways by the prophets, but in these last days he has spoken to us by a Son. . . . He is . . . the exact imprint of God's very being." It may seem a little odd to put it this way, but it does not take too much reflection, in light of this passage in Hebrews and in light of Jesus Christ as the climax of God's revelation, to realize that Abraham did not understand as much of God as Moses, or Moses as much as Isaiah, or Isaiah as much as Jeremiah, or Jeremiah as much as Jesus. Such realization of the dynamics of Scripture has enormous import when it comes to development of a "biblical" or canonical view of any doctrine.

More-recent emphasis on the canon helps one see how each work contributes to a larger whole. It helps deal with how Ecclesiastes, whose theme is the emptiness and perhaps meaninglessness of life, and Esther, which does not mention the name of God, can fit into the canon as supplementary but not as central. A canonical approach will look to the center of gravity in the Torah and the major prophets in the Old Testament, and the Gospels and Paul in the New Testament, just as the early church did. The books of 2 Peter, Revelation, and Jude have their place in the New Testament, but as supplements and not as the center. At times, however, a book like Philemon may rise to the fore as a critique of slavery, or the book of Esther may rise, after the Holocaust, as a critique of genocide. Again, such an approach calls for a complex hermeneutic and more theological sensitivity than one might think. Discerning levels of importance in the canon is not a way of minimizing inspiration—it is a way of doing justice to it. It is following, one might say, the divine pattern of inspiration rather than imposing a neater, but distorting, pattern of our own liking or culture upon it.

The Two Horizons

An aspect of the incarnational nature of Scripture itself that is often overlooked and unrealized is the fact that the horizon, so to speak, of

Scripture may be quite different than that of later readers, namely, our own. The natural thing to do is to bring to the text our own horizon; we can do no other. As Gadamer has pointed out, this is not a bad thing per se. It actually gives us a foothold in understanding a text. We likely would not even be interested in reading Scripture apart from our contemporary horizon that values it so much. All understanding involves such a "fusion of horizons."[54]

The danger, however, is that we do this uncritically and unconsciously. We thus impose our own assumptions upon the text, transforming the text into something that it is not. This is actually a rather serious thing. If we are concerned for biblical authority and for understanding the word of God in God's revelation, it is important that we understand the text as best we can. By distorting the text through imposing our own presuppositions upon it, we can end up missing the meaning of the text and go away believing that we have understood the text when in fact we may have strayed far from it. Mark Noll, speaking of habits of evangelical reading of the Bible, similarly warns, "It is all too easy to allow forms of thought which appear to be only common sense in our century, but which are largely foreign to the world of Scripture, to dictate interpretations of what the biblical writers must have intended."[55] To make matters even worse, in thinking that we have understood the text and in trying to be faithful and committed to it, we may be rather forceful and dogmatic toward others, requiring or mandating that they share our understanding. We may, in fact, try to impose our understanding of the text upon them, identifying our understanding with the word of God itself, when we ourselves have seriously misunderstood the text. The stakes are high.

One of the first heresies in the church was the gnostic heresy, recently highly publicized due to the appeal to other gospels found at Nag Hammadi in 1945. The upshot of this heresy was that it had a difficult time believing that God could come close enough to the material world to become incarnate. In other words, a great gap looms between the spirit and the body. Most gnostics had a very difficult time affirming the true humanity of Jesus. The irony is that we may veer quite close to that heresy by understanding Scripture in a gnostic way. We do this when we do not do justice to its historical and contextual nature and presuppose that what we understand in our own historical horizon is the universal horizon for all people in all times. In other words, we take an ahistorical, atemporal, and disembodied approach to the text, which actually is gnostic but not Christian.

Such an approach cannot take account of cultural changes that impact our understanding of the Bible, such as the development of modern historiography and critical methodology. We have, for example, several assumptions about the way attention to history should be given. Modern historiography pays a lot of attention to factual detail, chronological development, and attention to supporting evidence. Along with developments in philosophy, this has resulted in a suspicion of symbolic language and of history that has an agenda.[56] Unfortunately, that means that we are not in a very good position to understand what the ancient writers were doing when they were treating history as compared to what we are doing. A fascinating example of this is the fact that in all of the literature about Jesus, including the canonical and the noncanonical material, no one at the time apparently thought that it was important to give any kind of physical description of Jesus. One of the first things that we would have done is something that apparently never crossed their mind. The huge gap in the story of Jesus between his birth and his ministry is another aspect we would have narrated. The ones telling the story then did not apparently deem it important. We may even have noticed that several of the accounts of Jesus, such as Mark, John, Hebrews, and the Pauline literature did not think it important to deal with Jesus' birth or with the prehistory to his ministry. This reminds us of how far removed their purpose and intent was from ours.

The use of heavily metaphorical language stemming from their oral culture is also not something that our dominantly print culture is prepared to appreciate.[57] Our tradition of actually being suspicious of the use of symbolic language not only means that we are inclined not to understand it very well, but we can easily misunderstand their language by assuming that their use of language and numbers should be taken literally. For example, in the classroom when we are investigating something, we usually assign research papers, which have a well understood structure: logical or chronological development, supporting evidence, and careful argumentation in literal language. It is striking that in virtually all of the Bible, no one took that as an appropriate way to convey truth. Perhaps it never even crossed anyone's mind that such a pattern would be a way to transmit truth. Yet it is our chief and first way, sometimes perhaps the only way, that we consider adequate in exploring truth. What happens then is that we may falsely assume that their use of numbers and their use of symbolic language is like our modern historiography and prosaic language. Hence, we have some of the great misinterpretations and distortions of Scripture, especially associated with predictions of the end of the world.

We may thus misread Scripture even with the best of intentions. Because we have a high view of Scripture, we want to take what it says seriously. But because we are not aware of the magnitude of the differences from their context, we interpret poorly. We may think that we are actually standing *under* the authority of Scripture, but subtly we have placed ourselves and our contemporary culture and horizon *above* Scripture. We may not realize that it is quite a difficult thing to "stand under the text." This is why the practice of biblical interpretation is a virtue: it is a practice that matures through hard work into excellence. The hermeneutical challenge is to let our presuppositions, our culture, and our horizon be challenged by a very different one. It involves trying to understand material written from a very different perspective and not to superimpose our standards and our assumptions carelessly upon the text.

This last point suggests another one of our challenges. Along with the developments in technology and the standard of living in the modern West, there is often a deep-seated assumption of superiority over other cultures. It is easy to go to the Bible and assume that our horizon is the only one or the best one. This may conceal from us actually the great difficulty that we may have in interpreting the biblical text. This is not to gainsay all of the benefits and developments that modernity has brought. Even when it comes to the Bible, we now have access to manuscripts unavailable to the church since the first few centuries. We can do computer searches and detailed analysis that the church has never been able to do. We now have access to translations and Bibles like few Christians in history. We could easily assume that we are in a far superior position.

On the other hand, because of our shaping by our scientific and technological tradition, we may actually be "biblically challenged" in significant ways. Because our textual culture is quite different from the kind of oral culture behind the biblical writings, we may have difficulty understanding what they were doing. We may not appreciate them and, at times, may not even understand them. We may have more difficulty following poetic language and narrative as a way of conveying the deepest truths than many other "less-developed" cultures, even in our time. Therefore, while modern Western persons may have some significant advantages, we also have some disadvantages, which probably could be said of any culture that has encountered the biblical story. So we should not underestimate the difference between the ancient biblical horizon and our horizon.

As soon as we are overwhelmed by these challenges, however, we can observe that Scripture has had an amazing capacity to speak to diverse people across the centuries. Despite the differences, Scripture deals with people who experience the very universal human phenomena of birth and death, joy and tragedy, hope and despair. They rejoiced over the birth of children and grieved over barrenness and the loss of children. They praised God and they questioned God. They wondered about the suffering of innocents and found strength in the midst of crises. They manifested jealousy, pride, and anger as well as compassion, humility, and peace. In other words, the strikingly down-to-earth nature of Scripture along with its universal themes, quite apart from a special sense of divine inspiration, have allowed it to speak powerfully again and again across millennia.

Hermeneutical Implications

Several implications flow from these reflections. One is that, in interpreting Scripture, we must pay serious attention to the historical context. This means, for example, that the language in which it was written is significant. It is not incidental that most of the Old Testament is written in Hebrew and that the New Testament is written in Greek. These books have to be understood in light of these languages, in those times, with all of the awareness of the imprecision of translation, as any bilingual person knows.

At the same time, Christians generally have not placed as much significance upon the original language as, for example, Muslims have with the Koran. In other words, believers regard translated Scriptures as being adequately the word of God. A good translation is thought to convey the word of God, and it is not a requirement only to use the Greek and Hebrew. Understanding the Greek and Hebrew certainly is helpful, even crucial, for providing an adequate translation and for understanding the meaning. The practice of the Christian churches shows that there is allowance for both sides of the issue.

A second implication is that we must be sensitive and appreciative of the way in which the biblical message comes to us in highly symbolic and narrative language that is distant from the way that we typically express and analyze reality. Fortunately, it is not totally different in that we do use symbolic language and narrative—perhaps just not nearly as centrally or as well as they did. We have to guard against the tendency to assume that the language being used is a kind of propositional description or a literal description without paying attention to the dynamics of a story such as plot, character development, and symbolic meaning. We have to pay due attention to the switches from one genre to another where, in many cases, "the medium is the message."

A third issue is to understand the historical development that takes place through the Old Testament and into the New Testament. A basically Christian understanding is that the fullness of God's revelation is in Jesus Christ. It implies that there was not the fullness of that revelation prior to Christ. While some would come to the Bible as a "flat Bible," this is a very ahistorical and unincarnational way to approach it. If we think in terms of what is called "progressive revelation," then we can understand that God is being revealed to people throughout the Old Testament in ways compatible with their ability to understand. John Calvin spoke of this as God "accommodating" the limitations of their understanding.[58] At best, he thought, God speaks baby talk to us because of our limitations. We should always be aware, therefore, that revelation does not mean utter and thorough explanation, but it is accommodated to particular places, cultures, languages, translations, and concepts. There were places where the Israelites had a dramatic understanding of God, and there were places where they pretty clearly did not grasp the way God is later understood in light of the revelation in Jesus Christ. For example, polygamy seemed to be seen by many in the Old Testament as consistent with God's will. Jesus pointed out in the Sermon on the Mount that the understanding of divorce in the Old Testament was not really God's intention. Genocide, under the name of holy war, was thought to be consistent with the will of God in some of the Old Testament, which is difficult to reconcile with the perspective of Jesus in the New Testament. Unless we have an idea of God changing in God's basic character, which is almost universally considered unorthodox among Christian theologians, then it is difficult to conclude that what happened was that God changed; rather, what it looks like is that the *understanding* of God changed and developed over the course of time. This is the meaning of progressive revelation.

While this approach enables us to avoid the seeming contradictions in the Bible and to make some aspects of interpretation quite a bit easier, it does represent a challenge. It puts a burden upon the believing interpreter to discern, in light of the whole canon, what is consistent with the nature of God and the purposes of God in places where they are not clear. For example, in the Old Testament, we have the commandments "You shall love the Lord your God with all your heart, with all your soul, and with all your might" (Deut 6:5) and also "You shall love your neighbor as yourself" (Lev 19:18). It is easy to see these as revelatory of God in the full and universal sense. It is much more difficult to see holy war, the practice of polygamy, or God hardening someone's heart (as with Pharaoh, Exod 10:1) as consistent with the understanding of God conveyed in Jesus Christ. Even harder is Psalm 137, where the prayer is that God will dash the enemy's children against the rocks (v. 9). In the context, there is no hint that there is anything wrong with this sentiment, and one can imagine someone taking from the psalm that we are to exemplify such a vengeful attitude. It is only in light of the wider message of the whole Bible that we would have a more critical perspective.

A fourth aspect of understanding Scripture is to realize that, obviously, Scripture does not say everything about everything. Sometimes issues are treated in Scripture that are not pertinent today, and sometimes issues that are very burning today are not addressed at all in Scripture. For example, the question of whether one should eat food sacrificed to idols receives extensive treatment in Paul (Rom 14; 1 Cor 8). Conversely, a woman's right to vote in political elections is not on the radar—and took twenty centuries to be realized. The challenge of interpreting Scripture is thus often taking issues that are treated, such as the former, and applying them to untreated issues such as the latter. What is even more disconcerting is that sometimes issues that are treated today seem to be addressed in Scripture, but in reality are addressed in a quite different way or are actually tangential to the contemporary issue. Various groups quickly read their traditional ecclesial practices into the instructions about women in 1 Timothy, into the selection of "deacons" in Acts 6, or into the laying on of hands in Paul and Barnabas' appointment as missionaries in Acts 13, yet do not realize the gulf between the two horizons. A more complex example along this line is dealing with the contemporary question of what happens to those who never had a chance to hear the gospel on the basis of Romans 1–2, when it is apparent that this current issue is not the focus. Paul is focused on the need to proclaim the gospel, not worrying about what happens if it is not heard. Without careful attention to the context in the Scripture, this difference in purpose and context can be missed and thus set up serious misapprehension. A heavy burden, therefore, is laid upon the interpreter.

Fifth, the case of Galileo, which we considered early in the chapter, reminds us that Scripture's purpose is focused upon God and God's relationship to the world and not the transmission of arcane scientific facts. In fact, if God were interested in revealing interesting scientific facts such as the location of the earth or the age of the universe, one wonders why God did not reveal much more helpful information such as the nature of germs, viruses, and their antidotes, which could have saved millions of lives. It is clear that such is not the nature of God's revelatory purposes. In this connection, two classic passages on inspiration are very helpful. According to 2 Timothy 3:16-17, "All Scripture is inspired by God and is profitable for teaching, for reproof, for correction, and for training in righteousness." This practical, spiritual, theological purpose—rather than what we would consider scientific—has been called inspiration in terms of "faith and practice." John 20:31 states, "But these are written that you might believe that Jesus is the Christ, the Son of God, and that believing you may have life in his name." This purpose of the Gospel of John also indicates the practical nature of special revelation. A phrase enshrined in several Baptist confessions, apparently coined by John Locke, says of Scripture: "It has God for its author, salvation for its end, and truth, without mixture of error, for its matter."[59] While this appears on the surface to be a "strong inerrantist" statement, it actually represents what one might call the "infallibilist" position.[60] At the time it was written, the confession was apparently reacting to the excessive claims about Scripture being made, even in terms of grammar and spelling. It specifically says that the purpose of Scripture is "salvation," and truth pertains not to the form, such as grammar—and perhaps one could add the cultural framework in which it was expressed, such as a flat earth and a geocentric universe—but to its "matter," again the salvific and practical content. Unfortunately, it is not always so easy to separate form and matter. Belief in God entails some things about the creation, as we shall see, such as it being good, not inherently evil, not an illusion, and not divine—all of which have been major philosophical and religious alternatives. In fact, one could argue that such theological beliefs undergird and support scientific investigation. There is overlap, just not where it has sometimes seemed to lie.

Sixth, this reminds us that even with the aid of Scripture, and as important as Scripture is, it does not relieve the church and the individual Christian from a significant challenge of understanding the word of God. We often come to Scripture looking for a quick-and-easy answer. Rather, much of the time, what we find in Scripture is more like background principles, a narrative context, or a guiding framework. Sensitivity then must be brought into play in a holistic kind of discerning, judgment about how Scripture applies today. This implies, of course, that a premium is placed on the understanding of current issues in order to relate them well to Scripture. The area of science and religion is littered with casualties of failures to do so. In the application of Scripture, limited or forced or even ignorant understanding of contemporary issues can be as crippling as similar failings when it comes to Scripture.

Sometimes Scripture does address issues fairly directly. For example, if you ask yourself the question, Should I love my enemy or hate my enemy? the answer is rather clear: we are to love our enemies (Matt 5:44). The difficult question that follows, however, is, What does that mean in this circumstance? Consequently, even in the case of a fairly explicit command, a great deal of discernment is often required in order to apply Scripture. This is the place for the phronetic thinking that we developed in the previous chapter, that is, practical wisdom. Aristotle thought that one could never come up with enough rules to cover the details of every case, much like we think of when legalists are never able to come up with enough laws. In the Christian context, what is needed is this kind of practical wisdom that is shaped by walking in the Spirit, Scripture, the Christian tradition, formation in the life of the church, and also knowledge of the contemporary world.

As we discussed in the previous chapter, all of these kinds of things come into play as in the Wesleyan Quadrilateral, even if understood in the more complex way that I suggested. The surprising benefit is that applying Scripture in the contemporary world in that kind of depth often boomerangs upon Scripture in such a way that we begin to understand the message of Scripture much more deeply through the very process of application. This would be true in the cases of Philemon and Esther mentioned above. Such a hermeneutical spiral is why someone like Gadamer could say that one can never separate the application part of the hermeneutical process from what is often thought of as the earlier stages.[61] One cannot neatly separate, as exegetes were wont to claim in the past, "what it meant" from "what it means." That is also why one cannot segregate theology from biblical exegesis.

Seventh, although one might be getting discouraged at this point, seeing all of the difficulties of interpretation that we have detailed as being a burden and a problem, one might look at it a different way. It can be seen as part of the adventure and pilgrimage of the Christian faith. The New Testament recognizes that the Christian faith involves a movement from infancy to maturity, from being babes in Christ to being adults in the faith. Some traditions put emphasis on this as a process of great growth over a long period of time. Others do not think that much growth is possible; others think that maturity or perfection can be reached in a short time, perhaps by a supernaturally bestowed second blessing. The view that I prefer is one that involves the Christian taking a long time, even a lifetime, in growth, which we will explore in the chapter on the doctrine of salvation. This seems to be the picture that is suggested by the apostle Paul in chapter 3 of Philippians. He says, in an almost paradoxical way, that those who are mature will think like him in realizing that they are not mature (v. 15). In other words, a mark of maturity is realizing that there is farther to go; Paul strains for what lies ahead so that he may reach the goal. In this light, we can affirm with Paul and 1 Corinthians 13 that we see in part and know in part (13:12). All of Christian life is a process of not only growth but, more importantly, getting to know God better and better—a process that, given the greatness and majesty of God, is something that not only can take a lifetime but might quite possibly take all of eternity (an issue that we will explore in the chapter on eschatology). It is upon this journey that we have the opportunity and gift to be able to embark in this life. With regard to Scripture, this means that the spiritual understanding and application of Scripture is a lifelong process of faith seeking understanding. For instance, our understanding of sacrificial love may deepen as we experience such love from others and then are called upon to exercise it ourselves. Can anyone, however, plumb the full depths of sacrificial love in a human lifetime?

Eighth, another dimension of revelation, therefore, is not just Scripture but the continuing understanding of God and of Scripture itself through the reflection of the church. This brings in and includes all of church history. This is because Scripture cannot be understood apart from interpretation that has been ongoing now for two thousand years, longer than that when one includes the understanding of the Old Testament. This raises what, for many Protestants, has been a dirty word, namely, *tradition*. Especially for Baptists and other groups who are similarly "restorationist," such as the Churches of Christ, the ideal has been to go back to the early church and emulate it. We could also probably include the Pentecostals here as well in their attempt to recover the charismatic gifts of the early church. Part of the antipathy toward tradition stems also from a residual anti-Catholicism as part of the strained legacy of the Reformation. With an almost stunning renewal of appreciation of tradition by Protestants in recent years, especially among some of those who have been most critical of it, it is easier today to recognize the fact that tradition is inescapable. As we discussed in the previous chapter, we need to consider where tradition fits in and how to estimate it, that is, how to be critical of tradition even while recognizing that tradition itself brings a critical dimension.

Renewed appreciation of the Christian tradition includes groups like the Baptists, who have not only gone back to the Protestant tradition of the Reformation but have started going back to the early Christian writers themselves.[62] The role of tradition, like that of theology, can be seen as valuable, even indispensable, but as having its own proper location. It does not take on the role of Scripture in the Protestant tradition, but it does serve as an unavoidable and indispensable means by which the incarnational nature of Scripture is received and understood. When we look at the doctrine of God and at the doctrine of Christology, we will see that even some basic things that most Christians now take for granted and find almost self-evident in the pages of Scripture were not so evident in the early church and, in fact, took several centuries to work out. In that sense, what we take to be the meaning of Scripture was not very well understood at the beginning and was something that is mediated to us through the Christian tradition. Much of our developed notions of our understanding of God's attributes, of the Trinity, of the atonement, and of the nature of the Christian life have taken more than a thousand years to be developed in such a way that most people take for granted today. Tradition, however, is not a seamless garment. We continue to re-examine tradition as well as Scripture and often find ourselves revising our understandings. In fact, some of the most remarkable shifts in understanding have occurred in the last hundred years, as we saw in the previous chapter.

Tradition, in the end, is not something we can avoid: as Gadamer points out, it is actually helpful. It gives us a foothold by which we actually can interpret. With a greater appreciation of tradition, we can return to our previous point, namely, the drama of interpretation. This means that the adventure of understanding God and of understanding Scripture is never ending. It involves the whole history of the church and, in Alasdair MacIntyre's phrase, is an "extended argument" over time.[63] It is structurally a narrative that continues to be written, a "never-ending story." All Christians, as they try to understand God and to live their lives in the midst of common human challenges, contribute in some way to this ongoing discussion in this ongoing story.

AN INCARNATIONAL VIEW OF GENERAL REVELATION

As mentioned above, revelation does not refer only to Scripture or to the Christian tradition. The traditional term "general revelation" refers to the knowledge of God available apart from God's "special revelation" through Israel and the church.[64] Even in the Bible, God's revelation, ironically, is portrayed as not only coming just to Israel or just to the church. The thrust of God's revelation concerning God's mission in the Bible itself is not just to a certain group of people but to all of the world. Even the call to the Jews is understood as God's way of reaching out to all of the world and being a blessing to all of the world. In the Old Testament story, this was not always understood, but a parochial and centripetal understanding of God's revelation was always criticized. In some of the most striking passages in the Old Testament, Amos reminds Israel at one time that God not only brought them out of Egypt, but God brought the Philistines also out of captivity (Amos 9:7). The first eleven chapters of Genesis, which one might see as the prologue to the rest of the biblical story (including the Christian story), clearly picture God as the Creator of all the world and the one who deals with and reaches out to everyone. Instead of Genesis 12 and God's call to Abraham being a break with that purpose, it is the continuation of it. Having tried in other ways, God is still reaching out to all, only now through a specific individual in the scandal of particularity. What does this mean for those, for example, who have never had a chance to hear the gospel of Christ?

The classic text for what we are considering here as general revelation in the New Testament is chapter 1 of Romans. In that text, Paul, who is not known for emphasizing the knowledge of God of sinners, says that God's invisible nature "has been clearly perceived in the things that have been made" (v. 20). As Paul strikingly adds in the book of Acts, quoting apparently from a Greek philosopher, he says, speaking of all people, "In him we live and move and have our being" (17:28). As critics of general revelation are quick to point out, Paul does go on in Romans 1 to indicate clearly that this revelation leads to the sobering conclusion, "All have sinned and fall short of the glory of God" (Rom 3:23). All revelation comes in an incarnational context, which, as Paul indicates, includes sin. This is reminiscent of the outcome of God's initial creation, which by the sixth chapter of Genesis already finds that the thoughts of all people's minds were "only evil continually" (v. 5).

Nevertheless, Paul does insist that the knowledge of God is available through God's creation and seems clearly to understand that this knowledge is extended to all people. In Romans chapter 2, in some admittedly obscure passages, Paul chastises the Jews for being overly proud of their privileges and revelation. He suggests that possibly, at least, there might be Gentiles who are circumcised in their heart and who are in a better position than Jews who would be circumcised only in the flesh—and he calls this the "real circumcision" (Rom 2:29). These passages in Romans 1 and 2 also indicate that general revelation does not just refer to a kind of passive knowledge available in nature. Since revelation is always personal, all revelation is in a sense "special," for it always involves the activity of the Spirit of God working in the inner recesses of the heart whether or not it has been privileged to hear the gospel of Christ. Both general and special revelation are thus personal and dynamic.

Whatever specifics Paul might mean in these passages, he seems again to open the door to the possibility of some rather significant understanding of God apart from God's special revelation. This only makes sense. God created the whole world and is reaching out through the Holy Spirit to the whole world. It would be odd if God were not interested in anybody besides Israelites between Noah and the New Testament—a view that the Old Testament itself undermines, as we have seen. The picture of God in the Old Testament and in Jesus' teachings, of the God who is like the shepherd who leaves the one sheep who is saved and goes looking for the rest (Luke 15:3-7), could hardly be understood not to be reaching out in all ways possible to all of the world at all times. The Holy Spirit does not belong to a certain group of people or even to the church; rather, the church belongs to the Holy Spirit. "The wind blows where it chooses," Jesus said (John 3:8). This theme belongs to the later discussion of the church, but just as God's whole self cannot be contained by the temple in the Old Testament (Isa 6), neither can God's spirit be contained simply by the Christian church, although we will see that the church is certainly crucial and focal for God's activity in God's mission in the world. The question, then, is not whether God is involved with the rest of the world or whether God's revelation is available to all of the world; the question is, how far does this involvement extend, and what does it mean?

Another way to approach this issue that may be helpful is to think of it in terms of what kind of knowledge Christians can appropriate from non-Christians such as non-Christian scientists. To put it this way almost makes it seem ridiculous to think that Christians cannot learn from non-Christians, given that Christians take advantage every day of technology and scientific developments derived from non-Christians. Certainly it does not require a perspective of faith to be a good biologist or physicist or doctor and to make significant discoveries that are helpful to everybody. One perspective on this is rooted in the Logos theology of John, where Jesus, as the Word of God, the Logos through which God created the world, is "the true light, which enlightens everyone" (John 1:9). As Arthur Holmes, longtime philosophy professor at Wheaton College, emphasized, all truth is God's truth, an implication of monotheism itself.[65] A related emphasis is from Calvin's conception of common grace, where God enables much knowledge of the world that benefits humankind. Mark Noll, a Reformed evangelical, emphasizes this idea, even in the area of biblical studies, for the church to be able to draw upon secular scholarship to better understand Scripture.[66] Again, looking ahead to the doctrines of God and of creation, we understand that God is the Creator and source of all things and that no other god or other ultimate source of truth exists. God is a God of truth, and no truth exists apart from God's truth. Human beings, obviously, "see in a mirror dimly" (1 Cor 13:12), and it is not always so easy to know what the truth is. It would seem to restrict the scope of God's sovereignty and God's range of influence, however, to say that there is some truth that pertains to God, and there is some that does not. This is another place where a more robust doctrine of creation can be helpful. God is not only the God of redemption, God is the God of creation who created all things and all people, who cares for all people, and who continues to work with all people.

The question is, how does this other knowledge extend to religious knowledge? The early church had two perspectives on this. One was negative, exemplified by Tertullian, who asked, "What indeed has Athens to do with Jerusalem?"[67] It was a rhetorical question, and the answer was "Nothing." Tertullian's attitude reflects a real strain in the Bible itself. On the one hand, there is a trajectory that calls for purity and separation from the world. In the Old Testament, this is exemplified by the books of Esther and Daniel. In the New Testament, the quotation from Paul is apropos: "Come out from them and be separate from them, says the Lord" (2 Cor 6:17). It can be argued, however, especially from the outgoing practice of Jesus and Paul themselves, that these passages are not referring to literal exclusion from the world or not learning from the world, but they express a very real concern to remain faithful to the truth.

The other tendency in the Bible and in the early church was more inclusive. In the Old Testament, it is reflected in the late books of Jonah and Ruth; in the New Testament by the Logos idea itself. This was expressed by early church fathers such as Justin the Martyr and Clement of Alexandria in the second century and early third century, who argued that philosophers such as Socrates and Plato were compatible with truths of the gospel.[68] They thought that Greek philosophy acted as a tutor to the Greeks, just as the law acted as a tutor to the Jews. Augustine expressed a more cautious approach but still an open one. In a striking analogy, he referred to the way the Israelites, when they fled Egypt, stole what they needed, such as utensils, food, and clothing, from the Egyptians. Likewise, Augustine argued, Christians should be able to appropriate from pagans whatever is useful, since whatever they have that is true ultimately stems from God.[69]

This approach draws on the Johannine emphasis on the Logos, who is the source of all light and truth, and on the general monotheistic perspective that God is the only God, namely, that there is no truth apart from God. It is then from a perspective within the church that one can be open to truth outside the Bible and the church itself. It is also important, however, to be discriminating. With the help of special revelation, which is now available, and also with the help of the indwelling Spirit of God, it is an open question where one may find truth. Clement of Alexandria aptly characterizes this openness: "The way of truth is therefore one. But into it, as into a perennial river, streams flow from all sides."[70] At the same time, even within the church, one must be aware of the effects of fallenness and sin on everyone. There is a place for openness and also a place for suspicion. One can evaluate whatever one sees, and if it is compatible with the truth, then it can be accepted. In many cases, insights from others may be partial truth, which may require even more discrimination.

It is then virtually a denial of the scope of God and of the Logos to restrict revelation and truth just to the church. This realization can increase appreciation for God's work with other people at the same time that it calls for discernment within the church, as always, of what truth is. While many in the church, including Calvin, are open to a degree of knowledge outside of the church, the issue of salvation is another question. The Reformed tradition has often put it this way: God gives enough truth to damn but not to save. Seeing it put that starkly virtually cries out for qualification if not correction. This is a vexing issue, especially in our increasingly pluralistic world, that we will take up in the final chapter on last things, eschatology. As is evident, much hinges on one's understanding of the nature of God, to which we turn more directly in the next chapter.

4

GOD
The Beginning and the End

The doctrine of God is surely at the center of any theology—if any doctrine can be considered central apart from the other doctrines. Yet it is often seen as the most formidable and forbidding, full of esoteric lists and discussions of properties, so much so that it is easy for a newcomer to theology to sympathize with the spirit of the message sewn in Pascal's cloak and found only after his death, "Fire. God of Abraham, God of Isaac, God of Jacob. Not of philosophers and scholars."[1] Yet such a dualism cannot finally be maintained, even giving all due respect to Pascal (1623–1662), one of the great philosophers in Christendom. For example, would it not be odd to affirm in philosophy an "uncaused cause" of all that is, who is a different being than the God of the Bible? Yet Pascal's passion underscores something that we cannot let ourselves forget in Christian theology, namely, that God is first and last a powerful presence, One whom we love and fear, One in whom "we live and move and have our being" (Acts 17:28), long before we can enumerate God's metaphysical attributes and properties. As Paul Tillich put it, God is our "ultimate concern"; theology thus has to do with our being and nonbeing.[2]

Yet seek to understand God we must. Revelation means little if we understand nothing. The great drama embedded in Scripture is of no avail if we know not at all who has saved us and whom we serve. As we have discussed in the previous chapters, theology is an essential and unavoidable aspect of the Christian life. Despite the fact that a separation between theory and practice runs deep in Western thought, reflection and life can be more integrated and, indeed, are more integrated. Fundamental beliefs shape our whole way of relating to the world. Perhaps theology and the doctrine of God per se would not be so forbidding if we thought of theology not so much as abstract speculation but, to use a common biblical image, as a journey into knowing and loving our Beloved more and more. In a marital relationship, love means little if it does not issue in greater understanding. In turn, understanding enriches the relationship and can deepen love. This is the sense in which a doctrine, an understanding, of God is pursued.

The rationalist quest in the West has also been driven by a drive toward exhaustive understanding: the Platonic seeing in the full light of day, the Cartesian "clarity and distinctness." Yet this will not do when it comes to God. As this dream is fading in the twilight of modernity, even with respect to knowledge of the natural world, the problems of such an excessive rationality have generally been understood all along the way with respect to God. Thomas Aquinas, for example, is often seen as the quintessential scholastic theologian who seems to know too much; yet in actuality Aquinas' thought about God is characterized by an impressive modesty. He sounds a frequent theme among theologians by saying that God is Being *qua* Being, He who is, not a being among other beings or creatures. Thus no category of thought or language can properly be applied to God. According to Aquinas, then, the first step toward the understanding of God is therefore the *via negativa*, the negative way, which involves denying the literal meaning of any concept that we apply to God. At best, we can use only analogical language about God because God is so supremely transcendent and beyond our capacities to comprehend. Again we are reminded of Pascal's appeal to the living God who comes to us as "fire," who transcends the attempts to be captured in philosophical or theological systems. Paul says that we "know only in part" (1 Cor 13:12). This is especially true when we focus our attention upon God directly.

The mystery of God is not just that God is too transcendent to grasp; it is that God is also so immanent as to be best "understood" in personal encounter. God is simultaneously too far and too close to be treated as an object. Remembering Ricoeur's hermeneutical arc, theology begins with the encounter of God, which "gives rise to thought" but then points us back again to renewed encounter. Luther's warning that theology should be done on our knees points to this reality. Theology first and last lives by prayer, or its reflection cannot avail. Even our personal relationship with others is a mystery that cannot be fully explicated, though our partial understandings can often be immensely helpful. It is thus not surprising that our personal relationship to God can only partially be "explained" and can only be "understood" in a holistic, empathetic (*phronetic*) way that can never transcend a significant tacit dimension. To use prophetic language, grasping God is more like attempting to grasp a whirlwind than an inert object (the paradigm so dominant in the rise of modern science) (Job 38:1). As theologians in the twentieth century so often reminded the church, God is always a *subject* and can never be fully turned into an *object*, or objectified.[3] This insight was shaped by the great Jewish thinker Martin Buber, who stressed that God is always a "Thou" and never an "It."[4] Again, like Pascal, perhaps such a cleavage is overdrawn, but it reminds us where the emphasis should be: not on the concepts by which we characterize (and sometimes caricature) God but on their efficacy in fostering contact with God. The Hebrew Bible itself perhaps scandalously underscores this priority of relationship by using the common euphemism for sexual relationships, "knowing" a person, for our "knowing" God.

Embarking on this journey of understanding God is like walking a narrow ridge, avoiding the precipice of saying too much on the one side and of saying too little on the other. Augustine expressed this challenge well in his classic text on the Trinity, when he virtually despaired of saying anything valid. He finally confessed that he spoke only because it was worse to be silent.[5]

In this chapter, we will begin with a startling case that reminds us of the importance of God and of the scandal of belief in God. This will help us grasp better in our context the challenge of knowing God. Then we will plunge into significant aspects of the nature of God by focusing on the issue of the renewed grasp of the suffering of God. This will point us to the revival of the significance of the Trinity for Christian understanding. At this stage, we will have realized that it is difficult even to think about God apart from God's creation, which we will explore here to some extent and further in the next chapter.

Case Study: Nietzsche's Madman and Arguments for God's Existence

One of the most discerning and poignant insights into the significance of belief in God in modern thought ironically came from one of the most notorious atheists, Friedrich Nietzsche. This passage is from *The Gay Science*, where he pictures a madman:

> *The Madman.* Have you not heard of that madman who lit a lantern in the bright morning hours, ran to the market place, and cried incessantly: "I seek God! I seek God!" As many of those who did not believe in God were standing around just then, he provoked much laughter. Why, did he get lost? said one. Did he lose his way like a child? said another. Or is he hiding? Is he afraid of us? Has he gone on a voyage? Or emigrated? Thus they yelled and laughed. The madman jumped into their midst and pierced them with his glances.
>
> "Whither is God" he cried; "I shall tell you. *We have killed him*—you and I. All of us are his murderers. But how have we done this? How were we able to drink up the sea? Who gave us the sponge to wipe away the entire horizon? What did we do when we unchained this earth from its sun? Whither is it moving now? Whither are we moving now? Away from all suns? Are we not plunging continually? Backward, sideward, forward, in all directions? Is there any up or down left? Are we not straying as through an infinite nothing? Do we not feel the breath of empty space? Has it not become colder? Is not night and more night coming on all the while? Must not lanterns be lit in the morning? Do we not hear anything yet of the noise of the gravediggers

who are burying God? Do we not smell anything yet of God's decomposition? Gods too decompose. God is dead. God remains dead. And we have killed him. How shall we, the murderers of all murderers, comfort ourselves? What was holiest and most powerful of all that the world has yet owned has bled to death under our knives. Who will wipe this blood off us? What water is there for us to clean ourselves? What festivals of atonement, what sacred games shall we have to invent? Is not the greatness of this deed too great for us? Must not we ourselves become gods simply to seem worthy of it? There has never been a greater deed; and whoever will be born after us—for the sake of this deed he will be part of a higher history than all history hitherto."

Here the madman fell silent and looked again at his listeners; and they too were silent and stared at him in astonishment. At last he threw his lantern on the ground, and it broke and went out. "I have come too early," he said then; "my time has not come yet. This tremendous event is still on its way, still wandering—it has not yet reached the ears of man. Lightning and thunder require time, the light of the stars requires time, deeds require time even after they are done, before they can be seen and heard. This deed is still more distant from them than the most distant stars—*and yet they have done it themselves.*"

It has been related further that on the same day the madman entered divers churches and there said his *requiem aeternam deo.* Led out and called to account, he is said to have replied each time, "What are these churches now if they are not the tombs and sepulchers of God?"[6]

Nietzsche grew up as a young child with a precocious faith.[7] As he navigated his teenage years and began exploring the wider world, he followed a common path in modernity of leaving God behind in the face of critical questions—or so he thought. As this passage indicates, he was aware that modern Europe, with all of its skepticism and atheism, was haunted by God. We find later, as in the parable of the Madman, that he himself was haunted by God and particularly by Jesus of Nazareth. Nietzsche was one of the first to point prophetically to the implications of widespread unbelief and skepticism. His prescience reminds us that, as Michael Buckley indicates about the beginnings of modernity, there once was no atheism.[8] Even in the mid-1700s, a prominent Enlightenment thinker like Voltaire could surmise that people were a little off their rocker if they did not believe in God. Even later in the century, David Hume, one of the greatest critics of religious belief in modern philosophy, is reputed to have commented to a French collection of philosophers that he had never met a real atheist. The reply was to the effect that he was dining with fifteen of them; the three others had not made up their minds yet.[9]

The legacy of modern doubt, exemplified at the beginning by Descartes who eventually proved God's existence, yielded toward the end a presumption of atheism.[10] Hans Küng in his study of the rise of modern atheism and nihilism reveals that disbelief in God on the part of these "masters of suspicion," such as Nietzsche, Karl Marx, and Sigmund Freud, was not a warranted conclusion at the end of their thought but more of an unproven assumption at the beginning.[11] Yet, as Nietzsche saw, the problem with God is that God will not go away quietly.[12]

The modern challenge to faith in God initially was epistemological, that is, God's existence could not be proved, *pace* Descartes, Augustine, Aquinas, and most theologians and philosophers. Traditionally, theologians had largely assumed that one could demonstrate by reason, in a coercive way, that there must be a first uncaused cause (the cosmological argument), that there must be a designer of the universe (the teleological argument), that a perfect being must exist (the ontological argument), and that morality presupposes a lawgiver (the moral argument). These modern critics pointed out how the traditional proofs for God's existence were not nearly so obvious or coercive. This criticism was so damaging that one could generalize that for most of Christian history, Christians had assumed that one could prove God's existence. But after the withering analysis of the eighteenth and nineteenth centuries, even most *theologians* did not think that God's existence could be proven. In fact, sometimes it has been theologians as much as philosophers who have argued that the proofs were not just weak, they were fallacious and misguided. The latter perhaps was the most damning.

Søren Kierkegaard was a fascinating counterpart and contemporary of Nietzsche. He is considered, along with Nietzsche, to be one of the two fathers of the later existentialist movement that developed in the twentieth century. In his hands, the proofs became an outright threat to belief in God. If one did found one's faith upon such a proof, it was a sign that one had no faith at all and had gone completely down the wrong track. Kierkegaard asks:

> For whose sake is it that the proof is sought? Faith does not need it; aye, it must even regard the proof as its enemy. But when faith begins to feel embarrassed and ashamed, like a young woman for whom her love is no longer sufficient, but who secretly feels ashamed of her lover and must therefore have it established that there is something remarkable about him—when faith thus begins to lose its passion, when faith begins to cease to be faith, then a proof becomes necessary so as to command respect from the side of unbelief.[13]

Kierkegaard thus is well known for picturing the believer as being suspended "over seventy thousand fathoms of water," relying solely on faith in God to prevent sinking into the depths.[14] This was greatly to influence later theologians such as Rudolf Bultmann and Karl Barth, who saw no rational or "natural theological" path to God but more of a "leap of faith" and an existential decision.[15]

Only in the late twentieth century have the traditional arguments made a comeback, now not as proofs but as more or less convincing arguments. Here Kierkegaard's dichotomy between passion and reason is modulated to a more integral connection. It is recognized that the efficacy of the arguments depends in part on one's epistemological presuppositions and is rooted in one's life experience. This means that the salience of these arguments will always be person dependent and context dependent. Another way of putting it is that evangelism or apologetics on these grounds might or might not be effective, depending on the particular presuppositions of each person—ruling out any kind of cookie-cutter approach to such efforts. Even evangelism has to be rethought in a postmodern age.

The legacy of late modern skepticism, so exemplified by Nietzsche's passionate vehemence more than by Descarte's half-hearted skepticism, is that such intellectual issues often dominate the discussion about God. Besides questioning God's existence, some raise questions about the very coherence of the notion of God.

What if the *concept* of God is not plausible, which means that the question of God's existence cannot even be asked? Questions are raised, for instance, about the coherence of God's omnipotence and human freedom. Does God grant a degree of self-determination and thus run a risk, as in Arminianism? Or would such "libertarian freedom," as it is called, be a threat to God's total sovereignty, as in Calvinism (strictly speaking, five-point or "strong" Calvinism)? If God has foreknowledge, as most Christians have traditionally believed, do humans have genuine freedom? The traditional companion beliefs that God is not only timeless but also neither changes (immutablity) nor suffers or experiences (impassibility) have been more recently challenged as incompatible with a providential God, as we discussed in the prolegomena. As philosophers have pointed out, if the conception of God is incoherent at the outset, it makes no sense to take the further step of arguing for belief in God's existence, which would be like looking for evidence of a square circle. These are serious issues.

If that was not enough, more recently, the issue that most feel is the major obstacle to belief in God is the problem of evil and suffering, technically, the "theodicy" problem.[16] How can God's perfect goodness (omnibenevolence) be defended in light of God's omnipotence and the fact of immense human evil and suffering? After the Holocaust, Stalin, Rwanda, Darfur—the names and places go on—this is no small question. In the past, it was thought that God's existence could be proven in a strong sense, so this question was minimized. Certainly few argued for God's existence on the basis of the problem of evil, but if one already could rationally prove that God existed on other grounds, it was no threat. If the proofs for God's existence have failed, and pressing questions about the coherence of the concept of God are raised, this issue looms larger. In fact, in light of the problem of suffering, it has seemed to many that one can prove God's nonexistence. A great deal of ferment has occurred in this area, showing that it is difficult to do one or the other. Thus a common perspective among theologians and philosophers is that they cannot prove God's existence, but neither can the problem of evil, when examined more closely, mandate God's nonexistence.[17]

What is clear is that conviction about God and faith in God are mysteries that transcend exhaustive rational unpacking. I would argue that this does not mean that it is a complete "leap of faith" in the face of all evidence either. It often is trust and commitment in the face of conflicting evidence, the result of a configured whole, a particular way of assembling a cumulative case based on irreducible personal experiences and judgments. It is a case where the whole is more than the sum of the parts. This reflects our situation in a pluralistic world with many religions and also many philosophical worldviews that assume no divine being at all. Phronetic practical wisdom is coming to a conviction that involves explicit rational grounds and yet more. In this, as we have seen, it is not unlike the rationality involved in every other field or area of reality. Its importance is magnified in this case because presumably no other dimension of reality can rival the complexity and mystery of divine reality. The modernist inclination in the face of this lack of objective certainty was to fall, in later modernity, into skepticism, relativism, even nihilism, which Nietzsche announced but struggled against. Moving outside the modern paradigm lessens that pressure and opens the door to "conviction and critique," or perhaps better, "mystery and critique." Rigorous thinking is as crucial as ever and can serve important apologetic purposes for non-Christians in understanding and even considering Christian faith. But reliance on supposedly neutral "proofs" that would be airtight, coercive arguments for anyone is as unadvisable as such proofs are unavailable. In this, Kierkegaard was right to warn against putting all of the Christian eggs into the rational basket. The significance of a postmodern context is to be able to move beyond such a false dichotomy between faith and reason, between theological mushy-minded wishful thinking and scientific harsh-minded rationality.

The haunting questions of Nietzsche's madman remind us of the stakes. Rather than seeing the disappearance of God as an opportunity for maturity, for freedom, or even for license, what Nietzsche saw was that God makes a difference—and God's "death" makes a difference. Here the believer may learn from the atheist. When the ground for meaning and purpose disappears, we might ask if there "is any up or down"? "Has it not become colder?" What happens when we "loose the sun from its sky"? Nietzsche reminds us that whether or not we believe in God, disbelieving in God changes everything. And believing in God changes everything. Why? Not just because faith in God is traditional or habitual—it is because of the meaning of who God is and its effect upon human reality. Nietzsche ironically reminds us, just when someone might think that belief in God is difficult, disbelief in God might be more difficult.

GOD AS HOLY LOVE

Who is the God in whom Christians believe, who makes the kind of difference that Nietzsche saw? When people reject God, they are always rejecting some particular conception of God. In fact, one can argue that one might well reject the perversion of God as foe of human flourishing often proposed by Marx, Freud, and Nietzsche, in effect agreeing with them, and yet believe in what one regards as a more authentic God. But what is the authentic nature of God? The fact is that the Christian understanding of God is unique; many religions understand God in different ways. One of the remarkable things about the Hebrews is that they came to understand God in a distinctive manner, over against the common understandings shared by their Semitic cousins and the Egyptians. Their background was polytheism, the belief in many gods. The Greek and Roman mythology with which we might be acquainted reminds us of how widespread this understanding was in the ancient world. In fact, the Hebrews expressed their understanding of God not in a vacuum but in contrast to those around them. The biblical center for the understanding of God is that God is love, yet it is love of the one, holy God. A look at the first chapter of the Bible unveils this distinctive view of God.

Genesis 1 and Christian Theism

If one looks at the creation story of Genesis 1 through 2:4 in this regard, it is an astonishing theological document. In its narrative-poetic form, it expresses beliefs that were in contrast to virtually everyone else's conceptions of God at that time. This account arose among a people not otherwise distinguished from those around them by their science, astronomy, mathematics, technology, architecture, warfare techniques, and so on. From a neutral perspective, they were not outstanding in anything except for their revolutionary understanding of God. Of course, it does not seem revolutionary to us because it is our heritage. We are so used to it that we can hardly appreciate its dramatic innovation. Later deists in the seventeenth century would argue that reason would lead anyone and everyone to belief in one God who created the world, rewarded virtue, and punished wrongdoing, yet it is evident that reason had not led even great thinkers to that conclusion before the Hebrews came along.[18] What does the first creation story in particular say, translated for our sakes from its poetic form into theological affirmations?

It maintains that there is one God who created the heavens and the earth. This God is clearly a personal being who cares about the creation, who is pleased to see that "it was very good" (Gen 1:31). Besides the contrast with the Hebrews' own polytheistic heritage and context, think of the widespread religions of the East without a personal god. Creation out of necessity was the widespread conception of God that haunted the early years of the church in the form of neo-platonism, which also represented the world as a necessary emanation of God's own self. This reminds us of how widespread it has been to think in terms of pantheism, where the world is divine in some sense, familiar also in some tribal and Native American religions. We can see in the Genesis account of creation, however, a personal act of grace, where God gives being to others not out of compulsion or necessity but as a free gift. The implication is that God exists in God's own self, from eternity, in joy. Creation is an act of neither need nor necessity but is a voluntary sharing of the joy that God already possesses.

A common understanding is that Genesis 1, in its current form, was developed in the time of Israel's Babylonian exile or shortly thereafter, thus in the sixth through fifth centuries before Christ. Genesis 1 appears to be a rejection of the Babylonian creation story, where creation is due to violent strife between the gods, the earth is created from the dead body of a god, and humans are created as servants and playthings of the gods.[19] Even a cursory reading of Genesis 1 shows how sharply it differs from that perspective. As John Milbank, one of the foremost contemporary theologians insists, the Judeo-Christian heritage refers to a creation out of peace, not violence.[20]

And there is more. God created in an orderly way out of chaos. Christians saw early that this was not creation out of some preexistent matter or out of the divine self but out of nothing (*creatio ex nihilo*). While this was not always the earlier Jewish understanding, Jewish theology later largely followed this interpretation.[21] The reference to chaos, probably reminiscent of the Babylonian creation out of warlike chaos, remains as a pointer to the finite fragility of creation and the way things so easily fall apart and seem to spin out of control. To the contrary, God is seen as the one who brings order out of chaos, reflected in the step-by-step, developmental, even rational, progression of creation. In modernity, faith has had its wars with reason as it has with science, but the creation story reminds us that they need not be pitted against one another. Early Christian scientists such as Galileo and Isaac Newton saw in the creator God ground and motivation for their searches into the hidden rationality, even mathematicality, of the universe.

From this biblical account, we have what is generally called "classical theism," the belief in one personal God who is the ground of all being, who created the world out of nothing in an act of freedom and grace, and who created with a purpose. This is contrasted with monism, which sees all of reality as one substance, and perhaps impersonal (pantheism, Hegel, Spinoza); dualism, which sees reality as made up of two ultimate principles (Platonic reason and matter; Zoroastrianism, which posits a virtually equal God and Satan); and polytheism (multiple deities).

In light of contemporary concern with the problem of evil and suffering, one of the striking things about these various understandings of God is that they all reflect different ways of coming to grips with the universal question of human suffering. Monism tends to downplay the reality of evil, for if there is only one reality, and it is evil, the result is a pessimistic view indeed. An example is the Hindu conception of suffering as illusory when one grasps that individuality is itself an illusion. Another is Spinoza, who sees suffering not as evil in itself but a result of how humans evaluate reality. Reality simply "is." Dualism represents one of the most successful responses to the problem of suffering and evil. One of the two ultimate principles is good, and the other is evil. As Plato put it simply, God is responsible for all of the good; "matter" is responsible for all of the evil: the problem is that God must work with recalcitrant material. Zoroastrianism would say that the problem is not so much matter but an evil rival of God. The intellectual coherence of dualism's response to theodicy is at the cost of incoherence elsewhere, for it forsakes the dearly bought insight of monotheism. Some would argue that the idea of two ultimate principles is itself incoherent. Polytheism, as one might imagine, posits multiple ultimate powers whose rivalry and competition yield the mess of the world, as in the Greek and Roman myths. Theism, which has the advantages of monism without identifying the world as itself divine, perhaps suffers its greatest intellectual challenge when it comes to theodicy, for it attempts to maintain together that there is one God who is omnipotent and perfectly good, and yet that genuine evil exists (and is not an illusion). It does not give up any of these affirmations, which is both its blessing and its bane. It is not surprising that theodicy is seen as the greatest threat to theism today—but not as much to other religious and philosophical conceptualities.

The biblical story portrays one God who desires intimate fellowship with humanity (Gen 2) and who continues again and again to reach out to estranged and rebellious humanity (Gen 3). God is angry and disappointed at the failure of God's creation as the creation turns to evil and begets suffering (Gen 6), yet God continues in judgment and grace to work with humanity (the rest of Genesis; indeed, the rest of the Bible). God makes promises and covenants toward a blessed future, undergirding the transformation of the view of time from a cyclical to a more linear view.

God as Ultimate Concern

The development over time among the Hebrews of the concept of one personal God who is the creator and ground of all being and value is one of the great religious insights in human history. God is not just one god among other gods, or one power above other powers, or one value among other values. As Tillich expressed it, God properly should be our "ultimate concern."[22] The idea of God's holiness points to this uniqueness of God. God is the one who, as Creator and origin of all that exists, is the answer to the great question, Why is there something rather than nothing? God is, one might say, "Holiness Itself." If anything finite, anything less than God, becomes our ultimate concern, our faith is inauthentic—or in biblical language, it is idolatrous. The first of the Ten Commandments is, "You shall have no other gods before me" (Exod 20:3). The third is, "You shall not make wrongful use of the name of the Lord your God" (Exod 20:7). While often misunderstood as just referring to misusing God's name in swearing, the latter actually means that anytime we take God's name lightly or bear it hypocritically, we are violating the commandment. This can happen in innumerable ways, in a technological twenty-first century C.E. setting just as much as in a pastoral biblical setting. Perhaps idolatry is unfortunately an even greater danger in a society like ours where a multi-billion-dollar advertising industry is designed to make many other things ultimate in our lives. It may actually be that our besetting temptation is thus as much a functional polytheism as was the ancient world. Tillich says that the language of ultimate concern is the translation of what Jesus saw as the great commandment that sums up all the Law: "You shall love the Lord your God with all your heart, soul, mind, and strength" (Luke 10:27).[23]

In this sense, the doctrine of God is not, first of all, an esoteric doctrine but is minutely practical, affecting every day and every aspect of our lives. Is God the center of our lives, or have we allowed something else boldly, or perhaps surreptitiously, to topple God from God's proper place? This claim is the force of Jesus' shocking statement, shocking in a time when Christianity is often identified with "family values": "Whoever loves father or mother more than me is not worthy of me; and whoever loves son or daughter more than me is not worthy of me" (Matt 10:37). Understand, Christians are called upon to love all people, certainly including the family. Jesus and Paul both castigate those who use religious excuses to evade familial responsibilities. Yet in the end, as tempting as it can be, it is not genuine love to put anyone or anything else in the place of God. They cannot bear it; neither can we. Only God can take that place. That is the amazing insight that the Hebrews were perhaps the first to realize, namely, that this is what we mean when we say "God." In a positive way, this is what Augustine understood when he prayed, "Thou madest us for Thyself, and our heart is restless until it repose in Thee."[24]

In the beginning years of Hitler's reign over Nazi Germany in 1934, when Karl Barth led the confessing church to sign the Barmen Declaration during a riveting sociopolitical situation, it was a striking expression of God's centrality as revealed in Jesus Christ:

> Jesus Christ, as he is testified to us in Holy Scripture, is the one Word of God, whom we are to hear, who we are to trust and obey in life and in death.
>
> We repudiate the false teaching that the church can and must recognize yet other happenings and powers, images and truths as divine revelation alongside this one Word of God, as a source of her preaching.[25]

This poignantly reveals the danger of nationalism in the modern world as a constant temptation to idolatry. While much good can come from being proud of one's country and striving to improve it, neither one's nation nor one's family can take the place of God.

In a more mundane way, although devastating for many who lost their retirements, the Enron debacle in the United States was led by a Baptist layperson who professed to sense God's call in his business but who, in the end, substituted profit for integrity and argued that his faith should not interfere with business.[26] Lest we be quick to judge, this attitude seems to be common for Christians in the developed countries. Conversely, the whistle-blower was willing to sacrifice her position for the sake of integrity and all the people who would be hurt by the company's fall, and who were devastated. Yet such whistle-blowers are often the most castigated. Who was following the first commandment in this case? What is the *practice* of the doctrine of God? It is letting God be God in ways great and small, not just in times of worship on Sunday but especially the rest of the week. Rather than being the most abstract of doctrines, it can easily be seen as the most practical.

Love and Power

While the theodicy dilemma focuses on God's omnipotence, the biblical emphasis on the covenantal God reminds us that the dominant Christian view of God is that God is a God of love: 1 John says simply, "God is love" (4:8). Since love is understood in myriad ways, this affirmation is filled in by the larger biblical narrative. In our culture, love can stand for spineless sentimentality, for natural filial affection, or for romantic thrills. For Christians, the meaning of love is chiefly specified by Jesus Christ as the central revelation of God's nature, giving us a picture of a God who is willing to suffer and die for the sake of humanity. Early Christians turned to a particular Greek word for this love, *agape*, that represented selfless, grace-filled giving and caring to set it off from other understandings of love. English perhaps suffers from having only one word to cover so many different concepts.[27] Part of the challenge of theology, then, is to develop a more precise and fuller understanding of love in the light of divine revelation.

As we have seen with many other things, Christians have struggled to live up to our own understanding. In a context of caesars and emperors, God's power came to be emphasized early, so that omnipotence came to be a dominant concept and was understood largely along the lines of imperial power—as domination and control. Along with other "omnis" such as omniscience and omnipresence—but not omnibenevolence—omnipotence came to govern the understanding of theism more than love. While Christians in late antiquity, with the best of intentions, were affirming God's ultimacy in terms of power, what they seem not to have done was to question the meaning of power. This is one of those places where unquestioned assumptions can slip easily into our theologizing and even determine it unawares.

This means that while omnipotence is a legitimate affirmation, like the concept of love, it all depends on how it is understood. As the ground of all being and as the Creator of heaven and earth, God is certainly powerful. As the One who can wrap everything up at any time in the final consummation, God is certainly powerful: otherwise, one would have dualism or polytheism. Virtually all Christians, as well as Jews and Muslims, therefore affirm that God is omnipotent (although some prefer the more biblical language of "almighty"). The problem is more subtle. It seems that at times power has been understood as a "zero-sum" matter, meaning that there is only a finite amount, and if one has some, another has less. What this has meant is that if God is limited in any way by the power of human beings, then God is not omnipotent. So God's power came to be seen, in the words of Arthur McGill, more as "dominative" than as "donative," more a matter of "control" than of "gift."[28]

It is difficult to understand disputes about predestination and providence apart from this issue. If God ultimately must be in full control in order to be God, then everything that happens must be seen as ordained by God from all eternity, as Calvin saw.[29] Augustine allowed more scope for freedom early in his career, but later in his life he saw that this freedom was meticulously controlled by God behind the scenes.[30] Contrast this view with the dynamic of the first chapters of Genesis, which present a God who creates with the best of intentions and then sees the creation go terribly wrong, so wrong that "every inclination of the thoughts of their hearts was only evil continually" by chapter 6 (v. 5). God is so disappointed and "sorry" for how things have turned out that "it grieved him to his heart" (v. 6). So the Lord moves to a new beginning, but even that goes awry (Gen 6–11). Again, God initiates a new beginning with Abraham, and with Jacob, and with David, and on and on. The picture is that God has given radical freedom to those in the divine image, implying that such freedom is part of that image, with the risk that it can be terribly misused—which it has been over and over again. Rather than God controlling what is happening and presumably eliminating what is so displeasing, God patiently, though with much travail, continues to work around, with, and through such radical freedom. In the Christian story, it comes to such a pitch that God in God's own self participates in human suffering and dies an agonizing death for the sake of reconciling these wayward humans. Despite much grief, disappointment, and suffering, God is never ultimately threatened—as in dualism—and ultimately moves toward a blessed consummation, but not without the possible precious loss of those in God's image who finally reject God's gracious overtures.

As one can see, these are two radically different understandings of power, in fact, so different that they are two incommensurable paradigms. What makes sense in one does not compute in the other. We will return to this issue when we treat the issues of freedom and salvation, but here I venture to say that this emphasis on unilateral power and control is a place where we have brought, one might say, a secular notion of power "unbaptized" into Christian theology. It is apparent that the idea of dominative power was the common view of power outside of the church in the Greek and Roman world, and it continues to be the worldly conception of power. More and more control is better; less control is worse. It pits everyone against everyone else.

Increasingly, theologians now argue that the Christian view of power is radically different. Giving up control may be more powerful. Granting power, empowering, is also powerful. Paul's great meditation on love in 1 Corinthians 13 makes little sense otherwise. Love "does not insist on its own way" (v. 5). Power is not seen so much as an issue of control but of benevolence, the power to give. God creates not just to dominate but to empower. The fact that this may seem counterintuitive is perhaps why Paul could say that the cross is "foolishness" to the Gentiles. It is difficult for a faith that has Jesus Christ and the cross at the center, as the supreme revelation of God, to understand power as dominative. Suffering love is not coercive love. Rowan Williams, former archbishop of Canterbury, expresses this well:

> The word "God," in Christian theology, does not name a being
> or reality of unfettered power, who has chosen to love—it does

not, that is, name a reality in which power goes deeper than love. Rather, it names a reality for whom—if I may put it like this—love goes all the way down. In the Christian picture, God's power always and only emerges from God's love—God's will from God's loving nature—and so love trumps power, every time. There is no shadow of power without love in God.[31]

In this sense, it is more fitting to speak of God as "Holy Love" than of anything else, such as "Holy Power." The uniqueness, holiness, of God lies preeminently in God's love. Even though holiness now is often seen as connoting morality, perhaps even a judgmental or legalistic sense of law, the canonical shape of holiness means that law, judgment, and divine demand is refracted through the primacy of God as Holy Love.

The emphasis here has been on reframing our understanding of power in favor of love because this has been perhaps the greatest area of need, where divine power has been understood in terms of worldly power rather than the other way around. I hasten to add, however, that there is also room for our worldly notions of love to be transformed by divine revelation. We are in our time aware of how love is often distorted as timidity, sentimentality, and codependency. Love does not always mean giving in or giving way. Even when it does, it is meant to foster a transforming initiative, as in "turning the other cheek" or "going the second mile" in Jesus' Sermon on the Mount.[32] Sometimes, though, the most transforming and loving response is resistance, as exemplified by those who signed the Barmen Declaration. C. S. Lewis also saw this in our expectation that God provides us whatever we want, a hedonistic paradise. When we do not get it, therefore, we are resentful. Lewis points out that God loves us too much always to give us what we want; rather, God loves us with a fierce love that wants our best, even when we do not. Sometimes we would rather God let us alone and not pursue us into the depths of hades, in the words of the psalmist (Ps 139:8). We would rather the Holy Spirit not convict us of sin, of righteousness, and judgment (John 16:8). We would rather God not desire our "soul-making," but leave us be in our "soul-unmaking." What we do not realize is that there is little that is more persistent and passionate than love's opposition to sin's damage, destruction, and distortion. Love forgives in ways beyond human imagining, but love sees also the *need* for repentance and forgiveness sometimes beyond human awareness. Nothing opposes oppression more than divine love, so the prophets say.[33] Children know this from the movie based on Lewis' book *The Lion, the Witch, and the Wardrobe*, concerning Aslan the lion as the Christ figure who is no "*tame* lion."[34] And when the wind of the Spirit is not a balmy breeze but a tempest, one can say, as Molly Marshall said of the Spirit that drove Jesus into "the searing silence of the desert," "Here is no sweet dove. This Spirit thing has claws, talons."[35] Understood in this way, the gap between love and justice is not so great, for justice is but another side of love's passion. God's power is refracted then not only through love but also through justice. God loves too much to run roughshod over ultimate human decision, but God also loves too much to yield easily. Divine power is respectful and patient but also persistent and passionate. Power is at the service of these dynamics, not the other way around.

One can say that God must limit divine power for this to be so, and the language of "self-limitation" is now a widely used theological concept. Insofar as the language of God's total sovereignty in Augustine and Calvin has been a minority theological position in the church, the church has always had a strong sense of divine self-limitation. In passing, one must note that, while the self-limitation of God's power is enmeshed in Christian theology, there is no such concept as the self-limitation of divine love, again suggesting its primacy. Even self-limitation of divine power is not an externally imposed limitation, however, but one deriving from God's own nature. In fact, the dominant Christian response to the problem of evil and suffering has emphasized human freedom and thus human responsibility for much evil. This is already a pervasive recognition of divine self-limitation throughout Christian history due to the fact that God's choice to create free beings is a choice not to control them. Even Aquinas recognized that it is no slight on God's power to say that God cannot perform logical impossibilities such as creating a square circle—or predetermining free beings.[36] Why?

Because God's own nature determines the limits of reality and what is conceivable. The appeal to free will in the face of evil is based on the understanding that it is contrary to God's nature to create free beings who are also predetermined. Divine self-limitation is thus a crucial theological concept to understand, indicating that God is omnipotent and the ground of being but that God does not meticulously control everything.

The issue of how to understand power has enormous implications throughout the whole range of theology. What one decides here determines much of the rest. If power is understood more within the framework of suffering love and as donative, then human beings have a great deal of say in their own destiny, which may be contrary to God's will. This means that God ran severe risks in creating a free creation, which indeed has turned out badly in tragic ways. The Christian gospel, good news, is thus that God offers redemption in the midst of such waywardness again and again even to those who resist God's overture. If we take a passage like 2 Peter 3:9 directly, that God is "not wanting any to perish," this may mean that God experiences the worst loss imaginable even though God experiences great joy in the salvation of others.

Such thinking does not even make sense if power is understood in a dominative way. In this latter way, God cannot experience great distress or loss. Then one is pulled toward the strong Calvinist view that God ultimately determines everything.[37] Grammatically, we might say, in this view it is forbidden to say that God "risks" or that God's will is not done. God's grace is "irresistible," as one of the five points of Calvinism says. From the other perspective, to say that God determines someone's choice yet that person is accountable makes no sense, or is ungrammatical. To say that God somehow wills someone to sin is contrary to the holiness of God. This sense of each side talking virtual nonsense in the terms of the other is a large part of what makes these debates so intractable and interminable. Communication therefore involves understanding from where each perspective is coming and appreciating what each perspective values. In the end, this is a place where each has to draw one's own determinative theological conclusions.

The strong Calvinist view claims that people are still free in that they actually "choose." They are thus still responsible and still deserving of eternal damnation for their sin. The other side of that equation is that God is not limited by free will and can determine free choices, which in contemporary parlance is called "compatibilism," that is, determinism and free will are compatible. Interestingly, this view also is represented by atheistic positions in which people are determined by genetics or by biology. It is usually argued by compatibilists of all stripes that people experience themselves as free; phenomenologically, experientially, and subjectively, we feel free, but objectively and ontologically we are not. "Theological" determinism claims somehow to maintain God's determination or ordination yet also human culpability. Proponents affirm that, though this seems paradoxical or contradictory, it is possible for God. For those who emphasize the unrestricted power of God, this is unsurprising: God can do anything, no matter how illogical or incomprehensible. To be omnipotent, God must be able to control anything, even free will. Opponents simply see this as contradictory. One cannot have it both ways, they say. Otherwise, one can make little sense of the human rebellion in Scripture that seems so displeasing and contrary to God's will. If God is controlling and determining everything, why are things so out of hand?

Incompatibilism, or libertarianism, is the view that genuine freedom means that some choices, to some extent at least, are within an agent's own power and not someone or something else's. This possibility, of course, is seen itself as a gift from God. It is usually regarded as a "self-limitation" on the part of God in order for humans beings to exist, to be free, and to love (which requires freedom). To put it positively, God is so powerful that God can grant being and freedom to others without being threatened. Human beings are created in God's image to have the capacity to fulfill the two greatest commandments, to love God and to love each other. In this way, they participate in the deepest way in God's nature as love (most fully seen in the light of the Trinity, as we shall see). In order to do so, however, they cannot be controlled or dominated but must have a certain independence or autonomy—not total but enough to be genuine individuals. This makes both the greatest and worst acts possible for human beings: love and sin. God is so great that God makes this possible. It is a divine self-limitation in one sense; in another it is the gracious gift of God, with God being strong and "secure enough," we might say, to withstand and not be threatened by rejection of God's love. In the tradition of dominative power, this makes God weak. In the tradition of donative power, it transposes God's power to a higher key. This is one of those places where neither position can be objectively proven; both can claim that they have a higher, more exalted sense of power. Rather, it is a place to exercise one's theological insight and intuition. The theological stakes are high because, again, what one decides here influences so much else.[38]

Freedom and Foreknowledge

These differing understandings of divine power have also resulted in a recent array of possibilities concerning free will, foreknowledge, and divine providence. These options are based, as in the issue of power, on another root theological judgment concerning the difficult issue of foreknowledge and freedom. Some do not understand how God could have foreknowledge, and our future actions nevertheless remain free. If God knows today what one will definitely do tomorrow, then these thinkers believe one's actions tomorrow are determined. The strong Calvinist view agrees with this but is committed to foreknowledge and thus ultimately denies genuine human freedom.

"Open theists," as they have commonly come to be called among evangelicals, agree with the strong Calvinists that foreknowledge eliminates freedom, so they swing to the other direction and deny divine foreknowledge.[39] In their view, they are not denying omniscience because they typically understand the future as something that cannot be known in principle. "Knowing the future" is thus, for them, something like a square circle. It is not actually something that could be done; it is a nonsensical statement. Thus, God has omniscience in that God knows everything that can be known. God does, however, in this view know everything that is determined in the future. If God has determined to return in the second coming at a certain time, then that event is determined. So, in their view, some events unilaterally determined by God can be foreknown. God, however, has chosen to create beings in God's image, who are thus free, which means that God has allowed that their free decisions cannot be precisely known until they are made. God can be an expert guesser, and would presumably have knowledge of all possibilities, so God is extremely ready and resourceful in responding to free decisions. In this view, a common analogy is of God as a master chess player who fully allows the novice chess player to move but is skillful enough to be thinking several moves ahead and to work around whatever the other player does.

Although another aspect of this view has not been developed as much, the same would apply to freedom in other areas of reality. If, as scientists generally indicate, genuine randomness exists in the natural world, perhaps both at the subatomic level and the level of everyday experience as treated by "chaos theory," then random acts also, by definition, would not be precisely known ahead of time by God. God could have created a deterministic nature where the future would have been foreknown. However, God chose not to create such a world, presumably because it would have lacked beings in God's image and the necessary natural conditions for such beings—and would have lacked many other things such as creativity, surprise, and so on. Thus it would not be as valuable or desirable a world. Open theists argue that God is never out of control ultimately because God has set the parameters for these diverse manifestations of freedom. God retains the power to "wrap it up," so to speak, at any point, even to the point of removing all freedom.

A third option rejects the assumption that foreknowledge and freedom are incommensurable. This is known as the traditional "Arminian" view, which was developed in the early seventeenth century by Arminius, originally a Calvinist who upon reflection rejected some of the strong Calvinist tenets.[40] A basic insight of broadly Arminian views is that God could have foreknowledge, and yet humans remain free. This is because God's knowledge is determined by future human choices, not the other way around. If humans were to make different choices in the future, then God would know that. So causation in the case of human freedom runs in the direction of humans to God, not vice versa. In this case, fore "knowledge" is not fore "determination." Neither strong Calvinists nor open theists grant this intuition and reject it as a philosophical judgment about reality, thus virtually "determining" their further theologies. Traditional Arminians accept this judgment, which "determines" their basic theological positions.

Traditional Arminians basically affirmed God's foreknowledge but perhaps did not realize that this really does not help in terms of God's providence.[41] If God only knows the future, then God cannot do anything differently in light of such knowledge. God could not guide someone to turn down a certain job because God knows how it would turn out because if the person did not take the job, then it would not happen and thus not be foreknown by God. God could only be a passive observer of what happens but would not be able creatively to alter the world in light of future knowledge of such contingencies. Yet the implication of much Christian practice is that God does act in light of some kind of knowledge of the future. For example, if people pray that God guide them in terms of a crucial decision, they often seem to be assuming something like this: God knows what would happen if they go to location A and what happens if they do not. If God knows that moving to location A would be a disaster, then God might lead them elsewhere. If God only has foreknowledge of the actual future, then God could not act to change what would happen in the future because then what God knew would not have been the future, and thus God would not have known it.

Because of this conundrum, a rediscovery of a sixteenth-century position has been offered by William Lane Craig as "the single most fruitful theological concept that I have ever encountered."[42] The theologian who developed this was Luis de Molina, so it is variously called "Molinism" or "middle knowledge." The latter characterization comes from the previously observed insight that God must possess more than simple foreknowledge in order for foreknowledge to be practically effective and more than just knowledge of all possibilities. What is efficacious is for God to have knowledge of what would happen, even if it never does in fact occur—as the prayer above assumes. Virtually any view understands that God has foreknowledge of all possibilities. What has not been understood is whether God has actual knowledge of what happens "between," so to speak, the knowledge of every possibility and the knowledge of the actual future. This "middle" knowledge is more precise than just the knowledge of possibilities because it assumes that if confronted with multiple possibilities and choices, God would know exactly which one a person *would* choose. This is knowledge in an odd sense because it sometimes includes knowledge of what never happens. In philosophy, it is therefore called "counterfactual knowledge."

In a theological context, it means that God knows, for example, whether John F. Kennedy would have won the 1964 presidential election if he had not been shot. God would have known also if Bobby Kennedy would have won the 1968 election if he had not been assassinated. To proponents, this view allows for genuine human freedom and for a great deal of influence of divine providence. Terrence Tiessen argues that it is a better expression of the kind of control that Calvinism desires because it allows for meticulous governance by God as well as freedom.[43] More typically, it is seen as allowing for a significant view of freedom to which God must respond and work around, engendering the grief and wrath displayed in biblical stories. Still, God has distinct advantages in responding. God would be able to take into account much more than God could from an open theist perspective. Lest one assume that more control is obviously desirable, to return to the theodicy issue, this means that God has more influence, but it makes God more liable for the amount and intensity of suffering in the world. God's power may be preserved at the cost of God's goodness. Most Molinists, however, like Craig, would argue that God still must work with true human freedom, which both significantly limits God's control and makes humans genuinely accountable for their choices. The challenge of theism, again, is somehow to hold together God's goodness and God's power. Molinists believe that this view strikes the best balance.

This treatment of options in foreknowledge hopefully not only introduces a prominent feature of the theological landscape, it also

shows how consideration of the divine attributes has major consequences for Christian practice, even Christian prayer, because each
view implies a significantly different way of praying. Tiessen actually considers at least ten different Christian models of providence
and indicates how each inculcates a different ethos in praying. A
strong Calvinist typically would pray more for acceptance; an open
theist would pray for God's guidance and influence and also for the
strength to face whatever comes; a Molinist would pray for God's
guidance in making the very best decision, already known by God.

Divine Suffering and Its Impact on Divine Attributes

Another related issue is the issue of divine suffering. As part of the
assumptions of the world around them, early Christians generally
took over the idea that God could not change (immutability) or suffer (impassibility). As discussed in the prolegomena, this view came
to be seen as orthodoxy until recently. As with power, it was not out
of suspicious or questionable motives that Christians affirmed that
God possessed all virtues in a perfect way. It was with the best of
intentions that God was praised as perfect. As in the case of power,
what they did not think to do was to question the meaning of perfection. For the most part, perfection meant power, not as shaped by the
biblical story but by the Hellenistic world, which could not imagine
a worthy God who was not immutable or impassible, significantly
like the God of Plato and Aristotle. Perhaps this is unfair; they came
to see the Bible through these lenses such that they understood the
Bible and these Hellenistic conceptions as synonymous. We also
must realize that we, too, are shaped by our culture and tend to find
in Scripture what we expect to find. This is the two-edged sword of
context and tradition.

An aspect of theism, then, has been that the personal, Creator
God whom we described previously has also been seen as omnipotent (in the dominative sense), immutable, and impassible. These may
all be questioned as inherent in theism—and their questioning at
the current time accounts for much of the ferment in contemporary
theology. Two related ideas were, one, that God is timeless because
time involves change. Since God is immutable, God cannot be in

time. For medieval theologians like Aquinas, a prior understanding of God was that God is "simple." The notion of divine simplicity, still sometimes defended, means that God cannot be composed of parts, hence cannot "come apart," or perish. It thus buttresses God's imperishability. The same argument was used by Socrates in the *Phaedo* for human immortality, where Socrates, in one last dialogue before drinking the poisonous hemlock to which he had been condemned, argued that the soul is simple, thus immortal. Divine simplicity means that all of God's properties are the same and interchangeable. Thus God cannot be mutable or passible because if some aspect of God is unchanging, then all aspects must be unchanging—since there are no aspects actually, just one simple being. God exists in one moment of eternity, with no before and after, having experienced everything all at once. For instance, God has already experienced for all eternity the consummation of all things in the distant future. Some in this view, such as Aquinas, argue that God consequently cannot be affected by humans but determines everything in one direction, from God to the creature.

These interlocking concepts have created great conundrums for Christian theology. One of the first questions that students ask about divine impassibility is, how can it be reconciled with the cross? The early Christians resolved this question in an ingenious way. As we will see later, in this same period, they were wrestling mightily with other issues about God and Jesus Christ as well. And to remind us that not everything that the early church borrowed from Hellenistic culture is problematic, most of the church considers the conclusions reached by the early councils with the aid of Hellenistic concepts to be extraordinarily insightful in Christology, especially given the tremendous political pressures of the time. One of these insights was that Jesus Christ is one person with two natures, divine and human. In this way, they maintained that Jesus Christ was fully human *and* fully divine, yet was not some kind of composite being (which would make him neither truly human nor truly divine). With this conceptuality in mind, theologians could say that Jesus Christ's human nature suffered but not the divine.[44] Even Jesus Christ's divine nature, therefore, never changed and is timeless and immutable. If these properties are essential to divinity, then this had to be the case.

At this point, questions usually begin to fly even faster. Does not the incarnation represent a change in God? How can timeless eternity be related to time? How does this view reconcile all of the passages in Scripture about God suffering, being upset, being pleased, and so on? Just like the immutability question, answers for each of these have been developed. In fact, we have had almost twenty centuries to work them out.[45] Still, they are troubling. It is striking to see how little of an issue they were for much of the history of the church, because the assumptions upon which they were based ran so deep. The founder of a seminary where I taught, James P. Boyce, who was trained by Princeton Calvinists, in the nineteenth century dealt with the question of biblical passages of suffering and change by saying that it was "sure" that passages of Scripture suggesting the suffering of God were anthropomorphisms and did not mean what they implied. Rather, it was "sure" that Scripture taught that God was impassible and immutable.[46] Sometimes it was so difficult to relate timelessness and the biblical story that theologians would appeal to mystery, saying that we cannot understand—but they must nevertheless be reconcilable. Perhaps all of us have to make such appeals at times, but we have to play that card carefully, because it quickly can open the door to virtually any contrary claim.

From the vantage point of many theologians today, it is "obvious" that the view of God as simple, timeless, immutable, and impassible is more of a picture of Aristotle's God than that of the Bible.[47] Ironically, this view is also much more consistent in Aristotle. Aristotle was not worried about God even caring or knowing anything about the temporal world. For him, God was a final cause who drew all things toward God, but God only thought and knew of God's own self.[48] When one takes that conception of God and adds incarnation and the cross, as well as the Trinity, as we shall see, the coherent Aristotelian picture is strained to the breaking point.

Conversely, if one drops the idea that God, in order to be perfect, must be simple, timeless, immutable, impassible, and dominatively omnipotent, the problems are lessened considerably. This seems to be behind the virtual sea change, almost overnight, in which many theologians have indeed abandoned those assumptions in the last half century.[49] Several advantages stand out. First, compatibility with Scripture is much more evident. While one still does not have to maintain that God thinks and feels in exactly the same embodied way that human beings do, one can see that these conceptions can have their ground in God in a meaningful way and are not evacuated of all content. It is striking that, in the Christian tradition, there has been a comfort level with ascribing thought to God but not emotions. Yet from our vantage point, this again seems to be influenced by the Hellenistic dualistic conception of the self that so prized the mind and reason over against threatening emotions. In other words, because the mind was so important, one could think of God as being "mind" and having "thought," but one could not imagine God having emotions or suffering. In the end, there seems to be no reason to privilege one over the other. All can be seen as truly grounded in God but in an analogous way, that is, in God's own unique way.

Second, a God who can change and is temporal is much easier to reconcile with the dynamic story of salvation in Scripture. God can be seen as initiating, responding, and adapting. God can be seen as a promising God who is faithful through changing vicissitudes of history. An important nuance is crucial here. If one is starting within the traditional paradigm, the first reaction is often that a changing God means that God must be getting better or worse — painting the troubling picture of a growing or a declining God. In fact, much of that assumption seems to have driven the Hellenistic affirmations of timelessness and immutability. Recent reflection indicates, however, that this is not necessarily so. God can be seen to be steadfast and even immutable in God's basic character, yet still have new experiences.[50] Failure to make this distinction made theologians fear that God was threatened by time and change. This went so far that Aquinas even followed Aristotle in maintaining that God does not think of us in terms of being affected by us. Rather, God affects us, but we do not affect God in any way. His example was the way an animal moves around a column.[51] To the animal, it looks like the column is changing. From the column's perspective, however, it is not changing. To be affected by people would be to disturb God and threaten God. What was wanted was a God above it all, so to speak.

An unperturbed God is bought at a very high price, however. It is a God who cannot deeply feel or grieve or even sympathize. The paradigmatic change can be seen here. From this newer perspective, one can see that God is even greater and more powerful to be able to be involved with people and yet remain God. As Walter Brueggemann points out, "The God of Israel is characteristically 'in the fray' and at risk in the ongoing life of Israel. Conversely the God of Israel is rarely permitted, in the rhetoric of Israel, to be safe and unvexed 'above the fray.'"[52] Who is the more powerful? The one who maintains equanimity by refusing to be involved, or the one who gets involved and yet retains equanimity? This is again one of those places for critical theological judgments that cannot easily be compared to one another.

A third advantage relates to timelessness, which implies the idea that even the future consummation has already occurred for God since God exists in "one moment" of eternity. Everything for God has happened all at once. There is no before and after in God. One can ask whether this does justice to the dynamic forward movement in the scriptural story. Can one imagine that God also looks forward to the consummation of all things? This sense of promise and fulfillment, suspense and satisfaction, is largely ruled out with timelessness. Does such a conception of timelessness not undermine the move toward the future that is so central in the Bible, which a temporal view undergirds? Of course, a temporal view also has enormous ramifications for eschatology, as we shall see. If God's life is timeless, it suggests that the afterlife is also a timeless state. While this may appear desirable, and has been a prominent conception, can a timeless state do justice to the visions of the final consummation, for example, in Revelation 21–22? Divine simplicity also poses a problem, for it forbids any new experience for God. In a sense, it seems to preclude a dynamic life in the sense of engaging and experiencing an other, in the sense of a world or human beings. Since

God is just one "thing," at least one aspect of which is unchanging, then no aspect of God can be changing or new. Besides this seeming very remote from the biblical picture of God, for many theologians, it seems artificial not to be able to say that some aspects of God are unchanging and some are not, which allows God to be the living God and ground of life.

Fourth, perhaps the most serious problem with these troublesome conceptions is impassibility, the denial of divine suffering. Here again, the scriptural picture of God, anthropomorphic (or anthropopathic) as it may be, is difficult to understand apart from a sense of divine suffering. More importantly, can the pathos of the cross and resurrection, central events for Christianity, be understood if God is unaffected, meaning that even Jesus Christ, in the divine nature, is also unaffected? Can this do justice to the passion of the Christ? Can a view of God as impassible do justice to the intense imagery of the book of Hosea, where God's sorrow over Israel's unfaithfulness is cast as the anguish of a husband whose wife is unfaithful or that of a parent of a rebellious child? Can it do justice to the emotions of the central figures in the parables of the Lost Coin, Lost Sheep, and Lost Son in Luke 18? Because these questions seem so unanswerable, this long-held affirmation of impassibility has been largely set aside by many theologians in favor of passibility.

Due to the interlocking nature of these concepts, this change points also to a God who is temporal and mutable as well as passible. It further urges a reconception of power in order to make sense of omnipotence compatible with suffering and weakness. Rethinking the nature of God in light of divine suffering brings love—and pathos—to the fore in a way that a focus on power does not. This reconceptualization is not a denial of power but is a significant transformation of the notion of power, a "baptism" of power if you will. The grain of the universe is thus not domination but donation.

It is fair to say that questions arising from this rethinking have not been resolved.[53] In this light, we should remember that the church has had almost two millennia to think through the previous paradigm, and we are just in the beginning of reformulation. It is also apt to remember that if we do not yet understand the nature of an atom, and may never fully do so, we will probably always struggle to understand the nature of God.

These reflections do not undermine a basic sense of theism that might be shared with Judaism and Islam, but they highlight the distinctiveness of the Christian notion of God. Christians put weight on the affirmations of a God who is monotheistic, personal, creative, loving, all-powerful, and purposeful—but these are subordinate to a God who exercises power through suffering, risking love. The Christian emphasis on love, moreover, points to the uniqueness of Christ, the cross, and resurrection. Ultimately, it points to the affirmation that most separates Christianity from Judaism and Islam, the Trinity.

THE TRINITY

To point to the Trinity as the outcome of our reflections on God as suffering love may be surprising because the doctrine of the Trinity is often seen as abstract, esoteric, and obscure, perhaps even insignificant. The renaissance of the doctrine of the Trinity, however, over the last century shows that this doctrine, properly understood, is not at the margins but at the center of the Christian conception of God—not an intellectual puzzle but a pastoral practice.[54]

Social or Individual Analogy

This may be seen first in the Trinity's relation to divine love in terms of a recent tectonic shift in the Western world concerning the doctrine of the Trinity.[55] For a variety of reasons, the Eastern church tended to understand the "threeness" of the Trinity in relation to the "oneness" of the God of monotheism along the lines of an analogy of three "persons" who are so much "one" that they actually are one, termed the "social Trinity" or "social analogy." This view obviously allows more room to think of love as the essence of God if God is eternally in loving relationship.

The Western church has tended, conversely, to think of the Trinity in terms of the analogy of a being who has different dimensions such as mind, will, and emotions, which has been called the "individual analogy." This does more justice to the oneness of God, to be sure, but makes it more difficult to think of God as being constituted by love apart from creation of others to love. In other words, love tends to become significant only in terms of creation, when there has been something to love, not as deeply determinative of God's nature. Traditionally, divine attributes have been distinguished in terms of those pertaining to God's being, apart from creation, properties *ad intra*, and those relational attributes pertaining to creation, properties *ad extra*. While these are rather arbitrary, this is a context where it may clarify differences between theological views. How can an individual being, with no other, love? Critics point out that this individualistic understanding of God dovetails with the excessive individualism of the West. It is thought also to provide crucial theological support at an earlier time for monarchical governments and the divine right of kings. The monarch represents the single power over society just as the pope, in the church, represents a single power over the church. Both in their own way picture the solitary God presiding over the world. Thus, there is a straight line from God to the monarch in a simple hierarchical system.[56]

Things are usually not that simple, however, and this clear contrast can be mitigated. The Eastern church has tended to emphasize the dominance of the Father over the Son and Spirit, resulting in their own support for monarchy and hierarchy. The social Trinity also has a ground in Augustine, whose views have been so dominant with respect to the individual Trinity. Later, the medieval Western theologian, Richard of Saint Victor (d. 1173), developed a form of the social Trinity emphasizing love between the persons in a more mutual way than most in the Eastern church.[57]

Nevertheless, most recognize differences in the two traditions and that our conceptions of God do have deep influences on how we approach the world. The dramatic shift of Western theologians recently to a recovered social Trinity can undergird a stronger view of love as the essence of the divine. For theologians such as Jürgen Moltmann and Stanley Grenz, this understanding runs throughout their theology in that a social view of God also implies a social view of the self, a stronger communitarian view of the church, and a more social view of eschatology.[58] This is in contrast to the influence of radical individualism in the West that has worked against all of these tendencies. In this sense, the emphasis on the social Trinity is an aspect of postmodern theologians' criticism of the damaging effect of radical individualism on the church and a recovery of the priority of love and community.

The rise of the social Trinity in the Western church has probably also been influenced by the fall of Communism and the new openness of West and East to each other. The creative ferment as a result of this leavening has seen an emphasis on the equality of persons in the Trinity as well as on the mutual love between them. This is actually an appropriation of a traditional term for the Trinity, perichoresis, often translated as "interpenetration." The members of the divine life engage thus in a divine dance (drawn from a related Greek word) in which humans are invited to participate.[59] Theologically, the persons of the Trinity, who may differ in terms of function, are best understood as equally divine, which, as we shall see, is in accord with the developing intuitions of the early church against understanding the Son or the Spirit as not fully divine. Here, the understanding of the oneness of God is crucial in seeing that any action of God is always the action of the whole Trinity. One cannot thus compartmentalize the Trinity, which would be a form of tritheism rather than monotheism. The early church expressed a formula for this: "the works of the Trinity ad extra (in creation) are indivisible."[60] At the same time, the Trinity is distinguished in light of the "economy," that is, in light of the history of salvation. The differentiation thus between Father, Son, and Spirit is not an artificial and peripheral understanding of the immanent Trinity but discloses it.

The attraction of grasping perichoresis in relation to a dance helps one imagine the divine Trinity as an eternal dance of communal love.[61] While this does not deny anything about God's power as Creator and Consummator, one can see how significantly this approach moves away from "dominative power" as being the first words to say about God. Rather, understanding God in terms of cooperative dance rather than dominating control helps one see how in fact "God is love" are the first words. Power becomes a subordinate way of expressing the divine dance in creation and redemption. As we shall see, this conception, which allows for divine action and suffering in a more robust way, opens up fresh insights into the nature of the passion as the Father suffering the death of the Son in the Spirit.

Developing Conceptions of Christ

The conclusions that the early church reached after several centuries of arduous travail over the doctrine of the Trinity have been so convincing that it is often difficult for Christians of any stripe to understand what all the fuss was about—but fuss there was. We so easily read the fifth-century conclusion at the Council of Chalcedon (451) into the New Testament that present-day students of Scripture often are stunned to discover that even two centuries after Christ the church still had not arrived at what is now taken for granted. In fact, at that point it does not appear that anyone had yet developed in much detail what later came to be considered orthodoxy.

As one reviews the history of the attempt to give an answer to Jesus' question to his disciples at Caesarea-Philippi, "Who do you say that I am" (Mark 8:29), what is striking is that virtually every possible answer was given in a significant way at some time by a substantial group of people. Before the New Testament was written and then canonized, of course, the problem was sharper. The four centuries of canonization correspond roughly to the time it took to hammer out the church's orthodox understanding of Christ. Initially, then, some of the alternatives rebounded on the issue of what Scripture is. Soon, however, in the second century the core of Scripture with the Gospels and the major Pauline Epistles was available to most of the church, but it still did not resolve things; it was only the beginning. Along with Scripture and its claims for Christ, the church continued to worship Christ as Lord. This put enormous strain on the Jewish foundations of the Christian faith and upon its basic monotheistic stance. Virtually all wanted to maintain monotheism—but they also desired to support the church's practice in worshipping the Christ. To some extent, holding these together remains a mystery.

At the beginning of the second century, four major views had made their way from the Eastern church to Rome.[62] One option was to hold firmly to monotheism and to Jesus as a human being. Various forms of adoptionism began with Jesus as human but saw him at some point as adopted or raised to higher status, perhaps at his baptism or resurrection. The Ebionites appeared to be an early remnant of Judaizing Christianity who thought that Christ so fulfilled the Law that God chose him to be the Messiah. The author of the *Shepherd of Hermas* of Rome (110–140) similarly saw Jesus' obedience rewarded by being chosen to be a partner of the Holy Spirit, yet Jesus was still but a forerunner of the rest of us. A later second-century adoptionist movement is sometimes called dynamic monarchianism because it preserves the supremacy of the Father. This was a reaction against an emphasis on the Fourth Gospel that had such a high view of the Word (the *logos*) as divine, which was stronger in the Eastern church than in the Western. These *alogoi* (anti-Logoists) stressed the subordination of Christ. Theodotus the Tanner from Byzantium, for example, taught in 190 in Rome that Jesus was a man upon whom the Divine Christ or Holy Spirit fell. Some of his followers denied divinity to Jesus, but others thought he became in some sense divine at his resurrection. Theodotus was finally excommunicated by Bishop Victor of Rome. Paul of Samosota, bishop of Antioch around 260–272, thought of the Logos or Son of God as an impersonal attribute of the Father, by whom Jesus was filled or indwelt. Thus Jesus was united to God in will by his love but was not one substance with God. The union is moral but inseparable. In this way, Jesus Christ has a kind of delegated divinity. These views were considered by three synods between 264 and 269, and the last excommunicated him. Paul of Samosota represents a tradition at Antioch that persisted in emphasizing the human side of Jesus and a functional union between the divine Logos and the human Jesus rather than an essential or ontological union. In other words, the relationship is more of a heightened form of the kind that any human could have rather than a unique difference: to use other language, it is a matter of degree rather than of kind. It may be good to remark here that, while this approach came to be considered heretical, one recalls from the chapter on revelation that it is this school's more literal approach to biblical interpretation that is usually championed by

Protestants over against the Alexandrians' allegorical approaches—but whose views on the Trinity came to be more favored. This Antiochan alternative on Christ has also remained a live option for much of the church up to the present day.

Conversely, a second option emphasized the divinity in relation to the humanity. A major approach that accentuated the divinity was the Logos Christology rooted in the Gospel of John. The Johannine school, centered in Ephesus where apparently both John and Paul worked, combined the two in a way that focused on the incarnation, union with Christ, and life with Christ. These emphases remained distinctive of the Eastern church as opposed to the Western church's emphasis on the side of Paul that stressed legal reconciliation more than mystical reconciliation. This view emphasized that Jesus Christ was the incarnation of the Logos. Justin the Martyr (d. 165), probably converted in Ephesus, saw Christianity as the true philosophy. He emphasized the Logos at the expense of the earthly Jesus. Still, the Logos is subordinate to the Father, yet one with him in some indefinite sense. Irenaeus (ca. 140–200), who was brought up in Asia Minor where he had contact with Polycarp and who knew John, saw Christ as the second Adam, who restores what Adam lost by recapitulating the stages of Adam's fall. The Logos, of course, is preexistent and became human so that "what we had lost in Adam . . . we might recover in Christ Jesus."[63] Tertullian was a Western thinker with a legal mind who coined the term "trinity" (trinitas) from "tri-unity (unitas)" and also presciently anticipated later formulations in seeing Father, Son, and Spirit as three "persons" (personae) but still one substance (substantia). The Son and Spirit are nevertheless subordinate to the Father, a tendency that remained in Logos Christologies until Augustine in the fifth century and continued in the Eastern church.

A third view that emphasized the divinity of Christ in another way was "modalistic monarchianism," which understood Christ's activity as a divine mode of the one God. In this view, the one God is manifested sometimes as Father, at others as the Son, and at others as the Spirit. This was a major alternative because most wanted to emphasize the oneness of God against heathenism, and the Logos

Christologies and dynamic monarchians seemed to undermine it. It arose in the East, like dynamic monarchianism and the Logos Christologies. Noetus taught from 180–200 "that Christ was the Father Himself, and that the Father Himself was born and suffered and died."[64] This problematic formulation led to the charge of "patripassionism," which was declared a heresy because it seemed to claim that the Father, not just the Son, died on the cross. Praxeas taught these ideas in Rome around 190, of whom Tertullian said, "He put the Paraclete to flight and crucified the Father."[65] Sabellius also taught these views in Rome around 215 to such an extent that it is often called "Sabellianism." He was excommunicated in Rome but had a large following in the East. His identification of Father, Son, and Holy Spirit was rejected, but the implication of the basic equality of the three ultimately triumphed in Augustine. As one can see, the refinement of understanding of the Trinity was a complex conversation that included and sometimes benefited from many who are now considered heretics.

Besides the obvious problem of dealing with Jesus' prayers to the Father, the modalistic view seemed to make the revelation of God in Christ a temporary one that does not reveal God ultimately. The "economic Trinity," which refers to the revelation of God in a three-fold way in salvation history, is then contrasted with the "immanent Trinity," God as God is in God's self. The two Karls, Karl Barth and Karl Rahner, perhaps the preeminent Protestant and Catholic theologians, respectively, of the twentieth century, particularly emphasized that Christ could not be the supreme revelation of God if he were only temporary. The principle that the immanent Trinity is the economic Trinity, and vice versa, has come to be known as "Rahner's Rule."[66] In making this emphasis, they were contending against a tendency to favor the immanent Trinity since the early centuries of the church.

In terms of an overemphasis on divinity or on the Father, a fourth option denied the genuine humanity of Jesus. This extreme view was an earlier great rival to the orthodox position in the second century— and perhaps even in the first—namely, the gnostic movement that has recently come to the fore with the discovery of lost gospels and other documents at Nag Hammadi in 1945–1946. The Gnostic Gospels represent movements in early Christianity that hallowed Jesus but in a dualistic, Platonic way. They sharply distinguished, as did Plato, between spirit, which is good, and matter, which is the source of evil. This kind of thought was very dominant in the early centuries of Christianity, much like democracy is part of our thought-world.[67] It represented a grave rival to what we now call the orthodox view, but at the time, views did not come neatly labeled as orthodox and heterodox: they had to be hammered out. An early form of this general view is called "docetism," which thought that Christ only seemed to be human. What is clear is that there were major groups of Christians who thought that the gnostic, docetic understanding was the true and best interpretation of Christ and represented not a minor but a major alternative. In fact, as we have seen, there are scholars who today argue that the wrong view won and that much was lost with the demise of the gnostic alternative. We are following here the line of reasoning that led the church to reject such alternatives as not doing justice to the genuine humanity of Christ.

Up to this point, at the end of the second century and before the crucial first Council of Nicea in 325, several startling observations can be made. Several different ways of understanding the humanity and divinity of Christ had already emerged and were followed by significant contingents, often rooted in geography. The response of excommunication raised the ante. The issue became, then, not just of who predominated in theological discussion with the best argument but an issue of identity, fellowship, and even damnation for the loser. Moreover, the views typically gravitated toward Rome, which was soon to become central to the Western church, as we know. In Rome, however, at the end of the second century, there were several major attempts to understand Christ, all of them having some strengths but not even one of them representing what later came to be considered orthodoxy.[68] In other words, almost two centuries after Christ, the orthodox interpretation of Scripture on Christ that for centuries has seemed virtually self-evident had not been seen by anyone as far as we know. This serves as a reminder of how crucial the role of theological reflection has been in the history of the church.

Another generalization is that most of the views originated among Eastern theologians, who were said to have had subtler minds and better analysis—but less consensus. The most influential theologian of the East, Origen of Alexandria (ca. 185–254) could be interpreted on both sides of the issue of the divinity of the Son. He taught the "eternal generation" of the Son, which comes from the language of Jesus as the "only-begotten (generated) Son" (John 3:16). Instead of the Christ coming to be as a creation of God at some later time, the Son could be seen as eternally generated. Still, at times he implied adoptionist ideas in seeing the Son as a second God and as a creature.

The Conciliar Development of the Trinity

A fateful controversy, the Arian, then erupted and corresponded with one of the major paradigmatic shifts in the history of the church. From a persecuted sect, Christianity became the adopted faith of the Emperor Constantine in the early fourth century. Soon it would be virtually the official faith of the Roman Empire. It is still debated whether this was a boon or bane, but it certainly brought about a change in status and nature so dramatic that some thought that the millennium, the one-thousand-year reign of Christ in the world mentioned in Revelation 20, had arrived. One of those changes was that the emperor would become heavily involved with the affairs of the church, because division within the church could become a division within the empire. While this led sometimes to dreadful meddling, it also led to the rise of the great early councils of the church that provided the doctrinal bedrock for virtually every major Christian group. The Reformation, for example, did not touch the results of the first four major councils of the church, which stretched from 325 to 451, councils to which both the Western and Eastern churches appeal since they predate the church's split.

In Alexandria, in 320, Arius, who had adoptionist influences from his study with Lucian of Antioch, thought that Origen believed Christ to be a created being, not of the substance of God, but made of nothing. Arius even developed a catchy jingle that helped further his views: "There was when he [Christ] was not." This meant that, in some sense, Christ is a lower god, neither fully God nor fully human. It was a way of preserving the immutability of the Father and placing mutability in the Son. Arius' bishop, Alexander, held the other side of Origen's teaching, that the Son was eternal, of the essence of the Father, and uncreated. Arius enlisted support from the powerful bishop of Nicomedia, Eusebius, who had been a fellow student with him of Lucian. The resultant turmoil caused Constantine, who had won control of East and West in 323, to call the Council of Nicea in 325, a strategy he had earlier employed in the Donatist dispute, which concerned whose baptism was valid. Only six bishops were from the West; all the rest were from the East. One small party represented the Arians. Another small group supported Alexander. Most supported Origen and had little notion what to make of the issue. Of course, Constantine was a major participant who primarily wanted peace and unification.

Eusebius of Caesarea, the famous church historian, offered a creed from his church that pre-dated the controversy. To it were added such phrases as "begotten, not made," "of one essence (*homoousion*) with the Father." The council rejected Arian phrases such as "there was when He was not," and "He was made of things that were not." They used words such as *essence, substance* (*ousia*), and "*hypostasis*" as equivalent, which later were seen as quite different. The relevant passages are the following:

> We believe in one God, the Father All-sovereign, maker of all things visible and invisible.
> And in one Lord Jesus Christ, the Son of God, begotten of the Father, only-begotten, that is, of the substance [*ousias*] of the Father, God of God, Light of Light, true God of true God; begotten, not made, of one substance [*homoousion*] with the Father, through whom all things were made.[69]

These phrases, as we have seen, already had acceptance in the West, so Constantine seemed to like the idea of the West agreeing with a part of the East. With his direction, all but two of the bishops signed it. The two and Arius were banished.

One might think that debate was over, but it was really just beginning in the East. The Arians rejected the use of the word *homoou-*

sion. To others, it seemed Sabellian, not allowing for distinctions in the Trinity. Eusebius of Nicomedia, Arius' friend, then gained great influence over Constantine. The great defender of Nicea also came on the scene, namely, Athanasius, who had been a young secretary to Bishop Alexandria at Nicea. As bishop of Alexandria, Athanasius defended the tenets of Nicea, if one can imagine, through five different banishments. Typical of the East, Athanasius thought the issue was one of salvation, which underscores the way that Trinitarian and christological doctrine was not driven by speculative impulses but by the practical issue of salvation. Only by true divinity taking on full humanity, he thought, could humanity be saved: "He was made human that we might be made divine." This formulation, called "divinization," or *theosis* (becoming God), which rings strange in Western church ears, did not mean that humans would become fully divine in a Hindu or Mormon sense but basically means what Western Christians call "becoming Christlike." In 335, Constantine supported Arius' restoration and Athanasius' banishment. The night before the ceremony in which Arius was to be restored, however, in 336, Arius died. Then Constantine died in 337.

The empire was divided between Constantine's sons, Constans in the West and Constantius in the East. They became even more involved in the religious issues than their father and caused the spread of the Nicene controversy from the East to both empires. First, they allowed exiled bishops, including Athanasius, to return in 337, but when Eusebius (the Arian) was promoted to bishop of Constantinople, he had Athanasius banished again in 339 and replaced by an Arian bishop, Gregory. Arianism seemed dominant in the East.

What is important to realize, given our sense of theology long secured and noncontroversial, is that a view such as Arianism prevailed at certain times. If history had stopped at several points, the church's official doctrine would have been Arianism, as strange as that may seem, given that Arianism saw Christ, from our eyes, as semidivine, a creature created, "begotten," by the Father—but not fully God. Arius could appeal to a literal interpretation of Scripture: God gave "his only-begotten Son" (John 3:16). He could appeal to

divine immutability and was concerned to protect the true divinity of the Father. The Son was the one who could be mutable and
passible. In the end, his views seem an odd compromise—yet they
almost became official doctrine.

To return to the story, in the West, the bishop of Rome, Julius,
called a Western synod and protested the banishment of Athanasius
(who had fled to Rome). The East responded by trying to do away
with the Nicene Creed itself. Then in 341, Eusebius the Arian died.
When Athanasius' rival, Gregory, died, Constans got Constantius
to allow Athanasius to return. Then a rival emperor to Constans
arose, Magnentius, whose supporters killed Constans in 350. In
353, Constantius conquered Magnentius and became sole ruler of
the empire. In the meantime, Athanasius' aggressive promotion of
Nicea in Alexandria fostered a backlash by the Arian, Aetius (d.
ca. 370), who baldly stated that the Logos is "unlike" the Father.
In addition, Constantius came to see Athanasius as a troublemaker.
He caused Athanasius to be banished again in 356 and brought the
Western bishops to support the East. At a synod held at the emperor's
home in 357, terms like *ousia, homoousios,* and *substantia* were forbidden as unscriptural, which meant the end of Nicea and the triumph
of a kind of adoptionism. They called the Son "like" (*homoios*, rather
than "same" *homos*) the Father and thus were called the *Homoion*
party. This great dispute over the letter *i* (*iota* in Greek) is actually
the source of the expression "not one iota of a difference," but in
this case, it threatened the Trinity itself. Again, by 360, Arianism
seemed to have won as official imperial orthodoxy.

At this time, the vast majority were actually not happy with the
Arians and joined forces with the Niceans. This compromise party
actually preferred the term *homoiousios,* meaning not the same substance but a like or similar substance with equality of attributes.
They were also beginning to distinguish between *ousia* (substance
or essence) and *hypostasis* (subsistence), not making them equivalent
as in the Nicene Creed. Then they could support Origen's affirmation of three hypostases but still see them as one essence in some
way. Athanasius, however, from exile argued strongly for a compromise, stating that *homoousion* protects the unity of God but did not

mean that the Son is identical with the Father. Athanasius' qualification of the meaning of *homoousion* did justice to the interests of both sides and supported the Greek formula of the Trinity being one *ousia* (being) with three *hypostases*. This coalition between Asia Minor and Alexandria eventually overcame the Arians.

Constantius died in 361 and was succeeded by Julian, the last heathen emperor. Since Julian wanted to foment problems in the church, he let Athanasius return in 362 but then banished him within the year because Athanasius was so successful at converting heathens. When Julian was killed the next year, his successor Jovian allowed Athanasius to return again. Jovian's short rule ended in 364 and was succeeded by Valentinian I. He put the East in the charge of his brother, Valens, influenced by the Arians, who then promptly exiled Athanasius for the fifth time in 365. Athanasius was able to return soon, however, and died in 373, "old and full of years" and fame. In the meantime, two other influences were arising.

One is that the nature of the Holy Spirit came into the picture. It seemed logical that if the Son was *homoousios*, then the Spirit should be *homoousios* also or "consubstantial" with the Father. Arians, however, who saw the Son as the chief creature produced by the Father, consistently saw the Spirit only as the chief creature produced by the Son.[70] Just as there was a tendency in Arius to place the Son in a mediate position, once the Son's full consubstantiality with the Father was established, the Spirit was sometimes seen as in a mediate position between them and creation. In 362, a synod held in Alexandria, where Athanasius was working out the compromise on *homoousios*, also condemned those who made the Holy Ghost a creature and separate from the essence of the Father and the Son.

In the early fifth century, Augustine suggested that the Spirit proceeds from the Father "and the Son" (*filioque*), a great change from the Nicene Creed. This suggested, on the one hand, a superiority of the Father and the Son over the Spirit, but on the other hand, more of an equality of the three persons against the primacy of the Father over the Son and the Spirit. These disputed interpretations became a major bone of contention between the West and the East (which rejected the *filioque*) and a major reason for the subsequent split.

The second influence was that of the three great Eastern theologians, the Cappadocians, the brothers Basil of Caesarea (the administrator) and Gregory of Nyssa (the theologian) and their friend Gregory of Nazianzus (the preacher). The victory of the new compromise Nicene movement is attributed primarily to them. They in fact built upon Athanasius but had influenced Athanasius' understanding of God as one being with three hypostases. Concerning the Holy Spirit, Gregory of Nyssa clarified that the Spirit is distinguished from the Son by *proceeding* out of the Father *through* the Son. The Son is eternally *generated*; the Spirit eternally *proceeds*.[71] They are seen sometimes, though, as modifying Athanasius' emphasis—which is more typically Western—on one God leading a three-fold personal life to three divine hypostases who have the same nature. For the Western theologians, the threeness was the problem. For the Eastern theologians, the unity was the problem. For example, the Greek *hypostasis* indicated subsistent modes of being, thus highlighting the threeness. The Latin *persona* did not connote the modern idea of an individual but a mask, so it highlighted the oneness of God "behind the three masks." Ironically, in the modern period, "person" now connotes three individuals, closer to the Greek idea, if not actual tritheism.

Back to imperial influence! Valens died in 378, leaving Gratian as the ruler. Gratian appointed Theodosius governor of the East and eventually ruled for a time the whole empire. Theodosius, who was born in Spain, preferred the theology of the West, the Nicene. With Gratian, he issued an important edict in 380 that made Christianity officially the one religion of the empire and the type of Christianity the new Nicene one, namely, one essence (*ousia*) in three hypostases in the East, or one substance (*substantia*) in three persons (*personas*) in the West.

Under Theodosius, a council was held at Constantinople in 381. This council rejected Arianism, reapproved the Nicene Creed, and supported the consubstantiality of the Holy Spirit. Perhaps most notably, it also rejected Apollinarianism. As attention turned to the relation of the divine and human in Christ, Apollinaris, bishop of Laodicea (d. ca. 390), was an important figure. As an Eastern thinker, he thought Christ had to be fully divine to save humanity. Apollinaris moved to say that Jesus had the body of a person, but his reason or animating spirit was that of the Logos. These views so elevated Christ's divinity that they had long-lasting influence in Eastern thinking. The problem was that they seemed to deny Christ's true humanity by not seeing Jesus Christ as fully human. Thus, they were condemned at this Council.

After the crucial Councils of Nicea and Constantinople, then, we have two basic Trinitarian formulas of God as one substance in three persons (the Latin form) or one being in three hypostases (the Greek form). Nicea affirmed that Christ was fully divine, Constantinople that he was fully human. Developments in Christology and the next two major councils will await that chapter, but more can be said about the Trinity at this point.

This historical narrative is given to indicate that doctrine developed in the early church much as one sees it now in the church—in the midst of boiling pots of politics, dissension, rivalries, personalities, but also of careful thinking and sincere intentions. Theology also emerges from incarnate life. Perhaps we learn much about providence from looking closely at history. We can often be discouraged at the omnipresence, it seems, of such human pettiness and fallibility in the midst of matters of great moment; history can remind us that, just as in the biblical story, so in the church's story, God is present, and that, over time, truth can be gained despite such failings.

In the renaissance of reflection upon the Trinity in the last century, other major issues crystallized—for most theologians, if not for all. Rahner's Rule has already been mentioned. Perhaps motivated by the rise of the social Trinity, clear emphasis upon the equality of the persons of the Trinity emerged, although this still arose from an ancient formula (all the works of the Trinity are indivisible). From both East and West has arisen an emphasis on sociality and love. With this insight and allowance for divine temporality, greater emphasis on the eternal dynamism of the Trinity can be seen. A favorite image is the eternal divine dance that in creation extends outward and invites all to participate.[72] Eschatology then becomes the expectation of all creation joining in the divine dance in eternal celebration.

With the emphasis on equality, how can distinctions be made? Here is the place for continuing reflection. One response is to see that the differences in the persons of the Trinity simply lie in their relationships. The Son is not the Father, nor the Father the Spirit, nor the Spirit the Son. Sometimes this goes so far as to suggest that the three are pure relations without a "related," which perhaps stretches even an analogy to a breaking point.[73] It does, however, remind us that the Trinity is unique and not literally comparable to any finite thing. A second response is to see differentiation but not dominance in the eternal relationships of the Son being eternally begotten of the Father and the Spirit eternally proceeding from the Father (and the Son?).

A third response has been to express the activities in the economic Trinity as integrated activities. An existential way of expressing this is to see the Father as Primordial Being or Letting-Be, the Son as Expressive Being, and the Spirit as Unitive Being.[74] Barth's formulation was God as Revealer, Revelation, and Revealedness.[75] Another could be the Sayer, the Said, and the Saying. A more traditional Augustinian view is to see the three as the Lover, the Beloved, and the Relationship between the two, which again tends to leave the Holy Spirit in a nebulous, almost insubstantial, position. A very recent one is Source, Wellstream, and Living Water.[76] These are better attempts than some traditional attempts such as Sun, Ray, and Heat (Tertullian) because, as suggestive as it is, they can be separated. Another problematic example is water as ice, liquid, and steam, which actually appears to be modalism. An opposed criticism can be given to traditional ways of distinguishing them in terms of Creator, Redeemer, and Sanctifier. Although these are enshrined in the Apostle's Creed and the liturgy of much of the church, as well as in many theologies, they can threaten the rule of interpenetration or *perichoresis*.[77] The Son is involved in creation, as is also the Spirit. Likewise with redemption and sanctification. This will be important, for example, in reviewing a traditional substitutionary model of the atonement, where it tends to separate the Father's intention (wrathful) from the Son's (reconciling).

In Christology, we will look more closely at recent reflection on the cross in light of these newer views of the Trinity. Instead of seeing the divine Father and Son as impassible, the mystery of the Trinity enters the mystery of the cross, where the Father suffers the death of the Son but is not the Son. The Son experiences death before the Father, but is not the Father. At this point, the role of the Holy Spirit must be included, but it is easy to see how a dynamic Trinitarian formulation can move us more deeply into the pathos of the death of the Son of God on a cross. We will return to this momentous event after further consideration of other important councils, of Christology in general, and of atonement.

This dynamic approach to the cross points also to the renaissance of the doctrine of the Holy Spirit in the last few decades. The interpenetrating role of the Holy Spirit in the cross points to the way we both comfort and suffer the suffering of others—in the presence, comfort, and power of the Spirit. The New Testament, particularly in the last discourse of Jesus in the Gospel of John in terms of the "Paraclete," indicates several roles of the Holy Spirit, which is important because the paucity of attention to the Holy Spirit, apart from the new Pentecostal and charismatic traditions, tends to impoverish our grasp of the breadth of the activity of the Holy Spirit. The Spirit comforts and convicts, trains and teaches. As the Spirit of God and of Christ (in both John and Paul), the Spirit combines, in a dynamic tension, the breathtaking power of new creation as difficult to control and corral as the wind with the dove-like ministrations of peace, nurture, and comfort. Both sides are important. Creativity and conviction are not always experienced as comfortable or controllable. The dynamic guidance of the Holy Spirit points to the situational sense in which the Spirit leads, at the right time and in the right way, to give the apt word and fitting gesture, whether it be a word of judgment or an embrace of peace. The church has often sought to define and legalize the delicate tension between faith and works, grace and law, judgment and compassion. The Holy Spirit reminds us, as the Spirit of Jesus Christ who did the same in the first century, that legalism never works; we can never transcend our finitude, our seeing in part, or the need for the judicious reliance on the timely whispering of the Holy Spirit.

An initial reaction of other denominations to the rise of Pentecostalism in the early twentieth century was almost denial of the Holy Spirit altogether. With the explosive growth of the Pentecostal and charismatic movements worldwide, expected to continue in exponential growth in the next century in the Southern Hemisphere in Latin America, Africa, and Asia, fresh attention is finally being paid to the crucial role of the Holy Spirit in the "last days."[78] Peter's famous sermon at Pentecost announced in fulfillment of Joel's prophecy that in the last days young women and young men, old women and old men, would be prophesying and visioning under the power of the Holy Spirit (Acts 1:17; Joel 2:28). The implication of Acts is that we have been in the last days for twenty centuries. According to John, it was better for the church for Christ to depart this earthly life; the Paraclete is the Spirit of Christ indwelling anyone who will receive the Spirit, which is even better than Christ's earthly presence (John 16:7). The Spirit continually leads the church toward life beyond legalism as a dimension of the way the Spirit as the eschatological Spirit leads the church into the future. The Spirit unites (Eph 4:3) even as the Spirit convicts (John 16:8). One can hardly understand the more recent interest in spirituality and mysticism as well as lively worship apart from a fresh interest in the Holy Spirit.

THE TRINITY AND GOD-TALK

Such "thick description" of the Trinity reminds us, as little else can, of a common understanding across the history of the church of the limitations of our language about God.[79] Emphasis among Protestants upon revelation and Scripture, combined with the modern fascination with the clear and precise, can easily make our God "too small," in the ringing words of J. B. Phillips.[80] We can miss the fact that most theologians have stressed the frail grasp that we have on God. As the Trinity reminds us, God is unique. The most dominant way of thinking about our "God-talk" sees that our best language, even based on special revelation, is analogy. Aquinas is seen as an originator of scholastic theology that surely tried to peer too far and claim to know too much. As we have seen, however, Aquinas' first step in the understanding of God was to agree with the "negative" theologians that we must initially deny that anything we say of God can be literally true.[81] While he did not stop with the *via negativa*, he agreed that it contained an essential insight. In his terms, God is Being Itself (Being *qua* Being), while language arises from beings, the world of finite things. As such, our language must be stretched almost to the snapping point to try to grasp God. Even then, Aquinas startles us by saying that we can only know "that" God is, not "what" God is.[82] Eastern theologians make this point by saying that we know God's energies but not God's essence.[83] God's inner being is forever beyond our best grasp. What these theologians underscore is the way our understanding of language, which we touched on in the prolegomena and revelation chapters, is more clearly seen as theologically shaped by our doctrine of God.

Some contemporary thinkers, with better understandings of the creative power of metaphor, describe all of our language about God as, at best, metaphorical.[84] Like any metaphor, such language always must be affirmed and denied. For every "is," an "is not" must be whispered. It is important to realize that this is not the result of an unbelieving skepticism, which would be laughable to apply to premodern theologians like Aquinas. It is the reflection of an immense humility and modesty before the majesty of God.

Such reticence with its "is not," however, also contains an "is." Here Aquinas could not remain within the strictures of the negative theologians that were strong in the early church, influenced by a metaphysics of a Being beyond being that perhaps owed more to Plato than to the Bible.[85] In this sense, rather than language being a constraint, permission is given to the fecundity of language almost to explode in images for God. Theology itself perhaps has played a part in restricting the luxurious play of language in Scripture that abounds with images of God, from human images of mother, father, parent, and lover, to animals from lion to hen, to innumerable objects such as mountains and fortresses, even to tiny seeds and grains of salt. Theology tends to thin the undergrowth of language about God in Scripture, but even our more disciplined theological language leads us astray if we do not remember its roots in figurative language. Even our theological language is figurative all the way down.

As we indicated in the prolegomena, Paul Tillich, using the language of symbol, pointed out in what was a revolutionary thought in the philosophy of language at the time that sometimes things can be better said in symbols than in any other way.[86] Sometimes theology turns to prosaic explanation, not to replace symbols, but to enable us better to understand the symbol as symbol. At other times, a symbol or metaphor is "explained" by another metaphor, which seems to be the preferred biblical mode and one preferred by Jesus. How often did he picture the kingdom and then offer another picture? Theology cannot escape its roots, but in the sense of theology as part of a hermeneutical spiral, it must not replace the figurative but rather point us back to the figurative, now understood in a richer and deeper way. Understanding the metaphors of God as "Abba" or of the kingdom of God can take a lifetime. As mentioned before, if even our hardest of sciences can now be seen to have inevitable recourse to metaphor precisely because of the mystery with which it deals, we should not be surprised if the language of God strains our human conceptions even more.

As mentioned, many in the early church were drawn to the *via negativa*. They thought that this did most justice to the transcendence of God as well as underscoring a mystical form of spirituality that meditatively turned away from the outer world, with its literal objects and words, and toward an intense encounter with God that was beyond expression in words (ineffable). This earnest spiritual tradition in the church is unfortunately often neglected as people who are hungry for prayer and meditation seek a deeper spirituality but do not find it in the church—and thus turn to other traditions, Eastern and New Age in particular. As Aquinas pointed out, however, this negative way forestalled another option. While being correct to reject the literal or univocal way, the negative way did not grasp an analogical way. Fortunately, the rich explosion of reflection upon figurative language in the last half century helped us realize that figurative language need not be reduced to literal language to be understood. It does not hurt to have a literal explanation, as preachers have long understood. On the other hand, sometimes the meaning is facilitated better by a story or symbol than an involved prosaic explanation—as preachers have also long understood. This new appreciation of the disclosive power of figurative language, as we saw in the previous chapter on revelation, has borne much fruit in a new appreciation of the nature of figurative language about God that so dominates Scripture.

With this portrayal of religious language in mind, it may help us to bring into focus more easily a contentious contemporary debate about the use of feminine imagery for God. The Bible and the church itself have generally existed in patriarchal cultures, making the issue more pressing of whether the traditional inhibition about feminine language for God is genuinely biblical or a contingent, cultural issue. If one begins with the above theological reflection about language, developed without reference to this issue, it dissolves much of the problem. The basic theological issues are these: (1) Scripture itself sometimes uses feminine language for God, along with a multitude of other images (Ps 139:2; Hos 11:3-4). (2) All language is at the very least analogical or "stretched" when it comes to God simply because of God's transcendence and uniqueness. (3) Thus, all language, including masculine and feminine images for God, must be denied as well as affirmed. In other words, any language for God must be understood in terms of strengths and weaknesses, capacities and limitations. (4) Women and men are both clearly in the image of God (which we will explore further in the doctrine of humanity). In fact, it may take both to express the image of God fully. This is a crucial point, for it means language that is one sided and exclusive cannot do justice to the revelation of God in Scripture, on Scripture's own terms. This is a pertinent point that Elizabeth Johnson, a devoted Roman Catholic theologian, makes against Thomas Aquinas in her book *She Who Is*.[87] Aquinas' favorite characterization of God, drawn from Aristotle, is "He who is." As we have said, Aquinas makes clear that no term literally applies to God. Because God is Creator, any creature can in some way analogously represent God. There is no reason, therefore, to deny that "she who is" is an appropriate description of God, especially given Aquinas' belief that both men and women are created in the image of God. It would be invalid if Johnson made the same mistake on the other side and only allowed "She who is." Johnson, however, desires more, rather than fewer, figures for God. She is able to show, on Aquinas' own terms, that it is contrary to his and thus most traditional theology to restrict the understanding of God to "He who is."

In the end, Christian practice has sometimes been more impoverished and restricted than biblical usage. The result has been to rob Christians, especially the half (or more than half!) of the church who are women, of rich resources for understanding and relating to God. One can argue, of course, that such deprivation harms men as well as women, since both miss out on a fuller understanding of God. Another result has been to foster by implication a heretical theology that women are somehow not in the image of God and that God is somehow male but not female, when proper theology understands God to include but transcend both. One need read no farther than the first chapter of the Bible to understand this (Gen 1:26-27), but it is not the first time that the church can be pulled far from its roots by its surrounding culture.

When one adds to these biblical and theological reflections the sad history of the church in which the dominant practice of theologians, virtually all male of course, has been to diminish women's being in the image of God or to see women as "misbegotten" men as did Aquinas, again following Aristotle, one sees the vital importance of sound theology.[88] I have experienced women who did not believe that they were in the image of God due to the church's teaching. I have seen young girls wonder why God is a man, feeling distanced from God. In an earlier time, men were thought to represent and include women in themselves, so God as a male could naturally be thought to represent all people. As Daphne Hampson countered, however, in a historic article, "Today men are not in the same way held to represent women: there are two sexes and women represent themselves."[89] To continue to think of God as only male is thus not just to misrepresent Scripture but to omit and often alienate women. To misunderstand God is often to mistreat people. To understand God as a tyrant fosters human tyrants. To understand God as only male fosters male dominance and the suppression of women. It means depriving the church of the multitude of spiritual gifts that God has richly provided but which have been locked away, much like the man who hid all of his talents in Jesus' parable (Matt 25:14-30; Luke 19:11-27). Is it too much to imagine that just as the master in the parable was quite displeased, that God is displeased with the church's squandering of God's gifts?

More social-psychological arguments indicate that when exclusively male language is used, even when consciously understood to be inclusive, it is subconsciously understood by both men and women to mean male and not female. The historical denigration of women, as practiced in the church and in society, that has stereotyped them as not fully rational, much less in the image of God, and as incapable for much of modernity of not even being able to vote, shows the powerful impact of our images of God. The pressing question for the church is whether its language does justice to its theology, or is it subverting its theology by its language for God, with detrimental consequences for men, women, and the understanding of God?

Some argue that Jesus called God "Father" and thus gave Father as the name for God.[90] A little reflection shows how odd such an argument is. "Father" is more of an image, not a name. If it were a proper name, it would be a designator but not a descriptor. My name does not necessarily give any description of me. So if "Father" functions as a proper name, it does not indicate necessarily any properties, any more than, say, "Jesse" tells one anything without actually knowing the person. It seems evident that "Father" is a way of understanding God just as one can address God as "Lord" or "Mighty Fortress" or "Rock" or "My Shepherd." "Father," of course, is a powerful image for God and has its own strengths and weaknesses. It is misunderstood if taken without any qualification, leading to absurdities such as God literally fathering children.

One must also note that the most startling way that Jesus referred to God, agreed upon even by skeptical historians, is not "Father," but "Abba," which is close to our affectionate word "Dad." This use, at the very least, points to a warm, familial context rather than a distant, patriarchal one. To be sure, it still has male connotations, but at the time, it shocked people by its intimacy and sense of nurture and compassion, so much so that people were both amazed and drawn to Jesus' way of praying. Given the contrast to the sense of distance and transcendence of God at the time, one can argue that today one of the best ways to communicate the meaning of what Jesus did is to call God "Mother."[91] This conveys today the shocking sense of intimacy, nurture, and compassion that "Abba" connoted in Jesus' time. Of course, it seems to convey to some people other things, such as a rejection of Scripture and of traditional faith. One of the lessons to learn from this reflection on language is to focus on what the other person understands by one's words rather than just what oneself understands. Arguing that had Jesus wanted to allow other words he would have used them is to box oneself into a real corner. There are many places where Jesus fit his culture; this is part of what an incarnational faith means. If one followed this slavishly, Christians would still have to follow the Judaic law, walk around in robes and sandals, and speak in Aramaic. It would be a mistake to disregard the New Testament as Holy Scripture since it does not use Jesus' words but is a translation into Greek. The church today obviously does many things differently than Jesus did, and rightly so. The question is whether its practices are consistent, not the same. Even the use of the same word as translated into another language often has a very different set of connotations and perhaps even basic meaning, as translators know well. As we have already seen, the word *love* is a well-known example where our one word functions to cover at least four Greek words. One has to be careful with it so as to keep it consistent with the church's use of *agape*, a Greek word different from Jesus' Aramaic, and also a word used differently by the church than by the surrounding Greek culture. "Father" itself does not always have the same range of connotations in every culture. While there is a degree of commonality, characteristics that are supposedly masculine and feminine change widely from culture to culture, so we must be careful in legalistically using for God one limited term whose meaning varies even from the biblical context. Ironically, we may end up conveying a very different meaning by using the same word. A simple example is *dunamis*, the Greek word for power from which we derived the word *dynamite*. The meanings are related but still quite different. Another example is Ephesians 6:4, where fathers are called upon to discipline their children without provoking them to anger, but mothers are not mentioned. In our more recent culture, we might well have seen mothers as having a primary relationship to the discipline of children instead of fathers. In any case, few would want to exclude mothers from a major responsibility in raising children. In this sense, the Greek is sometimes loosely, but appropriately, translated as "parents," reflecting the difference in our culture from the first century. In relation to God, a similar dynamic is true, as Frank Tupper emphasizes in relation to Christ: "The issue is the quality and character of the relationship of God to us disclosed through the self-revelation of God in the story of Jesus. This relationship is not masculine in contrast to feminine but comprehensively parental."[92]

In characterizing God, the challenge is not to find the few exact terms, which is likely impossible, but to allow many appropriate terms, as has actually been the case in Scripture and in the church, and always to reflect critically upon them to see if they are adequately conveying what they are meant to convey about God. In the end, it may take the full panoply of terms, parables, and stories even to approach "the hem of God's garment." For the reasons I have just given, my practice will be to avoid pronouns that refer to one gender, often referring to "Godself" rather than "himself" or "herself." Even in our everyday language about God, we cannot escape theology!

Our understanding of God and our language of God reveals much of what we think and feel about ourselves and about others. As we shall see in the next chapter, on creation, our understanding of God also reveals much of how we relate to the world around us as well as to one another. Monotheism means that because God is so central, our understanding of God impacts everything else.

5

CREATION
The Beginning

The breathtaking progress in technology over the last four centuries, along with the increased concentration of people living in cities, makes nature a foreign concept to many such urban dwellers: a place to visit on holidays perhaps, and even then not as preferable as a human-designed Disney World or Las Vegas. The tsunami of 2004, shortly followed by Hurricanes Katrina and Rita in 2005, brought vividly to the forefront of such urban consciousness the notion that nature is still a force to be reckoned with and can only be ignored to our peril. Greater awareness of the way an expanding population—of almost seven billion people, racing toward ten billion—has consequently become ever more vulnerable to the fluctuations of global warming, massive consumption, and simple periodic changes of weather renders the sharp delineation between human and nature no longer tenable. The chaos of which the ancient Hebrews were so clearly conscious, as in Genesis 1, now appears not so ancient. The doctrine of creation has long suffered in relation to the more robust development of the doctrine of redemption. We are learning that we can no longer endure such a rigid demarcation and subsequent theological anemia concerning creation.[1]

As we saw in the previous chapter, it is difficult to understand God apart from consideration of God's creation. In actuality, every section of theology is necessary to understand God and will continually deepen our grasp of God, especially as we consider Christology and redemption. The doctrine of creation, however, gives us a first in-depth look at God's relationship to the world, which culminates ultimately in its consummation in a new heaven and a new earth.

We will first reprise Genesis 1, now from the creation side, to deal especially with the ecological challenges that threaten the long-term existence of the world in unprecedented ways. A century ago, people were often optimistic about the twentieth century being the Christian century and looked forward to a millennial reign of Christ on earth. A century later, my experience is that many people are not optimistic that the human race will survive for another one hundred years, largely because of our consciousness that we may make the planet uninhabitable.[2] Secondly, we will examine the vexing relationship of religion and science through the lens of a case study. Third, we will look more closely at the even more perplexing issue of evil and suffering, especially what is called "natural evil," the suffering that arises not from human malfeasance but from natural occurrences provocatively called "acts of God."

AN ECOLOGICAL THEOLOGY?

Now viewed from the perspective of creation, the first chapter of the Bible reveals the universe as created by the one personal God, planned by God, ordered out of chaos by God, and blessed by God. Creation as such is neither divine nor made out of divine "stuff" (pantheism) nor is it evil or the source of evil, as in much of Platonism and Gnosticism. As material, it is neither an illusion nor unreal, as in much of Hinduism and Buddhism. It has its own creaturely reality and integrity. Despite Christian language of depravity and fallenness, it is inherently good and cannot ever be totally evil. The fuller metaphysical language is that evil is *parasitic* upon the good.[3] If something were to be wholly evil, it would cease to exist. Evil, as we shall discuss further later, is always perverted good. At the end of the first creation account, God in fact seems as pleased as at any time in the biblical story: "God saw everything that he had made, and indeed, it was very good" (Gen 1:31).

This is ironic because the Christian tradition, as we have noted, has suffered from a gnostic and dualistic gravitational pull inherited from the first centuries of the church. Its occasional despising of this world and longing for the next world is itself a perversion of God's intention for human dwelling in creation. This is another area that in just the last few decades has fostered the recovery of a more sound biblical theology of creation—one that unfortunately has been only a minor chord in Christian history. As many point out, this change is not as benevolent as it is desperate. The world is threatened as never before, and more and more people realize that if we do not take care of our earthly home, we will suffer and expire along with it. But this is a new story and a new realization. Perhaps earlier agrarian cultures countered the "gnostic drift" to some extent because they felt this rootedness in the good earth in their bones; but, especially in modernity, with a massive shift of populations away from rural areas to the cities at ever-increasing rates, it has been easier to remove the world as an object to master and dominate as wholly other than human reality. Perhaps the greatest example of this was, again, Descartes, the father of modernity, who actually separated reality into two substances that could hardly relate to each other: physical and mental (spiritual).

Only in the last half century have humans realized a couple of sobering, even bitter, truths. One is that humans for the first time in history can destroy not only all of themselves but all other life on the planet—and not just in one way but in several. I grew up with the consciousness that the world could be destroyed a hundred times over by either the Soviet Union or the United States and that such a nuclear holocaust could erupt at any minute—the great fear was that an errant pigeon could be misread on a radar screen, catapulting us all into oblivion! That fear seems to have faded from consciousness only to be replaced by an awareness that we can destroy ourselves in other ways as well, such as by overpopulation and overconsumption, leading to mass starvation and pandemics. Germs or viruses may erupt by natural causes or by warfare to end it all for human beings and perhaps other life. Excessive destruction of the rain forests can deprive the world of sufficient oxygen and has already led to all of us living with lower oxygen levels than a century ago. Damaging emissions, again from overconsumption, can upset the delicate balance of nature, whether by destruction of the ozone layer that protects earth from destructive solar rays or by global warming that can transform productive cropland into vast deserts or, ironically, lead to sudden Ice Ages, as vividly depicted in the movie *The Day after Tomorrow*. These work together in almost demonic ways, because modern overpopulation and massive concentration in cities along seacoasts make any kind of natural disaster all the more catastrophic. Lists like these rival the book of Revelation in their apocalyptic terror.

The second truth is that, unlike the Enlightenment assumptions of the unencumbered self, separate from others and the world, we realize that we are all intertwined in a complex ecological system. This is no longer an idiosyncratic liberal or conservative belief but the common understanding of all—a radical change in itself over the last fifty years. No one doubts that humans are enmeshed in the world and vulnerable to its changes, to mention again the recent tsunami and Hurricane Katrina among a multitude of others.

The realization of both of these truths means that we no longer have the luxury of a decrepit doctrine of creation. For too long, we have tended to separate the God of redemption from the God of creation, almost as if God wars against creation. Ironically, in this way Christianity has not escaped the snares of one of its first heresies, the Marcionite heresy, described in chapter 3, that so radically separated the Testaments that it saw the God of creation and of the Old Testament as a different God than the God of the New Testament. Some of this divide in evangelical theology is the result of the modern warfare between science and religion. Some of it is defense of the miraculous against a scientific understanding of nature that seems inexorably to encompass everything within natural law. Some of it is frankly self-serving, not wanting any impediment to rapacious exploitation of the earth for short-term profits. Thus, much of the land has often been despoiled and ruined for further use. Finally, however, the piper is demanding payment. Short of an amazing advance in space exploration and discovery of another habitable planet, there is basically no more land over the next hillock to use up once this is gone. In the 1960s, Lynn White made headlines by suggesting that the Judeo-Christian heritage itself was largely at fault and that we have no hope unless we jettison such threatening cargo. He appealed precisely to the chapter that we have emphasized, Genesis 1.[4]

The idea that troubles him is the focus on humans to subdue the earth and to have dominion. He is right to point out that these ideas, stated explicitly in Genesis 1:28, have often been used (misused?) to mean "exploit" the earth. He is also right to say that we cannot afford such messages anymore if we are to survive. The question is whether this is an adequate interpretation of the passage. In actuality, Genesis can provide a profound, balanced ecological theology, even for a technological, twenty-first century society.[5] As with any passage, one has to read it in context; one cannot understand these commands, with their forcible language, without understanding the previous language of humans being made in the image of God and, to be sure, without understanding the entire canonical context. In our chapter on humanity, we will examine more closely the meaning of the image of God, a crucial concept that, however, is nowhere explained. Nevertheless, at this point we can mention that part of the meaning is likely that humans are to represent God, bearing God's image as an ambassador might bear a ring or some other sign of the king's image to show that he or she is a representative of the king. At the very least, if the image of God is seen more as standing in relationship to God, it points to responsibility before God.[6] Whose creation is it? Even in this passage, it does not suggest, as it is sometimes taken, that God gave the world to humans in the modern sense of ownership. This would mean, as some think, that it is ours to do with as we wish, to waste or exploit if that is our desire. To the contrary, the implication of Genesis 1 is that the world is created by God and remains God's. Humans are, to be sure, the crown of creation but are clearly part of creation. Humans are "stewards" who actually are meant to rely upon the earth, not in the sense of "despoiling" but in the sense of "taking care of." This is also evident when one turns to Jesus' numerous parables that picture a steward who is responsible to a master (Matt 21:33-41, 24:45-61, 25:14-29). Over and over again, the question is how well the steward has taken care of the land when the owner returns to inspect the stewardship. Genesis 1 implies the same relationship. The serious message of Genesis 1 is actually a pertinent ecological one. When God returns, as in the Christian hope, will God find not only faith on earth (Luke 18:8) but also the earth itself? Will God be pleased with human care of God's world?

To these reflections, one should add that much theology has been quite androcentric, focused only on humans and particularly on men. As mentioned, Genesis 1 supports the special dignity of humans—all humans. What it also does, which is not as often noticed, is emphasize how pleasing the world is to God quite apart from humans. God sees that the creation is good many days before humans appear on the scene. Humans do not even have their own special "day" but are part of the creation of ground creatures on the sixth day. Animals, too, are "living souls," which means in this context that they are alive. In short, already in Genesis one finds the kinship of humans with the rest of creation of which it has taken modern science several centuries to remind us.

When we gain more awareness, as we have in the last hundred years, of the vastness of the universe in time and space, we may appreciate this theological point more. The universe has only recently been more closely pinpointed in age as being more than thirteen billion years old. Light from the universe as it was nine billion years ago has actually been seen, meaning that it took the light nine billion years to get to earth. There are billions of galaxies each with billions of stars, light-years away from each other. We may ask anew with the psalmist, "When I look at your heavens, the work of your fingers, the moon and the stars that you have established, what are human beings that you are mindful of them?" (Ps 8:3-4). Modern homo sapiens emerged on this planet apparently a little more than 100,000 years ago. As long ago as that is, it is only the equivalent of a second if the age of the universe is compared to a twenty-four day. Do we actually think that God is only interested in this last second and only with human beings? This is not to deny the special place of humans as being in the image of God and the crown of creation. It is not to deny the psalmist also answering, "Yet you have made them a little lower than God" (Ps 8:5). It is, however, to question the incredibly parochial and short-sighted focus on ourselves as if even God were wasting time until humans came on the scene. In other places, Scripture gives hints of the appreciation that God has of all of nature, including all of animal and plant life. If we can appreciate the beauty of a sunset, a flower-studded field, and the grace of an antelope, do we think God cannot? So part of a fuller doctrine of creation and an ecological theology is to attempt to see things from God's perspective and to appreciate God's enjoyment of God's creation for its own sake.

This puts a greater onus upon humans to take our stewardship seriously and to take creation seriously. It is not just about us! A part of spirituality, therefore, is how we treat the earth. A canonical practice is thus ecological practice. Grasping the spiritual significance of creation does not necessarily provide easy answers to all of our questions. It cannot decide in a particular case whether to sacrifice access to water for preservation of an endangered snail or whether drilling for oil is too damaging to a particular landscape. It can provide a common framework for approaching such issues. It can direct us to the pertinent values with which to make such decisions. For the rest, the application of practical, spiritual wisdom is necessary, as in all cases.

In another direction, eschatology has often been privatized as something involving only humans—in fact, only human souls and not even human bodies. Paul seems to slap this tradition in the face in 1 Corinthians 15 when he says that what perishes is the "soulish" body and what is transformed is the "spiritual body" (15:44). The soul, in a sense, is what does not last, but the body does! A correction of such a dualistic theology is already ongoing to better appreciate the biblical affirmation of humans as embodied and of resurrection as a "spiritual body." A part of that ongoing correction is also, however, to take more seriously the image of a "new heaven and a new earth," where the new Jerusalem is not found in heaven but comes down from heaven, where the saints dwell with God in peace—not in aethereal heaven—but in a luxurious new embodiment of earth (Rev 21:1-5). Perhaps the transformation of earthly bodies is the first fruits of a similar transformation of this entire universe. The shadow of the gnostic ghost upon Christian theology is a long one, and this is one area where new light is opening up fresh theological panoramas.

RELIGION AND SCIENCE

Modern science has severely challenged biblical hermeneutics with new issues that did not need to be confronted in quite the same way as before. After four centuries of the development of modern science, the debates rage as fiercely as ever. Relations between the church and science got off on the wrong foot with the Galileo episode in the seventeenth century. Early in the twenty-first century, there is continued stumbling. Yet another landmark case represented theology going to court just before Christmas of 2005, when a federal judge—a Republican Christian appointed by George Bush—in *Kitzmiller v. Dover* ruled against the requirement to teach the concept of Intelligent Design (ID) in the public schools. ID is the newest permutation of so-called "creation science," most known for claiming that the universe is only about six thousand years old.[7]

Case Study: Kitzmiller v. Dover

In an unusually long decision, 139 pages, the judge hoped to decide the issue of the requirement to teach ID in the public schools of the United States once and for all. After all of the testimony, lasting for several months, with leading experts on all sides, he drew two major conclusions. One is that ID could not be taught as science because he could not find one professional article that had been accepted in its defense or any reputable evidence in its support. This meant that it had no more standing in the scientific community than any number of other views that might be religious but not scientific, such as New Age, Hindu, and Native American views of origins, implying that an ancient view of the world as riding on the back of a turtle has as much scientific standing.

These court cases are often much more complex than they are seen in the religious community because in court they are not simply theological issues: they are legal issues that must face the strictures of U.S. law for what is acceptable in public schools that include people of many beliefs. The judge's conclusion implied that if ID were acceptable, hundreds of other views of origins might also have a claim to be taught in science classes since they would be just as worthy, having no scientific credentials either. One would then face the prospect of never having any science taught, because equal time would require all of the innumerable other views to be allowed. This particular aspect of the case points to a principle that can be helpful in adjudicating the issue even outside of the courtroom, namely, that any view that wants to claim to be scientific must prove itself in the relevant scientific community; it cannot take shortcuts through political entities such as local school boards or state legislatures to circumvent the normal scientific process. To do such an "end around" means entrusting scientific education to politicians rather than to scientists. Neither is perfect, but few have argued that politicians are credible in the scientific arena. Other scientific views have had to face the tough sledding of proving themselves to critical scientists. This is said with full awareness of a more up-to-date understanding of science, where science is communal and not totally objective or perfect in its judgments.[8] Many views, such as relativity theory, chaos theory, plate tectonics, and the Big Bang have all had to overcome initial bias against them—but their proponents did persevere and won their way eventually by the force of evidence. What is odd is that both ID and creation science claim to be "more scientific," not "religious," and to be acceptable only on the basis of scientific evidence.[9] Yet even their own proponents deplore the lack of scientific study on their behalf and the hard work of doing what other theories have done, that is, overcome resistance by pointing to publicly accessible evidence.[10] This at least means that any claim to science in theology must be straightforward about its claims. The judge seemed most perturbed by the dishonesty of confessing Christians claiming more about their position than was warranted—and rightly so. To win one's way through deception and dishonesty is to win a battle but lose the war—especially on Christian grounds, one would think. If the scientific evidence is lacking, honesty demands that this be acknowledged. Even if people believe that they have found some evidence, honesty demands that when others, perhaps virtually all others in the pertinent scientific field, reject it, it should be acknowledged forthrightly. In the end, a Christian judge judged other Christians to have brought a case of "breathtaking inanity"— not common words in the sphere of public court.

The second major conclusion that the judge drew was that ID is a religious claim and not a scientific one. This meant that he found overwhelming evidence that ID was proposed on religious and not scientific grounds. As such, it is unconstitutional. The judge pointed out, however, that his ruling does not mean that ID is false nor that it could not seek to validate itself in the future as a scientific view. The case, however, does raise the question whether such enormous amounts of energy and money should be put behind such a venture.[11]

Implications for a Theology of Religion and Science

Several theological issues are relevant. The church—presumably— learned from the Galileo case that the Bible should not be seen as a science book. This has generally been accepted across the board in the theological spectrum, since no one is defending a flat earth or geocentric universe. This was a valuable advance hermeneutically in understanding the nature of Scripture. A crucial issue is always to consider the purpose of Scripture in interpreting a passage. What is perplexing is the resistance to applying the same hermeneutic to other scientific cases such as the age of the universe or the development of life. It is problematic if not quixotic to apply one hermeneutic to one case and not apply it to another, not because of textual or scientific reasons but because the conclusions are less palatable to tradition. We should remember how distasteful Galileo's conclusions were at the time. The church, however, made a huge mistake at that time, as is generally agreed, by wrongly using the Bible to reach scientific conclusions. As we have seen, this is to confuse the place of both Scripture and science. Both have their own purposes and parameters.[12]

This means that we should not comb Genesis and other parts of the Bible to find scientific facts that allow us to skip physics or biology class. They are not what the Bible is about. We have already seen how profoundly Genesis provides a theological framework for understanding both God and creation, as well as ecology and, later, humanity and sin. These, however, are not scientific findings but truths about the nature of God and humans. They are focused more practically. As Walter Brueggemann points out, "Creation is not to be understood as a theory or as an intellectual, speculative notion, but as a concrete life-or-death discipline and practice, whereby the peculiar claims of Yahweh were mediated in and to Israel."[13] In so doing, these claims actually provide a sophisticated and nuanced theological and philosophical *basis* for science itself, though the framework does not offer particular *results* of science. Even though Lynn White deplored it to some extent, he recognized the significance of Scripture for the rise of science. Others as well have argued, with some validity, that the rise of science owed much to this framework in that many early scientists were Christians who were motivated by their faith to discover more about God, indirectly, through their science. Like Galileo, however, they did not look to the Bible for the results of their research but to motivate their research. Moreover, one could look to the troublesome passage in Genesis 1 about subduing the earth to find a basis for a mission to do science. Again, the point is not to yield the results of science but to motivate it. It is as if permission, if not encouragement, is given, but God is saying, "It's up to you to find out how it was done."

What we find is that scientific information has indeed been left up to human investigation—and it took an enormous amount of time to find out very much, given that science is barely centuries old. If God was interested in conveying helpful scientific information, we could have benefited from much more than arcane information about the beginning of the universe. Looked at in this light, it is evident that this is not the purpose of revelation. We often are unaware of how recent are our basic understandings of the nature of the earth, the body, the mind, and so on. The discovery of the Big Bang is barely a half-century old. The insights into the great age of the earth (about 5.5 billion years) and the universe (more than 13 billion years) are barely a century old. On the other hand, we do not necessarily understand any better than the biblical writers the dynamics of God's relationship to the world and to humans, which was their purpose in conveying revelation—we may even have regressed in our understanding. In any case, a grasp of these hermeneutical principles makes the contemporary uneasiness on the part of some toward the age of the universe and evolution rather straightforward to treat.

The simple implication of the hermeneutic that the church universal learned from the Galileo episode in relation to modern science is that neither one of those issues is a matter of biblical teaching— they are issues of science. Such a straightforward application initially in relation to both would have saved the church an enormous expenditure of time and resources—and will continue to do so. Early in relation to the evolution controversy, many in the church, including evangelicals, did not see a particular problem. They did, in fact, apply the "Galilean hermeneutic" rather well.

As historians have pointed out, creation science was not a significant view a century ago among evangelicals.[14] Ironically, as evidence has increasingly accumulated for the billion-year-old age of the universe and for evolution, especially in chemistry and genetics, support for creationism has grown. Likely because of the so-called Scopes Monkey Trial in 1925, which was such a disaster for evangelicals, the age of the universe and evolution became identified as a kind of scapegoat for the humiliation and frustration of many evangelicals, leading to the rise of fundamentalism.[15] Aggressive marketing based on such fears has led many lay evangelicals to identify this as a make-or-break issue for faith.[16] While this is virtually a wholesale attack on all of science, since the issues in the age of the universe and evolution are assumed in so many other disciplines such as astronomy, physics, chemistry, biology, and psychology, this one particular theory is identified as the sole problem. The judge rightly pointed out in the Dover case that there is no basis for singling out evolution and not these other areas of science.

Theologically, it is inappropriate to take only one of the four major theories, all held even by inerrantists, of Genesis 1 and make it a crucial issue for Christian faith. Most views try not to clash with the evidence for an older universe. Some have held to the day-age theory, where days are seen as representing an indefinite period of time.[17] This was the most popular view among evangelicals a century ago. The gap theory posits a great period of time between Genesis 1:1 and Genesis 1:2, where Satan fell and affected the universe. Of course, this is anachronistic in positing a view of Satan in a text where the view of Satan as an enemy of God had not yet developed. It also is highly speculative in piling so much into a supposed gap that is not even in the text. At one point in my denomination, the official Bible study teacher's guide maintained that the gap theory was the only theory that Christians can hold—again showing the dangers of overreaching. The view that I would favor sees Genesis 1 as having theological import through the medium of a liturgical narrative but does not intend to teach specifics of anything that we today would call science. Early inerrantists did not necessarily see a conflict between Genesis and science. For example, B. B. Warfield, who has been called the "father of inerrancy," could say of himself that he was a "Darwinian of the purest water."[18] Ironically, William Jennings Bryan of the Scopes Monkey Trial did not see the "days" as literal.[19] It is not that Genesis teaches a scientific theory; it is compatible with a variety of findings of science. That is not its point; rather, its point is the theological framework that we have identified. Incidentally, there is virtually no controversy at all about this theological framework, which is widely agreed upon as the intended theological meaning of the text. It is only when dealing with the text's relationship to modern science—which obviously was an issue far in the future for the Old Testament writers and most of the history of Christianity—that people have mined the text for scientific theories.

Creation science per se is the only view of the four that is in stark conflict with modern science because it posits a universe only six to ten thousand years old, perhaps as much as sixty thousand years old. Even the latter does not help much in relationship to billions of years. What this means is that anyone who holds this view must undermine virtually the whole of modern science, which presumes an "old earth" rather than a "young earth." The striking thing about ID, which sometimes is seen as in league with creationism, is that it soundly rejects a young earth and thus with it most of the criticism of evolution. To try to show that all of the many dating methods, which strikingly concur from so many vantage points such as geology, oil deposits that took millions of years to produce, stars that are billions of light years away, and genetics whose history can be traced over millions of years, are grossly mistaken is a huge burden of proof. Especially to make this a condition of faith, on a par with the resurrection of Christ or salvation by grace through faith—a sad ploy that I have witnessed—is to raise a false stumbling block for prospective Christians and for new Christians.[20] Having been in settings of higher education, when young people are told that they must choose between a questionable reading of Scripture—which in fact is only one of several views held by conservative Christians and the evidence of science—and science, many choose science. There are legitimate stumbling blocks identified in Scripture: the willingness to take up one's cross and deny oneself, to rely on salvation by grace through faith, to affirm the resurrection of Christ and of the dead, among others. Holding a particular theory about the relation of Genesis 1 and science is not one of them. The seriousness of this issue comes from a stern warning of Jesus about placing false stumbling blocks before vulnerable people: "If any one of you put a stumbling block before one of these little ones of mine who believe in me, it would be better for you if a great millstone were fastened around your neck and you were drowned in the depth of the sea" (Matt 18:6). This reminds us of the levels of significance in Scripture. Some beliefs are held by almost all Christians. The rejection of these might be considered make-or-break issues—such as the confession of Jesus as Lord, salvation by grace through faith, and the resurrection. Many others involve differences that should not break fellowship, even though they are significant. At the very most, these scientific issues should be in the latter category.

With this perspective, one can approach science with affirmation and caution. As a Christian, one can affirm the effort to understand and probe God's universe. It can be seen as a legitimate calling for young people and can be blessed by the church. It has the promise, as in medicine and agriculture, to be of enormous benefit to the most needy. It can be a modern way of offering a cup of cold water (Matt 25:35). At the same time, this potential benefit does not rule out the need to bring theological and ethical criticism to science. The place for theology to enter the discussion is at the level of the philosophical (and theological) presuppositions of science, the use to which science is put, and the relative importance placed upon it. One of the reasons most likely for the reaction of the church against science is some scientists' overreaching just as much as some Christians. Notable antireligious statements by some scientists hit the press regularly, implying that science proves that faith is outmoded or infantile. Recently, Richard Dawkins has argued that religion is a dangerous virus; he prefers sticking to scientific knowledge.[21] This, of course, should be recognized as just as much bad science as it is bad theology to substitute the Bible for chemistry class. At this point, these scientists, perhaps notable in their field, have gone beyond science to become philosophers or even theologians of a sort—perhaps "a-theologians" is the right description. Given the clash between religion and science, it has been pointed out that scientists rarely get training in the philosophy of science and certainly not in theology.[22] It is not surprising then that when scientists step outside of their training and expertise, they are not necessarily any better qualified than an athlete giving an ad for the chemical superiority of one brand of soap over another. Étienne Gilson, the great Catholic philosopher, in speaking of agnostics makes a point relevant to such scientists: "The trouble with so many of our contemporaries is not that they are agnostics but rather that they are misguided theologians."[23] This, however, should also give pause to theologians who presume that they can pronounce on complex areas of science for which they have no training. It is important for both sides to realize that science and theology have their own purposes and limits with respect to each other. After Galileo, and perhaps after *Kitzmiller v.*

Dover, we should not make the same mistake over again. We are both misunderstanding and misrepresenting the Bible to the world when we claim for it what it does not claim for itself—and apparently what God in inspiration never intended for it to be.

Theology and Genesis

To return to Genesis, understanding the text in its context and in terms of its genre significantly aids in avoiding what appear to be contradictions at a literal level. It then shows how the two creations stories in Genesis 1 and 2 actually are remarkably complementary, which should not surprise us since they were chosen to be complementary by, on virtually all accounts, one of the most gifted religious writers or editors in ancient history. This is not to mention the perspective of faith that sees their collection in just this canonical form as inspired. Problems of harmonizing the two creation stories on a literal level have been seen since the beginning. People have long wondered how to reconcile the two very different stories on a literal level and how later Cain found his wife (was it his sister?) in other cities that had suddenly sprung up outside of the family of the circle of Adam, Eve, Cain, and Abel—on such a literal reading presumably the only humans alive at the time (Gen 4:17). In the early church, it was not always an issue because these passages were sometimes interpreted allegorically. With the rise of a more historical understanding of the development of Genesis, the two stories are seen to come from different hands, different settings, and different times. Unless we think the brilliant editor (redactor or redactors), who collected the accounts in Genesis much as the Gospel writers collected accounts of Jesus in the New Testament, was almost unbelievably blind or clumsy, we must think that the problems that we see on a literal level were not intended, nor were they apparently seen as such by early readers. Our problems are precisely that—*our* problems and not necessarily those of the text, which apparently stands well on its own. In this case, the problems of Genesis 1—picturing creation as emerging from watery chaos versus Genesis 2 as from a desert; of human beings created last in the first chapter and the man (Adam) being created first in the second chapter; of Cain finding a wife and cities after killing Abel when supposedly there were no other humans around—all can be seen as taking the stories too literally. A similar, although not exact, comparison would be taking Jesus' parables as having to be literally exemplified and all literally compatible. Genesis 1, in fact, does not specify the creation of just one man and woman but of humankind, male and female. Adam and Eve in chapter 2 represent human beings in their intended fellowship with God and also provide amazing insight into the dynamics of sin and brokenness: all, however, in narrative form and not in the form, as we might expect, of a theology treatise.[24]

When seen as complementary narratives conveying truth about God and the human and world condition, Genesis 1 and 2 first of all strongly parallel each other.[25] God is seen as creating by bringing order out of chaos. Genesis 1 was apparently given its final form during the exile. With this in mind, as Brueggemann says, "The world given in these liturgical utterances is a 'contrast-world,' compared to the world of exile that holds threat, anxiety, and insecurity."[26] God's activity brings about an orderly, one might even say, rational, creation. In Genesis 2, God brings life from the desert. In both, it is a process that is very lifelike, with water, trees, animals, and humans who procreate—and who are tempted. Humans are closely related to the animals, being created on the same day in Genesis 1 and naming and finding fellowship with them, however finally fulfilling it might be, in chapter 2. Yet humans are also the crown of creation in both. They are created last in the first chapter. They are created first and last in the second. Strikingly, given the patriarchal culture, there is equality among humankind. There is no endorsement of racial, economic, or gender bias in either. Compare this to creation accounts that favor a particular race or people, a particular gender, or a particular aristocratic group, or even just the king. In Genesis, inequality does not occur except as a result of sin in chapter 3. The emphasis in both is on mutuality between the sexes, without denying biological differences. In Genesis 2, the woman is fitting for the man, but the word does not suggest inferiority or subordination.[27] Both narratives, of course, affirm one God, one people of God, a creation that is neither divine nor evil but which has its own pre-fall goodness, and a blessing on human labor and fruitfulness. (One must note that work is a mandate before the fall in both accounts.)

Second, they are complementary in that the first chapter, seen usually as coming from priests, emphasizes the *transcendence* of God, even the distance of God from creation. God creates by a word. The second chapter has an emphasis on *immanence*, where God is as intimate with humans as we see Jesus with Abba in the New Testament. It is difficult to exaggerate the theological power of the picture of God coming to walk and talk over the day with the humans in the coolness of the evening—a scene that is vivid to us in the desert-like conditions of West Texas. God bends down personally to fashion the humans from the dust of the earth rather than speaking from a distance. If we persist in imposing our tendency toward literal readings upon ancient literature, we create contradictions where there need be none, which in turn has often presented hermeneutical stumbling blocks that cause moderns to shun the Bible as not worthy of regard. Interestingly, Augustine spoke strongly to this point in regard to science in his time:

> Now, it is a disgraceful and dangerous thing for an infidel to hear a Christian, presumably giving the meaning of Holy Scripture, talking nonsense on these topics; and we should take all means to prevent such an embarrassing situation, in which people show up vast ignorance in a Christian and laugh it to scorn. The shame is not so much that an ignorant individual is derided, but that people outside the household of faith think our sacred writers held such opinions, and, to the great loss of those for whose salvation we toil, the writers of our Scripture are criticized and rejected as unlearned men. If they find a Christian mistaken in a field which they themselves know well and hear him maintaining his foolish opinions about our books, how are they going to believe those books in matters concerning the resurrection of the dead, the hope of eternal life, and the kingdom of heaven, when they think their pages are full of falsehoods and on facts which they themselves have learnt from experience and the light of reason?[28]

If we try to appreciate them on their own grounds, they are amazing theological documents, presented in a poetic, liturgical mode

(Genesis 1) or narrative mode (Genesis 2). Again, there is little debate about the theological meaning on these terms; debate arises when we persist in bringing our assumptions about what kind of literature that this *must* be to the text. We will return to the special nature of Genesis 1–11 when we treat further humanity and sin, but the foundation must be seen as already laid by understanding their theology of creation.

CREATION, EVIL, AND SUFFERING

Would that such a harmony were possible to construe from the texts on the issue of evil and suffering! While this issue, and even the philosophical dimension of it, predates Christianity, Christian theism faces this challenge perhaps more than any other kind of religious or philosophical view. This is because theism attempts to hold together the belief in one personal, loving God who is omnipotent and perfectly good on the one hand, and the reality of evil and suffering on the other. If one denies any of these terms, which many religions and philosophies do, the problem of understanding diminishes, although not the problem of experience. No theological or philosophical account, however brilliant, can remove the trauma of actual sin and suffering. It is possible, though, that some understandings can, and have, led people either to spiritual strength or to despair just when they needed divine comfort the most, hence the great attention to this issue from all sides over several millennia.[29]

Theism and Other Faiths

It is often a shock for those immersed in a Christian culture, and sometimes for those who are not, to realize that the intellectual problem of evil is rather readily solved apart from a theistic context. If one denies the reality of evil and suffering, as in some religions and philosophies, the problem is less. If one does not see God as Creator but as a being, as in Platonism or modern process philosophy, having to deal with recalcitrant material that is as ultimate as God, then the problem is less. God is consequently the source of good; evil is the result of "matter" or perhaps a malevolent being, as in the Persian Zoroastrianism that may have influenced

Judaism during the exile. The view of God having to deal with chaos is behind Rabbi Kushner's bestseller, *When Bad Things Happen to Good People*.[30] His book represents well earlier Jewish theology that understood God to create out of chaos.[31] Similar to what process philosophy maintains, God's answer to Job in Kushner's view is that God is dealing with a complex and difficult world the best way possible. Humans must accept much that happens in the world not as willed by God but as part of the complex universe that God did not create and cannot totally control. This reminds us that Christianity very early emphasized *creatio ex nihilo*, an understanding that protects the uniqueness and ultimacy of God even as it intensifies the problem of evil.[32]

If one thinks that this world is evil or of little worth, as in the Gnosticism that seriously challenged early Christianity, the problem is less. One would then despise the world and have little to do with it. If one thinks that something necessary in God compelled God to create, as in the neoplatonism that also grew up with Christianity, it would be less. God then had no choice. The theistic view is that God could have chosen not to create or to create, say, a beautiful diamond swirling through space, thus no evil. Yet God, on purpose, chose to create a world that ended up like ours.

If one thinks of all reality as divine, then evil is seen as a human construct and not part of ultimate reality, as in pantheism in general and in philosophies such as those of Spinoza and Hegel specifically. In other words, if there is only one reality, as in these "monistic" views that see all reality as just one thing such as Spinoza's Nature or Hegel's Spirit (*Geist*), it would be exceedingly pessimistic to identify the only reality there is with evil. These views are often deterministic as well. The usual tendency for monists is to minimize, if not eliminate, the reality of evil. Major forms of Hinduism and Buddhism are close in seeing everything in reality as one; in Hinduism this is expressed as Atman (the individual soul) is Brahman (the one reality).[33] This individual reality with its physical suffering is an illusion, *maya*. Buddhism may be the only religion that begins with the reality of suffering.[34] The First Noble Truth is: suffering exists. The Second Noble Truth answers the question, why is there suffering?

Answer: craving or desire. The Third Noble Truth deals with the question, how do we overcome suffering? Answer: Cease craving. The Fourth Noble Truth answers the question, what is the way to cease craving? Answer: to follow the Noble Eightfold Path, which includes disciplines of self-control. Evil and suffering are thus seen as problems of perspective or attitude that can be changed.

Three Major Christian Approaches

In order to mitigate the problem of evil for theism, then, one can reject any one of the three major terms that form its challenge: one can deny God's omnipotence, God's omnibenevolence, or the reality of evil and suffering. Over against these radical responses, the challenge of theism is to affirm all three. Theism also implies the belief that God did not have to create or could have created innumerable other creations. God could have created a land with beautiful waterfalls but no sentient creatures, as perhaps exists in other parts of the universe. There would then be beauty but no evil and suffering. Yet theism is committed to the belief that God chose just this creation that has turned out like this—when there were many alternatives—presumably having a great, if not exact, idea of how it would turn out.

To make matters worse, theism affirms the reality of evil and suffering and their terrible nature. This is part of the horror of sin and injustice that is so displeasing to God and, in Christianity, ultimately leads to the atonement at the center. This complex and troubling constellation of ideas is the challenge of theism that is not faced by most other religions and philosophies. Yet it is one that must be faced by the Christian theologian. It cannot be comprehensively approached without "the whole armor of God" (Eph 6:11), so to speak, so we will approach it when we deal more fully with sin, redemption, and eschatology. Here we will focus on the development in recent years of reflection on the issue that relates most to creation, that of natural evil, which is also connected to the rise of scientific understanding of natural law in a quite new way that was not common to the biblical worldview or to most of Christian history. In order to understand this newer approach, however, we need to understand the main traditional approach, along with a significant minor chord, the Calvinist tradition.

The Augustinian Free-Will Defense

The dominant approach to evil and suffering in the Christian tradition is the Augustinian tradition of a free-will defense, which involves also the idea of divine self-limitation. A crucial assumption is that God cannot do things that are logically impossible. Thomas Aquinas noted that this dispels some logical conundrums, such as, can God create a square circle? or can God create a stone too heavy for God to lift?[35] These actually are not possibilities that God could or could not do; they are incoherent thoughts, impossibilities. One might wonder, who or what determines what is logically possible? Christian theologians would not say that there are logical laws outside of God that limit God; rather, logical limits are inscribed within God and are based on the nature of God. Thus, these are not limits to God's sovereignty but, in a sense, expressions of it. What is possible in reality is ultimately rooted in the nature of God. This is an important point in most views when it comes to giving an account of how God and evil are both possible, which is called "theodicy" (literally, a defense of God).[36] The free-will defense, the centerpiece of the dominant approaches to theodicy in Christian history, sees that freedom and determinism are incompatible.[37] Because of the nature of God, to put it correctly, even God cannot create free beings whom God then determines or coerces. Thus God must limit God's power or control in order to make room for freedom. God could presumably have chosen not to create a world with free beings, but if God did choose to create free beings, then God runs the unavoidable risk of them going wrong. This is what it means to be free, or perhaps more specifically, to have significant moral freedom.

In current terminology, as we saw in the previous chapter, this understanding of freedom is called "libertarian," "indeterministic," or "incompatibilistic." Contemporary strong Calvinists, or five-point Calvinists, who represent another significant tradition, deny this notion of freedom. Calvin himself thought it would be better just to do away with the notion of freedom.[38] Calvinists, in this sense, argue that freedom and determinism are compatible, so their view of freedom is called "nonlibertarian," "deterministic," or "compatibilistic."[39] Obviously, their view of freedom rules out a free-will defense since free will is no limitation on God's ability to control human choices. As we shall see, they have to turn in a different direction for theodicy and actually represent a quite different paradigm of not only freedom but of interweaving conceptions of power and sovereignty. For instance, they generally do not accept that God is limited by logical impossibilities, as does most of the Christian tradition. The irony is that Augustine and Aquinas, usually placed in the camp of a free-will theodicy, in some ways support the Calvinist tradition in that both affirm predestination of individuals to salvation or damnation. Immediately one wonders, if God has this much control, enough to guarantee free choices, then why is God limited by freedom, and is God removed from responsibility for evil as the free-will defense argues? It is not the first time that people could go different directions based on the thought of the same theologian!

With this in mind, the free-will defense then indicates that freedom is of such a great value that it is worthwhile for God to run the risk of evil and suffering. If God had chosen not to create free beings, then the creation would have been immeasurably impoverished. This can be seen more clearly if one sees that genuine freedom is essential to genuine love. Some have questioned whether freedom is all that it is cracked up to be. A powerful challenge is given by John Roth, who appeals to the novel and movie *Sophie's Choice*, where Sophie is confronted by a Nazi guard in a concentration camp concerning her two children. He claims to grant her freedom by allowing her to choose which of her children will live. Roth portrays this tragic scene as saying, "In a word, our freedom is both too much and too little."[40] Whether or not such a grotesque choice is the paradigm of freedom or a terrible perversion of it, it points out the limitations of freedom taken by itself. But what if freedom is not all that is at stake? Is it possible to have love without freedom? If love is coerced, can it be genuine? Is not "coerced love" another one of those logical contradictions? If so, to put it biblically, then the two greatest commandments, to love God and to love each other, affirmed in both Testaments, would not have been possible apart from free will. Additionally, if somehow freedom and love are essential to being in the image of God and thus being human, then freedom is the cost of human existence altogether. Creation therefore would have been deprived of humans as the crown of creation apart from God running the risk of freedom. According to this thinking, the stakes are much higher than just freedom. The question is whether there should have been any beings at all in God's image, persons as such, and whether love was to be a reality in God's good creation or not.

This means that when the poignant question arises, was it worth it?[41] we are asking whether it would have been better, not only for us never to have existed, but also for everyone else never to have existed. It is important for us to realize that some of the greatest spiritual figures in the Bible came to the conclusion that it was not worth it for them to have been born, particularly Job and Jeremiah (Job 3:3; Jer 20:14). The dark night of the soul, as the spiritual tradition realizes, is not a malady only for weak or nominal Christians. Searing questions such as these cut to the heart of the best of us. The striking thing is that this is recognized in the Scriptures. We have a tendency to see these questions as contrary to faith, but in the Bible they are a part of an intense dialogue with God. They are not threats to God, even though they may be threats to ourselves. Wrestling with God, evinced so clearly in the story of Jacob, is a part of the Christian pilgrimage in the Scriptures (Gen 32:22-32). Such strenuous dialogue with God can threaten our faith but can also be a part of greater faith. It is difficult for me to think, for example, of any "spiritual giant" who has not suffered greatly or wrestled with God deeply.

We often think of the question, put inimitably by Ivan Karamazov in The Brothers Karamazov, was it worth it? as occurring in this individual context, asking whether I might not have been created and the world have been better?[42] Could not things surely have gone better for me or that child over there? This is a tough question in itself and part of the struggle with theodicy. Both Jeremiah and Job thought it would have been better if they had not been born, but they did not necessarily answer the question for all others. For example, the speeches in Job begin with Job saying, "Let the day perish in which I was born, and the night that said, 'A man-child is conceived.' Let that day be darkness!" (3:3-4). The question is much more difficult than what an individual laments for himself or herself. It is one thing to speak for oneself; it is another to speak for everyone. Yet this is what is ultimately at stake in this context of a free-will defense. A world for any genuine human being, one who is free to love authentically, may not have been possible apart from the risk of the suffering that is possible and, in fact, exists. If so, who among us could unequivocally desire that it would have been better for none to have existed? Perhaps only God could make such a choice. From the perspective of faith, God did make such a choice.

What the free-will defense brings to light is that such a choice may have been more agonizing for God than we imagine. We see God in anguish over a recalcitrant creation afterward. Like any parent, would God not have known that bringing new life into the world runs the risk of significant suffering and brings a poignancy even to the creation of new life? This is only a dim analogy, but I have often thought that in the modern world—where, with contraception, having children is more of a planned choice than ever before in human history—the questions that some couples have about bringing children into such a perilous world give us some dim insight into God's own creative act.[43] It means that the later divine suffering, revealed so vividly in the case of Hosea, for example, was not a surprise for God but already a part of the original act of creation. Sadness does not only arise late in the story.

This adds a tragic note to any discussion of suffering in creation. Genesis 1 and 2 cannot be understood apart from chapters 3–11. God's proclamation that creation is "very good" in the first creation account is countered by God's regret for creation in Genesis 6. Generally, theologians have avoided the note of tragedy, which parallels the resistance to seeing any suffering in God. God has been preferred to be seen as imperturbable, above it all. Certainly, there is a place to trust in and understand that God is not threatened in God's being by sorrow or change and that "the peace . . . which surpasses all understanding" (Phil 4:7), which can be possible in the midst of the storm in human life, is surely true for God. God may be thought to hold together blessed peace and serenity along with agony in a way that is not possible for God's creation. But the desire for strength and repose in God on the one hand is not a reason to deny God's distress on the other. The theological tradition has had its difficulty in holding complex things together, often falling for false dualisms. God either suffers or does not. God's will is always done or God is weak. God saves those whom God wants or God cannot save anyone. And so on. In this case, there is no overriding reason to think that one cannot trust in God's steadfastness and also do justice to God's intense care for the creation—both poles of the dilemma being clearly affirmed in Scripture.

If this is true for God, even the best theological account of evil and suffering can have its own tragic note. Burton Cooper points out that C. S. Lewis' by all accounts great theodicy in *The Problem of Pain* seemed to some too facile.[44] It perhaps was too easy to say that "pain is God's megaphone." Yet Cooper notes that when Lewis suffered the death of his wife, related in *A Grief Observed*, a note of tragedy and poignance entered that was lacking before, a dynamic portrayed in the film *Shadowlands*. Lewis says, "It has been an imaginary faith playing with innocuous counters labelled 'Illness,' 'Pain,' 'Death,' and 'Loneliness.' I thought I trusted the rope until it mattered to me whether it would bear me. Now it matters, and I find I didn't."[45] Job and Jeremiah might have said the same. A theological account does not take the place of living; it can help deal with pain but cannot do away with pain. To my mind, this does not mean that Lewis was necessarily wrong in his general theological account beforehand; I draw heavily on Lewis' account in my own theodicy. Yet the actual living out of one's faith is a test for all of us. There are moments when any of us might cry out, "My Father, if it is possible, let this cup pass from me" (Matt 26:39). What this does mean, however, is that any theology that does not contain a note of tragedy is not only untrue to life, it is untrue to the God of Scripture and to genuine theology. Frank Tupper calls this the scandal of providence.[46] It means that there are no easy answers and no easy ways. The poignance that we sense, and that Lewis experienced, is matched by God's own anguish in creation over the cost of creation and the fate of God's beloved creation. Arthur McGill called suffering the test of theological method.[47] We will see how this test applies to the following theologies.

From this crucial point of the justifiability of the creation of freedom, the Augustinian rationale is that the rest is human fault. God created the world perfect, with a capital P, one might say. Augustine exaggerates and intensifies even the idyllic picture that one has in Genesis 2 into an environment where nothing "could produce in him [Adam] any unpleasant situation."[48] When one thinks about this, one can see that Augustine has gone far beyond the Genesis text's description itself, a move that seems theodicy driven. If the environment were perfect, then God is not liable. He also seems to be shaped by the more Greco-Roman notion of perfection than of the Hebrew notion of goodness. As commentaries point out, the Hebrew word for goodness, *tov*, does not mean absolute perfection but a more functional sense of something being what it needs to be in order to fit its purpose.[49] As we shall see, this Old Testament view of goodness is much closer to the other major free-will approach of another church father who actually precedes Augustine by a couple of centuries, Irenaeus.

Augustine's picture is a clear and dramatic one from this point, which helps account for its wide acceptance and historical impact. God created the world perfect. Inexplicably, Adam and Eve chose to rebel even though they had it all. Such a heinous act thus merited a severe punishment. Otherwise, God would not have been just. This meant that what we call "natural evil," the suffering that comes from nature, is primarily due to God's punishment for the human misuse of free will. The world was originally meant to be without natural evil, but natural evil is now seen as deserved punishment. When one adds the Augustinian notion of original sin (meaning original guilt), where Adam acted for everyone else, then everyone, even infants, come into the world deserving of natural evil and of eternal condemnation. All humans, due to Adam's sin, deserve eternal condemnation, seen as literal torment.[50]

This means that for Augustine there is no innocent or horrendous suffering. The problem of innocent suffering, especially in massive ways as in the Holocaust, is perhaps the most extreme form of the problem of evil in the contemporary context.[51] It is important to see how the issue of horrendous or gratuitous evil has *not* historically been a major issue under the impress of the Augustinian framework. For Augustine, all suffering is deserved, even for infants before what free churches call the age of accountability.

As Augustine also emphasizes, God predestines from God's one timeless moment of eternity all those who are to be saved, leaving the rest to the condemnation that they so richly deserve (called "single predestination").[52] Calvin follows Augustine closely to this point but insists that God does not just "leave" the rest to damnation but specifically ordains or predestines both to salvation and damnation (called "double predestination").[53] Those who are saved thus show God's amazing, unmerited grace, and those who suffer in hell show the propriety of God's justice. These last theological points perhaps reveal the cultural imprint of Roman culture, with its emphasis on proportionality and balance. Augustine even speculates that God chose just the number of humans to make up for the angels who fell in a pre-cosmic fall.[54]

Several observations are in order to give an idea of why this framework has been by far the dominant historical view but has less credence nowadays. One stems from appreciating the simple and dramatic nature of this account. It is more a narrative than a theory. Yet at the same time, it provides an answer for virtually every question. It is not difficult to grasp why it has had such a hold on the Christian imagination. Several problems, however, arise in terms of contemporary understanding. With the rise of Believers' churches and the emphasis on believer's baptism, coupled with the much greater sense of individuality in the West in the last half-millennium, the cogency of such a view of original sin—or perhaps more accurately, original guilt—is severely lacking. If theodicy is to give us an idea of God's justice, then to many it seems patently unjust to hold others, especially infants, accountable for Adam and Eve's sin. While this was not largely questioned for most of Christian history, it perhaps raises more questions than it answers for contemporary Christians. In fact, instead of explaining God's justice, it tends to undermine it.

More-recent developments in biblical exegesis raise more questions. Augustine's view of a perfect paradise is now seen as a significant extrapolation from the biblical account rather than a straightforward rendering of it. It is an interpretation, as is every other theology, and may well be the best, but it cannot claim that it is simply relating the biblical story. The Genesis account is now seen as more this worldly and down-to-earth than Augustine's perfectionistic account. Many of us are so influenced by the Augustinian tradition that we find it difficult to distinguish Scripture from our Augustinian lens. In addition, a major exegetical issue is that the linchpin of Augustine's exegesis, Romans 5:12, has been shown to be based on a mistranslation. He read it in the Latin Vulgate as saying that Adam was the one in whom all sinned and thus in whom all are guilty. It is now commonly understood that this is a poor translation and should be read as all people being guilty because they sin *like* Adam.[55] Certainly, this latter reading fits a Believers' church model much better. People are guilty and deserving of condemnation only when they are old enough freely to choose for themselves. Infants are not seen as guilty but as going to heaven if they die before they can make a decision for themselves. Only those who have reached the age of accountability are old enough to have sinned like Adam and thus are guilty on their own account. The irony is that many Believers' churches tend to espouse an Augustinian framework although their theology undermines it at the center. Augustine could still develop his view based on larger theological considerations such as his views of divine power and of free will, but it is now not so easily "read off" the text.

In addition, as one may have already wondered, how does predestination fit with the free-will defense? For many, the answer is simple, it does not. This represents a deep incongruity that cannot easily be resolved without going the strong Calvinist route of making freedom and determinism compatible. The problem with the compatibilist answer, however, is that it sabotages the free-will defense altogether. To see this more sharply, one has to realize that, according to Augustine and the strong Calvinist tradition, God can so guide a person's free decisions that God can guarantee that a person whom God has elected will make the choice for God (or will be born in a Christian family so that he or she is baptized as an infant and later is confirmed). If God has this kind of control, one may ask, and desires all to be saved, according to 1 Timothy 2:4, then why are not all saved? Why could not God prevent much of the suffering and evil in the world, which seems to fly against God's holiness? Why does God seem to be upset over what God could easily have prevented? In light of these questions, the thrust of the free-will defense is that sin is not God's will and is human responsibility as a misuse of God's gift of freedom—precisely because God does not and cannot control free acts without evacuating human responsibility. Therefore, this Augustinian kind of divine control or guarantee is not what is meant by the libertarian freedom that undergirds the free-will defense.

At this point, some have turned to perhaps another alternative altogether, namely, an appeal to paradox or mystery. The idea is that freedom and determinism are incompatible, but God can resolve such contradictions in a way beyond our ken. While all realize that there is a great degree of mystery in any theology, it is always crucial where one places it. Is it giving up on rationality altogether, or is it recognizing, in a sense, the "reasonable" limits of reason? If one undermines reason completely, then one could not do any theology. For example, one could claim that God is both good *and* evil or that we are saved by grace *and* by merit. If logic does not matter, then anything goes. It is clear that theology is based on an assumption of a minimal level of rationality. Generally, apart from the Calvinist tradition, the appeal to paradox at this point is seen as allowing outright contradiction that would undermine most other claims in theology as well. The free-will defense becomes no defense at all if God could mysteriously work around freedom to guarantee that people do exactly what God desires. As we shall see, the other Calvinist response was to reject the idea that God desires all to be saved, so that sovereignty is protected at the expense of human responsibility. This is the reasoning behind the extraordinary turn to the idea of "limited atonement" in strong Calvinism, which means that Christ did not die for all people because God did not desire for all to be saved.[56] If God had desired for them to be saved, they would have been, so the reasoning goes, because human freedom is no impediment to divine control. Obviously, the free-will defense is now out the window, and one must turn in a different direction altogether in theodicy, which contemporary strong Calvinists, to their credit, recognize and do.[57]

A final major contemporary concern with Augustine has to do with science. The idea of a perfect paradise that operates differently than anything that we see now in the physical world does not make as much sense as it might have before the rise of modern science and the understanding of natural processes and laws. The common understanding of the universe now—as beginning with a Big Bang more than thirteen billion years ago, gradually cooling until planets could be formed, then the earth coming to its present form through billions of years of volcanoes, movement of tectonic plates, and erosion by wind and rain, long before humans appeared on the scene about one hundred thousand years ago—does not fit very well with Augustine's paradise, to say the least.[58] Greater appreciation for the complementary nature of the two creation stories, not as blow-by-blow scientific accounts but as theological documents that presuppose a very this-worldly picture of the earth, alleviates this tension. This change also raises a major question about the advisability of vesting all of one's theological capital, so to speak, on a young and perfect earth contrary to our current scientific understanding. In other words, if one has to run against the grain of almost all of modern science in order to believe the Bible or to have an Augustinian theodicy, then the Christian mission is probably in serious apologetic trouble. Are we, first, interpreting the Bible correctly and avoiding the mistake that the church made in the time of Galileo? Second, are we raising unnecessary stumbling blocks for those to whom we are proclaiming the gospel?

The Irenaean Free-Will Defense

In light of these concerns, the general direction of thinking in theodicy has moved dramatically in a different direction, in many ways representing another free-will defense that antedated Augustine but that has been neglected in the West until the last century, namely, that of Irenaeus (140–200). John Hick is perhaps the one who was most significant in putting Irenaeus back on the map, but he points out that he is resurrecting an older theology and also one that fits with the ideas of the father of modern theology, Friedrich Schleiermacher (1768–1834). Schleiermacher was, interestingly, one of the first to try to develop his theology to be consistent with modern scientific understandings of the universe. Irenaeus, in the second century, heavily influenced Eastern Orthodox theology in terms of a more developmental approach to creation, so the resurgence of influence and interest in Eastern Orthodox theology in the West after the fall of the Iron Curtain has also contributed to an increase in the interest in Irenaeus.

Ireneaus thought that Adam and Eve were more like children, young and immature, rather than being perfect already, as Augustine pictured them.[59] The "Irenaean intuition," as we might call it, is that God could not make already formed, "pre-fab" saints, so to speak.[60] This is one of those logical impossibilities to which Aquinas refers, akin to the impossibility of people being both free and determined. Irenaeus referred to the contrast between image and likeness in Genesis 1:26-27 to distinguish between creation as potential to become what God desired rather than already being created in such a state. While most see this as inappropriate exegesis, where image and likeness are seen as roughly synonymous in terms of Hebrew poetic parallelism, the idea can be expressed in a defensible way as representing the larger movement of Scripture on the distinction between the image of God in creation and the image of God realized in Christ.[61] Emil Brunner saw this as the difference between the "formal image" and the "material image."[62] All people are in the formal image of God, which already grants respect and dignity and being loved by God. People by their own choices, however, can respond to God's grace and love in being transformed into the material image of Christ. While Irenaeus obviously had no thought of modern science, the attractiveness of his approach is that it is more compatible with a contemporary scientific understanding, as well as a more Old Testament conception of the initial goodness of creation as serving God's purposes rather than having already fulfilled God's purposes. As this view has been developed, the major distinction from the Augustinian view lies in the way that natural evil is treated. For Augustine, natural evil was a *consequence* of the misuse of human freedom. For the Irenaean view, it is a *condition* that makes human freedom possible.

Not all such thinkers who make this turn concerning natural evil always call themselves Irenaean, but there is a pervasive common pattern among many contemporary theologians in giving a very similar account of natural evil. A number of these contemporary thinkers have explored more fully what it means for humans to have significant freedom and being. C. S. Lewis argued that one needs the ancient category of "matter," a medium that allows people to relate and interact with each other and a world.[63] God cannot be changing it willy-nilly all the time because we would never learn how to interact with it. Thus, it must have a certain "relative autonomy," its own integrity, even as it is sustained by God. This means that a rock that may be a stumbling block for one person could be a stepping stone for another. To make significant moral choices also calls for such an environment. Lewis points out that if God constantly intervened to make things turn out right, we could never make a choice that had any harmful consequences; we would never have to make a decision about a choice being beneficial or damaging. Again, this points to a certain reliability and dependability of nature, or relative autonomy. Hick suggests that if God were transparent to us, then we would be overwhelmed, as is pictured in several biblical accounts such as Isaiah in the temple and John in the book of Revelation. Thus, we need "epistemic distance," knowing distance, so that we come to God out of love and not out of coercive evidence or logic. In order for there to be genuine freedom, Hick then adds, the world needs to be "religiously ambiguous."[64] This does not mean that God cannot be known but that it must be possible for God to be rejected. This is the import of Moses only being able to see God's back, not God's face, even for Moses, whose face would shine in the presence of God (Exod 33:23). This is perhaps seen in the fact that the greatest revelation of God for Christians, Jesus Christ, was not only seen and rejected at times but was identified with Satan (Matt 10:24, 12:24). Another factor is greater realization of the immersion of humans in the physical world and the way the world interacts with humans. Stephen Hawking actually suggested that the key to discovering why we exist is for scientists to figure out the way the four basic forces interrelate to all physical reality. Then, he says, "we would know the mind of God."[65] While this is a gross overstatement as well as an overemphasis on a scientific understanding of reality, it points to the deep way in which the world is interconnected in lawlike ways. As John Polkinghorne, one of the most prominent theologians at the science-theology interface, suggests, we thus need a "free-process" or "free-nature" defense as much as a free-will defense.[66] In other words, freedom at the human level is deeply related to every other level in nature since humans are naturally embodied beings. The interplay of necessity and freedom (or chance or randomness) at the natural level correlates with human freedom at higher levels of complexity. When you add these various insights together, one has a theology that looks very different from the Augustinian approach. They convey a synergy that points to a world much like ours, even with its natural evil, at the outset.

In any case, on this contemporary Irenaean account, our world seems to fit the bill. It is what is needed to make possible—though not necessary—soul-making. This means that perhaps, given God's purposes in creation, God *had* to create a world something like ours from the beginning. This does not mean that the human interaction with natural processes could not have gone better if people had walked in harmony with God. In his inimitable way, Lewis imagines that if the "Paridisal man now could appear among us, we should regard him as an utter savage, a creature to be exploited or, at best, patronised." Before sin and the fall, however, he imagines that if we "would glance a second time at the naked, shaggy-bearded, slow-spoke creature," we "would fall at his feet."[67] He imagines that Adam might have had an intuitive relationship with nature, much like animals do, and even the kind of body control evinced by yogis who are able to heal themselves. Certainly, a greater spiritual connection with God could have given greater direction and access to healing powers. The risk of freedom, however, is that once sin entered the world, the fragile harmony was broken, with ripple effects throughout the world. The fall is thus a natural consequence of a failure to walk with God in what could have seemed "a garden of Eden." Now, we all live "east of Eden" (Gen 3:22-24).

Given free will—and perhaps the reality of chance at the quantum level and, in terms of chaos theory, at the level of everyday experience—the world, once created, can go in a number of directions that are not determined unilaterally by God. No one can prove that some other, safer world could not have been possible. As Alvin Plantinga has pointed out, however, one cannot prove either that such a world could have been guaranteed by God operating within the constraints of freedom, given the realities of human and perhaps natural freedom.[68] And such a burden of proof is not what is required. What we are looking for is some way to understand how an omnipotent and perfectly good God *might* have created a world that ended up like ours, rather than this being an obvious fact that undermines Christian belief.[69] Both the Augustinian and Irenaean traditions provide such accounts of how the significance of freedom might account for the evil and suffering in the world. All people must determine for themselves how plausible these theologies show themselves to be.

This contemporary adaptation of the Irenaean view has strengths in its greater openness to modern science and more consistent reliance on human freedom, without, for example, relying also on predestination. It is important to see that this is an adaptation of Irenaeus. Eastern orthodoxy certainly extended Irenaeus' thought in terms of infant baptism in a way that does not fit as well a free-will defense. Irenaeus himself was certainly not engaging modern science.

Another difference between the Augustinian and Irenaean free-will defenses can be seen in their spiritual implications. For this, we need to say more about providence. General providence is the way that God sustains the world in its being and can be seen as God's sustenance of the natural processes themselves. We saw this in the Irenaean model, where natural processes are part of God's good creation that God has a stake in preserving. Even Augustine saw that God preserves the fallen world in its being and in its integrity.[70] This dimension of providence is often ignored. With it, we can help bridge the gap that we have mentioned that often exists between the God of creation and the God of redemption, close to the early heresy of Marcionism. Yet the world is God's creation. It is not difficult to see that the proper functioning of our environment is crucial to our existence. Some scientists have argued that there must be life on other planets because of so many galaxies and so many stars with so many planets. Others have argued that so many fortuitous things occurred to make life possible on our planet that the odds are extremely low that life could exist anywhere else, even from a naturalistic perspective. A striking example is that it seems that the presence of the moon being just about its size is crucial to our planet's being stable enough for life to have developed over billions of years. If the moon had been much larger or much smaller, it would not have helped. Its size helped stabilize a natural wobble that in most planets would have made things too chaotic and unstable for life to have survived.[71] Add to this that the moon seems to have been created as a result of a chance collision with a celestial object long in the past that broke off part of the earth—so the moon once was part of the earth. If that had not happened when it did, neither too early nor too late, and had the results that it did, neither too large nor too small, we would likely not be here, scientifically speaking.[72] This is just one of many innumerable, unpredictable, chance events that are crucial to human existence. Faith sees these as part of the providence of God creating and sustaining a nature that is the framework for human life—and human redemption. The fact is that these fortuitous events had to occur for beings like us to be possible. Creation is the presupposition or framework for redemption; both are grounded in God's grace and good purposes. The importance of the general preservation and guidance of the natural world cannot be minimized. Hence we could say, the God of creation and providence IS the God of redemption; the God of redemption IS the God of creation and providence.

The question is, how does general providence work? Under the influence of the Augustinian view, with its view of God being able to control even free human decisions, this providence has been seen as "meticulous."[73] In other words, even in nature, every particular thing happens because God desires that particular thing to happen—from all eternity. This may sometimes imply a looser view of divine "permission" for us to go ahead and sin or for an earthquake to happen and not be due to divine intervention. However, it is clear that if God did not want something particular to happen, God could prevent it. This implies that anything that happens to us, especially in terms of natural evil, is somehow God's direct will. If we are upset about it or angry about it, the implication is that we should realize that it was ultimately God's will, and we should bring ourselves into acceptance of it and thus into conformity with God. This actually licenses, as a logical consequence of theology, people to say that natural catastrophes are "God's will." This kind of spirituality is of course much more emphatic in the Calvinist view, but it is also important to see that it is a consequence of the typical Augustinian free-will view.

The Irenaean view runs in another direction. General providence operates nonmeticulously. Nature is supposed to have a relative autonomy, as we have seen, and it is so interlinked, as we have realized more in accord with science, that natural events are not typically targeted or directed. This means that hurricanes and tornadoes happen as a part of nature. We experience this as suffering and as natural evil when we get in the way, but there is nothing evil per se about natural processes. They are the same processes that make the world habitable for us. An appeal might be made here to Jesus' saying, "God causes the sun to shine on the just and unjust, and it to rain upon the just and unjust" (Matt 5:45). Some things just happen. This is part of what makes the world religiously ambiguous. If only bad people experienced natural evil, and good people did not, then it would be obvious and not epistemically distant that God is involved. This does not mean that such an event is desired specifically by God. God, too, can regret such a thing as part of the cost of creation and see this as the "groaning of creation" as it awaits a more perfect consummation in the future (Rom 8:22). Especially if moral evil is involved, God can be seen as opposing it through the conviction of the Holy Spirit. As happened numerous times in the biblical story, God may then be saddened and outraged at the outcome. So when we feel distraught and even angry at some things that happen, instead of seeing these as God's will, we might understand our sorrow and anger actually as bringing us closer rather than farther from God, because they are not God's will.

In the contemporary world, we understand things as part of nature in a way that was not possible throughout most of Christian history. This is a crucial difference between our assumptions and the biblical perspective, no matter how conservative or liberal our theology. A storm or an earthquake that we would accept as having natural causes would have seemed to ancients as surprising and inexplicable, more directly an act of God. Their category of "miracle," for example, would not have included a dimension of being contrary to natural law since the idea of natural law did not yet exist. Unfortunately, the modern category of miracle, developing at the same time as the rise of modern science with its early picture of a Newtonian world that operated in terms of strict mechanistic laws, almost inevitably implied some kind of notion of intervention or contravention of natural law. We are actually in a better place today, with the significant changes in the scientific worldview over the last century, to make room for a more biblically based notion of the miraculous that is also consistent with scientific developments. Such thinking is desperately needed to avoid unnecessary conflicts again with science. It is also needed to help the normal Christian better to make sense of God's activity in the world, instead of people struggling with some direct sense of God causing and targeting natural catastrophes or God not being involved at all. Rather than succumbing to this dilemma, the openness in the world due to greater understanding of the interplay between chance and law gives room for God to work in terms of special providence within God's creation and not "against" it or "in spite of" it. After all, it would be surprising if God the Creator did not leave room for God to work within God's own creation. The approach of a more Irenaean, nonmeticulous view of providence gives room for the general functioning of nature, general providence, that provides a ground for human existence, but it needs to be religiously ambiguous—which it is. Whatever one's theology, the fact is that the world is religiously ambiguous. For the believer, it can manifest the glory of God, but not so clearly for the nonbeliever. God's special providence, as some theologians attest, is "in, with, and under" God's creation, not contradictory to it.[74] The category of intervention, therefore, is probably not the most helpful way to think about it. When God acts, as God did in Jesus, it may be seen as God's work, but it may also not be seen as God's work. During this life and this "fallen" existence, this more hidden and veiled way seems to be God's chosen way of providence. In any case, it fits the demands of an Irenaean theodicy and the contemporary scientific understanding of the world.

Both approaches, the Augustinian and Irenaean, in a sense allow for permission and see evil as part of the cost of freedom in creation. The Augustinian approaches it through Adam and Eve, who were the only ones who were ever free enough to make an accountable choice and sees permission as meticulously granted. The Irenaean approach understands all human beings as making free, account-able choices that determine whether they are separated from God or not. For the Irenaean, permission is nonmeticulously granted in that God grants freedom in nature and in human beings in a general way as part of the cost of creation. The question of special providence in light of such a greater emphasis on general providence must be treated further, but this can be done better in the context of salva-tion and the Christian life. In the meantime, our account thus far provides a way of understanding truths both about God and the world, of the nature of God and of creation, that supports and points to redemption and eschatology.

The Strong Calvinist Theodicy

One more major approach, very different in not relying on the free-will defense, can now be considered, namely, the strong Calvinist. This has been a significant trajectory in Christian thought although not the major one. Even when affirmed, as we shall see, it was often half-hearted in simultaneously appealing to some extent to a free-will defense. Generally, the Roman Catholic

Church and Orthodox Church have put more emphasis on the reality of free will—sometimes, however, inconsistently allowing for predestination. In fact, reading the theological tradition often is a matter not of quoting chapter and verse but of picking up on the main emphasis. It is sometimes surprising to find that deep fissures and tensions exist in even great theologians, perhaps attesting to the challenge of wrapping our feeble minds around a reality as complex and majestic as God. Aquinas is a good example in that he affirms predestination and even at one point, in conjunction with his understanding of God as immutable and impassible, stresses that God affects us but that we cannot affect God. This implies to some that God determines everything from one moment of eternity. Aquinas, however, would say that God determines free actions as free, which some consider to be a mere sleight of hand, an incoherent notion.[75] Whether or not Aquinas is consistent is thus a major issue, but many Thomists put Aquinas on the free-will side of the ledger in the end due to his endorsement of the reality of free will. Contemporary Presbyterians also largely back away from "strong" or "Five-Point" Calvinism. This latter was the Calvinism that drew, to be sure, heavily upon Calvin but by the seventeenth century had developed more of a heavy emphasis on God's sovereignty and predestination in a logical system. This view is commonly framed in terms of the TULIP acronym: Total depravity, Unconditional election, Limited atonement, Irresistible grace, and Perseverance of the saints. As one can see, these stand together in pointing to God's determining, meticulous ordination. Calvin himself argues strenuously at times that God ordains everything, even the slightest movement of a branch in the wind or the dryness of a mother's breasts.[76] He would rather do away with the ideas of permission and freedom because they just confuse things.[77] Calvin also affirms that God determines both the saved and damned, namely, double predestination, from the foundation of the world. Interestingly, this view has had a resurgence among evangelicals in recent years, especially among my own tradition of Baptists of the American South.[78] When I first began teaching, I did not need to deal with strong Calvinism very much because the students were uninterested. Now, many students come with strong Calvinist assumptions.

Clearly, though, the free-will defense will not do for Calvinism. If free will is not an impediment to God's ordination, then appealing to human responsibility does not get God off the hook with respect to evil and suffering. Contemporary strong Calvinists actually see some of the inconsistency in Calvin and draw out this conclusion more stringently. They affirm that such Calvinism is compatibilist, thus undeterred by human freedom. Even though they will state that people are free and are responsible in some mysterious way, in the end God determines what people freely do and is unconstrained by human freedom. This is why opponents of Calvinism argue that God's goodness is what is at stake.[79] Calvinists counter that sovereignty is at stake. This is one of those areas that come down to one's fundamental theological intuitions. How one understands God indeed makes a difference.

The strong Calvinist view of freedom is therefore a different conception, a nonlibertarian concept in contemporary parlance, which is often confusing in reading contemporary theology because theologians are often using the same word, freedom, with different meanings. Calvin himself at times inconsistently appealed to Adam's sin as a way of affirming human responsibility over against divine responsibility. Like Augustine, he thought that Adam acted for all, thus Adam and Eve were the only free humans; all others are rightly condemned to hell as a result, even at birth. Given his strong views of sovereignty expressed elsewhere, this appeal to Adam having what appears to be libertarian freedom is incongruous, which contemporary Calvinists see. One might argue that Calvin, trained as a lawyer, saw the inconsistencies in Augustine and followed out the logical conclusions more rigorously. Contemporary Calvinists see the small remaining inconsistency in Calvin and follow out even more consistently the logical implications.

How is this done? Perhaps the most straightforward way is to argue that God is so sovereign that humans have no rights over God. I heard this best expressed in an oral presentation by a William of Ockham scholar—Ockham being a theologian who similarly emphasized divine sovereignty and who greatly influenced Martin Luther's high view of sovereignty. The analogy was to a picnic where someone sees ants heading toward one's peanut butter sandwich. The assumption is that ants have no rights over humans, so you can step on the ants or you can exercise unmerited grace and let the ants pass, perhaps by moving the sandwich. On this analogy, whatever God does is just, by definition, in relation to humans because humans, like the ants, have no rights or claims against God. Appeal is often made in this connection to Paul's reference to the pot having no claims against the potter in Romans 9:21.

As to how God can determine human actions and yet humans deserve to go to hell rather than God being responsible, this is difficult to comprehend—so difficult that this is where Calvinists usually appeal to mystery or to paradox and non-Calvinists get off the Calvinist boat. The idea is that God is so sovereign and powerful that God is able to do what seems inexplicable to humans. Again, strong Calvinism is not only assuming a certain limited view of freedom but is also assuming a logically prior conception of power itself as dominative rather than donative.

In their favor, Calvinists draw out the logical implications of a view of pure, unmitigated power and thus often have appeal to the rationally minded, despite the heavy appeal to mystery in light of paradox![80] In one of the few self-revealing passages in Calvin's writing, he himself finds it reassuring that God is in complete control of everything.[81] That is more comforting to him than to allow for genuine freedom or chance. Calvin makes it clear, to be sure, that he does not expect everything to go well for a Christian. The catastrophes that he lists are terrifying. Yet even attributing these traumas to God is preferable to him than attributing them to randomness. I think most would have some sympathy here. This again points to divergent paths in theology and spirituality. If we want God to be completely controlling everything, as in meticulous providence, we have to accept with that security the implications that God is behind everything that has created the problem of evil and suffering. This means that, despite divine opposition to sin, God could have prevented any atrocity without violating human freedom and yet has not done so. Obviously, such an implication is what creates the worst kind of problem of theodicy. What happens is that one protects a certain perspective of divine power at the cost of grave challenges to divine goodness. Sometimes this pressure has been dealt with in terms of the left and right hand of God, or the manifest and inscrutable will of God. John Piper, a popular contemporary Calvinist, speaks explicitly of having to accept two such wills in God: one that looks like Jesus Christ and one that actually can will sin and suffering.[82] The almost overwhelming strain to hold these together has driven most in the Reformed tradition—following Karl Barth, as much as he loved Calvin—to reject this aspect of Calvinism. Rather, Barth insisted that Jesus Christ is the one who reveals the nature of God as no other. One cannot look behind Christ for a secret and actually master will.[83] Without taking on the whole of process metaphysics,[84] Christians can affirm that God's omnipresence means that God knows in the biblical sense of knowing, not a distant and removed "knowing that," but an experiential knowing and experiencing of all that occurs, which includes a level of divine interaction with everything that occurs. Polkinghorne expresses well a Christian perspective:

> He [God] is not a spectator but a fellow-sufferer, who has himself absorbed the full force of evil. In the lonely figure hanging in the darkness and dereliction of Calvary, the Christian believes that he sees God opening his arms to embrace the bitterness of the strange world he has made. The God revealed in the vulnerability of the incarnation and in the vulnerability of creation are one. He is the crucified god, whose paradoxical power is perfected in weakness, whose self-chosen symbol is the King reigning in the gallows.[85]

This theology, however, does mean that during this in-between time, between creation and consummation, the world is religiously ambiguous, and God works mostly in hidden, persuasive, noncoercive ways. Hence the cross.

Theology makes a difference. It shapes our way of being in the world and thus our basic spirituality. This means all of theology, however. This chapter on creation reveals how the pathway through understanding the nature of God and creation cannot be bypassed by simply jumping to soteriology or even to Christology. A split between the God of creation and redemption cannot be sustained. Soteriology and Christology cannot be understood apart from the framework of creation and providence. It is also true, as we shall see, that we will further develop the understanding of God and creation in light of redemption and eschatology. More immediately, appreciating the greater significance of creation sets the stage for taking a fresh look at the nature of humanity and human embodiment, with all of its implications for rethinking the nature of sin.

6

HUMANITY AND SIN
Rising and Falling

If God is a mystery, so are human beings. Perhaps the mystery of God is only matched by humanity as the climax of God's creation, named in the first chapter of the Bible as being in God's image, and having to do with the mystery of personhood itself that both share in common. The nature of the self, of course, is not something of interest only to Christians or to religious people. Everyone, obviously, has a stake in understanding the nature of the self, but fault lines of understanding in general run across this doctrine more than some others. What is the self? Are we dualistic or holistic beings? Are we free or determined? Were Adam and Eve free but no one else? Are human beings essentially good, or have we lost the image of God? How malleable are human beings? What difference does sin make? What does it mean to be spiritual or holy? Can human beings survive death? The answer to the question, what is the self? is the key to the answer of almost all religious questions. This way of putting it may come across as too subjective in the postmodern context. Interestingly, though, John Calvin, known to be anything but a subjectivist, himself began his landmark *Institutes of the Christian Faith* with the memorable lines, "Nearly all the wisdom we possess, that is to say, true and sound wisdom, consists of two parts: the knowledge of God and of ourselves."[1] Pascal sounded a similar note just a century later, albeit with more pathos:

> When I consider the short span of my life absorbed into the preceding and subsequent eternity, . . . the little space which I fill and even can see, swallowed up in the infinite immensity of spaces of which I know nothing and which knows nothing of me, I am terrified, and surprised to find myself here rather than there, for there is no reason why it should be here rather than there, why now rather than then. Who put me here? On whose orders and on whose decision have this place and this time been allotted to me?[2]

With the rise of a modern focus on individuals, along with the greater understanding deriving from scientific understanding, Calvin's and Pascal's insights are only accentuated.

We will begin by looking at cases of what the church has thought of as exemplary spirituality to begin seeing the implications of our views of the self. Then we will turn to the important issue of the image of God, followed by the newly appreciated understanding of the self as holistic, embodied, and social. These reflections will provide a broader perspective for us to consider the self's fragility, fault, and the resultant dynamics of sin.

ROSE OF LIMA

Kelley Pigott, the chaplain at my university, tells this story of Rose of Lima, coupled with his own, about growing up spiritually in the church.

> Isabel de Flores, born in the sixteenth century, had two things going for her: she was beautiful and rich. However, her mother became very concerned when Rose, as the family called her, did not seem interested in men. For some reason she preferred to hang out at the church and befriend nuns. When other girls were talking about dresses and romance, Rose was talking about sin and suffering. The family, and her mother in particular, spent ten years trying to get Rose to give up her austere interests, but to no avail. Rose had even gone so far as to take a vow of vir-

ginity, which, if kept, pretty well ruined her chances of getting married. In 1606 Rose joined a convent and became a Dominican of the Third Order. At this point Rose's pursuit of God took a bizarre turn, though there were already hints that she was deeply disturbed about something. For example, rather than flaunt her beauty, Rose did everything in her power to make herself look ugly, from the clothes she wore to the caustic lime she'd smear on her face to splotch up her skin. When she became a nun she chose a very strict life of seclusion, relegating herself to a hut in her family's garden. There she donned a silver studded ringlet which dug painfully into her head; she slept regularly on a bed of broken glass, stones, potsherd, and thorns. Rose believed that by subjecting herself to such torture she could draw closer to God and earn grace for her fellow sinful countrymen.

Perhaps more bizarre than Rose's masochistic tendencies was the reaction from the church which eulogized her. She became a role model of piety for other young women. And the people of Peru, especially, embraced her as a spiritual super hero. Unfortunately, Rose's lifestyle took a toll on her health and she died at the young age of thirty-one. Several miracles occurred soon after which were attributed to Rose, so that in 1668, Pope Clement IX beatified her, declaring Rosa of Lima to be the patron saint of South America.[3]

To her credit, Rosa of Lima pursued God with a serious tenacity that is to be admired. And her chosen lifestyle is consistent with the penitential theology of the Roman Catholic Church. So in speaking of Rosa I do not want to seem disrespectful or antagonistic. Even today, her life continues to deeply influence the lives of thousands who look to her for spiritual guidance. But I am deeply disturbed by the message for which she lived and died—a common notion existent in both Catholic and Protestant circles that misery equals piety. In other words, Kingdom of God is about suffering.

As a young Catholic attending parochial school, I remember the teacher placing a large picture of Jesus above the blackboard. His face looked contorted and in pain. On his head sat a crown with long, pointy thorns, some of which were clearly embedded in his skull. Blood drained down the sides of his face in dark crimson lines. And every now and then the nun would point to the picture and warn us that each time we did something bad we pushed another needle into Jesus' head. The thought horrified me as a six-year-old. And I remember staring for long periods of time into the face of Jesus, wondering why he was perpetually upset at me.

As I read the New Testament I get a very different vision of Jesus than what I was led to believe in parochial school. Shockingly, Jesus developed a sullied reputation of being a glutton and a drunkard. Understand, Jesus never committed the sins of gluttony or drunkenness, but he obviously loved eating and drinking and hanging around those who did the same. Yet the very thought of this unnerves people today, as it did when he walked the earth.[4] They can't imagine a savior mingling, laughing, or even telling a joke, much less drinking. Nor can they fathom Jesus actually encouraging such behavior.[5]

One could add to Dr. Pigott's reflections that this tension between Jesus and Christian practice is not just true of the Roman Catholic Church, it is pervasive in Protestant piety as well. While not always true, the caricature of Puritan piety forbidding, in Max Weber's words, "the spontaneous enjoyment of life and all that it had to offer" points in a similar gnostic direction rather than a Jewish or Christian one.[6] This world-hating tendency, as Nietzsche characterized it, can be found over and over.[7] We have seen that such self-flagellation was part of Luther's attempt to be spiritual as a monk. Lest we leave out Eastern orthodoxy, a grim scene is portrayed in *The Brothers Karamazov* of admiration of a monk largely because of his depriving himself of earthly pleasure.[8]

The question that this raises has to do with the value of the created world, in the first place, and the nature and status of humanity, in the second. We have seen already in the previous chapter how wrongheaded is such an attitude toward God's good creation. We will see in this chapter how the church has similarly missed the mark with respect to humanity. In other words, the only thing that matches this astounding pattern of extreme asceticism in Christian history is its near absence in Scripture. To be sure, there is self-discipline. Fasting is encouraged. The difference is that it is encouraged for the sake of healthy self-control and spiritual focus but not out of a negative attitude toward the body or the world. We will also certainly have to take into consideration the way sin mars God's good creation but not so much that it should cause either God or us to turn away from creation. In fact, as one can see by the image of "missing the mark," perhaps the dominant view of sin in the Bible, one can miss the mark by despising God's handiwork just as by overindulging. Sometimes we can sin by thinking that we are overcoming it; we can be most unspiritual in striving to be spiritual. The stakes again are high, and the key lies in the answer to the question, who are we?

THE SELF IN GOD'S IMAGE

The first thing to be said about the doctrine of humanity has to do with the basic standing and value of humanity. This has been traditionally located in the understanding of humanity as being created in the image of God. Scripture affirms that human beings are in the image of God numerous times, but it does not specify the nature of the image of God. Thus, there has been much speculation in Christian history about what it entails. The *locus classicus* on the image of God is the powerfully poetic passage in Genesis 1:26-27:

> Then God said, "Let us make humankind in our image, according to our likeness; and let them have dominion over the fish of the sea, and over the birds of the air, and over the cattle, and over all the wild animals of the earth, and over every creeping thing that creeps upon the earth." So God created humankind in his image, in the image of God he created them; male and female he created them.

In the first creation story, human beings are created last, apparently underscoring their special dignity. It should be kept in mind, however, that land animals are also created on the last day. Human beings thus do not have a special day unto themselves, reminding us that humans are clearly on the creaturely side of the Creator-creation divide. Humans are special but are closely allied with other creatures and the rest of creation. A similar theology is found in Psalm 8:

> When I look at your heavens,
> the work of your fingers,
> the moon and the stars
> that you have established;

what are human beings that you are mindful of them,
    mortals that you care for them?
Yet you made them a little lower than God
    and crowned them with glory and honor.
You have given them dominion
    over the works of your hands;
    you have put all things under their feet,
all sheep and oxen,
    and also the beasts of the field,
the birds of the air,
    and the fish of the sea,
whatever passes along the paths of the seas.
O LORD, our Sovereign,
    how majestic is your name in all the earth! (Ps 8:3-9)

This careful configuration of humanity's place is important to see in these ancient texts, which recognize both the humble and exalted status of humanity in a more perceptive way than has often been the case in Christian history. Especially in modernity, the difference of human beings from their biological background was emphasized along with an extreme dualism, as if humans are not really on earth, but standing somewhere between earth and heaven. More recently, we have understood ourselves to be biological beings who are related to the rest of creation, ironically bringing our understanding back in line with the Genesis text from more than two millennia ago.

As we have noted so often, the challenge in theology is not just to get something right but to get it in the right balance. This is crucial here. After a long period of overestimating the difference between humans and the rest of creation, we are recovering the deep sense of immersion in the world that is not a curse but a part of the blessing of human life. Since we inherit a legacy of distinguishing humans from the animals, exacerbated by the evolution debates, this repositioning can feel awkward, like a putdown. In the biblical sense, it is more like finding one's proper groove than trying to perch on a pedestal that was never meant to support human beings.

Even as we continue to do justice to the creaturely, earthy side of human beings, which is humbling, we cannot lose our balance on the other side and forget that humans are the only beings described as being in the image of God. Quite apart from the various ideas about what exactly the image of God is, it is very clear that human beings have a special value and dignity in being in the image of God. Much more can be said of this that is also theologically rich. In Genesis 1, it is not just the few elite human beings—or one human being who is semidivine—who are esteemed, but all human beings are seen to be in the image of God, male and female. One could argue that the political implications of this simple but radical view were not reached until the French and American revolutions in the eighteenth century, and even then the revolutions did not attain to the level of Genesis 1 because they did not include people of all colors and women. Martin Luther King Jr., repeated the logic given for black inferiority for so long after the revolution in the United States:

> All men are made in the image of God;
> God, as everybody knows, is not a Negro;
> Therefore the Negro is not a man.[9]

Ancient Israel certainly did not fully measure up, either, to the profundity of the first chapter of the Bible. Dealing with such a distorted gap between belief and practice will occupy us in treating the nature of sin.

More specifically, the striking thing about the Genesis account of the image of God is that it is not described.[10] Humans are in the image of God, but it is not clear what this means, resulting in manifold historical debates. In many ways, it has been identified as something that distinguishes humans from the animals, from the upright stance of humans to the more common view of the human soul or mind. All of these have the character of being a property that humans possess.

A slightly different perspective has been common in the Eastern church, based on Irenaeus' interpretation of the "image" as our capacity for God and the "likeness" as our actual conformity to God. It corresponds to the view that Adam and Eve were more like children and not fully formed rather than being created perfect. Unfortunately, the passage represents Hebrew parallelism where image and likeness are likely two similar ways of describing the same thing. This dynamic view can be better expressed from a Christian perspective as the image of God referring to human potentiality to be in the image of Christ or to be Christlike. As such, Irenaeus' view may be poor exegesis but reflects good canonical theology. This refiguration makes another important point, namely, that the measure of true humanity is not Adam and Eve but Jesus Christ, a conception that we will develop further in the chapter on Christology. Emil Brunner expressed this as the image of God being the "formal image," the potentiality, and Christlikeness being the fulfilled or "material" image.[11]

A variation of the dynamic that takes it a step further is an eschatological view, where the image of God is not found until it is complete in Christ in heaven or the eschaton.[12] This view corrects the tendency to look backward to Adam and Eve as the human ideal and underscores that the future kingdom of God is the standard. The danger in this view is that not regarding all humans as by nature in the image of God and only potentially in the image of God can weaken the affirmation of the worth and dignity of all humans. It can also support a dangerous misunderstanding of the idea of "total depravity" in Reformed thought as the loss of the image of God altogether. These views are difficult to sustain from the text since humans after the fall of Genesis are still described as in the image of God in Genesis 9, specifically to stress the inherent value of all humans beings before God.

Another major development especially based on Karl Barth's insights is that the image is relational. The image is not so much an individual possession as it is a relationship between humans and God and each other. He took as one of the only clues in the text that the depiction of humans in the image of God is immediately followed by humans being described as male and female.[13] While relationality is of course not circumscribed by male-female relations, it is a potent symbol of the basic relational nature of human beings. Claus Westermann similarly argues that the image is not any particular property but that humans are created to "correspond" to God, "so that something can happen between God and man."[14] As will be seen in the next section, this emphasis chimes in with a rediscovered sense of the ineradicably social nature of the self. Since the meaning of the image is not spelled out in Scripture and must be grasped in light of the larger canon and message, this view surely has much to commend it. It suggests that the image of God has to do with the first and second commandments, namely, to love God and neighbor. While being seen as relational, it suggests a capacity to love that may or may not be realized. It can be seen as an aspect of Augustine's notion that "You have made us for yourself."

A related view mentioned in the previous chapter is representational.[15] Humans thus represent God by bearing God's image, perhaps as an envoy would bear the image of the king. As we have seen, this approach resonates with the general canonical sense of humans representing God on earth and being accountable to God for their stewardship of God's creation, an idea strongly reflected in Jesus' parables (Matt 21:33-41, 24:45-61, 25:14-29). As we saw in the previous chapter, dominion follows from being in the image of God and being in some sense God's representative; however, it should not be construed in terms of freedom for exploitation but in terms of responsibility. Westermann notably points out that dominion does not extend to other humans but to nature.[16] Whether or not this particular view is correct, it conveys at least some of what it means to relate to God and to walk with God; this surely also means being responsible before God for God's creation.

One can pull together these various views about the image of God by placing within the dynamic view a sense in which humans are ineradicably in the image of God and oriented toward a destiny of being in relationship with God now and in the eschaton. The image is thus both endowment and summons.[17] All human beings have worth by being in the image of God. The fulfillment of the image is not a foregone conclusion, however, as we see in the fall in Genesis 3. In fact, from a Christian perspective, the consummation of the image is only enabled further as salvation by grace through faith in Jesus Christ. Human beings together, as relational beings, have an inherent calling and responsibility to which they may or may not respond but are not left alone. The God who graciously creates and bestows worth graciously keeps calling and gifting, not to a pristine past but to a "beloved community" in the future.[18] The understanding of the image of God is thus not complete from the first chapter of the Bible but only from the last.

THE HOLISTIC, EMBODIED SELF

A second question has to do with the nature of the self. In that light, one of the great shifts over the last century has been the turn from understanding the self as dualistic to understanding the self as holistic.[19] This shift occurred in large part due to greater scientific understanding of the deeply embodied nature of human life. People could think in earlier times of the mind and thought as working almost separately from the body. As we have seen, one of the first offshoots of orthodox Christianity was a gnostic Christianity that later combined with neoplatonism to see the spirit as good and matter—the body as well as nature—as the source of evil. This tendency, while ostensibly rejected, has deeply affected the church in its spiritual practices, like a magnet drawing the church toward an asceticism for its own sake and a mindset that was suspicious of the goodness of earthly life. Even in modernity, Descartes saw soul and body as two distinct substances and could never quite figure out how they could interrelate.

As we now increasingly understand, thought occurs in the brain; the mind is in the brain. If the brain is damaged, thought is damaged. Short-term memory can be lost, as in the movies *Memento* or *Fifty First Dates*, where a person can have memories of the past but cannot hold recent memories. One's personality can be altered by brain damage, which can be specified in great detail. While some see the understanding of the brain as only just beginning, equivalent to Galileo's seventeenth-century understanding of science, enough has been understood for all to acknowledge how deeply embodied we are. Much of philosophy, with its Platonic roots just like Christianity, assumed that rational thought was distinct from the body and emotions, but now it is evident that even critical thinking is dependent upon emotions and the body.[20]

Philosophers thus increasingly have reconceived the immersion of the mind in the body. Maurice Merleau-Ponty described how we "are involved in the world and with others in an inextricable tangle."[21] What he saw was that not only are we entangled in the body, we and the body are entangled in the world. Perhaps our language fails us because we continue to speak in quasi-dualistic terms when distinguishing between ourselves and the body. Rather, we *are* our bodies, and our bodies *are* ourselves.

Martin Heidegger is a major figure in this respect in saying that we are "beings-in-the-world."[22] He was reacting against the modern skeptical question of whether we can know that our bodies exist or whether the external world exists. He argued that this is a nonsensical question, for our very capacity to think about it presupposes our embodied "being-in-the-world."[23] He was saying, in other words, that one cannot give a good answer to a bad question. The modern skeptical question is misplaced.[24]

Since most of Western thought, philosophy, and theology has presupposed dualism, this recent shift to holism presents a major challenge to rethink theological categories such as faith and reason, which we treated in the prolegomena, and the self and sin, which we treat in this chapter. It will lead us in new directions in understanding salvation, the church, and the afterlife as well. With a virtually gnostic approach to the self, the church has not always done justice to human embodiment. Pastoral care, preaching, and teaching have often been directed at people as if they were pure minds but not also fully feeling, physical beings. If the latter dimension was treated, it was that it should be minimized or depreciated. If we are holistic beings, however, one has to think of retraining, formation, and integration—very different tasks. Holism is grounded in the goodness of creation and implies that redemption is not just of the soul or spirit, understood as disembodied, but is for the transformation of the whole self. The practice of discipleship, then, is rooted in bodily training, if you will. Habits, abilities, and feelings must be trained as well as the mind.

Another way that our bodily being-in-the-world shapes us is in our sexual identities. While much of what we have had to emphasize in recent years is the equality between the sexes and the way culture shapes gender roles, we still must recognize the physical basis of who we are. On the one hand, this can lead to an appreciation of the unique contributions that each gender can make. For example, the church has missed out by its silencing of women's perspectives borne out of their experience of childbirth and pain. Our identities are too interwoven with who we are as physical beings—in many ways, not just gender—to make embodiment only peripheral.[25] On the other hand, we have to realize that we all differ from each other in our being-in-the-world in many ways, all of which contribute to our identities and our capacity for contributions to the church and to the world. Even basic personality types seem to be genetically based, which impacts the way we express our spirituality. Some prefer inward contemplation of images; others prefer outward actions. Some tend toward an imageless mysticism; others prefer rational articulation.[26] James Fowler has supported an approach to differing stages or styles of spiritual development that are rooted in common intellectual and moral development.[27] The fact that people are at various such stages, all within one church or one Bible study, greatly affects how a church as a whole processes issues. These differences are also a part of missions because the same stages impact people outside the church. Our differences, which are so rooted in our embodiment, as well as our various cultures and traditions, have often been neglected and even denigrated in our desires to be pure minds or spirits. The biblical view, on the other hand, seems to bless these earthy differences as part of the goodness of creation. As we shall see, human sin and fallenness distort everything, so this natural goodness can sometimes only be recovered in redemption. Part of this recovery may well be, however, overcoming a depreciation of our embodied being-in-the-world.

So, over the last century, science and philosophy have moved toward an understanding of the self as holistic and embodied. What is remarkable is that the same shift occurred in biblical studies at about the same time, seemingly independently, and the confluence of these various waves made this shift a powerful and relatively sudden force.[28] Suddenly, biblical scholars began to see that the language suggestive of dualism in the Bible, such as "mortify the flesh," should be read in a Hebrew context rather than a Greek. It was clear that the Hebrew view of the Old Testament was holistic. All creatures are "living souls" in Genesis 1. The soul is not something separate from the body. Rather, the soul is the embodied self. As we will see in the chapter on eschatology, the Hebrews so assumed this that they could hardly conceive of an afterlife after the body has died. The Sadducees in Jesus' time continued this denial of an afterlife.

There is now a large consensus that Paul, "a Hebrew of the Hebrews," continues this thought-world in the New Testament. Like the Pharisees, he could conceive of bodily resurrection—and perhaps some kind of intermediate, incomplete existence until the final kingdom of God—but he seemed in general to think in terms of a holistic self. When Paul speaks of "sins of the flesh," he can include envy, which is usually thought of as a sin of the spirit, not of the flesh. This is a clue that something else is going on. Paul speaks of "the world" and "the flesh" at times not as something totally distinct from the self but as an inclination of the self away from God, of the old way of life in contrast to being a new creation of the Spirit.[29] The import of all of this is that these various movements represent a confluence toward conceiving of the self in a holistic way and toward seeing this as the more warranted biblical view. As indicated, this calls for rethinking virtually all of the themes of theology and the practices of discipleship and spiritual formation.

Theologically, the importance of embodiment is justified not just in terms of the doctrine of creation, which affirms the goodness of embodied human life, but on the basis of the centrality of incarnation. John, of course, puts it most bluntly: "The Word was made flesh," likely a flat rejection of gnostic tendencies already at work. Graham Ward is just as direct in spelling out the implications, not just for Christ but for all human beings: "Human beings have to participate in becoming flesh as He became flesh. Human beings are not truly themselves, are not truly flesh, until they have become flesh as He became flesh."[30] With the church's nearly two-thousand-year-old flirtation with Gnosticism in mind, it is safe to say that we have only just begun to rethink the meaning of spiritual and ecclesial practices in light of such a truly canonical anthropology.

THE SOCIAL SELF

This rethinking is extended when we understand that the self is not just embodied in the world, but that the self is a social self. The self cannot be understood as primordially isolated and unencumbered, as in modernity, but it is ineradicably a social self. In Ricoeur's words, we must understand "oneself as another."

This is a dramatic shift from the modern ethos, although in this case not so much from the premodern. The ancient world often thought of the self in a collective sense. In the Old Testament, we can see this in the punishment of Achan, including the putting to death of his wife and children as well as his livestock and belongings: all were him! We also should note that there was a shift toward individual responsibility, especially in Jeremiah and Ezekiel, but there still remained much more of a social sense of the self than is common in the modern West. This view still prevails in much of the world, especially in the East. Jesus' radical actions are all the more striking for putting himself outside the social structure. Paul likewise was remarkable in setting out on his own.[31] No wonder that some thought that each one, Jesus and Paul, was mad.

We can appreciate some gains in modernity of individual dignity and rights. One could argue that these are finally the outworkings of the implications of the egalitarianism and dignity of each person implied in Genesis 1 and in much of the rest of Scripture. Jewish-Christian origins were behind much of the move toward respecting the basic worth of each person. Yet it is also evident that modernity went so far in the direction of the individual that it became an era of radical individualism. The autonomy of the sufficient self became a presupposition. Perhaps we are now in a place to find a happier balance between the two extremes.

We can now see that the solipsist challenge of modernity is misplaced, that is, in terms of the question of whether other selves exist. Heidegger's response to this question, besides pointing out that we are beings-in-the world, was to point out that we live in a "with-world." This point is backed up extensively by psychology, which indicates that our very identities are shaped by growing up in a social setting. We would likely not be able to use language or think about such things apart from a human world. Depriving infants of significant social interaction can even lead to their death. The fact that we can speculate about the reality of other selves is possible only because of identities and language formed by a social world. Helen Keller is a dramatic instance of the role of language in making possible a reflective world. She was struck with deafness and blindness at the age of two. With the help of her teacher, Annie Sullivan, she was introduced to language. After a stormy childhood incident in which she took a doll, which had been a gift, and trampled it underfoot, her teacher took her outside:

> Some one was drawing water and my teacher placed my hand under the spout. As the cool stream gushed over one hand she spelled into the other the word water, first slowly, then rapidly. I stood still, my whole attention fixed upon the motions of her fingers. Suddenly I felt a misty consciousness as of something forgotten—a thrill of returning thought; and somehow the mystery of language was revealed to me. I knew that "w-a-t-e-r" meant the wonderful cool something that was flowing over my hand. That living word awakened my soul, gave it light, hope, joy, set it free!
>
> I left the well-house eager to learn. Everything had a name, and each name gave birth to a new thought. As we returned to the house every object which I touched seemed to quiver with life.[32]

Language is itself an aspect of the social world, which undergirds individual consciousness. It is true that an amazing thing about human beings is that once they have received the gift of self-identity, language, and thought from others, they can question whether others and all of the rest of the reality even exist. Built upon the foundation of the social world, humans have the capacity of transcendence. In a positive way, humans can criticize their social world and sometimes rise above it. Often, ironically, this is with the help of previous traditions that provide another perspective or point in a different direction. The kingdom of God can function this way by pointing to alternatives to the status quo. Even Jesus drew on earlier traditions, admittedly in a profoundly creative way, to live out a quite different role of Messiah.

The point is that we are in a position to understand the self in a way that avoids the alternatives of collectivism, on the one side, where individuality and transcendence are lost. On the other side, we can avoid radical individualism, where the self ironically becomes a god to itself and becomes severely impoverished at the same time. The postmodern context at best preserves the gains of modernity while correcting its excesses. At worst, it also lapses into the unfettered self of late modernity. An apt characterization is to understand the self as the self in relationship or the self in community. The Christian gospel values each individual so much that each is seen in the image of God, as equal before the cross, and as the one for whom the Good Shepherd would leave the ninety-nine safe sheep to seek. The priesthood of the believer, so valued by Believer's churches, emphasizes the importance of each person owning one's beliefs and being responsible for the welfare of the church. Yet the individual is always seen in relationship to God and to others. A priest is one who cares primarily for others, not just for himself or herself. As we soon shall see, relationships can be distorted and broken, yet they still define the self. At best, the self functions in relationship to the body of Christ, as valuable as any other in the body but no more valuable.

The Fragile Self

With this fuller understanding of the self as holistic and social in mind, we can add one of the contributions of existentialists. They rejected dualism while at the same time recognizing a kind of two-foldness to human beings. In Søren Kierkegaard's classic words, "A human being is a synthesis of the infinite and finite, of the temporal and the eternal, of freedom and necessity, in short, a synthesis."[33] Human beings are unitary beings but live in a two-fold tension, one might say, between the heavens and the earth. As Genesis 2 indicates, humans are clearly earth creatures. Failure to accept finitude, however, is entangled in the first sin of Adam and Eve in attempting to overcome their limits.

As soon as we begin to appreciate this earthiness of the self, we are reminded of the infinite dimension of the self. In fact, we would not likely be anxious about finitude if we were not capable of transcending it. As Hegel saw, one cannot grasp a boundary unless one is in some sense already beyond it, in awareness at least. In a way that far surpasses any animal that we know, humans are self-aware. Humans are conscious of the past and the future. This is not only the source for enriching memories and encouraging hopes but debilitating grief and enervating despair. Humans are finite—but know that they are finite. This capability is both our agony and our ecstasy. It means that humans have the capability of sufficient abstract thought to think of God and of what our relationship should be to God. We do not just live but are aware that we are living. We are also aware that once we were not and one day we will be no more in this life. This is the occasion for wise planning and judgments about what is most significant in life as well as deep anxiety, even a "sickness unto death."[34] The fact that we can imagine "forever" casts a shadow on the thought of death. Eternity is both promise and peril.

This two-fold finite-infinite relationship, a dyadic but not a dualistic one, is the fault line for humans. It is itself not sinful but is the occasion of sin. It is our "fallibility" though not yet our "fault."[35] This is a crucial Christian insight to realize. Humans are not inherently sinful. Fallible, yes; at fault, no. This delicate balance is the source of our blessing as well as our bane.

Our capacity for self-transcendence and imagination allows us to imagine God. It enables us to see that we can be different and better. It allows us to repent in favor of a different life. It enables us to imagine a different way of being for society and the church. When Martin Luther in the sixteenth century imagined that the pope could be wrong, he brought about something new. When Thomas Helwys called for church and state to be separate in the early seventeenth century, he was imagining something way ahead of his time. When James Madison in the eighteenth century sketched out a new constitution, in Abraham Lincoln's words, of government of the people, by the people, for the people, it changed the world.[36] When women in the early twentieth century agitated for the right to be one of those people, it was something new, going against the grain of centuries.

When the imaginative capacity for the new, infinite side of the self does justice to the finite side of the self, we can walk with God. We realize legitimate needs for nutrition, rest, and shelter, which have led to emancipation of the enslaved and more-just labor laws. Appreciation of our embodiment opens up appreciation of the goodness of this physical world and of being alive in it. It can lead to enjoyment of beauty and of productive, fruitful work that blesses all around. This was the intention of God as illuminated in the second creation story where God walks with Adam and Eve in the cool of the day after they after have tilled the garden.

If this relationship between God and creation, between infinitude and finitude, were programmed in us so that it was instinctual, we would not have a problem. We might not be human, but we would also not sin. Our freedom and potentiality is our agony and our ecstasy. As Mark Twain pointed out:

> Of all the creatures that were made he [man] is the most detestable. Of the entire brood he is the only one — the solitary one — that possesses malice. That is the basest of all instincts, passions, vices — the most hateful. . . . He is the only creature that inflicts pain for sport, knowing it to be pain. The animal kingdom, as brutal as it is, does not lead to atrocities like humans commit.

Human beings have the capacity to become like Christ, but they can sink lower than animals.[37]

Wolfhart Pannenberg has also emphasized the way that humans are open to the world.[38] We do have instincts and physical drives, but the striking thing about humans is their flexibility. We have to learn so much, which is part of the unusually long childhood for human infants. It allows for the brain and body to develop over time, but also allows for the necessary social learning and adaptation to occur in order to make one's way in the world. It is not already programmed. This has provided the flexibility that has led to our incredible success as a species; it can also lead to our downfall. This necessity of openness, we can say, means that we have to forge our identities, and we do so amidst a maelstrom of competing needs and desires. Jean-Paul Sarte put it famously: "We are condemned to be free."[39]

To deal with this perilous gift, we need to place ourselves in the right relationship to God and the earth. This involves doing justice to needs for food, shelter, sex, and procreation while striving to be just and compassionate. It means to preserve our lives by spending endless hours providing for our earthly needs but also realizing that physical survival is not everything. Higher values exist. We have a legitimate concern for ourselves, but we also care for others. We must prepare for tomorrow, but not to the detriment of today. We must be ambitious and aggressive enough—but not too much. None of this is determined but is something all of us must figure out for ourselves. The difficulty of working all of this out in proper balance can seem almost impossible—and it has been. Very traditional societies with strict rules and customs take the load off the individual, but often to the detriment of the individual. Societies with a great deal of freedom struggle with crime, addiction, and delinquency. There is a balance between self and other, but it is a fragile one. This challenge has been addressed by modern philosophers and artists, and it is also portrayed in page after page of the Bible. It is the story of creation's good intentions yet tragic fall.

THE FALLEN SELF

The Christian view of things is complex. God created a good world, yet a tragic rupture runs through all of creation. Neither humans nor the material world, however, are purely evil. Redemption is real but exists in a world already with a fateful combination of goodness and evil. Tillich's surprising, but apt, word for this is "ambiguity."[40] To appreciate fallenness and sin, this complexity must be borne in mind. As we have considered the goodness of creation and of humanity, we will now take a fresh look at the fall, then at the dimensions of sin in light of the two-fold nature of the self, and then at larger dimensions of sin and evil.

The Biblical Falls

One of the first things to realize in looking anew at the fall is to realize that there is not just one fall in the Bible. The long shadow of

Augustinian theology has actually obscured the canonical emphasis. It is as if Christians had decided to adopt just one gospel. How anemic and distorted would our Christology be? Yet this is what has occurred in relation to sin.

When one examines Genesis, it is clear that Genesis 1–11 is a unit that sets up the call of Abraham in Genesis 12. Chapters 1–2 are creation stories, as we have seen, which give us complementary perspectives on the goodness of creation much like the different gospels give us mutually enriching perspectives on Christ. Chapters 3–11 portray in vivid ways what has gone wrong with God's good creation—not just in one way but in several ways.[41] In fact, in Judaism and even in the early church, the Adam and Eve story was not always the one most emphasized. Sometimes the flood account was stressed when it came to the fall; others stressed human responsibility and/or Satanic influence.[42] The Tower of Babel story, too, is a crucial story about collective sin. Each one adds its own note, and together they yield a full, subtle understanding of the human situation that even modern perspectives from the sciences hardly rival.

When we see that Genesis 2 emphasizes positive relationships— the relations of humans to God, to each other, to animals, and to the earth—we can better understand the profound dimensions of what happens in Genesis 3. Often this fall is referred to as Adam's fall, yet it is clearly a mutual affair. In fact, the most prominent actor is Eve, who is often portrayed as weaker and more sinister. The traditional picture is that after being tempted and falling, she then lures her partner into being an accomplice. Adam can seem even magnanimous in not desiring to leave his partner alone in her transgression. This is where reading the actual story can be enlightening. In the story, Adam and Eve are both present. Adam says nothing and apparently weakly goes along. Both are drawn into the dynamics of sin. As 1 John summarizes it, they are tempted by "the lust of the flesh, the lust of the eyes, and the pride of life" (1 John 2:16, KJV). They desire to eat the fruit; they are drawn by its beauty; in accordance with the serpent's spin, it is desired to make themselves wise, perhaps even like God. Remove these three occasions of temptation in life, and there is little left: the pull of illicit physical desire, the desire to possess what is attractive for oneself, and pride. The Western church has emphasized pride as the root sin, and with good reason. Perhaps its root lies in this drama. Humans desire to be more than they are, even to be gods. Yet as crucial as pride is, there is more to be said about sin.

In the Genesis 3 account, the effect of sin ripples through all human relationships. First, Adam and Eve hide from God, leading to one of the most poignant questions in all of the Bible, "Adam, where are you?" Far from eagerly walking with God in the cool of the day, they tremble in the bushes lest God find them. They are not only estranged from God, they are estranged from each other. Adam blames what happened on Eve—and perhaps on God. He says, "The woman whom *you gave* to be with me, she gave me fruit of the tree, and I ate" (Gen 3:12, emphasis added). Passing the buck has a long tradition. Just a short time before, Adam had been overjoyed at the gift of a companion. Eve in turn blames it on the serpent.[43] As Miroslav Volf points out, people usually either deny their wrongdoing outright or rationalize it. Even worse, "at times apologies even transmute perpetrators into victims."[44] Adam and Eve now see themselves as being abused by God.

Because they are now ashamed at their nakedness, God provides clothing for them from animals, intimating a break in the harmonious relationship with animals of the previous chapter. Part of the curse is that the work will now turn to hard labor, and the woman's labor in childbirth will be increased. Estrangement breaks in everywhere: between each other, God, animals, and the earth. Every positive relationship that they had is now marred and broken. The ancient Hebrews realized something we often find difficult to comprehend with the advances of science: nothing escapes the ravages of sin. Anything humans touch can and probably will be deformed by human wrongdoing. When one looks at the potential of modern science to provide cheap energy and food for all people, yet the same technologies have been transferred into means of killing ever larger masses of people and actually leading to greater starvation than ever before, the lesson is clear. With all of the goodness of creation in chapters 1 and 2, never underestimate the damage that can be done to it by human sin.

After the heyday of Christian liberalism in the nineteenth century, with its optimism about human nature and inevitable progress, what is usually called the neo-orthodox movement reacted sharply by recovering "Christian realism," in Reinhold Niebuhr's words, about sin and evil.[45] This was not meant to be *pessimism* to counter liberal *optimism*. It was an attempt to rediscover the clear-eyed grasp of human reality that is found already in the third chapter of Scripture.

Genesis 3 has traditionally also been interpreted in a couple of ways that have had enormous impact but which now are not so well supported. One has been to overemphasize the role of Eve in the fall. Eve is blamed for the fall in this respect, thus giving warrant to prevent women from having leadership positions, from being thought capable of higher rational thought, or from being thought worthy even of having a political vote. As we know, through most of church history, women were seen as not deemed worthy of being priests and mediating grace.[46] Because this "original sin" has often been interpreted in sexual terms, as if Eve were seducing Adam (implying that sex in their relationship was somehow wrong), even sex in marriage has been denigrated as being less spiritual than a celibate life. To be spiritual enough, then, to mediate grace through the sacraments, priests could not be married, that is, have sex with women. The influential early church father Tertullian could fix the blame of the fall on women as "the devil's gateway," implying that men would have been okay if women were not around always to seduce and tempt them.[47] The story is a sad one, especially since it is so little biblically based.

The Hebrew culture was patriarchal, with a generally low view and treatment of women. It is all the more remarkable that in these sacred passages they saw Adam and Eve as being equal and complementary before the fall and mutually implicated in the fall. Ironically, we repeat one of the first sins by passing the buck either to women *or* men for the fall. If anything, this story teaches us that it is too easy to scapegoat someone, or some gender, for our problems. Again, ironically in light of the sad history of pinning the blame on Eve and thus subordinating and subjugating women, the first mention of domination and subjugation is a result of the fall, not God's purpose before the fall.[48] God says to the woman, after telling her of the increased pain in childbearing, that she will still desire her husband, "and he shall rule over you" (Gen 3:16). This has been interpreted as God desiring that this be so, as a command. Yet the nature of what God is saying is not so much a command as a consequence. Despite God's good intention, human sin has brought about not what God desired but what God did not desire! If humans are to honor the various results of the fall not as consequences but as commands that God desires, it would mean not trying to make farmwork easier or to alleviate pain in childbirth. Yet we commonly attempt to undo the results of the fall in these cases. This is not the only place where we have had selective interpretation, taking part of a passage one way and part of it another way. If we have been sufficiently trained in canonical discernment of sin, it is not difficult to see how self-serving it has been for men to strive to alleviate the sweat of the brow but insist that ruling over women is God's good will. In general, the consequences should not be overly pressed in terms of a modern scientific perspective, which was far from the minds of the writers and their early audience. As with many of Jesus' stories, the details are not so important as the main message. And the main message is clear: sin makes everything worse and tarnishes whatever it touches.

Another consequence is that Adam and Eve were expelled from the garden and left "east of Eden." What a powerful description of where humans live—east of Eden. The implication is that this is the story of every man and every woman. Apart from the Christian confession of Christ's sinlessness, this is a statement about the universality of sin, which Paul could express in Romans: "All have sinned and fall short of the glory of God" (3:23). An important nuance is that these passages do not intimate that sin is necessary; humans are not fated to sin in a way that destroys human freedom. Rather, the Hebrew insight is that humans inevitably fall into temptation.

Modern readers often recoil at what seems to be the arbitrariness of God, which is part of the problem of evil and suffering. While not minimizing these concerns, as we have seen in the previous two chapters, it would be a very wooden reading of this kind of genre to press it to be a modern philosophical, scientific, or historical tract. We want to ask, Why was there a tree of good and evil in the garden? Why was there a serpent who could tempt the humans? Why weren't they created so that they could resist temptation? Could not an omnipotent God have created free creatures in such a perfect environment that they would have never freely sinned? Why did they have to be kicked out of the garden? Isn't that unfair to their descendents? And we are not even to the question of where Cain got his wife and where all of the civilizations suddenly came from. Just to ask these questions alerts us to this being a different genre than we might expect. The ancient Hebrews were not so much explaining those kinds of questions about the past as explaining the dynamics of sin in the present. They were not trying to explain, in a modern historical or scientific sense, where evil came from and why it is present, as much as how it works—from the beginning until now. And in so doing, they were incredibly perceptive in a way that challenges our often facile modern understandings.

With the foregoing in mind, we can turn to another interpretation of this passage that has had great consequences but is increasingly questioned as an adequate reading of the text. As we saw in the previous chapter, Augustine is generally credited with reading this as the one fall story where Adam sinned for everyone, and thus all—even newborn infants—are guilty and merit the condemnation of hell.[49] This is what is usually understood as "original sin." In this account, Adam (and Eve) were the only humans (apart from Christ) who were ever free. All others are in bondage to sin and are "not free not to sin." Humans are so much in bondage that God can only save those whom God has elected or predestined by a supernatural act that is irresistible. We recognize this as a view of compatibilist, nonlibertarian freedom for all humans apart from Adam and Eve, who were the only humans to have libertarian freedom. Augustine assumed that he was following Paul, in all good conscience, based on a mistranslation of Romans 5:12; this view, even though arising some centuries after Christ, came to be seen as the only scriptural view.[50]

The only problem is that this view is neither very scriptural nor very Pauline. It represents just the kind of misconstrual of the genre that we have mentioned. It is to read both the original text and Paul's treatment of it as a quasi-historical, metaphysical account. There actually is in neither passage a suggestion of Adam acting for all human beings in a coercive way, any more than his counterpart, Jesus, acts in a coercive way for all. Adam, as the representative first human, sins *like* all others sin, according to Romans 5:12. He portrays the human race in its lost potential. Christ, the second Adam, portrays the human race in its realized, God-intended potential. In both cases, there is not a loss of free will. People are guilty because they sin as Adam did; Adam is indeed thus their symbol and representative. Others can be in Christ if they have faith and confess Jesus as Lord. Christ thus becomes the representative of saved humanity. Adam and Christ are not identical in what they do. Adam was not, in Trinitarian terms, the second person of any kind of Trinity. Adam was not the means of sin for all in the way that Christ atoned for all.

The implications of Genesis 3 and Paul in Romans is that all humans have sinned. One could say that Adam *and* Eve both represent all human beings. All of us in our own way are guilty and in need of justification because *we ourselves* have sinned—not because they sinned. The meaning of original sin is not original guilt but that all people sin, from the first humans until now, and thus all are born into a broken and fallen world. Theirs is original in one sense in that they represent the first sin but also in that the effects of sin are passed down, which is something that we tragically see around us. Children do not inherit the guilt of their parents, as Ezekiel and Jeremiah had to point out six hundred years before Christ. They do, unfortunately, bear the brunt of the consequences of the guilt of their parents. Thus, we are all born, not in Eden, but east of Eden.

Reading Genesis 1–11 as a unit means that one is immediately plunged after chapter 3 into chapter 4, the fratricide of Cain. The story is tragic: a family of four, with only two brothers, and out of jealousy one of the brothers murders the other. The story becomes darker. Adam and Eve ate forbidden fruit; Cain murdered his only brother. How far have things fallen from God seeing that all was "very good"? Together, these two fall accounts show the irrationality of sin and also its recklessness, the sense of its being out of control. The violence becomes actually wanton. In the Song of Lamech, the descendant of Cain boasts, "If Cain is avenged sevenfold, truly Lamech seventy-sevenfold" (Gen 4:24).[51] This is a master storyteller, as the reader has to fill in much of the detail. We have to surmise much of what went on and thus are pulled deeply into the narrative. We have to imagine the scenario, which suggests that Cain did not bring an offering as valuable as his brother's and was jealous of his brother. We are not even told why Cain's offering was not as acceptable as Abel's. What is clear is that, repeating the responses of his parents, he fails to take responsibility but blames his brother for his own failings. Rather than deal with his own problem, he projects his anger toward an innocent bystander, so to speak. Instead of solving the problem, he compounds it. He could have given better offerings; he can never bring back his brother. Some wrongs can be forgiven— but cannot be undone. We learn this by chapter 4 in the Bible.

Genesis 6 is one of the most mysterious chapters in the Bible. The flood story is clear enough; the cause of the flood is not. The first passage, verses 1–4, intimates more than indicts as it describes the sons of God who "took" the women that they wanted for wives. It implies that in some way the result was the "Nephilim," who "were the heroes that were of old, warriors of renown" (6:4). This would not be clearly a problem if it were not followed by the next passage, likely from a different original source, verses 5–8. The damning judgment is this: "The Lord saw that the wickedness of humankind was great in the earth, and that every inclination of the thoughts of their hearts was only evil continually." It could hardly get worse than this. Even the Cain and Abel story pales in comparison. In light of this drastic turn of events, one re-reads the first verses of chapter 6 as implying a breaking of boundaries, violence, depradation, probably rape. This is accentuated in verses 11 and 13, where God specifically names "the filling of the earth with violence" as the reason for its judgment. One gets the picture of marauding hordes sweeping across the landscape, raping and pillaging, as has been the case too often in history. Immediately we hear one of the most poignant statements in all of Scripture: "And the Lord was sorry that he had made humankind on the earth, and it grieved him to his heart" (v. 6). So much for the God who does not feel or suffer! For the God who planned everything to happen just as it has occurred! One can feel here the agony of the Creator whose attitude toward the creation was at first to be very pleased, then a scant few chapters later regretting, "repenting" as some translations have it, of the very act of creation altogether. One can hardly understand the drama of redemption in Scripture apart from a due regard to this low point. It adds an entirely new narrative depth to Paul's summary theological statement, "All have sinned and fall short of the glory of God" (Rom 3:23). It not only speaks to the pathos of God but also to the radical freedom and risk of creation. God gave to humanity so much freedom that humans could go as wrong as this. Only a parent, to whom God is so often compared, can relate to the pathos of regretting what one has conceived; and yet it has come to this by chapter 6 in the Bible.

Much like the message of Genesis 1 is often missed by the misplaced focus on how it relates to modern science, the significance of this passage is often missed by speculative questions, which themselves reflect an attitude of modern science, of how the flood occurred and where. Much like the questions we would ask about the garden of Eden and of Cain's wife, the passage is eerily silent about the specific cause and rationale of God's judgment. Despite the attraction of the fascinating account of the flood, with the animals, the forty days and nights of rain, and the olive branch of the bird to connote salvation, the major point is elsewhere and is often missed. Despite God's dismay at the waywardness of creation, God looks to begin again on a new basis. God picks presumably the most righteous man on earth and his family and starts afresh. Very soon, after a drunken celebration, the youngest son looks upon his father naked, obviously violating a taboo, which we see later is a characteristic of Hebrew law (Gen 9:21-22). We are thrown back to Adam and Eve again. The new beginning has not worked any better; Noah and his family are still east of Eden. The turn to Abraham in chapter 12 cannot be understood apart from these failed attempts at redemption for the whole human race, with Adam and Eve, with Cain, and now with Noah.

The third fall story has moved to a corporate level beyond the family of Adam and Eve, involving collective evil. The final fall story takes this further. Human beings can sin enough on their own; there is almost no limit to what evil they can do together. This story, too, can be easily misunderstood. It can be read as opposition to any collective, technological effort, which would be bad news for the modern West. Since there has already been recognition of civilization and technology in earlier chapters, without particular approval but also without evident blame, this reading does not seem to fit. As with all of these stories, the Babel account is understated and makes great demands on the reader to enter into the story and interpret with discernment. The implication is that humans were using their unity—their unified language—to succumb to the serpent's temptation, namely, to become like God. The early Hebrew readers (centuries later) would almost certainly have thought of the lofty and imposing ziggaurats of the hated Babylonians, who had driven them into exile. These were imposing edifices that might have been seen as pagan attempts to control their own fates magically. This was yet another case of humans not accepting their place, this time on a collective rather than individual basis. The confusion of tongues is a recognition of the way that different languages and the pervasiveness of interpretation can limit collective human efforts. This is a phenomenon still played out around us, especially in the Middle East where Arab and Israeli seem to inhabit different worlds, not only different languages, and Westerners continually misread their cultures to their own peril. This story is often read as the diversity of languages being a curse, but it can be read, in contemporary terms, as a blessing to prevent the way some humans use a single ideology to oppress everyone else. In other words, their unity was not a real unity but one that was imposed and oppressive.[52] In contrast, the miracle of Pentecost in Acts is an obvious sign of the kingdom of God bringing a unity that does not do harm but good. True unity is thus the gift of the Spirit, which in Acts and in Paul nevertheless allows for diversity.

In any case, even after the new start from the flood, humans were failing drastically again—on an individual basis, as with Noah and his sons, and on a collective basis, as with the Tower of Babel. Instead of God again being driven to grief at this point, as one might expect, a surprising thing happens. God begins again, this time not with the most righteous person but with a person of faith—and with a people. But this is the rest of the story of the Bible—and the story of redemption.

Understanding the fullness of the fall accounts provides a realistic picture of human beings in their goodness and yet "depravity," to use Calvin's word. It is not just an individual offense or just a matter of pride, it is collective depradation and many other failings. Fallenness affects every aspect of being human, yet it does not destroy the image of God.[53] It drives God to grief, yet it does not destroy God's purposes. To draw on Jesus' parables, Genesis 1–11 is a lengthy counterpart to the prodigal son, whom the father does not give up on, and the lost coin and lost sheep, whom the woman and shepherd do not just wait for but actively seek (Luke 15). God first finds Abraham, then Israel, and continues looking for all others. The fall accounts parallel—most likely quite consciously since they were given in their written form at the time—Israel's fall into exile, living in subjugation (east of Eden) even after the exile, and yet hoping for the future.

Through the rest of the Bible, the major description of sin is "missing the mark" (*hamartia*). This can only be understood in light of God's purposes in creation. One can only miss if one is aiming at a goal. Sin is not a fulfillment of human nature but a perversion, as in the reference in Deuteronomy 32:5 to a "perverse and crooked generation." The various words for sin gain their fuller meaning by the narrative backdrops of passages like those in Genesis 1–11.

With this biblical background in mind, we can make a crucial point: Christian faith enables us to "name" sin. It is not just being a pessimist in noticing the negative. It is difficult to desire salvation without realizing one's bondage. This is the meaning behind Paul's somewhat perplexing remark, "If it had not been for the law, I would not have known sin" (Rom 7:7). Paul does not mean that there was no sin apart from the law, which would contradict what he had said about all having sinned in chapters 1 and 3. The gift of the law, however, as he interprets it as a Christian, is that it helped him to know better and more clearly what sin is. Part of the deceitfulness of sin is to disguise itself as good or normal. An aspect then of the law and also of the gospel is to help us to sift discerningly through the fog of deceit to name sin for what it is. This is not only true before becoming a Christian; if anything, it intensifies as one grows in Christ. Walking in the Spirit should enable a Christian better to identify the many ways in which we miss the mark.[54]

The Dynamics of Sin

With the above accounts in mind as being the story of every man and woman, we can turn back to the dyadic account of human nature to further grasp the dynamics of sin. We have seen how human beings are a delicate balance of the infinite and finite, which are held together at best in a healthy tension. In sin, we fall out of this precarious balance every which way. We are especially accustomed to seeing how we miss the mark of both the infinite and finite in overdoing both.

Concerning the infinite, we imagine ourselves to be more than we are. In other words, the sin most commonly emphasized in Western Christianity, pride, stems from our capacity of self-transcendence beyond the self. In itself, as healthy self-esteem, pride is a good thing but easily gets out of hand. We want to be more than we are; we want to be more than others are. We want to be more than we can or should be. This sin is seen in Adam and Eve desiring to be like God.

What has not so often been stressed is the opposite, namely, thinking less of ourselves than we should. We can use the wonderful gift of imagination to amplify others and minimize ourselves. Kierkegaard saw this as "in despair not to will to be oneself."[55] One imagines that if one were like that other person—taller, stronger, more beautiful, smarter, with better parents, more money, in a better place—all would be well. The grass is greener on the other side because we imagine it so. Like Moses, we then try to talk ourselves out of following God. We think we cannot possibly do what God is calling us to do. This could be called the sin of timidity, or lack of courage, expressed in Paul's admonition to Timothy, "For God did not give us a spirit of timidity but a spirit of power, of love, and of self-discipline" (2 Tim 1:7, NIV). This problem has not only not been clearly identified in Christianity, it has been exacerbated sometimes by Christian theology. The concern to deal with pride has gone overboard, and theologians have consequently stressed how worthless people are. We sometimes preach what is called a "worm" theology, emphasizing that humans are of little value at all. Ironically, even a worm probably has more worth than this. We do not have to make God look good by making humans look bad. Sin is harmful enough without exaggerating human worthlessness. The admonition to be "meek" is thus often misunderstood to mean weakness and capitulation. Actually, meekness has the idea of being strength under control, like a horse is "gentled," made meek, by being made responsive to the rider's touch. The goal is not to "break the spirit" of a horse but to "gentle" it. Feminist theologians have pointed out that one might see pride as more of a male problem because society has so elevated males; it is not so much a problem in women as is the problem of timidity, that is, of not thinking enough of oneself to follow Christ.[56] It is like the servant who hid his talent in the ground, thinking he could never please the master (Matt 25:14-30). He was afraid to use his "talents." This, too, is a sin. The dynamics of codependent relationships are due not to healthy solicitude but often to lack of self-esteem, which undermines healthy relationships. Whether men or women are more prone to overvalue or undervalue the self, the point is that it is sin either way. Overemphasizing and underemphasizing the value of the human self wrecks relationships with God and with others.

All humans struggle at times with each. In fact, these two problems may be more deeply connected than we realize. How often is arrogance due to a sense of inferiority, not thinking enough of oneself, so that one boasts in order to bolster one's lack of self-esteem? The challenge of Christian discernment is to value oneself appropriately. One can so emphasize self-esteem that there is no place for sin.

One can also lack genuine, healthy self-esteem so that all of one's efforts and relationships are crippled. It is ironic that sometimes the first thing we say in reaching out to non-Christians is that God loves them and values them; as soon as they respond, we then say that they are worthless. Healthy self-esteem is an aspect of being willing and courageous enough to follow Christ. The church has not discerned well the distinction between healthy self-esteem that is supported, even enabled, by God's grace in creation and in redemption from destructive and dysfunctional pride.[57] Faith should encourage healthy self-esteem and ground it, not discourage it.

Concerning the finite dimension of the self, the sin of concupiscence, or lust, has been emphasized, which is the overemphasizing of the physical. Lusts of all kinds wreak enormous havoc, even within the church. The inability to discipline the sex drive, or the hunger drive, or the desire for riches causes damage within and outside the church. The freedom and opportunity of modern Western society has opened up enormous problems of addictions of all kinds. It seems that the body can addict itself even without abusing a substance as in gambling, sex, or shoplifting. There is no end, it seems, to the possibility of such bondage. Reinhold Niebuhr points out that sensuality is also, in its own way, a kind of despair of not wanting to be a self, when one, "having lost the true centre of his life" ends with "a plunge into unconsciousness."[58]

Our greater sense of the essentiality of our embodiment allows us to grasp the nature of lust even more. We are our bodies. We become addicted physically to things in such a way that we are virtually enslaved to them. This is the modern form of bondage to sin. Often, these things are tried when we are young, when they may seem fairly innocent. They are tried at a time when strong developmental urges encourage rebellion and risky behavior with peers to find identity and separation from parents. Before we know it, we are addicted, and then it is much harder to stop because it is physical—but we *are* our physical bodies. It may be almost impossible to overcome. The streets are littered with sad cases of people with tremendous potential and support who began an addiction in their teens but in their forties and fifties cannot transcend their addiction.

The demonic side of sin, as well as the insidious craftiness of it, is seen here. The body becomes so habituated, the brain so rewired, that even with recovery there is usually a vulnerability or weakness that never goes away. This is behind the claim of alcoholics that, even after years of recovery, they are still alcoholics.

Some sins of lust, such as gluttony, are especially difficult because one cannot go "cold turkey." One cannot be a "teetotaler" when it comes to food. One must eat something to survive; the problem is eating well and stopping after starting. In a country that spends more than the entire national budget of some countries on advertising that uses the best of modern science to figure out ways to entice people to lust and to consume, it takes Christian discipline and discernment at a whole new level of maturity to be "in the world" but not "of the world" (John 17:15-18).

Conversely, one can underemphasize the finite side of the self, but this, like underemphasizing the infinite side, is not nearly as recognized and appreciated as a failing. In fact, the response to lust has often meant overreacting in the other direction. This would mean depriving and depreciating the physical. Extreme asceticism has, in fact, sometimes been affirmed as a sign of greater spirituality. Depriving oneself of comfort and food has been seen as a sign of maturity, as we saw in the case study of Rose of Lima. Celibacy has been advocated as the only way for anyone to be spiritual enough to be a priest and mediate the sacraments. As an example of this tendency, the great church historian Peter Brown says of the late-fourth-century church that so influenced Augustine: "The integrity of the virgin state was the highest pinnacle of Christian virtue. Married sexuality lay in shadow of that one bright peak."[59] Even the mixing of the soul with the body, for Ambrose, was for it to have become "effeminated," not a mark of praise.[60] Brown summarizes Ambrose's influence:

> For him, human sexual feeling stood out in dark silhouette against the blaze of Christ's untouched body. Human bodies, "scarred" by sexuality, could be redeemed only by a body whose virgin birth had been exempt from sexual desire. It was a heady antithesis, with a long future ahead of it in the Latin church.[61]

By going too far in encouraging self-mortification, one ends up not with healthy spirituality but with dysfunctional rejection of God's good creation. Rather than appropriate discipline, this extreme is actually rejection of the physical, representing a slide into Gnosticism. The challenge is to find the right, healthy balance. This is so challenging that it is not difficult to believe the Christian affirmation that "all have sinned and have fallen short of the glory of God."

Paul says that he learned how to abound and how to suffer want. He did not suggest that one look for opportunities to suffer want. In fact, he seemed to be fighting an incipient Gnosticism already when he sharply rebuked those in the fledgling church who would practice unnecessary kinds of asceticism. The call to self-control and discernment is the practice of finding the appropriate discipline of appreciating, but not being enslaved to, God's creation. This truly demands practical wisdom that comes from walking in the Spirit.

Collective Sin

The ineradicable sociality of the self also has implications for sin. The church, especially in modernity, has tended to emphasize the individuality of sin. Sin is seen as a matter between the self and God. Evangelicals, especially in the United States, have often made sin a private, spiritual matter that hardly affects the outer world at all, except as it might make someone anxious rather than at peace

Principalities and Powers. In response to this extreme aberration, another major shift in theology in recent years has been to give fresh attention to the collective dimension of sin, the brokenness manifested in society and culture in ways that far transcend any individual and any individual's capacity to control or change. In actuality, this has meant a return to a better canonical emphasis, which has a fuller sense of the holistic and social dimensions of sin as well as human life in general. In other words, one may repent and turn things around in one's own life, but this may have little effect on the larger world where grotesque savagery and brutality may abound. How do these relate? Is such social sin a matter for the individual at all? This is a place where positive developments of separating church and state and granting more freedom of religion to the individual have also been distorted by sin. Nothing escapes, it seems, its corrosive effects. Some Protestant groups have gone so far as to insist that politics is outside the purview of the Christian and that one should pay little attention to it. It is a matter, at least, that should never come up in the church. The reaction against this extreme has led not only mainline denominations but even evangelical Christians to become increasingly engaged in politics. What does this mean for rethinking the nature of sin?

John Howard Yoder was a Mennonite who had great influence in reminding that Jesus' message was not just spiritual but was strongly political.[62] Jesus was, after all, crucified as a political criminal. The agitation about him came largely from the volatile effect he might have on the crowds in the political situation of the day. He said that his kingdom was not from this world (John 18:36), but this meant that he had no designs on Caesar's job, not that Jesus' kingdom had nothing to do with the world. Liberation theologians similarly have stressed that while Jesus' ministry was not identified simply with a political revolt against Rome, he was interested in liberation in this life. The tumult caused by his words and works was genuine because it upset the cultural status quo. He broke social barriers in order to include people. He emphasized the value of the marginalized by saying that "the last will be first, and the first will be last" (Matt 20:16). As he showed in his practices, such reversal already begins in this life. It is especially supposed to be manifest in the church, which is to be an advance outpost of the coming kingdom (see the chapter on the church). The clash with worldly structures and mores was real. Jesus' message was holistic; he had great concern for physical needs. He reserved some of his sharpest criticism for the way people used the rules to perpetuate injustice. In this, as many have pointed out, he was following in the footsteps of the great prophets. No wonder that most people thought he *was* a "prophet."

Walter Wink is another who has emphasized the importance of corporate evil. He stresses the Pauline categories of "principalities and powers" as a dimension of human sinfulness. These are the larger social structures that have a life of their own that can be forces for good but also, as everything human, can be deformed and broken. These powers, as all of God's creation, are essentially good, as in Romans 13 where Paul actually speaks of the Roman Empire as being ordained of God. As Wink points out, the principalities and powers have an objective, institutional structure but also a subjective, spiritual nature.[63] There is a corporate culture, a transpersonal system, that permeates even individual interactions. Given the pervasiveness of sin, the powers, like human beings, are inevitably flawed—often so much that they fall into being what Wink calls the "domination system." Sometimes, as in the time of Nero's Rome, Nazi Germany, Rwanda, extermination of Native Americans, all in the name of official authority and power, the social structures become demonic. This is illustrated by Revelation 13, speaking of the same Roman Empire that has become a "beast": "It opened its mouth to utter blasphemies against God, blaspheming his name and his dwelling" (13:5-6). Wink's point is that the demonic should be reserved for such combinations of individual human sinfulness and perverse social structures. Miroslav Volf prefers to speak of the "exclusion system" rather than the domination system, for the usual purpose of dominating corporate cultures is to exclude.[64] At the most basic level, it can mean excluding others from food, shelter, and life. At other levels, it can exclude people from medical care, from jobs that pay enough to sustain a family, and from education that enables others to get those jobs. As in personal sin, as we have seen with Adam and Eve, corporate evil never wants to see itself as evil but only as good and benevolent. What makes it more sinister is that it has so much power, is so invisible, and is so subtle. It is often so effective in "doublespeak" that to oppose a destructive "corporation," in this sense, is often framed as being disloyal, lazy, unpatriotic, or not a good worker or a good citizen. Jesus ran headlong into such an exclusion system, which framed him, its savior and redeemer, as a menace to society, as in cahoots with the devil.

It is now possible to destroy more people than ever before in history, not because people are more evil, but because the combination of immense population growth, individual sin, and wider structures and technology make it possible. Partly it is the result of the blessings of developments in agriculture, medicine, technology, and architecture that have allowed more people to live and survive. It is also the result of scientific and technological advances that could provide other enormous benefits to the earth. Yet this same science and technology in the hands of powerful nations with great resources and energy has made it possible to destroy the world in multiple ways—and, in the case of nuclear weapons, hundreds of times over. We ignore this corporate dimension of sin, as complicated as it is to get a handle on, to our peril.

The other side of the social dimension of selves is the point behind the well-known saying "give people a fish, and they will eat for a day; teach them to fish, and they can eat for a lifetime." Often in our concern for individual, momentary aid, we lose sight both of the sinful principalities and powers that have brought them to this plight and also of the great redemptive structural possibilities for doing God's will "on earth as it is in heaven." Great evil and great good can be done corporately.

The frustration is that many people seem to be able to identify the problem. It has been recognized that just a few days worth of the military spending of the United States alone could provide food to all of the world. Medical care similarly could be provided to everyone with just a small portion of annual U.S. military spending. As Jürgen Moltmann says, "The success story of 'the First World' has never gone unaccompanied by the story of the Third World's suffering," and adds, "Modern times—the 'new time'—have called for both modernity and sub-modernity."[65] People lament the fact, but has anything changed? Sometimes it seems virtually impossible to change. This is the strange dynamic of social and collective evil. It has a power and force of its own that outstrips human control. It often has a downward drag toward abuse and exploitation of the most vulnerable: poor women, children, and foreigners. This is why the Old Testament, in the Law and the Prophets, again and again refers to concern for the widow, the orphan, and the resident alien, who then and now still represent the most vulnerable and exploited in society. The stories are endless; the plot is similar.

Principalities and powers aid and abet individual choices to raise to an exponential level the devastation of evil. Jesus' own death is a prime example. As we shall see when we turn to the atonement, his death is often seen in the context of atoning for individual sins. It occurred, however, in the context of a social, structural evil that could kill a good and great man, whom some now see as the best man who ever lived, in good conscience as an evil. Jesus himself warned of the danger of mistaking good for evil as a great danger (Luke 11:14-23). Systemic evil is a master at just this reversal. It sucks individuals into its wake with such seductiveness that they do not even notice—or notice at a level that they only recognize later when it is unmasked before all. For instance, most Baptists today can easily decry racism while their forebears embraced it. This is why there is no response when people cry out, "Thou art the man." After the Holocaust, what could one say? In looking at the genocide of Native Americans, what can Caucasians now say? In looking at slavery, what can Southern Baptists say? The mark of such evil is that it seems so justified at the time but so unjustified in the end. Repentance is the response to sin, but what does it mean in these cases?

This is where we need to remember the full canon, namely, the Old Testament, which some groups of us tend not to, and go to school with the prophets. Again and again the prophets emphasized two primary benchmarks, or plumb lines, to use Amos' imagery (Amos 7:7-9), by which God judges a nation and individuals: purity of worship and social justice. This is so obvious in Scripture that it should hardly need saying if we had not had another case of the occlusion of systemic evil that has especially blinded evangelical Christianity in the United States. Probably the dominant trait among evangelicals for years has been to castigate concern for social justice as liberal and as a threat to the pure gospel. Those who most protested that they were preserving the pure gospel were actually criticizing any concern for one of the issues that in Scripture is dearest to God's own heart. Of course, on the other hand, the perversion was so great that liberal Christians sometimes condemned concern for individuals being born again and converted as a threat to the gospel. The truth is that both are in Scripture. How could we have come to such an impasse? It is just more testimony to the seductiveness of sin, and especially structures of tradition and vested interests, that blind us both to the personal and collective dimensions of sin.

Because matters are complex, however, does not mean that they should be ignored. In fact, one of the beguiling temptations in this area is to rationalize that since we have such little power, we have no responsibility and even no need to concern ourselves. Instead, we must think of levels of responsibility and guilt. The person whose little influence largely consists of one vote among millions bears little, although some, responsibility—depending on their vote. Going along with and promoting a culture of racism makes one more responsible than someone who goes against the grain of a larger cultural wave, even if he or she did not hit the streets to march in protest. The question of whether one is doing enough to resist injustice is always a difficult one. People face this with respect to concerns about abortion, about capital punishment, about war, and about poverty, among a multitude of others. A little thought shows that we cannot give full resources to every issue of need. Still, can we say that we have done enough? The need for the balance of practical wisdom is again paramount. In this as in other cases, the challenge is to find the critical edge between taking the question of responsibility seriously but also resting in the grace of God. Taking on too much responsibility smacks of a God complex. Yet avoidance can be a tempting sin. When we take up the issue of grace, salvation, and forgiveness, we will return to the complexity of repentance and forgiveness in the face of social evil.

Then there is the matter of doing enough to be aware of hidden, ideological sins, whose very nature is to be disguised as the normal and even the good. Were the leading Baptists in the South culpable for not going against the grain of their culture on slavery when virtually everything around them supported such a view? Did they do enough? Today descendants of those same Baptists see that they were terribly wrong—but they did not know it at that time. Were those who exploited Native Americans, feeling justified by killing them and taking their land—often in response to their violent retaliation—culpable for not seeing the larger issues that we so easily see today? How responsible were not only Germans but also Allied countries in not following up information and leads to know more about the Holocaust and doing more to stop it earlier—when it was very possible? It is easy to point the finger at others, but as we are reminded, three fingers are always pointing back at us. And what about sins that future generations will see in us of which we are just as unaware? Will those a century or two hence feel the need to apologize for Western countries, especially the United States, consuming far more than our share of the world's resources? For the way in which the relation of the pay of CEOs to labor in most countries is 30:1, but in the United States it is 400:1—and growing? As we give larger and larger tax breaks to the wealthiest and at the same time rail against those who want to provide medical care for all children? The nature of social sin is that it lulls people to sleep, and if perchance they half-awaken, suggests that they have such little power that they need do nothing.

The Satanic and Demonic. You may have noticed that my language about sin sometimes has been personalized. It is not just an abstract force; it is deceptive, seductive, deceitful. This moves us to the issue of the personification of evil in the New Testament, though not so much the Old Testament, the figures of the devil—Satan—and demons. Why here? I suggest that the place where we begin to see evil in terms that go beyond the individual is the proper place. Rather than making the devil a speculative curiosity about the origins and geography of hell, the devil and the demonic have their *Sitz im Leben*, their proper context, where evil reaches its highest pitch. Just as in the book of Revelation, as we shall see in eschatology, the proper context for it is not armchair speculation for math majors to determine the time of the end of the world, the place for demonology is at the place where evil is most destructive, which is where it seems transpersonal. I suggest that the site of the demonic is where personal sin is enmeshed in structures that multiply and intensify it. This can include the lethal combination of natural forces and human malfeasance, leaving people at the mercy of hurricanes or floods. Frank Tupper refers to this danger of natural evil as "chaos," also a deep biblical theme.⁶⁶ These can fatefully ally with corporate principalities and powers, which can work for good but can function as government and corporate structures that paralyze escape and relief efforts as well as prevention in the first place. So sin, natural forces, and principalities can join forces to form a "perfect storm" of lethal violence and evil. Tupper says of this deadly confluence:

> Human sin and responsibility are practically indefinable in the darkness of the demonic. The sin and responsibility of humanity can hardly begin to be stretched across it, and chaos cannot contain its seemingly bottomless depths. It usually dwarfs human sin and natural disaster. Unlike the randomness of chaos, moreover, the demonic can be selective and calculating. While chaos simply erupts and destroys wherever it happens, the demonic can target its victims. It can twist chaos into a perversity beyond the chaotic and wrest chaos insider the borders of the demonic domain. The demonic is always a killer, almost always a mass murderer of some kind or the other. Its names are legion: Auschwitz, Nagasaki, the Gulag, Khmer Rouge, Jim Crow, apartheid.⁶⁷

Even more insidiously, the demonic, which seems so obviously evil only in retrospect, if then, functions to make evil seem good and good seem evil. Responding to one situation where Jesus' healing actions were themselves called the work of the devil, Jesus related the unforgivable sin seemingly to such confusion where one calls the greatest good the greatest evil (Matt 12:22-32). Things can get no more upside down than that! Perhaps here is where one has no hope of extrication because the very means to repent are removed. When powerful forces combine in such insidious ways to make possible the murder of millions, the starvation of millions, the bondage of millions, made possible by advanced technology and brilliant minds, and no one seems to be at fault, one sees the demonic at work.

In approaching the issue of Satan and demons, one must keep one's scriptural grounding. There is hardly mention of Satan in the Old Testament, any more than there is a strong affirmation of an afterlife with a heaven and a hell. Later Christian speculation developed an elaborate mythology that is often read back into Scripture, but there is always a place to question it critically. On the other hand, the New Testament clearly makes Jesus' encounter with demons a significant aspect of his ministry of liberation and wholeness, much more than the figure of Satan. Satan is referred to a few times in the Gospels and elsewhere in the New Testament. At the same time, there is little explanation or elaboration of what the references mean. It is much like the presence of the serpent in the garden of Eden and the tree of Good and Evil. They are simply there, with no explanation. One should realize in this connection that the original context of Genesis 3 hardly relates to the idea of Satan at all, but the connection is largely later Christian speculation. So how do we approach Satan? The Bible would suggest very carefully, and so we shall.

The first step is to reiterate what was just said. We should approach the issue in the proper context and attitude. The issue is one of larger forces of evil that go beyond the personal human being and that are the most threatening and sinister of all. They are the more sinister the less we are aware of evil or the satanic, as in the cases of much corporate evil.

The major approach has been to see Satan as a personal figure of some sort with minions of demons. These are thought to be originally angels who fell. While the Bible barely intimates such a thing, it has surprisingly good theological grounding. The theological insight behind it is the belief that God would not create anything wholly evil. As Paul said, "Everything created by God is good" (1 Tim 4:4), so nothing can be evil per se, which is sometimes the way Satan is conceived. Even Satan and demons have to be seen as perverted goods, which is another reason to see them in connection with principalities and powers, structures that are supposed to be good supports of wider human and earthly life that easily get twisted into threats to life on this planet. They are seen in this view as so personal and so much as beings with free will like humans that some, like the great early theologian Origen, have thought that they might repent and be saved in the end—which actually would be consistent with what we know otherwise of God's dealing with free beings. Nevertheless, the whole area is shrouded with such obscurity and mystery that it is difficult to know how far one should go in thinking in personal terms and of falling and repentance at all.

Even with the idea of fallen beings with great power, it is important to see that they are understood only to have the power to tempt, and even then very subtly and distantly. Many people are never aware of such temptation. James can say that no one is tempted by anything but one's own desires (Jas 1:14). The fall stories in Genesis clearly place responsibility squarely on human shoulders and nowhere else. Whatever we finally make of the mysterious references to Satan and demons, they are not major players in the cosmic drama when compared to God and humans. When I was in college, my friends and I became very fascinated with demons. At one point, it was implied that if we did not ward off demons on a daily basis, we could become possessed of a myriad of demons at any moment. The range of demons of sleeping late, putting off homework, being jealous of others smarter and better looking, not concentrating on school, and so on, made the concerns certainly relevant. Still, I became aware at one point that our focus was on Satan and not on God, which is never the biblical emphasis even when there are warnings to be wary of Satan. So a test of one's proper attitude is not whether one is afraid of Satan or is thinking of Satan; rather, it is whether one's mind is set on things above (Col 3:2) and whether one is walking in the Spirit and grace of God (Rom 8:4). A spirit of fear is exactly what Satan would desire (1 John 4:18). In this view, the great danger is for the person to give themselves so over to evil that they become possessed by an evil spirit. The responsibility here lies clearly on the human side, so there does not seem to be the idea of being overpowered by another spirit. It is akin to the biblical language of one's spirit being "cauterized" so that one can hardly be conscious of the good. M. Scott Peck, a psychiatrist who investigated the My Lai massacre and reflected on his own practice, concluded in the end that such a category of "evil people" should be placed in the main psychiatric manual of psychological disorders. The only remedy he could find was casting out of demons.[68] The main symptom he noticed, it should be reminded, was that these people were viciously mean and destructive but were brilliant in making themselves look good and others bad. They can rise to the top of organizations and thus have the means of great social power that they are skillful in manipulating. Here again is the locus of the demonic, whatever one thinks of it in detail.

The other view is to see the satanic and demonic as impersonal, transpersonal powers, which are personified in order to deal with them. They are the personifications of principalities and powers, better termed thus by Paul. The richness of this theological theme is that the more evil, the less personal. The more evil an entity, the less it is a personal being.[69] The essence of evil is impersonality. As Paul Ricoeur pointed out, the earlier symbols in Scripture and in many other sources are like stain and defilement, more like a virus than a personal choice.[70] While there is great gain in grasping more clearly the sense of personal choice in responsibility and guilt, something of this impersonal dimension remains. Marcus Borg expresses this position well in his book *Jesus* but finds it difficult to avoid a personal dimension altogether:

> Is Satan real? Is there a devil? That some people have experiences of an evil power or powers is clear. But what ontological conclusion should be drawn from such experiences? I am skeptical myself that there is an ontologically real evil power. But the personification of evil as Satan does reflect the fact that evil is "bigger" than any of us. Evil is not simply the product of free individuals making free bad choices. In many ways, the world is in bondage to evil powers. . . . But whatever one thinks about the ontological status of Satan, some people have visions of Satan.

He goes on then to discuss the spiritual significance of Jesus, as a holy person, having such visions and experiencing spiritual warfare.[71] Philip Jenkins has pointed out that this personalist perspective will only become more central, not less, with the shift of the center of the church to the Southern Hemisphere, dominated by a Christian faith and worldview that takes the former, personal view of the demonic to a level hardly imaginable in the developed Northern Hemisphere.

In any case, the proper context is all the more important. Just as in eschatology the precise theory of the afterlife is not nearly so important as being ready for the afterlife, in this area the precise theory about it is not so crucial as the practical issue of how to deal with it. On this the Scripture is rather clear and the theology straightforward. First, the focus is not on the demonic but on the grace of God. If one is walking in the Spirit and in faith, one is both safe and prepared to deal with sin and evil of all kinds. The focus is on God and the good, not preoccupation with evil. Second, a part of growth in the Christian life is nevertheless growth in keen discernment toward sin and deception of all kinds, including matters of personal choice as well as larger ideological structures. A hermeneutics of trust is thus paired with a hermeneutics of suspicion. Prophetic suspicion is then not an enemy but a friend of faith and goodness. It is an enemy of course to evil, the satanic, and the demonic, whatever their manifestations. Third, the element of spiritual warfare is very real in the Christian life. It hardly needs to be said that evil is destructive and deadly. Much of the Christian life involves resistance to it. Again, this may occur best by focusing on good, but that is part of the struggle. Also, this does not just mean a battle with personal temptation, which is crucial, but also a battle for social justice.

CONCLUSION

Paul Tillich is known for a correlation method in theology. He argued that theology "answers" the "questions" that arise from human existence.[72] In this sense, we may see our exploration into the nature of humanity and fallenness as raising the question that Christ and salvation powerfully answer. We must add, however, that this picture, while illuminating, is too simple. It is not as if we have described human nature and fallenness from a neutral perspective, and now we are turning to a theological perspective. Rather, even the understanding of human nature and sin is shaped by the perspective of revelation. In a sense, our questions get reworded by the answers. This is again a reminder that each doctrine cannot be understood apart from all of the others. For Christians, the North Star that orients all the other doctrines is Christology, to which we now turn.

7

CHRIST
The Light of the Way

Jesus of Nazareth has unquestionably had as great an impact on history as any other individual. This is not a statement of faith but one of observation, made all the more remarkable when one considers his growing up untrained as a professional spiritual leader, a Mediterranean Jewish peasant in the words of one scholar, in a small village of a few hundred people in Galilee in the north of Palestine in the first century.[1] Many other figures made the world tremble at the time with their royalty and their power. None make it tremble today like the carpenter from Nazareth. Yet no one thought to describe what he looked like; his public ministry according to the Synoptic Gospels may only have lasted about one year; little is known about his earlier life; and he died the most shameful death possible at the time, his followers in utter disarray around him. Yet his message of a God who loves everyone with a fierce passion without regard to social standing, who calls upon all to forgive exorbitantly and to love even enemies, whose enjoyment of the simple pleasures of the day and yet radical prayer for change in light of his utopian hopes for the morrow impresses even those who deem him impossibly idealistic. Where did he and such a message emerge? Its roots are in Judaism, which has too often been forgotten; but like the monotheism that arose in Israel, its radical message of love came as a countercultural bolt from the blue. The New Testament and the following two thousand years of church history have been an attempt to answer that question more fully.

In the post 9/11 context, another, darker part of the picture must be painted. With the attraction of Jesus as a force for amazing good, one also must consider the way that enormous enmity has risen against Christianity, the movement that bears his name. This is in part a response and reminder of the evil that has been done in his name, so much so that some claim that Christianity and other religions in general—with Islam well in mind, too—are a danger to the long-term survival of the human race.[2] With forced conversions by imperial soldiers; the Crusades; Christians slaughtering other Christians in the Reformation and its aftermath; Christians fomenting anti-Semitism for centuries; Christians supporting colonialism, destruction of Native Americans, and segregation—all in the name of this same Jesus—the question of who he is becomes sharper. As we have repeatedly seen, what we believe makes a difference. Theology makes a difference.

We are not far from the central passage in the Synoptics, where Jesus has withdrawn from Galilee after disillusionment with the response to his ministry, spends the night in prayer, and asks his disciples, "Who do you say that I am?" (Mark 8:29). They respond with traditional options, with the wider horizon including the possibility of Jesus leading a violent revolt against Rome. Their options are not the same as our present options, but they are not far from it. The question of Jesus' identity has been long with us, beginning during his own ministry. In fact, as we shall explore, a fascinating question is, how did Jesus himself come to see things so differently?

The approach to Jesus historically has occurred in a variety of ways. Roman Catholics often focus on the cross of Christ and his suffering, picturing him hanging from the cross or suffering in a coffin. Evangelicals, too, focus on the cross as payment for sin. Liberal

Christianity has focused on Jesus' life as a moral example. The Eastern Orthodox Church has focused more on the incarnation and resurrection.[3] Despite this variety, however, Christians have generally approached Jesus "from above," especially seen in the conclusions of major ecumenical councils that emphasize his preexistence, his nature, and his relationship to the Trinity. Sometimes this preoccupation overshadowed everything else, so much so that Jesus' life and teachings have been eclipsed. In other circles in the modern period, conversely, there has been incredible interest in approaching Jesus "from below," trying to understand as much as possible of the Jesus of history. This focus has been driven both by pious fascination with Jesus' earthly life but also by skeptical and revisionist concerns to undermine the Gospel accounts. The rise of historical-critical methodology in biblical studies is motivated in large part by its application to the understanding of the Jesus of history. Over the last two centuries, three major quests for the historical Jesus, as they have been called, have emerged. These have their skeptical sides but have also enormously enriched the understanding of Jesus' historical context. As a result, there is greater understanding on several fronts of the significance of Jesus' life and teaching.

Following a case study of one of the early councils will introduce some of the perennial issues in Christology. Our approach will be to begin with Jesus' life and these new developments. In the process, we will hopefully see how a more balanced approach that considers Jesus' life and teachings, the cross, and the resurrection helps put all of them into better perspective. Then we will look at the conclusions with their greater emphasis on Christology from above as well as further implications such as the preexistence and postexistence of Christ. We will close this chapter by considering the issue raised by liberation theology of the identification of Jesus with every group, of whatever race, ethnicity, or gender, especially the oppressed. Theologically, how do we tread that landscape? Can James Cone stress that Jesus is black? Can one answer positively the poignant question from women, "Can a male savior save women?" We need to traverse some significant theological ground to respond.

CASE STUDY: NESTORIANISM AND THE THIRD
ECUMENICAL COUNCIL

The Second Ecumenical Council of Constantinople in 381, which
we considered in the chapter on the doctrine of God, concluded that
Christ was *truly* human.[4] The decision was against Apollinaris, who
was understood to say that Christ was *mostly* human, but the divine
Logos replaced the human reason or will, providing its animating spirit. This expressed, in an extreme form, what is called the
"God-flesh" trajectory in early Christology, rooted in the Johannine
tradition. The story does not stop there, however. Apollinaris was
opposed by Diodorus (d. 394) of the Antioch school, which emphasized the full human life of Jesus more than the Alexandrians.
Diodorus thought, somewhat similarly to the earlier Antiochian,
Paul of Samosata, that in Christ there were two persons in a moral
rather than in an essential union, which is called the "God-man"
trajectory. The union of human and divine is thus like that of body
and soul or husband and wife. In terms of understanding the relationship of the divine and human in Christ, this is a comprehensible
solution, a likely reason for its continuing attraction. Jesus is clearly
seen as human like other humans. His likeness to God is his special
openness to the Spirit, as a model for others. In other words, Jesus'
difference is more of degree than of kind. If one has difficulty with
one person being fully human and divine, a mystery at least as great
as that of the Trinitarian three-in-one to which it is obviously closely
related, then this is an attractive option. It still gives precedence to
Jesus as more fully filled with the Spirit than anyone else but not
so as to give rise to conundrums of being both human and divine.
The perplexity is not new. Apparently, it is what drove the Antioch
school toward the idea of a moral rather than an ontological union.
Does this say enough? This is the question that engaged the church
after the Council of Constantinople.

Later disciples of Diodorus were John Chrysostom, Theodore
of Mopsuestia, and Nestorius. Theodore was the greatest theologian of Antioch, who criticized with acuity the Alexandrian tendency to diminish the humanity of Christ. Although he continued

the Diodoran idea of a conjunction of will between the Logos and the man Jesus, he preferred the image of the Logos "indwelling" or "tabernacling" humanity as in John 1:14. Nevertheless, he moved further toward the Alexandrians in affirming that Christ was somehow still one person (*prosopon*). How this worked he did not explain well and left his thought "open to dangerous exploitation at the hands of his less cautious disciples."[5]

One of those disciples was Nestorius, a monk and presbyter of Antioch, who was made patriarch of Constantinople in 428. He was charged with teaching that Christ was two persons rather than one. The historical Nestorius perhaps did not explicitly do so but did see the unity in terms of an intimate conjunction of will. He said, "God the Word is also named Christ because He has always conjunction with Christ." In other words, the human Jesus is so one in spirit with the Logos, we might say, that he *is* the Logos. Whatever the actual Nestorius taught, however, he was taken to imply a crude union of "two Sons" adjoined in a moral union.

Cyril, patriarch of the rival see of Alexandria, was jealous of Constantinople's prominence and schemed to get Nestorius condemned in order to raise Alexandria's fortunes over against Constantinople's. Cyril's view was actually quite close to Apollinaris (whose views had been already deemed heretical). At the time, he thought that Christ had only one nature rather than two (called a "monophysite" position, literally meaning "one-naturism"), which of course implied that Christ could only be one person as well. The issue was thus posed: the Antioch position implied two persons, the Alexandrian position one person.

The debate was clouded by the way the participants tended to equate the number of persons with the number of natures, an issue that the fourth great ecumenical council, the Council of Chalcedon in 451, would take up. Part of the problem lies in the different understandings of the word *nature*. Cyril took it in a concrete sense, so of course there could only be one nature. Others took it in the later Chalcedonian sense of abstract properties, so there could conceivably be two natures in one concrete person. As J. N. D. Kelly observes, "Every alert reader must have noticed, and been astonished by, the extent to which theological divisions at this time were created and kept alive by the use of different and mutually confusing theological terms."[6] At the time, Cyril's view actually implied that Jesus was not truly human, which had already been ruled as heretical; the Logos simply took a human element. This supports the divinization of humanity that was so important to the Alexandrians (and much of the East). Cyril said, "One *physis* (nature) of the Word, and it made flesh." "From two natures, one." Despite his own heretical views, however, he won the political battle.

Cyril and the Alexandrians referred to Mary as *Theotokos*, the bearer of God. To Nestorius, this did not do justice to the human, so he criticized it. He thought that it was more correct to say that she was the *Christotokos*, the Christ-bearer. Theologically, he was probably more on target in distinguishing between the incarnate Logos and the full Trinity. This is similar to the earlier distinction we have seen, where the church condemned patripassionism, the modalist idea that God the Father suffered on the cross. The criticism was that patripassionism does not discriminate sufficiently between the second person of the Trinity, the Logos, and the first person of the Trinity. Nestorius was making a similar distinction. Although Nestorius was willing to use the term Theotokos in a guarded way, he offended popular piety. Cyril saw his chance and went on the attack against Nestorius on this basis—not the first time that piety has been used for political purposes. He charged that Nestorius' views destroyed the entire basis of salvation. He sent his concerns quickly to the emperor, the empress, the emperor's sister, and the pope. Those who affirm Cyril today see the issue as a defense of the full divinity of Christ. Did Mary bear just a human or also the Logos? In fairness, the Antiochene position, in seeming to distinguish between two persons in Christ, the Logos and the human Jesus, gave rise to this concern. If one takes the Eastern position that what Christ did not assume, Christ could not save, then the issue is major. If the Logos did not become fully human, being borne by Mary, then humans cannot be saved. These are fine points, but no finer than later debates about free will, grace, or even modern church music.

The pope surprisingly ruled against Nestorius despite the similarities between their views. Probably a shared political interest between Rome and Alexandria in working to humble Constantinople prevailed. Cyril was also more respectful and flattering in his address to the pope. An additional factor is that Nestorius, who was politically more clumsy, had been somewhat indulgent to the Pelagians, who were suspect for not giving grace its due. Even though Nestorius did not agree with them, his affirmation at this time did not help his cause.

The result was the Council of Ephesus in 431. Cyril and his followers arrived first, promptly met, and condemned Nestorius. When Nestorius' group arrived a few days later and found out what had happened, they met and condemned Cyril. No surprises there! Emperor Theodosius II of the East did not know what to do. At first he imprisoned the both of them. Politics soon prevailed, however. Nestorius was sacrificed (retired to a monastery, then banished to Egypt to live a miserable existence) in return for Cyril conceding something to Antioch in a creedal formula. The compromise formula was vague. It stated, "We therefore acknowledge our Lord Jesus Christ . . . complete God and complete man. . . . A union of the two natures has been made, therefore we confess one Christ." And of course, it affirmed the Theotokos. In truth, both Cyril and Nestorius probably could have signed this in good faith, but it meant the demise of Nestorius as orthodox. In the end, however, Nestorius' legacy lived on and later entered China and India, with churches still in Turkey, Persia, and India, a fact often neglected when we think of worldwide Christianity. Even in the most orthodox conclusions, and it is difficult to find more consensus than in these first four councils, the universal church has not always agreed, thus calling for continual discrimination and theologizing.

This significant account in the life of the church reveals several things. First, it shows that the church was still struggling to grasp the relationship of Jesus to God almost four hundred years after Jesus' death. This reminds us of the important role of the church and of theological reflection in understanding the meaning of Christ and of the scriptural accounts. It also reminds us, as Søren Kierkegaard did in the nineteenth century, that the incarnation is a mystery that we should not underestimate or present as simple. There is a place for continual reflection on its meaning, and it is such a rich and complex event that there will always by a place for further reflection. It should give us a certain humility in the process, where room is allowed for exploration and a degree of disagreement.

Second, the process was a very human, social, and political one. The church's theologizing is itself incarnational even as it reflects on the incarnation. The context of finitude and fallenness continues even in the life of the church as well as outside the church. As Jesus saw in his own context, sometimes sin is most subtle and difficult to deal with in the context of religion.

Third, the universal church has largely ratified the decision reached, despite the human—all too human—process. This is a salutary reminder that God continues to be redemptive as the Spirit works in the midst of the brokenness of the world. The assumption is often made that God only works or dwells where things are pure— in the Holy of Holies, in a sacred space, in the best people, in the best processes. If so, we are in a lot of trouble! As we can learn from church history, God is everywhere and perhaps most at work in the worst of situations. This is important to realize for the sake of the church and for our own sakes. God is willing to get involved in the messiest of situations even when we are not.

The conclusion that the Council of Ephesus reached is that there is a genuine uniqueness about Christ. While Christ represents the truly human, there is a unity with the second person of the Trinity, which John calls the Word, the Logos. The one person, Jesus Christ, is the incarnation of the Logos, John says. As we shall explore, this does not answer all of the questions, and the Council did not intend for it to do so. They were ruling out some specific wrong answers but not providing all the right answers. For instance, to be truly human, Jesus had to learn and grow—through suffering, as the book of Hebrews says. In other words, he was not omniscient or omnipresent or omnipotent. Many of the orthodox theologians at the time did not really affirm this, sometimes suggesting that Jesus even feigned ignorance when he really knew everything.[7] Paul, in the second chapter of Philippians, early in the church, perhaps quoting an even earlier hymn, says that the Christ "emptied himself" to become human. This, too, does not explain everything, but it helps us to see how the early church attempted to appreciate the genuine humanity of Christ, which the church historically often has downplayed.

Fourth, this immersion of the Spirit in the world does not diminish the summons of the Spirit of Christ to follow Christ. If we are scandalized by the pettiness involved in dealing with theological issues of such moment, it is a good sign; we should be. The call to follow Christ is not just for our personal lives, it has implications for life together in the church and in the world. The church is called to a better way even though she has "spots and wrinkles" (Eph 5:27). Sometimes it is seen at its worst in the midst of weighty theological issues. At best, the church represents the Lord as it often did in the first few centuries, when pagans could say in grudging admiration, "See, . . . how they love one another."[8]

CHRISTOLOGY FROM BELOW

In terms of the understanding of Christ as fully human and fully divine, it is deemed heretical to deny either. Certainly non-Christians who nevertheless admire Jesus deny the divinity of Christ while accentuating his humanity. Even in the church, Jesus' humanity has often been emphasized to the detriment of his divinity. This was characteristic of early church movements such as the Ebionites and dynamic monarchians, who saw Jesus as one who was remarkably in tune with the Spirit. For the adoptionists, this set the stage for God's affirmation, or adoption, of Jesus as his unique Son, perhaps at the baptism or perhaps at the resurrection. While making Christ easier to understand and placing him in a long line of prophets and Spirit-filled persons, this could not do justice to the confession of Jesus Christ as Lord and the emerging worship of Christ.

A more nuanced position was Arianism, which, as you may recall, was a powerful movement that virtually won the day at several junctures in the fourth century. Arianism held Christ to be the supreme created being but still not fully divine. The resultant notion of a semidivine being was finally judged unsatisfactory by those who, like Athanasius, deemed that the Savior must be wholly divine and wholly human.

Modern liberalism has also tended to emphasize the human side of Christ. The enormous influence of Immanuel Kant included a largely symbolic approach to Christology, understanding Christ to be a significant image or archetype of a morally good person.[9] While Kant neglected the historical Jesus, his conception of Jesus focused on Jesus' humanity as a moral person who did his duty. This emphasis on Jesus as a premier moral teacher was characteristic of much of the liberalism of the nineteenth and early twentieth century. To this day, it continues to be a way of understanding the significance of Jesus for some Christians and non-Christians who have high regard for Jesus but find highly problematic what they see as the mythology of a divine human.

Perhaps in reaction against this, more-conservative churches accentuate Christ's divinity. In general, those who have clearly affirmed Christ's divinity have not done justice to the humanity of Christ. We shall see that major church fathers, bastions of orthodoxy such as Athanasius, sometimes held views of the relation between humanity and divinity that virtually undermine the humanity of Christ.[10] Especially among evangelical churches, any tendencies toward heresy commonly lie in the direction of denying Christ's full humanity. This is not just a technical or scholarly issue. It often means that the Gospels, which do appreciate the humanity of Christ, are not given their canonical due. Preoccupation with the passion accounts in the Gospels themselves can involve misunderstanding by isolating them from the context of Jesus' life. The book of Hebrews claims that if we do not understand how Jesus "learned obedience through what he suffered" (5:8) and was "tested as we are" (4:15), then we miss a spiritual benefit for our lives. In other words, ironically, the desire to exalt Christ by focusing on his divinity, his sacrifice on the cross, and his resurrection can lead, in light of the fuller canonical picture, to an anemic and impoverished spirituality derived from Christ. It is worthwhile, therefore, to take some time with the historical Jesus, just as the Gospels do. The incarnational foundation we lay here in Jesus' teachings will undergird the fuller development in the next two chapters on salvation and the church.

The Quest for the Historical Jesus

With the rise of modern biblical criticism, the historicity of Jesus was placed on the front burner. What is known as the first quest for the historical Jesus began in the nineteenth century.[11] As often happens in the first stages, optimism far outstripped evidence. By the end of the century, Albert Schweitzer, whose book is thought to have effectively ended the first quest, said, "Those who are fond of talking about negative theology can find their account here. There is nothing more negative than the result of the critical study of the Life of Jesus."[12] On this basis, George Tyrrell said of Adolf Harnack, the great nineteenth-century liberal church historian and, by implication, others in the first quest, "The Christ that Harnack sees, looking back through nineteen centuries of Catholic darkness, is only the reflection of a Liberal Protestant face, seen at the bottom of a deep well."[13]

Already, we are alerted to some key features that are important in understanding the search for the historical Jesus. One is that it is more of a historical than a theological investigation. To put it another way, it is a search for what modern historiography might yield, not what faith might yield. Given the criteria of modern historiography, which have developed only in the last few centuries, the restrictions are high. Since there is more data, for example, for Jesus and the early church than for most figures of ancient history, one expects some confident historiographical results—and then is puzzled when they are not forthcoming. We will thus have to sort out the difference between a historiographical study and a canonical study.

A second feature is that, in this area perhaps more than in other areas, even in historiography, presuppositions matter. As we saw in the prolegomena, an aspect of the end of modernity is the understanding that presuppositions affect everything, even science. The idea of total objectivity is illusory and actually distorts the conclusions themselves in that it claims more certainty than is possible. This does not rule out the quest for knowledge or truth but does help in sorting out various claims that are sometimes asserted on the basis of "the assured results of modern research." It is not surprising that scholars of orthodox faith tend to come up with more-positive results, or that the first quest ended up with a Jesus much like the questers, or that scholars who do not believe in God come up with more-skeptical results. Historiography, particularly, is now recognized to be "constructed" in nature, a product of historical data, to be sure, but shaped creatively by the productive imagination.[14]

Third, the historical investigation has a positive role to play, despite its limitations. A part of the first quest was Schweitzer himself pointing out, in a self-correcting way, the limitations of the nineteenth-century quest in terms of historiography. Christianity claims to be rooted in history; attention to history keeps its feet on the ground. While we need not and should not be limited to a consensus of historical results, historiography can provide a sense of what is historically available and also provide a degree of honesty to those who do not share faith. A common mistake is to claim more than can plausibly be claimed, in the end actually harming the cause because those outside recognize the dishonesty. Historiography can also illuminate the biblical texts by providing more background. What did it mean to live in the first century? In Palestine? Under Roman rule? Sometimes historiography can shed light on the text itself. As we shall see, it can also provide a check on biases. For example, historiography can remind us that Jesus' context was Jewish, which is important in light of the centuries-long tendency to drive a wedge between Judaism and Christianity.

The second quest is said to have begun in the 1950s when Ernst Käsemann, a student of Rudolf Bultmann, called for new attention to the historical Jesus. This is important because, after Schweitzer, the authority of Bultmann had been thrown behind the idea that virtually nothing could be known about Jesus and that what we have is a product of the early church. Käsemann's call led to new studies by several scholars, such as Joachim Jeremias, that were more defensible in terms of history. Nevertheless, they still yielded limited and contentious results. One of the major issues that arose in this time concerned the assumptions of historiography itself. For example, one assumption is the principle of analogy, which means that the historian should not count as historical anything that is not analogous to current experience. While this is easily applied to legends of talking dogs or claims of magic, it is not always noncontroversial. If one has not experienced the miraculous today, it will be discounted in the past. More to the point, if one has not experienced resurrection today, then it will be discounted in the past. With this criterion, then, the foundational testimony of Christianity to the resurrection of Jesus is ruled out ahead of time, even before investigation. This seems, well, unscientific! This was the point made by Wolfhart Pannenberg. It seems that such a conclusion should be reached at the end, not at the beginning, of the discussion. In fact, in his significant work *Jesus: God and Man*, Pannenberg's conclusion was that the best explanation for the evidence that we have, and for the behavior of the early disciples, was that Jesus actually rose from the dead.[15] This is a conclusion recently reached by another major New Testament scholar, N. T. Wright, who sees it—perhaps more carefully than Pannenberg—as a historiographical conclusion that cannot be separated from faith.[16]

We should immediately recognize that their conclusions have not carried the day. Other scholars, especially non-Christian ones, are dubious. Other hypotheses abound, as we see even in the Gospels themselves, which point out that some thought that the disciples stole the body and made up the story. The point is not that history can prove—or disprove—the resurrection. The modern investigation of history can probably do more, or less, than we often expect. It can point to possibilities of something as astounding as the resurrection or even Jesus' healing miracles, but it cannot prove such astounding phenomena, whose very nature makes them striking and unusual. There is too much debate about the very nature of historiography and its criteria to put as much weight on it as has been put. Skeptics appeal to historiography to discredit the claims of Christianity, claiming more than it can provide. Christians sometimes claim that historiography proves, beyond the possibility of doubt, the claims of Christianity, also putting more weight on historiography than it can support. In the end, it is important to understand the nuances of the nature of historiography: it is modern and recent; it is disputed in terms of its basic criteria at times; it can do some things well and other things poorly; and it is not the same as faith. In fact, there is a place to exercise great caution in confusing faith and historiography, for such reliance on historiography—as notable theologians have pointed out—may end up harming and distorting faith altogether.

With this dispute about the nature of historiography in mind, we reach the third quest, which is ongoing. It is thought to have begun in the 1970s and has benefited from advances in research into the first-century Middle Eastern context. Perhaps the most famous, or infamous, aspect of this new turn is the so-called Jesus Seminar. This is a group that has "gone public," so to speak, and tried to advertise their work to a popular audience. Their often-sensational results have led to a great deal of press—and much misunderstanding, some of it their own doing. Perhaps the most prominent feature is their voting on the historicity of sayings of Jesus, which are then color coded. They cast colored beads in a box to vote. If a saying was seen as certainly authentic, it was coded red. If it was seen as probably authentic, it was coded pink. If it was seen as probably inauthentic, it was coded gray. And if it was seen as certainly inauthentic, it was coded black. Eventually, they published a color-coded Bible.[17] The implication is that they represent a cross-section of scholarship and are providing objective results of scholarship. We are familiar enough with the claims of objectivity to cruise cautiously in these waters. In fact, the group, for good or ill, represents a small group of scholars heavily tilted toward a skeptical or liberal attitude at the outset. They use criteria that are defensible but also sometimes controversial and limiting.

One example is multiple attestation. This makes sense in historiography. The more diverse the witnesses to a thing, the better. In these ancient texts, however, it is not so clear how much multiple references outweigh one. Because something appears only once, such as the parable of the Good Samaritan, is it thereby discredited? Another controversial aspect is the Seminar's high priority on the *Gospel of Thomas*, which is usually dated later in the second century. The Jesus Seminar tended to take it as early, perhaps earlier than the canonical Gospels. It is thus used as another source of attestation on a par with the canonical Gospels. Because the Gospel of Thomas does not include a passion and resurrection account, they have taken it as evidence of less historicity for these accounts. While a historian can draw such conclusions, one can easily see how other historians could draw very different conclusions—and do. Most see the Gospel of Thomas as coming much later.[18] The lack of a passion account may not indicate disbelief or even disinterest.

In some ways, the extreme conclusions of the Jesus Seminar have had the salutary effect of spurring many other studies, so we all benefit from having a genuinely broad cross-section of scholarship. One of the things that others have pointed out about the Jesus Seminar, besides the above features, is that they tend to arrive, surprisingly, at a non-Jewish Jesus. This is surprising because the general trend has been to plant Jesus firmly in his Jewish context, which has actually led to greater understanding.[19] Perhaps because of the undue influence of the Gospel of Thomas—which is a collection of sayings, often mystifying, without a narrative—the Jesus Seminar often pictures Jesus as a sage who is in some ways more like a traveling Greek philosopher than a Jew whose locale was largely Nazareth. It also is surprising because some in the Jesus Seminar have contributed to the understanding of the historical context. Studies of the life of Mediterranean peasants, while not necessarily telling us specifics about Jesus, place his words and deeds in a denser framework. As I mentioned earlier, the tendency of conservative Christians is to deny the humanity of Christ. We do this when we diminish the incarnation, which entails Jesus' particular placement in space, time, and culture. Perhaps historiography is reminding us of something that we should have known anyway, but it certainly has been helpful nonetheless on this score.

One more comment on the Jesus Seminar is important before turning to other aspects of the third quest. In some ways, the Jesus Seminar's approach has been a throwback to modernity rather than being postmodern, which is ironic because it developed concurrently with postmodernity. A major aspect of the third quest overall, in fact, is that it benefits the postmodern critique of modernity's limitations. The Jesus Seminar, however, by and large does not. This is reflected in the way that their assumption is that what is important and authoritative is the result of historiography. Thus, if a saying receives a grey rating, it should not be considered so highly or authoritatively. Moreover, the very passion to find the historical Jesus behind the Gospels, the world behind the text, is one of the limitations of the modern period. This is because it replaces the text that we have with a hypothetical text that is a speculative construction of the individual historian. It represents an obsession with *historical* fact, or what the criteria of historiography can allow as probable, over the *meaning* of facts. To return to our discussion of the nature of Scripture in the chapter on the doctrine of revelation, Scripture has an incarnational and factual basis, but it is much more than bare facts. It is not "an encyclopedia of uninterpreted facts," as some thought in the nineteenth century. It is so much more. The texts that were approved by the early church as canonical were chosen because they were so powerful in conveying the meaning of what happened in Jesus Christ. The early church was certainly aware of the difference between fact and fiction but was more concerned with meaning. We could say that it did not separate the imaginative, configurative power of fiction so distinctly from the idea of bare facts, as modernity was wont to do. That ideal of bare fact has itself been seen as a fiction. The world of the text was their concern, which they saw, we might say, as configuring the meaning of the world behind the text. Sometimes, for example, the Jesus Seminar and others can reach probabilistic conclusions about the Aramaic behind a Greek saying of Jesus. Should that replace the canonical text?[20] Perhaps a historian who is seeking the historical Jesus would prefer it. But is this what a believing Christian should prefer? Should the scholarly speculation be granted more authority than the canonical text? To do so is to mix apples with oranges, in a sense. It is to confuse two distinct enterprises, yet this is what the Jesus Seminar often gives the appearance of doing.

From a Christian perspective, the canon is the authority for a variety of reasons. One of those is to realize how much poorer we would be if we did not have the ability of the four evangelists in conveying the meaning of the Jesus event; the historical basis is crucial, to be sure, but where would we be without understanding its meaning? Even N. T. Wright, who thinks history strongly supports the resurrection, points out that apart from the context of meaning, even a dead man who was raised and appeared would be a curiosity, an entry into Ripley's *Believe It or Not*, but would not necessarily have meant anything for the salvation and resurrection of anyone else. The canon is significant as the authoritative interpretive framework. Other studies supplement, illuminate, and support it, but cannot replace it. This is another way of clarifying the difference between a modern historiographical approach, which is interested in the world behind the text, and a theological approach, which focuses on the world of the canonical text.

In general, the quest for the historical Jesus shares the former approach and is thus inherently limited for theological purposes. It serves a purpose and has a place, but a limited place. This is true even for scholars such as Wright, Ben Witherington, and Luke Timothy Johnson, reputable historians but Christians who are much more positive in their historical results. Even the more-skeptical approaches have gone beyond previous conclusions, such as those of Bultmann, in seeing a basic historicity in much of the accounts of Jesus. The surprising thing, given the skepticism that one can bring to history, is that any of Jesus' sayings received a red coding!

As indicated, the third quest more generally has emphasized the Jewishness of Jesus and the Jewish context for understanding Jesus, for example, how the notion of resurrection had a quite particular meaning and context in his time. Not all Jews believed in it, such as the Sadducees. Not all Jews affirmed bodily resurrection, such as Philo who affirmed more of a Platonic notion of a disembodied spirit. Yet apparently all understood that, if there were a resurrection, it would happen at the consummation of history when God's kingdom was to be established. What the early disciples understood to have happened with Jesus was thus totally unexpected, occurring in this matrix of ideas but at the same time exerting tremendous pressure upon it. Jesus' distinctiveness, which led to him not only being proclaimed as Messiah but worshipped as Lord in an unprecedented fashion for a Jewish context, can hardly be understood apart from understanding that context. Historiography has a major role to play, even in the theological enterprise.

Much attention has been paid to the nature of first-century society as an honor-shame society set in a domination system. This means, first of all, that issues of cleanliness are not so much about hygiene but about religion and had tremendous social implications quite difficult for modern, individualistic societies to grasp.[21] Jesus' breaking of many of those taboos had consequences far beyond that of being a social rebel marching to his own drummer, which is the way he might be viewed in a modern Western context. Paul's break with his training as a Pharisee was similarly convulsive in a way difficult for us to imagine, but it cannot be interpreted simply as a move toward individualism.[22] The domination system refers to the dynamics of a social system where most were poor, and a few, about ten percent, were the ruling and wealthy class.[23] Again, it is difficult for modern Western society, with its strong middle class, to understand those dynamics. For instance, Jesus' actions in such a society took on threatening and deadly political overtones that we easily miss, leading us often to characterize Jesus as nonpolitical and only spiritual.

Another contribution has been to bring out the sense of Jesus as a sage, a wise man, albeit Jewish and not Greek. Traditional categories for grasping Jesus have been as prophet, priest, and king—all of which are still significant. To this, however, should be added sage, which helps to bring in the important role of the Wisdom literature of the Old Testament canon and which has been somewhat neglected in understanding Jesus.[24] The Wisdom tradition supports Jesus' role as a teacher, as one who was gifted in aphorisms and telling parables. Interestingly, exorcism had become an aspect of the Wisdom tradition.

In looking now at the canonical account of Jesus' life, we will draw on these rich studies of the historical Jesus. By now, it should be clear that our primary reliance is not on these historical studies but on the biblical accounts. We are interested primarily in theological meaning, not in speculative historical reconstructions that replace the canonical accounts. But historical studies are helpful, as we have seen, in providing clarification, context, and sometimes support for our theological understanding.

A theological account is thus one that approaches Jesus from a perspective of faith. My own approach is characteristic of much of the church in giving pride of place and authority to the canonical configuration of the meaning of Jesus. It also gives great weight to church tradition as well as valuing historical studies. Compared to a historical approach that attempts to be neutral or that might have a predisposition against faith, a theological approach is closer to the historian who approaches the Gospels with a postcritical conviction of God's reality primarily revealed in Jesus Christ, of meeting the risen Christ through the Holy Spirit, of being forgiven through the death of Christ, and of walking in the Spirit of Christ. Perhaps this person has experienced or witnessed providential acts of God and miraculous healing, similar to accounts in Scripture. This person obviously is going to be much more open to the historicity and veracity of the Gospel accounts than someone who does not believe in God or any kind of transcendent realm and has not experienced any of the above. For a host of reasons that cannot be explicitly proven or laid out on a table, such a theologian is already convinced of the basic canonical and church claims about Jesus, as well as the authority of Scripture. The issue of a historical basis for the Gospel accounts is rather easily accepted, even on historiographical grounds; the more important quest for the theologian is not even the third quest but the theological quest of understanding the significance of Jesus for the believer.

Jesus' Words

Historians have generally agreed that three things are characteristic of the historical Jesus: he proclaimed the kingdom of God, he spoke in parables, and he called God "Abba" (father).[25] These actually represent well the heart of Jesus' teaching.

The Kingdom of God. The kingdom of God particularly has received much attention over the last century. It was the theme of John the Baptist's message and called out to Jesus as well. At the beginning of his Gospel, Mark summarizes Jesus' message after his baptism and temptations in the wilderness as saying simply, "The time is fulfilled, and the kingdom of God has come near; repent, and believe in the good news" (1:15).

It is now emphasized that the kingdom of God connotes more the lively reign or ruling of God than a spatial location.[26] With the context of kingly domains and even the rule of the church through much of Christian history, it was often easy to miss this dynamic character. Perhaps God's kingly rule is a better understanding. Since kingship is not so transparent to many moderns and is easily misunderstood, perhaps it is better to take Jesus' cue and understand it as happening when God's will is done. The idea of power is present, but as we have seen, we must be sensitive to the way Jesus often turned ideas upside down. To refer to one of Jesus' aphorisms, Jesus' ideas are like new wine: pouring them into old wineskins explodes the wineskins (Matt 9:17); or, as Paul would say, the weakness of God is more powerful than human strength (1 Cor 1:25). Martin Luther King Jr., interpreted the kingdom as "the beloved community": the kingdom of God, the rule of God, the will of God, is where there is "beloved community."

Another gain in understanding the kingdom of God has been to appreciate its nature as a symbol, as a metaphorical image. The nature of God is deeply mysterious and thus deeply metaphorical. When it comes to language about God, as we have seen, it is always limited in doing justice to the reality of God. The kingdom of God is a powerful image, but it can be misunderstood in societies that give meaning to their words largely in the context of dominating, worldly power. Rather, Jesus was transforming worldly notions. If God is love, it is safe to say that Jesus' notion of the kingdom of God is better understood from that perspective than from worldly domination. To draw on the much later understandings we dealt with in the chapter on the doctrine of God, if the Trinitarian God is understood as loving community already, from all eternity, God's purpose is to draw all of creation into the circle of divine love, into the divine dance.

Debates have also centered around the timing of the kingdom. Was it wholly in the future? Much of Jesus' teaching assumes a future kingdom that greatly reverses the present world, where "many who are first will be last, and the last will be first" (Matt 19:30). It will abound with surprises. "Not everyone who says to me, 'Lord, Lord,' will enter the Kingdom of heaven, but only the one who does the will of my Father in Heaven" (Matt 7:21). Perhaps the most startling are those in Jesus' parable of the Sheep and the Goats who are unaware that they are serving Christ but, as the king says, "Just as you did it to one of the least of these who are members of my family, you did it to me" (Matt 25:40). Jesus urges people to be ready for the kingdom, for it will come like a thief in the night (Matt 24:33). It will begin with the marriage feast of the new bride and groom of the kingdom of peace, longed for in the Old Testament as a time when "they shall beat their swords into plowshares" (Isa 2:4). This certainly is not yet the case.

Nevertheless, as the passage in Mark implies, Jesus could see the kingdom as being "at hand" (Mark 1:14, optional reading). Thus, some have thought that Jesus taught a realized eschatology rather than a futurist eschatology. Jesus certainly seemed to do so at times. The Gospel of John especially emphasizes that eternal life has already begun: "Whoever believes in the Son *has* eternal life" (3:36, emphasis added). Yet John also clearly points to a future fulfillment. Jesus tells the disciples in his last discourse that he is going away, he is going to "prepare a place" for them, but they will have the Paraclete, the Spirit of Christ, while he is gone (John 14:3, 6). A strong consensus has thus emerged that Jesus assumed an "inaugurated eschatology," a "now but not yet" dynamic. The power of the kingdom is present in Jesus' ministry and continues to be present through the Holy Spirit, yet the fullness of the kingdom, where the nature of God's reigning will be fully manifested, is still to come. Paul's image is that of "first fruits" (1 Cor 15:20). The initial signs of the kingdom have already occurred, and continue to occur. We should not mistake the present evil age, however, with its sorrow and brokenness, for the true harvest of the kingdom of God. The Beatitudes read in this way: "Blessed are those who mourn [now], for they shall [then] be comforted" (Matt 5:4); in Luke, "Blessed are you who are hungry now, for [then] you will be filled" (Luke 6:21). The blessedness is assumed to have begun already; its fulfillment, however, is obviously in the future. The significance of the disciples becoming convinced that Jesus had risen bodily from the dead is that this was the great sign, as "everyone" knew, of the fulfillment of the coming kingdom. The kingdom must then already be initiated.[27]

Jesus' Parables. Jesus' wider teaching and his works dovetail with the message of the kingdom of God. Some would say that the structure itself of Jesus' teaching, properly understood, points to the kingdom, where "the medium is the message." As John Dominic Crossan points out in relation to the parable of the Good Samaritan, "The hearer struggling with the contradictory dualism of Good/ Samaritan is actually experiencing in and through this the inbreaking of the Kingdom."[28] One of the most striking things about Jesus' teaching in the Synoptic Gospels is the parables. This is all the more revealing when we see that none of his followers, such as Paul, seemed to emulate him, and they do not even show up in the Gospel of John. While historians also stress that this seems to be one of the most verifiable things about Jesus, it has taken some time to appreciate their nature fully, in some ways not until the last decades of the twentieth century.

In order to understand this, we must look at the history of parable interpretation. Obviously, much of the meaning of the parables has always come through. The meaning of the parable of the Prodigal Son, with its great challenge to the mores of almost any time and place, is difficult to miss—and also difficult to follow. Parables of the importunate widow, the lost sheep and lost coin, the mustard seed, and of the pearl of great price can quickly be grasped—although again they may take a lifetime to follow. Nevertheless, the general tenor of the parables has largely been misunderstood. For much of Christian history, they were understood as allegories, where every point was mined to make a theological application. In the parable of the Good Samaritan, every aspect of the story was thought to have a hidden meaning. While such speculation was supposed to be constrained by the rest of the canon and the rule of faith, it still left room for individual flights of fancy limited only by the interpreter's imagination. As creative and evocative poetry, this approach can be appreciated. As attempts to understand the textual meaning, it is suspect.

The Reformers in the sixteenth century were critical of the allegorical approach in general, being suspicious to the point of there being little hermeneutical control. In the twentieth century, the case was made that allegory was not the correct genre for understanding the parables. Rather than finding points in everything, the idea was that these are simple stories with one main point. This could be the lavishness of grace or the supreme value of the kingdom.[29] In the 1970s, however, came intensive focus on the parables in light of developments in understanding metaphor.[30] A major insight emerged against a long tradition that rich metaphors cannot be translated into prose. The assumption had been that in order to understand a metaphor, one must translate it into literal language. Especially in modernity, literal language became the only way to express truth with the appropriate "clarity and distinctness," to use the Cartesian terms. But what if one cannot fully translate the metaphor into prose? What if one does not need to do so in order to understand it? As we have seen in the prolegomena, one of the aspects of the postmodern shift was this sea change with respect to the priority of literal language. Sometimes it is not just that the metaphor cannot be translated, it is that the metaphor expresses truth *better* than the literal language. Literal exposition can help in interpreting a metaphor, but the prosaic explanation does not necessarily exhaust the meaning of a metaphor. In some ways, the medium is the message. There is a surplus of meaning in a rich metaphor that gives rise to endless interpretation.

With this change occurring, especially in the 1960s and 1970s, New Testament scholars turned again to Jesus' parables, now seeing them as extended metaphors. First, they saw that the idea of representing the meaning of a parable by a prose paraphrase was the same attempt to translate metaphors into prose—it cannot be done, and the effect is to domesticate the power of the message by changing the medium.

Second, as scholars investigated especially the parable of the Good Samaritan, they saw that the parables, like metaphors, have a "semantic impertinence" that "orients by disorientation." In other words, they disrupt one meaning to erect another in the rubble of the first. In Crossan's words, parables first of all "shatter" worlds.[31]

This can be seen in the parable of the Good Samaritan.[32] Besides being fodder for creative allegory, it was long understood as an example story. It showed how one should act through illustration. If one gave it a point, it was to show compassion for those in need. As such, one could argue that it did not challenge convention so much as support it. It was not basically offering a new ethic as much as reminding of the old. After all, "love your neighbor as yourself" is in the Old Testament. Rabbis also told parables at times, but they tended to fall into this category of illustrating the world. If one follows the parable as it is told, taking the place of the hearer, one imagines a crowd of common Jews identifying with the man in the ditch on the well-known dangerous Jericho road. They would be wanting someone to help the poor fellow, themselves, in the ditch. As they heard about a priest walking by on the other side, one can imagine them shaking their head as they saw how religious rules keep people like themselves not only from being seen as holy as the spiritual leaders but from being aided by spiritual leaders. Then as now, while there was respect for religious leaders, there could also be criticism and resentment for those in higher positions who look down on others. Preacher jokes are popular for a reason! Then a Levite also passes by the wounded man. Again, one could imagine them identifying with the point they anticipated that Jesus was making. Fellow Jews are not helping other Jews in need, and they are using religious excuses to boot. They knew Jesus as a critic of the abuses of the religious status quo; they appreciated him calling people back to the true meaning of the Jewish law, especially as seen in the Prophets, that revealed God's special concern for the poor and needy. They might anticipate a common Jewish person walking by, giving aid, and showing even the priest and Levite the meaning of true religion. But that is not what happened. If it were an example story, that is what should have happened. At most, a shocking twist would have been to have a Samaritan in the ditch and have a Jew helping someone whom they all would not want to touch or to help, not just the priest and the Levite. When Jesus had a Samaritan come by as the helper, the one who proved most religious, the genre was turned inside out. The wineskin burst. One can imagine them being left speechless, their anticipated "Amen" caught half-formed before it was sounded, and some going away angry. The story would have to be written today with a Muslim helping a wounded Jew, a black man helping a white in the Old South, a Sunni helping a Shiite in today's Iraq. It is difficult to underestimate the shock of this parable in its context. As some have said, the sign of a true parable is that the listener goes away either glad or mad; indifference is not an option. The effect of the parable was to shatter their world, not piecemeal but as a whole. The question they were left with, as identifying with the wounded man lying in a ditch, was whether they were willing to receive aid from a totally unlikely quarter, from a direction that they could hardly imagine, even one they might detest. When one remembers the wider context of Jesus' presenting himself as a messenger from God as a source highly unlikely, a carpenter from Nazareth, whose understanding of the fulfillment of the law was one that came across as lawbreaking, and who saw himself as pouring new wine into new wineskins, the parable becomes virtually a messianic parable. If God comes, through the Messiah, in an unlikely, even shocking manner, how will he be received? How will God's aid be welcomed, if it arrives as someone the equivalent of a hated Samaritan?

As other parables were reexamined, they fit this structure of disorientation. No wonder they were often puzzling, even to the disciples. In this way, Jesus' parables were quite unlike the rabbinic tradition of parables. Crossan tended to see parables as only disorienting.[33] Paul Ricoeur and others saw parables as also reorienting through disorientation.[34] They undo, but they also point, however vaguely, in another direction. This characterizes at least the parables of Jesus, which gesture toward the kingdom of God. It is thus difficult to appreciate the uniqueness of Jesus apart from his parabling.

Abba. Another unsettling feature of Jesus was his calling God not only "Father" but the more intimate term "Abba." While this can have the connotation of "Daddy," it was also used by adult children of their fathers. Nevertheless, it seemed to be unusual for Jesus to use it to refer to God. It represented the general intimacy that he apparently felt and portrayed, so much so that people asked him, "Teach us to pray" (Luke 11:4). Marcus Borg sees Jesus as a "spirit person," who like other charismatic religious figures had a spiritual presence, an aura, about him that drew people to him.[35] He conveyed a closeness to God that is all the more appealing because of his message of God's extravagant grace, revealed in his parables and in his actions of inclusion of people normally seen as marginalized and outcast. He seemed to know God well and conveyed a God who was more interested in all people than society had led people to believe. Here again, Jesus' teaching of the kingdom of God and his parabling come together with his relationship to God. The kingdom of God is one where God is like a parent to his children. As the book of Revelation puts it in its magnificent metaphorical vision of the end, "The home of God is among mortals. He will dwell with them as their God; they will be his peoples, and God himself will be with them" (21:3).

With Jesus' parables in mind, as well as his calling God "Abba," it is worth mentioning here that the effect of this term for God was to convey the familial warmth and intimacy of God through an unusual term for God, not the gender of God.[36] As mentioned in the chapter on the doctrine of God, women suggest that a similar effect comes from calling God "Mother." The Bible itself licenses feminine imagery for God. With the understanding that all language about God is limited and partial, one may see the value of the metaphorical usage of "Mother" for God, which suggests in our culture a warmth and intimacy of God that is somewhat shocking—much like "Abba" did in Jesus' time. In fact, we are so used to "Abba" that it conveys little shock; perhaps the closest to experiencing a similar impact today is hearing God called "Mother." It is possible that people may hear this with unintended meanings, but Jesus was also understood to be meaning things he did not intend, such as being charged with being a "glutton and a drunkard" (Matt 11:19). In the end, the point is for all to be able to relate to God as Jesus did, which represents the kingdom of God, the "beloved community."

Jesus' Works

One of the contributions of the third quest has been to emphasize the significance of many of Jesus' actions—his works—and particularly his eating. This seems strange, but nothing is more human than eating. Jesus' "commensality," as it is called, was part and parcel of his message.[37] Especially in a highly stratified, honor-shame society, with close attention being paid to those with whom one associates, eating together could become a prophetic and even political statement. It could be a judgment on the present kingdom and a sign of the inbreaking new kingdom of God. Jesus' crossing of boundaries in his table fellowship was a symbol of the kingdom, a symbol that continues, or should continue, in the central practice of Communion. As such, it was a serious and sobering prophetic practice; at the same time, we should realize that the meals were not just rituals. They were apparently times of fellowship and enjoyment, just as we might think of enjoyable food and fellowship today. It is apparently here that Jesus was charged with being a glutton and a drunkard (Matt 11:19). This does not sound like the picture of somber, serious meals with no levity and joy. People apparently enjoyed being around Jesus. The ones who did not enjoy him seemed to be the ones most interested in preserving the rules and the status quo. This could be said about most of Jesus' practices. Jesus' deeds in general fit his message. Jesus not only told parables, he was a parable.

More widely noticed as a countercultural, iconoclastic practice is Jesus' "breaking" the Sabbath rules. "Breaking" is in quotes because apparently in Jesus' mind, he was completely in accord with Sabbath observance; he just understood it in a different way. The opposition to Jesus reflects the continuing tendency of religious people to lapse into legalism, a tendency that haunts Christianity as well. A religion that has grace at the center is sometimes unfortunately most known in the culture for being legalistic and judgmental.[38]

Jesus' practice thus displayed a strong aversion to legalism. As he classically put it, "The sabbath was made for humankind, and not humankind for the sabbath" (Mark 2:27). When Jesus was faced with healing someone on the Sabbath, he did not hesitate, even if it was "work" and not "rest" (Mark 3:1-6). On the other hand, there is no indication that Jesus was an iconoclast in the sense that he thought that the fourth commandment had no meaning. All indications are that his practice also was to worship and rest on the Sabbath, insofar as it was for humankind. We can learn from Jesus a caution about religious rules: they may have validity as general guidelines, a reflection of pooled wisdom, but we should be careful of making rules into absolutes. Here again is a place for practical wisdom and spiritual discernment to guide us when the rules cannot determine what is best to do.

Jesus' Worship

Under the heading of "Jesus' Worship" is included Jesus' spirituality, his discipleship. Strange words, these. Could Jesus have been a disciple? The root meaning is a "learner." Did Jesus have to learn? Common piety suggests that he did not. The divine nature is so emphasized that we struggle to do justice to Jesus' humanity, yet our reticence is not shared by the New Testament. Luke's brief account of Jesus as twelve not only mentions what we highlight, namely, that the teachers in the temple "were amazed at his understanding and his answers" but also that Jesus was "listening to them and asking them questions" (Luke 2:46-47). Presumably he was not just testing them but was wanting answers for himself. This is confirmed by Luke's later summary, comparing Jesus to young Samuel: "And Jesus increased in wisdom and in years, and in divine and human favor" (1:52; cf. 1 Sam 2:26). A little reflection helps us realize that of course Jesus was not born already knowing Aramaic, much less Greek, Latin, modern English, or modern physics. If he had known about modern anatomy and medicine, he could have helped multitudes of people over the centuries. There is no indication, however, that Jesus had any of that kind of knowledge. However we understand the relationship of humanity and divinity, the importance of the Gospels is that they show that Jesus was clearly human. He surely grew and developed in normal ways as other children. He learned to crawl, walk, and talk gradually. He surely went through the "terrible twos"! His brain ostensibly developed the capacity for abstract thought at the normal time, around adolescence. His parents had to discipline him for him to learn self-control, just as in any other parent-child relationship. If this seems strange, it is likely because we are impoverished in our understanding of Jesus' humanity and thus miss out on the importance of it.

The book of Hebrews, with one of the highest Christologies in the New Testament, is clear on this subject: "He learned obedience," the writer says emphatically (5:8). Not only that, it adds he learned obedience "through what he suffered." One might think that he is referring only to the cross, but likely not. That is late to be learning! This is made more clear by other blunt remarks—blunt, however, only to our impoverished, docetic sensibilities when it comes to Jesus' humanity. "For we do not have a high priest who is unable to sympathize with our weaknesses, but we have one who in every respect has been tested as we are, yet without sin" (Heb 4:15). If we are uncomfortable with thinking of Jesus as being weak and being tempted, note that the writer of Hebrews says that it is only through this that we are therefore to "approach the throne of grace with boldness, so that we may receive mercy and find grace to help in time of need" (Heb 4:16). Just to further clarify the point, Hebrews says, "It was fitting that God . . . should make the pioneer of their salvation perfect through sufferings" (2:10). Odd, is it not, that we so often think it unfitting that Jesus should have been truly human and thus have grown and developed as other humans? "He had to become like his brothers and sisters in every respect, so that he might be a merciful and faithful high priest in the service of God. . . . Because he himself was tested by what he suffered, he is able to help those who are being tested" (Heb 2:17-18).

If grasping the reality of the way that Jesus was truly human in growing and learning through trials and suffering is the key to our receiving spiritual aid from the risen Christ, then our spirituality is likely deeply lacking. In my experience, Christians are uncomfortable with Jesus' being human in these ways. Being without sin, which is the testimony of the church, does not mean being inhuman. Hebrews makes it clear that a part of being human—and being the Christ—in this fallen world is to grow, to learn, to suffer, and to face temptation. Temptation is not sin; yielding to it is. We learn from Gethsemane that Jesus did not play with temptation. Rather, it is deadly serious. If we think of spiritual warfare as real, as Paul did, then we must think of Jesus' experiencing it not less than we do, but probably more. Our failure to take in the full dimensions of Jesus' humanity deprives us of vital spiritual resources—yet it is common in the church. Such a limited view of Jesus means that he cannot be our example of humanity; he becomes the great exception, which we might adore but cannot learn from or emulate.

With full appreciation of Jesus' humanity, we actually can esteem what he did even more. After all, in the way that we may unconsciously think, he was divine; his miracles should have been easy for him. What if they were not? What if he was like us? If he was, then we can, from the human perspective, value more highly what he did as a Palestinian peasant—and still confess his divinity.

As mentioned, Jesus seemed to have a spiritual aura that impressed and drew people to him, a remarkable thing for an uncredentialed layperson. He "taught them as one having authority, and not as their scribes" (Matt 7:28). Cursory attention to Jesus' humanity can give people the impression that since Jesus Christ was of two natures, divine and human, he did not need to worry about communion with God; it happened as a matter of course. In reality, what we see in the Gospels is Jesus as an *example* of someone who was dependent upon God through prayer and meditation, not as an *exception* to every other human being. In this, as in other ways, we are called to follow him.

We find Mark saying of Jesus, "In the morning, while it was still very dark, he got up and went out to a deserted place, and there he prayed" (Mark 1:35). Luke says that "he was praying in a certain place" when one of his disciples asked him, "Teach us to pray," presumably impressed by the prayer practice of Jesus (Luke 11:1). Luke also adds that before the great question that Jesus asked after he had retreated from Galilee to the north of Caesarea Philippi, "Who do you say that I am," Jesus had been "praying alone" (Luke 9:18; cf. Mark 8:27; Matt 16:13).

Presumably when he went into the wilderness, driven by the Spirit to fast for forty days, he was not doing it just for show; he needed it (Mark 1:12). He apparently longed for the time in prayer and reflection at the beginning of this new stage in his life and in his calling. It is not surprising then that the temptations he experienced were messianic in nature. It is important to see that, for the most part, they were not temptations to do evil; they were temptations to be the "good" Messiah that most expected (Matt 4:1-11; Luke 4:1-13). They fit the assumptions that virtually all would have had of the Messiah, ones which Jesus surely had been taught. His own understanding of the Messiah fit nobody's expectations. It was new and was hardly understood even after the resurrection, with the benefit of hindsight.

No wonder that the encounter at Caesarea Phillippi was so significant. It seemed to be precipitated by the crowds drastically misunderstanding the significance of Jesus' miracle of the feeding of the multitudes, so much so that around this time Jesus asks poignantly of the disciples, "Do you also wish to go away?" (John 6:67). Jesus apparently thought some things through in the wilderness after the baptism; he apparently needed to retreat and pray some more at the middle of his ministry, most clearly in Luke, which sees the turning point in Jesus' ministry coming soon after Caesarea Phillipi when Jesus "set his face to go to Jerusalem" (9:51). The encounter is revealing in that this seems to be the first time that the disciples and Jesus call him, or dare to speak of him as, the Messiah. Yet we see in Matthew, as soon as Jesus says to Peter perhaps the most approving thing of anyone in the Gospels of Peter, "Flesh and blood has not revealed this to you, but my Father in heaven. And I tell you, you are Peter [the little rock], and on this rock [bedrock] I will build my church" (16:17-18). Jesus then says perhaps the worst thing he says of anyone, again of Peter, "Get behind me, Satan!" (16:23). Why? Jesus had just revealed to them that the meaning of the Messiah was to "be killed." Remarkably, Peter then "took him aside and began to rebuke him" (16:22).

We can have some sympathy for Peter because what Jesus was saying made no sense to anyone. The understanding of the Messiah was to be an earthly, triumphant deliverer who would bring in the kingdom immediately. Jesus is likely the first ever to have put so clearly together the messianic passages and the Suffering Servant passages. Up to this point, they were seen as referring to two very distinct phenomena. They were not linked in the Old Testament. Moreover, the messianic prophecies never spoke of two comings at all, much less one for suffering and one for triumph. No wonder that Jesus needed time and prayer to think things through—not just once during the time in the wilderness but later at Caesarea Phillippi—and we have not yet mentioned Gethsemane or the cry of dereliction on the cross. We fail to appreciate this marvel and Jesus' need for prayer and reflection only if we do not do justice to his humanity. Failure to do so robs us of Jesus as an example and model and leaves him only as a divine being that one can behold at a distance but can never truly follow. Paul could say, "Be imitators of me" (1 Cor 11:1), but if we rob Jesus of his true humanity in the fullness of all of its dimensions, we cannot allow Paul to add, as he did, "as I am of Christ."

With all that Hebrews says about Christ's humanity, it adds, "Yet without sin" (Heb 4:15). One might imagine that this is surely not relevant to Christ's humanity but only to his divinity. This, however, is to say that essential human nature is sinful, which has been denied, officially at least, by theologians. Such a claim is inconsistent with God creating everything good. Essential corruption would be true perhaps of Platonism and some forms of Gnosticism, yet it runs contrary to Jewish and Christian theology. In this sense, sinlessness is actually a manifestation of Christ's true humanity. In fact, we can say that he, not Adam and Eve, is the first truly human being. Especially if we understand Adam and Eve as being representative of the first humans who are potentially but not actually truly human, this is so. It is true, however, that the incarnation occurs in the midst of a fallen world and partakes of the fallout of fallenness. It is all the more significant then that in the midst of brokenness, we find wholeness. It is perhaps not surprising that the clash of wholeness with brokenness resulted in the brokenness of the one who was whole.

Christ's sinlessness should not be understood as something that can be historically proven, any more than the virgin birth. As Stan Grenz has pointed out, it is not a foundation of faith but is dependent upon faith.[39] Because of the conviction that this one is God's chosen one, the Messiah, attested by his resurrection from the dead, we confess that he was sinless. This seems consistent with what we are told of his life; but as representing a statement about his inner thoughts and motives, quite inaccessible to us, it is a confession, not a proof. In addition, we should be careful not to identify sinlessness with the absence of temptation. As we have seen, Jesus struggled with temptation apparently as greatly as we do. His temptations were perhaps different than ours in detail, but the point of Hebrews saying that "he was tempted as we are" is not that he is identical but similar. Which is greater? To be so above the human context that one can make light of temptation or to face it squarely, "yet without sin"?

Such a walk with his Abba did not just happen by chance, as we have seen. Jesus practiced spiritual disciplines, we could say. He meditated upon Scripture and prayed regularly. He seemed to have a striking intimacy with God that was notable even among extremely religious people. We are in the realm of mystery here, but perhaps we can imagine someone who, to be sure, grew and developed, even suffered in his growing and developing, yet was without sin. What does this mean? It conjures the sense of someone who enjoyed a fellowship with God that we can only imagine, an intimacy that we might experience intermittently—yet without the brokenness and pangs of separation, much like Adam and Eve hiding in the garden. Rather, it was like their walking with God in the cool of the day. What could it mean then for someone with that unbroken sense of communion to have it shattered—for the first time, in the time of one's greatest agony, while dying? Is this the existential sense, the human sense, of the cry of godforsakenness? Jesus' very spirituality, his closeness with God, made the end all the more bitter.

Jesus' Cross

For some Western Christians, Jesus' death on a cross overshadows everything else. Hardly anything else is even emphasized, not his teachings or even his resurrection. It was on the cross that Jesus "paid it all" and perhaps did it all, in this view. As important as the cross is, this near-exclusive emphasis does not represent the canonical placement of the cross. In order to approach the mystery of the cross, we will come to it here in the context of Jesus' life and resurrection and will probe it further in the next chapter, on salvation. In many ways, what Protestants think about the cross of Christ took more than a millennium of reflection to work out. This obviously points more to a perspective of a Christology from above than below, with a great deal of retrospective theologizing, much as we see in reflections on the Trinity—only more so. Thus, we will treat what is called "the work of Christ" in distinction from the "person of Christ" in a fuller way in the context of soteriology. Whatever we say about the cross of Christ, however, should be framed in light of the actual event, especially as it is portrayed in the four Gospels, where it is placed as the tragic ending of his ministry, followed quickly by his resurrection and then the beginning of the church. All of these notes must be sounded along with the cross for it to ring true.

We must first avoid a tendency to overspiritualize Jesus as someone whose kingdom was so "not of this world" that he could hardly have offended anyone. How then did he end up clashing with authorities, both Roman and Jewish, so that they fervently desired to put him to death? Second, by sometimes coming to Christ and the cross too much "from above," we may think that his cross was so predestined by God that all of the drama and the thick, incarnational context is wholly lost. Seeing it "from below" helps us appreciate the wider ramifications. This is crucial because the implication is that the import of his mission for us cannot be so easily compartmentalized, and thus domesticated, within a tiny portion of our lives. The command to love God with all of our being can be understood better in light of the way that Jesus loved God with all of his being—and ended up risking everything about his life before it was over. We can miss what should be one of the plainest facts, namely, that Jesus died as a political criminal. How odd that in many evangelical contexts, Christians strive to deny any political implications of Jesus, so much so that they charge such a thing with being liberal. Yet it is part of the stark reality of Jesus' death. The cross means more than that—but surely not less than that.

From the human perspective, the cross moves us with the extent of Jesus' suffering. The movie *The Passion of the Christ* graphically displayed this, although it is important to note that the movie went far beyond Scripture. The biblical stories rather matter-of-factly indicate that Jesus was flogged, he staggered, he was hung on the cross, he was mocked, and he died. One of the models of atonement that we will consider in the next chapter, the moral-influence theory, reflects the sense in which during Communion, on Good Friday, and at other times, we are compelled by Jesus' suffering to take up our cross and follow him. This is a central motif in the New Testament and can hardly be appreciated without approaching the cross from a human perspective.

What happened on the cross in Jesus' life is ultimately a mystery, perhaps focused more than anywhere on his cry of godforsakenness shortly before he died (Matt 27:46; Mark 15:34). Apparently it was so shocking that only Matthew and Mark mention it. Later commentators have softened it, rightly, by pointing out that it is the first verse of Psalm 22. This psalm uncannily reflects Jesus' experience on the cross in ways such as "I am poured out like water, and all my bones are out of joint" (v. 14) and "They divide my clothes among themselves, and for my clothing they cast lots" (v. 18). Jesus surely was aware of this and also that the psalm ends on a more positive note: "For dominion belongs to the Lord, and he rules over the nations" (v. 28) This has wrongly been taken to suggest that Jesus really was not experiencing anything to lament, even though this is a psalm of lament; he just could not get to the end of the psalm! This is to misunderstand the psalms of lament in general. They telescope experience such that within a short psalm, one might move from despair to hope rather quickly. In life, this might take hours, days, even years.

With recovery of the significance of God's experiencing travail and suffering, new dimensions in understanding Jesus' experience on the cross have opened up.[40] If God the Father can suffer deeply, it is not surprising that the incarnate Son could suffer deeply. If we did not also have Gethsemane, we might be more strongly tempted to minimize Jesus' existential agony, but we are almost overwhelmed, as he was, with the extent of his travail in the garden. In that light, a cry of lament on the cross is not incongruous. Also with a stronger sense of the social Trinity, theologians have probed the cross more deeply. In the main Christian tradition, God did not suffer and neither did Jesus in his human nature. Now, one can see that the cross was a Trinitarian experience, but it was not entirely the same for each. The Father suffered the death of the Son, and the Son suffered death as separation from the Father. Later theologians have pointed out that one must include the dimension of the Holy Spirit. As the incarnation is seen as the Father sending the Son through the Spirit, the bitter end must be understood as the Father and Son's brokenness through the Spirit. If this seems complicated—it is! There is surely a mystery here that cannot fully be plumbed any more than the incarnation itself. Yet Gethsemane and the cry of godforsakenness remind us of the real spiritual agony that coincided with the physical. Perhaps Jesus experienced for the first time a sense of separation from God. In some way, he apparently felt what great spiritual guides have called the absence of God, the dark night of the soul. On the cross, perhaps he experienced such felt absence for the first time. We speculate—but something gave rise to such a cry. Clearly, Jesus did not die the peaceful death of a Socrates. He begged in the garden not to have to drink the cup (Matt 26:39); in the end, he drank it to the bitter dregs.

In Moltmann's classic work that "landed like a bombshell on the playground of the theologians,"[41] he pointed out how realization of the suffering of God opens up a true Trinitarian understanding of the cross, but it is centered upon the cry of dereliction. He could say:

> Basically, every Christian theology is consciously or unconsciously answering the question, "Why has thou forsaken me?," when their doctrines of salvation say "for this reason" or "for that reason." In the face of Jesus' death-cry to God, theology either becomes impossible or becomes possible only as specifically Christian theology.[42]

Doing justice to the suffering of God in the Father and the Son on the cross is the test of any theology, just as suffering is. Moltmann adds, "By the standards of the cry of the dying Jesus for God, theological systems collapse at once in their inadequacy."[43] Given the recent turn toward affirming God's suffering, our theology is just now coming to grips with its meaning. Will it take the next three or four hundred years to grasp this mystery as it did to formulate adequately the basic understanding of the Trinity? In any case, it allows us to consider the way God takes within Godself the deepest darkness of humankind. When early theologians argued for the true humanity of Christ based on the idea that what God did not assume, God could not save, they still assumed that God did not suffer. What would this formula mean if God can suffer, that the Father can suffer the death of the Son on the cross? It would mean, again with Moltmann, that this "'bifurcation' in God must contain the whole uproar of history within itself."[44] Somehow salvation and the highest hope is tied to the deepest loss and despair. Rather than seeing, as have many early theologians, that Christ's divinity lay in his deeds of power and his weakness in his humanity, one can see from the perspective of the cross, as Moltmann says, "God is not more divine than he is in this humanity."[45] Here we are closer to Paul when he says, "God's weakness is stronger than human strength" (1 Cor 1:25).

We should also remember, however, that many others were crucified, and, of course, many have died terrible deaths. What made Jesus' death special was not just the physical suffering but presumably also the spiritual; it was something manifested in his whole life, especially the resurrection. However one understands the two natures, the cross had to do with the understanding that "in Christ God was reconciling the world to himself" (2 Cor 5:19). It had to do with Christ's calling to be whom he was called to be, realizing that it would bring him into deadly confrontation with the principalities and powers of his day, leading ultimately to a tragic death. In some way, God was in Christ at the cross, suffering also the cost of creation—and redemption. God experienced in Christ the destructive powers loosed in creation and fallenness and took them into the divine experience. The Christian confession is that this occurred in a unique way in Christ. The union of the divine and human at the cross nevertheless involved the anguish, tragedy, and loss of death. We hear it in the Godforsaken death cry of Jesus. Part of Jesus' agony is that he hears nothing from God—until later.

Jesus' Resurrection

Jesus' death would have represented another failed messianic hope, along with several others even in his own time, apart from what happened next. His followers were dismayed and disillusioned at Jesus' death. However little clarity there is about the awareness of details that Jesus knew ahead of time, and scholars debate this question, it is clear that the disciples had no hope of resurrection at the cross. They could well have been comforted by belief in Jesus' life after death in some kind of intermediate state awaiting the final resurrection.[46] Their grief was that Jesus had not been who they understood him to be; he had not been vindicated and upheld by God.

The shock that they experienced was that the unexpected and unbelievable occurred, according to the testimony enshrined in the New Testament—Jesus not only was alive in an intermediate state, he had been resurrected. But resurrection was not supposed to occur until the consummation of the kingdom that Jesus had preached, for the hope of which they had given up everything. Nothing had been able to dissuade them from the common presupposition that the Messiah was connected with the final consummation and the final resurrection at that time. And why would they? Only perhaps if they had been able to have "ears to hear." Despite Jesus' teaching, they had not changed their presuppositions on that point. Their breakthrough had been to accept Jesus as the Messiah but not to change their conceptions of the Messiah or of resurrection.

Whatever they experienced, there is consistent testimony in the early church that they experienced Jesus as resurrected, which was only to happen at the consummation of the kingdom. This also clearly meant, contrary to their doubt and despair, that God must have vindicated him after all; Jesus was, in fact, the Messiah. Talk about new wine being poured into old wineskins! Little wonder that it took several hundred years just to work out the basics of what happened. Initially it was all that they could do just to accept these two things, two things that both fit and did not fit their theologies. The Messiah had been resurrected, that could fit. That the Messiah had been resurrected in the midst of history, that could not fit. They possessed the concepts of Messiah, consummation, kingdom, and resurrection, all of which were supposed to happen together. Somehow these had been torn apart temporally, and they had to put them back together theologically. The resurrection of Jesus had already occurred, which meant that Jesus had been vindicated, which then meant that he was indeed the Messiah, which also meant that the kingdom had in some sense already begun. Who said that matters of faith do not involve logical reasoning?! Of course, they also realized that the kingdom in its fullness was not yet, and the general resurrection of the dead had not occurred, and the Messiah had not been clearly revealed to all. Never was the demand for theology greater.[47]

The varied details of the resurrection cannot obscure the consistent testimony of the early Christians. Jesus had been raised bodily from the dead; he was not only alive as in an intermediate state like all the faithful, he was the first fruits of the coming general resurrection. The experience of Jesus would have made little sense apart from the concepts that allowed the early Christians to interpret it. It made little enough sense as it was. What we see is that, despite the bursting of their wineskins, enough was left over to grasp the larger significance of what had happened. It was not just that they were happy about what had happened to their friend. They knew that what had happened to Jesus portended something of universal significance for all of them. The coming kingdom of God had broken into history in an unprecedented way, rivaling the exodus, rivaling the Davidic kingdom in the promised land, rivaling the return from exile. Like the powerful smell of the anointing oil when the flask was broken to anoint Jesus' feet by the unnamed woman of the street, never had the flavor of the consummation of history so flooded history itself.

The significance of resurrection can hardly be appreciated apart from the stress and strains of this larger story. When one adds that this was the resurrection of the crucified one, who just a few days before had died the most ignominious death possible, one can hardly imagine their first attempts to put "Humpty Dumpty back together again." It makes us appreciate the basic nature of God as the Spirit who is uncontrollable, which like a wind blows where it wills (John 3:8). Concerning the amazing and miraculous return from Israel's exile in Babylon, God says, "Do not remember the former things, or consider the things of old. I am about to do a new thing; now it springs forth, do you not perceive it?" (Isa 43:18-19). We often minimize the question, wondering why the disciples did not perceive it more easily. When we "live into" the experience of these first disciples, in turn despairing, then mystified, then hoping beyond hope, we can appreciate the significance of this question. Can we ever keep up with God?

The resurrection is the resurrection of the crucified one. The crucified one is the resurrected one. These balancing confessions lay at the heart of the Gospels. Forgetting or neglecting either is to miss essential dimensions of the Gospels. Of course, in light of our concentration on Jesus' life, we should add that the crucified and resurrected one is none other than Jesus of Nazareth who told parables, who did parables, and who was a parable of the kingdom of God. The words and works of Jesus were part and parcel of his being the crucified and resurrected Messiah.

The purpose of theology is not necessarily to provide an apologetic or proof for the resurrection. Given its nature, it could hardly be affirmed apart from faith and wider considerations. For example, if a naturalist was already convinced that there was no God or transcendent reality, one would not get very far appealing to witnesses of the resurrection. On the other hand, for those who are open, the witnesses provide, not proof, but a grounding for faith, including the startling reference in Paul that the risen Christ "appeared to more than five hundred brothers and sisters at one time, most of whom are still alive" (1 Cor 15:6). We do not have videotape confirmation or lengthy explanations of what happened. Scholars debate whether it was a historical event or a nonhistorical event. If one follows the accounts, it fits neither. The important thing was whether resurrection happened—and on this the early disciples did not waver.

What we do have, even for some who are more skeptical, is a situation in which a plausible reason—perhaps even the most plausible reason—for the accounts is that Jesus actually rose from the dead. As we pointed out, most of his followers would not have been surprised that Jesus experienced an afterlife, that he was still alive, and might even have appeared in dreams or visions. They would not have expected his resurrection before the end of the age. In this light, what is so striking is that there was no debate about what it was that Jesus had experienced, namely, resurrection. Such conviction provides a foundation that it was indeed an experience of the risen Lord that produced such a transformation. Nevertheless, even as Calvin pointed out, the evidence is insufficient apart from the experience of the risen Lord through the "internal testimony of the Holy Spirit."[48] Other explanations such as the disciples stealing away the body (then being willing to die for a deception), mass hallucinations, confusing the tombs, are not very convincing either. For a historical faith, the historical basis is what one would expect. The life, cross, and resurrection of Christ are the proper places to find the strongest historical roots and warrants. The historical roots *are* there, which is better than them *not* being there: for example, no evidence apart from Scripture that Jesus ever existed (say, for several centuries, as in the case of the Buddha), great disagreement on whether it was resurrection, significant evidence that Jesus was later seen as obviously resuscitated and not resurrected (as *The DaVinci Code* desires), and so on; but the claim of resurrection also requires more than a neutral historical assessment. It requires openness to God, an experience with God, and in the end, faith.

Jesus' Birth

It probably strikes the reader as odd that Jesus' birth is placed here, *after* the events of Jesus' life, rather than at the beginning. The reason is to situate it in its canonically *theological* place. The rest of Jesus' life is given primary emphasis. The earliest witnesses seem not to mention or possibly even be aware of what we call the virgin birth. It is not in Paul or Mark; it does not appear later in Hebrews or John, both of which have probably the highest Christologies in the New Testament. The virgin birth, or better, the virginal conception, then is likely best placed within the background of the rich texture of the rest of Jesus' life in mind. Grenz makes a good point in light of this that, unlike the life, death, and resurrection of Christ, the virgin birth is not so much a *ground* of faith as an *object* of faith.[49] Its happening could hardly appeal to witnesses at the time, and later did not have witnesses, even in the canon. On the other hand, given that it does appear in two of the Gospels, what is its meaning?

This question is colored by the fact that for evangelicals, belief in the virgin birth was placed as one of the five fundamentals of fundamentalism, a place that, as we have seen, it does not have even in the Bible.[50] This misunderstanding makes it difficult for conservative Christians to consider its canonical shape. Another misunderstanding is to think that the virgin birth was necessary for Jesus to be divine. This would put Jesus on a par with the Greek and Roman mythologies of semidivine beings fathered by one of the gods. Some think that Mark and John might have avoided dealing with it altogether precisely to avoid this implication. Rather, it seems that Jesus could easily have been conceived in a nonmiraculous way and still have been incarnate, just as he was incarnate in being born at all, being born poor, or being born in a stable. In fact, in the early church, the virgin birth was used not so much to support the divinity of Christ but to support Christ's true humanity. Later, it was seen as heresy to deny Jesus' full humanity. We can come close to doing so if we misunderstand the virgin birth as making Jesus somehow not fully human. Another historical misunderstanding has been to think that Mary had to be sinless herself, and even her womb was not opened in the birth. This view again reveals an inability to accept Jesus' full humanity, his full incarnation, and further extends to make even Mary not fully human. This tendency partakes more of the gnostic deprecation of the physical than of God's blessing of the material world.

Positively, what does the virgin birth mean? It reflects, it seems, God's affirmation that this child is the truly incarnate one. Perhaps it helps to pair it with the baptism, where a dove alights upon Jesus, designating him as the Son in whom God is well pleased. Both are miracles that affirm Jesus' calling and destiny. Neither was necessary in an absolute sense; neither made Jesus less than fully human; neither made Jesus divine. Both testify to who Jesus is and foreshadow the destiny of Jesus. Ironically, one best understands both from the end, not the beginning. Perhaps both are best understood starting with a Christology from below.

CHRISTOLOGY FROM ABOVE

The church soon moved to consider Christ, however, not from below but from above. Their question was how to understand the divinity of Christ. Their conclusion was that Christ's divinity did not detract from his humanity; rather, as we saw in the opening case study, they supported each other to such an extent that they affirmed Christ as one person. Unfortunately, this understanding was more often the ideal than the reality. The idea of divinity often overwhelmed the idea of humanity. Such overemphasis sometimes went so far as to be named heresy. At other times popular piety, with good intentions, minimized Christ's humanity and made it difficult for Christians even to imagine Christ as fully human. The strong gnostic influence throughout the history of the church exacerbated this natural tendency, leading to the official denial of the reality of divine suffering—even on the cross. The "work" of Christ, then, is actually attenuated for most Christians. The biblical witness becomes not only undermined, its purpose is short-circuited. The ideal expressed by the early councils, beyond what even they could imagine, was that only by doing justice both to Christ's divinity and humanity could one understand and appropriate what Christ did. Perhaps only a transformation of worldly values can enable an intimation of how Christ's divinity is expressed in the suffering and weakness of his humanity. Even after two millennia of reflection, in some ways we are just beginning to realize the import of the ecumenical confessions. We have looked closely at relatively recent developments in doing justice to Christology from below. In order also to do justice to "Christology from above," we shall review the conciliar conclusions and then their implications for aspects of the divinity of Christ.

The Council of Chalcedon

As we saw in the chapter on the doctrine of God, the Councils of Nicaea and Constantinople, through severe exertion, concluded that the church could not avoid affirming both the divinity and humanity of Christ.[51] The Council of Ephesus, as we saw at the beginning of this chapter, concluded that Christ was unique in his oneness with the Logos. Rather than his being just a person who was very Spirit-filled, only more so, he was at all times one person as human and as the Logos. It was in his being one with the Logos that he was a Spirit-filled human who becomes our example of someone who walks with God. The question, however, returned again concerning whether Jesus Christ was an amalgam of humanity and divinity or whether he could always be seen as fully divine and fully human. In the way it was put at the time, was he "out of two natures" or "in two natures"? That question led to the fourth great ecumenical council, the Council of Chalcedon in 451.

It may help in preparation for understanding this council to note that two tendencies had been dominant in Christology from the Nicene Council. We have seen different emphases in the Alexandrian and Antiochene traditions. The former's view has been called a "Word-flesh" Christology, which tended to see the Word (Logos) as taking on the flesh of humanity but not full humanity. This more Platonic view, with its dualism of soul and body, preserved the "one person" but had difficulty with the two natures. It tended to see the Logos as providing the soul or mind of the physical body. Both Athanasius and Cyril, for example, basically had this view. On the other hand, the Antiochene school had what has been called a "Word-man" Christology, which tended to see the fully human and fully divine coming together in a moral union. They were more Aristotelian in seeing the body as incomplete without a soul. Thus, one could not have a full human nature without a full human mind and soul. They did justice to the two natures but had difficulty seeing Christ as one person. While the Alexandrian school leaned toward the heresy of Apollinarianism, the Antioch school leaned toward the heresy of Nestorianism. This tension is similar to the tension that we have seen in the Trinitarian discussions between those who emphasized oneness and those who emphasized three-ness. What the church labored to find was a way to do justice to the strengths of each while avoiding the weaknesses—all the while in the midst of politics and petty rivalry.

Cyril had been successful in preserving the emphasis on the one person of Christ. After Cyril died, his successor Dioscurus also schemed to advance Alexandria by theological means. Dioscuros supported Eutyches of Constantinople, a partisan of Cyril and also a friend of Chrysaphius, the imperial favorite minister for Theodosius II. Eutyches was charged with confusing the two natures of Christ. He said, "I confess that our Lord was of two natures before the union, but after the union one nature."[52] He was understood to mean that the natures resulted in a semidivine being, but he could also be understood as representing Cyril's view, namely, that the incarnation represented a being of one person and one nature. Perhaps Eutyches himself was unclear, which was the verdict of Leo who said that Eutyches was a "confused and unskilled thinker."[53] Anyone who has attempted to work through the subtleties of these arguments may well have sympathy with Eutyches. In any case, Eutyches was con-demned by the successor to Nestorius in Constantinople, Flavian, whose sympathies seemed to be with the Antioch school. At this point, the focus against Eutyches was on preserving the integrity of the two natures as the way to maintain the divinity and humanity of Jesus Christ. This point, of course, had been well established in the first two councils of Nicaea and Constantinople.

To Dioscuros' surprise, when the case went to the able Pope Leo I, he supported Flavian and wrote the famous "Leo's *Tome*" in 449. Pope Leo represented the view of the West—virtually since Tertullian—that "there was born true God in the entire and perfect nature of true man, complete in his own properties, complete in ours."[54] Dioscuros then turned to the emperor, who called the so-called "robber's synod" at Ephesus in 449. Here Dioscuros' support for Eutyches temporar-ily won the day. Eutyches was restored. Flavian was condemned and died soon after, rumored to be as a result violence at the meeting! The alliance between Alexandria and Rome had been ruptured. Leo tried and got nowhere with Theodosius II, but he had influence with the emperor's sister Pulcheria. Then, as fate would have it, Theodosius accidentally died, leaving Pulcheria and her husband, Marcian, on the throne. The theological tables turned.

The new emperor called the Fourth Ecumenical Council at Chalcedon in 451. Dioscuros was now exiled and soon died. The Ephesus Council of two years earlier was rejected. A new creed was adopted. The new creed stated that Christ was "truly God and truly man," "*homoousion* with the Father" and "*homoousion* with us according to the manhood," "in two natures," "one person (*prosopon*) and one subsistence (*hypostasis*)." This council thus completed the classic formulation of the early church, largely agreed upon since by both the Eastern and Western churches, as well as by the Protestant churches, namely, that Jesus Christ is fully divine and fully human, one person in two natures. The emphasis of the Alexandrians that Christ was one person after the union was affirmed, while the important Antiochene tenets of Christ's full humanity and full divinity after the incarnation were also affirmed.

The compromise of the Chalcedonian Council did not fully satisfy adherents of either camp. As we have mentioned, Nestorianism continued. In the East, dissatisfaction with the "two-nature" doctrine continued. In the seventh century, the Eastern church asserted that Christ had one will and energy, called "monothelitism" (one-will-ism). The Western pope used this against them to reassert Western primacy (and two wills corresponding to two natures) in the Sixth Ecumenical Council at Constantinople in 680–681. This council declared that Christ had "two natural wills or willings . . . not contrary one to the other . . . but His human will follows, not as resisting or reluctant, but rather as subject to His divine and omnipotent will."[55] Despite the politics, this asserted the way that the divine works through the human and that it does not just override it. The monothelite position emphasized the human as a passive, and perhaps not genuine, instrument of the Logos.

The effect of these deliberations over several centuries was momentous once one considers the diversity at the beginning of the third century. A full Trinitarian and christological position had been laid out, with hard-won fine-tuning of the way any affirmation could be misconstrued if not balanced by a statement on the other side. These reflections thus underline several key factors. One is the importance of paying attention to balance in any theological reflection. After several centuries of such speculation, rooted in soteriology as it was, one can be forgiven for the impression that abstract theology had left simple discipleship of Jesus of Nazareth far behind. This is probably true, even appreciating the gain in the understanding of Christology that it represented.[56] The long-lasting effect has meant that movements in the church have tried again and again to pull the church back to its roots, much like the current "emergent church" movement, sometimes swinging to an antitheological extreme.[57] What is needed is not one or the other but the right balance. A second need is the acknowledgement that theological reflection always takes place in an incarnate situation, which includes the presence of human frailties and politics but also human desires for truth and "to get it right." A third is to recognize that the early councils did not fully explain everything but were carefully establishing parameters for further reflection.

The Divinity of Christ

With the divine dimension of Christ in full view, we can consider some aspects of Christology that could hardly be treated with a focus on his humanity.

Preexistence. By the preexistence of Christ, we refer to the reasoning reflected in the Gospel of John, Ephesians, and Colossians that the implication of Jesus being Lord is that he could not have begun to exist at conception. As mysterious as the incarnation itself, John's identification of Jesus as the Logos connotes that the Christ relates to the word by which God spoke the world into existence in Genesis 1 and to Wisdom, who was personified as God's partner in creation according to Proverbs. The divine nature that constituted the one person of Christ in the later Trinitarian reflections thus is the second person of the Trinity. As a "person" of the Trinity, of the one God, this "person" could not have failed to exist from all time. This is an important part of the meaning of the rejection of Arianism, which saw the Logos as the supreme creature but begotten at some point in time ("there once was when he was not"). Colossians puts this even more strongly, if possible: the one in whom "all things hold together" is this Christ (1:17).

As we have seen, this does not detract from Christ's full humanity. However one understands the incarnation, perhaps as kenotic emptying or laying aside of some divine attributes (based on Phil 1:7), we can still affirm Christ's humanity—and must. Yet this same human is affirmed as fully divine and worshipped as Lord, which could not be appropriate for anyone less than God.

Christ's preexistence has another oft-neglected implication. John and Colossians tie the preexistence of Christ to creation, which supports again the significance of creation and its basic goodness and value. It meshes with the incarnation itself. The one through whom God created the world became flesh, became fully "en-worlded," if you will. With the divine creation and the divine becoming human in the incarnation, the implication that Christianity is a most "worldly" religion is undergirded. It underscores the irony in the way that Christianity has often taken on the more Platonic tones of being otherworldly.

John also says that this incarnate one, as pre-existent, is the "true light, which enlightens everyone" (John 1:9). This gives a cosmic dimension to Christ and expands the meaning of the later words in John, "I am the way, the truth, and the life" (14:6). Because of the significance of preexistence in John 1, one cannot confine or even tame these words into a private, religious sphere. Certainly one could not go to the extreme of some medieval thinkers who believed that religious truth and philosophical truth could be incompatible. Rather, they point in the direction of Arthur Holmes' words, "All truth is God's truth." Wherever truth is found, it is rooted in the preexistent Logos.

The Descent into Hell. An even more mysterious dimension of Christ is affirmed every Sunday in church after church. The Apostles' Creed testifies that Jesus "descended into Hell," which was apparently not part of the early kerygma to which Paul refers in 1 Corinthians but is alluded to elusively in 1 Peter (3:19; 4:6).

Historically, there has been little uncertainty about this confession, being taken rather literally and simply as Christ after death entering hades and emerging triumphant over it. This could refer to the hades of the Old Testament that was the holding place for all of the dead. In this sense, it was often thought, following 1 Peter's implication, that Christ proclaimed the gospel to all of the dead, including the righteous dead from Old Testament times, who had looked forward to the Messiah in faith as the book of Hebrews said (11:39-40). These then followed Christ out of hades into heaven. Some thought that this might include even righteous Gentiles who responded to the gospel, perhaps having the "circumcision of the heart" to which Paul alludes in Romans 2. Others have thought that Christ simply proclaimed his triumph to the wicked in hell, which is taken more in the New Testament sense of the place for the wicked. The lack of a clear biblical basis makes this strongly traditional confession more speculative than preexistence.

We will look more closely at its implications for life after death when dealing with eschatology, but at this point we can emphasize its symbolic value as representing that Christ died in the fullest sense. He was not only fully divine and fully human, he was fully dead—he experienced fully the "sting of death," and the triumph did not come until resurrection.

Ascension and Postexistence. Another area of mystery and speculation is the ascension. The Gospels and Acts attest that after the resurrection, Jesus Christ ascended into heaven. Matthew has the risen Christ saying to the disciples, "All authority on heaven and on earth has been given to me." Later in Acts, at Stephen's death he sees Christ "standing at the right hand of the Father." At the time, it was pictured as Christ simply rising into the clouds, which fit their cosmology but not ours: people do not think of Christ simply as being up in the sky; again, the meaning lies in its symbolism. It represents a break between the resurrection appearances and the later spiritual experiences of the risen Christ. This is significant in apologetics in that sometimes the resurrection itself is seen as being much like current spiritual experiences of the presence of God in Christ.[58] To the contrary, the early disciples clearly distinguished between the experiences of the risen Christ and their later, ongoing experiences of being "in Christ." Even Paul, who claimed to have been the last to experience the risen Christ on the Damascus road, saw him only that once and not in his continuing sense that "Christ lives in me" (Gal 2:20).

Moreover, it points to the sense in which the kingdom of God, which as proclaimed by Jesus had a "now and not yet" quality, continues that dynamic relationship. Something happened in Christ. The powers of the kingdom continue to be available just as in Jesus' ministry, even though they appear hidden and even nonexistent in the eyes of the world. The power of forgiveness, of new life, and of the mission of the kingdom of God continues through the Christ who is exalted at the right hand of God. This reign has often been understood in triumphalist terms, as the coercive reign of the church, often with the aid of the sword of the state. This is what Martin Luther called the theology of glory. Yet Christ's reign can hardly be understood apart from the paradox of power, where God's power is not manifested as worldly power but as weakness. Christ is powerful as the resurrected one, to be sure, but always as the crucified one. Luther called this the theology of the cross. The establishment of the kingdom of peace, the "beloved community," is the "not yet" of the kingdom. The "now" is the cross-marked presence of the power of Christ in the midst of a world that Paul still saw as "groaning in labor pains" (Rom 8:22). Christ has risen and ascended but still serves—even as Christ's body the church continues to suffer. This is human weakness as the power of God.

The Spirit of Christ. We will focus on the Holy Spirit more in the next two chapters, but there is a place here to see the Holy Spirit as especially the Spirit of Christ in light of the risen Christ. One cannot grasp the significance of the risen and ascended Christ apart from the Trinitarian context of the Spirit of Christ. Such a connection is intimated by Paul, where he can refer in one verse to the Spirit, the Spirit of God, and then to the Spirit of Christ (Rom 8:9). John, too, powerfully depicts the Spirit as the Paraclete, another Counselor, who takes Jesus' place and represents his presence in a transforming new way (John 14–16).

The Spirit of Christ, like the cosmic Christ, must be understood as larger than the visible church. Neither God the Creator, the Christ, nor the Comforter can be limited to the church, although we will understand the church as the special focus of divine activity. For missional purposes, this helps us see that missionaries do not first bring Christ to unreached groups. Through the Holy Spirit, Christ is already there. The Creator Christ has always been there. The cosmic Christ, the Spirit of truth, has always been there. The risen Christ, through the Paraclete, continues reaching out, convicting, and drawing all to himself. This is an encouraging word to missionaries of all kinds. Their work is crucial, but they cannot take God's place. God is always already at work, and we are called not to begin but to join in the dance, so to speak.

THE LIBERATING CHRIST

Paul Tillich, in his classic *The Courage to Be*, indicated how the gospel is an answer to existential questions.[59] He thought that the question of finitude and mortality of the ancient world was answered in the resurrection of Christ. The medieval preoccupation with sin and guilt was answered by the cross of Christ. The modern questions of meaning were answered by the teachings and life of Christ, as well as the future hope. Along these lines, this overview shows that Christology has never been an academic exercise; it has always been a matter of salvation, liberation, and hope. For Christianity, Christ is the center of such hopes. In recent years, liberation theologians in dire situations of physical suffering have reacted to the emphasis on the inner suffering of guilt and meaning to outward issues of liberation. At best, they have not rejected these other aspects of liberation or their centrality but have called for recovery of the full implications of Jesus' salvation as manifested in Jesus' own life and ministry. The nature of the incarnation and Christ have been central in these concerns. We will explore in the next chapter the wider extent of salvation, but at the end of this focus on Christ, it will be helpful to look at the significance of Christ's identification with all of the needy and oppressed. This is crucial because of the constriction of

Christ sometimes to the rich and powerful of this world rather than to the poor and weak.

Liberation theology especially thinks of Christ as identifying with the oppressed.[60] The poor think of Christ as poor. African-American theologians have emphasized further that they can understand Christ as black.[61] This is a further step since the historical Jesus was indeed poor but presumably brown, not black—even though this might come as a surprise to many Caucasians who picture Jesus as being blond and blue-eyed. Black theology does not deny the historical particularities of the incarnation but stresses that the risen Christ identifies with the particularities of all people, especially with the needy and marginalized—just as God did, according to the prophets, and Jesus did, according to the Gospels. Rather than assuming that Jesus' physical characteristics, whatever they were, were privileged, the point is that God identifies through Christ with all people. Thus, one may not prefer brown skin color over black, or black eyes over blue, or any other particularity of the incarnation in the Middle East.

Recently, a study was done by forensic anthropologists to discover what Jesus looked like. They proceeded by coming up with an average, composite first-century male in Palestine. The result is a broad-faced, black-haired person about 5'1" and 110 pounds. This may be what Jesus looked like, but even if it were known what Jesus' appearance was, it would not matter. Theologically, the point is that his historical particularity does not prevent his identification with others but actually fosters the way the risen Christ can identify with any particular person. God not only makes humans in God's own image but also takes on that image as the incarnate and risen Christ in order to reach oppressed persons at the very core of their identity.[62]

Moreover, theological implications arise on two sides. One side gives permission for all cultures, as they have tended to do anyway, to picture Jesus in their own image. If the incarnation had occurred in their culture, Jesus would have looked like them. The physical particulars are contingent, not necessary. The other side prevents anyone from privileging their cultural appearance over others, which is also what all cultures have tended to do. It is crucial to be able to identify Christ as one's own color—but also as every other human color. Perhaps this is why, in the providence of God, we have no physical description of Jesus.

A logical but further implication has been drawn by feminist liberation theologians. Just as the risen Christ can be seen as a short black-haired black man or a tall Chinese man, the risen Christ can be seen as female.[63] There is no reason to privilege gender over skin color or hair color or any other contingent particularity of incarnation. People are quick to point out that a woman would not have had a hearing in Jesus' day, a likely reason for the historical Jesus being male. This is probably true, but it is also an important thing to realize that this fact is contingent, not essential. If the incarnation had occurred in a matriarchal culture, presumably the Christ would have been incarnated as a woman.

Oddly, the church has historically been quick to see that other aspects of the incarnation were contingent but has fastened upon gender as the one exception—with devastating results to women. The church itself has often taken the lead in suppressing rather than liberating women, even though particular Christians have taken the lead in liberating women. Since women are seen as fully in the image of God in Scripture, it is surprising that Christians presume that the incarnation had to be male. This was part of the reasoning that led to a male priesthood. Yet when one examines this reasoning theologically, it contradicts several central emphases of Scripture. Such myopic thought has been used to see women as less in the image of God, closer to evil, and less spiritual than men, who were therefore thought to be able to mediate grace and thus be priests in a way that women could not. If there are reasons for women not to be full leaders in the church, they should not be located here, in Christology. Neither can they be found in terms of the image of God. Such reasoning contradicts the central point of the incarnation as God's identification with humanity, all humanity. Women should be able to identify with Christ as fully as any other human, who might perhaps look different than the historical Jesus, as most do in one way or another, but who still could imagine Christ as having been incarnate in them.

Eleanor McLaughlin uses a powerful illustration from C. S. Lewis' *The Lion, the Witch, and the Wardrobe*. She says:

> The most pleased of the lot was the other lion, who kept running about everywhere pretending to be very busy but really in order to say to everyone he met, "Did you hear what he said? *Us lions*. That means him and me. *Us lions*."[64]

McLaughlin then adds, "Women yearn for the experience of the newly freed lions of Narnia, to hear the icon of God say, 'Us *women*.'"[65]

The emphasis of Christology is that "we love because he first loved us" (1 John 4:19). God took the initiative in coming to all people through the historical specificity of an incarnation in Jesus of Nazareth. The point of the incarnation, as Jesus' entire life, death, and resurrection so clearly showed, was not to exclude anyone but to identify with and embrace everyone. Christ became incarnate not just for a certain culture, a certain race, a certain skin color, or a certain gender—it was to represent all. This is not a generic, tasteless "all," however; it is that each person, especially "the least of these," can identify with Christ because Christ has identified with them. The christological issue is that Christ has identified with all people; the soteriological question is whether people in turn are willing to identify with Christ, and to that question we now turn.

SALVATION
The Way

Besides Christology, no other area of systematic theology draws more attention than *soteriology*, the doctrine of salvation. Practically speaking, it draws the most interest. If Paul Tillich is right that our ultimate concern, God, has to do with our being and nonbeing, then the meaning of our understanding of God is focused on the issue of salvation. This is the existential question of questions. Sin reminds us of our brokenness and estrangement; salvation provides hope that there is an answer.

Early Christians did not refer to themselves as Christians; they referred to themselves as followers of the Way (Acts 9:2). Salvation has to do with being able to embark upon the Way, continue upon the Way, and arrive at the destination. Interestingly, in the New Testament, salvation is described as happening in the past, "we have been saved"; as happening presently, "we are being saved"; and as happening in the future, "we will be saved." Unfortunately, in some conservative traditions that emphasize conversion, revivalism, and evangelism, such as my own Baptist tradition, salvation has been seen only in the first sense, as the beginning. More accurately, it is described as punctiliar, as happening all at once, beginning and ending, as it were. The result has been an anemic understanding of the Christian life or discipleship, called "sanctification." Sometimes following the Way, living the Christian life, is presented as an option: You have been saved; if you wish, you can follow Christ. Salvation and discipleship have been cleanly separated, an example of the human propensity of tearing asunder what God never imagined as separate. One would have to search long and hard in the Bible for such a separation. We will explore in this chapter some of the reasons for this distortion and see how they are closely related to the images or metaphors that we habitually use for salvation. In part, we have a truncated vocabulary and imagination. Rather than employing the plethora of images that abound in Scripture, we tend to coalesce around one or two and then suffer the limitations of any image. This problem is exacerbated by the fact that the most dominant image among evangelicals has perhaps contributed the most to a truncation of understanding the Christian journey; we will have to consider how fair and valid these criticisms are.

On the other hand, some groups, especially in the Wesleyan holiness tradition, so emphasize the Christian life that sinlessness is posited as expected, often as a result of a miraculous second blessing. The result sometimes is a fear of losing one's salvation, over and over. Again, we will explore the various images of salvation to understand why this emphasis might occur and also its strengths and weaknesses.

In probing the theological understanding of the doctrine of salvation, we can never lose sight of its existential meaning. The beginning of the Christian life can involve the anguish of repentance and regret along with the miracle of forgiveness, new spiritual life, and hope. It cannot avoid the question, however, of the challenge of becoming more Christlike, which continues to involve struggle with sin and failure as well as growth in peace and other fruits of the Spirit. The Christian emphasis on grace supposedly transcended a religion of legalism, but Christians constantly have lapsed back into legalism, exemplified especially by Galatians in the New Testament. The struggle that Christ had with legalism in the New Testament has been constantly replayed throughout Christian history. It is likely a besetting temptation to any Christian. What are the expectations of growth in the Christian life? How does one balance the centrality of grace with strong assumptions of growth, even works? What is the difference between works in the sense of meriting salvation and works that are expected fruits of salvation? What is the place of practices that are a part of Christian transformation into the image of Christ? And can one begin to understand the Way of Jesus Christ in this life apart from the context of expectations for the consummation of salvation, namely, eschatology? Do such eschatological hopes help or hinder the practice of faith in this life?

We will begin to explore salvation with a couple of case studies, one drawn from Scripture and the other from contemporary life. Then we will look at the divine side, we might say, of salvation with the understanding of what has been called "atonement." What did God do for us in Christ? We will follow with the meaning of atonement for us, for the beginning of the Christian life and then for its continuance in sanctification.

CASE STUDY: THE PARABLE OF THE PRODIGAL SON

Drawing on the parable of the Prodigal Son (Luke 15:11-32) as a case study might be surprising since it is already a biblical example, not a contemporary one, and, as a parable, it is not even purportedly an actual event. Nevertheless, since the significance of the images for salvation have been so crucial, as already intimated, it is important to keep grounded in the New Testament. It is not that images are bad; every view of salvation is rooted in a metaphor. The question is more of where one places an image in relation to other images, that is, what image is more central, and how is it balanced by other images?

It is therefore difficult to dispute the centrality of the parable of the Prodigal Son for understanding salvation because it crystallizes so much of Jesus' message and practice. Despite this significance, as we shall see, sometimes the meaning of this parable can be almost wholly eclipsed by other images.[1]

The parable is striking in several ways. The younger son's plea for his inheritance was already a slap in the face of the father, virtually a wish that his father were already dead. The extravagance of the father's later response is intensified already by the excessive ill will and foolishness of the son. The father surprisingly accedes to the request, whereupon the prodigal becomes in fact a prodigal, following a pattern often seen today of people receiving a great wealth, thinking it will last forever, and finding it soon gone. In Jewish eyes, he fell as low as possible, not only in his moral bankruptcy but finally in caving in to feed swine and then in desperate hunger to crave even their food for himself. Again, the son's extremities serve to highlight the drama of his desire to return. When he "came to himself" (Luke 15:17) and desired to go back home, wondering if his father at least might be prevailed upon to take him back as a hired hand, it is likely that the quick reply that would jump to most hearer's minds would be "fat chance." In wonderment, we return to the father who, while his son was still far in the distance, sees his son and actually runs to him—the father does not walk or wait (v. 20). The suggestion is that the father has been waiting and gazing into the distance; this much we can understand. The rest we cannot. Before the son can utter his repentance, the father embraces him and kisses him. The father orders that the son be clothed with the best clothes and that a fatted calf be killed, "for this son of mine was dead and is alive again; he was lost and is found!" (v. 24). In a society of honor and shame, with great attention to rules and protocol, all the rules are broken. Rather, they are shattered by an extravagant love and forgiveness. In many of Jesus' parables, the elements of excess and shock are present. When humans encounter God's love and grace, in Jesus' eyes, they can hardly take it in. It bursts the wineskins.

In the attempts to make sense of salvation and atonement, we cannot lose sight of this surplus of grace, for our human tendency is always to rein it in; we will see this even in prominent theories of atonement. Here we take up the rest of the story, who some see as the main character of the story, the elder brother. He is the one who wants to make sense of things, to bring things back into perspective, to make them proportionate and manageable. And he has a point. While many want to identify with the prodigal, and can at some level, most will likely resemble the elder brother, the one who wants what he has coming and resents someone else getting something for nothing, especially one who receives far beyond what he deserves. Yet it is the elder brother who is reprimanded; he is the one who is called upon to forget his calculations and "celebrate" (Luke 15:32). Christianity again and again has been marked by this explosive, uncontainable surplus of grace—in Christ, in Paul, in Augustine, in Luther, in Wesley—yet it is also easily lost or misunderstood, even in the church, which has constantly fallen back toward legalism and what we call "works righteousness."

This parable is accentuated by the parables of the lost sheep and lost coin that precede it in Luke 15; the former is also recounted in Matthew 18:12-14. The stories are deceptively simple. The first begins, "Which one of you, having a hundred sheep and losing one of them, does not leave the ninety-nine in the wilderness and go after the one that is lost until he finds it?" (Luke 15:4). While this might be true of sheep, it was not true in the religious realm. The Jewish practice might receive proselytes but would not generally go seeking them. Again, the story is surprising, shocking, and excessive. The shepherd seeks "until he finds it." Then he calls others to "rejoice with me" (v. 6). The woman who has ten coins (each worth a day's wage) and loses one, then desperately searches until she finds it, makes a similar point (vv. 8-10). The Johannine tradition, consistent with these parables, intimates that of all the things that one can say of God, the most direct is "God is love" (1 John 4:8).

It is difficult to transcend the simple power of these stories and their picture of a loving Heavenly Father (or Mother with the image of the woman with the lost coin) that even the church has struggled to exemplify. Much needs to be said as a supplement, and much more is said in the New Testament itself. The point is that our commentary should support—not replace, distort, or undermine—these parables. They will serve as a crucial touchstone because it is easy to lose our way as we track the church's continuing struggle of faith seeking understanding of complicated issues of salvation that have absorbed the church ever since—the nature of atonement, Christian beginnings (conversion), and Christian growth (sanctification).

CASE STUDY: FORGIVENESS IN SERBIA

A more pointed, as well as more contemporary, case study concerns radical forgiveness as derived from theologian Miroslav Volf's immersion in the complex conflict of the former Yugoslavia as it fell into civil war.[2] Decades of Communist totalitarian rule had held in check centuries-long ethnic and religious unrest. In the aftermath of the fall of the totalitarian government, it became evident that such conflict had not dissipated but only simmered. Neighbors and classmates went to battle against each other in barbarous ways that eventually drew in all the major powers of the world.

Volf grew up in the Croatian home of a Pentecostal preacher. He did his doctoral work with Jürgen Moltmann in the German Reformed tradition and then went to teach for several years at Fuller Theological Seminary in Pasadena, California, one of the major evangelical seminaries in the United States.[3] He then went to his current position in systematic theology at Yale Divinity School. Besides exemplifying dramatically the picture of Christian faith as a journey in the midst of the worldwide church, he has grappled with the issue of forgiveness.

This was brought home to him especially by his teacher Moltmann after Volf had spoken of forgiveness. These are his words:

> After I finished my lecture Professor Jürgen Moltmann stood up and asked one of his typical questions, both concrete and penetrating: "But can you embrace a *četnik*?" It was the winter of 1993. For months now the notorious Serbian fighters called "*četnik*" had been sowing desolation in my native country, herding people into concentration camps, raping women, burning down churches, and destroying cities. I had just argued that we ought to embrace our enemies as God has embraced us in Christ. Can I embrace a *četnik*—the ultimate other, so to speak, the evil other? What would justify the embrace? Where would I draw the strength for it? What would it do to my identity as a human being and as a Croat? It took me a while to answer, though I immediately knew what I wanted to say. "No, I cannot—but as a follower of Christ I think I should be able to."[4]

Jesus' teachings on forgiveness are not meant for coffee-table discussion. They are meant in the context of his journey to the cross and in the midst of crises like the Balkan war. As Jacques Derrida put it, "Forgiveness forgives only the unforgivable."[5] This paradoxical statement means that forgiveness takes place where incommensurable harm has been done. There is no reciprocity here, no equivalence. The "economy of exchange," of tit for tat, quid pro quo—all are shattered. Law and obligation begin to lose their meaning, for forgiveness is not a legal requirement but an act of excessive grace. It does not belong to the impersonal arena of a law court but is a deeply personal, spiritual movement. In contexts like that of Volf, people testify that the capacity to forgive is itself an act of superabundant grace.

Even more significantly, forgiveness is at the heart of Christian salvation, for salvation means God's forgiveness of us, also unexpected, lavish, transforming. And the point is drawn as much as Jesus makes any point. If we expect to be forgiven by God, we should be willing to forgive others. It is almost too blunt: "If you do not forgive others, neither will your Father forgive your trespasses" (Matt 6:15). Forgiveness is something we receive that begins the journey of salvation and is a constant practice on the journey, as we are called upon to forgive others—and to be forgiven by others. It speaks to the meaning of atonement, what Christ has done for our salvation. It then speaks to our response, as we are continually taught to pray, "Forgive us our debts, as we also have forgiven our debtors" (Matt 6:12). How crucial is our repentance, and that of others, for forgiveness? What does it mean to forgive those who have no desire to repent? How does that relate to the demands of Christian justice? And to Christian love? Forgiveness is all about relationships; the personal dimension cannot be lost. Its purpose is to restore relationships. This will be significant as we reflect on the great models of atonement and salvation. But does forgiveness mean no repercussions? Volf was attempting to sort through all of these issues, which were inescapably real and concrete for him.

Keeping our eye on this central dimension of forgiveness will help us keep our focus also as we also consider the dimensions of salvation; in turn, considering the full nature of salvation will help us return, at the end, to these questions in connection with the Christian practice of forgiveness.

ATONEMENT: THE WORK OF CHRIST

Since the Reformation, a particular theory of atonement, the penal-substitionary, has been dominant, especially among evangelical Protestants. In that group, in fact, it is so dominant that it has come to be synonymous with atonement, and many would not be very comfortable even in terming it a "theory." A theory suggests limitations and implies other possible approaches. The rise of Fundamentalism almost a century ago further specified that this approach was one of the five fundamentals of the faith, making it synonymous with atonement per se.[6] In other words, rather than atonement being central, the penal-substitionary theory was named as central. This move has become problematic for several reasons, and further reflection on atonement has made it one of those areas of rich theological reconsideration.

The General Approach to the Atonement

An earlier version of the penal-substitutionary theory had been advanced by Anselm in the eleventh century.[7] Instead of being based on a legal metaphor, it was rooted in the medieval context of honor, where satisfaction must be given if someone's honor has been offended. The basic logic, however, of the penal-substitutionary view was already delineated in Anselm. Already in the medieval period, Abelard saw significant weaknesses in Anselm's theory and thus formulated the moral-influence theory. In a landmark work in 1930, Gustaf Aulén pointed out what should have been obvious, namely, that the satisfaction theory itself was a relative latecomer and had been preceded by another theory for the first millennium of the church, which he called the "classic" theory.[8] While not as thoroughly worked out as the later ones, it was still rich in detail. It was based on the metaphor of someone paying the ransom price for another to be freed from slavery and then developed in terms of Christ's war with, and defeat of, Satan.[9] This prominent role of Satan was one of the reasons that Anselm rejected it in favor of his model. Aulén and other proponents, however, emphasize more the spiritual warfare motif that also involves structural evil than "buying off" Satan.

Further, the new dialogue with Eastern orthodoxy has brought to the attention of Western theologians the fact that yet another model was also prominent in the first millennium of the church and has been significant ever since in the Orthodox Church, and that is the divinization model. Irenaeus saw this as "recapitulation."[10] This was a view that we have seen as being tremendously influential in the christological, conciliar debates, where it was understood that what Christ did not assume, Christ could not save. In other words, Christ, as fully divine, had to become fully incarnate, fully human, in order to save humans.

Several things are probably evident at this point. One is that the church has had several theories of atonement, not just one. In fact, the reflection on atonement is almost as varied as the christological debates. Second, *theory* might not be the best word because in our scientific context, it connotes something of somewhat factual and mathematical precision. Atonement models are based on metaphors that are then elaborated with varying degrees of detail. Third, the metaphors are rooted in their cultural context and make sense in that light. As metaphorical models, recalling our earlier discussion of metaphors, they must be seen as having strengths and limitations. Any metaphor must be affirmed and denied at certain points. So rather than being theoretical "scale models," they are "metaphorical models," which are illuminating of a mystery without necessarily dispelling it. In fact, the reliance on metaphors points to a reality so rich that it can hardly be spoken of in any other way and perhaps can never be exhausted in its rich metaphorical meaning and certainly not by literal language. Fourth, these models are all rooted in particular biblical metaphors. When one pays close attention to this dimension, one realizes that the Bible contains multiple metaphors that are neither drawn upon nor exhausted by any of the models taken singly or together. So one of the most important insights is that the Bible offers a reservoir of images that is even broader than the classical models.[11] If one is not already overwhelmed, these reflections suggest, fifth, not a limitation of models but an encouragement of more models to grasp such a rich and complex reality. Finally, in that spirit a new model has arisen in the contemporary Western context that fits well its context, namely, a relational model.

What this complex history suggests, besides the fact that a conciliar consensus never developed around models of the atonement as it did in Christology, is that in this area, a profusion of models is better, not worse. Rather than the impetus being to find the one and only model, it is better to discern the strengths and weakness of each model. The models then become complementary rather than competing. This situation is perhaps analogous to the situation in physics where models of electrons as waves and as particles are seen as distinct but complementary. This background also suggests that new models that speak powerfully to new and different contexts might erupt, without invalidating the older models. With this complementary rather than contradictory approach in mind, we will explore the major models mentioned above in their historical order.

The Ransom Model

Irenaeus in the second century is the major early source for this view. The world is in the thrall of the evil one, and Christ paid the necessary ransom to free humans from Satan's grasp. The root metaphor is that of paying a fee, a ransom, to free someone from bondage, much as Hosea in the Old Testament ransomed his wife Gomer from the slave block. It is rooted in Jesus' saying, "The Son of Man came not to be served but to serve, and to give his life as a ransom for many" (Matt 20:28). It is closely related to the image of redemption, where a price is paid to redeem someone from bondage. In this, as in most other cases, it is important to recognize that these images in the New Testament do not necessarily carry the theoretical freight of later theories. They are usually suggestive and open-ended rather than dense theoretical arguments. Most of the theories trade on the notion of sacrifice, as this one does for instance, but the idea of sacrifice, while pervasive, is never clearly explained in either the Old Testament or the New. The basic idea of giving up something valuable, especially lifeblood, as part of being in good relation to God is never fully developed. It is sometimes frustrating, in fact, to see so much detail in *how* to sacrifice but virtually none concerning *why*. This is where further theological reflection is virtually demanded by the very nature of Scripture itself.

This open-endedness of symbols such as sacrifice and ransom calls forth creativity but also critique. In the case of the ransom theory, early theologians—even someone as critical as Augustine—delighted in one of its extreme manifestations, called the "mousetrap theory."[12] The idea is that the humanity and cross of Christ were the bait, and the divinity was the trap, and so God caught Satan. Obviously, it implies that Satan was tricked and that God may have had to resort to such a trick to win—not the best model to emulate. This crude extreme was partly why the theory was so soundly rejected by later theologians like Anselm, who took Satan out of the picture altogether.

At best, the image points to the drama of spiritual conflict and the bondage of sin and evil. God is not subject to Satan but works within the parameters of freedom that God has set in creation to redeem humans through the power of suffering love. In its earlier form, it occurs somewhat abstracted from human life, as an event between God and Satan. In its modern form, especially as appropriated by liberation theologians, it is set firmly within history and portrays the constant way in which God is a liberator who battles with God's people to free people from all kinds of bondage. Justo González thus points out that it is a dynamic, historical, and practical view.[13]

The Recapitulation (Divinization) Model

Conjoined with the ransom theory was a view also held by Irenaeus, namely, that Christ takes on fallen humanity in order to reverse the process and bring redemption, thus recapitulating the story of humanity. This insight was parlayed into the christological debates as the key soteriological reason for affirming Christ's full humanity and full divinity. As Saint Gregory Nazianzen put it, "What has not been assumed has not been healed."[14] This view obviously puts great emphasis on the incarnation, while atonement is often connected just with the cross due to the popularity of substitutionary models. Proponents of this view did not deny the significance of the cross as a dimension of Christ fully assuming human nature, but their emphasis on the entirety of incarnation—including the resurrection—is a powerful complement to exclusive interest in the death of Christ. While not always affirmed, there is even the implication that if Adam and Eve had not sinned, the incarnation would still have been necessary, which is an intuition far different from substitutionary approaches.

In the Eastern church, recapitulation was formulated in terms of God's purpose being *theosis* or "divinization." This emphasis is usually misunderstood by Western theologians as affirming a kind of Eastern religion monism, where humans become submerged in God, losing their identity. In contrast, Eastern theologians were careful to maintain the ontological difference between God and humanity and never saw humans as becoming God in the way that Jesus was fully divine. They meant something like Western theologians mean by the call to be "Christlike" or "godly."[15] Nevertheless, the East has tended to have a more mystical, spiritual approach to atonement and thus has emphasized more the sense of dying and rising with Christ (Rom 6:1-11), of Christ living in us (Gal 3:20), and of being one with God as a fulfillment of Jesus' high priestly prayer in John 17. As mentioned before, the Western church has tended to emphasize the legal side of Paul, and the Eastern church emphasizes the spiritual. The new cross-fertilization with the Eastern church, along with a greater emphasis on spirituality in the West, has led Western Christians to find deeper meaning in this more comprehensive approach to atonement.

Substitutionary Models

As Aulén pointed out, the first millennium of the church did not work out atonement theories in great detail, including either of the ones aforementioned. That work was left to Anselm in the eleventh century. In his groundbreaking work *Cur Deus Homo?* (Why the God-man?), Anselm rejected the ransom theory as being too crude, too anthropomorphic, and for being too "luciferous," that is, giving too much place to the devil. Instead, he argued in terms of medieval life: if someone's honor is offended, it must be "satisfied." If God is the one offended, then the satisfaction must be ultimately valuable. No human could suffice, even as sinless, but all humans have sinned anyway. Only God could pay a price sufficient to satisfy God's honor, but since humans were the offenders, the one paying the price must be human, but a sinless human; hence the God-human. The cross of Jesus Christ is thus the only logical answer to the deep human crisis of sin. All in all, the "satisfaction-substitutionary" theory was a theological *tour de force.*

This essential logic was formulated later in the shift from feudal life to more abstract legal national and legal relationships. The Reformed tradition especially saw the problem in more-impersonal legal terms. God is the great lawgiver, and humans have broken God's law. Only God could pay for such a crime, but only an innocent human could offer it. Again, the God-human is required. This penal-substitutionary theory came to be so dominant that among evangelicals it sometimes serves as the only theory that they have heard of and thus the only valid one. It is often called an "objective" view because it has more to do with changing God than with people: God had to do something about it. It also draws on the powerful image of vicarious sacrifice, where an innocent person offers his or her life to save another's, reminiscent of Jesus' saying, "No one has greater love than this, to lay down one's life for one's friends" (John 15:13). Paul adds to this, "While we were yet sinners, Christ died for us" (Rom 5:8). This model supports, as we shall see, the Reformers' emphasis on justification by faith, where God looks at a person, sees Christ, and pronounces the person innocent. It allows one to capture vividly the sense of other passages where the sins of the whole world are placed upon Christ, seemingly as the scapegoat (2 Cor 5:21).

Despite these strengths, troubling questions have arisen. It seems to some to posit a split between the Father and the Son. My doctoral professor, Dale Moody, put it this way: "God was mad, but Jesus made him glad." This view is based on an emphasis of some in the evangelical camp that Christ's sacrifice was a propitiation to appease an angry God. Others, like Anselm, would deny such a split, insisting that it is the Father's love that sends the Son. All proponents defend the view that God is hostile to sin and requires a price to be paid for it. Against this, others are uncomfortable with the idea of God being angry until a sacrifice is made, rather than seeing atonement as a matter of God's grace all the way through.[16] Hostility toward sin can be affirmed but only as subject to the primacy of the God of love. They argue that expiation is a better concept. In any case, if any view sunders the will of the Father and the Son, it cannot be defended. Salvation is due to the initiative of the Trinitarian God. Our earlier reflection on the Trinity would not allow one part of the Trinity to be contrary to another.

More disconcerting problems arise in relation to the requirements of legality. The model suggests that if the price has been paid, then forgiveness is obligatory. It cannot be withheld. The danger here is that atonement is reduced to a legal transaction that puts God in a bind. It is crucial to keep in mind our point that the center of Jesus' teachings is the extravagant grace in the parable of the prodigal son. Divine grace and forgiveness is a gift, not an obligation, which is central to Paul's great influence on the West through Augustine and the Reformers. One could argue that the initial sending of the Son is an act of grace, which is a point well made. Still, the reign of law seems to dominate in this view rather than being superseded by grace. Ironically, this view, most associated with those affirming *sola gratia* (grace alone), is in some tension with grace.

It has been pointed out that the basic analogy fails at a crucial point. On the one hand, a reason that the model still speaks powerfully is that an impersonal legal system dominates modern societies. On the other hand, the legal system would not allow an innocent person to take the place of a guilty one—and it certainly would not be for the judge who came down from the bench to do so! Perhaps an innocent person could pay a fine in a civil case, but the power of the analogy rests more on the resemblance to a criminal case. Vicarious suffering is still a resonant image in our society. It occurs, however, not in the legal system but in the arena of personal relationships, where someone can step in to take another's consequences.

Another weakness of this model, as well as the traditional form of the ransom model, is the reduction of salvation to a punctiliar act, a judgment at one point from guilty to not guilty. This model is insightful in pointing out what people are saved *from*; it is not so helpful in indicating what people are saved *for*. The common notion that salvation is a one-time decision separable from discipleship perhaps stems from a heavy reliance on this model, as if one can be saved apart from following Christ. This model powerfully indicates that one is forgiven and set free—but for what? The contemporary appropriation of the ransom model, conversely, stresses an ongoing, dynamic conflict with the forces of evil that will only be complete at the end of history.

A further major question has been raised about this model in light of the pathbreaking work of René Girard, who argued that the New Testament story precisely works to deny the common human failing of scapegoating.[17] The Gospels resist the unconscious victimization of Christ by stressing his innocence and pointing out the injustice of those who killed him. As Girard says:

> The true Resurrection is based not on the mythical lie of the guilty victim who deserves to die, but on the rectification of that lie, which comes from the true God and which reopens channels of communication mankind itself had closed through self-imprisonment in its own violent cultures. Divine grace alone can explain why, after the Resurrection, the disciples could become a dissenting minority in an ocean of victimization—could understand then what they had misunderstood earlier: the innocence not of Jesus alone but of all victims of all Passion-like murders since the foundation of the world.[18]

The sense of taking others' sins upon himself was not necessary in the sense of a legal obligation but represents God's willingness to face human sin in order to transcend it. It is more of a voluntary, gracious act than a forensically mandated one.

Along this line, feminist theologians in particular have questioned whether the necessity of suffering in order for God to be able to forgive, or even to cease being angry, says too much. Does it make God a divine child-abuser? a serious question indeed. Elie Wiesel, the Nobel Prize laureate and Jewish survivor of the Holocaust, has wondered whether a religion that "glorifies suffering will always find someone to suffer."[19] This criticism perhaps stems to some extent from the weaknesses of this model, but it misses the emphasis in the New Testament—and in the Old Testament in the person of the

Suffering Servant. The issue is not one of God making someone suffer unnecessarily. Rather, it is the willingness of people to resist sin and evil to such an extent that they face and endure suffering. An analogy is perhaps to think of Martin Luther King Jr.'s father pleading with him not to go back to Montgomery because, as he said, "They gon' kill my boy." In the end, King's father let him go, which was consistent with his own resistance to racism throughout his life.[20] This is not child abuse, but the willingness of people with spiritual strength and courage to give their lives—and to bless their adult children giving their lives—for good. This aspect of the cross is perhaps better seen in other models, particularly the relational one that we will soon consider; but even in this model, it is not arbitrary but a matter of God willing to pay the price to forgive humans. The weakness of this model is that the price seems a matter of impersonal law that somehow stands apart from the personal dimension of God, something to which God must yield rather than something that reveals God's excessive willingness to go to the far country, find the prodigal, and bring him home.[21]

As one can see with so much debate about this one model, theologizing about atonement continues and is as sharply contested as ever. With the complementary approach toward metaphors of atonement that we are taking, we can appreciate the emphasis that each model brings, but we must also be alert to the places where any model is limited and when it begins to run contrary to the basic spirit of Christ.

The Moral Influence Model

Close to the time of Anselm, another great medieval theologian, Abelard (1079–1142), saw some of the problems of the substitutionary model and proferred another, more subjective model in the early twelfth century. Abelard has often been seen as giving another stand-alone model, although he probably desired himself just to give a complementary model. He was concerned that the objective nature of Anselm's model did not do justice to the way that Christ moved people to follow him by consideration of his love and sufferings. So his view emphasizes more a change in people than in God.

Certainly the experiences of many Christians during Communion and Holy Week testify to the devotion aroused by meditating upon the suffering of Christ for their sake. The strength of Abelard's view is to maintain an integral relational dimension throughout that preserves divine initiative. The weakness of the view, taken alone, is that it tends to see Christ as an example to emulate but not making a unique sacrifice for humankind. In the New Testament, it seems more evident that the latter is the basis for the former, rather than being optional.[22]

González has argued that early church emphases on Christ as offering a kind of special knowledge, *gnosis*, emphasized by Clement of Alexandria and Origen, is akin to this view.[23] Christ is not so important in himself but is the true philosopher who imparts wisdom to others. This may be considered a different approach altogether, emphasizing wisdom rather than love or morality, but it is similar in seeing Christ more as an example and downplaying the significance of the cross per se. It also runs the danger of an elitism in knowledge that is inconsistent, for example, with Paul's emphasis on an egalitarian body of Christ that values everyone and even the foolishness of God that is wisdom.

A Relational Model

In the spirit of offering a model that speaks to contemporary times much as the other models have spoken to their times, D. M. Baillie in the 1950s suggested that one might think of atonement in terms of restoring broken relationships.[24] Often one thinks of the offender being the one who must sacrifice pride to find the humility to repent, but Baillie points out the pain that the offended must bear in restoring a relationship, especially in taking the initiative as Jesus calls for in the Sermon on the Mount (Matt 5:21-26). One must think here of serious breaches of a relationship such as unfaithfulness in a marriage or a close friend embezzling one's retirement money late in life. Although it is not a matter of breaking a previous relationship, one might think of the recent tragedy where the Amish quickly forgave the gunman who stalked into their school and murdered their children. As the Amish scholar Donald Kraybill remarked, "The blood was hardly dry on the bare board floor of the Nickel Mines School when Amish parents sent words of forgiveness to the family of the killer who had executed their children. Forgiveness? So quickly and for such a heinous crime?"[25] Here is where Derrida's adage rings true: "One can only forgive the unforgivable." In these cases, one cannot command forgiveness; it may even seem beyond human possibility. Certainly forgiveness cannot be conceived apart from the dynamism of a journey of forgiveness, as Fiddes underscores.[26] In other words, the movement from shock, denial, and anger may first have to be traversed. In the case of the Amish, the way may have to be cleared by a whole lifetime and ecclesial history of preparedness to forgive.

Baillie highlights both an objective and subjective dimension to this journey. The subjective anguish is obvious; objectively such reconciliation is not possible apart from the offended taking the cost of the breach upon himself or herself. There is no cost-free reconciliation; in this sense, such costly reconciliation is always a sacrifice on the part of the offended for the sake of the offender. The objective dimension thus is not an arbitrary imposition of impersonal law but the unavoidable cost of reconciliation.

This view draws upon the somewhat neglected theme of reconciliation in the New Testament, as in 2 Corinthians 5:19: "In Christ God was reconciling the world to himself, not counting their trespasses against them, and entrusting to us the message of reconciliation."[27] Atonement is placed in the context of ongoing relationships. The "for what" is clearer in this model. Reconciliation does not imply something important only in the past but opens up a new life together in the future. One would not think of salvation apart from discipleship in this model. The attraction also is that this approach should speak to a "psychological age," one that craves relationships, small groups, and therapists, just as the other models spoke to their age. This view also expresses the extravagance of grace that goes beyond law, placing it fully within the desire of God. In these ways, it has advantages over the substitutionary model.

What the relational model does not do so clearly is emphasize the importance of the incarnation, as in the recapitulation model, or the strife against bondage, as in the ransom model, or the centrality that the cross of Christ has in the New Testament. The latter can be seen, perhaps, as the extent to which God is willing to go to reach out in reconciliation. This view of the cross, avoiding the sense in which it had to happen in order for God to be able to forgive, may actually be seen as an advantage. The cross is therefore the price that God is willing to pay, if necessary, for reconciliation, not the means for God's anger to turn to love.

SALVATION

These rich approaches to the multifaceted nature of the "work of Christ" are the crucial backdrop to turning to the way atonement works out in human life. The very nature of salvation that follows from atonement is related to how we conceive of conversion and sanctification, as we shall see. Sometimes one has been emphasized to the neglect of the other. On the one hand, the moment of conversion has been so emphasized that sanctification is seen as optional. On the other hand, a second blessing, often paired with the risk of easily losing one's salvation, has been emphasized so much that conversion has been overshadowed. The magisterial reformers Luther and Calvin stressed justification by faith; radical reformers emphasized holiness of life. The Reformed tradition has tended to place so much weight on justification that perseverance was guaranteed. The later Arminian, Methodist, Holiness, and Pentecostal traditions have tended to place so much weight on sanctification that apostasy is a looming possibility.

In order better to deal with these perplexing issues, a few reminders will help us keep our bearings. One is that we can lose ourselves in the trees of these complex alternatives, so we must keep clear sight of the forest of atonement and what it implies about salvation. To put it differently, atonement is based on the divine initiative and purpose for human beings. The emphasis, as in our leitmotif of the parables of the Prodigal Son and the Seeking Shepherd, is finally on the Father and the Shepherd. That is the light that clarifies the situation of the son and the sheep. Yet a second view "from the forest," so to speak, is to keep in mind that salvation in the New Testament is referred to in three tenses: past, present, and future. Sometimes it speaks of "having been saved" (Luke 7:50; Eph. 2:8), sometimes of "being saved" (Phil 2:12), and sometimes that we "will be saved" (1 Pet 1:5). The comprehensive term *salvation* then includes all dimensions of the Christian life and matches the comprehensiveness of the term *reconciliation* from the side of atonement. Yet a third vantage point is to keep in mind that all of these aspects of salvation that follow, while they seem to be focused on the individual, only occur in the context of the church—the body of Christ. In other words, they are never merely individualistic but are inseparable from the tissue of the wider body of Christ. This last will be brought out more in the next chapter, on the church.

Conversion

In the New Testament, the typical pattern of the beginning of salvation is repentance, belief, and regeneration, which later is referred to in the classical term of the Reformation: "justification by faith." While virtually any Christian group will affirm the basic meaning of all of these, once one probes more closely, they are distinctly shaped by basic intuitions that we have discussed concerning the power of God and free will.

Repentance. In the beginning of Mark, after noting that John the Baptist was "preaching a baptism of repentance for the forgiveness of sins (1:4), Jesus is baptized by John and begins his own ministry with the injunction "Repent, and believe in the gospel" (v. 15). The Old Testament term means "turn" (*shuv*), and the New Testament term means "a change of mind" (*metanoia*). Both imply the kind of commitment symbolized by a baptism of immersion, where the implication is that one dies to one way of life as one is submerged and begins another as one arises from the water. The corollary imagery is new birth from the waters of life. Paul in Romans 6 draws on such imagery in the oft-cited baptismal formula, "We were buried therefore with him by baptism into death, so that as Christ was raised from the dead by the glory of the Father, we too might walk in newness of life" (Rom 6:4). The layers of symbolism in these passages, as an aside, are rich, pointing to birth, death, Christ's cross, and the believer all at once, reminding us that an imagination that cannot appreciate the disclosive power and truth of symbols will struggle with Scripture. The committed change of life that these symbols imply gives the lie to any divorce between salvation and discipleship. The very first step of repentance points from the way of death to lifelong walking the way of Jesus Christ.

At this point, some are concerned that too much is given over to the human. This appears as something that humans do and accomplish before God enters the picture, seeming to be human "works-righteousness" rather than "salvation by grace through faith." In the history of the church, such a view is considered to be "Pelagianism" or "semi-Pelagianism," referring to Augustine's antagonist concerning the issue of grace. Pelagianism refers to the idea that a human is created with the capacity to trust God and be sinless without special aid from God, even after the fall. Semi-Pelagianism refers to moderated views that allow humans to take the first step apart from grace, while acknowledging that salvation is ultimately due to the grace of God.[28] This issue, which has caused the Western church to careen from the ditch on one side of the road to the other throughout its history, repays careful attention. The strong Calvinists are so concerned about works that they reverse this order of salvation (*ordo salutis*) altogether, placing regeneration even ahead of repentance and faith. The assumption is that people are so totally depraved and in bondage to sin, they are helpless to do anything for themselves. Linked with their strong views of irresistible grace and double predestination, the clear implication is that saving grace must be provided before anything else can happen. This is a revealing example of how a host of theological intuitions coalesce to imply a rather startling conclusion, namely, that one is first "born again," then repents, and then believes.

A more Arminian approach retains the ostensible biblical pattern yet affirms the centrality of grace. It may help to remember that Jacob Arminius (1560–1609) was a Calvinist who came to differ on predestination with its implication of what we nowadays call a "compatibilist" view of human freedom. Arminius likely continued to think of himself as Reformed with a high view of grace. How does an Arminian view grace? Since they agree with the Reformation insistence on *sola gratia* (grace alone), they have to insist that even repentance is based on the enabling grace of God, but they distinguish it from saving grace by calling it "prevenient grace" (grace that precedes or goes before salvation).[29] This preserves the idea of the shepherd whose seeking always precedes the finding, that is, God's initiative in atonement always precedes actual atonement. Another approach in John is the Holy Spirit convicting someone of their sins (John 16:8); another approach in the Johannine Revelation, much loved by evangelicals, is the image of Christ knocking on the door of one's heart, waiting to be invited in[30] (Rev 3:20). Repentance is thus already a response to grace that both convicts and calls.

Faith. The process of turning away from the way of death and toward the way of God is already one of faith or belief. In much of the Christian tradition, faith has had the same cognitive connotation as belief in philosophy. Faith is, according to Thomas Aquinas, primarily assent to true propositions about God.[31] While faith has a cognitive component, such an intellectualist view can hardly do justice to the biblical context that is much more focused on will and action. The view of a holistic self, which we are presupposing, cannot separate these things out so cleanly. "Faith" (*pistis*) in the New Testament often has the connotation of "faithfulness" (Rom 1:8; 1 Thess 1:8).[32] The issue is trust in the context of a personal relationship. In this sense, faith has both a dimension of knowledge and lack of knowledge. Just as one may be willing to trust another's word for something unknown, one may trust God. This is not trust out of ignorance or a leap of faith but trust because one does know enough about the other person based on previous experience to see them as trustworthy. In a relationship, the knowledge is not just of objective facts but the dense weave of relationship that is much more holistic than instrumental reasoning. Modernity, to be sure, tended to place such holistic, tacit awareness out of the category of knowledge, but as we have seen, we have had to put it back. To draw on the category of practical wisdom, *phronesis*, again, such personal knowledge involves external factual knowledge but also "thicker" personal, holistic awareness. On this basis, one trusts and commits oneself to another. Seeing salvation in instrumental, transactional terms makes it very difficult to keep this personal dimension at the center of faith. Without it, faith can be seen as simply accepting a transaction completed a long time ago—and that is all. One keeps the "contract" in a closet until needed at death, reminding oneself occasionally—by going to church at Easter or for funerals—of the security in the lockbox. The Reformation emphasis on *sola fides* (faith alone), while warranted against the abuses of semi-Pelagian understandings of salvation like those that led the young Luther to whip and starve himself in order to deserve forgiveness, has sometimes led to this truncated, transactional understanding of faith. Faith, to the contrary, is not just accepting what someone else has done, although it includes this, it also involves the movement of personal relationship toward that one to whom one entrusts oneself and one's future. It is belief, trust, and practical commitment all rolled up together. Repentance and faith cannot be fully separated. The practical action of repentance is thus an integral part of the movement of faith.

At best, justification by faith points to the sense of atonement that placed the emphasis on God paying any and all costs for salvation—that salvation is something that God desires and offers. Inspired by Paul's forensic analogy in Romans, it powerfully points to images such as a judge looking toward a guilty party but finding no one because all he or she can see is the innocence of Christ or, in a different image, one who has paid the debt in full. This has been called "positional" or "forensic" righteousness in that it is not a righteousness that one has attained but righteousness that has been given as a gift.[33] Such an understanding has been liberating—in Paul himself, in Augustine, in Luther, in Wesley, and in many others. Over and over, people with an accusing conscience have struggled to find the answer in the one and only adequate one who can forgive. As Jesus suggested concerning the sinful woman who anointed his feet with her tears, the one who is forgiven much loves much (Luke 7:47). History thus has made it clear that one cannot compromise on this dimension of faith. To confuse the grace of salvation with efforts to earn or merit God's favor can never avail. At the same time, the faithful response to this incredible reality is not simple assent but the response of one's whole life, like the woman anointing Jesus' feet. Here the forensic model of atonement has to turn back to the more central reconciliation model. The whole purpose is to restore a relationship that one is then graciously enabled to have and to live. It is not a wearisome burden or obligation that one has now incurred; rather, it is a quality of new life that conversion makes possible. This reminds us of fresh perspectives on Paul and on justification that set it firmly in an eschatological context. God's fulfilling of God's prom-ises has already begun; God has already acted to bring creation to its consummation. The "now and not yet" quality of the kingdom of God manifests itself precisely here. New life begins now, through faith, because the future has already begun.[34]

We are now at the vexing intersection of faith and works that has so challenged the church. Unfortunately, like some Pharisees of Jesus' time who bedeviled him, zeal for God keeps lapsing into keeping external laws in order to gain God's favor. Christians have fallen again and again into a reliance on works after being saved by divine grace. The whole relationship, while a delicate one, is seen as living the life that has been granted as a gift. Such a life naturally involves "bearing fruit," the happier image of Paul that is less mis-leading than "works." Even James already in the New Testament, it seems, had difficulty with the abuse of the idea of salvation by grace alone. A perhaps too simplistic analogy is one of a person drowning. As he is going down for the last time, he cries out yet again, "Save me! Save me!" At that moment, someone, a powerful swimmer who had leapt into the water, reaches him and lifts his head out of the water. As the drowning person begins to gasp for air, he has just enough breath to query, "I am so grateful that you've saved me, but do I have to breathe?!" The ridiculous nature of this "parable" is actually to the point. The whole reason for being saved from death by drowning is to be able to live, that is, to breathe. God must be as nonplussed by us as we are of the victim in this story when we wonder, "I appreciate being saved, but do I have to follow you? Do I have to live the Christian life?" For God, ostensibly, there is no other life but living it with God. The whole point of repentance and belief is not just to accept a transaction but to enter into a relationship of life instead of decaying towards death.

Belief, then, or faith, has the elements that were developed out of the Reformation. There is information (*notitia*), assent (*assensus*), and faithfulness (*fiducia*).[35] What is different in keeping reconciliation at the center is that *fiducia* is not an add-on at the end but is the heart of faith. Faith *is* faithfulness. Faith is based on knowledge that is credible, but it is not merely logical assent to a good argument. No such argument can do justice to trust in personal relationships. It is not that the arena of relationships is too subjective to be cognitive; the arena of logic and factual data is so impoverished that it cannot do justice to the richer cognitive dimension of personal relationships.

In addition, trust has a future dimension that goes beyond the factual. People trust others even when they do not know everything and certainly not the future. Spouses trust their spouse in the sense that they do not have to know or "spy on" everything the other is doing. Humans can betray such a trust, but it does not change the nature of trust—it undermines it. Humans may decide not to trust, but relationships are impossible without it. In Christian faith, we are called to one who will not let us down. It is a reasonable faith based on what is known to trust where less is known.

Perhaps we can better understand the full panoply of dimensions surrounding faith when we relate it to the great commandments: to love God with all of one's heart and to love one's neighbor as oneself. In many ways, to "faith God," using the word *faith* as a verb the way it is sometimes used in the New Testament, is largely the same as to "love God" with all of one's heart. The Old Testament notion of "heart" as the center of mind, will, and emotion points to the holistic nature of its counterparts of love and faith in the New Testament.

Out of the divinely inspired human responses of repentance and faith come forgiveness and reconciliation. The human experiences of these are powerful. Think of someone like the prodigal son who desperately desires forgiveness, but the nature of forgiveness is that it cannot be required or often even expected—yet it occurs. One might think of a married couple whose relationship is fractured by unfaithfulness. Even in Matthew, adultery is cause for divorce, so one cannot mandate reconciliation (Matt 5:32). In this case, forgiveness does not even necessarily entail restoration of the marriage relationship nor should it—but it might. Genuine repentance occurs, and the relationship is restored based on genuine forgiveness. Life together, which might have been lost for good, is renewed. These human situations point to the power that comes from divine forgiveness and the establishment of a new divine relationship based on faith. The biblical images are potent, significantly rooted as much in the Old Testament as in the New:

> Come now, let us argue it out, says the Lord:
> though your sins are like scarlet,
> they shall be like snow;
> though they are red like crimson,
> they shall become like wool. (Isa 1:18)

> Seek the Lord while he may be found,
> call upon him while he is near;
> let the wicked forsake his way,
> and the unrighteous their thoughts;
> let them return to the Lord,
> that he may have mercy on them,
> and to our God,
> for he will abundantly pardon. (Isa 55:6-8)

Just as John identified the central characteristic of God as love, a central understanding of God in the Old Testament is of one who forgives and restores the one who turns to God in faith.

Regeneration. Speaking of new life in a new relationship indicates another crucial dimension of conversion that also goes beyond notional assent to facts, namely, regeneration or transformation. This is perhaps most vividly expressed in Jesus' frustrating nighttime attempt to explain to a prominent teacher of the Law, Nicodemus, that he must be "born from above" (John 3:3). This vivid image goes beyond what a human can do, even through repentance and trust. As we have seen, Paul also understands salvation to mean dying and rising again, already beginning in this life. Here we have moved from forensic images of atonement to mystical images of "new creation," as Paul puts it in 2 Corinthians 5:17. The Christian witness is that reconciliation with God involves spiritual rebirth and a sense of inner transformation. With this regeneration is associated peace that reflects newfound harmony with God. Paul links such peace with justification: "Therefore, since we are justified by faith, we have peace with God through our Lord Jesus Christ" (Rom 5:1). This is more than an external legal "fiction," as it is sometimes called; the life of the early church reflects this as an inner spiritual reality, as mysterious as it is. If the Christian story is true, a people made in the divine image for fellowship with God—who are then cut off from it but then begin to be who they are created to be—should experience life at a new level. Paul describes this consistently as being "in Christ," but also as "living by the Spirit" or "walking by the Spirit" (Rom 8:1-11; Gal 5:16). The renewed spiritual craving manifested in our own secular society points to such a dimension not satisfied by technological conveniences. As Augustine put it in his prayer at the beginning of the *Confessions*, "You have made us for yourself, and our heart is restless until it finds its rest in you."[36]

A question that has likely been coming to the fore at several places may not be able to be stilled at this point, namely, What we have described fits an adult, like many in the New Testament, who has converted, but what about those born in the church? Most Christians in history have been baptized as infants. How do words such as *repentance, faith,* and *regeneration* describe a baby? This is a major source of division in Christendom and is striking since much of church practice does not fit the prototype that I have just presented. After a few centuries, the church moved to practice infant baptism, which prevailed until the Reformation. Even then, it continued in most Protestant churches. The Radical Reformation, however, moved to restore the idea of believer's baptism as a conscious confession and commitment. In England a century later, Baptist churches also moved in this direction, followed by numerous other groups such as the Christian and Pentecostal churches.

Typically, "paedobaptist" churches, those who baptize infants, understand that regeneration actually does occur in the child based on the implicit faith of the child or the actual faith of the parents or godparents. Often this is tied to a sacramental view of baptism, where the baptism conveys grace to the recipient. It also implies belief in original guilt deriving from Adam's sin, which is washed away by the baptism. Otherwise, if the child died unbaptized, he or she would go to hell or to limbo, the latter of which is not quite hell but not heaven either. The understanding is that such rebirth will be confirmed later, usually around the age of twelve, when a conscious profession of faith is made.

If we leave the centrality of the context of an adult turning toward God, which seems to be what the New Testament writers have in mind, then the basic understanding of salvation subtly can be changed. It can come to be seen as occurring apart from human response or as conveyed more by the church or by the priest than received by the recipient. The argument that infant baptism is a better model for salvation than believer's baptism stems from such a transformation because it clearly shows that the recipient contributes nothing.[37] Yet surely this alters the dynamic picture of reconciliation that is at the center of salvation as we have described it. One cannot imagine reconciliation by oneself; at least two must be involved. Believers' churches have insisted, therefore, that salvation and baptism involve conscious repentance and faith.

Of course, believers' churches have also had to deal with the issue of children and infants, which for the fledgling New Testament church was apparently not yet an issue to be addressed. Generally, Believers' churches regard those who die before the "age of accountability" as going to heaven. This practice is complicated by not having any settled conception of when that age occurs; moreover, it has moved to being younger and younger over the last century, from older teenagers even sometimes to preschoolers, raising the question of how far it is from infant baptism. When we turn to the issue of the church in the next chapter, we will come back to the baptismal question, but one can see that both approaches have had to move from the clear prototypical pattern of salvation in the New Testament to a more complex picture. Paedobaptist churches have made infant baptism the norm. Believers' churches have kept closer to the prototype but have moved closer and closer to infant baptism, all the while seeing infants in a different situation altogether. It is also true that children raised in the church, who easily move from life in the church to a profession of faith, do not fit the New Testament model very well either. For it is a picture of moving from an adult who "is dead in trespasses and sin," who then repents with great sorrow, and whose life is subsequently transformed. No matter which direction one goes, one cannot escape the necessity of theology! One must think through a more complex situation based on the biblical foundations in light of the traditions of the church. This complication also reminds us again that nothing we have treated so far occurs apart from the church. As we turn to the issue of growth in salvation, the ecclesial context will continue to be significant as we will treat the issue more from an individual perspective in this chapter and more from a corporate perspective in the next.

SANCTIFICATION

The image of new birth should immediately imply a natural process of growth—but it has not always worked that way in the life of the church. In fact, especially in those influenced by the Lutheran and Reformed traditions, followed by American revivalism, there has been a tendency to emphasize conversion at the expense of discipleship. Dale Moody would tell the story of an oilman that he visited while doing a revival in Texas who responded, "I was saved when I was a kid. Why do I need to do anything else?" In the flush of mass revivals like those of Billy Graham, many were concerned about the number who would make "decisions" at the revival meeting but then would never be seen again in any of the churches. On the other hand, some have been attracted to a second blessing that yields maturity or even a kind of perfection almost instantaneously. Between these two extremes, how should one think of sanctification?

Discipleship in the Spirit. Sanctification (in the New Testament, *hagiasmos*) is related to consecration. Early in Israel's religious history, it meant something set aside for God and not necessarily a higher moral quality. As time went on, it came to characterize a person not only as belonging to God but as being "godly." The purpose of salvation is not therefore just to be converted but to become transformed into the image of God and, more specifically, of Christ. As we saw when discussing the "image of God" in creation, the Irenaean view that has dominated the Orthodox Church is that humans are created with the potential to become transformed into the image of Christ. This is the process of sanctification. Another prime biblical word, instead of sanctification, is *discipleship*, or becoming a *disciple* (*mathētēs*). In the Great Commission in Matthew 28:19-20, the risen Lord said, "Go therefore and make disciples [*mathēteusate*] of all the nations, baptizing them in the name of the Father, and of the Son, and of the Holy Spirit, teaching them to obey everything that I have commanded you." This passage actually puts more emphasis on discipleship than appears in English. It should read, "Going," or "As you go," make disciples. The instruction is not just to make converts or to baptize but to train and teach converts to become like the disciples themselves.

It is odd that there was ever a question about the necessity and normalcy of Christian growth. It is likely that this distortion stems from a variety of stresses. One is the emphasis on grace that was a reaction to perhaps too much emphasis on Christian works, to the neglect of grace. Another was the revivalist context where grace apart from discipleship was emphasized along with a great emphasis on numbers. The image that comes to mind in the Southern Baptist context is of megachurch pastors phoning each other as soon as possible on Sunday to see who had the highest numbers. Another is a church that did not want to invest in ministry to a hospice because there was not much promise to add numbers to the church. Another result is the common emphasis in my youth of a sharp distinction between salvation and the call to discipleship. The latter was desirable but optional. It was thought of as rare, so the status quo was that most Christians would be saved but would not desire to follow Christ. Another influence that we have noted was the emphasis on a transactional view of the atonement that made it seem like taking out an insurance policy in a punctiliar event.

A passage like the one just cited from Matthew indicates how aberrant such views are and how inseparable salvation is from discipleship or Christian formation. Here is where more-expansive views of atonement may help. The relational view that sees salvation as reconciliation and the opportunity to be in relationship with God naturally implies continuance and growth in the relationship. John's image of fruit abiding in the vine is another view that suggests that it is either growth or death (John 15:1-5). Either one is nourished by the vine, or one withers and dies.

Perhaps resistance to an emphasis on sanctification has come from the fear of works-righteousness; if so, it is perhaps an understandable but unfortunate overreaction. Paul, the great apostle of grace, clearly emphasizes works: "He will repay according to each one's deeds" (Rom 2:6), and "It is not the hearers of the law who are righteous in God's sight but the doers of the law who will be justified" (2:13). James, who is so often presented as being opposed to Paul, could not have said it better, but perhaps James has the better nuance: "Show me your faith apart from your works, and I by my works will show you my faith" (Jas 2:18). In other words, faith and works are not opposed but integral to each other. It is crucial, however, to integrate them in the right way. Works are to reveal faith, not the other way around. In fact, perhaps the better analogy, given the constant misunderstandings surrounding the idea of "works," is "fruit." Paul, of course, appeals to the "fruit of the Spirit" as being expected of a growing Christian life (Gal 5:22-23). In Philippians 2:12-13, Paul connects God's initiative of grace with works in a telling way, noting that it occurs in a communal context:

> Therefore, my beloved, just as you [plural] have always obeyed me, not only in my presence, but much more now in my absence, work out your own salvation with fear and trembling; for it is God who is at work in you, enabling you both to will and to work for his good pleasure.[38]

The works thus produced are not meritorious products that earn God's favor; they are in fact products of God's grace at work in us, sometimes helping us just to be willing, at other times helping us actually to do things. The implication is that this is a process that may take time, is not easy, and is the result of a prayerful walking with God. One of the most significant Christian practices, is learning, almost paradoxically, how to "work hard" to "abide in the vine" (John 15:5), which requires effort in Christian disciplines such as prayer, participation in a church, and service in ministry. Yet its success does not succumb to pride or hypocrisy or frantic striving to earn God's favor. Finding the right *phronetic* balance is itself a matter of Christian learning and discernment. It is crucial to discipleship, judging from the way that the church has struggled in this area.

Another perspective is Jesus' parable of the undeserving servant:

> Will any one of you, who has a servant plowing or keeping sheep, say to him when he has come in from the field, "Come at once and sit down at table"? Will he not rather say to him, "Prepare supper for me, and gird yourself and serve me, till I eat and drink; and afterward you shall eat and drink"? Does he thank the servant because he did what was commanded? So you also, when you have done all that is commanded you, say, "We are unworthy servants; we have only done what was our duty." (Luke 17:7-10)

While the relationship to servants is a not-so-happy analogy in our more egalitarian age, in the context of Jesus' parable it makes the point that doing a job, works, does not necessarily merit a reward; it can rather be seen as just doing what was expected. Thus, to live the eternal life that has already been given and has already begun should not be seen as an onerous obligation, a burden, or a payment, but rather an opportunity. From God's perspective, the querulous question, "Do I have to?" must seem like the murmuring of the Israelites in the wilderness right after their miraculous deliverance (Exod 14:1-12). Life with God is not so much what one *has* to do but what one *gets* to do. It is like after nearly suffocating, getting to breathe.

Paul does not therefore see discipleship as a matter of merely human effort to do the impossible. It is the natural result of life in the Spirit of Christ. He describes this life in Romans 8 after seeing it as being set free from bondage (7:13-24) and condemnation as, alternately, "walking according to the Spirit," "living according to the Spirit," and "setting the mind on the things of the Spirit" (Rom 8:1-9). This is the mystical or spiritual dimension of sanctification. Of course, Paul also describes it as being "in Christ," and having been "crucified with Christ," and having Christ now living in him (Gal 2:20). Paul often calls the Holy Spirit the Spirit of Christ (Rom 8:9). Discipleship is not thus a matter of learning rules and following them; it is living in concert with the Spirit of God. Since this dimension has been highlighted in the last century by the Pentecostal and charismatic movements, which are the fastest growing part of Christendom worldwide, we will turn our attention to it but then also to the place that discipline, even rules, might have.

Filling of the Spirit. Fresh attention to the Trinity over the last century led, toward the end of the century, to a renewed interest in the neglected doctrine of the Holy Spirit—neglected, that is, by most churches.[39] Conversely, with the rise of the Pentecostal movement, the last century has seen perhaps the greatest emphasis on the Holy Spirit in Christian history. On January 1, 1901, in Topeka, Kansas, Charles Parham laid hands on Agnes Osman, who then prayed in tongues, which he interpreted as the baptism of the Holy Spirit.[40] Parham then influenced an African-American Holiness preacher named William J. Seymour, who began a three and one-half year revival, 1906–1909, that included what was considered to be baptism of the Spirit attended by speaking in tongues. The Assembly of God denomination developed out of this movement and believes that speaking in tongues is a necessary sign of the baptism of the Holy Spirit, understood as a baptism of empowerment subsequent to salvation.[41] After mid-century, the movement spread to many other denominations, including the Roman Catholic Church and Episcopal Church, where enthusiasts emphasized the idea of the baptism of the Holy Spirit as a second, empowering experience usually, but not always, accompanied by tongues. Charismatics, as the "second wave" of Pentecostalism, began to stay in their denominations rather than separating into Pentecostal denominations. From only about 10 thousand Pentecostals at mid-century, Pentecostals and charismatics have now increased in number to about 130 million worldwide, the fastest growing part of the church in the United States and in the world. A "third wave" of Pentecostalism began in the late twentieth century with a greater emphasis on other spiritual gifts of power such as miraculous healing and exorcism.

Such a movement, often castigated and even demonized at first by older denominations, can hardly be ignored.[42] It offers a simple message that salvation is one thing, empowerment is another. This empowerment is not something that one can produce oneself but is a gift of God. Millions now witness that such experiences have made a dramatic difference in their lives, and the trend is expected to increase throughout the century. What do more-traditional denominations make of this?

First of all, it is crucial that the central importance of the Holy Spirit for Christian growth and empowerment be disentangled from the question of speaking in tongues, especially, and to some extent, the question of a "second" experience of the Holy Spirit.[43] The Holy Spirit is clearly tied to Christian life and empowerment in the New Testament. In John, the new birth is being born of the Holy Spirit. In Luke and Paul, the Way of Jesus Christ is life in the Spirit. It is often suggested that Acts be retitled as "The Acts of the Holy Spirit." Likewise, as we have just seen, Paul cannot envisage the Christian life apart from walking in the Spirit. Perhaps other Christians are in a place now, after the first response to Pentecostalism, not to be reactionary, and even hysterical—on both sides—but to give a considered, reflective theological response. Sometimes the reaction was so strong that the doctrine of the Holy Spirit, so often neglected in any case, was actually avoided so as not to be Pentecostal or charismatic. This would be catastrophic in theological terms. The Christian life *is* life in the Spirit. The New Testament consistently sees the presence of God in the believer's life as the presence of the Holy Spirit. New birth, spiritual transformation, and prayer are inconceivable apart from the Holy Spirit. So the essential place of the Holy Spirit in Christian life cannot be minimized, even if one considers that the doctrine of the Holy Spirit has been abused.

Second, the above reflection indicates another important benchmark. The implication of Pentecostal theology of the baptism of the

Holy Spirit is that it is later and not true of all Christians. This is to make the same mistake that others have made with respect to discipleship. One cannot separate Christian life and life in the Spirit. Theologically, it is much more appropriate, following Pauline theology, to understand conversion as baptism in the Holy Spirit. Water baptism is thus a symbol or sacrament of baptism in the Holy Spirit. New Christian life, however mystical or spiritual one understands it, is made possible by the Holy Spirit, and both John and Paul connect this with salvation itself. In 1 Corinthians, Paul says, "For in the one Spirit we were all baptized into one body—Jews or Greeks, slaves or free—and we were all made to drink of one Spirit" (1 Cor 12:13).[44] In Ephesians, Paul says that there is "one faith, one baptism" right after speaking of "one Spirit," which he connects with the "one body" of the church (Eph 4:4-5).[45] This connection with new life is also clear in Romans 6:4, which we have already cited, and Colossians: "When you were buried with him in baptism, you were also raised with him through faith in the power of God, who raised him from the dead" (Col 2:12). Paul would not be able to conceive of new life in God that was not at the same time new life in the Holy Spirit, not to mention that such an idea undermines Trinitarian theology. It seems best then to reserve the idea of baptism in the Holy Spirit in Paul for the beginning of the Christian life. On the other hand, Paul does have the idea of later being filled with the Holy Spirit. He seems to see this as something that may or may not be the case, depending on the spirituality and maturity of the believer. He thus encourages, "Do not get drunk with wine, for that is debauchery; but be [repeatedly] filled with the Spirit" (Eph 5:18). This should be aligned with the profuse metaphorical language that we have seen him use of believers and the Holy Spirit in terms of walking, living, thinking, and now being filled.[46]

While it is more complicated, it is crucial to see that Acts is more descriptive in theology than normative and also reflects a quite chaotic time in the early church.[47] The Day of Pentecost in Acts 2 seems to connect with the saying of John the Baptist in Luke: "I baptize you with water; but one who is more powerful than I is coming; I am not worthy to untie the thong of his sandals.

He will baptize you with the Holy Spirit and fire" (Luke 3:16). It is also foreshadowed in Acts 1:5 before Christ's ascension when Jesus says, "For John baptized with water, but you will be baptized with the Holy Spirit not many days from now." Pentecost however, is ambiguous in that it represents, in Lukan theology, the first coming of the Holy Spirit "in the last days"; thus, it is connected at least as clearly with conversion as with further empowering. Moreover, in Acts, Luke uses a variety of terms that are not clearly worked out. He refers on the day of Pentecost not to baptism but to "filling" or "pouring" of the Holy Spirit (Acts 2:4, 18). In addition, Peter's sermon speaks of receiving "the gift of the Holy Spirit," which again seems to tie in with the beginning of the Christian life, not with something added later (2:38).

The caution about Acts being more historical is pertinent in the next occasion in Acts, where the Samaritans had been baptized with water but had not yet received the Holy Spirit (8:15-16). In other words, while Paul is manifestly trying to teach theology at times, Acts is more historical and at least more suggestive and subtle, which means that we must be more cautious in theologizing on the basis of Acts. It is not at all easy to reconcile this passage, for example, with the rest of the New Testament. It does not mention speaking in tongues, although Pentecostals argue that something was so visible that Simon the magician wanted to buy it, *ergo* it must have been speaking in tongues (8:18-19). Another aspect of this passage is that it depicts the spreading of the gospel to the Samaritans, a great breakthrough prophesied in the aforementioned reference to baptism in the Holy Spirit by Christ, just before the ascension, that through this power, "you will be my witnesses in Jerusalem, in all Judea and Samaria, and to the ends of the earth" (1:8). The gift of the Holy Spirit, often with tongues, accompanies fresh breakthroughs to new areas in Acts.[48]

Acts raises more questions on this subject than it answers. (1) It is not so much normative, as descriptive, as we said. (2) There is no clear sequence or terminology when Luke does refer to the Holy Spirit and tongues. (3) We should not forget that Luke does not mention tongues in many of the episodes of conversion. (4) Most typically, Luke connects the Holy Spirit with conversion. (5) We should add that Pentecost seems to be a special event where the coming of the Holy Spirit and even the experience of speaking in tongues is somewhat unique. In that case, the miracles seemed to be one of hearing: "Each one heard them speaking in the native language of each" (Acts 2:6). This does not seem to be the later experience in Acts or the writings of Paul, where the tongues appear to be unknown. Thus, it is difficult to rest too much weight on Acts apart from the general testimony of the New Testament that the Spirit of God enables salvation and power in the Christian life.

When one turns to Paul's more theological treatment in 1 Corinthians, a clear but different picture emerges. Paul does not seem to imagine everyone as receiving the gift of tongues (12:30). Some do; some do not. He urges them to strive for the "greater gifts" rather than tongues (12:31). They seem to be unknown languages, so another gift of interpretation must be correlated in public worship for translation. Paul prefers not to have tongues at all in public worship, but he would allow two "or at most three, and each in turn; and let one interpret" (14:27). Note that this is the only place in all of Paul's letters where he even refers to speaking in tongues. Elsewhere, as we have seen, he sees the Holy Spirit as essential for salvation. One can argue, as charismatics do, that Paul affirms that speaking in tongues is a case where "my spirit prays," and Paul commends such praying in the Spirit as something that "builds up." (14:17) If one conjoins this idea with Paul's claiming not to speak in tongues in public worship but still more than them all, then one is led to infer that Paul has a "private prayer language."[49] The wider inference is that this might be possible for all, although such a conclusion is only implied, at best, in the texts that we have. The larger picture is that Paul does not refer to speaking in tongues in any other of his epistles, and it is not totally obvious that what he is referring to in first century Corinth is the same as the modern twentieth and twenty-first century phenomenon. I would grant that it is similar enough, but it is a question mark. There is evidence that people spoke in tongues in other religions in Corinth before becoming Christian, and so it was natural to expect to do so in a "superior" or "true" religion. Another very important issue for Paul is that he places the gifts of the Spirit in a far second place compared to the fruit of the Spirit, particularly love. This is evidenced by the fact that he placed the great "love chapter," chapter 13, in the middle of his discussion of gifts, saying that love is "a still more excellent way" (12:31) and that without love, spiritual gifts are "nothing" (13:1-3). This does not mean that he thinks spiritual gifts are unimportant. As Gordon Fee, a Pentecostal exegete, states concerning the gift of tongues, "Although trying to cool their ardor for congregational tongues-speaking, he does not disparage the gift itself; rather he seeks to put it in its rightful place."[50]

The Pentecostal and charismatic movements have rightly emphasized the urgency for each Christian to seek to be filled with the Spirit and the importance of spiritual gifts for the vitality of the church. The important thing is to keep spiritual gifts rooted in spiritual growth, the subject of the next section. Corinth reveals that one can be spiritually immature and yet have great spiritual gifts. The gifts of the Spirit, therefore, are not strongly correlated with spiritual maturity; "fruit of the Spirit," however, is. All Christians, in order to be Christians, are enlivened and empowered by the Spirit—but they may not be filled with the Spirit. In Paul's language, how much they are filled with the Spirit or walk in the Spirit is up to them. What is crucial to remember, at the same time, is that Christian growth, like the gifts, is a matter of grace, not of merely individual effort, and that this grace is mediated through the presence of the Spirit.

Maturity and Growth in the Spirit. Much in the New Testament emphasizes growth or maturity in Christ. At one place, Paul castigates those who are still "infants" in Christ (1 Cor 3:1). The writer in Hebrews reprimands his recipients for still needing milk, like infants, not solid food (Heb 5:13-14). The image of reconciliation that we have emphasized brings out that the point of salvation is a continued, intimate relationship with God, which implies a growing relationship. This relationship springs from grace and continues in grace. We have seen that it is not a matter of keeping external rules and regulations but is "life in the Spirit" and "walking in the Spirit." The analogy of physical growth is widespread, however, and apt. Physical growth is natural and is not labor, but it also requires sustenance. A balancing analogy is one of athletics, where growth requires training and discipline.

Perhaps Jesus' striking analogy is even more illuminating. Probably the most consistent problem that Jesus faced, and over which he became most angry, was legalism. He consistently drew attention to the spirit of the law rather than the letter of the law. Yet at one point, Jesus said, "Come to me, all who are weary and are heavy laden, and I will give you rest. Take my yoke upon you, for my yoke is easy and my burden is light" (Matt 11:28-30). One would not think of "taking up a yoke" as easy, but the implication is that for which we were designed. Walking in the Spirit of Christ and abiding in Christ are spiritual realities that are fulfilling. It is, as John says, not just better physical life but "abundant life," using not bare life, *bios*, but another word denoting quality of life, *zoe*. Yet it is taking up a yoke. There is an effort involved to remain in the vine, to continue being filled with the Spirit. Perhaps more simply, one cannot consciously turn food into energy in the body, but one does have to eat it. The mysterious relationship between receiving life and a relationship with God as a gracious gift, and "working out" our salvation with fear and trembling is a delicate balance. It is not surprising that the church has constantly teetered from one side to the other, but if rightly poised, the yoke is supposed to be easy and light. While opposing legalism, Jesus continued to practice Judaism and to advocate practices such as giving, fasting, and praying—just doing them in the "right spirit."

Such an equilibrium has been threatened from both directions. Tendencies have existed on the one side to emphasize desperate sinfulness and depravity so much that little growth is possible. Conversion is stressed so much that the rest of the Christian life is neglected. On the other side, the church has desired a second blessing that would instantaneously bring one to maturity along with exaggerated demands to reach a final sinless state. The dominant pattern in the New Testament, however, is in between, finding the right balance, which again is more precarious. In Philippians 3, Paul expresses such a balance in almost paradoxical fashion: "Not that I have already obtained this or am already perfect; but I press on to make it my own, because Christ Jesus has made me his own" (v. 12). Philippians is generally understood to have been written toward the end of Paul's life. I think most would agree that if any Christian were mature, Paul should be in that camp. Yet Paul does not regard himself to have arrived. In fact, the word translated as "perfect" might better be translated as "mature," so Paul does not even think of himself as mature—but the plot thickens. A few verses later, Paul writes, "I press on toward the goal for the prize of the upward call of God in Christ Jesus. Let those of us who are mature be thus minded; and if in anything you are otherwise minded, God will reveal that also to you. Only let us hold true to what we have attained" (vv. 14-16). The word *mature* used here is a variant of the same word translated as "perfect" above. In a sense, Paul is saying, "Those who are mature will realize that they are not mature," or, "Those who are perfect will realize that they are not perfect."[51] His language is reminiscent of Socrates' concluding, after much investigation, that he was indeed the wisest man of his time, as the Oracle at Delphi had said, because others thought that they were wise and were not, whereas he knew that he was not wise and therefore was.[52]

One might point out that Paul is not talking of sin but perhaps only of perfection. One might imagine being sinless yet not perfect, which seemed to be John Wesley's idea of "entire sanctification" and that of many in the later holiness tradition that ensued.[53] At this point 1 John is helpful, making a point that is almost as paradoxical.[54] For most readers of the Bible in English, 1 John is perplexing initially, seeming to contradict itself. For example, 1 John 1:8 says, "If we say that we have no sin, we deceive ourselves, and the truth is not in us."[55] It then adds a response to personal guilt: "If we confess our sins, he who is faithful and just will forgive our sins and cleanse us from all unrighteousness" (1:9). The problem is that 3:9 says, "Those who have been born of God do not sin, because God's seed abides in them; they cannot sin, because they have been born of God." This is not a case of tension between different books but within a brief letter. Greek grammar helps here, as do larger theological considerations. The first verse is a clear statement that

Christians are deluding themselves if they think that they have no sin in their lives. This is surely true if we remember that sin is not just a particular conscious act but can also consist of attitudes that are enmeshed in larger webs of corporate injustice. The problem with those people, like Wesley at times, who thought that one could attain sinlessness is that they usually heavily qualify it so that sin is a conscious, intentional act against God. Spiritual teachers, however, often confess that as they mature, the deeper issue is often in actions that are not clearly intentional. Perhaps we have so rationalized our actions that at the time they seem acceptable; only later do we wonder how we were duped—or were able to dupe ourselves. Moreover, it is often only in greater maturity that one becomes aware of more-subtle tendencies toward envy and pride, for example, that were completely masked earlier, perhaps when our attention was fixed on more-obvious sins. There seems to be great wisdom in 1 John 1 that we should always be aware of our vulnerability and not have a false sense of accomplishment.

On the other hand, 1 John 3 seems fully to support the Wesleyan ideal of entire sanctification. The tense is continuous, however, so it is better translated as, "Those who have been born of God do not habitually, repeatedly, continually commit sin." The idea seems to be that sin cannot be an accepted habit about which one is not concerned. If so, there is no fear and trembling. Thus, in the first chapter, the emphasis is on whether sin is ever committed. The latter chapter is on one's immersion in sin. The assumption is one of growth and maturity—but not attainment.

The expectation is that life with God will result in Christian growth, which is a lifelong project. Growth is a natural outgrowth of life. Since we are not literally plants or vines, but humans, such growth involves commitment, effort, discipline, and goal-setting. In that sense, it may not seem so natural. As we noted, Paul said, "I press on toward the goal" (Phil 3:14). In Colossians, he said, "Set your minds on things that are above" (3:2). Yet he bases such admonitions on the fact that "you have died, and your life is hid with Christ in God" (3:3). This tension reminds us of the tension between the now and not yet of the kingdom of God.

The long and short of it is that one cannot conceive of Christian life and growth apart from such a spiritual, mystical dimension that is the gift of grace. The mistake is then to assume that it is magical and spontaneous with little correlation to effort or discipline. Paul, however, can also make comparisons with an athlete or a soldier who requires strenuous training. The Epistle to the Hebrews is perhaps more startling. After chastising the recipients for still needing milk, the writer says, "But solid food is for the mature, for those who have their faculties trained *by practice* to distinguish good from evil" (5:14, emphasis added). This suggests that spirituality is something that takes practice and time—one can get better at it. In other complex areas, studies suggest that it takes ten to fifteen years to become an "expert."[56] It also takes immersion in the area so much that much of the knowledge and skill becomes second nature. The scientist Michael Polanyi, you may recall, called this immersion in an area "indwelling."[57] In a simple way, it is how the more skilled driver is able to drive a car without thinking about it. An expert chess player, it was found, has less to preoccupy the mind than a novice because so much is taken in at a glance. While relating to God is not just another field of expertise, is it any simpler? Even something as basic as learning Scripture so that it becomes a guide to one's life can take years of indwelling for it to come to mind in the way that it came to mind in the story of Jesus' temptations in the wilderness. In recent years, interest has grown in the Protestant world in spiritual disciplines. These are not seen as works that threaten grace but as practices that foster the unleashing of grace in our lives. The popular Christian philosopher Dallas Willard captures the difference by distinguishing between "trying" and "training."[58] Another comparison is to the way that any marriage relationship requires work in order to grow and not stagnate and die. Yet the focus is not on the work per se but on how it contributes to a vibrant, natural relationship. To think of the spiritual life apart from discipline is to have a discarnate view of sanctification.

Before turning more specifically to the question of how to incarnate spirituality, however, two cautions must be given. First, Christian growth is not an individual phenomenon. We will focus on the church in the next chapter, but Christian growth, true growth, always requires community. Spiritual growth is, to be sure, growth in awareness of God and in Christlikeness, but this is manifested in relationship. Love of God is always correlated with love of neighbor. The Way of Jesus Christ is always life together.

A second caution is similar in that we are not thinking of wrestling just with inner, personal sins. Rather, part of Christian growth is becoming more aware also of our larger entanglement in social sin. A sign of Dietrich Bonhoeffer's spiritual discernment, along with others of the confessing church in Germany, was that he was able to see through the web of deceit that most Christians, in this sense immature Christians, did not.[59] A measure of his maturity, and others, was his courage to face social oppression. Martin Luther King Jr. almost despaired of white preachers, whom he thought would be his greatest allies, many of whom fought against him.[60] Some were with him; today we see those as the spiritually mature ones. Blindness to social sin is a sign of spiritual adolescence, if not infancy. Not seeing connections of one's faith with social issues is the kind of thing that also frustrated Jesus. Responding well with practical wisdom to social issues in one's own time is greatly challenging and a mark of spiritual maturity. Some do not see social evil at all. Some see the social sin but do more damage than good in their rash responses. Others see it but do not wrestle with the issues enough to know how to respond. A mark of patience is not just a matter of being patient within one's personal relationships; it also relates to the patience to deal with intractable social evils. Individualism in the West has sometimes privatized and internalized spirituality so much that spirituality itself can become a sinful preoccupation, turning people away from others and blinding our eyes to the wider sin around us. Jesus' harshest words seemed to be reserved for those who outwardly wore the garb of spirituality but did not address real needs (Matt 25).

Practices in the Spirit

As we have seen, the incarnation is at the heart of Christianity. We have realized more fully in recent years both the embodied nature of the Judeo-Christian faith and the embodied nature of human beings. It is not surprising that this should play itself out in the redeemed life as well. We will thus look at some Christian practices that are crucial to the Christian life. We cannot look at all, for there are many, and they can change. In different times, for example, preaching as a horseback-riding, circuit-riding preacher might be a spiritual practice whereas hosting a Christian radio program might be similar in another age. An aspect of an incarnate faith is that it is rooted in its context. While Bible study, prayer, and proclamation might be universal, they are inevitably localized.

Bible Study. An ancient practice and one that is dominant in Believers' churches is Bible study. This is something that has long been a part of preaching and teaching in public ways. In many churches, children and adults engage every week in Sunday School that is mainly Bible study, year after year, of books of the Bible. With the rise of printed books, beginning in the fifteenth century with the Gutenberg press, it also has become an individual matter where people are encouraged to read their Bibles every day and to memorize Scripture verses. Some traditions prefer the term *contemplation* to *study*. The ancient practice of *lectio divina*, contemplative Bible study, is growing in Protestant circles as well as Roman Catholic. The emphasis in this practice is not just on reading and memorizing but imaginatively "living into" the text and then "living it out."[61]

With Scripture being the primary authority for virtually every Christian group, such Bible study is a foundational Christian practice. It is the backbone of Christian evangelism, preaching, and social action. It is crucial to another practice that we will consider, Christian discernment. How does one know the will of God? The response usually begins with considering what the Bible says. In understanding this practice, we must remember all of the things we said about the nature of Scripture in the chapter on revelation, but it may be helpful to treat several additional misconceptions.

(1) One misconception is that it is enough just to read and learn the facts of the Bible. Some of the most conservative, Bible-centered evangelical groups fall into this approach, especially under the influence of modernity. As we saw in the chapter on revelation, Scripture

is far more than an "encyclopedia of facts." One must appreciate its narrative and symbolic nature; interpret it in its historical context; set each part in the wider canonical context; and, as we have emphasized in this chapter, glean the spirit of the law, not the letter. Scripture is not a gnostic document, dropped out of heaven, detached from its context. Scripture is about the incarnation and is itself incarnational. It takes study of facts, but it takes far more indwelling than that to become canonically formed. The goal, as Kevin Vanhoozer puts it, is finally not just to learn the script of Scripture but actually to perform it.[62] As the so-called Yale School of theology loves to say, in the best sense, we must finally let the modern world be absorbed into the biblical world rather than vice versa. In the end, our lives are to be transformed into the canonical pattern, of course, by the Spirit. Here again, we have the Spirit and word working together, not pitted against each other. This requires a movement from learning facts and context to following the story to imaginatively indwelling the whole canon. Like the expert in other areas of life, the one who really knows the Bible is the one for whom the right thing comes to mind almost without thinking. This is seen when one lives out Scripture often as the natural thing to do, without having to search or strain to figure it out. This is when it truly becomes a "lamp to my feet, and a light to my path" (Ps 119:105).

(2) A second misconception in the modern period is that Bible study is something one does alone and is about one's private interpretations. This has led people to think that having the Bible is sufficient apart from a community of faith, perhaps even sufficient without living out the faith. It has certainly led one after another to think that the Bible is a source of puzzles that anyone can creatively solve to their heart's content, whether or not their interpretation is grounded in a contextual understanding of Scripture or is consonant with the basic historical affirmations of the Christian faith. The truth in this misconception is that one should study and ponder Scripture on one's own. It is also true that one is responsible for one's faith and must decide about God for oneself. The individual can stand against church authorities on the basis of Scripture, even as Martin Luther did. Yet this kind of individual responsibility, an

aspect of the priesthood of all believers that we shall look at in the chapter on the church, must be understood in an ecclesial and not a modern, privatistic sense.

Even if one can read the Bible on one's own, which is to be encouraged, in the church this is not necessarily private. The very fact of having a translation, for example, means that one is benefiting from the work of others, often other Christians as a part of the body of Christ whose very translations are interpretations. As we discussed in the prolegomena, we bring our traditions to the Bible, which do not have to be seen as a hindrance but as a help. The Bible can hardly be understood without a historical study of the context, which is helped by study aids and teachers, again contributions often from the wider body of Christ. The vast array of seminaries and divinity schools around the world, as part of the body of Christ, are gifts to provide resources for so-called "private" Bible study. This theology book itself hopes to be such a resource. When one is studying the Bible alone, one is not really alone.

Moreover, the most important difference from private, individualistic biblical study is that a Christian reads the Bible not just to hear one's own voice but to hear the voice of God. In addition, one reads to be better members of the body of Christ. One does not read it just for oneself but for others. Thus, there is an obligation to check one's understanding with others in the church, whether alive or dead, in a humble and not prideful way. Even the proud tradition and practice of dissent in Believers' churches is not a matter of the individual going one's own way but is a service to the church as one loyal to the church. Dissent arises out of love for the church, not out of disdain or disregard. Bible study is an aspect of the self that is a self-in-relation, as we saw in the chapter on the self. The larger pattern is thus one that ideally combines individual Bible study and contemplation, group study, preaching in worship—all in relationship to living out the word of God.

(3) A third misconception is that Bible study is sufficient. Some assume that one need not worry much about walking in the Spirit if one really knows the Bible. One need not study theology or church history or even the modern world; all one needs is the

Bible. Ironically, Scripture itself points beyond itself toward God. It is not meant as a rival to the Holy Spirit but is meant to help disciples become spiritually receptive to the Holy Spirit. The Bible itself, for example, teaches us to rely on the Spirit and to be discerning in new situations where the Bible does not give a specific answer. The Bible is not an answer to every question but provides a basis for responding to every question with God's help. It even helps us deal with the times when no answer is forthcoming. The Bible also points us toward learning about the world and does not claim to tell us everything about the world. Scripture is the primary authority, as we have seen, but it is more of a foundation for consulting other authorities and sources of truth. Perhaps the picture is a little overwhelming, but in trying to discern the will of God, we need not only to know Scripture well but also to know the guidance of the Spirit and our present context well. Wisdom is always incarnational, wisdom in a context.

The practice of Bible study is a lifelong indwelling of Scripture in order to be canonically formed in one's context. The test of knowing Scripture is not how many Bible verses one has memorized or even how much one knows of a particular context of a passage but finally how scripturally formed one has become.

Prayer. A second crucial and pervasive practice of the church is prayer. If salvation is being reconciled to God, then prayer—communication with God—is its lifeblood. Of course, this should work hand-in-hand with Bible study if one understands Scripture as divine communication. Prayer is that time, however, when communication becomes most direct. One may in this sense "pray" Scripture. Prayer, too, is a broader-based practice than is often thought.

Prayer is both individual and communal. With the emphasis on the responsibility of the believer for his or her own faith, especially stressed in Believer's churches, prayer must be individual. According to Jesus, just as God knows even when one sparrow falls to the ground, God desires for each one of us to know God (Matt 10:29). The parable of the lost sheep has to do with the shepherd looking for the one that is lost (Luke 15:4). An amazing aspect of the Gospel is the love of the God of the entire cosmos for each individual. Yet it is also God's love for *all* individuals, calling them into community and caring for each other. Prayer is not just a matter of internal navel-gazing, working on our own problems, but it draws us away from ourselves to God and then to all that God cares about, which is true of any loving relationship. Prayer is not private because it is a relationship with the most communal (Trinitarian) being there is. Prayers of petition should thus often be for others. Even for ourselves, a tacit purpose of petitionary prayer is to prepare us better to befriend and serve others. Prayer is not a private line, so to speak, but a party line. It is a web of relationships.

Prayer is both spoken and felt. Sometimes prayer is thought of as explicit verbal communication, which may be rather brief. Yet the Scripture points to the Spirit praying for us with "sighs too deep for words" (Rom 8:26). Pentecostals would certainly point to a private prayer language in this respect that goes beyond words. In addition, we are called to sense the peace of God and to let the peace of Christ guide us (Col 3:15). All of this is not possible apart from a sense or awareness of God that is a tacit foundation for explicit words. The dearth of meditation and contemplation in much Protestantism may be due in part to the modern emphasis on explicit words as the essence of communication. In any deep relationship between humans, though, much is nonverbal and "felt." In relationship to other persons, these are physical and visual cues. With God, there is a felt relationship that is more mysterious and spiritual—yet faith testifies that it is real. For much of Christian history, the attraction to Platonism was its recognition that the "spiritual" realm was actually more real than the physical. The mistake was sometimes then to denigrate the physical. The healthier balance is to see that the spiritual is real but is mediated through the physical. We are spiritually incarnate beings, open toward the physical and the spiritual.

Prayer is both responding and asking. Sometimes there is tension between those who emphasize prayer in terms of thanksgiving and praise while others seem to think only of prayer in terms of petition. Both are emphasized in Scripture. To take the Lord's Prayer as what it seems to be, a model prayer, both are present, although petition is rooted in praise and thanksgiving. Petition has its place, but its place is in the context of recognizing, thanking, and loving God. Petition comes quickly, however: "Our Father in heaven, hallowed be your name. Your kingdom come" (Matt 6:9-10). What an audacious request! No more powerful or comprehensive petitionary prayer can be uttered. Perhaps the closest in audaciousness is Jesus' prayer to the Father that the church might be one (John 17:23). Neither prayer has yet been realized, often in painfully blazing ways. Yet both are desires of God that are to be our desires. As prayers of Christ, they are our joint prayers with God. Sometimes, too, they are realized in this world in amazing ways, "far more than all we can ask or imagine" (Eph 3:20).

Petitionary prayer is often misunderstood. Our literalist print culture comes to Jesus' words to ask whatever we wish, "and it will be done for you" with little sense of the context (John 15:7). These words take their place in the entire canon, in fact, in the entire context of a theology of creation, sin, and redemption. They are related in other places to asking "in Jesus' name," which implies asking according to the spirit and tenor of Jesus (John 14:14). They are closer to the ideal, "Love God, and do whatever you want."[63] In this case, it would be, "Love God, and *ask* whatever you want." Our requests of God, until the final kingdom of God, will not undo this creation. If people take a libertarian view of free will as essential to love, they will not override free will. Our prayers, however, in a mysterious way, open up both ourselves and perhaps reality to the working of God's Spirit, who is usually working in persuasive, not dominating, ways. The story of Jesus Christ is the chief pattern. God worked mightily through Christ but did not save Jesus from the cross. We are similarly called to take up our cross and follow. Resurrection has not ended this world but is promissory beyond this world. It points to the finger of God that may be sometimes manifested in this world, usually through prayer, but not to the full revelation of God. The implication is that petitionary prayer makes a difference, always, in opening the world up to God, but it does not guarantee the final kingdom. Sometimes it may enable us, as we discussed with respect to providence in connection with Romans 8, to see that even if we suffer famine, nakedness, peril, or sword, "we are more than conquerors through him who loved us" (Rom 8:37). Such petitions are inseparable from thanksgiving and praise. Paul says, "Rejoice always, pray without ceasing; give thanks in all circumstances" (1 Thess 5:16-17). The key phrase seems to be "in all circumstances." We are not to be thankful *for* everything, for some things grieve even God. By implication, we are not to rejoice *for* everything, but in the midst of prayer, we might find, even in our deep sorrow, "peace which surpasses all understanding," for which we can rejoice (Phil 4:7). Prayer without ceasing is thus not uttering words of prayer at all times but implies a constant state of awareness of God, where communication of words or not is a natural flow. Christian maturity is learning how to pray and what to pray.

Discernment. These two Christian practices are spiritual disciplines that undergird every other Christian practice. Another practice that supports everything else is Christian discernment. Some might call this "knowing the will of God." An emphasis in early Believers' churches was the role of discernment. Perhaps this was most manifest in the Quaker meetings, which called for prayerful listening and community consensus. This was not just an appeal to a unanimous decision versus a majority vote, or to the right of one person to hold the rest hostage to their whims and fancies. It was a call to labor together as a community that highly respects each other to come to a spiritual agreement, which might mean everyone changing before the final consensus is reached. Discernment had long been rooted in monastic practices of spirituality, usually coupled with spiritual guides and directors. It is, however, not reserved for the privileged few, not just a matter for popes, priests, or pastors. Any Christian who is responsible to the Spirit will search to discern the will of God. Those who emphasize congregational church government especially see each member of the body of Christ as equally responsible for the direction of the church. Whether a decision of the church to begin a ministry, to call a pastor, or a believer's question about a vocation or spouse, discernment is as common as breathing in the Christian life.

At times, discernment has lapsed into legalistic judgmentalism, noticing the speck in the other's eye but not the log in one's own. As such, as a communal practice, it has fallen out of favor and practice in many churches. Recovery may be aided by seeing it in a broader way, as including much more than negative judgments about others. James McClendon connects it with "soaring" in the Christian life in a fascinating way:

> We must accept soaring as an adventurous stage in principle less predictable than any other aspect of the Christian life. Hence the "sign" to which it best relates is the practice of communal discernment. Discernment not preoccupied with sin and fault and exclusion may find a better task in the church, the task of recognizing vocations, acknowledging and encouraging gifts, and helping the gifted to see their role with the rule of God.[64]

Common directions given for discerning the will of God are to triangulate the decision in terms of how it lines up with Scripture, how the Spirit is leading, and how it fits circumstances. The first two are practices in themselves, as we have seen. Concerning the leading of the Spirit, the emphasis is on direction from the Holy Spirit, which is not usually verbal or direct, although these experiences do happen occasionally. Sometimes such experiences happen in tandem with Scripture. One of the most famous is Augustine's conversion, where he heard a child chanting and calling out, "Take up and read." He then opened up the Scriptures and felt the Spirit speaking directly to him in the words, "Put on the Lord Jesus Christ, and make no provision for the flesh, to gratify its desires"[65] (Rom 13:14). These became words of power to him, enabling him finally to sacrifice all in following Christ, including becoming celibate. The reason for various guides is that the Spirit usually does not work in that direct of a way. Sensitivity to the Spirit through a life of prayer is crucial for sensing the more subtle direction of "letting the peace of Christ guide" (Col 3:15). The comparison that my pastor made once was thinking about his family calling out as they came in the door of their house. As soon as he heard them, he knew them. With all due regard for how much more mysterious the Spirit's calling is, this familiarity is the basis for mature discernment.[66] Because this process is complex and mysterious, canonical maxims and patterns provide stability. Maturity in understanding the Bible, and the spirit of the Bible, as well as maturity in discerning the difference between the Holy Spirit and one's own spirit is crucial.

Facility in being aware of the seductiveness and treachery of sin is also crucial. In fact, the greatest mistakes are to rationalize one's own selfish or prideful desires as the leading of the Spirit or the words of Scripture or to mask one's fears or timidity behind the Spirit or the Bible. As the book of Hebrews says, mature Christians are those "whose faculties have been trained by practice to distinguish good from evil" (Heb 5:14). All that we have said about social evil comes into play. Just as Bible study is crucial, "social study" is required in order to discern social dynamics. Reinhold Niebuhr reminded a whole generation of the way that institutions have strong tendencies to dehumanize and preserve themselves by sacrificing individuals. If one does not understand this, one can hardly "be wise as serpents and innocent as doves" (Matt 10:16). This is not to demonize institutions or "the establishment," which many Christians did in the 1960s and still do, but it is to be as alert to social sin as we are called to be alert to individual sin.

Like Bible study, discernment is not merely an individual practice, something that we do by ourselves for ourselves but a social, ecclesial practice. The passage in Colossians that calls for letting the peace of Christ act as a guide is immediately followed by the words, "to which indeed you were called in the one body" (3:15). The "peace of Christ" is not just an individual matter of my inner being but is related to the peace of the body of Christ. It is in the next chapter that we focus upon the church, but what a difference this might make for the church if everyone understood personal discernment in such ecclesial terms. Ultimately, discernment is for the sake of the coming of the kingdom of God. We do not just discern for the well-being of our own lives but for our own lives as part of God's will "being done on earth as it is in Heaven" (Matt 6:10).

Another aspect of the social dimension of discernment is that this discernment must reflect the humility to check with others and to listen to their responses. It does not mean to abdicate one's own responsibility and to pawn it off on others, but it means that we realize that we see "in part" (1 Cor 13:12), that following God is perhaps more complex than anything else one might attempt to do, and that part of being the body of Christ is that we rely on the gifts of others. If we do not exhibit openness and humility, then we are not engaging in the Christian practice of discernment. It is easy to confuse the Western emphasis on individual rights and freedom to make up our own minds with Christian discernment. This is not to denigrate the human rights tradition, which is a great gain and often offers space for Christian freedom. In the end, though, it is not full Christian discernment that is ecclesial discernment for the sake of the kingdom of God. Christian discernment is before God and before the church, not just for the self.

Discernment may not be individualistic, but it is always local. When we are called upon to love God and love our neighbor, it takes discernment to know how to do that in particular situations. This does not mean that we are a blank slate; we are not bereft of guidance. We have large Bibles and two thousand years of church history to guide us. We neglect such guidance to our peril, falling prey to the common saying, "Those who cannot remember the past are condemned to repeat it." Yet just studying the past and what happened is not sufficient, any more than knowing what the Bible says is sufficient. We must be discerning of what was good and bad in the past as well as how to apply biblical patterns in the present. Kevin Vanhoozer, in emphasizing that we are to perform the Bible script in the present, has to concede that this is "improvisatory theater."[67] The performance must be creative and somewhat "on the spot" to relate to the current situation. Sometimes it is a matter of *which* biblical pattern is appropriate. Sometimes we might be called upon to honor our parents and provide for them. At other times, we might be called upon to "hate our mothers and fathers" (Luke 14:26). At times, we are to obey the laws of the land as in Romans 13. At other times, we must rebel against them as in Revelation 13. Practical wisdom, *phronesis* again, the ability to apply general principles to specific situations, becomes spiritual discernment in the Christian context. It is a practice that takes practice.

Reading circumstances is as complex as relating the Bible to the situation and sensing the Holy Spirit. It requires an entire theology of providence. Apart from a view of providence that sees God as orchestrating everything, the nonmeticulous view sees God committed to a creation that has its own regular laws, a nature that has its own genuine randomness, and the free will of people, as well as God's persuasive luring. It means that God's will is not always done, in fact, that it is often not done, but God is immensely creative in responding and working with God's creation in providential ways. When Paul in Acts 16, for example, came from the east, the door was shut to the north and south, "forbidden by the Holy Spirit" (Acts 16:6). The Macedonian called in a dream for him then to go west, which opened up Europe for the gospel. We do not know how this happened. The Holy Spirit's speaking may have been through circumstances. It has been suggested that the road might have been blocked for Paul to go north. Others have wondered that vehement opponents to Paul blocked another path. Yet the way that was still open became an open door that God used in other powerful ways. Discernment is full of such language about "knocking on the door" and "seeing if it opens." "That door was shut, so I tried another." It takes faith, and sometimes imaginative creativity, to rebound from rejection and disappointment to be open to walk through, much less see, another open door.[68] It also requires discernment to distinguish between an obstacle that must be resisted and overcome and a "door that the Holy Spirit has closed." Sometimes there are open doors through which we should not pass. "The gate is narrow" that leads to life, Jesus said (Matt 7:14). Sometimes difficulties and suffering attend the will of God, not an easy and painless path. Yet we must discern whether an option has been closed or not.

Moreover, others can fail to do God's will, which impinges upon us. God may have wanted us, for example, to go to that church, to have that job, to minister to that person, but it is not possible. There is a place, as Jesus said, to wipe the dust off of our feet and go to the next town (Luke 9:5). The door is closed. The "serenity prayer" by Reinhold Niebuhr, for good reason, has been a benchmark for many: "God, grant me the serenity to accept the things that cannot be changed, the courage to change the things I can, and the wisdom to know the difference." Spiritual discernment is thus an individual-communal Christian practice that is exceedingly complex yet practiced every day.

Forgiveness. The next practice is as central as all of the other practices that we have considered—Bible study, prayer, and discernment—which actually are preconditions for it. With our wider look at salvation, we can return to the practice of forgiveness that we began with in Miroslav Volf's case.

It is not surprising that forgiveness would be stressed so much by the historical Jesus, before the cross, before the resurrection, and before centuries to develop atonement theology. Forgiveness is at the heart of salvation, and the forgiveness that we receive is to be extended to others. This ongoing practice grows out of the basic meaning of salvation and the Christian life. The forgiven are enabled to live a new life in reconciliation and relationship with God. With the inevitable sin and mistakes that come in this broken, groaning world, the forgiveness that is received is to be offered to others—and received from others. Since forgiveness in salvation is not a legal requirement, not a part of the economy of exchange, but a gift, the practice of forgiveness inhabits the space between an obligation and a voluntary act. We are commanded to forgive by Christ, but its nature as a gift means that such a command is not a legalistic, external one.

Paul Fiddes speaks of the "voyage" of forgiveness.[69] Just as we recognize that in prayers of lament the culmination in praise of God is not instantaneous but a process, sometimes one of hours, weeks, and months, forgiveness is a process. We must recognize that people who have been deeply wronged do not automatically leap to the ideal stage of Christian practice. Sometimes there are stages of forgiveness, just like there are stages of grief, which in fact are closely related. The wrong that elicits forgiveness is a loss—a loss of friendship, of love, of trust. Forgiveness does not necessarily restore the loss. It makes much restoration possible, but not necessarily all. In drastic cases, when someone has murdered a loved one, forgiveness cannot restore the loved one. Someone who has embezzled one's life savings, or criminally lost them as in the Enron case, cannot always replace them. Forgiveness allows good to come from evil. It does not put things exactly back where they were, but it allows for redemptive, transforming initiatives such that new possibilities can emerge. Paul thought of himself as the chief of sinners because he had persecuted and killed Christians (1 Tim 1:15). He was reconciled, however, with the Christian community and became a great leader. This did not bring back the martyrs, like Stephen, whose execution Paul (Saul) "approved" (Acts 8:1), or alleviate Paul's feeling of being a great sinner. Yet, "he loved much because he was forgiven much." Forgiveness opens up redemptive possibilities.

Opening up those possibilities takes time. Moving from shock to anger to grief to a willingness to forgive can take time. From a human standpoint, forgiveness of the murderer of one's child or one's rapist cannot be legalistically commanded. This distinction is much misunderstood. The call to forgive has its home not in the external law court but in the personal relationships with God and with others. It can be solicited and prayed for, but the desire and ability is a gift of grace: "For it is God who is at work in you, enabling you both to will and to work for his good pleasure" (Phil 2:13). This allows the Christian community to call forth forgiveness but also to be understanding of the voyage of forgiveness that is as unique as each individual. Sometimes the individual and the community must "wait upon the Lord" (Isa 40:31)—and each other—as they move toward readiness to follow Christ in forgiveness.

Much criticism has come from some with regard to the Christian call to lavish forgiveness because it may work against the equally strong call to justice and to care for the oppressed. It is often the oppressor who demands forgiveness and acquiescence just to continue oppression. An example would be a wife in an abusive situation who is asked to keep forgiving her husband and thus continues taking the abuse. Sometimes what is required is to resist abuse and not to acquiesce. Using forgiveness to promote oppression is obviously a perversion of the spirit of forgiveness, but responding to the problem is complex and provides the necessary place for practical spiritual wisdom.

One helpful perspective is to place forgiveness within the higher command to love our neighbor, even our enemies.[70] While we forgive and are willing to put the past behind, we still must think about what is most loving toward the other. Then the question is whether it would be loving or in the other person's best interests to put someone in a place of great temptation, one for which they have shown they are not ready. This might be helpful also in understanding how the spouse of someone who is unfaithful might take the other back—or might not. Forgiveness means one is willing to consider it. Doing the loving thing for all concerned is a larger question and might mean that one should not. Forgiveness places recrimination aside for what happened in the past; failures in the past must be taken into account in thinking of what is best for the future. In many ways, the spirit of what is done is what is crucial. Are one's actions motivated by resentment and revenge, or are they motivated by genuine care for the person and others who might be affected by his or her actions? Sensitive discernment is inescapable. To apply a rule that does not take into account particulars becomes legalistic and even damaging.

Considering the larger issue of love also aids in another issue. Sometime the choice seems to be between forgiveness and hostility, even when the other is unrepentant—and in fact would be offended if it were suggested that they needed to repent. Think of a racist who feels justified. Or a corporate CEO who justifies harsh treatment because it serves the financial bottom line. The problem is not whether someone can forgive them. They do not want forgiveness or believe that they need it. Forgiving such that one tries to keep a positive relationship with someone who is being abusive can lead to more abuse. It can be destructive of both persons and can actually impede the abuser from coming to repentance. So forgiveness may not be what is needed. Some who appeal for forgiveness in every case—no matter what—sometimes justify it for "selfish" reasons. Forgiveness is not for the offender but for the offended. It prevents one from destroying oneself in bitterness and hate. The recognition that bitterness harms the one who is bitter more than the cause of bitterness is insightful. Yet such a rationale misunderstands the nature and spirit of forgiveness. Forgiveness is not primarily about oneself; it is other directed. To make it selfish is perhaps to follow the letter of the law but not the spirit.

This rationale also is blind to the wider dimension of love of neighbor. Even if an abuser is unrepentant, a Christian is summoned to love. Perhaps Jesus' most shocking teaching was love of enemies (Matt 5:44). If one loves a person, one cannot be bitter or hateful toward them, even though the journey to transcend these feelings can take time. Everyone is thus called to desire a situation of forgiveness, but it is not always possible. If one understands that the primary meaning of forgiveness is relational, this makes sense. As Fiddes says, "Forgiveness, unlike a mere pardon, seeks to win the offender back into relationship."[71] Therefore, one can no more normally forgive by oneself than one can get married by oneself. Reconciliation takes two. Love appeals to reconciliation with accompanying repentance and forgiveness, but it does not guarantee it.

More can be said about something as complex as forgiveness, but this is to give an idea of what such a Christian practice involves. It draws from biblical revelation and Christian tradition, one's own experience of being forgiven by God, the intrinsic particularities of a situation, and the discerning application of these various dimensions. One might also draw on the insights of psychology. Often the social dimension is far broader than two people. Children might be involved in a quarrel between parents. Churches might have factions at odds with each other. Whole denominations can experience strife where reconciliation and forgiveness involve people who hardly know each other. Counsel with spiritual friends should be a part even of torn relationships between two people. Gregory Jones places forgiveness within the church, which, as he says, is the proper locale for practicing the "craft of forgiveness" as a Trinitarian community.[72] The emphasis thus lies not simply on an atomistic act of forgiveness but especially on the character and community of the one forgiving. Such character and craft, he insists, are learned from the scriptural narratives and others. As we turn to the next chapter, on the church, this is a place again to remember that everything discussed in this chapter always occurs in a wider social and ecclesial context. Forgiveness transforms one's self and the other, and then many others.

9

CHURCH
Walking Together

The early Christian movement was called the Way, a path, a journey (Acts 9:2). It was never seen as a solitary path, however, but as a Way for people to walk together. The early church quickly took the term *ecclesia*, a gathering, a community of people joined in a common undertaking. With the rise of Constantinian Christianity in the fourth century, the church sometimes became a heavily hierarchical, oppressive institution, to Christians and non-Christians alike, so much so that it has split innumerable times as a result of protest movements. With the rise of modernity's turn to the self, the church commonly has taken a back seat to the individual's religious journey. The church became an option, an afterthought. Just as discipleship became separated from salvation, the church became separated from the Christian. Increasingly, both of these splits are disastrous breaches in the true meaning of the Christian faith. While Christ and the church are not identical, neither are they fully separable. After much time in which the church's role has taken the background, if not slipped completely out of sight, it is coming to the fore again in Western thought. This is not a return to the hegemony of the Constantinian or Western medieval church, however, for it affirms the individual more strongly. Along with a greater realization of the priesthood of all believers, of all Christians equally called to God's mission, it represents a truly postmodern rather than premodern sense of the community of faith. This new sense of the essential communal shape of faith and mission is rooted in a renewed sense of the social Trinity and the social self, interlocking with them as the missing piece of the puzzle. This renewed and transformed conception of the church will be the theme of this chapter.

We will first look at a case study of the rise of the Baptist movement as one of the beginnings of the burgeoning Believers' church movement worldwide. Also called the free church movement, it is centered around every member who has made a conscious profession of faith being baptized as a believer and regarded as spiritually equal to every other member. As we shall see, in its beginnings, the Baptist movement was not so much centered in a person as in a local community of faith. Such a look will, at the same time, bring to the fore the greater sense of individuality and freedom that marks this movement and also the modern world. In fact, the Baptist tradition was birthed virtually at the same time as modernity and has flourished in modernity, so much so that, ironically, the Baptist church has often been eclipsed to leave only the "free" individual.[1] The transition to postmodernity, along with many other theological challenges, however, has presented new challenges to the Believers' Church movement just as it has to the older denominations that began as "establishment" churches. The Protestant split from the Roman Catholic Church, along with its bewildering diffusion into innumerable other groups such as the Believers' churches, has constantly raised afresh the question, What is the church? What are its characteristics? What does it mean for the Christian to follow Christ in the church? These questions will be treated in light of this continuing tension between the sense of Christianity as one faith and one church—yet the reality that the church today exists in "many churches."

Perhaps in no other place in theology is one's own context and tradition so evident than in the doctrine of the church, ecclesiology. Sometimes one cannot tell the background of a theologian when dealing with the Trinity or the properties of God or the self; it is usually unmistakable, however, when it comes to the church. In this sense, one's ecclesiology seems more personal and confessional. One's true colors come to the fore, so to speak. This does not mean, however, that no theologian writes for the whole church. Each theologian does so as much here as elsewhere. Yet it may be that the incarnational sense of theology, which is so essential throughout, becomes more obvious here than elsewhere. In this context, one's convictions about God, the self, and salvation coalesce in a practical way. At the same time, the theologians' ecclesiologies help us see more clearly the import of the rest of their theology. It is not just of interest to those of their own confession but a contribution to the ongoing theological task of the entire church. At a time when perhaps the most creative ferment in theology lies in the nature of the church, sometimes not in reflection as much as in practice, every theologian's ecclesiology becomes significant for the whole church.

An Emergent Church: The First Baptists

As a premier exemplar of the Believers' or free church movement, which James McClendon designated the "Baptist" movement, Baptists have sometimes had an inferiority complex theologically, for they could not assign their origins to a famous theologian or even a famous leader.[2] Some "Landmark" Baptists tried valiantly but foolishly in the nineteenth century to claim John the Baptist as their forebear, trying to trump even the Roman Catholic Church's claim of apostolic succession to Peter.[3] Yet such a grandiose assertion could not be maintained historically and is suspect theologically, as we shall see. Nevertheless, Lutherans have Luther, Presbyterians have Calvin, Methodists have Wesley. Even the Christian churches that emerged after the Baptist church could claim Alexander Campbell. Baptists have had their heroes from time to time, but at the beginning they had none of that caliber. The closest perhaps was Roger Williams, who represented Baptist distinctives of religious liberty and separation of church and state in the New World as early as the 1630s, but he was a Baptist only a short time.[4] What Baptists did have, which perhaps even better exemplifies the free church tradition, was not so much great individuals as great congregations.

While the Reformation was raging on the continent in the early sixteenth century, a different reform was occurring in England.[5] Because of conflict between the king of England and the pope, England split from the Roman Catholic Church but more slightly and subtly. The Anglican Church that was born of the rupture (known as the Episcopal Church in the United States) remained close to the Catholic Church in many respects. Nevertheless, the continental Reformation exerted its pressure so that by the end of the century, England, too, was experiencing division even within the Anglican ranks. Some desired change but remained in the church and were called Puritans. Others felt that the problems were so severe that they must leave and were called Separatists. These tended to emphasize the importance of a committed church membership—as opposed to all being in the church by virtue of being baptized as an infant— and thus practiced congregational church government, which called for all in the church to be responsible for the local church. Yet they still practiced infant baptism.

In 1606, one of these Separatist churches was meeting clandestinely in the village of Gainesborough out of fear of reprisal by the state church. King James I, sponsor of the King James Version of the Bible, had threatened to "harry them out of the land" unless they returned to the state church. Some of the key leaders were John Smyth, Thomas Helwys, William Bradford, and William Brewster. As they grew, they divided into two congregations in order to avoid detection: the Smyth-Helwys group met in Scrooby, and the Bradford-Brewster group continued to meet in Gainesborough. The tension became so great that both congregations resolved to move to Holland in 1607.

Can you imagine whole congregations moving for the sake of their faith? This is a sign of the emphasis on the covenantal community and the local church at the heart of Believers' churches. The essence of the church, so to speak, is its incarnation in a local community of believers committed to each other. Many from these two churches set out to continue as churches in a new country, with a new language. Another fascinating characteristic was to hold together commitment to scriptural authority, *sola scriptura*, as in the continental Reformation, together with an openness to new insights into Scripture, which were coming with breathtaking rapidity. Before they left England, Smyth drafted a covenant wherein they resolved to "walke in all his wayes, made known, or to be made known unto them."[6] In this brief aphorism, they revealed the kindred challenges that face any Christian of any age to understand God's revelation in light of the Wesleyan Quadrilateral. They desired to be faithful to "his ways made known"—Scripture and tradition—with openness to how they might be made known in light of new experiences and reflection in light of the creative Holy Spirit. It reveals an eschatological dimension of openness to the future that we will stress in the next chapter. All of this was happening, of course, not in a utopian mountaintop experience but in the midst of real life, real families, real politics, and real dangers. For example, Mrs. Helwys stayed behind in England.

While in the Netherlands, these congregations were likely influenced by the Mennonites, "Anabaptists" as they were often called, who had already moved to believer's baptism as the practice more consonant with the practice in the New Testament and more symbolic of the new birth that is consciously chosen by someone old enough to make a profession of faith. Such practice also put a premium on a committed and pure church that was composed of a regenerate church membership, that is, only of those who had made conscious, adult professions of faith. As such, it represented the reaction against what many saw as a corrupt and worldly church that inspired all of the Reformation movements. Soon, therefore, Smyth led his congregation to believer's baptism. Somewhat clumsily, he baptized himself by pouring water on his head and then baptized the others in the congregation who were willing. Only much later did they move to the practice of baptism by immersion. Such was born the first Baptist church in 1609.

Very quickly, however, the flighty Smyth became convinced that succession in baptism was important, so he led some to join a Mennonite church. Helwys and others did not agree and remained as a smaller church. The issue was significant. Many churches, such as the Orthodox and Roman Catholic, have maintained similarly that succession must be literal, so to speak. It must be capable of being traced physically back to an origin. Helwys' church thought that continuity with the true church was crucial, but the continuity was spiritual, not literal. Apart from such a momentous theological move, the proliferation of free churches could not have gotten off the ground. It has led to greater emphasis on the local church, rather than connection through an official succession of official clergy in a hierarchy that transcends the local church. It is mostly in these nonsuccessionist churches where great growth is occurring in the Protestant churches. For good or ill, the small beginnings among Anabaptists and Baptists in the sixteenth and seventeen centuries provided the foundation for the monumental changes in the church of the modern world.

In 1611, Helwys led the group back to England, to Spitalfields near London. Representing the spirit of the priesthood of all believers, he had moved from laity to clergy rather easily due to his gifts, yet another harbinger of things to come. As observers have noted, Smyth was brilliant but unstable. Helwys was the lawyer with a steady hand with finances that stabilized the group. One record said that if Smyth brought oars, Helwys brought sails. Rather than rising to leadership due to official training or accreditation, Helwys was called by the congregation, who recognized his gifts. The decision to return was historically significant, for it led to the establishment of the Baptist church on English soil. Part of his reasoning was that if they did not go back, who would be a witness to their fellows in England? Also he had left his wife and children behind.

In any case, they returned. In 1612, Helwys wrote apparently the first document in the English language explicitly appealing for liberty of conscience with the implication of the separation of church and state.[7] The reason is that since no one can stand before God on our behalf, no one on earth should be able to force our conscience. He was long before his time; for such outrageous writings, he was thrown into prison until he died in 1616. He was followed by yet another lay person, John Murton, a furrier. He, too, is credited with writing one of the first works in the English language on religious liberty, appealing to the very nature of salvation as its basis.[8] Since each person must respond to God individually, no one should coerce another's faith. Murton similarly was ahead of his time, was thrown into prison, and died in prison in 1626. While their views made little sense at the time, they bore fruit a century and a half later when, inspired especially by Baptist lobbyists with James Madison, the new United States of America made freedom of religion one of the linchpins of the new society, a principle that is increasingly recognized around the world.[9] While many take it for granted today, its humble beginnings were born not that long ago and in sufferings such as these. Langdon Gilkey, longtime professor of theology at the University of Chicago Divinity School, expresses today the deep connection between this insight and a political structure of separation of church and state, "The First Amendment is important not only to guarantee the rights of alternative religions and of non-religious persons in society; it is also important in setting the only possible legal and social conditions for the creative health of serious religion itself. This my own tradition—the Baptist (as well as that of the Quaker and the Unitarian)—has held from its own early beginnings on this continent."[10]

Oh, yes, the other congregation, the Bradford-Brewster congregational church, decided also to leave—but to go to the New World as what we know as the Pilgrim church that founded Plymouth.

This story is not to glorify Baptists. Baptists and free churches have their own demons, as we have already pointed out from time to time. It does, however, paint in vivid colors how a very different way of being the church arose that, for the sake of a vital church, has emphasized believer's baptism, the centrality and autonomy of local congregations, democratic church government, the priesthood of all believers, and the separation of church and state. All of these are arguably interconnected with the emphasis on individual freedom and responsibility that arose in step with similar ideas in the larger world with the rise of modern nation-states, democracy, and individual rights. Such a movement is increasing rather than decreasing, even when, ironically, such churches born of oppression and marginalization have become dominant in many parts of society such as the U.S. South and have often become repressive of other groups. Many throw up their hands in the face of what they see as the splintering of the unity of the church into a multitude of churches that are better at splitting and fighting than of serving and cooperating. The challenge that this movement brings cuts to the heart of what it means to be the church, even to what salvation means. Trying to find a stable place to stand in the midst of these changes requires examining again the biblical foundations for the church and a further look at the historical development of the church.

The Centrality of the Church

We live in a time of other emergent churches striving for vitality in a changing time, and the church is experiencing something of a renaissance. The church had been relegated to secondary status due to the rise of individualism in the West. Its situation has been worsened by being identified with impersonal hierarchies—its identification with business models only aggravating the problem—and scandals of prominent clergy from virtually every group. Despite all of these forces, a cry for genuine community has arisen in part because of the poverty in relationships bequeathed by modernity, and the church has responded.

As we have developed several theological themes, it is easy to see how central the church is to theology and to the Christian life. Rather than being an option or just a practical area, it is integral to an understanding of Christianity. This is seen most clearly in the greater emphasis placed on the social Trinity. When God in God's own self is seen as deeply relational—of course, without detracting from monotheism—and humans are seen as created as deeply social beings in God's own image, the church becomes the human expression of redeemed humanity. Being isolated individuals is a sign of human estrangement from human purpose. Manifesting and living out true community is not tangential to salvation but is an essential expression of it. As humans are "selves in relationships" the healing—salvation—of such selves is the healing of relationships.

It is not surprising then that major biblical images for the church are living, organic ones expressed in Trinitarian fashion. The church is the "people of God" who are chosen, elect, by God (Judg 20:2; Heb 4:9, 11:25). Like Israel, the original people of God, they are chosen not because of merit or accomplishment but out of God's own love and desire for them: "We love because God first loved us" (1 John 4:19). Like Israel, which was formed from an agglomeration of slaves into a people, the church, as part of the progression of Israel's calling into the calling of the entire human race, is "the beloved community," in Martin Luther King Jr.'s words, which receives inwardly and proclaims outwardly God's love for all people. It embodies this calling as it has been received and molded into a self-conscious people. The biblical and traditional word for the community that is formed is the "city of God," made famous by Augustine's book of that name. Drawing on the Greek tradition of the *polis* (city), Augustine meant more the idea of a city that bonds people together in a common covenant and commitment. The primary sense of a "local church" represents the spatial focus of the city of God, but it may rival a secular city that occupies the same place. Augustine distinguished between the city of the world and the city of God; both exist together. Barry Harvey calls this "another city," a city that never blurs into the world but is always a distinctive "people."[11] Another image is the people of God as "an outpost of Heaven."[12] This captures the eschatological dimension of the people of God as always on the way to the future. They are a people not so much in light of the past as in light of their destiny. "Outpost" expresses also the sense of community—but one that is located in somewhat alien territory. In history, the church has been tempted to combine the city of God with the city of government and use the governmental power of the sword to coerce faith and doctrine. The great gift of the Radical Reformation was to show this for the temptation it was and to display how contrary it was to the spirit of the gospel. Faith must be sincere and come from the heart, and not be imposed by external forces matched by grudging consent. Mere assent is not the same as personal, conscientious conviction. Of course, as the descendants of the Radical Reformation gained power, such as Baptists in the Bible

Belt of the United States, they have shown that they are equally susceptible to the desire to merge the two cities. The people of God are a people who not only are shaped by God's moving graciously toward them but wend their way toward others in like fashion. They are enabled to do this because they are a people, a community, another city that forms the citizens of their commonwealth to be the light and salt of the world around them, rather than, in Jesus' image, to lose their saltiness (Matt 5:13). This image shows that the way in which salvation comes to the world is not just in the isolated individual beloved by modernity but through an alternative community, a social practice so different that it may be seen, in Harvey's words, as "the invitation of Jesus to a holy madness, to a life of truthfulness in a parallel *polis*."[13]

The church in Paul is seen as the "body of Christ" (Rom 7:4; 1 Cor 12:27; Eph 4:12). Christ cannot be represented by one person alone. The whole church is Christ's body. The many gifts and energies of all the people of God make the church at the local level and at the universal level one body that is to be Christ's hands and feet. In this sense, one cannot understand atonement or salvation apart from their fulfillment in the church as the body of Christ. In an almost literal way, this image underscores the fact, so often missed in a hyperindividualistic culture, that following Christ is not possible apart from relating to Christ's whole body, including the historic church and the global church. This also means that the church is under Christ and serves the mission of Christ. Thus, the church is always subject to judgment in light of the gospel of Christ. The church has often fallen captive to other lords, but it only has one Lord. Faithfulness to the church sometimes is best seen in terms of dissent rather than acquiescence. Unity does not mean uniformity or automatic agreement.

The third great Trinitarian image is the church as "the fellowship of the Spirit" (Phil 2:1). The church is neither primarily an external organization nor an impersonal hierarchy nor a visible collection of people; it is a fellowship before all of those things. Insofar as fellowship is lacking or recedes into the background behind those other aspects, one can say that the church has become unbalanced.

A fellowship cannot easily be measured or described, but it can fairly easily be felt. It is easier to experience than to describe. This is why, in the end, virtually every group has moved to see the local fellowship as the central locus of the church. The church is thus a spiritual, living reality that must be incarnate, for example, in giving a cup of cold water to one another. This image also means that the church does not live by its own power as if it must muster up energy and courage to go on but lives by the enlivening power of the Spirit of life.

These images help us keep central what is central. The church is people in relationship, not buildings or structures. The latter are expressions of a church, not the church. In popular parlance, people often speak of a church building as the church or the worship service on Sunday as church, but the church is the people wherever and whenever they are; and it is not just the people by themselves but people in actual, real relationships. Insofar as the church fails in this regard, it fails to be the church. This is crucial in keeping the proper balance, as we often discuss in theology. There are strong pulls in organizations to place the organization above people, buildings above congregations, and budgets above needs. The instinct for self-survival is as strong in institutions as in people, which can lead to an institution's abusing the people who compose it. As we shall see, as incarnational, groups of people nevertheless need structure and organization. Good ones serve fellowship as well as love and justice.

As in all things human, however, a broken and sinful world pulls in the opposite direction. One manifestation of human brokenness, in terms of loneliness and alienation, is the distortion of the healthy need of relationships, which often leads to anger directed at oneself and others. Another manifestation, however, is that even when humans gather in organizations to overcome such loneliness, the organizations dehumanize and sacrifice them for the sake of the organization. Sinfulness strikes everywhere, and as we saw in the reflection on sin, corporate sin can become demonic. The church at best pulls against these tendencies. As in individual lives, however, the church as a whole has succumbed to and propagated evil rather than resisting it. In fact, any Christian wrongdoing is an action of the church. The individual call to discipleship and sanctification in fact cannot be individual but is part and parcel of the church's striving for discipleship and sanctification. Following Christ thus takes place in the context of Christ's body, both within and outside the church.

As we saw in connection with the self, the self is a self in relation. The self is not lost in the community, nor is the community sacrificed to the self. In this sense, modernity has represented gain as well as loss. The greater sense of self-responsibility and respect for the individual conscience is deeply rooted, and in fact presupposed, in Scripture. The idea that one could coerce faith or mandate faith from outside does not respect the individual's relationship to God. This move to authentic individuality is presupposed in Jesus' call to discipleship as well as by prophets like Jeremiah and Ezekiel who saw that one could not blame others for one's own decisions. The criticism of hyperindividualism in modernity does not evince lack of respect for individual responsibility or equality. Rather, they are part of the unfinished business of modernity because such ideals have only partially been realized, and they have been taken to extremes that actually threaten genuine community. The challenge of the church, in our time of greater recognition of the excesses of the Enlightenment, is to find the balance between the individual and the community. Modernity tended to oscillate between individualism and totalitarianism. Premodernity did not do justice to the individual. The Christian ideal is none of these. It is one always of a self in relation but not of a self lost in relationships, coerced by relationships, or subjugated by relationships. The stain of the premodern church was to convert at the point of a sword or a bonfire. The stain of modernity was to loosen the self from any commitments whatsoever—and thus any genuine relationships. Paul Tillich expressed this tension well: the Christian ideal is neither *heteronomy* (where the self is dominated by an outer law), nor *autonomy* (where the self recognizes no transcendence), but it is *theonomy* (where the self voluntarily commits internally to One who fulfills the self).[14] It is often expressed in the Bible as a paradox in relationship to God, namely, slavery to God is perfect freedom.[15] In relationship to others, a similar dynamic exists. Only when one cares about others and commits to others can one fulfill one's own self. To care only for oneself dooms one to an atrophied and impoverished life, a less than human existence. As Jesus put it, "For those who want to save their life will lose it, and those who lose their life for my sake will find it" (Matt 16:25). To be in community is the way that we were made, according to a Christian view of creation. This is what we corrupt, according to a Christian view of sin. This is what is redeemed in the church, according to a Christian view of salvation.

THE NATURE OF THE CHURCH

Not just any community, however, is identified as the church. Beyond what we have said already, how does one understand the specificity of the church? With a myriad of groups claiming to be the church, and more arising every day, is there any guidance for sorting out such a question? At times, the church was identified as an institution. The Roman Catholic Church would say, "No salvation outside the church," meaning the Roman Catholic Church.[16] Others have said practically the same thing. This was further specified in terms of certain beliefs. If one did not share the right beliefs, one could be executed or banished or otherwise punished. In the past, the power of the sword, whether wielded by the church or by the state for the church, was used to enforce the structural boundaries of the church. Besides such an approach being almost impossible in today's world, is it, was it, ever promising? Was it ever consistent with the basic nature of the gospel?

In its better moments, the church confessed several other "marks" of the church. Every Sunday, in the Nicene Creed, most believers have confessed their belief in the "one, holy, catholic, apostolic church." These have been central guides to the nature of the church and still are—yet take on fresh meaning in the contemporary context.

THE UNITY OF THE CHURCH

The unity of the church has been a vexing issue from the outset. As the early church quickly moved outward from Jerusalem, it proliferated in ways recently highlighted by the Nag Hammadi findings, which showed that in the first few centuries there were many other versions of the gospel that differed from the orthodox version. Even in the New Testament itself, Acts gives witness to disputes between Hellenistic Jewish Christians and those native to Israel. Later, conflict erupted concerning whether Gentile Christians should become Jewish. With the decision, in essence, to burst the boundaries of Judaism and its land, the church spread around the Mediterranean. In each place, local churches took on characteristics of their local culture. Paul's letters to the Corinthians indicate how much diversity could exist in one church and how difficult it was to hold it together.

As time went on, consensus emerged around a canon of Scripture and central confessions. Even a certain common structure emerged, which, however, was never universal. Later church history has smoothed over the rough edges of the story, suggesting a Roman Catholic Church or an Orthodox Church with little divergence until the Reformation, yet there were always local differences, sometimes manifested in larger ways such as the significantly different ethos between the Eastern Greek-speaking churches and the Western Latin-speaking churches. "Unorthodox" churches continued to exist, such as mostly Jewish churches, gnostic churches, Arian churches, Nestorian churches, and Monophysite churches.

The unity of the church has been commonly confessed but little understood—and little realized. The church has existed in various locales, yet these have been confessed as one church. Sometimes this has been done by dismissing competitors. Catholics dismissed the Orthodox, and vice versa. Landmark Baptists and the Churches of Christ dismissed all others. The Reformers sometimes castigated the Catholic Church as apostate, a false church. Radical Reformers rejected Magisterial Reformers. On the other side, efforts have been made more recently in the ecumenical movement to restore the organizational unity of the church but with little success. How do we understand the question of the one and the many with respect to the church when the church is confessed as one but is undeniably many? In this section, we will treat the relationship of the many different church groups with the confession of the unity of the church. In the section on the universal (catholic) church, we will treat the issue of the relation of the local church to the universal church, which is an issue even within one confession such as the Roman Catholic Church.

Perhaps a cue can come from the New Testament with relevance for both issues. In 1 Corinthians 12, Paul speaks of the metaphor of the body of Christ clearly with reference to the local Corinthian church. Here he is concerned with unity in one local church. Significantly, he does not see unity as uniformity. The very image of the body suggested to him that members would be quite different from one another yet would contribute to the well-being of the whole. Each member had gifts and was as crucial as any other—just different. In Ephesians, Paul again turns to the imagery of the body of Christ but clearly refers to the whole church as one body of Christ. This letter was likely a circular letter to be sent to numerous churches, and here he is reminding the churches of their common unity. There is one Lord, one faith, one baptism, one head, and one body (Eph 4–5). Even here, he refers again to many gifts in the church that do not threaten but instead contribute to the unity of the body.

The upshot is that the New Testament has a sense of both the local, concrete body of Christ and what is called the "universal" (catholic) body of Christ. We will explore that confession in another way, below, but in this sense, it helps us understand the meaning of the one body of Christ. There is a sense in which everyone who has been "born again" and is a child of God is a part of the family of God. This is the one, universal church that is mystically connected through the Holy Spirit. There is also the concrete manifestation of the body of Christ in a local church that takes on the full functions of a church in caring for one another and ministering to the world around it. This local church has priority in that it is the most clearly incarnational manifestation of the church. The universal church is patently not manifested in an organizational sense yet exists in a spiritual sense.

The two major Christian groups in the early church, the Eastern and Western, saw themselves as one church oriented around a common Scripture, a common tradition (the rule of faith), and a loose relationship of prominent bishops in major centers such as Rome, Alexandria, Antioch, and Constantinople. After the Constantinian revolution, they also were united to some extent by ecumenical councils such as the Nicene and Ephesian councils and the political Roman Empire due to the influence of the emperors. After the split between the Eastern and Western churches, both have thought that they were the one church. Even though they both claimed a kind of spiritual or mystical unity, this unity was based on an outward organizational affiliation. It was particularly embodied in a succession of physical ordination that was supposed to go back to the apostles. While this may be true for both the Catholic and Orthodox churches, since their split, neither one can maintain it very well in light of the other's existence.

This kind of external unity, therefore, already not a unity in fact from very early on, has been even more clearly decimated after the Reformation. To insist on this kind of unity would be to undermine the unity of most of Christendom because many Christians are neither Catholic nor Orthodox—and neither one of them has full standing in light of the other. In the West, this problem has been accentuated with the recent prominence of the Orthodox Church that has perhaps greater claim, on these grounds, to be the one church than does the Roman Catholic. One could see this kind of organizational disunity, as these traditions do, as the sinful break from the one church on the part of all of the other confessions, allowing only for restoration of the true unity with the return of all of these other groups into organizational unity with the one church. A recent case at a prominent Baptist university had a faculty member, who was also president of the main inerrantist theological society, rejoin the Catholic Church. He gave this reason: "It seems to me that if there is not a very strong reason to be Protestant, then the default position should be to belong to the historic church."[17] The problem with this reasoning is that the Orthodox Church may well have a better case than the Catholic Church to be the "historic church," and it also assumes that the unity of the church means organizational rather than spiritual unity. It is not impossible, as Luther and Calvin thought, that the historic church could lose its spiritual way, and the church would better be represented in its true unity in churches that are in spiritual continuity with the church of the past. Besides it being extremely unlikely on a large scale that all Christians would return even to one of these two churches, Orthodox or Catholic, other groups have made similar claims to be the one church, as already mentioned, such as the Landmark Baptists and the Churches of Christ.

If the church's unity is based on this structural or physical unity, then unity is not actual and has not been actual, yet this is supposed to be an essential mark of the church—not optional but an aspect of the nature of the church. At best, this would be a confession of an eschatological hope, not a confession of the historical church. Confession of the "one" church in this life would virtually be hopeless.

To the contrary, one of the things to learn from the Protestant Reformation is that unity should not be based on outward matters but on spiritual matters, which theologically should have been central all along. In other words, the very nature of the gospel, emphasized by Jesus himself, has always been on the inner, spiritual reality more than the external. A theological principle then is that the primary emphasis should be on the spirit and not the letter, on the inward truth rather than on external forms. Theology and history thus point away from finding unity in a unified organization.

The incarnational nature of the gospel, of course, means that the inner must be incarnated outwardly in some way. The question is whether the primary emphasis should be on external organizational forms. Rather, the theological principle of unity in diversity, exemplified in the body of Christ image, suggests that the unity will not lie in organizational uniformity but in diversity that nevertheless reveals spiritual unity. In this light, diversity is not necessarily a threat to unity. One can actually confess true unity in the midst of great structural diversity.

When Christians of various local churches and denominations gather together in worship, service, or fellowship, they manifest the one church. When Christians of various groups bear witness to the gospel of grace based on the cross and resurrection of Christ, they manifest the one church. When diverse Christians serve together to bear witness to Christ and to serve others in Christ's name, they manifest the one church. Christians often give witness to rich experiences of fellowship with other Christians who are not in their local or denominational group. Ironically, while there was great strife within my own denomination, I sometimes found greater fellowship with Christians of very differing denominations. Yet this wider fellowship should not be a surprise, for it reflects the reality of the one body of Christ.

This emphasis on spiritual unity is not to bless, however, factionalism or strife based on petty envy, pride, and jealousy. It is not to hide one's face from the ugly divisions in Christianity where Christians sometimes refuse to associate with or serve with one another at all. Many times, other Christian fellowships have been portrayed as unchristian and apostate, even when they share the basic confessions of the faith. All differences and all divisions are not just mere diversity in the body that contribute to the whole. Sometimes they rip and tear and shred. Often they have undermined the gospel of Christ itself by exhibiting a spirit of hatred and judgment rather than of love and grace. This means that when any group claims for itself the mantle of church to the exclusion of others who bear witness to the basic claims of Christianity, they are actually undermining their own claim to be the church by denying the one body of Christ.

These reflections indicate two things. First, it is impossible to conceive of more than one Christianity, that is, one church. There is one head of the church and one body, to use Paul's image. This unity is not threatened by, but rather is supported by, the manifestation of the one church in many and various localities, all of which take on their local incarnational characteristics. In principle, the local does not undermine the global in terms of the church. Second, therefore, any such privileging of one's own organizational group undermines the unity of the church. To claim that others who lay claim to these basic beliefs and who give witness to the fruit of the Spirit are not Christians because they do not share the particularities of one's own convictions is actually to move oneself farther from the church— for the church is one. History witnesses that this exclusionary tendency has been quite common in the past, so it is a salient reminder. Typically, Christians come to more-specific ways of understanding salvation or providence or even the structure of the church and then claim such a universality for these claims that it actually undoes Christian unity.

This does not mean that one cannot or should not have deep convictions about such matters. They do matter; in fact, they are contributions to the well-being of the whole church. If one believes that a certain theological conviction, say, about free will or sanctification, is the truth and would benefit the church, then it is important. Yet it does not have to exclude others from the church altogether. Such conviction can recognize that others of good will can differ in their convictions. All difference does not have to be chalked up to sin. Some is due to the ways of God being difficult to grasp, to our seeing only in part, and to inevitable influences of our incarnational immersion in various contexts. Theology is itself a journey, and concord is not reached in a day. Perhaps some deeply complex issues such as freedom and sovereignty, faith and works, infant or believer's baptism, will never be finally resolved for all of the church. New issues and new perspectives on old issues continue to arise, as we have seen throughout this study of theology. Reaching consensus, if it is possible, will not come by suppressing differences but by continuing to work through them with good will.

This perspective can help us see that the differences in the church that include the various denominations reflect not just sinful division but Christians on a theological journey to understand better the ways of a God so majestic that God's ways are "not our ways." These differences attract different people and meet different needs. They are contributions to the overall reflection of the whole church on what the right and best path might be. Respecting different denominations is as valid as respecting individual Christians who are assessing their beliefs at different times in their lives, sometimes maintaining, sometimes changing them. Especially from a free church perspective, one must respect each one's responsibility and integrity in working things out for themselves, even if in "fear and trembling" (Phil 1:12). Even if one thinks that he or she is in the position of being the "strong" Christian whereas others are "weak," Paul counsels that people must follow their consciences (1 Cor 8). In this case, he calls for respect even of those weak Christians with whom he differed. Far beyond what Paul could imagine, the church exists in different cultures and vast numbers with manifold issues. Some will not be able in good conscience to be a member of a Calvinist church or an Arminian church, a church that elevates the clergy to sacramental status or a church that does not, a church that practices infant baptism or one that does not. Yet in other ways beyond the local church or a particular denomination, one can respect another's judgment and work together in many other ways, wherever it is possible. This has occurred over and over in evangelistic crusades, in movements over social issues, and in mission projects. In this in-between time, while we see "in part," this is not surprising and does not have to rend the unity of the church based on the more fundamental confession of Christ as Lord and Savior.

The Holiness of the Church

Another mark is the holiness of the church. This does not mean, however, what most people would think of initially, that is, that the church is fully mature or sinless or perfect. As we saw in the previous chapter, this is a misunderstanding of the Christian life, which is an epic pilgrimage from new birth to a completeness that is never attained in this life. Traditionally, the holiness of the church was seen especially in terms of the bishops, who were sanctified, trained, and ordained to be set apart for God. Since grace was mediated through the bishops, who were in a line of succession back to the beginning, this preserved holiness even when the church often seemed unholy. The diversity in the church has also made this view almost impossible to maintain. Yet the traditional view emphasizes two aspects of holiness that need to be maintained.

One relates to the root meaning of holiness, which means those "set apart for God," or "consecrated" to God. In this sense, Paul called all Christians, even the immature Christians of Corinth, "holy ones" (saints) (1 Cor 1:2). All Christians have been set apart for God, reflected in baptism, participation in a church, and in their commitment to follow the way of Jesus Christ.

The second aspect of holiness as being ethically pure is thus the fruit of the earlier sense. The doctrine of justification similarly points first to righteousness that is a gift of God's forgiveness; it then issues in actual transformation or sanctification. The shift in emphasis to moral holiness has led the Holiness tradition, as we saw in the previous chapter, to have a high view of sanctification, expecting that it should mean sinlessness. Thus, the church should be sinless. Often, non-Christians share this same view, perhaps more than Christians do, reflected in the harsh condemnation of failures in the church. Drawing on the previous chapter, such a view of holiness is actually misleading. It is not surprising, then, for those outside to misunderstand it.[18] The holiness of the church has more to do with the commitment and incipient transformation of sinners than with the perfection expected in the consummation—and perhaps beyond, depending on one's view of heaven. The church is still holy in that it is set apart for God and is committed to God even though sometimes faltering in that commitment.

Yet without expecting full maturity in every way, there still should be an ethical edge to the church. The church is not perfect—but it is never satisfied with being less than perfect. The church should be the focal point of the "now" dimension of the kingdom of God. While the church does not always realize this calling, at best she enables people to see God. As in the early church period, believers were called "little Christs," Christians, because they reminded people of Christ. People should at least be reminded of Christ when they experience the church.

A church should never be complacent about sinfulness. The large role of confession in worship should include the failings of the church as a whole, not just those of individuals. Especially when a church fails, such as Baptists on the issue of slavery and the Catholic Church on the issue of sexual abuse by priests, the response should never be one of coverup or defensiveness but one of confession and genuine repentance, which means action to right the wrongs that have been done. The mark of the holiness of the church entails a virtue of not just doing what is right but of reacting properly when wrong is done.

The holiness of the church thus undergirds the central place of discipleship as one of the major practices of the church, as we shall see. The call to "be holy, as I am holy" is not necessarily fully realized in this life any more than the kingdom of God is fully realized in this life, but it should be a noticeable dynamic in any living church. In this sense, the call to discipleship on the part of each Christian stems from the call to the church as a whole. The individual's discipleship should not only manifest but serve the holiness of the church. For example, one's own sacrificial service to God will include sacrifice for the sake of a church and other Christians to realize their holiness. The holiness of the church in turn promotes its role as "another city" that serves as a prophetic protest to social injustice.

Since we are thinking of the communal dimension of Christianity, we should not think of holiness as something merely private or moralistic or interior, certainly not something that is forbidding, stern, or unforgiving. Rather, holiness is an expression of God's nature, so the expression of holiness will be manifested in the church's love, forgiveness, and inclusion. It is marked by joy and cheer as much as moral earnestness. It is addressed to social justice as well as to individual piety.

Insofar as judgment is given, it is the judgment of love against destructive powers. This means that the church exhibits its holiness when it joyfully proclaims the good news of grace and healing but also courageously resists principalities and powers that wound and destroy. The holiness of the church has often been manifested in speaking out against corruption and abuse. This can include dissent within the church, not as an intrusion of a foreign, secular element within the church but as an expression of the church's call to holiness. Unfortunately, those in the church have had to speak out against the church. The church itself has been a power that wounds and destroy. Just as some in the church led the fight against slavery, others supported it. Just as some resisted anti-Semitism, others supported it. Thus, dissent is not necessarily a mark of individualist separation from the church but is an expression of loyalty to it and to the holy God it serves.[19] The writer of Hebrews says that "the Lord disciplines those whom he loves" (Heb 12:6). As we have seen, God's work often takes place through the church. The discipline of abuses in the church as well as outside often comes from those protesting from within the church itself. As we have mentioned, the Reformation motto was *ecclesia semper reformanda*, "the church always reforming herself." This reform is driven by holiness.

The Universality of the Church

The "universality" or "catholicity" of the church reflects the unity of the church in its geographical breadth. It points to the sense in the early church of beliefs that were held everywhere by everyone. Even though this pertains only to the most basic and central beliefs, it supports the fact of one church spread across the earth. More importantly, it points to the spiritual connectedness of all the church. The universal church then includes all those who have been forgiven and received new life in Christ. While this is usually obvious, only God knows in the end who are in the body of Christ. This confession is recognition that the church includes those who are alive in God through confession of Christ, not just those who agree in theological particulars.

To return to the Pauline sense that the body of Christ is both local and universal, we can see that these do not threaten each other. Some have emphasized the universal church, usually with the idea that the connection is structural and that theirs is the one church. Others have rejected this emphasis to stress the local church to the point that the universal church was denied. It was a sensation for Baptists when the Southern Baptist Convention in 1963 added belief in the universal church in *The Baptist Faith and Message*. Both are crucial.

Even sacerdotal churches now tend to emphasize the local congregation as the focus of the church because this is where Communion is shared.[20] In fact, this is where the life of the church and of the Christian is lived out if the church is an incarnate church. The local church is where people are committed to each other and express these commitments. Here is where, in the thick tissue of everyday life, one's faith is lived out to the realities of life, of birth, death, jobs, love, and loss in close relation to other Christians—where baptism takes place and Communion occurs. This is the place of the daily or weekly participation in worship and fellowship with other believers. Free churches like to think of the local church as the outcropping or expression of the church universal, which does not exist apart from its incarnation in localities.

The confession of the church universal bespeaks a humility that realizes that one's local church is not the whole of the church, that the universal church and God's work is much bigger and broader than one's locale. Conversely, God's church and work does take place in the local church; this is where it should take place. It always takes place in particular, incarnate situations. The local church and the universal church mutually implicate each other and are not contrary to each other.

The Apostolicity of the Church

Treatment of the issues of unity, holiness, and catholicity are incomplete apart from the mark of apostolicity. While this may initially give rise to thoughts only of apostolic succession, it means much more than that; it means succession, in accordance with the emphasis here, in more spiritual rather than physical terms. In Roman Catholic and Orthodox terms, it refers to apostolic succession that is understood as being passed down in unbroken organizational succession from the early church, or Peter, until now.[21] Even for those churches, succession also means continuity with the apostolic teaching. In the face of early threats of divergent teaching to the church, the response in the second century was to appeal to the rule of faith, perhaps even more than Scripture, which had been passed down from the apostles to the later bishops. In the words of Vincent of

Lérins, a key to the unity and purity of the church was to "hold that which has been believed everywhere, always, and by all people."[22]

Even then, continuity had more to do with content than with personal, physical connection, and the content was not in specifics but in the main teachings of the church. The challenges at the time were gnostic teachings that denied the humanity of Christ and Marcionite teachings that were similar but also separated the God of Christianity from the God of the Old Testament. These are theological viewpoints that obviously cut to the heart of the Christian faith. In that sense, the issue of apostolicity has to do with these central teachings of the church rather than to particulars over which there has been great diversity and conflict. Apostolicity is one of the ways, therefore, that the one universal church is manifested in the many churches.

It is not the only way, in that the deeper meaning of the one universal church is a spiritual unity. The latter is one that is more difficult to determine, which only God can truly judge. Apostolicity, however, is easier to see. Again, this means that we are thinking of basic beliefs—or it would not be easy at all. These are, for example, the beliefs of the existence of a personal, triune God who created the world, sent Jesus Christ to die on a cross for salvation by grace, and who will return again to inaugurate a new heaven and a new earth for the redeemed to dwell with God.

The mistake is to extend apostolicity to those middle-level beliefs that can be seen as legitimately Christian but over which Christians sometimes vehemently disagree. This leads to the many attempts to rule huge numbers of Christians out of the church altogether on the basis of a narrow, sectarian belief. Apostolicity has to be construed broadly or it cannot be a true criterion of the whole church. Failure to do so has led to the unseemly splits within the church that have so damaged its testimony.

Affirming apostolicity in this broad sense, however, is not opposed to diversity of kinds of churches within the church. Agreement on essentials allows, as we have indicated, for genuine differences on details, as important as such details are. The traditional saying is "agreement on essentials, tolerance on matters of indifference (*adiaphora*)." While we should be tolerant about indifferent matters, it is not easy to find something that people find "indifferent." If it is a matter of debate, people are not indifferent! These other matters such as the *filioque*, which point to serious theological issues, baptism, and issues of freedom and providence can have enormous implications for the practice of the church. The very nature, for example, of missions and evangelism is shaped by issues of freedom and providence. It is not that these middle-level beliefs are indifferent, it is that they are not the basis of unified belief in the church. They are not close to what the church has "always believed everywhere." While apostolic beliefs are not as a whole believed by every entity that calls itself a church, they are close to what are widely recognized by legitimate Christian churches. On matters of importance that are not apostolic, the church may differ in an ongoing conversation. Sometimes such issues become settled over time. The controversy over the full humanity and divinity of Christ gradually became settled. The canon of Scripture became largely settled apart from the distinction between the New Testament, which all accept, and the Apocrypha, which not all accept. In recent years, even the Calvinists have agreed that compatibilistic freedom does not rule out missions and evangelism, which some believed it had done at times in earlier centuries. New issues may arise, such as believer's baptism in the sixteenth century, dispensational premillennialism in the nineteenth century, and Pentecostalism in the twentieth, which are still being debated. The marks are intended to represent essential aspects of the entire church and not just a minority of the church.

In light of this, it is important to see apostolicity in terms of basic beliefs and not in terms of ordination or priestly succession. If the latter are held as universally apostolic, then the church is rent asunder because most Christians are not today in such succession. What this does is put the matter of organizational succession into the middle level of belief rather than at the top level. In other words, this is an issue over which Christians may disagree but which should not lead to dismissal of the other as Christian per se.

In addition, apostolicity should not be identified just with basic beliefs but also with the apostles as sent to convey the gospel. The church cannot be apostolic and rest satisfied in comfortable church buildings. The church is only apostolic when it is on a mission. The mistake at times of Israel in the Old Testament was to understand God's election *of* it as only *for* it. Rather, the election of Israel was for the purpose of electing the whole world, just as Christ's atonement was for the whole world. God's focal activity in the church is not an end in itself, but the church exists for the mission of God that is reaching out to all of the world. This emphasis on mission points to the next section, on key practices of the church. So with the understanding of these essential marks of the church in mind, which are admittedly broad and vague, we now turn to consider more specifically what the essential practices or functions of the church are.

KEY PRACTICES OF THE CHURCH

At the time of the Reformation, with churches breaking away from the Catholic Church right and left, the question became urgent: what is a true church? The question had been easy to answer in the West: it was a church in good standing with the Roman Catholic Church with all of its practices. Now that answer would no longer suffice. The first basic answer was that a church is where the word of God is rightly preached, and the sacraments are duly administered. The Radical Reformers on the continent and Baptists in England added that it should be a covenantal community with discipline. The question has only become more difficult to answer with the proliferation of even more denominations, parachurch organizations, and community churches. The question arises sometimes in a university context: "My dorm Bible study provides greater fellowship and community than any church I may be a member of and attend for Sunday worship. Isn't this dorm group my church?" In order to more fully answer these questions, we need to look at what constitutes the practices of a full-fledged church, which apply virtually to any denomination whatever the larger structure.

Mission

A contemporary watchword for the church is that it should be missional, a timely and appropriate call to renewal.[23] The idea is that mission is not just one part of a church's function or one program of a church but is an aspect of all that the church does. It also means that the church in a sense is not the focus but serves the larger Trinitarian mission of God to save and serve the world in moving toward the kingdom of God.[24] The Spirit of God is moving on mission in the world; in Moltmann's words, the church is caught up in this movement and goes in the power of the Spirit.[25]

Moreover, an additional key emphasis is that every Christian is called to mission, not just missionaries or ordained Christians. In this sense, being missional is not equivalent to supporting missionaries "over there." In a sense, it means that every Christian is called to be a missionary right here. The latter emphasis chimes in with the Believers' church emphasis on the priesthood of all believers. As such, it echoes a perennial appeal in these—and other—traditions for every member of a church to be considered a "minister." All are called to follow Christ and to minister in Christ's name. All will be judged, as Matthew 25 indicates, in part by how they minister to those in need. Decades ago, Findley Edge and Elton Trueblood called for "the greening of the church" and an "incendiary fellowship," where the church would have revolutionary impact due to every Christian following and serving Christ.[26] In contemporary words, they thought that we could hardly imagine what the church could do if all were missional. It appears that the postmodern younger generation, Generation Y, or the Millennials, are much more tuned into this dimension of the church. This may seem a welcome change but not to a church comfortable and complacent. As Jimmy Long, longtime campus minister, says, "For the first twenty years of my ministry, I had a vision to prepare our InterVarsity students for the church. For the last ten years to the coming ten years, my vision is to prepare the church for our 'emerging postmodern students.'"[27] This means that even being missional in one's familiar locale can be uncomfortable because it means reaching out to the unchurched away from the pull toward herding together in a gospel ghetto.[28]

Even though this movement still sputters, if a group is not "on mission," it can hardly be considered a church. Even with limited effort, it is difficult to imagine a bona fide church that is not reaching out to others in the spirit of Christ. This is a criterion that might question the legitimacy of a dorm Bible study being a church, as important and valuable as it can be. The question is, is the group also on mission together? Or do they leave and go their separate ways, perhaps doing service or not.

Another misconception is that the church is a building, a place to gather. While such a sacred space may be important, as we shall see, it is not the church. The church is where the people are, and the people are always to be on mission. In *The Emerging Church*, Dan Kimball argues that we must revise our language because language is always powerful and telling. He mentions the confusion that came when he tried to explain that "We can't go to church because we are the church."[29] In *The Missional Church*, Darrell Guder argues that the Reformers are partly to blame because, in trying to identify the church, they saw the church as where the word is rightly preached and the sacraments rightly administered.[30] Relating this to mission, it is not that we go to church to gather but that we gather to go. The Reformation emphasis can easily make the church building a place where the church sometimes happens rather than the church being people who always are on mission.

Being missional includes all aspects of the church, but it especially takes two forms, namely, evangelism and service. Sometimes these are divided into totally separate categories, but the missional emphasis is wise in holding them more closely together because, in the North American context, they have been too sharply divided. Sometimes in other contexts, too, as occasionally in liberation theology, they have been separated. They are closely wedded, if not in fact virtually identical, because they are both ministering to the deep needs of others in light of the gospel. They are both missional; they are both liberating.

Evangelism. As we considered in the previous chapter, God's great purpose is to be reconciled with all human beings. This is every person's deepest need and greatest fulfillment. Inviting and helping someone to be "saved" is thus to aid them in the best way possible. It is to help them for now and eternity. A paradigm case would be someone who is wracked with guilt, who sees no meaning to life, who is "broken" in many ways. It is not difficult to imagine the rejoicing in heaven—and on earth—that occurs when any lost one is found, as in the parables of the lost sheep and lost coin. In this light, there should be no apology for wanting to be "ministers of reconciliation" (2 Cor 5:18) for all the world to be reconciled to God. This has come to be known as evangelism because it is proclaiming the good news of such salvation to all people. It represents the dimension of "witness" (marturia) for any Christian. If one believes the basic Christian message, this appeal for evangelism must be at the heart of any church's concern. When Jesus called the fishermen Peter and Andrew, he said, "Follow me, and I will make you fish for people" (Matt 4:19). We have emphasized that every Christian is called to salvation, which includes discipleship. As Eddie Gibbs puts it in connection with evangelism, "Following and fishing are closely linked."[31]

Since God has worldwide concern, this cannot be just a local interest or an interest just for people like us; it should extend to all. The risen Christ puts it this way: "But you will receive power when the Holy Spirit will come upon you; and you will be my witnesses in Jerusalem, in all Judea and Samaria, and to the ends of the earth" (Acts 1:8). Witness begins at home and then quickly becomes global.

This appeal of Christ reminds us also that witness is empowered by the Holy Spirit. It is not something that one does to merit the presence of God; it should be a natural fruit of the indwelling presence of God. As a Christian walks with God, witness inevitably happens. As with any practice, one can get better. A church can improve. Improvement may mean being more clear and more winsome in witness. It may mean being more intentional. But it also may mean being less coercive and intimidating. It may mean integrating witness more with the entire holistic mission of the church. Evangelism itself, though, should not be neglected or despised, for it is clear that it is at the heart of what the gospel, the good news, means.

Having said this, it is heartbreaking to see the divide in the Western Christian world over evangelism and service.[32] Evangelism is often seen as conservative or even fundamentalist; service is seen as liberal. Sometimes both groups disdain the other's practice. Sadly, this is to rip apart what should not be separated. Both groups are at fault in offering too narrow a view of both evangelism and service. Evangelism is sometimes conceived in a limited way—as buttonholing strangers with an in-your-face question of whether they know they will go to heaven when they die. In our pluralistic world, some have little idea of what is being asked, or they might have the wrong idea of what is being asked. Whatever such a short-term "prospect" would say consequently means little. Perhaps worse, the very process of such evangelism may contradict the spirit of it. Someone who might have been open could be much more closed after such an encounter.

Evangelism offers good news of God's love and redemption for people. It also partakes of the personal dynamics of the way God relates to people. It is not trying to foist something on people that they do not want. In the end, no foisting is possible. Both the means and the ends of evangelism must be congruent, which all too often they are not. As Rob Sellers, longtime missionary and missions professor says, we have to move "from monologue to dialogue" and "from pronouncement to testimony."[33] In light of the way that salvation was described in the previous chapter, God is not coercive. God woos rather than forces. God wants the inner heart, not outward acquiescence. This can only come from genuine desire and not external compulsion. God is a personal being and relates to humans in God's image as personal beings.

Sometimes the analogy is given that a Christian is like someone with a cure for cancer who should batter down the doors of cancer patients with the cure. While this analogy captures the joyful spirit of bringing good news, it is too simple. It does not recognize that the issue is restoration of a personal relationship where there is already alienation, and not a physical problem. It is more like trying to be reconciled to one's estranged teenager, perhaps, or to someone already suspicious of you, than like offering a cure for someone already desperately open to finding one. This means that one must deal with all kinds of cultural and traditional barriers, prejudices, and inhibitions, which vary from person to person. It means that evangelism is inherently particularistic, which we could also call incarnational. It cannot be a one-size-fits-all approach, which is more appropriate to machines than to people. The approach called friendship or relationship evangelism is a basis of any appropriate form of evangelism because it reflects the nature of people and the nature of God's approach to people.[34] Sometimes the problem of the theology of evangelism is that it is inconsistent with the rest of our theology—but it cannot be.

In this view, evangelism should not be separated from holistic care for the other. Jesus' ministry reveals his concern for every aspect of a person. In respecting the incarnational nature of persons, and thus of evangelism, we must realize the way that all needs are integrally connected. The love for others that offers them good news of reconciliation with God is part and parcel of loving them enough to give them food, water, and clothing; to help with emotional needs of depression and grief; to be concerned about their families and jobs; and to care about political oppression and brutality. Fertile ground for evangelism is often best prepared by ministry to the whole person. It may be through helping provide food, daycare, and employment opportunities. It may be through standing up for someone's civil rights or helping with legal advice. As successful missionaries have long found, providing healthcare and education gives long-term credibility for sharing the gospel.

Despite this integration, there is a place to distinguish evangelism from service. Ministry to others should not have ulterior purposes. It would be to put the emphasis in the wrong place to say that one only cares for physical needs to get an open door for evangelism. Caring for others is an end in itself.

It is also true that one can distinguish between the relative value of this life, with all of its great joys, in comparison to eternity. Sometimes people make this life an absolute. The Christian view values greatly this life and undergirds giving "a cup of cold water," as Jesus taught. Nevertheless, a Christian view should recognize that this life might be sacrificed for a greater, eternal good, such as maintaining one's integrity even in the face of martyrdom. This means that reconciliation with God is an eternal good, crucial in this life and beyond. This realization puts things in perspective but does not mean valuing one and not the other. At best, they naturally relate to each other as ways to care for a whole person.

Service. With such a relative distinction, one can see that a church cannot just do evangelism; service to others is an essential practice of any church because all people have many needs. With the church being the primary "hands and feet" of God in the world, one can understand that, as God cares for all the needs of all people, knowing even the numbers of the hairs of each person's head, God would seek to work through the church to reach out to others.

This includes special care of those in a local body of Christ, not because they are more important than others but because if we cannot care for those who have most committed themselves to our care, how can we have integrity in caring for others? Being incarnational means being spatially located. It is all too common to have concern for needy people across the world somewhere, even to desire to be a missionary to them, but to have little concern for the same needs nearby. The incarnational principle implies that we have the greatest responsibility for those closest to us. A local body of Christ has special responsibility for its members. It has special responsibility then for those in its own locale. Responsibility begins at home and extends outward. This is often called the Acts 1:8 principle: "But you will receive power when the Holy Spirit has come upon you; and you will be my witnesses in Jerusalem, in all Judea and Samaria, and to the ends of the earth."

Service should not be undertaken for ulterior, say, evangelistic purposes. Jesus' parable of the sheep and the goats implies that the best service may be quite unintentional in serving God. The "sheep" actually wondered if they had ever ministered to Christ. Glenn Hinson once called them just "downright good" people because they seemed to do good without concern for their benefit.[35] As Christians mature in the Spirit and become habitually spiritual, goodness becomes an instinct, something that one does not have to force oneself to do but something that is natural, even joyful. In this fallen world, as we discussed with respect to sanctification, we are rarely at that level of maturity. Yet it can happen. We marvel at people for whom it commonly happens. Too often in evangelical churches, evangelism is emphasized so narrowly that one can hardly conceive of service that is not primarily evangelism. Then there is disappointment when our efforts are "wasted" when people we have helped do not convert.

Yet we cannot totally pull apart our care for people. If we care, we will help with all of their needs. If service opens a door of testimony, we should not slam it shut. We should also realize that love for the whole person is virtually a prerequisite for evangelism because salvation includes the whole person. Evangelism that excludes service is empty; service without openness to evangelism is blind. If our approach to people comes across as having selfish hidden motives of really wanting something from them, then we have missed the boat. If we come across genuinely wanting their best, then we have succeeded in being in tune with the Spirit of God.

Worship

Mission is an intrinsic practice of the church, perhaps more important than all else. Sometimes worship, too, is seen as the greatest practice. It is a crucial practice but not the only practice. Loving another is seen as loving God, which is the greatest commandment. The mission of God to the world is not a lesser practice. Worship, however, cannot be minimized. It is a direct way of loving God. Here, we do not indirectly but directly say that we love and praise God. It is the most intense, direct dimension of a relationship with God. Jesus said that he did not come to make us servants but friends. Worship is thus akin to friends enjoying one another, communicating with one another, and caring for each other. As in a marriage, sometimes it is important to say, "I love you"; worship is similar for the Christian and the church.

Worship is much more than such intense personal human relations, however, for it is relation to God the Creator, the Ground of Being, the Source of all that is. God is personal but not just another person. From the perspective of Christian faith, God is the one who completes us. Augustine reminds us that we find true rest and freedom only in God. As Jesus indicated, taking up his yoke is easy. We were made for a relationship with God that involves the only appropriate response of love and praise and worship. From outside, worship has been criticized as reflecting an egotistical being demanding strokes, but this is to confuse the Creator with the created. God does not need praise. Praise is a reflection of a healthy and life-giving, not codependent and destructive, relationship with the Creator. The deepest desire of the human heart, however tacit and hidden, is to worship God. It is worship not of a power-hungry tyrant but of one who gives away power; it is of one who is most deeply love, who gives of God's own self in suffering for the sake of those who are not God. Worship of God is worship of one who cares for the lowly as a physician who does not come to the healthy "but to seek out and to save the lost" (Luke 19:10). Worship is therefore worship of the "Good" in the highest, redeemed sense. It is not surprising then that a constant in all churches is worship.

The church continually aligns itself with the true "grain of the universe" as it regularly worships God. For all of the importance of private prayer and worship on one's own, in one's closet, corporate worship is special. Jesus said that in some special way, "where two or three are gathered in my name, I am there among them" (Luke 18:20). Public worship orients not just the individual but the whole in a common direction. In a mysterious way, the many support and enable the individual. This reflects the social dimension of the self as created in God's image and becomes a way for many people, who might struggle to feel close to God on their own, to enter more easily into the presence of God.

Worship is extremely varied, as are people and cultures, yet the embodied nature of human beings means that the incarnate setting is itself important. Church buildings are not the church, but they can powerfully foster worship. Some find that certain church buildings, usually Gothic (!), almost demand worship. Music is as powerful as anything in the realm of the spirit, and it is not surprising that music is usually central to worship. This may vary from classical music, to

Gospel hymns, to praise songs, to Pentecostal tongues, but it all has led people to transcendence. Because people do become habituated, certain rituals, sights, and sounds can function almost as "triggers" to foster a spiritually receptive state.[36] Catholics have emphasized the Eucharist, the Orthodox have emphasized ritual drama, and Protestants have emphasized music and the sermon, but each has met the deep needs of many hearts.

Because worship is a human practice, it can be dampened, diverted, and distorted. Worship is an excellence, so it can be done poorly or well. Or better, a church can foster worship in poor or excellent ways. A church must intentionally consider its worship practices. This is not to program worship, for worship is of the Spirit, "which blows where it wills."[37] Yet one should not separate the body from the spirit. Church leaders should consider their traditions, their culture, their people, and their context in preparing for worship. Since worship is not just for leaders, the congregation must also prepare itself. Each person contributes to worship by being prepared and alert. This is an ideal rarely realized, but it is a dimension of the priesthood of all believers. Worship depends on the worship of all and is from all. God cares about each person equally. Worship is intensely important for each person in a congregation.

Much criticism arises today for a consumer mentality where people attend worship to have their needs met. The worship leaders are seen as performers whose goal is to entertain the congregation for the sake of their institution. Success is measured by increasing numbers. In order to achieve those numbers, the worship is geared toward satisfying the customer "who is always right." Far be it for a church then to challenge or to make a consumer uncomfortable! Insofar as these dynamics prevail, it is true that the church has become captive to culture and has sold its birthright for a mess of pottage.

The opposite mistake, however, can also be made. That is not to consider the needs of the congregation and to promote a worship that is more for Platonic reason than for embodied humans. It is to assume a certain cultural standard of worship from the past and expect that everyone today should accommodate it.[38] This has led to freezing worship into a certain language, into a certain time, into a certain kind of music, into a certain kind of preaching—no matter how the culture has changed around it. It is to confuse the contextual form of worship with the universality of worship itself. When these frozen practices have been broken in history—by worship being in the vernacular, by relating to contemporary music, by changing the form of preaching—the result has often been spiritual revival, not slavery to culture. Worship needs to be contextual. That is why the church has been so successful in adapting to so many cultures. This is just another expression of the incarnational principle of the faith.

Contextualization, however, does not mean sacrifice of the message and meat of the gospel. Søren Kierkegaard's famous image expresses this well. The congregation is not the audience but actually the performers, the leaders are the prompters, and God is the audience.[39] Worship is about God more than anything else. Yet this, too, can be distorted. It is about the worship of the God by those whom God loves. To be focused on God is to be focused on what God loves. It is human worship of God, who cares deeply about us and others. It is therefore also about human beings, when kept in the proper perspective. It is to be the great joy of human beings to worship God, and a church does well to foster genuine worship. In light of recent "worship wars," which ironically have split churches and inhibited worship, these parameters are crucial. When it is kept in mind that worship is primarily about God and all of God's people; when it is about edification of the entire body, not just of a part; when it can be endlessly diverse as long as it leads toward God; when it is accepted that it will likely be continually changing in its form but not its matter; the problem becomes manageable. Immaturity, selfishness, and worldliness will be perennial challenges. Growth in discipleship and understanding is a great antidote, however, for such attitudes of "babes in Christ."

What is important in worship? The Lord's Prayer is a guide for corporate worship as in private prayer. Praise, thanksgiving, confession, and petition are all important. Sometimes worship implies only praise, but actually it is much richer, partaking of the range of any healthy relationship. Since it is the majority part of Israel's hymnody in the psalms, lament should be added to the above. Lament can be seen as grieving with God over the damage done to God's creation just as we are called to "weep with those who weep" (Rom 12:15). It is also a way of bringing ourselves corporately into line with God's desires for God's creations. The groanings of creation are joined with the Spirit's groaning and our groaning, as in Romans 8. The diversity of ways to do this in Christendom is not necessarily a sign of the church's disunity but a sign of the rich resources of the church.

When worship is approached in the right way, there is a place to consider, say, in moving to a new city, where one and one's family worships well. This is a recognition that our context is sometimes different from the first century, when often only one church existed in a small town. Now, looking for a church in which to participate may involve considering tens if not hundreds in some places. Of course, worship is not the only consideration. One first of all seeks God's calling, which involves seeking where one can minister as well as be ministered unto. In such a situation, considering which church will conduce to healthy worship and healthy spirituality is just wise and is not necessarily "consumerist," though it could be if one is only thinking of oneself. In many cases, though, I have seen that such a decision in a new setting is one of the most important decisions a family makes, involving much time in prayer and thoughtful reflection. It is often made in light of what is good for a family, not just for one individual. It is not wrong for the individual and a family to seek a church with healthy worship; neither is it wrong for a church to consider those who might be seeking healthy worship. No church, however, can be all things to all people. Each church must seek to find its own way, which is perhaps different from others but also as spiritual. There are many ways to worship God and many ways to be spiritually mature. Most of the time, churches are a mixture of maturity and immaturity and are in transition from one way of doing things to another.[40] This is a part, however, of the journey of faith for churches just as much as for individuals. The challenge for Christians is to be discerning but not consumerist. Especially after one has committed to a church, it is important not to "church hop" whenever something does not go one's way. The culture encourages this, but here is a place for the Christian to be countercultural.

Fellowship

One of the prominent themes in the Bible concerning the church is that the church should be characterized by "the fellowship of the Holy Spirit," as we saw earlier. Both the "people of God" and "body of Christ" themes underscore the centrality of fellowship. In fact, it is difficult to imagine a church existing at all without some degree of fellowship, but Christian "fellowship" (*koinonia*) has several levels and meanings that may differ from assumptions.

Fellowship does not mean a church is a good social club. Fellowship does not just apply to a time to shake hands in the worship service or to come to Wednesday night meals. It certainly should not mean that people are comfortable with each other because they are so homogeneous and exclusive that they keep out those who are different and disturbing. The local church is often pulled in this direction. It has been said to the church's shame in the United States that Sunday worship time is the most segregated time in the week. Part of the downside to having so many choices in churches is that people gravitate toward those who are similar and comfortable and thus do not experience the inclusive nature of the church as a fellowship that is diverse and breaks down barriers. Seeker-sensitive churches sometimes try too hard to be homogeneous and comfortable. Fellowship, however, is actually a serious and challenging word, not a comfortable word. It is perhaps more like the fellowship of a family that is made up very different people who are accepted here—but maybe nowhere else.

Fellowship is the outgrowth of being baptized into the one Spirit and sharing a spiritual unity as well as a common commitment to the canonical and apostolic faith. As those who have emphasized the social Trinity have maintained, the integral connection is that the self is a social self, and the church thus becomes the community of faith rooted in Trinitarian community, the sharing of God's own eternal nature as love. Fellowship is then not an optional activity for the church; *koinonia* expresses the church's very nature. Moreover, fellowship is not merely abstract or vacuous, for its primary meaning lies in the local covenantal community where believers "rejoice with those who rejoice and weep with those who weep" (Rom 12:15). Its meaning is rooted in the incarnational density of people who know each other well enough to "bear one another's burdens" and even to restore those who stumble (Gal 6:1-2). Just as with the incarnation of Christ as described in 1 John 1, *koinonia* is being close enough— even to those very different but who have been adopted into God's family—to hear, to see, to look at, and, appropriately, to touch with one's hands the other person. Its primary locus thus is in the local church, and it grows symbiotically out of other practices of the church, in worshiping together, serving together, rejoicing over the lost one who is found together, and growing up in the faith together. It involves being side by side and hands on.

Hugh Wamble, a Baptist church historian, described the major contribution of various denominations.[41] Surprisingly, he identified the Baptist contribution not as religious liberty, which was dear to his heart, or believer's baptism, but he called Baptists "the denomination of Christian fellowship."[42] He meant that Baptists prized the friendship of being in church together. He observed, "No group has done more than Baptists to popularize such terms as 'church members' and 'church membership.'"[43] Baptist churches in the past were not identified as much by worship services as by "fellowships," by the Sunday school where adults as well as children have been involved for years in lifelong "small groups," and by worship services themselves that are so social that they seem raucous to higher-church worshipers.

Fellowship, however, can take on many forms. High-church worship, where the worshiper comes, takes Communion, and leaves without speaking to anyone but the priest can coexist with fellowship in other ways. Conversely, an emphasis on church socials may devolve into an exclusive club. In the end, however, fellowship is meant to meet the deep craving of the human heart for intimacy and to do it in a Christian way. This means that it is a fellowship around the mission of God in the world, invigorated by the Holy Spirit, and taking up the yoke of the Christ. It should be a place that welcomes all the redeemed, where all the dividing walls have been broken down, where wounds can be bound up, and where people can share their joys and successes.

At this time, an emphasis among the emergent church movement is that the younger generation craves fellowship more than size, intimacy more than glitter. The megachurch, with a professional performance to behold, is not as desirable as smaller groups who serve together. In general, sociologists emphasize that the dislocation and mobility of modern society, along with the breakup of the traditional nuclear family, has produced for the foreseeable future a deep desire for intimacy.[44] Fellowship, of course, as with any practice, can take many shapes and forms, but it may be that this function will rise to greater prominence as it answers a great need in the society around it. The Christian belief is that God has created people not only for God but for the community of the church, and it fulfills therefore one of the main longings of the human heart. It is not just to be any community but the one distinctive community formed around the deepest reality of God and God's purposes.

The church struggles with this high calling. James already dealt with those who gave preference to the rich over the poor (Jas 2). Paul had to deal with divisions between Jewish and Gentile Christians, which are also portrayed in Acts (Gal 2:11-21; Acts 15). Jesus himself was familiar with the way religion could create divisions between people rather than removing them. Church history is replete with similar struggles. How often have I heard divorced people say that the church is the one place where they experienced the most rejection? As pastors who counsel their church know well, the sunny appearance of all is well that greets them on Sunday morning conceals hurt and pain in virtually every family. The church is often the place where people feel least able to be honest and authentic. People in the church often deem it their job to make people feel guilty and ashamed, when usually their lack of commitment or spirituality is not the problem at all, especially for those who are inclined to come to a church service. Rather, the need for those who are thus broken is for those who will be merciful, who will forgive, and who will bend down to give them a helping hand. The need is for the church to be the hands and feet of God, people who touch people with healing and forgiveness rather than with pointing finger and feet that walk away. It has so often not been so. The few times that Jesus pointed the finger were precisely at those who were judgmental, not the judged. Somehow we have confused Jesus with those Pharisees.

The church is not yet "without spot or wrinkle," but the church should always be striving toward the goal of being the fellowship of the redeemed, where it could be said many times, not just sometimes, as it was said of the early church, "My, how they loved one another." While witness is not the primary purpose of fellowship, any more than it is of service or worship, one of the greatest witnesses is simply a healthy, vibrant church. In John, Jesus says simply, "By this everyone will know that you are my disciples, if you have love for one another" (John 13:35).

Formation

To become such a community requires "training in righteousness" (2 Tim 3:16). One of the essential practices of the church is the formation and discipleship of Christians. We dealt with this in the previous chapter as something that cannot be separable from salvation. If salvation is reconciliation with God, discipleship is walking in that relationship and being gradually transformed into the image of Christ. For some time in the day of mass evangelistic crusades, there was a tendency to focus on the conversion experience itself. The problem was that conversion was not only divorced from discipleship but also from the church. Just as babies need families, so infants in faith need a family. In this context, discipleship is something inherently ecclesial, not individual. The church is to be that community that forms its members into a certain likeness, the likeness of the one who is the essence and spirit of the community, Christ.

When David Gushee did a study of why some Christians, but not most, helped Jews during the Holocaust, the answer came back that most of the time such strength of character was rooted in their Christian communities.[45] They had been in the kinds of churches that formed people to be able to do such things. This graphic case illuminates what this practice of the church is about, forming disciples to walk in the Way of Jesus Christ even when it is difficult. It is to be the kind of community that enabled the Amish, as we saw in the previous chapter, to be able to forgive their enemy so readily.[46]

The challenge today is that the Amish way is not likely to be the dominant way. Most churches are entangled in the world, yet still are called to form disciples. In the modern period, this has often been seen in a rationalistic way as teaching, as propositional, and as informational. In a postpropositionalist theology, as Kevin Vanhoozer puts it, one must understand the function of formation more holistically. It must include training in emotions, habits, and attitudes as well as in thoughts and ideas. Sometimes propositions are apt, but knowing the proposition "Christians should love their enemies" is only the beginning. At other times, this function has been identified for Protestants almost solely with preaching. Adults would not go to Bible study or Sunday school, just to the service that centered around the pulpit in the center and the sermon. The sermon itself would often focus on expository preaching that was highly didactic and propositional.

As we have discussed in relation to the nature of Scripture and of the self, a much more comprehensive and holistic understanding of ecclesial formation is important. A crucial part of formation is making the story, or stories, of the Bible one's own story, namely, being absorbed by the biblical world. To return to the theme of the earlier chapter on revelation, Scripture's authority has been understood in terms of right propositions that one must believe. It is probably more helpful to understand its authority as the formation of disciples. And Scripture's formative power is not just something that concerns the individual. In this light, we can say with David Cunningham, "Every reading of the Bible is an *ecclesial* reading, in which the reader is never a solitary individual but is formed in particular virtues and animated by the life of the reading community."[47] Even when one is reading or meditating upon Scripture alone, one is not really alone. We are ecclesially formed to read Scripture well. This does not require lockstep understandings, however, but allows for dissent and should encourage critical and prophetic "readings" of the community on the basis of Scripture as well as always testing interpretations of Scripture.

The exposition of Scripture also should happen more through narrative and symbol than through literal explanation, as Jesus illustrated. This does not mean that propositions, and certainly not systematic theology, are thrown out and do not have their place, as we have discussed, but that their place is shifted from center stage to the wings. The intellect must learn and grow; it is sad to see adults whose intellect has grown in science and computers but who are infants when it comes to the understanding of their faith. It is as crucial, however, that the emotions, habits, and attitudes also grow. It perhaps is even sadder for adults with responsible positions who act out emotionally in the church. As we have seen, all of these aspects are ultimately inseparable for a healthy human being. The church inculcates such growth in a myriad of ways. All of the other practices support such formation: mission, worship, and fellowship. In fact, as is often said, faith is "more caught than taught." Sometimes it is best to see faith lived out holistically. Children learn unconsciously by being around their parents; so do disciples with their parents in the faith. Seeing someone forgive when it is hard, accept someone whom others reject, go the second mile when others are stopping at the first mile—these powerfully form faith. This is again why the local church is so crucial; it takes such a thick tissue of teaching to convey not only the explicit but the tacit, not only the verbal that might be read in a book, but the nonverbal that cannot.

Moreover, "teaching" in this sense includes the verbal sermon but also includes all of the other aspects of worship. High-church worship knows this well. Roman Catholics are immersed in the Eucharist, which teaches them regularly about the nature of the faith. The Orthodox see portrayed in dramatic form in every service the saga of faith in a panoply of senses: sight, sound, touch, and smell. As mentioned, architecture and art do the same. Some churches have the Communion table at the center and the pulpit at the side. Others make the pulpit and the sermon central. In the medieval period, when most were illiterate, the gospel was taught through the rituals of worship, the stained glass windows, even the Gothic architecture that lifted the sight up to the heavens. These represent distinctive emphases, but they all teach. Through listening, seeing, smelling, responding, singing, kneeling, and praying, even the physical acts of rousing oneself to get up from bed to go to a church service, faith is holistically formed.

Baptism

Baptism and the Lord's Supper could be included under worship, but their importance makes them distinctive practices of the church in their own right. Almost nothing else is more distinctive of the church than these, called "sacraments" by many churches that emphasize their intrinsically holy character and called "ordinances" by others that emphasize more their symbolic character. Both unite the church on the one hand and divide it on the other, not because others in the main do not practice them but because of differences in understanding them.

Both are distinctive commands of Jesus, which in this case the church has faithfully followed. John the Baptist's baptism of repentance pre-dated Jesus' own ministry. Jesus himself was baptized by John, then called for his own followers to be baptized (Matt 3:13). The Great Commission includes baptism as a central aspect of discipleship, "Go therefore and make disciples of all nations, baptizing them in the name of the Father and of the Son and of the Holy Spirit" (Matt 28:19). The practice of John, Jesus, and the early church appeared to be immersion of those who had repented and committed themselves to the message, in other words, believer's baptism. The word *baptizo* means to immerse, which along with the practice of the very early church was a reason for the early Baptists to move to believer's baptism. There is no explicit record in the first two centuries of infant baptism.[48] Churches that practice infant baptism will often point to the baptism of the Philippian jailer "and his household" as implying at least the possibility of infant baptism (Acts 16:31-33). The requirements of training of a catechumen, however, before baptism as well as the confession expected at baptism imply that the candidate was older.[49] The lack of firm historical information about the first century of the church, however, softens historical arguments and points to a larger theological consideration.

At some point by the late second century, however, the practice of baptizing infants began, probably due in part to the issue of dealing with children born into believer's families. Augustine, however, codified a theology for the practice in the fourth and fifth centuries by seeing baptism as washing away original sin. Thus, in order for an infant who died to be able to go to heaven, he or she must have been baptized. Only just recently has the Catholic Church allowed that unbaptized infants might still be able to go to heaven—and not to limbo.[50] Paedobaptism became the dominant practice until the rise of the Believers' Church movement in the sixteenth and seventeenth centuries.

The Catholic approach, as one can see, is sacramentally based. In other words, the baptism, when properly authorized, conveys grace and represents the regeneration of the infant. The Reformed tradition, which also practices paedobaptism, understands baptism as covenantally based. Baptism is a sign of the covenant or agreement that God has made, but the effect is the same: baptism conveys grace and regeneration. As we saw in the previous chapter, Calvin argued that infant baptism better represents the nature of salvation as irresistible grace than believer's baptism and better corresponds to its counterpart in the Old Testament, circumcision.[51] Churches that practice infant baptism usually have a confirmation time, often around twelve years old, when the growing child is expected to study and "confirm" their baptism by a more mature profession of faith.

Believers' churches have insisted that the meaning of baptism as representing one's repentance and faith cannot possibly happen for an infant. Generally, it was understood as adult baptism and took place in later teenage years. This practice was part and parcel of the turn to a renewal movement of a regenerate church of people who were covenanted together, such as the Scrooby and Gainesborough churches. For such "baptist" churches, ironically, with all of its importance, baptism has not been seen as sacramental but as symbolic. Baptism becomes an outward symbol of what has already happened inwardly. One is born again of the Holy Spirit. Then one is baptized in water to confess to it, portray it, and experience its effect.

As we shall see with the Lord's Supper, such differences have been exaggerated in the modern period, when the meaning of the word symbol has been nearly evacuated of meaning. Something is never "merely a symbol." Symbols are so powerful that people fight and die over them. Symbols instigate and portray spiritual experiences perhaps more than prose. Part of the emphasis now in Believers' churches is to realize that such symbolic practices are, or should be, at the same time powerful spiritual experiences. Baptism all at once represents death, rebirth, cleansing, new life, and total commitment. Whatever one's views, baptism has been a powerful time of worship where the Holy Spirit has come.

The challenge for paedobaptists is for the infants to grow up and be committed to the faith. The sense that this was not happening after the Reformation, when everyone was supposedly a Christian because they were baptized as an infant, led to believer's baptism as a renewal movement toward a committed church. The challenge on the side of Believers' churches is also what to do with the children. Generally, since baptism is not sacramental, and infants and children are regarded as going to heaven if they die, there is no urgency about baptism for infants. But since no particular age is mandated as in paedobaptist confirmation, there is great flux in practice as to the "age of accountability."

Children who have grown up in the church do not always have a sense of being "lost" and then repenting and being saved, yet they are expected to have these experiences. Under the influence of revivalism in the United States, dramatic conversion experiences have been prized, which has pushed the church to expect such children in the church to have these notable experiences. When they do not, often they later question their salvation, or others question it. Since the emphasis is on baptism, little recognition is given to the importance of faith development and nurture before baptism, especially when compared to paedobaptist traditions. As Temp Sparkman pointed out, "First among the weaknesses of believer's baptism is that faith is not seen as beginning until one is converted."[52] What is needed is much greater affirmation of the growing faith of children before they are ready to make an adult commitment.

To make things more complicated, the twentieth century pushed the age of baptism regularly downward so that four- and five-year-olds are being baptized, as compared to older teens at the beginning of the twentieth century. Is this believer's baptism or paedobaptism? Often these earlier baptisms are repudiated when teens have more vivid experiences later, leading to the phenomenon of multiple baptisms. Just as paedobaptist churches have become more open to believer's baptism, Believers' churches have had to grapple more seriously with the role of children's faith development in the church. More recognition has been given to a gradual process of faith development for those growing up in the church where they move from childhood faith to more mature faith without a clear sense of demarcation. Baptism then becomes that time when they are ready to make a public commitment and declaration of their faith, preferably in late childhood or adolescence, yet faith and spiritual experiences are recognized and encouraged all the while.[53]

Paedobaptists have emphasized the meaning of baptism as cleansing. Believers' churches have emphasized baptism as more symbolic of the believer's death, burial, and resurrection. Immersion obviously pictures this more strongly than sprinkling. Glen Stassen has argued that the Baptists in England in the seventeenth century likely derived this understanding from the Mennonites on the continent with whom they had contact, for cleansing was the prevalent meaning in the Reformed tradition that had so influenced them.[54]

Baptism is also understood as entry into the church. It should first be interpreted as at least symbolizing rebirth. Our understanding of the inseparability of the Christian from the church makes its connection with the church obvious. The beginning of the Christian life is itself entry into the universal church. It should then naturally lead into membership in a local church. Baptist churches usually require that someone be baptized before they can be accepted as members.

For Believers' churches in the present pluralistic situation, questions arise about how strict to be about acceptance of different baptismal practices. Landmark Baptists went beyond sacramental churches, who usually accept other church's baptisms, by saying that only Baptist baptism counted, even if someone had been baptized by immersion as a believer.[55] For a group that understands baptism as symbolic and not sacramental, this puts far too much weight upon it, undermining the unity of the church and its "one baptism." Some Baptist groups, in recognizing the importance of these theological principles, will recognize infant baptism although they themselves would not practice it. Most Baptist groups require believer's baptism, not as "rebaptism" but, in their understanding, as the initial baptism. A more vexing issue is a case of someone "sprinkled" as a believer. Some Baptist churches will accept such baptism in order to preserve the significance of the one baptism of the church and also in light of their view that baptism does not save. Yet most have not. It is a matter of balancing one theological theme against another. Each church faces its own issues on this score, but this illustrates how theologically complex such practices are. It also again reveals what a transitional time this is and thus the corresponding urgency of theological reflection. At certain times, these practices were rather fixed, but this is not one of those times.

Lord's Supper

The Lord's Supper, for those who see it as symbolic, or as the Eucharist, for those who regard it as sacramental, is perhaps a greater symbol of the unity of the church, for almost all churches regularly practice it. Yet it has perhaps been the center of even more controversy. Ironically, a unifying practice that is to welcome all believers to the Lord's Table has become one of the greatest moments of exclusion in worship.

Rooted in the memorable and traumatic "Last Supper" of Jesus and his disciples, the Lord's Supper early became a regular practice of the church. In the earliest materials of the New Testament, Paul attests to its centrality in worship as part of a "love feast" where he masterfully points out that it is a remembrance of the passion and cost of salvation for Jesus in the past; it is a sign of the "new covenant" that is manifested in the present; and it is an expression of hope for the future, as we "proclaim the Lord's death until he comes" (1 Cor 11:24-26). All of these dimensions are important to remember since the emphasis on Communion as remembrance in Baptist churches tends to emphasize the past; the focus on renewed sacrifice in the Catholic tradition has tended to place attention on the present. The element of joyful celebration oriented toward the eschaton is certainly muted. The context of a love feast in Corinth reminds us that the Lord's Supper likely grew out not only of the Last Supper but the fond memories of the glad fellowship (koinonia) that the disciples regularly shared with Christ. It is notable that by the second century the common name was the eucharist (thanksgiving), which saw it as a joyful thanksgiving.[56]

The issue of sacramentalism and symbolism has been even more sharply debated with respect to the Lord's Supper. The Roman Catholic tradition had developed at the time of the Reformation into a view of "transubstantiation," where the bread and wine were understood literally to be changed into the body and blood of Christ, that is, into his real presence. This was undergirded by Thomas Aquinas' appropriation of Aristotle's philosophy whereby one could understand the "accidents" as remaining bread and wine but the "substance" as changing.

The Reformers responded to this view, as did the Orthodox Church, by seeing it as too magical and too philosophical. Martin Luther, once a Catholic monk, continued to put great emphasis on the sacramental significance of Communion and emphasized that Christ was in some special way *with* the elements, so his view has commonly been called "consubstantiation." John Calvin had a slightly different view, yet also growing up Catholic also had a strongly spiritual view, one might say, of Communion. He thought that Christ reigned in Heaven but was spiritually present at Communion. His view has much to commend it in emphasizing that Communion should certainly be an experience of the Spirit.

Another major option at the time of the Reformation was the Swiss Reformer Ullrich Zwingli's symbolic view. He insisted that the words "This is my body" should be taken as a metaphor and not literally. While he emphasized that the Lord's Supper should be a spiritual experience, the reaction against the sacramental and literalist views was so strong that sometimes this approach has been understood as saying that it is only a memorial, implying that it is not a present experience of the Spirit. Sometimes this has been called pejoratively "the belief in the real absence." The shame was that the united front of the Reformers was broken over the inability of Luther and Zwingli to agree on the meaning of the Lord's Supper, and thus a fateful breach began in the Protestant ranks that rivaled the breach from the Catholic Church—all over the failure to agree on the meaning of the word *is*.[57]

This may be one of those instances where Christians agree to disagree, but the larger issue at a later time is whether Christians outside of a denomination can partake of other's experiences of the Lord's Supper. After Vatican II, Catholics began to allow others, such as the Orthodox, to share in Communion. The Orthodox, however, do not allow others to share with them. Landmark Baptists are similarly exclusive about allowing only those in their own church (closed Communion) or only of "like faith and order" (close Communion) to participate. Sometimes Communion has been a use—or abuse—of church discipline by the pastor and/or deacons allowing and disallowing people to partake, not seeming to notice the words of Paul in 1 Corinthians: "Examine yourselves" (11:28).[58] Some have been all too willing to judge others in this instance.

While each fellowship must determine their own practice, it is an irony that the groups who most emphasize the unity of the church have been quickest to break it at this point. Here is a concrete place where the confession of the one, catholic church can be manifested without requiring agreement on all particulars. The Lord's Supper is the Lord's, and the one loaf symbolizes, at least, the one body of Christ. Theologically, it seems strange to deny access to the Lord's table to those who are the Lord's. If one wants to reject others as Christians altogether, such a practice might be consistent, but nowadays few would want to go that far. But if others are recognized as brothers and sisters in Christ, how can they be denied the hospitality of sharing in the Supper of the one Lord, one faith, one baptism, one body?

STRUCTURE

When people think of a particular church or denomination, they likely think of different organizational structures. If they think of a denomination, including the Catholic and Orthodox Churches, it has to do with how they are structurally linked. The questions in these churches inevitably reflect their structures. Is the pope infallible? How are the Episcopalians, Presbyterians, and Methodists dealing with their controversial issues, which are debated and decided at high levels beyond the local church? How can Southern Baptists divide but not split when there is no authority over the local church? Who speaks for them anyway? In other words, one of the first things that comes to mind when people consider the church has to do with structure, yet I have delayed it. Why? Part of the reason is that church structure has played too important a role. Another is to keep the particularities of the churches from overshadowing the unifying issues of the church. A third is that it is easier to treat the matter of church structure with the above background already firmly in hand. In looking at church organization or polity, which does have its place, we will look at the general issue of structure and then at the major alternatives.

Church Organization

The tendency historically has been for churches to locate their structure in the New Testament or early church and identify theirs as the only valid structure. Catholics appealed to the passage about Peter being the rock to justify papal authority; the Orthodox Church appealed to the importance of early bishoprics and councils; Episcopalians and Methodists appeal to Paul's appointing elders or bishops (*episkopoi*); Presbyterians emphasize the role of multiple elders (*presbuteroi*) and authority beyond the local church; Baptists appeal to the churches in Jerusalem and Antioch making major decisions by the whole congregation.

What has been difficult is to see that the church in the New Testament period was in flux, was developing, and varied from place to place. No other church seemed like the Jerusalem church or the Corinthian church. One must be cautious in appealing to the practice that developed over the first few centuries as the authoritative answer to these questions because it may or may not be defensible in every respect. Protestants later questioned severely some of these developments such as the authority of the bishop of Rome, as did the Orthodox Church themselves. Catholic, Orthodox, and free churches, for example, differ in how they assess this early history—at times even differing concerning the "facts." For example, does papal authority go back as early as Peter? Were bishops—in the later sense—that prominent in the early church? Did the early church practice only believer's baptism by immersion, or was infant baptism practiced from the beginning? The answer to the structure question cannot be answered apart from appeal to scriptural precedent as well as this early church history, but it cannot be answered definitively by such appeal. The latter conclusion is fairly widely held today, which is much different than in yesteryear. There is much greater realization now that the New Testament provides principles and tendencies, but it does not clearly delineate a definitive practice.

As we discussed in connection with Acts and tongue-speaking, much of what we have in Acts is more descriptive than doctrinal. This is true also of structure. It is not easy to tell just how far we are to take the practices in Acts as mandatory for all of the church for all times. Even in other parts of the New Testament that are more theological, as in Paul, the references to church structure seem more descriptive than prescriptive in laying out a theological blueprint for all churches of all times. Paul's advice to the Corinthians may not have been the same to all churches. If we take the Pastorals as from Paul or at least as being "Pauline," we know that he did not give the same advice to all the churches. Corinth was much more loosely structured and allowed women to prophesy; his advice to Timothy in 1 Timothy for the churches under Timothy's care was that women should not. As we indicated in discussing this issue, however, his advice in 1 Timothy is in the same section as advising women not to braid their hair or wear jewelry, which is largely now seen as contextual and not universal by most evangelical churches in the United States. This suggests, for the sake of consistency, that the advice on women and authority should be taken as similar—but it often is not. Here is a place where people may have strong convictions based on exegetical conclusions. Yet those who are so convinced also must realize that the evidence is not as clear to others. The dizzying variety of church structures bears witness to that conclusion. These issues are not as evident in Scripture as the call to forgive and to love one's enemy. They are not as clear today even as the views of a suffering God or a holistic self, even if these represent significant changes in recent years and are not unanimous.

What shall we conclude? I suggest that we pay attention to the patterns in the New Testament and the early church, but the decisions we make should be based on larger theological conclusions. One's own tradition and background will play a significant role; even one's wider cultural horizon makes a difference. The free church tradition slightly preceded the modern turn to democracy—and perhaps contributed to it, as we have seen—but grew up in its context, making democratic church government as well as separation of church and state more plausible today than it was for fifteen hundred years of church history. We all must take these various influences into account. It will be easier to see some of the pertinent theological issues in considering the specific approaches.

Hierarchical Structures

Most churches have a top-down, hierarchical structure where the main authority rests in bishops or representative bodies beyond the local church. Episcopal structures that emphasize a bishop (*episkopos*) are various. In the West, the best known is the papal structure of the Roman Catholic Church. The pope is considered to be the chief successor to Peter, who was appointed by Jesus to be the rock on whom he would build his church (Matt 16:18). The pope is the vicar of Christ and thus has unique authority over the church. Papal infallibility when making official statements, *ex cathedra*, only became a dogma in 1870 at Vatican I, but it was an assumption for much longer. The bishops (*episkopoi*) and priests are also crucial. There is no church in actuality without the pope and the bishops, for they have sacramental significance in mediating grace to the rest of the church. Cyprian states this early. First, he said, "He can no longer have God for his Father, who has not the Church for his Mother."[59] And he adds in another place, "There is one God, and Christ is one, and there is one Church, and one chair [the bishops] founded upon the rock by the word of the Lord."[60]

Other churches with episcopal structures appeal to Paul and Barnabas at the end of their first missionary journey appointing "elders," seen as corresponding to bishops, in each church. (Acts 14:23) and to Paul counseling Titus to "appoint elders in every town" (Titus 1:5). Paul and Timothy's role is also seen as being like that of a later bishop. The Orthodox Church rejected the supremacy of the Roman bishop but still emphasizes the supremacy of the bishops of the other five main centers from the ancient world: The bishop, or patriarch, of Constantinople, is seen as "first among equals" (*primus inter pares*). Like the Catholics, they see official relations with their bishops as the measure of the church, and thus other churches are not technically churches. The Anglican or Episcopal Church has a looser structure but one still focused on bishops and apostolic succession. The laity are better represented. The Methodists also emphasize bishops but not apostolic succession and also delegate authority to an annual conference made up of wider representation from local churches. Presbyterians draw on the word for "elders" in the New Testament for a "presbytery" that has a pastor and elder from each local church who have authority over the church. They also have wider general assemblies and "sessions" or "consistories."

The strength of these approaches is that one can have checks and balances from a variety of perspectives beyond the local church. In other words, a local church can be checked in its mistreatment of a pastor or a member or in extreme theological deviation. Theological decisions are often made in consultation with experts, though the decisions can end up being very political and emotional, just as we have seen throughout the history of the church. Wise leadership at higher levels can guide the church, but the weakness is that poor leadership can have undue effect. As a Baptist friend of mine who became an Episcopalian priest once said, "Being Episcopalian is great as long as you have a good bishop!" The clergy-laity split is often very great and insuperable due to the sacramental nature ascribed to priests. In other words, laity do not have full access to God apart from the clergy. The laity in a local church do not always have a strong voice and sometimes are seen as being "second class" in the church.

Congregational Structures

With the rise of the free church movement after the Reformation, churches with congregational polity have increasingly multiplied, applying to Baptists, Christian churches, and some Pentecostals and community churches. These churches have a bottom-up structure, with primary authority resting in the local church. In fact, usually no organization above the local church has any official authority over it. The churches within themselves place final authority on the whole congregation, with each member having a vote, so they are considered to have a democratic church government. Originally, they functioned much as one might think of New England town hall meetings, where the whole church decides every item of business, but in fact the New England town halls were modeled after the congregational churches. Generally, though, responsibility is delegated. Increasingly, with larger churches, the staff, committees, elders, or deacons may have a large amount of responsibility, with the church as a whole only occasionally having business meetings. Still, the leaders are accountable to the whole congregation. This approach takes to heart the priesthood of all believers, emphasizing a fundamental equality of all Christians. The clergy are, in principle, not any more "priests" than the laity. The clergy's function, in accord with Ephesians 4:12, is to equip the laity for ministry, not to do the ministry by themselves. This is their preferred translation of Ephesians 4:12, which has traditionally been interpreted to mean that the clergy are appointed to do "the work of ministry." It is now generally understood to mean that the clergy are gifted to equip the saints so that the saints, all of them, can do the work of ministry.[61] Thus the leaders do not have a sacramental but a symbolic view of the clergy and of the ordinances. The church is a reality even without ordained clergy, which was often the case in the westward expansion of the United States where churches would meet even when clergy were not available. Some, in fact, do not affirm ordination" at all as a biblical idea. Despite the emphasis on the local church, many of these have associated with larger groups in significant ways. For example, at one time Southern Baptists had as large an organization for seminary training—even though education is not required in order to be ordained or to become a pastor—and missionary organization as any Protestant group. There are local associations, state conventions, and national organizations that have authority over their own functions—but none have official authority over the local church or each other. This is why those familiar with hierarchical structures are so puzzled in understanding these structures. For instance, observers often talked of a split in the Southern Baptist Convention in the last years of the twentieth century, but there can be no formal split because the convention has no authority over local churches. Local churches that feel unrepresented do what they desire to do, as they always have done. The national convention, however, goes with all of the agencies and assets to the simple majority.

The strengths are that this approach puts most weight on the local church, which is central in any view, and highlights the priesthood and equality in discipleship of all Christians. Obviously, many Christians would not value overcoming the clergy-laity split, but this approach goes the farthest in this direction. It puts authority where the greatest responsibility lies, namely, in the local church. As with any structure, things do not always work out this ideally. The clergy-laity split has often been just as great in these churches. Sometimes charismatic pastors or deacon bodies have ruled the local churches and left congregational government as only a facade. Probably the greatest problem is that there is little check-and-balance beyond the local church. Renegade churches can do great damage, and little can be done. Pastors or members can be abusive to one congregation and just move on to another, often without a good way for other congregations to know.[62]

In the end, any structure should be biblically and theologically based on sound principles. The structures throughout church history have varied widely from the early church, which itself varied widely. Perhaps at this time all can agree at least on the following principles. Any structure should support a vibrant local church, the calling of all Christians to follow Christ, and checks-and-balances or accountability. The latter derives from the understanding that even Christians are vulnerable to the temptations of the big three—money, sex, and power.[63] Christians with much power and little accountability rarely handle it well. Gifted and mature Christians can make any structure work well; ungifted and immature Christians can sabotage the best of structures. Yet good structures can protect some good people from falling into devastating temptation and from doing damage to other people. All Christians do well to follow Paul's advice to the Thessalonian church: "Do not quench the Spirit, . . . but test everything" (1 Thess 5:19-21).

LEADERSHIP

The nature of leadership in the church is ingrained in one's wider ecclesiology. If one has a more hierarchical, successionist, sacramental view of the church, then the leadership usually represents a strong clergy-laity split, with the church being identified closely with the clergy. Ordination separates clergy from laity and implies a unique capacity to mediate grace. Usually more authority is given to clergy over the church, ruling out congregational church government. Congregational polity implies a basic equality between clergy and laity, where the former are equippers for all the saints to do ministry. Ordination is more relative and sometimes not affirmed at all. In general, the church has reserved the ordained clergy for men, with the Roman Catholic Church especially emphasizing the requirement of celibacy as well. This is often related to Christ being male, to the apostles being male, to women being incapable of exercising such authority, to women being morally weaker, and/or to women being assigned a more domestic role.

Hierarchical churches tend to have categories of bishops, local priests or pastors, and deacons. Increasingly, a group of elders serve together in a church as pastors. Baptist churches, as an example of a congregational church, usually have just pastors and deacons. The deacons often played a governing rather than servant role, which in all practicality made them more like elders. The ideal, however, has been for deacons—following the Acts 6 example—to serve the church in roles other than pastoring and teaching.

What can be said about church leadership in general? The following observations obviously reflect my free church orientation but hopefully point to wider principles. One of the places where the church has followed culture rather than vice versa has been the role of leadership and power. Jesus dealt with the issue of understanding leadership in terms of power and prestige when the mother of James and John came to him privately to request privileged places for her sons, to sit at his right and left hand. She obviously at this time was thinking of Jesus as a traditional messiah who would come in power over this earth. It is likely that James and John understood the same. It shows that even in Jesus' inner circle, the worldly way of power prevailed. Jesus said about as clearly as it could be said:

> You know that the rulers of the Gentiles lord it over them, and their great ones are tyrants over them. *It will not be so among you;* but whoever wishes to be great among you must be your servant, and whoever wishes to be first among you must be your slave; just as the Son of Man came not to be served but to serve and to give his life a ransom for many. (Matt 20:25-28; emphasis added)

Despite this, it has been so among us. Over and over, the church has not only emulated worldly power, leaders have outdone worldly leaders. What an irony and what a scandal for the church. Even more ironic, women, who have been seen as playing the role of servants, have been denied leadership roles, which are supposed to be servant roles, because of the argument that leadership involves power and authority not becoming to them. No wonder that Jesus came to turn so many ways of the world upside down. In this light, much is gained if Christian leadership is understood from a genuinely theological perspective. As we saw with respect to God's sovereignty, the church has often brought in worldly notions of power "unbaptized." The same has been done with respect to leadership and power. Jesus' notion was, rather, that leaders are servants. If anything, one might see clergy as *less* than laity, playing a support role for those who are supposed to be on the front lines.[64] This probably goes too far in instituting positions of privilege the other way, but it underscores how incongruous it is to think of clergy as being superior or privileged in a Christian context. Rather, the vision is of all Christians being equally called to follow Christ and having gifts that are equal in value in God's sight, even if they are varied and diverse. As Jim McClendon put it, "On this view bishops are part of the laity; on this view every Christian is a cleric."[65] A church thus unleashed is what Findley Edge called "the greening of the church." He hoped for it in the 1970s. We are still waiting.

If one has an understanding of Christian leadership as servant-leadership, then questions about clergy become transformed. It is no longer a question of power, privilege, or access to God. It becomes a question of who is gifted and equipped to themselves become effective equippers of other Christians to do the work of ministry. The role of pastors as shepherds of a flock is still valid. Pastors, bishops, popes, and elders have a special responsibility to serve the flock by nurturing, protecting, and empowering them. It should not be a question of having power "over" but of "em"-powering others.

This is not a denial of a role for structure and even strong leadership. It transforms the nature of the leadership, however. Too often the aims of leadership in the church are little different than in the secular world. The goal of Christian leadership, rather, is to empower and equip the laity in accordance with Ephesians 4:11-12. In today's world, this often requires a lifetime of training and education. It is important for the Christian leader to be expert in the Bible and the tradition and in relating them to contemporary culture. This does not happen in a day. It involves gifts and training of those gifts. This, of course, can happen in numerous ways, but there is little room to avoid the equivalent of higher theological education to be prepared in today's world. So the commitment of most denominations to ministerial education is valid; if anything, it is more imperative than before. The forms of such education change, but the need does not. Free churches often prioritize the call to the individual and the local church before such education. This is defensible in order to emphasize the priority of the local church and the Spirit's work, allowing for God to do unusual and unexpected things as is God's wont. Yet this again should not be seen as a substitute for a leader of the church not to "do your best to present yourself to God as one approved" (2 Tim 2:15).

Ordination is defensible as a development in church tradition, though not explicitly spelled out in Scripture, to emphasize the significance of good church leadership that is called and anointed by God.[66] It should not be seen, however, as something that depreciates the sense in which each and every Christian is equally called before God to special tasks. Plenty of evidence shows that God calls people to full-time Christian service. The church is blessed by such callings and gifts; if anything, the church has lagged in "calling out" such "called" in recent years. Such ordination should also represent, at least in a symbolic way, the fact that the individuals have been anointed by the Spirit in a special way for such ministry. An ordination service, like baptism or the Lord's Supper, should itself be a spiritual experience of empowering. It should not be seen as the only time of empowering, for the minister, as any Christian, will need repeated fillings of the Spirit to continue along the Way.

Calling, as we have seen more recently, can be very diverse and can change over a lifetime. God is endlessly creative, and society is increasingly complex. It is not a surprise that people need to always be "on their toes" and "lightly packed" so as to follow God's new callings. Someone who is a pastor might end up later in a secular job, serving God through it and around it, just as all Christians are called to do. They might have still a special call to equip and shepherd others. Some are called to pastoral ministries later in life. Circumstances such as physical debilitation or responsibilities for family can change what is possible. As we saw in the discussion of providence, God always works in an incarnate way, thus always working in and with the actual and realistic circumstances of a world that is both created by God but also groaning in its bondage where it does not serve God's purposes. Christian leaders are not exempt from such incarnational immersion in such a world.

The issue of women's leadership also becomes transformed when we "baptize" the idea of Christian leadership. While traditional roles can be defended by specific texts, it is difficult in the larger picture to avoid the impression that women's subordination is more cultural and contextual than a universal principle.[67] The fact of women's leadership in prophesying and ministry in the Bible itself, in very patriarchal cultures, is unavoidable. The basic equality of women before God as being fully in the image of God; the fact that women appear to be fully gifted in the ability to exercise leadership, proclamation, nurturing, and teaching; the fact that Paul does not distinguish in the gifts between genders; and the example of so many women who by the fruit of their ministries give testimony that they are genuinely called—all support the unleashing, not only of the laity, but of half of the church to fully exercise their gifts of leadership. This is leadership not as a place where women now get to have the power and privilege that has been denied them, but in the church it is a place where they get the chance to serve and minister in ways that have been denied them. In a time when most Christian groups are crying out because of a dearth of leaders, it seems a tragedy that so many who are capable and gifted—and straining at the bit—are excluded. The greening of the church might erupt yet.

Looking to such a hopeful future may seem unrealistic, but the church's goal is not to be realistic about the present but to live in light of the reality of the coming kingdom. Everything, in fact, that we have said about the church and other doctrines is in light of the coming kingdom, that is, eschatology. It could have been first, but it is also fitting for eschatology to be last not because of its relegation to secondary status but because of its climactic importance.

10

LAST THINGS
The End

If the understanding of God and of Christ in terms of the Trinity was diverse in the first centuries of the church, the understanding of last things (eschatology) was even more so. Besides basic affirmations of the second coming of Christ, of resurrection, of heaven and hell, and a final judgment, details varied tremendously. The idea of an intermediate state developed slowly and took various forms, from its denial in an immediate judgment and resurrection to holding places for both the wicked and the righteous, to purgatorial ideas, sometimes for all people in the direction of universal salvation. Toward the end of the second century, the idea of a literal millennium on this earth flourished, often adorned with vivid earthy luxurious lives, only to be largely dismissed as too crass and crude by the fourth and fifth centuries. Sometimes the disembodied soul was thought to exist after death while waiting for the final resurrection, where the physical body would be miraculously reassembled from all of its fleshly parts, whatever their fate. Others took the body to be transformed immediately since it was to be more aethereal and spiritual anyway. Others thought the dead slept until awakened. Hell was pictured as literal, physical torment, forever, while others saw it as more spiritual and internal, perhaps not lasting forever—even for Satan. Some thought the final state came immediately; others thought it came with stages of development, perhaps lasting forever, except perhaps for the greatest saints.

The difference from the Trinitarian and christological issues is that these issues were not settled so consensually. We have virtually the same live options vying for attention in the present—with a few added. As has been stated already, eschatology has consistently been the area of liveliest theological activity, sometimes with the amount of speculation in direct proportion to the lack of evidence. Here is the theological place for the dictum, "Fools walk in where angels fear to tread." It calls for the greatest theological caution precisely where there has been historically the greatest theological activity. Minefields abound, but the ground must be traversed. Everything leads to this point, and if we falter here, everything we have presumed so far is called into question. As Paul said, "If for this life only we have hoped in Christ, we are of all people most to be pitied" (1 Cor 15:19). In this case, we might say, "If Christ is not returning to bring a new heaven and a new earth, then we are of all people most to be pitied."

In order to tread carefully, we will first consider a couple of case studies that illuminate these issues, then move to the contemporary renewal of eschatology, to personal eschatology, to historical eschatology, and then to cosmic eschatology.

CASE STUDIES

The Millerites

On October 22, 1844, numerous Christians in the United States awaited the second coming of Christ based on the careful mathematical calculations of one William Miller, an erstwhile bibliophile, successful farmer, Baptist, and math teacher. Perhaps a million had attended Millerite camp meetings, and one hundred thousand prepared themselves for the great day when they would be saved while the world was destroyed by fire. Some farmers were so sure about the date that they did not plant their crops that spring and abandoned their animals as the time drew near. Some merchants closed their stores and gave their goods away.[1] Some sold their property; other gave up their jobs. It has been said that some gathered on the highest hilltops in white robes so as to be just a little closer to meeting the Lord when he came.[2] When the "Great Disappointment" occurred, that is, when Christ did not come as designated, another date was set, followed by yet another disappointment. Some of the group then came to be especially influenced by a charismatic, miracle-working young woman named Ellen White. When she argued, or rather saw in a vision, that Christ had indeed come to the inner sanctuary—but in heaven, not on earth—the movement was saved and went on to become the Seventh Day Adventist church, only to spawn yet another date-setting movement, the Jehovah's Witnesses, based on the ideas of Charles Taze Russell, who had first become an Adventist.[3]

Martin Luther King Jr.

During a heavy storm, weary, dispirited Martin Luther King Jr. was prevailed upon to address a crowd in Memphis, Tennessee, the evening of April 3, 1968.[4] He spoke without drawing upon a script, in a voice filled with sadness. He reflected on the significance of the time. If God had given him a choice in eternity of where he would spend his days, he said, he would have bypassed great ages of the past, of Moses, of Plato, of Martin Luther, and of Lincoln. He would have sped past them all to have spent a few years in the last half of the twentieth century. This is strange, he said, since it was such a troubled time, but he added, "Only when it's dark enough can you see the stars." Then he reminisced about a decade earlier when he had been stabbed so close to the aorta that a doctor told him that if he had but sneezed, he would have died. In a cadent refrain, he spoke of all that he would have missed, if he had sneezed. He would have missed freedom rides, African-Americans in Albany and Birmingham stirring a nation, the chance himself to give voice to a great dream at the Lincoln Memorial, and now the opportunity to join a community in Memphis contending for justice. He was glad that he had not sneezed. With great responses from the audience, he intoned, "It doesn't matter. It really doesn't matter what happens now." He told them of a bomb threat just that morning and reiterated,

> We've got some difficult days ahead. But it really doesn't matter with me now. Because I've been to the mountaintop. Like anybody I would like to live a long life. Longevity has its place. But I'm not concerned about that now. I just want to do God's will. And he's allowed me to go up to the mountain. And I've looked over. And I've *seen* the Promised Land. And I may not get there with you. But I want you to know tonight that we as a people *will* get to the Promised Land. So I'm happy tonight. I'm not worried about *anything*. I'm not fearing any man. Mine eyes have seen the glory of the coming of the Lord.

Then he ended with words familiar from that speech in Washington:

> I have a dream this afternoon that the brotherhood of man will become a reality. With this faith, *I* will go out and carve a tunnel of hope from a mountain of despair. . . . With this faith, *we* will be able to achieve this new day, when all of God's children— black men and white men, Jews and Gentiles, Protestants and Catholics—will be able to join hands and sing with the Negroes in the spiritual of old, "Free at last! Free at last! Thank God almighty we are free at last."

By the next evening, his voice was quieted by the bullet of a sniper's gun.

Two visions, Miller's and King's. Both had drunk from the same well. At that point, they took sharply different paths. One focused on mathematical speculation about a future life, giving up this life to advance to the next. The other spent a life bringing the future to bear on this life. They portray the very different ways in which eschatology makes a difference. The former type of approach was sharply criticized by Karl Marx as providing the "opium of the people."[5] It was a way of escaping this life and making a bitter peace with the injustices of this world. The latter was invigorated and inspired to do more to bring about justice in this world than even he could have dreamed. Eschatology is central to Christian faith, enshrined in the earliest confessions. It is unavoidable even as it has always been highly potent, but like any central belief, it can be a force for good or ill, depending on how it is understood.

Because of the influence of Marx's critique, enshrined in the Marxist governments of most of the world's population for much of the twentieth century, Christian eschatology often has a bad name and has been downplayed even by Christian theologians. King, however, portrays the power of eschatology in a healthy way. Rather than causing one to turn one's back on the problems of this world, it can empower one to face such problems. Precisely because of hope for the future, one can have the courage to risk all in resisting problems. If this life were all there is, such risk would pale in comparison to the drive to accommodate and extend this life as long as possible.

Even more significantly, the vision of the future, King's translation of the kingdom of God as "the beloved community," gives not only inspiration but shape and direction to efforts to transform this world.[6] Rather than eschatology encouraging passivity and quiescence, it should stir disquiet in light of the way that the affairs of this world fall short of the peaceable kingdom.[7] King was inspired by the Old Testament prophets who themselves were stirred to protest against the status quo in light of their vision of what God desired. Perhaps above all, King was driven by Amos' prayer, "Let justice roll down like waters, and righteousness like an ever-flowing stream" (Amos 6:24). Rather than being an opiate for the people, as expressed by Marx and often by Christian leaders themselves, as King described in "Letter from a Birmingham Jail," eschatology in this vein is expressed in the title of another of King's works, *Why We Can't Wait*.[8]

The power of eschatology, moreover, is not just that a vision is provided in the imagination, it is based on the sure promises of God for the future. It is not just that such a dream would be attractive if it could be realized; it is based on the fact that, for faith, it is the shape of things to come, the "grain of the universe," as it were.[9] As we shall see, much has to be said in working out this relationship of present and future, but the contemporary renewal of interest in eschatology, which is fed by the post-Marxist realization of the positive power of Christian eschatology, is hard at work on just such issues.

CONTEMPORARY RENEWAL

Eschatology adds other significant dimensions to the full range of Christian theology. It helps, as much as any other doctrine, to put this life and this world into a larger perspective and framework. We have already seen the dynamic pattern that moves from creation, fall, and redemption toward the promise of a future fulfillment. Eschatology helps us look not just from the past to the future but *from the future to the past*. In this sense, it represents one of those major theological revolutions that have occurred in the last one hundred years that we are highlighting. Because of the problems of eschatology and its misuse, eschatology in modernity in some ways had been put aside and neglected—apart from certain groups such as the Millerites that ran wild with it, thereby making the point that this is an area to be avoided. Generally, the approach in theology had been to move from the past, specifically, creation and the ensuing major events of salvation history, to the present, and then into the future. When the eschatological theologies of Wolfhart Pannenberg and Jürgen Moltmann erupted on the theological scene in the 1960s, all of this changed.[10] In slightly different ways, they both stressed that God is "the power of the future." Whereas the mainline theology of an earlier time had been influenced by Immanuel Kant's (1724–1804) philosophy, namely, liberal theologies of the nineteenth century and neo-orthodoxy of the twentieth century, these newer eschatological theologies were influenced more by Georg W. F. Hegel's (1770–1831) philosophy that put more stress on the end than on the beginning. Hegel stressed more the dynamism of history, the immanent presence of God within history, and the way that truth lies in the whole of history. To express the latter in a more striking way, one cannot understand the present apart from the perspective of the future. Given the significant place that the promise of the future has always had in Christian theology, namely, the "blessed hope," it was natural to begin rethinking theology in light of the future. As we have already seen, this enabled Pannenberg to stress more strongly Jesus' coming as a "prolepsis" or "first fruits" of the future.[11] As we discussed in the chapter on Christology, the very significance of Christ is eschatological and can be understood, or can best be understood, only from an eschatological perspective. My doctoral supervisor in theology, Dale Moody, at about the same time in the sixties that Pannenberg and Moltmann were publishing their books, also focused on eschatology, publishing a major work on it.[12] Perhaps more significantly, the influence showed up in his systematic theology, published in 1981, where he approached virtually every doctrine from the future first, and then worked backwards.[13] He followed the traditional order, similar to the one followed in this book, but his approach showed that it is difficult, for example, to understand creation without first thinking of the new creation. It is difficult to think of humanity without thinking of Christ and even of fulfilled humanity in a new heaven and a new earth. It is difficult to understand the meaning of salvation, similarly, apart from its eschatological purpose. Salvation is not just to recover what was lost but is a movement toward future potentiality.

All of these theologians conveyed the picture of God as not moving from the past to the future but of coming from the future to the present. For Pannenberg, particularly, this was tied in with the traditional notion of God's timelessness. This may seem odd at first, given his sense of God as the power of the future, but the idea that God is outside of, and transcends, time helps one to see how God is already in the future and looks at the present in light of the whole. We have seen, however, that there are significant philosophical and theological problems with the notion of divine timelessness. For example, we noted how simple foreknowledge of the future is not very helpful. If God simply knows the future, then God cannot do anything about it in terms of projecting that knowledge of the future toward the past. If it affected the past, making the past no longer the past that it was, then God would not know, of course, the past that never happened but would now know the alternative. In terms of the theology emphasized in this work, it seems like here again a notion of transcendent divine temporality would serve just as well or better. It provides deep ontological grounding for a sense of movement of past to the future and a great sense of expectation as well as the hoped-for blessed consummation in the future.

If God has already experienced the end, in a sense, being out-side of time, and if we have already experienced consummation as well due to our future eschatological state of being timeless, the sig-nificance of time and hope seems to be undermined. The fear that has caused caution about divine temporality, I think, stems from identifying time too much with the finite human experience of time. We are very aware of the fragile nature of human hopes and the lack of control that humans have over the future. In other words, hope is less substantial and ephemeral than reality in the present and in the past for humans. But this is to project human experience upon divine experience. Presumably, in this case as in many oth-ers, God is different. There is a substantiality and validity in God's plans for the future that are very different from human plans. For one, given our understanding of who God is and God's powers and abilities, God can do much more about the future than we can. As we have discussed, if God wants to consummate all of reality at a certain point in time, God can. God is presumably not subject to being pulled to and fro as humans are and so God's planning and desires for the future can be more reliable and trustworthy. In this sense, we can say that everything that has happened from creation on can be grounded in God's steadfast plans for the future, in other words, divine eschatology. All that God does can be seen as teleo-logically or eschatologically directed. God works with a plan. God does things with something in mind. Everything that is done then takes place in the shadow of the future.

One of the gifts of Judaism to the world was a stronger sense of linear time. The ancient world, especially in the area where Judaism developed, was dominated by a circular view of time. The present was generally seen as worse than the past and in continuous decline. People had little hope of an afterlife to console them. As it devel-oped in Platonism, it represented an escape from the world alto-gether. There was not expectation of an ultimately better future for the world, merely a continuous recurrence. Into this world Judaism came with its understanding that God began something in the past that was moving toward a future that was new, not a return to the old. The fact that it is difficult for us to relate to the circular view reveals how much impact this Judeo-Christian worldview has had on the West.

In the modern period, this view of time became secularized and also became, with the rise of science and technology, an expectation that things would continually get better in this life. The fact that this current generation of youth in the United States seems traumatized by the likelihood of being the first generation in U.S. history to be worse off financially than their parents shows how deeply a secular view of progress has been grounded. Moltmann is correct, however, to point out that this simple linear view of time is not identical with a Christian theological understanding of time. It certainly has been influenced by the Judeo-Christian faith, but in the end, it is a far cry from eschatological hope and fulfillment. The Christian eschatological hope is not just the movement of the past into the future, it is the coming of a better future into the present. It is not just more of the same—only a little better. Christians anticipate a radical transformation of reality, akin to the expectation of resurrection for the individual. Moltmann calls this "advent" rather than the "future."[14]

One might contrast the Christian view with the secular hope that progress in technology and medicine might enable people to live a very long life, perhaps hundreds of years. For some, this would be heaven. Such a hope is probably only possible in the developed West, where people, some people, have the means to enjoy many of the good things in life and are young enough to have had good health and have access to medical care enough to have not suffered immeasurably. Perhaps if there is no other hope, the most one could desire is the continuation of this life. A bizarre example of this was the family of the great baseball player Ted Williams, who tried to preserve him in the hopes that with developments in science he might be resuscitated. In the bizarre end of this story, he even was decapitated so that he could be preserved for the future.[15] Again, this is a far cry from Christian hope.

As mentioned earlier, it is striking to see scientists speculate, almost frantically, about how human life might be preserved in the far-off future, not just a few billion years into the future to survive the death of the sun of our solar system but trillions of years to survive the death of the entire universe (set at around 10 to the hundredth power of years into the future!). Due to the law of entropy, the universe will definitely run down. Some have thought that the wisdom of the human race might be placed on a computer chip, floating in space. Entropy, however, would even afflict that chip due to the slight amount of energy that it uses. Others have thought that there might be "multiverses," other universes, to which humans might be able to tunnel through "wormholes." In light of string theory with its postulation of eleven dimensions, others have thought that toward the end of the universe, the four dimensions of which we are clearly aware might collapse as the others expand. Humans might be able to jump at just the right time to the expanding ones and thus survive. It might be possible, some surmise, even to create a "baby universe" of our own.[16] After all of this, Christian eschatology is not as farfetched as one might have originally thought! For a naturalist, behind such existential *Angst* about the distant future seems to be an investment in the survival of the human race at some time as the only hope there is. In the end, this seems to be a pale substitution for personal and cosmic eschatological hope. It is to place value on continuation of human earthly existence beyond what it can bear.

The Christian view, as we have seen in earlier chapters, includes the great value of human life and of all creation. It expects Christians to be concerned about vulnerable and innocent life. Sometimes, though, Christians have been pulled in this direction so far as to make the present life virtually sacred. This would be to value it above all else, which is certainly not the Christian hope. The biblical story as well as Christian history, with its suffering, sacrifice, and martyrs, shows that Christians value this life but not above all else. Something more than biological life itself is important.

This is what eschatological hope undergirds. One, it indeed points to the value of human life and of the world, both of which are not lost but transformed. Second, it points to a perspective in which one might think about sacrificing one's life on this earth because of transformation in another life. Third, it points to the fact that one loses this life in hope of eschatological life, so that one is always thinking not just about how things appear in this life but how they will appear in eternity, and, one might say, in the final judgment. Ludwig Wittgenstein spoke of the significance of the peculiar logic of living one's life in light of this picture and not another.[17] The Christian desires to live this life in such a way that one can be blessed in the future, in the eschatological future. This does not mean capitulation and aquiescence to the status quo, as Marx thought, but can mean courage for resistance and change, as King saw. In this sense, many earthly values are not degraded or minimized but are relativized or, one might say, "eschatologized."

One can see how eschatology can lead, not to escapism, but to persistence and revolution. It can lead people to sacrifice many things in this life and to reject the easy way out, such as compromising, yielding, and submitting to injustice and oppression, all for the sake of the values of the kingdom of God. One may find a person like a Mother Teresa or Martin Luther King Jr., who risk their lives and give up many of the possibilities of ease and comfort for the sake of higher values. In the one case, Mother Teresa lived a long time. In the other, Martin Luther King Jr., led a short life. It is difficult to imagine either one of them taking the road that they took in this life apart from a future hope and the idea that they were living this life within the larger framework of an eschatological life.

As in all things, there has to be a balance, and the Bible is full of flashing yellow caution lights around these issues, which are very important because these caution signs have been run through many times. Paul warns in his earliest letters against those who, apparently because of thinking that Christ was coming soon, were not working or were not planning for the future (1 Thess 4:11; 2 Thess 3:10). This of course has happened many times in Christian history, as with the Millerites. It should be clear at this point, after twenty centuries, that the dramatic tension must be maintained between being ready at any time to meet one's Maker, so to speak, but also to plan for the future. One of Jesus' temptations was to presume upon God and to tempt God in a similar way (Matt 4:5-7). This is a place where we must avoid tempting God as well, but, unlike Jesus, we have often succumbed.

Another caution is not to minimize the goodness of this life. This is another area that has been abused over and over again in Christian history. The fact that sometimes the blessings in this life must be sacrificed for greater values does not mean that they are not good things or that God is not pleased when it is possible to enjoy the good earth. Paul again expresses it well when he says that he has learned how to have little and how to have plenty in all circumstances—for he can do all things through Christ who strengthens him (Phil 4:12-13). This is also expressed in 1 Timothy 4 against undue asceticism: "For everything created by God is good, and nothing is to be rejected if it is received with thanksgiving" (v. 4). Another caution is to avoid so dreaming of heaven that one cannot pay due attention to the blessings of this life. Jesus' admonition to pay attention to the concerns of the day, rather than inordinately living one's life in the future, is important (Matt 6:34). And as soon as we bring up this caution, we need to bring up the yellow light on the other side, that one should not just think about today but have due, balanced regard for planning for the future. It is crucial to plan properly as Jesus exhorts us to do—as any military commander does when he or she goes to war—in terms of how it is going to go and planning accordingly (Luke 14:31-33). A good steward is someone who considers the future in a proper, balanced perspective. There is that word again, *balance*. Christian wisdom, which takes judicious discernment because there are not enough rules, is in finding that balance.

The apocalyptic genre that is so crucial in eschatology differs from its common appropriation by Christians who live fairly well in developed countries. Rather than being somewhat like armchair speculation about the timing of the end of the world, suitable for a comfortable, leisure class, these writings emerged from people subjugated, exploited, threatened, and desperately needing to match tremendous threats with tremendous faith, courage, and hope. Again and again, when Christians have been severely threatened, apocalyptic scripture has come to the fore.

Apocalypticism is not without its abuses, however, as was seen in the time of the Reformation when, in light of eschatological hopes, some attempted at Münster to establish the New Jerusalem. Polygamy was established, and opponents were slaughtered.[18] This came, by the way, to be identified with the Anabaptist movement and tarnished that movement for quite a long time. The Millerites reflect another escapist abuse. At its best, apocalyptic literature is, as Moltmann says, literature "not written for 'rapturists' fleeing from the world, . . . it was meant for resistance fighters."[19] It is akin to the Revolutionary War pamphleteering by someone like Thomas Paine. It is meant to galvanize, not narcotize, as Marx complained. Moltmann adds:

> The dumb suffering of those who have been defeated and subjected finds no place in the annals of the ruling nations. Only apocalyptic, which sprang up out of Jewish and Christian martyrdom, lends these people a voice, a hope for redemption, and the power to rebel at the proper times. . . . Judaism's specific contribution to the history of humanity is to be found in the apocalyptic of the oppressed, and in the messianism of the conversion of time.[20]

Perhaps this point can be put most bluntly in saying that if one is not more prepared to be a martyr after reading the book of Revelation, then one has not understood it.

This material is very symbolic, and the images, as images typically do, slide from one usage to another. An example is the image of the abomination of desolation, which had a historical instance, pointed to in Daniel (9:27), but then it gets taken up again and again to point to future times (Mark 13:14). Another example would be the foe from the north, which represents various foes from the north of Israel over time to the final enemy of God and humans. Gog of Magog in Ezekiel (38:2, 14-15) becomes Gog and Magog in the book of Revelation (20:8). In Isaiah, the expectation of a future golden age where people still live, die, and have children that have a comfortable life (2:1-4; 11:6-9) is transposed in the book of Revelation into a new heaven and new earth for those who are resurrected from the dead, who do not die, get married, or have children (20–22).

One could argue that the basic nature of eschatological hope functions in much the same way and does not significantly change; but the underlying picture radically changes, indicating why a literal interpretation can cause one to go so wrong and actually create unnecessary problems for the integrity of the biblical message. At the very least, what we should learn is that any kind of heavily literal approach to eschatological and apocalyptic material is almost sure to misconstrue it. Unfortunately, some in the United States and in much of the world have fostered the idea that the default position is always the literal and so passages must be taken literally unless it is clearly to be taken otherwise. Ironically, as we have seen, this is probably a legacy of modernity and was not really part of the context in which Scripture emerged. In this apocalyptic genre, precisely the opposite should be the default, namely, that a symbolic approach should be preferred unless it is very clear that something should be taken literally. If one is not adept and familiar with interpreting symbolic language, then one is likely headed for hermeneutical shipwreck in this area. I suggest sometimes that the students who are probably best prepared for reading the Bible are English majors who at least are trained in reading poetic, symbolic language. The disadvantage in that tack is that we often take poetic language as fiction and thus not as true. The biblical authors, to the contrary, had the idea that poetic language was often the best way to convey truth.

If one understands that the language is symbolic, the details are not so significant as the main message, the point of which is not to give details but to provide sufficient grounding for future hope in order to live in the present. If this is the starting point, then we have a chance to interpret biblical revelation in this area very well. A helpful example has been to compare prophecies of the future to approaching a faraway mountain range. From a great distance, the peaks look like they are right next to each other and are too shrouded in fog and clouds to make out exact details. As one gets closer, what seemed to be close together becomes far apart so that the actual details look quite different. For example, in thinking about the Old Testament expectations of the messiah, it is striking, as we have indicated, to realize that the Old Testament nowhere speaks of two future comings of the messiah—not to mention three, as in the rapture of dispensationalism. The straightforward expectation that one would have in reading the Old Testament is that, if the idea of the messiah were highlighted at all, the messiah would come and establish the kingdom on earth in short order. Moreover, it was unclear how the Suffering Servant in Isaiah or the Son of Man in Daniel might connect.[21] It was not even apparent to everyone that the Suffering Servant was an individual figure and not the nation of Israel or a remnant of Israel. In the first century, as you may recall from the chapter on Christology, there were varied expectations concerning the messiah but none that fit what happened in Jesus.[22] Only in retrospect is it possible to re-read the Old Testament in such a way as to see a prediction of two future comings of Christ, the first one a suffering one. Jesus himself may have been the first to put these three figures together in a new way. Still, Jesus' disciples, who spent a great deal of time with him, did not understand this at all. This should give us pause and caution as we look at passages about the future when we are tempted to point out some kind of blueprint or schematic for how things are supposed to go. What if we will be as surprised at how things turn out as the disciples were surprised after the resurrection of Christ?

PERSONAL ESCHATOLOGY

An existential question for most in the West at the point of death is, is there a future beyond death? As Ivan Illych puts it in Leo Tolstoy's short story "The Death of Ivan Illych," this is no speculative question. When it was a matter of a distant acquaintance's death or the issue of mortality in general, it was one thing. But when it was a question of Ivan's death, it was another matter entirely. It is all the more poignant when gathered at the graveside of a spouse, family member, or especially a child. More than once, longtime Christians nearing death have asked me the question, what happens? The basic hope of Christians has been resurrection at the last day, but it has been joined with the ensuing question, what happens if I die before then? identified as the issue of the intermediate state.

The Hope of Resurrection

Christians tend to take for granted the hope of a personal afterlife as an integral aspect of the gospel without realizing that many, if not most, religious people do not even desire it. I am speaking of course of the fact that most people in the world are influenced by the Eastern religious idea of longing to get off the wheel of birth and reincarnation and to merge with the One or the All. To appeal to such a person that Christianity offers the hope of a person living forever might come across not as heaven but as hell! Even some in the West have seen it as a selfish desire, not worthy of a Christian.[23]

To complicate matters even further, the ancient Hebrews seemed to have had little hope of an afterlife. This is the dominant view in the Old Testament, with only a few hints of more of an afterlife that seem to come at the end of the Old Testament period and then became stronger in the intertestamental period.[24] Even in the first century, however, the belief in a resurrection for the righteous was not unanimous. To this day, the belief in an afterlife is not always a major emphasis in Judaism. Sometimes the Old Testament does speak of "shades" in Sheol. The shades appear to be a wispy shadow of earthly life bespeaking a slumbering existence. Sheol is the underworld where the shades go, where all go. It is not the dwelling of God or a place of reward or separation of the righteous and the wicked. Psalm 88 is illustrative:

> For my soul is full of troubles,
> and my life draws near to Sheol.
> I am reckoned among those who go down to the Pit;
> I am like those who have no help,
> like those forsaken among the dead,
> like the slain that lie in the grave,
> like those whom you remember no more,
> for they are cut off from your hand.
> You have put me in the depths of the Pit,
> in the regions dark and deep. . . .
> Do you work wonders for the dead?
> Do the shades rise up to praise you?
> Is your steadfast love declared in the grave,

> or your faithfulness in Abaddon?
> Are your wonders known in the darkness,
> or your saving help in the land of forgetfulness?
>
> (Ps 88:3-6, 10-12)

Job likewise reflects this view:

> Why did I not die at birth,
> come forth from the womb and expire? . . .
> Now I would be lying down and quiet;
> I would be asleep; then I would be at rest,
> with kings and counselors of the earth
> who rebuild ruins for themselves,
> or with princes who have gold,
> who fill their houses with silver.
> Or why was I not buried like a stillborn child,
> like an infant that never sees the light?
> There the wicked cease from troubling,
> and there the weary are at rest.
> There the prisoners are at ease together;
> they hear not the voice of the taskmaster.
> The small and the great are there,
> and the slave is free from their masters. (Job 3:11, 13-19)

Job later asks the question:

> As waters fail from a lake,
> and a river wastes away and dries up,
> so mortals lie down and do not rise again;
> until the heavens are no more,
> they will not awake,
> or be roused out of their sleep.
> Oh that you would hide me in Sheol,
> that you would conceal me until your wrath is past,
> that you would appoint me a set time, and remember me!
> If mortals die, will they live again? (Job 14:11-14)

The assumed answer to some of these rhetorical questions is, from a Christian perspective, surprisingly, "No." N. T. Wright, after looking at several of these passages, sums up the dominant Old Testament view:

Sheol, Abaddon, the Pit, the grave. The dark, deep regions, the land of forgetfulness. These almost interchangeable terms denote a place of gloom and despair, a place where one can no longer enjoy life, and where the presence of YHWH [Yahweh] himself is withdrawn. It is a wilderness: a place of dust to which creatures made of dust have returned. Those who have gone there are "the dead"; they are "shades," *rephaim*, and they are "asleep." As in Homer, there is no suggestion that they are enjoying themselves; it is a dark and gloomy world. Nothing much happens there. It is not another form of real life, an alternative world where things continue as normal.[25]

Christians throughout history have generally not taken this view in the Old Testament seriously—either through ignorance or through too-easy assimilation to the New Testament view. It reminds us, however, from deep within Scripture itself, of the distinctiveness of the hope of resurrection. Of course, we must also point out that the idea of resurrection sprouted late in the Old Testament and flourished in the intertestamental period, so the New Testament view of resurrection, while distinctively Christian, is also thoroughly Jewish. In one interesting case, the roots of the Saducean denial of an afterlife are based on the two arguments that we have already seen: it had not been taught in the Law or the earlier tradition, and it is a selfish desire, like "slaves serving the master for the sake of receiving a gift." Against this, the Pharasaic tradition countered with the hope of resurrection in the future after an intermediate state, going so far at times to say that one reason for not sharing in the blessed age to come is to be like the Sadducees, namely, not believing in the resurrection of the dead.[26]

Nevertheless, it is not as though the ancient Hebrews had no future hope. In fact, future hope was firmly rooted in their theological DNA, one might say. As we have noted, their general outlook is more corporate, more social. They obviously do not reflect a sense of modern individualism. They could then take comfort in the hope of the nation and their descendants finding rest at last in the land, when, in the words of both of the eighth-century B.C.E. prophets, Isaiah and Micah:

> In days to come the mountain of the Lord's house
> shall be established as the highest of the mountains,
> and shall be raised above the hills;
> all the nations shall stream to it.
> Many peoples shall come and say,
> "Come, let us go up to the mountain of the Lord,
> to the house of the God of Jacob;
> that he may teach us his ways
> and that we may walk in his paths."
> For out of Zion shall go forth instruction,
> and the word of the Lord from Jerusalem.
> He shall judge between the nations,
> and shall arbitrate for many peoples;
> they shall beat their swords into plowshares,
> and their spears into pruning hooks;
> nation shall not lift up sword against nation,
> neither shall they learn war any more. (Isa 2:1-4; cf. Mic 4:1-4)

This passage represents great expectations for the future, which are centered not only on peaceful dwelling in a land flowing with milk and honey, as promised to Abraham, but a land whose center is Jerusalem, whose center in turn is the Temple. Note, however, that this is a very this-worldly vision, not an expectation of resurrection for those who have died to dwell anew in the land. It is not a hope for Isaiah personally to share in this fruition but for his descendants to enjoy this blessing on this earth in a "normal" earthly, mortal life—but a blessed one. Such corporate hope is satisfied with fulfillment, not for oneself but for one's descendants. It is probably better to say that one's personal fulfillment is indeed satisfied in the blessing of one's descendants. Such a corporate hope is likely difficult to grasp for modern Westerners so oriented toward individualism and shaped by future hopes of individual fulfillment in an afterlife. Yet it seemed to suffice for the Hebrews for centuries.

It is a future hope, nevertheless. In fact, its dynamic is so similar to the pattern of the New Testament that it could be transposed without a break in rhythm in the book of Revelation, where resurrected believers, to be sure, not just descendants, dwell on "a great, high mountain" in the midst of "the holy city Jerusalem coming down out of heaven from God" (Rev 21:10). Even the nations are still mentioned in this transformed vision, where they are seen as walking by its light (coming from God) and enter in and out of its gates (21:24-25). The leaves of the tree of life in that city are "for the healing of the nations." In this way, the Christians could see their future resurrection, transformed as it was by their experience of what happened in Christ, as taking up in a new key the ancient Jewish hopes for their land, their nation, and their city. There is significant change, to be sure, but there is also significant continuity. Even before Christ, the dominant beliefs of the Jews at the beginning of the first century had already made the basic transposition of their hopes to include themselves in a future resurrected land and city. The movement from this-worldly corporate hope to eschatological personal hope (still very corporate) can be seen as a comprehensible progression but not a necessary one.[27] Most of those in the Old Testament apparently did not make that move—yet had vibrant faith.

What this reflection indicates is that an afterlife should not be taken as a matter of course, as an expectation that is almost seen as a right, as Western Christians shaped by Christianity might assume. There is no "natural immortality of the soul" here, such as one finds in Platonism, which was sometimes taken over into Christianity itself. Rather, there is "a sting of death" that marks the threat of possible dissolution altogether (1 Cor 15:55). One cannot argue logically or easily for an afterlife. It is contingent, a possibility, maybe even a long shot. This is what the Old Testament background reminds us. Rather than being a philosophical problem that is overcome by fleeing to the more Platonic notion of a natural immortality of the soul, belief in the resurrection underwrites in yet another way the centrality of grace. The New Testament view of an afterlife is thus one of sheer gift, total grace. Resurrection is a special salvific act of God that is not a matter of course but extraordinary. Such unmerited love is to be received as we do all of God's gifts, in Paul's words, "with thanksgiving by those who believe and know the truth" (1 Tim 4:3).

We can learn this lesson about the contingency of life from modern science. We are aware now more than ever, as we saw in the discussion of the holistic nature of human beings in the chapter on the

self, that humans are physically embodied beings. Our consciousness, our memory, our sense of self is only an accident, a disease,
a stroke away from being lost. One thing that has been clear to all
peoples, and we did not need modern science to teach it, is that we
die and our bodies decompose. In this sense, there has always been
a question mark about an afterlife. The initial evidence tells against
it! There is indeed an anxiety about our being-toward-death, to use
existentialist terms. There is an anguish that arises especially from
young lives cut short, possibilities cut off by death. It arises from
the parting of loved ones, of friends, whose absence, even in the
presence of robust Christian hope that sees it as temporary, represents a void, a loss, over which one legitimately grieves. If one says
goodbye to friends with no expectation of ever seeing them again in
this life, it is cause for grief. It is a sharper pang in saying goodbye
through death. Ironically, this tremor before death supports the New
Testament vision, which recognizes the sting of death yet emphasizes
the graciousness of the gift of the afterlife, as opposed to its logical
inevitability in the Platonic tradition. Against this, Christians are
often more Platonic, we might say, than Christian. Recovery of the
fragility of life, then, is an important part of coming to understand
the significance of Christian hope.

One classic way of dealing with such grief is to minimize attachment. This is the way of Buddhism and Stoicism. Cease desiring
another. Recognize that another person does not matter so much
after all. All is destined. Accept one's own karma and that of another.
Then it is not so painful. This, however, has not been the Christian
way. Marked as it is by the scandal of the cross, the Christian stance
has been one that encourages the attachment of love, frank recognition of the reality of loss, and yet hope beyond loss and death. It is
a narrow way, however. One can so focus on the afterlife that one
minimizes the importance of this life. One can experience a shock so
painful that it drives one to minimize loss and avoid attachment and
love. One can be pulled down by a grief so great that hope is lost,
and despair or cynicism prevails. The Christian approach winds its
way through all of those minefields. It can rejoice in this life as if
celebrating a wedding feast. It can be shrouded in gloom on Good

Friday. It can look forward to Easter hope. Sometimes, it can do all of these at once in a complex but discerning alchemy. Such is the life of a mature disciple; such is what it means to be canonically shaped into Christian eschatological practices.

The area of a personal afterlife has been one of the places where the Platonic influence upon the church has been most evident. A major understanding of the afterlife involved integrating the afterlife with God's timeless eternity. Even though Christians had to affirm bodily resurrection in accordance with 1 Corinthians 15, the after-life sometimes came to be conceived of as very ethereal, virtually disembodied. This was consistent with the Platonic ideal state as disembodied. Aquinas, drawing on Aristotle's philosophy, was able to justify embodiment to a stronger degree because of Aristotle see-ing that one needed form and matter, soul and body, to be a full or complete person. Aquinas, then, presuming that the full embodied state came only at the eschaton as in 1 Corinthians 15, saw the inter-mediate state as a disembodied one and therefore incomplete. With the Platonic view, one could wonder why one would ever want the embodied state. With this more Aristotelian understanding, how-ever, one could see why a psychosomatic whole (in Aristotle's terms, a hylomorphic, matter-form whole) was important. A dominant view is also that the saved (after Purgatory) exist in eternity worshiping God. Aquinas' term for this was aptly called the "beatific vision," which suggests the idea of one permanent gaze at God.[28] In the medi-eval period, of course, one could get to that point only after endur-ing purgatory—for almost everyone—a time of being cleansed and purged of sins. This was a recognition that people are not completely sanctified at death and need a time for both a kind of punishment and refining in order to prepare one for the final state of heaven.[29]

In contrast to this more dualistic tone in the church's tradi-tion, recovery of the idea of a holistic self and the importance of incarnation has renewed emphasis on bodily resurrection. Even the heavenly state, including the intermediate state, is seen as incarna-tional. There is a mystery here, which one grasps by considering 1 Corinthians 15. This passage strongly affirms that the resurrec-tion life is embodied, contrasting a physical body (a soulish body) and a spiritual body (1 Cor 15:44). Embodiment is what continues.[30] Nevertheless, in perhaps the most extensive treatment of the nature of the individual heavenly state in the Bible, Paul ends up suggesting that we know little about it. His point is that God will provide a transformed body. His comparison is the way a seed differs from its mature tree or flower (15:37-38). This is well and good if we are aware of both, but in this case, we know only the seed. This leaves us "seeing through a glass darkly," to say the least, in imagining the future flower with only the seed in mind.

It is clear that even with a spiritual body, we are pointed to dependence upon God and God's grace for our hope, rather than a natural argument for immortality. As we shall see, this incarnational turn sends a ripple throughout the rest of eschatology that affirms in new ways the continuity of not only this bodily life to the next but this cosmic life to the next.

The Intermediate State

This incarnational approach to the afterlife, particularly the intermediate state, is focused especially on a particular interpretation of the key passages of 1 Corinthians 15 and 2 Corinthians 5, which together raise the issue of an intermediate state between death and the second coming of Christ, the Parousia. The intermediate state is a question not discussed explicitly in the New Testament but lurks in the background. It is an unavoidable issue that arose in the early church when it was considering that the Parousia might occur far into the future. For example, Paul is clearly talking about the Parousia in 1 Corinthians 15 when he speaks of the last trumpet (15:52) and identifies the bodily resurrection as occurring at that time. In 1 Thessalonians 4, he is apparently responding to questions of the church to the effect that those who had already died might not participate in the final resurrection, so Paul replies that those who are alive shall not precede those who have fallen asleep, but they would all be caught up together to meet the Lord in the air (1 Thess 4:13-18). Here Paul seems to be thinking from the perspective of someone who will still be alive at the Parousia and is not giving much detail about the situation of those who are "asleep."

This euphemism for death has given rise to a major understanding of the intermediate state, soul sleep, which we will treat shortly. In contrast, in 2 Corinthians 5 Paul seems to be thinking as one who probably will die before Christ returns. In this complicated passage, he appears to suggest that death will bring the resurrected state immediately. Paul raises the idea of being "naked," or disembodied, but then dismisses it almost with horror, expressing a fairly common Hebrew dismay at the idea of being disembodied. This predictably has been misunderstood since the Greco-Roman legacy has been to prefer a disembodied state. So it is not surprising that the Hellenized church has often taken the language of the New Testament in a dualistic way that was likely not intended or even implied. This passage is a prime example. It has traditionally been understood along Thomistic-Aristotelian lines as implying a period of disembodiment but in the end receiving a resurrection body. First Corinthians 15 speaks in favor of this interpretation in that it implies that the resurrection body comes at the Parousia, not at death. It is possible, however, for Paul to be understood as referring to a different situation or to be speaking from a different perspective in 2 Corinthians 5—speaking as one who might die before the time of the Parousia. Paul attests that between the writing of the two letters, he almost died: "We were so utterly, unbearably crushed that we despaired of life itself" (2 Cor 1:8). Assuming Paul's Pharisaic background of embodied resurrection, he would hardly conceive of a disembodied state as being either possible or desirable and thus could be affirming some kind of embodiment at death.[31] In Philippians, Paul is clearly contemplating his own death, providing a model of Christian hope that is difficult to attain. He says, "My desire is to depart and be with Christ, for that is far better" (1:23). He does not specify the nature of this presence, but it certainly appears to be an expectation of being immediately in the presence of Christ and ruling out something like soul sleep. One might think here also of Christ's promise to the thief on the cross next to him: "Today you shall be with me in Paradise" (Luke 23:43).

With the assumption of dualism in the past, the idea of the disembodied state actually has been easier to accept. One could imag-

ine the soul being only loosely connected with the body to begin
with, surviving quite well apart from the body during a disembodied existence. With a reaffirmation of a holistic, embodied self, however, has come advantages and disadvantages. It has enhanced the
understanding of human life in this world but has made the question
of the intermediate state more difficult. In fact, under the pressure
of this recovery of holistic self, some have suggested that at death
the whole self truly perishes and is resurrected only as a replica of
the former self. This would be a version of soul sleep. In this case,
the person dies, and the next thing one is aware of, one is raised in
a new, spiritual embodiment that is like, or a replica, of the former
self. As John Hick intimates, the analogy is like moving software
into a new form of hardware.[32] In this case, the software is remembered by God, who is able to instantiate it in a new kind of embodiment. As Oscar Cullmann emphasized, this actually underscores
the greater Hebraic sense of the sting of death as opposed to a more
Greek notion of the immortality of the soul, whereas for Socrates,
and for most Christians thereafter, the soul is pictured as simple
and therefore indestructible, thus guaranteeing immortality.[33] The
Hebraic notion of Paul seems to imply that the soul can really die
and can only continue in life by the power of God. Since Paul seems
to think that this continuance can only occur in an embodied form,
albeit a spiritual body, this raises large questions for the intermediate state.[34] My own inclination is to think that in 2 Corinthians
5 Paul's thought implies a resurrection body at the point of death,
which is further completed and fulfilled in the full transformation
of the entire universe in a new heaven and new earth, thus giving
due weight also to 1 Corinthians 15.[35] Donald Bloesch develops this
same idea further in the sense of such resurrected bodies existing
in "Paradise" until the final transformation of heaven and earth,
in which such selves are more fully completed in an appropriate
environment.[36]

If one affirms the timeless view of God, of course, the problem
of the intermediate state could disappear. One simply arrives at the
point of death at the consummation of all things and has a bodily
resurrection. In short, there is no intermediate state. Conversely,

Moltmann thinks that this view of immediate resurrection discon-nects human fate with the fate of the world, an individualistic rather than a holistic turn that Moltmann prefers to avoid. He says against Karl Rahner's advocacy of this view, "Our bodily solidarity with this earth would be broken and dissolved. But is not every grave in this earth a sign that humans beings and this earth belong together and will only be redeemed together?[37] Of course, such a timeless view gives rise to all of the problems that go along with conceiving of God and eschatological life with God as atemporal. If one imagines the fullness of life with God as involving continuing activity in some ways such as worship and even growth in one's understanding of God, one cannot conceive of the eschatological state as timeless.[38]

Along with fresh emphasis on the importance of embodiment has come, strangely, a revival of the older idea of soul sleep. With Martin Luther, soul sleep was rather a simple idea, based on a reference to those who are asleep in 1 Thessalonians 4. He seemed to think that death was literally very much like sleeping, so that one dies, and the next thing one knows, one is resurrected at the Parousia. This involved raising the body and transforming it into a resurrection body, in whatever shape it was. This simple form, in light of further understanding of what it means to be embodied, will not do, quite apart from the possibility of the physical body being totally consumed by flames or spread to the far winds. The body is largely replaced every few years anyway, so one has to consider what it means to restore the body. The early church already was asking these kinds of questions about any kind of simply physical resurrection. As mentioned, Hick could imagine that the person dies completely, perishes, and at the Parousia or some other time be recreated as a replica. The replica idea, however, raises all kinds of philosophical issues about whether the replica is the same self as this person or just similar. Hick and others do not seem to be too worried about this, thinking that it is similar enough. Others, like myself, have more worries and prefer to emphasize direct continuity between the self at all times.[39]

Even with this idea, some have moved to a modified version of soul sleep in the sense of the spirit being preserved apart from the body. Because embodiment is so crucial, however, even according to these thinkers, the spirit is in a kind of dormant or comatose state, resting in God one might say—or as Stan Grenz says, "held by God."[40] Moltmann seems to suggest a similar idea also based on the incompleteness of spiritual existence from full embodiment.[41] It seems to me that this is a halfway house that is unnecessary. If one affirms that embodiment is essential to selfhood, following what seems to be Paul's Hebraic mindset, then it seems better to think of re-embodiment occurring at the point of death. This is a likely idea that Paul is suggesting anyway in 2 Corinthians 5 and avoids the problems of trying to imagine a disembodied state that otherwise seems to be impossible.

Heaven and Hell

The nature of the cosmic consummation of all things will be treated later, but the issue of a final judgment on the individual in terms of heaven and hell can be treated here. As in many aspects of eschatology, this is a minefield of fanciful if not grotesque imaginations. Sometimes it seems that Christians have gloried more in the sufferings of those in hell than in the joys of heaven. In the medieval period, in fact, part of the joy of heaven was supposed to be a delight in the suffering of those in hell.[42] Since one thing should be clear, namely, that salvation is by unmerited grace, such a spirit of gloating seems more diabolical itself than anything Christian—it at least reflects how much sensibilities have changed about retribution.

Although strong Calvinism has argued that God predestined from eternity those to go to heaven and those to go to hell, determining that their fate was sealed by the inscrutable decree of God, such a view has had to wrench us forcefully from passages like the parable of the prodigal son, which I have taken as a guiding center in soteriology. It has had to change utterly the meaning of passages like 2 Timothy 2:3: "[God] desires all to be saved and to come to the knowledge of the truth." This passage must be taken as referring only to God's manifest will but not God's hidden, unfathomable will, or taken inescapably to mean that one must insert words into the text as in, "God desires all *kinds of people* to be saved."[43] Here we are back to our fundamental conceptions of the nature of the power and love of God, which direct us in very different directions. I have argued that one does not have to undergird God's power by assuming that God always gets what God wants. If one conversely understands the love of God as desiring all people to be saved, but not forcing them, as in the parable of the prodigal son, then one cannot be so cavalier toward the lost. If one is like God, one seeks the lost and mourns over the prodigal. If we can accept the suffering of God, consistent with our previous theological reflections, then we can only imagine God's concern over the possible loss of those whom God loves.[44]

This leads us to a first firm place to stand in this area, namely, that we, like God, should desire the salvation of all people and grieve if it does not occur. Baptist theologian Bernard Ramm thus concludes, even for conservatives, "Every sensitive evangelical is a universalist at heart."[45] The meaning, it seems, is that this must be the hope of any Christian who is a person after God's own heart, for this is what God desires even if it does not occur due to human rejection of divine grace. In approval of this statement, Donald Bloesch cites Ezekiel 18:23: "Have I any pleasure in the death of the wicked, says the Lord God, and not rather that he should turn from his way and live?" Bloesch adds 2 Peter 3:9: "The Lord is . . . not wishing that any should perish, but that all should reach repentance."[46]

A second important principle should stabilize us as well, that is, the precise way in which the final destiny of all people is settled is not clearly set out in Scripture and remains a matter of speculation — theological and earnest speculation, but speculation nevertheless. Questions abound about the nature of heaven and hell and especially how it relates to those before Christ and those after Christ who never had a chance to hear the gospel. For instance, numerous theologians, especially in the Reformed tradition, who have a high view of sovereignty, have argued for universalism.[47] For a strong Calvinist, it is a short step from double predestination to taking literally passages such as 2 Timothy 2:3 and universalism. If God always gets what God wants and God wants all to be saved—as this and numerous other passages attest—then the outcome of universalism is settled.[48]

Strong Calvinists and Augustinians, of course, have long insisted on a double destiny, determined in the beginning by God.

Those more affirming of libertarian freedom and Arminianism have also allowed for a double destiny based on people's responses to God's offer of grace. The problem here arises with respect to those who never had a chance to hear the gospel—which probably includes most people who have ever existed in the world. This raises the question whether we might take away with one hand what we gave with the other. In other words, if one assumes that confession of the name of the historical Jesus is the only way to salvation, itself offered by a gracious, loving God, and yet people are condemned to hell without a chance even to respond to God's offer of grace, then one may undermine not only the justice but also the love of such a God. A theological conclusion that undermines God's love and justice is surely unacceptable. Whatever speculative conclusion that we might draw, we should be able to stand together on the ground that God is fair and loving. Otherwise, we contradict the central Christian hermeneutical principle that Jesus Christ is the supreme revelation of God. As we discussed in connection with soteriology, this is not to take sin or evil lightly—not at all. To do so would undercut the costliness of God's response to it. Yet surely we must do justice also to the seeking, reconciling, indefatigable love of God that is God's response to sin and evil. In being concerned about justice, we must do justice to that.

A mistake often made in this connection is to assume a clearly delineated biblical and Christian response to the issue of what happens to those who never hear a bona fide proclamation of the gospel, but a third theological guide is to realize that there is none. The Bible does not directly address this question. The interest in the New Testament is in the gospel of God and witnessing to it, not in worrying about what will happen if people are not reached. Helpful and tantalizing hints are given in passing as other subjects are treated, but no clear explanation is given. The issue is not even raised. As we have seen, various responses in church history, such as the Calvinist responses of double predestination (if they were elect, they would have been born in a better place), and universalism and the Arminian responses (Christians should proclaim the Gospel, but what if they do not) have been given; and there are others. In this area, no conciliar consensus exists. There is not even the presence of carefully worked out alternatives, as in atonement. In some ways, the issue has only fairly recently been seriously addressed due to the awareness of the scope of so many humans who have not realistically had a chance to hear the gospel and our closer encounter with such people. As always, personal encounters with others concretize an issue much more than dealing with it in the abstract.

Several responses have been given in this light, all affirmed by evangelicals with high views of Scripture.[49] One is simply to consign all who did not have a chance to hear the Gospel to hell. This might raise the question of who should go to hell: those who did not respond because of never having a chance or those who did not give them a chance! As Alister McGrath points out, "A human failure to evangelize cannot be transposed into God's failure to save."[50] Ultimately this comes back to God, who is responsible for a world where they have no chance. I remember a classmate in college who rejected Christianity because he could not believe in a cruel God like this. I had to confess that I also could not affirm a cruel God. Most who take this view resort to high views of sovereignty and to God's inscrutable mystery such as in strong Calvinism. In other words, if they were supposed to be saved, they would have been born where they had a chance to hear the gospel. This is usually tied to a view of original guilt based on all deserving to go to hell in Adam anyway, tied in with infant baptism as the removal of such guilt. Believers' churches, however, cannot rest easy with such a view. They can affirm that people are responsible for their sin, even without knowing Christ, but cannot rest easy with people suffering eternal separation from God without ever having a chance to respond to the gospel. Especially when God is affirmed by God's supreme revelation, Jesus Christ, as the seeking God who leaves the safe and seeks the lost until they are found, such a view seems inconsistent with the basic and clear revelation of God's nature.

Where do the more Arminian-minded go? Usually several other options are suggested. One draws on Paul's hints in Romans 2 that some Gentiles, who did not have the law, were nevertheless circumcised in their hearts before Christ (Rom 2:25-29). Combining this view with John's theology of the eternal Logos—who is the source of all truth and light from creation itself, "the true light that enlightens every man" (John 1:9)—some see that God reaches out to all through the Logos (ultimately through the Holy Spirit). Through the natural light of creation and conscience and the Holy Spirit, people might respond by faith in the grace of God. They may not know of the historical Jesus, but they have responded to the Spirit and reality of the one to whom the name attests. The Hebrew notion of the name not just being sounds or letters but standing for a personal reality is crucial. People can say the sounds of the word Jesus or the various ways it is translated. What has power is what the word means. That reality is now known through the Spirit of Christ and might be available today as that Spirit was known before the incarnation.

Thus, a further dimension of this approach is to relate those who never had a chance to hear the gospel to those before the incarnation who responded in a saving way to God. This includes the Hebrews like Abraham (and Melchizedek, Heb 5:10) who even preceded Moses and the Law, who did not understand much in terms of theology, but who, according to Paul, responded to God's overtures of grace by faith (Rom 4; Gal 3–4). This view is not envisaging another way of works-salvation, which is impossible according to Paul. It is salvation by grace through faith, which Paul says has always been the case, all the way back to Abraham (Rom 4:9-12). In the Old Testament, those like Abraham and Melchizedek and those before them were virtually like Gentiles in coming from their polytheistic religions, yet they came to know God. In Romans 2, Paul seems in general to allow for Gentiles without the Law to be in a saving relationship to God. This possibility might be extended still to all those who have not had a chance to hear the preaching of the historical Jesus.

Yet another possibility rooted in the early church, and perhaps in 1 Peter, is the idea of a postmortem opportunity to respond to the gospel. This is based on the idea of Christ's descent into hell after his death to proclaim the gospel to those in hades, seen as the holding place for all people before Christ, and giving all a chance to respond. "For this is the reason the gospel was proclaimed even to the dead, so that, though judged in the flesh as everyone is judged, they might live in the spirit as God does" (1 Peter 4:6). These passages are notoriously difficult to interpret, but it is important to see that they were interpreted in this way by notable theologians from the early church to this day.

This could be expanded in more creative ways like those of a C. S. Lewis and Donald Bloesch to imagine God seeking always to reconcile all to himself, even beyond the grave. In *The Great Divorce*, Lewis imagined that hell is simply a place where people get what they want. It is a bleak existence so far from God that it is next to nothingness. Occasionally, people have a chance to visit heaven, but they are put off by its size and solidity—its viscous reality. They are usually put off even more by the love and fellowship that radiates there. Occasionally, one might respond to the continual lure of God and still be transformed. Usually, however, people in hell are so persistent in their choices that they sink ever more into their resistance to God. This is why Lewis can say that the gates of hell are locked from the inside, not the outside. Hell is where people get what they want, as far from God as they can, which means almost nonexistence, by necessity. In fact, one can see in his vision that heaven seems like hell to the denizens of hell, whose perceptions are so deranged as to see good as evil and evil as good. They end up having a perverted happiness in their misery, misery that can only be seen from the heavenly perspective. While such speculations should be seen as what they are—namely, speculations—they do indicate how one can hold together the picture of God's ever-reaching love, yet with free will that is necessary to true love, and the meaning of the biblical symbols of heaven and hell.

As Lewis would himself say, these ideas do not offer another way besides that of Jesus Christ. It is not that people can be saved by some other god. If the Trinitarian theology of the church is correct, there is no other god than the God of the Father, Son, and Holy Spirit. If people in any way encounter God, they are encountering

Christ. If the church's understanding of the atonement is correct, if anyone is saved, it is based on the incarnation, life, death, and resurrection of Christ. This is the basis of God's offer of forgiveness; there is no other. What is not so clear is whether people can respond to the Spirit of Christ and welcome Christ into their lives—the reality of Christ—without knowing of the historical Jesus. Since this seemed to happen in the Old Testament, clearly one could say that biblical revelation itself points to its possibility.

Envisaging such possibilities is not to deny the surpassing value of the gospel story. Paul thought much of Abraham, in fact, that "faith was reckoned to him as righteousness" (Rom 4:9). Yet he was clear about the surpassing value of knowing the mystery finally revealed to the saints. The writer of Hebrews thought much of Abraham as well, seeing that he "died in faith," but the writer also saw that he and other Old Testament saints did not fully "receive what was promised, since God had foreseen something better for us, that apart from us they should not be made perfect" (Heb 11:39-40). Consideration of a "wideness in God's mercy," therefore, should never cause one to minimize what happened in Jesus Christ, the gospel, or missions, or evangelism.[51] This would be like saying that if Abraham was already justified by faith, then the incarnation was neither necessary nor desirable. In response to such a thought, Paul would likely have responded the way he did when people believed that grace suggests one should sin more. "By no means," he said, which is probably not as strong as it should be translated in English (Rom 6:2).

Lewis' ideas underscore yet another dimension of the response to this issue. A Christian's conception of hell can undermine the goodness of God. The fantastic imagination of hell as a place of unending physical torture by God that is to be enjoyed by God and Christians in heaven seems again to represent a sub-Christian rather than a Christian view of God's nature. Augustine even speculated that God might have to resurrect the wicked in bodies that could continue to burn without being burned up in order to continue their torture.[52] In our time, it is significant that even evangelicals protest against such views as being beneath the revelation of God's nature in Christ. The key is that the symbols, used even by Christ, must be understood as symbols, as they likely were in the first century. The problem is that people have taken them literally. The New Testament itself undermines such an approach, or at least indicates that they should not be taken literally, by the use of symbols that would be contradictory if taken literally. Jesus refers to hell in terms of fire (Matt 13:49-50; cf. Rev 20:15) *and* of outer darkness (Matt 8:12, 22:13, 25:30; cf. 2 Peter 2:17; Jude 13). One is a place of intense heat. Outer darkness presumably suggests being out in the cold, away from the heat![53] As in the eschatological symbols for heaven, which we shall see are presented as a garden and as a city, these symbols point to a symbolic but not literal reality. The city of God in Revelation, for example, is described in terms of precious jewels of that time but leaves out something like diamonds that we would use if describing it in our time. Hell then can be understood, much as Lewis did, of being outside of the presence of God. It is desperately to be avoided, just as one would avoid falling into a fire or being lost in the dark far from the warmth and protection of a campfire. Here, as always, the whole canon must be considered so as not contradict major confessions about the nature of God by misinterpreting the genre and meaning of particular symbols. In the area of eschatology, as we have noted, there has been probably more misinterpretation along this line than in any other area.

Another view of hell, also held by some evangelicals, is that the meaning of Jesus' teaching was more along the lines of annihilation. Dale Moody used to talk about confusing the worms and fire with people.[54] The worms and fire are what do not die and are not quenched (Mark 9:48). Such worms and fire mean that whatever they are attacking will be totally destroyed, which to some seems more merciful. If people choose to absent themselves from God, it means nothingness.[55] As we have seen, this is close to Lewis' vision. Others see such destruction as unworthy of God, especially if God desires continually to woo everyone to God.

Through this long consideration of various speculative possibilities, there is a place for caution and humility. Boldness, however, is always appropriate concerning such central affirmations of the love of God for all people and God's ultimate love and justice and fairness. We have been given an amazing hope by the amazing grace of God that can and should be proclaimed to all, without apology. Whatever our detailed theological speculations, we should sound a clear message that God can be trusted to be gracious and loving and caring for all people—and for each individual person—far beyond what any of us can imagine; in other words, that God is really like the father of the prodigal son, like the shepherd seeking the lost sheep, like the woman who lost a coin—or so Jesus said.

HISTORICAL ESCHATOLOGY

Keeping the preceding theological framework in mind will help us as we consider the most vexing aspect of eschatology, historical eschatology, better known as "millennialism." This has been the battleground where the close relation of eschatology to history has been played out. As one might already surmise, if the idea of the millennium leads in our theological dance, it almost inevitably leads to dancing disaster. Conversely, if one lets the wider eschatological theology provide the prism to consider the millennium, letting the millennium follow, as it were, the chances of stumbling drop considerably. This is in accordance with sound hermeneutics in general in the sense of allowing the dominant canonical themes to configure the minor notes rather than vice versa. Perhaps the worst case of getting these out of order, almost from the outset, is the topic we are about to consider.[56]

Historical Premillennialism

I say this keeping in mind the revival of turning to the early church and its premillennialism, even among some of my own teachers,[57] but even here, the early church did not get everything right or speak with one voice. We need only to read Paul's letters to the Thessalonians and the Corinthians to acknowledge this possibility. As mentioned, the earliest view of the millennium was "left behind," so to speak, after the Constantinian shift, only to experience something of a revival along with its recent cousin, dispensational premillennialism.

A common view of the millennium in the late first and second century was clearly a version of premillennialism as in the "Left Behind" view, but it was different than the more contemporary version in significant respects. One of its advantages was that it could read the book of Revelation, not literally, but directly, as applying to its own time (called the "preterite" [past]) interpretation. Revelation appears to be addressed to Christians of the late first century suffering under the ravages of imperial Roman power, offering them hope of deliverance to come. Probably they expected it soon along with the watchword that closes the visions, *Maranatha* ("Lord, come quickly")[58] (Rev 22:20). In terms of the dominant picture of the New Testament, Christians expected the Lord Jesus Christ to return again in glory (once) followed by the final judgment and final kingdom. According to this view, Revelation adds that after the coming of Christ would come the millennium, a one-thousand-year reign of Christ upon the earth, followed by a brief rebellion, then the final judgment, and "new heaven and new earth" (Rev 20:4). This view is called "pre"-millennial because Christ comes before the millennium. It is a pessimistic view because these early Christians thought that the world was getting worse, especially in light of their persecutions under Rome, and only the coming of Christ could supernaturally establish any kind of kingdom, whether millennial or not. Like contemporary dispensational premillennialism, they expected a literal millennial kingdom; but unlike it, they expected that the church would go through the final, severe persecution (this was not difficult since they already seemed to be in it). They did not expect a "rapture" to save them from persecution or to take them out of the world before the coming of Christ in the future. The rapture mentioned in 1 Thessalonians 4 referred simply to the one future Parousia of Christ. Moreover, the future millennial reign of Christ represented the reign of Christians, rather than being focused upon the reign of Jews as in contemporary dispensationalism.

The attractiveness of historical premillennialism waned as time passed. Much of what drove this view was the expectation that Christ would come soon in light of the suffering of the last days. Especially with the success of the church in the Roman Empire in the fourth century, it became difficult on both counts to maintain the imminent expectation and pessimism of this view. Obviously, a revival of historical premillennialism in the twentieth century was not going to share the same kind of imminent expectation. It did, however, take over the same kind of pessimism and simple formula that things would get worse just before the end, that Christians could expect persecution, and that when Christ came the millennium would be established upon the earth, focused upon Christians. A significant change in emphasis therefore does occur with the contemporary form of historical premillennialism. The attraction still remains, however, that historical premillennialism claims to represent perhaps the dominant early emphasis of the church and the basic pattern, apart from a literal millennium, that one finds throughout the New Testament.

Amillennialism

As mentioned, a huge change occurred with Constantinian Christianity, with Christianity becoming the favored and then the official religion of the Roman Empire. For some, this *was* the arrival of the millennium. It was thought that surely the church had won and so joy and enthusiasm greeted the notion that the kingdom of God had come upon earth. It was, therefore, difficult to maintain the deep pessimism of premillennialism. The second factor was a theological one, which was already occurring, namely, that theologians were reacting against the massive literalism of the millennial view, feeling like it was not sufficiently spiritual and too materialistic to be suitable for a proper Christian hope.

Amillennialism, which literally means "no millennium," means two things. One is that it denies a literal reign of Christ after the Parousia, which both forms of premillennialism affirm. It thus follows the simple and general New Testament formula of the Parousia, followed by the new heaven and new earth. Second, saying "No literal millennium" allowed for a symbolic interpretation of the reference to the millennium in the book of Revelation. Given the heavily symbolic nature of Revelation, there is much to be said for assuming a symbolic meaning at the outset, although the question of the meaning of the symbol is still a question.

The millennium, then, may refer to the present church age, perhaps the reign of Christ after the resurrection at the right hand of the throne of God, or beginning with the church's change of fortune under Constantine in the Roman Empire. As mentioned, some were quite enthusiastic at first about what this might mean for the wellbeing of the church. It was all too easy to identify Christ's reign with the reign of the church. As Moltmann points out, this often led to the amillennial idea being an ideological prop for abuses of power.[59] Amillennial theologians then became hostile to any other kind of millennialism, which suggested the need for a change. For this reason, Moltmann is quite critical of amillennialism in general.

For the Reformers Luther and Calvin, however, amillennialism could not be viewed as an affirmation of the rule of the Roman Catholic Church. Rather, they understood the millennium to refer to the reign of Christ at the right hand of God or in the hearts of true believers. It also can be seen as the reign of the saints in heaven in the intermediate state. Amillennialism continues to be very strong among Protestants with these meanings.

For some nowadays, amillennialism perhaps is a way of expressing reticence about the meaning of the millennium altogether. There is good reason for this position. The idea of the millennium is mentioned once in the Bible and only then in a difficult section of perhaps the most symbolic, difficult book in the Bible. This should give hermeneutical pause at the outset in investing much theological weight in the idea.[60] This is especially so when a literal interpretation implies a picture of things quite different from the rest of the New Testament, namely, a coming of Christ at the Parousia, then a reign of Christ upon the earth, then another battle with another coming of Christ in final victory. This means that the burden of proof, so to speak, is on the one who wants to make much theological hay with the millennium. When one considers that the book of Revelation involves significant symbolic parallelism, in accordance with typical Hebrew poetry where ideas are accentuated by being repeated in slightly different ways, the idea of a separate millennium is further called into question. Revelation 19–20 can easily be read as parallel, not speaking of two comings of Christ and two battles but rather of one conflict from different perspectives—not unlike Genesis 1 and 2.[61] This fits better the style of Revelation and also the theology of the rest of the New Testament.

Some form of amillennialism thus has been the most dominant interpretation in the history of the church and is still probably the most prevalent view of biblical and theological scholars. As a form of caution against making too much of the idea of a millennium, it is easy to defend. It can at least point to the "now" side of the kingdom of God where "all authority on heaven and on earth" has been given to Christ—already. It must be questioned, as Moltmann reminds us, when it does not do justice to the "not yet" side of the kingdom of God and when it gives rise to complacency and serves the vested interests of the powerful in the church.

Postmillennialism

The next major view that emerged powerfully on the scene came a millennium later (!) with the rise of modernity and the Enlightenment. It reflected a more optimistic tone of what was possible for the kingdom of God to accomplish upon this earth and a slightly different perspective from either of the preceding views. This view came to be called postmillennialism because it held that the kingdom of God would come upon the earth, and only afterward (post) would Christ come to establish the final kingdom. In a sense, this was almost the view of those at the time of Constantine who thought that the kingdom of God had already come with the church reigning over the Roman Empire. This later form, however, associated especially with the thought of Jonathan Edwards in the seventeenth century, was based upon the idea that the kingdom of God would gradually grow, like a mustard seed or leaven, and dominate the earth. At the beginning of the twentieth century, for example, the prominent Baptist theologian A. H. Strong thought that "the kingdom of Christ is steadily to enlarge its boundaries . . . and a millennial period is introduced in which Christianity generally prevails throughout the earth."[62] Another significant Baptist proponent of postmillennialism was B. H. Carroll, the founding president of Southwestern Baptist Theological Seminary in Fort Worth, Texas.[63] As we have seen in our theology of the church, this represents great optimism about overcoming sin even among Christians in the church. This view reflects, therefore, not only optimism about conversion but also optimism about sanctification. Another form of this, known in the early twentieth century as the social gospel, thought that the kingdom of God might come upon the earth as a result of social change and the improvement of the lot of humans. Thus, the prominent Christian magazine the *Christian Century* was named at the beginning of the twentieth century in recognition of these expectations.

In retrospect, it did not take long for these kinds of hopes to be dashed. World War I—supposedly the war to end all wars—came, and within a generation an even worse one erupted, World War II. This of course was followed by the Cold War, with the prospects of the whole world being ended at any time, which is still with us. It is thus difficult nowadays to find this kind of optimism among Christians.

Dispensational Premillennialism

In the early 1800s, a phenomenon much like Millerism arose, except in reverse. One account is that a young woman, much like Ellen White, in 1830 had a vision of Christ returning in a "secret rapture" to take Christians from the earth and then later returning in judgment.[64] This may have been the source of the rapture view clearly expressed by John Nelson Darby among a small group of Plymouth Brethren in England in the 1830s. This was one of the first times, if not the first, that Christians thought of two future comings of Christ. In this case, the visionary was followed by a mathematician like William Miller. This time, it was Nelson Darby who worked out details of the two Parousias. Like the Millerite movement, it also benefited from tremendous marketing and expanded far beyond its biblical grounding. Clarence Larkin's dispensational charts became almost synonymous with forecasting the end times, and the Scofield Bible, an Oxford Bible with C. I. Scofield's notes, became the Bible *du jour* for evangelicals in the United States for several generations. What happened is that people did not always distinguish between the notes and the scriptural text, both being "in the Bible." The movement accelerated after World War II with the pessimism spawned by the Cold War aftermath of World War II, as well as acceptance of the little-questioned interpretation of the "fig tree blooming" in Matthew 24:32-34 as being fulfilled by the restoration of the nation of Israel in 1948. Then Hal Lindsey's *The Late Great Planet Earth*, published in the 1970s, became a bestseller worldwide in the twentieth century. Lindsey predicted that since Jesus had said after the reference to the fig tree that "this generation will not pass away until all of these things come to pass," the rapture must occur no later than 1984. This was based on a biblical generation being twenty to forty years and allowing for the rapture to come in the middle (three and one-half years) of the seven-year tribulation rather than at the beginning (a "mid-trib" position). The final coming of Christ would then have to occur no later than 1988 (forty years after 1948), so the rapture had to occur at least three and one-half years earlier. Suffice it to say, the failure of this prophecy, much like the Great Disappointment of the Millerites, undermined this millennial view. Just as it suffered this blow and also suffered severe challenges to its questionable exegesis as the result of popular attention, it took on new and greater life with the Left Behind series of novels and movies—and shows no signs of abating.

Dispensational premillennialism thus became the latest significant millennial view. It is premillennial in its pessimism about history, positing that things must get worse before the end. In World War I, some were very consistent in this belief as demonstrated by not wanting to fight against Germany because democracy was a sign of the corruption of the end, and the end was nigh![65] Since that time, however, dispensational premillennialism has combined in an uneasy tension with American nationalism—uneasy because the same people who are dispensationalists and presume that the world must become worse and that the rapture will happen soon are often "bullish" about the future of America and its prospects.[66] It is premillennial also in its advocacy of a literal one-thousand-year reign of Christ on earth after the Parousia. As such, it shares features of historical premillennialism.

Nevertheless, dispensational premillennialism diverges sharply from historical premillennialism at numerous points. The most notable area of divergence is the idea of two Parousias. When one steps back from the intricacies of the view, it is striking that nowhere in the New Testament are two future comings of Christ even slightly indicated. At best, they are inferred from the tension between passages. Of course, sometimes inferences are legitimate, but this raises a question mark at the outset. Part of the justification for the pretribulation rapture is to prevent Christians from suffering the great tribulation in the book of Revelation. The problem is that it seems the Christians at the time of the writing of Revelation thought that they were already suffering those tribulations or at least those much like the imminent tribulation. In addition, it is extremely difficult to find the idea that God guarantees protection from suffering for Christians. If anything, it is predicted. For example, in the Beatitudes of the Sermon on the Mount, Jesus actually says, "Blessed are those who are persecuted for my sake" (Matt 5:10). In Matthew 24, one of the main apocalyptic passages to which dispensationalism appeals, Jesus describes the idea of some being taken and others left:

> Then they will hand you over to be tortured, and will put you to death; and you will be hated by all nations because of my name. Then many will fall away, and they will betray one another and hate one another. . . . But the one who endures to the end will be saved. . . . Woe to those who are pregnant and to those who are nursing infants in those days! Pray that your flight may not be in winter or on a sabbath. For at that time there will be a great suffering, such as has not been from the beginning of the world until now, no, and never will be. (vv. 9-10, 13, 19-21)

This passage seems clearly directed toward believers, actually being addressed to the disciples in front of him following the point that there will be "wars and rumors of wars" so that they would not be alarmed and would realize that the end is "not yet" (24:6). There is no suggestion that disciples will be rescued, only that the days will be "shortened," not avoided (24:22). The import of the passage, as is common with apocalyptic, is not that they might not have to suffer but to prepare them for the suffering—in accordance with the beatitude, "Blessed are those who are persecuted" (Matt 5:10). This is one of those places where Sigmund Freud's criticism that Christians engage in wishful thinking seems all too true.

Perhaps the most striking difference between the types of pre-millennialism, which is less well known, is that traditional dispensationalism focuses upon the Jews above the church. The millennium is actually about the reign of the Jews and not the church. The church age, that is, Christian history, is seen as a parenthesis in God's primary dealings with the Jews. The current popular version of dispensationalism does not emphasize this feature, and many Christians enamored with the view are dumbfounded when apprised of it. Yet it is a deep feature from the outset. The idea of dispensations, from which it gets its name, is based on seven dispensations clearly divided and governed by different covenants. While the Bible obviously emphasizes covenants, the general picture is of two broad covenants that cannot be so clearly demarcated. As we have seen, the relationship of Christianity to Judaism has had to be rethought in terms of closer ties, but this does not change the Christian view of Jesus as the Messiah who fulfills the covenant with Israel in such a way that the church can be described as a "chosen race," like a new Israel (1 Pet 2:9). There is little indication in the book of Revelation that the millennium does not concern the suffering Christians to whom the author was writing.

With these major problems, what is the attractiveness of dispensationalism? As already mentioned, its pessimism fits well the tragedy of the twentieth century. The seeming fulfillment of prophecy in Israel's becoming a nation cannot be underestimated. In terms of its popular appeal, its emphasis on being ready to meet God at any time actually chimes in with several of Jesus' parables and as such can foster a healthy spirituality. The shadow side of this beneficence is that the fear of avoiding the rapture and being left behind to a miserable fate has been used as nightmarish scare tactics for innumerable teenagers. It also appears to be an understandable, although misplaced, desire to be rescued from suffering. This seems especially true for well-to-do North American Christians, among whom the view is most popular, who have suffered comparatively little. Here it fosters an unhealthy spirituality. It may be said to offer a creative way of resolving the tension found in the New Testament, for example in Matthew 24, between an emphasis on being ready at any time for the coming of Christ and also to be able to read the "signs of the times." These seem to be contradictory on the surface, and the resultant tension accounts for divergent strains in eschatology. After the Millerite fiasco, Christians in North America were somewhat wary of date-setting. Ironically, in light of Lindsey and friends' date-setting a century later, dispensationalism initially offered a way to avoid date-setting, helping to account for its attractiveness at that time. In fact, it ingeniously implied that one could not know the time of the rapture and thus must be ready at any time—and also to prepare as if it might not happen for some time. Nevertheless, it showed how, after the rapture, the signs of the times could be read. This is based on the idea that the church age is a parenthesis of indeterminate time, dating from Christ until the rapture. After the church is raptured, the eschatological clock, given in Daniel, starts ticking again, and so the signs of the times can be read at the period of the seven-year tribulation.

While one can acknowledge the difficulty of this tension, it is now often explained as the tension between two issues being intermingled. One is the fall of Jerusalem and the temple around 70 C.E., which did occur within one generation of Jesus. The other is the final Parousia. Jesus consistently avoided date-setting and emphasized being ready for the Parousia that might come at an unexpected, unpredictable time. In fact, the key verses in this passage used to support the idea of the rapture actually mean the opposite. When Jesus talks of one being taken and the other left, the analogy is to the times of Noah when being taken refers to being destroyed, not being saved as in a rapture (Matt 24:37-41).[67]

As mentioned already, the one passage that mentions the millennium, read literally, does not directly indicate a rule on earth of raptured Christians, as many popular adherents suppose, or of the Jews, as the founders of this theology believed. It says that only those who did not take the mark of the beast during the tribulation would be raised during the millennium (Rev 20:4-6). Whatever this means, and it is probably deeply symbolic, it actually does not literally support *any* of the views mentioned. The upshot is that none can then be said to take the high ground, as each group is often wont to maintain, of taking the Bible most literally or most seriously.

A new form of dispensationalism called "progressive" dispensationalism has arisen in part because of the aforementioned problems. It plays down the numerous dispensations, the priority of Judaism over the church, and even the importance of the pretribulation rapture. The question one might ask is, why not just turn to historical premillennialism?

After this journey through historical eschatology that has so heavily influenced the church, what can we conclude? Surprisingly, we see that the category of historical eschatology is of dubious value. If it includes the basic understanding of the kingdom of God as "now and not yet," of looking expectantly for the kingdom to break forth and be manifested, yet realizing that this world remains a world in travail where Christians suffer and die along with everyone else, then it is legitimate. Beyond this, it may actually detract from what seems to be the main import of the New Testament, namely, to live dynamically the Spirit-filled life of the church in this world, being responsible both to plan for the future and to be ready for the Parousia in the present—in a healthy balance. The above views have at times led to paralyzing pessimism and foolish optimism. As we have seen, even the amillennial view that eschews a literal millennium has relaxed the tension of the "not yet" so as to foster complacency and acceptance of worldly domination. If one avoided millennial speculation and followed the rest of the New Testament, one would end up with the above, simpler emphasis. When apocalyptic material fulfills its original function, expressed through highly symbolic means generally understood by imaginative cultures, it is, in Moltmann's words, a "picture of hope in resistance, in suffering, and in the exiles of this world."[68] It can even be prophetic to comfortable Westerners hoping to avoid suffering, by challenging all Christians to live a faith so seriously that one can face death "for righteousness' sake." When it is used, however, to do what Jesus never did and warned his disciples against—namely, setting dates and speculating more about when the end would come than being ready for the end—it is best avoided (Matt 24:36; Acts 1:7-8).

Despite its problems, any premillennial view reminds us that we must recognize that within this world, which groans in its bondage in the last days, we cannot expect the kingdom of God and the new heaven and the new earth to be realized (Rom 8:21-22). At the same time, we should not underestimate the fact that the powers of the kingdom are already manifest among us, and there are possibilities for God to do far beyond all that we can ask or think, even in this life (Eph 3:20). Postmillennnialism, with its weaknesses, engenders evangelistic and reformist zeal. We should not minimize the way this has resulted in human life being improved in significant ways, even as we are not naive enough to miss how in some ways the world has been made worse and more dangerous. Perhaps, again, all millennialism "hopes" to find an appropriate balance between optimism and pessimism. Much as we discussed in terms of the doctrine of creation, we should not despise the earth in this life and should appreciate the basic goodness in it. There is a place to pray for it and to work within it, depending on the powers of the kingdom of God. We also need to have the spirit of the cry at the end of the book of Revelation, Maranatha, "Lord come quickly." This reflects our sense that the true kingdom of God can only be established by Christ. It is not until the very end that there will be no more mourning or crying or pain anymore, and all tears will be wiped away (Rev 21:4).

COSMIC ESCHATOLOGY

An aspect of such theological grounding for future hope is the mortality of this world. As mentioned above in relation to personal eschatology, due to the law of entropy, this entire universe is expected to wind down in 10^{100} years. Long before that, however, in just a few billion years, our sun will begin to burn out and make life uninhabitable on planet Earth. Hopes of the human race traveling to another solar system, light years away, are still pipe dreams. In natural terms, the human race is fated, along with the universe, to face a natural death. Dreams of tunneling to another universe or hopping to other dimensions are as wishful as the desire to avoid suffering. This calls into question even the ancient Hebrew faith that did not rest upon an afterlife. At least they expected that the nation, their descendants, would continue and experience blessing in this life and world in the future—but that is ruled out by the natural mortality of the universe. Ironically, the great scientific success that has granted such amazing understanding of the universe, longer life, and better health indicates no hope for the future of the human race—and a bleak one for the cosmos as well. This understanding raises in a fresh way the question that Job raised in his suffering but did not clearly answer: "If mortals die, will they live again?" (Job 14:14) For an incarnational theology that values creation and this world, this question must be answered in a way that is inseparable from the fate of the universe. Will the universe live again?

Despite the emphasis at times on the individual in an aethereal relationship with God in Christian tradition, the New Testament points to a transformed universe. To be sure, in 2 Peter, the language is that the present universe will be destroyed by fire before the advent of a new heaven and a new earth (2 Peter 3:10). In Revelation, however, the implication is more one of transformation. In either case, we should not miss the point that the destiny is not heaven but rather earth. Perhaps our language of "going to heaven" should change then to "going to Earth"! This emphasizes the embodied dimension of the afterlife. Just as there is a new realization of embodiment for the individual in this life and in personal resurrection, there is a new realization of cosmic embodiment. These, of course, are interlocked. In the end, it does not make sense to think of embodiment for the individual apart from an environment. Embodiment implies life in an environment.

Nevertheless, things are not that simple, either for the body or the cosmos. As we noted earlier, in 1 Corinthians 15, Paul is very elusive about the state of the spiritual body. Though a body, it is as like the physical body as a seed is to the flowering plant. If we continue the parallel with the cosmos, we should expect the same. The new spiritual earth could be as like—and as different—from this one as the spiritual body is to the physical. Again, the details of *what* it is like are probably not as important as its *meaning*—and here we have significant images to guide us.

The book of Revelation conveys two significant figures. One is that of a new garden of Eden. Revelation 22 begins, "Then he showed me the river of the water of life, bright as crystal, flowing from the throne of God and of the Lamb" (v. 1). The writer adds:

> On either side of the river is the tree of life with its twelve kinds of fruit, producing its fruit each month; and the leaves of the tree are for the healing of the nations. Nothing accursed will be found there any more. But the throne of God and of the Lamb will be in it, and his servants will worship him; they shall see his face, and his name will be on their foreheads. And there will be no more night; they need no light of lamp or sun, for the Lord God will be their light, and they shall reign for ever and ever. (vv. 2-5)

No longer is humanity outside the garden, "east of Eden" (Gen 3:24). One could imagine that as Yahweh walked with Adam and Eve in the cool of the day in Genesis 2, this kind of intimacy with the Creator is restored.

The image is also more down-to-earth than one might think. A river for drinking and washing, fruit for the eating, and seasons of the year do not point to the timeless, wispy heaven of much of the tradition.[69] On the other hand, taking our cue from 1 Corinthians 15, we should not press the images, which are clearly symbolic, too much and too literally as giving us a snapshot of the eschaton as much as giving us its quality. Obviously, blessed, whole, healthy life in intimate relationship with God is the intended human destiny, whatever its literal shape—perhaps beyond human imagining. More than one has suggested that the nature of eschatological life may be as unimaginable to us as life outside the womb is to a baby inside it. Perhaps little that we can imagine can do justice to the future of God, hence Paul's analogy of the seed and the fruit. Perhaps the most that we can do is what these images do, namely, convey the meaning if not the nature.

The same could be said for the other great image in Revelation that also recasts the image of a new garden, for the new garden is actually set within a new city. As soon as the new heaven and new earth is mentioned in chapter 21, the seer sees "the holy city, the new Jerusalem, coming down out of heaven from God, prepared as a bride adorned for her husband" (v. 2). While many utopias have pictured humans as returning to a primeval paradise, a state of nature, it is interesting that the dominant image of the consummation of all things in the New Testament is a city. This image likely grows out of the strong social sense of the Hebrews that sees humans as made for community—a community living and worshiping God at that most holy place where God's presence is especially found, Jerusalem. The passage continues:

> And I heard a loud voice from the throne saying, "See, the home of God is among mortals. He will dwell with them as their God; they will be his peoples, and God himself will be with them; he will wipe every tear from their eyes. Death will be no more; mourning and crying and pain will be no more, for the first things have passed away. (vv. 3-4)

Probably no other passage in the New Testament surpasses this one for the comfort and hope it gives in times of despair and death in this life. It is not individualistic for it conveys the image of dwelling with God in a city. Neither does it suggest, as some theologies do, that everything that happened was good or necessary. It does not suggest a cost-benefit analysis that implies that all evil was legitimated because it is now balanced by good. Rather, it conveys simply the fact of deliverance. It acknowledges tears, crying, pain, and death. It says simply that they are "no more." Perhaps no more can be said than this, but this may well be enough.

As we saw when discussing theodicy, some have tried to justify every event. This approach has been severely questioned, perhaps nowhere more poignantly than by Ivan Karamazov in Dostoyevsky's *The Brothers Karamazov*. Ivan questioned whether the suffering of children somehow is justified by heaven in the end, in a kind of calculus. He rejects such an equation. Maybe Ivan is right; one cannot put the goodness of life, the sorrow of death, and life with God in the eschaton in a formula. The book of Revelation does not attempt it. It acknowledges the reality of sorrow and pain; it simply promises that it will be removed—forever.

In Revelation 22, the new garden and the new city come together. "The river of the water of life" is described as "flowing from the throne of God and of the Lamb through the middle of the street of the city" (vv. 1-2). Paradisiacal promise is now blended with communitarian fulfillment—with rivers in the streets no less!

Whatever these images promise, they suggest more than timeless individual encounter with God, as blessed as that may be. When people speculate, as I have often heard, that they will be able to meet loved ones and talk with them, that they may meet other people, perhaps famous people of the past, and converse with them, that they may meet God and continuously get to know God better, it fits these more social images. These do not convey a static life of doing one thing, even if it is singing in praise. Rather, they suggest a fulfillment of life, not a diminution. Perhaps here even the purpose of labor, already envisioned in the garden, is now accomplished in some new and unimagined but endlessly fulfilling way. The Christian tradition has oscillated between the extremes of imagining the eschaton in perhaps too worldly a way and between perhaps too individualistic and aethereal a way.[70] Even Augustine moved from the latter vision in his earlier years to a more communal vision in his later years.[71] With the corporate dimension here envisaged, is it too much to wonder that there might not only be life together but even fruitful labor together? Is *labor* the right word since our human words, rooted as they are in our human, this-worldly reality, falter and fade?[72] Perhaps our greatest sense of refreshing fun and fulfilling labor flow together in ways that will then be indistinguishable. Is it possible that God is so majestic and mysterious that instead of seeing all in one beatific vision, we will continue learning of God, that is, growing in grace—forever?

My language is hesitant and questioning, for that seems to be the appropriate mode of understanding in this area. It is striking to note the paucity of detail on the details of heaven in the major confessions of the church.[73] They are not doubtful and denying, just hesitant on details but confident in meaning. Should one imagine at all? If not, we call into question the robust imagination of Scripture and Christian tradition, which have rarely been inhibited. We likely sell ourselves short spiritually, for we seem to be given license to imagine, just as Revelation moves in a luxuriant undergrowth of images. The images of Revelation may not be ours since they belong to the world of the first century; we may do them most justice when we transpose them into our own worlds. Nevertheless, ours must be fitting to theirs, must resonate with theirs. If so, if we find pictures of human and cosmic destiny as appealing as theirs were to them and as fitting as theirs were to God, we may find ourselves similarly encouraged and inspired to face life as they did. In the Johannine writings, we have one of the richest statements of full life on this earth, "life abundant" (John 10:10). In Revelation, we have perhaps the grimmest view of what suffering may come in this life, yet we also have the encouragement to face it with courage, even to the point of death. Why? In part because death is not the final word. As Karl Barth was wont to say, God's Yes is always beyond every human and worldly No.[74]

The profound theological balance of the New Testament that can only be finally appreciated in the light of eschatology is that there is a divine continuity between this world and the next. There is individual spiritual continuity, there is bodily continuity, and there is cosmic continuity. This gives value to this world and supports appreciation of its goodness and value. At the same time, this view looks squarely in the face of this world's temporality, its limitations, even its grotesque depradation. It sees that it will someday be no more, but not totally as if it had never been. No, it does not depreciate the tears or the lives—and perhaps not its sheer existence. Rather, the lives are redeemed, and the tears are wiped away—in a new earth. The meaning and purpose of this life is not depreciated but rather healed, transformed, and fulfilled in a life with God, with each other, with a new world.

As we have seen, Moltmann pointed out that traditional theology pictured God in creation positing something outside of God, a kind of masculine image of creation. Drawing upon the Jewish Kabbalah tradition, Moltmann thought a more appropriate image is that of God restricting, contracting, and making space within Godself for creation, a kind of feminine image of creation. Both have their strengths and weaknesses. A parallel can be drawn at the end as at the beginning. The first image suggests that God in the end draws what is outside of God back to God. The second image, which Moltmann again prefers, is that God "derestricts" and so fills everything again with God's presence.[75]

Neither image is meant to remove the integrity of the created as having its own being in the way an Eastern monism might do, as in the image of the drop of water finally falling into the ocean and merging with the All. Rather, the Christian image is that individuality continues, not in an "individualistic" way as a modern Westerner might think, but in the rich sense in which the Trinity might be three and one. Even there, the distinction between Creator and creature, Redeemer and redeemed, remains. Yet the image of unity is strong, stronger than perhaps Western theology has usually imagined. Here the West may be able to learn from Eastern Christian theology, which has always envisaged a greater union, described as "divinization."[76] Eastern Orthodox theologians have put more emphasis on the Johannine language that "they may all be one" and "also be in us" (17:21), although not to the denial of the continuation of personal identity. The self is not lost in others as much as finding, finally, its true fulfillment in relationship. Perhaps a Western sense of a distinct, radically individualistic self cannot do justice to the Christian vision. Only a stronger social sense of the self that preserves personal identity even as it stresses that personal identity is always in relationship can have a glimmer of a chance of doing justice to the final intimacy with God and with each other and with the cosmos.

The final thought concerns the question of whether the Christian emphasis on resurrection and an afterlife is really about God, or is it a clever disguise for a selfish desire of self-preservation? Is the eschaton really a transformation of human sin or perhaps an expression of it? This is a serious charge that has led some Christians to reject an afterlife altogether. The case begins with the observation, as we have noted, that for much of the time of the Old Testament, the Hebrews got along without a conception of an afterlife that is anything like the Christian one. Even when they had some vague ideas, it was not particularly desirable, not an improvement on this life, not a reward or punishment. In other words, they obviously loved God and were faithful to God without benefit of the promise of an afterlife. Is it then necessary? A popular Christian song has a haunting refrain about love of God without thought of reward. Is eternal life a reward? Is it selfish? Is it compatible with Christian agape? These questions can best be addressed only at this point, with the above fuller vision of the Christian end in mind.

I am convinced that if one begins from the side of human desire, that is, from below, one cannot find a satisfactory answer to this question. It is to get the cart before the horse from a Christian theological perspective. Rather, the proper beginning point is from above. One begins with the revelatory "fact" that "we love God because he first loved us" (1 John 4:19). Just as in salvation, the initiative lies with God: "While we were yet sinners, Christ died for us" (Rom 5:8). In this connection, we can affirm that even before creation, God desired to have fellowship with beings in God's image. In other words, what is at issue at first is God's desire. The desire that those in God's image could actually be called "friends of Christ" (John 15:15) finds its culmination in eternal life with Christ, where Christ and the Father are one as we are one with them—so goes the Johannine vision (17:22-23). In fact, eternal life has already begun for John, with the new birth (3:3). For Paul, our lives are already "hid with Christ in God," Christ already being seated at the right hand of God (Col 3:1-3). Life after death therefore is continuation in the most important sense of life before death. The progression is not cessation followed by another beginning as much as it is continuation and fulfillment of what has begun. One might as well deny the meaning of life with God *before* physical death, therefore, as to deny it *after* physical death. In this view, if salvation in eternity is denied, then so is salvation here and now.

Behind this dynamic temporal movement is the fact that eternal life is God's desire and God's gift. It is grace, unmerited grace, just as salvation is—for it is simply the fulfillment of salvation. It is not something that is deserved. It is not something that is logically necessary, along the lines of Socrates' philosophical argument for the immortality of the soul due to the soul's indestructibility. There is no logical or metaphysical necessity that can be the basis of a coercive argument, as some have tried. The very effort succeeds only by subverting the grace of the Gospel. One can only stand in wonder that such is God's desire. From God's perspective, apparently, the grand adventure that began with creation is aimed toward fellowship with God's creatures, as many as who so desire it. In this sense, eternal life is not initially about us as much as it is about God. Thus, we can neither prove nor deserve eternal life—we can only receive it. The issue of eternal life is then part and parcel of salvation and cannot be understood apart from it, as if it stood alone as an interesting speculative question about what might happen to humans after death.

With the first word being grace, from above, a second word can properly be said about such a destiny meeting the deep longings of the human soul. Perhaps because eternal life is contingent and not necessary, it is possible for humans not to see it or miss it, as apparently is the case among the ancient Hebrews and in many other religions. This desire, shaped as it is by the Christian tradition so much so that many Westerners can hardly imagine a religion that does not promise an afterlife, must first be seen as legitimately shaped and fostered by the divine initiative. At best, it is not a selfish desire but a dimension of following God. To desire eternal life in the truest sense means that one loves God with all of one's heart, mind, and soul. It is not surprising, if this is God's orientation, that humans are designed with a certain complementary, matching orientation. In other words, an afterlife is not deeply contrary or defeating of what it means to be most genuinely human. This accounts for the desire, often felt as a natural desire, for eternal life. It may be simply but profoundly felt at the loss of a loved one with the desire to see them again. It may be broken, partial, impure, as most human desires are. It would not be surprising for immature, beginning, "baby" Christians to think of the afterlife in selfish and egoistic ways. The importance of our reflection here, which is probably not emphasized enough, is that such thinking is immature and should be left behind for more grace-filled comprehension. If so, many of the above misunderstandings could likely be avoided.

Eternal life is a traditional aspect of Christian hope, but it is a hope that is not universal. It is rather deeply, integrally Christian, namely, based on grace and divine initiative. As I have reiterated, Augustine prayed at the outset of his *Confessions*, "You have made us for yourself, and our hearts are restless until they find their rest in you." It is apparently God's desire that that rest, for which God created us, be an eternal one.

NOTES

PREFACE

1   Shirley C. Guthrie, *Christian Doctrine*, 2nd ed. (Louisville: Westminster John Knox, 1994); Daniel L. Migliore, *Faith Seeking Understanding: An Introduction to Christian Theology*, 2nd ed. (Grand Rapids: Eerdmans, 2004); Ted Peters, *God–The World's Future: Systematic Theology for a New Era*, 2nd ed. (Minneapolis: Fortress, 2000).

2   Bill J. Leonard, *Baptists in America* (New York: Columbia University Press, 2005), 91.

3   Jürgen Moltmann, *The Way of Jesus Christ: Christology in Messianic Dimensions* (Minneapolis: Fortress, 1993); Dietrich Bonhoeffer, *Life Together: A Discussion of Christian Fellowship*, trans. John W. Doberstein, rev. ed. (New York: HarperCollins, 1992).

4   David R. Tankersley, "Scripture and Experience: A Postconservative Approach to Theological Method" (master's thesis in religion, Hardin-Simmons University, 2007).

CHAPTER 1

1   This incident refers to an actual student whose name has been changed.

2   Stanley Grenz and Roger Olson refer to "anonymous theologians,"

not in the sense that they are trying to recover from theology but because they are unaware of their implicit theologies. Stanley J. Grenz and Roger E. Olson, *Who Needs Theology? An Invitation to the Study of God* (Downers Grove, Ill.: InterVarsity, 1996), 13.

3 Cited in Timothy George, *Theology of the Reformers* (Nashville: Broadman, 1988), 61.

4 Plato, *Theaetetus*, 155d. See also Aristotle, *Metaphysics*, bk. 1, 982b.

5 Refers to the Greek word for church, *ekklesia*.

6 Eberhard Busch, *Karl Barth: His Life from Letters and Autobiographical Texts*, trans. John Bowden, 2nd ed. (Philadelphia: Fortress, 1976), 155.

7 When I refer to the free church movement, or Believer's churches, I am thinking of all of those denominations that emphasize believer's baptism (baptism only for those old enough to make their own decision) and a high degree of congregational church government (where all of the members of a local church have final responsibility in the governance of the church). This would include my own Baptist tradition, of course, but also the wider Christian churches (such as the Churches of Christ), Mennonites, and most Pentecostal churches.

8 Thomas Helwys, *A Short Declaration of the Mystery of Iniquity* (Macon, Ga.: Mercer University Press, 1998). See for background, G. Hugh Wamble, "The Background and Meaning of the 1963 Southern Baptists Articles of Faith on the Bible," in *The Proceedings of the Conference on Biblical Inerrancy 1987* (Nashville: Broadman, 1987), 331–54.

9 Traditionally ascribed to John Robinson, cited in J. H. Shakespeare, *Baptist Congregational Pioneers* (London: Kingsgate, 1906), 165.

10 Mark Taylor Dalhouse, "Jones, Robert Reynolds Jr.," *Notable Americans Who Died Between 1997 and 1999. The Scribner Encyclopedia of American Lives*, ed. Kenneth T. Jackson, Karen Markoe, and Arnie Markoe (New York: Simon & Schuster, 2004), 296–98.

11 Philip Jenkins, *The Next Christendom: The Coming of Global Christianity* (New York: Oxford University Press, 2002). See also the entire issue of the Summer 2006 issue (vol. 103, no. 3) of the *Review and Expositor* on "The Next Christianity."

12 Roger E. Olson, *The Mosaic of Christian Belief: Twenty Centuries of Unity and Diversity* (Downers Grove, Ill.: InterVarsity, 2002).

13 Olson, *Mosaic of Christian Belief*, 40, 44–45. Olson also talks of another level of belief that he calls "opinions," which are matters of dispute, and usually tolerance, even within individual denominations and

churches. Compare to the similar discussion in Grenz and Olson, *Who Needs Theology?* 73–77.

14   I heard this, in fact, from the director of Baylor University Press, Carey Newman, at that time a New Testament colleague.

CHAPTER 2

1   Serene Jones and Paul Lakeland, eds., *Constructive Theology: A Contemporary Approach to Classical Themes* (Minneapolis: Fortress, 2005), 9, represents the work of fifty theologians who see their work in this way, which they also call "theological geographies." Doctrines then are "collectively rendered maps." Interestingly, Thomas Kuhn, in his classic work that revolutionized the understanding of science and other disciplines, compared science to providing maps: "And since nature is too complex and varied to be explored at random, that map is as essential as observation and experiment to science's continuing development" (Thomas Kuhn, *The Structure of Scientific Revolutions*, 2nd ed. [Chicago: University of Chicago Press, 1970], 109). In turn, he points out that maps derive from larger-scale paradigms. "Paradigms provide scientists not only with a map but also with some of the directions essential for map-making." Largely because of this work by Kuhn, originally published in 1962 and its consequent influence, the word *paradigm* has become a common word in our vocabulary. What Kuhn says about science can be applied quite easily to theology, as he himself implies (*Structure of Scientific Revolutions*, 136). We will be exploring how to deal with the significant paradigm changes in theology.

2   Hans Küng identifies six different paradigms in the history of the Christian church. Hans Küng, *Christianity: Essence, History, and Future*, trans. John Bowden (New York: Continuum, 1998). Kuhn says, interestingly, that theology is different from the way that science obscures the complex dynamics involved in its development (Kuhn, *Structure of Scientific Revolutions*, 136). I think that he is wrong. Theology is often written in such a way that one does not appreciate the complex history and development behind it.

3   Cited in Mary Grey, "Feminist Theology: A Critical Theology of Liberation," in *The Cambridge Companion to Liberation Theology*, ed. Christopher Rowland (Cambridge: Cambridge University Press, 1999), 94. Refers to Adrienne Rich.

4   See Philip Jenkins, *The Next Christendom: The Coming of Global Christianity* (New York: Oxford University Press, 2002).

5   C. S. Lewis, *Mere Christianity* (New York: Macmillan, 1981), 132. Originally published in 1943.

6   The material on Descartes that immediately follows is largely excerpted, with permission from the *Review and Expositor*, from my article, Dan R. Stiver, "Much Ado about Athens and Jerusalem: The Implications of Postmodernism for Faith," *Review and Expositor* 91 (1994): 83–102.

7   René Descartes, "Discourse on the Method of Rightly Conducting the Reason," in *Descartes, Spinoza*, ed. Robert Maynard Hutchins, Great Books of the Western World 31 (Chicago: Encyclopedia Britannica, 1952), 44. The most helpful account of Descartes and the odd contradictions in his approach, which I am following here in its basic thrust, is Stephen Toulmin, *Cosmopolis: The Hidden Agenda of Modernity* (New York: Free Press, 1990), especially chaps. 1–2. See also the biography by Jack R. Vrooman, *René Descartes: A Biography* (New York: G. P. Putnam's Sons, 1970).

8   Descartes, "Discourse on the Method," 59.

9   Descartes, "Discourse on the Method," 52.

10   From a standard French reference work, *Le Grande Encyclopédie*, cited in Toulmin, *Cosmopolis*, 45.

11   Toulmin, *Cosmopolis*, 70–71. The reference to Bellah is on the back jacket of Toulmin's book.

12   Cited in Norman Kemp Smith, *New Studies in the Philosophy of Descartes: Descartes as Pioneer* (London: Macmillan, 1952), 33. This information is taken from Descartes' diary, which is not preserved, through notes of his diary by Adrien Baillet.

13   T. Z. Lavine, *From Socrates to Sartre: The Philosophic Quest* (Toronto: Bantam, 1984), 87.

14   This is the hope especially expressed in Nancey C. Murphy, *Beyond Liberalism and Fundamentalism: How Modern and Postmodern Philosophy Set the Theological Agenda*, Rockwell Lecture Series (Valley Forge, Pa.: Trinity Press International, 1996).

15   Nancey Murphy and Jim McClendon analyze these already in Nancey C. Murphy and James Wm. McClendon Jr., "Distinguishing Modern and Postmodern Theologies," *Modern Theology* 5 (1989): 191–214.

16   Antonio R. Damasio, *Descartes' Error: Emotion, Reason, and the Human Brain* (New York: G. P. Putnam's Sons, 1994).

17   Martin Heidegger, *Being and Time*, trans. Joan Stambaugh, State University of New York Series in Contemporary Continental Philosophy (Albany: State University of New York Press, 1996), 112.

18   Ludwig Wittgenstein, *On Certainty*, trans. Denis Paul and G. E. M. Anscombe, ed. G. E. M. Anscombe and G. H. von Wright (New York: Harper Torchbooks, 1969), secs. 341, 342.

19   Harold Bloom, *The American Religion: The Emergence of the Post-Christian Nation* (New York: Simon & Schuster, 1992), 217.

20   Eberhard Busch, *Karl Barth: His Life from Letters and Autobiographical Texts*, trans. John Bowden, 2nd ed. (Philadelphia: Fortress, 1976), 211.

21   A major treatment is Alvin Plantinga, "Reason and Belief in God," in *Faith and Rationality: Reason and Belief in God*, ed. Alvin Plantinga and Nicholas Wolterstorff (Notre Dame: University of Notre Dame Press, 1983). Many simply criticize "foundationalism" per se. Plantinga, however, gives a more careful delineation between a "classical foundationalism" with absolute foundations and a foundationalism that does not require objective certainty, which he himself would affirm.

22   Plato, *The Republic*, bk. 6.

23   Plato, *The Republic*, bk. 7.

24   Thomas Aquinas, *Summa Theologica*, 1a.12.12-13; 2a2ae.1.1-6.

25   Aquinas technically says that faith is a mean between science and opinion. Aquinas, *Summa Theologica*, 2a2ae.1.2.

26   Richard Dawkins, *The God Delusion* (Boston: Houghton Mifflin, 2006).

27   David Ray Griffin, *God and Religion in the Postmodern World: Essays in Postmodern Theology*, State University of New York Series in Constructive Postmodern Thought (Albany: State University of New York Press, 1989), 3.

28   Perhaps the most famous shot across the bow of this movement, Kuhn's *Structure of Scientific Revolutions*, actually suggested that science often moves forward by changes that are like religious conversions (150, 158, 166).

29   James K. A. Smith, "A Little Story about Metanarratives: Lyotard, Religion, and Postmodernism Revisited," in *Christianity and the Postmodern Turn*, ed. Myron B. Penner (Grand Rapids: Brazos Press, 2005), 140n65 (emphasis in original).

30   For fuller treatment of this point, see Dan R. Stiver, "Baptists: Modern or Postmodern?" *Review and Expositor* 100 (2003): 521–52; Graham Ward, "Postmodern Theology," in *The Modern Theologians: An*

Introduction to Christian Theology in the Twentieth Century, ed. David F. Ford, 2nd ed. (Malden, Mass.: Blackwell, 1997), 585–601.

31   Kevin J. Vanhoozer, ed., *The Cambridge Companion to Postmodern Theology* (Cambridge: Cambridge University Press, 2003), 20.

32   Kevin J. Vanhoozer, *The Drama of Doctrine: A Canonical-Linguistic Approach to Christian Theology* (Louisville: Westminster John Knox, 2005).

33   Brian McLaren does this in a popular, helpful way in Brian D. McLaren, *A New Kind of Christian: A Tale of Two Friends on a Spiritual Journey* (San Francisco: Jossey-Bass, 2001), chap. 4.

34   Aristotle, *Nichomachean Ethics*, bk. 6.3-7, bk. 10.6-8.

35   See, for example, Joseph Dunne, *Back to the Rough Ground: "Phronesis" and "Techne" in Modern Philosophy and in Aristotle* (Notre Dame: University of Notre Dame Press, 1993), 353. Vanhoozer, in fact, indicates that one of three aspects of his theology is that it is phronetic. Vanhoozer, *Drama of Doctrine*.

36   See, for example, Hans-Georg Gadamer, "The Universality of the Hermeneutical Problem," in *Philosophical Hermeneutics*, ed. David E. Linge (Berkeley: University of California Press, 1976), 3–17.

37   Susan J. Hekman, *Gender and Knowledge: Elements of a Postmodern Feminism*, Northeastern Series in Feminist Theory (Boston: Northeastern University Press, 1990), 135. In relation to Aristotle, Joseph Dunne makes the same point:

> It may be noted that the tension that I have been finding in Aristotle, as the first great systematic thinker of the Western tradition of reason, is one that has a strong resonance in contemporary criticism of the "logocentrism" of this tradition. Recent "deconstructionist" and "postmodernist" thought has taken issue strongly with a monopolistic reason defined as masterful, autonomous, technocratic and logocentric; and it has done so in the name of what has been suppressed by this monopoly: materiality, contingency, vulnerability, nature, and embodiment. That the kind of detailed exegesis of ancient canonical texts undertaken here in the second part of our study is not at all extraneous to this contemporary criticism should be evident from the fact that in quarreling with (what I have taken to be) Aristotle's rationalist account of techne I have found support for an alternative conception of it precisely by giving full weight to what he has to say

about matter, nature, and embodiment. I need to point out, how-ever, that if both phronesis and (the alternative notion of) techne have been elaborated over against a rationalist conception, they are not on that account irrational. The analysis here has not been inspired by, nor does it support, any desire to abandon the logos altogether." (*Back to the Rough Ground*, 335)

38 Karl Barth, *Church Dogmatics*, ed. G. W. Bromiley and T. F. Torrance, vol. 1.1, *The Doctrine of the Word of God*, trans. J. W. Edwards, O. Bussey, and Harold Knight (Greenwood, S.C.: Attic, 1975), sec. 6.

39 James K. A. Smith, *Who's Afraid of Postmodernism? Taking Derrida, Lyotard, and Foucault to Church*, The Church and Postmodern Culture (Grand Rapids: Baker Academic, 2006), 51.

40 Cited in Michio Kaku, *Hyperspace: A Scientific Odyssey through Parallel Universes, Time Warps, and the Tenth Dimension* (New York: Anchor, 1994), 111.

41 For example, see Michio Kaku, *Parallel Worlds: A Journey through Creation, Higher Dimensions, and the Future of the Cosmos* (New York: Anchor, 2005); Lisa Randall, *Warped Passages: Unraveling the Mysteries of the Universe's Hidden Dimensions* (San Francisco: HarperCollins, 2005).

42 Michael Polanyi, *Personal Knowledge: Towards a Post-Critical Philosophy*, 2nd ed. (Chicago: University of Chicago Press, 1962); Michael Polanyi, *The Tacit Dimension* (Gloucester, Mass.: Peter Smith, 1983). Polanyi does not use the language of phronesis or draw particularly upon Aristotle, but his independent understanding of the rationality of science is remarkably similar.

43 Jeffrey Stout, *The Flight from Authority: Religion, Morality, and the Quest for Autonomy* (Notre Dame: University of Notre Dame Press, 1981), 2–3.

44 Alasdair C. MacIntyre, *Whose Justice? Which Rationality?* (Notre Dame: University of Notre Dame Press, 1988), 360.

45 Hans-Georg Gadamer, *Truth and Method*, trans. Joel Weinsheimer and Donald G. Marshall, rev. ed. (New York: Crossroad, 1991), 270.

46 Richard Cunningham notes this immersion in life that shapes our thinking when speaking of philosophy, but if anything, it applies more so to theology. Richard B. Cunningham, "A Case for Christian Philosophy," *Review and Expositor* 82 (1985): 499–500.

47 "Literal Belief in Bible Down 10 Points in 30 Years," *Baptists Today*, July 2006, 25.

48 For fuller treatment of this shift that traces in detail the linguistic turn of the last century, see Dan R. Stiver, *The Philosophy of Religious Language: Sign, Symbol, and Story* (Cambridge: Blackwell, 1996).

49 For a helpful overview, see Norman Perrin, *Jesus and the Language of the Kingdom: Symbol and Metaphor in New Testament Interpretation* (Philadelphia: Fortress, 1976), chap. 3. Ben Witherington, III, points out how an oral culture with an emphasis on narrative and figurative language undergirds the understanding of Paul as well. Ben Witherington III, *The Paul Quest: The Renewed Search for the Jew of Tarsus* (Downers Grove, Ill.: InterVarsity, 2001), 232–37.

50 See below for the development of the idea of a "surplus of meaning" in Paul Ricoeur, *Interpretation Theory: Discourse and the Surplus of Meaning* (Fort Worth: Texas Christian University Press, 1976).

51 Paul Tillich, *Dynamics of Faith* (New York: Harper & Brothers, 1957), 42.

52 John L. Austin, *How to Do Things with Words*, ed. J. O. Urmson and Marina Sbisà, 2nd ed. (Cambridge, Mass.: Harvard University Press, 1975), 1.

53 Ludwig Wittgenstein, *Philosophical Investigations*, trans. G. E. M. Anscombe, 3rd ed. (New York: Macmillan, 1958), sec. 66.

54 Wittgenstein, *Philosophical Investigations*, sec. 67.

55 Wittgenstein, *Philosophical Investigations*, sec. 71.

56 Ludwig Wittgenstein, *Culture and Value*, trans. Peter Winch, ed. G. H. von Wright (Chicago: University of Chicago Press, 1980), 45.

57 E. Frank Tupper, *A Scandalous Providence: The Jesus Story of the Compassion of God* (Macon, Ga.: Mercer University Press, 1995), 428.

58 For all three of the traditional options in theology—the analogical, equivocal, and univocal—see Stiver, *Philosophy of Religious Language*, chap. 1.

59 Vanhoozer, *Drama of Doctrine*, 266.

60 Jon Meacham, "Pilgrim's Progress," *Newsweek*, 14 August 2006, accessed 14 August 2006, http://www.newsweek.com/id/46365.

61 Walter Brueggemann, *Theology of the Old Testament: Testimony, Dispute, Advocacy* (Minneapolis: Fortress, 1997), 84.

62 George Lakoff and Mark Johnson, *Philosophy in the Flesh: The Embodied Mind and Its Challenge to Western Thought* (New York: Basic, 1999), 3.

63 The most basic distinction was between what the text meant and what it means. Krister Stendahl, "Biblical Theology, Contemporary, 1," in *Interpreters Dictionary of the Bible* (New York: Abingdon, 1962), 419–20.

This is in part due to the depreciation of practice over against theory, but "application" has been crucial in the hermeneutics of Scripture and of law. Gadamer, *Truth and Method*.

64 Gadamer, *Truth and Method*, 306.

65 This is against a common misunderstanding of Gadamer's view that implies it is relativist, giving all the weight to the contemporary understanding, or revisionist, finding some middle synthesis between past and present. It allows that the present can dominate or that the past can dominate. Ironically, Gadamer has been charged both with extremely liberal and conservative views—both in actuality misunderstanding his point. In any case, the past text is always understood in terms of the present.

66 Gadamer, *Truth and Method*, 297.

67 This concept has great implications for the philosophy of education in a broad sense. It challenges the dominant Anglo-American influence of the empiricist philosophies of John Locke and David Hume that pictured the human as a passive *tabula rasa*, blank slate, on which information is inscribed. A powerful critique is in the novel by Charles Dickens, *Hard Times*, 2nd ed. (New York: New American Library, 1980).

68 Interestingly, this same insight is seen to be a key behind the most effective college teaching in Ken Bain, *What the Best College Teachers Do* (Cambridge, Mass.: Harvard University Press, 2004).

69 Ludwig Wittgenstein, *Zettel*, ed. G. E. M. Anscombe and G. H. von Wright, trans. G. E. M. Anscombe (Berkeley: University of California Press, 1967), par. 173.

70 Ludwig Wittgenstein, *Philosophical Investigations*, pars. 19, 23, 241.

71 From Goethe's *Faust*, I, cited in Wittgenstein, *On Certainty*, sec. 402, "Im Anfang war der Tat."

72 Polanyi, *Tacit Dimension*, 4.

73 Polanyi, *Personal Knowledge*, 59, 195.

74 Referred to in Timothy George, *Theology of the Reformers* (Nashville: Broadman, 1988), 59.

75 An example is William C. Placher, *Unapologetic Theology: A Christian Voice in a Pluralistic Conversation* (Louisville: Westminster John Knox, 1989). Ricoeur's thought itself relates to a variety of philosophical movements but also to psychology, sociology, and political science.

76 Vanhoozer, *Drama of Doctrine*, 216–31.

77 In this sense, I appreciate the traditional translation into Spanish of *logos* (Word) in John 1:1, as *el Verbo*!

78 Frederick Herzog, "The End of Systematic Theology," in *Theology from the Belly of the Whale*, ed. Joerg Rieger (Harrisburg, Pa.: Trinity Press International, 1999), 231.

79 Cited in Randall Balmer, *Thy Kingdom Come: How the Religious Right Distorts the Faith and Threatens America: An Evangelical's Lament* (New York: Basic, 2006), 17.

80 Herzog, "End of Systematic Theology," 231.

81 Jenkins, *Next Christendom*, 3.

82 Jenkins, *Next Christendom*, 7; Philip Jenkins, *The New Faces of Christianity: Believing the Bible in the Global South* (Oxford: Oxford University Press, 2006), 16–17, 27. Jenkins says of African-Americans who are simultaneously conservative but concerned about social and economic issues,

> When viewed on a global scale, African-American religious styles, long regarded as marginal to mainstream American Christianity, now seem absolutely standard. Conversely, the worship of mainline white American denominations looks increasingly exceptional, as do these groups' customary approach to biblical authority. Looking at this reversal, one is reminded of a familiar text: the stone that was rejected has become the cornerstone." (*New Faces of Christianity*, 13)

83 Meacham, "Pilgrim's Progress."

84 For discussion of this change among younger theology students, who are very syncretistic and emphasize spirituality, see Jones and Lakeland, *Constructive Theology*, 4, 42–43.

85 Thomas L. Friedman, *The World Is Flat: A Brief History of the Twenty-First Century*, 2nd ed. (New York: Farrar, Straus, & Giroux, 2006).

86 Jenkins, *Next Christendom*, 1.

87 See Bill Leonard's both positive and poignant note on Baptists in relation to globalism and pluralism, which form the last words of Bill J. Leonard, *Baptists in America* (New York: Columbia University Press, 2005): "Pluralism may well be the door, not the death knell, to spiritual vitality for all religious groups. But Baptists will surely divide over the meaning of pluralism in light of Christian particularism and the centrality of Christian revelation" (253).

88 Harry Lee Poe, "The Gospel in a Postmodern Culture," *Review and Expositor* 101 (2004): 500.

89 Wolfhart Pannenberg, *Theology and the Kingdom of God*, ed. Richard John Neuhaus (Philadelphia: Westminster, 1969), 56.

90 Jürgen Moltmann, *Theology of Hope: On the Grounds and the Implications of a Christian Eschatology*, trans. James W. Leitch (Minneapolis: Fortress, 1993).

91 Dale Moody, *The Hope of Glory* (Grand Rapids: Eerdmans, 1964); Dale Moody, *The Word of Truth* (Grand Rapids: Eerdmans, 1981).

92 James Wm. McClendon Jr., *Doctrine: Systematic Theology* (Nashville: Abingdon, 1994); Thomas N. Finger, *Christian Theology: An Eschatological Approach* (Scottdale, Pa.: Herald, 1989).

93 Jürgen Moltmann, *The Coming of God: Christian Eschatology*, trans. Margaret Kohl (Minneapolis: Fortress, 1996), 22–29.

94 Moltmann, *Coming of God*, 23.

95 Aquinas, *Summa Theologica*, 1a.13.7.

96 Ronald Goetz, "The Suffering God: The Rise of a New Orthodoxy," *The Christian Century*, 16 April 1986, 385–89. Again, Moltmann played a central role in another major work of the sixties, *The Crucified God*. Jürgen Moltmann, *The Crucified God: The Cross of Christ as the Foundation and Criticism of Christian Theology*, trans. John Bowden and R. A. Wilson (Minneapolis: Fortress, 1994).

97 Stanley J. Grenz, *Rediscovering the Triune God: The Trinity in Contemporary Theology* (Minneapolis: Augsburg, 2004).

98 Moltmann is again a theologian who has led the way. Jürgen Moltmann, *God in Creation* (Minneapolis: Fortress, 1993). See also Sallie McFague, *The Body of God: An Ecological Theology* (Minneapolis: Fortress, 1993); Vanhoozer, *Drama of Doctrine*.

99 Ricoeur treats this arc in several places, such as Paul Ricoeur, "The Model of the Text: Meaningful Action Considered as a Text," in *Hermeneutics and the Human Sciences: Essays on Language, Action, and Interpretation*, ed. John B. Thompson (Cambridge: Cambridge University Press, 1981), 131–44; Ricoeur, *Interpretation Theory*, chap. 4. For more elaboration on the significance of this arc for theology and its relationship to Ricoeur's later "narrative arc," see Dan R. Stiver, *Theology after Ricoeur: New Directions in Hermeneutical Theology* (Louisville: Westminster John Knox, 2001), chap. 2.

100 Paul Ricoeur, *Political and Social Essays* (Athens: Ohio University Press, 1974), 287–88.

101 Paul Ricoeur, *The Symbolism of Evil*, trans. Emerson Buchanan, Religious Perspectives, vol. 17 (New York: Harper & Row, 1967), 348.

494 / Notes to pp. 48–52

102 Cited in Friedman, *World Is Flat*, 305, of Hilarie Rooney, principal of Latyonsville Elementary School in Maryland.

103 Ricoeur, *Symbolism of Evil*, 349.

104 Paul Ricoeur, *The Conflict of Interpretations*, ed. Don Ihde, Northwestern University Studies in Phenomenology and Existential Philosophy (Evanston, Ill.: Northwestern University Press, 1974), 352.

105 Musicians tell me that they experience a similar phenomenon. For example, one may be drawn to a career in music through growing up in church choirs. After one's study, one may become impatient and judgmental of church choirs. It takes a certain discipline to recapture that first love and joy in appreciating the music as a worship experience.

106 Paul Ricoeur, "Metaphor and the Central Problem of Hermeneutics," in *Hermeneutics and the Human Sciences: Essays on Language, Action, and Interpretation*, ed. John B. Thompson (Cambridge: Cambridge University Press, 1981), 171.

107 Ricoeur, *Interpretation Theory*.

108 In the words of the title of Moltmann's *magnum opus*.

109 Roger E. Olson, *The Mosaic of Christian Belief: Twenty Centuries of Unity and Diversity* (Downers Grove, Ill.: InterVarsity, 2002), 56.

110 The formulation of Wesley's varied references in the more thematic Quadrilateral is recent, attributed to Albert Outler in the late 1960s, but is rooted in Wesley's usage. See Donald A. D. Thorsen, *The Wesleyan Quadrilateral: Scripture, Tradition, Reason, and Experience as a Model of Evangelical Theology* (Grand Rapids: Zondervan, 1990), 17–21. Thorsen points out how Wesley was influenced by similar Anglican approaches such as the so-called "three-legged stool" of Richard Hooker, made of Scripture, reason, and tradition. Thorsen also reveals the primacy of Scripture for Wesley. Recent debate among Methodists, ironically, has been more contentious. The concern is that the primacy of Scripture can be lost, and it is unclear how to relate them. Joel B. Green, "Scripture in the Church," in *The Wesleyan Tradition*, ed. Paul W. Chilcote (Nashville: Abingdon, 2002), 39; Ted A. Campbell and Michael T. Burns, *Wesleyan Essentials in a Multicultural Society*, ed. Robert Mulholland (Nashville: Abingdon, 2004), chap. 2. As will be seen, I share the concerns but do not see it in any case as a kind of calculus, guaranteed to churn out theological conclusions. It provides a map that helps one look in the right places, but there is no substitute for spiritual, theological discernment.

111 Roger E. Olson, *The Story of Christian Theology: Twenty Centuries of Tradition and Reform* (Downers Grove, Ill.: InterVarsity, 1999), 513.

112 See Stanley J. Grenz and John R. Franke, *Beyond Foundationalism: Shaping Theology in a Postmodern Context* (Louisville: Westminster John Knox, 2001), chap. 3, titled "Scripture: Theology's 'Norming Norm.'"

113 Alister E. McGrath, *A Scientific Theology*, vol. 3.1, *Theory* (Grand Rapids: Eerdmans, 2005), 177–83; Grenz and Franke, *Beyond Foundationalism*, chap. 4.

114 Nicholas Wolterstorff, "The Migration of the Theistic Arguments: From Natural Theology to Evidentialist Apologetics," in *Rationality, Religious Belief, and Moral Commitment: New Essays in the Philosophy of Religion*, ed. Robert Audi and William J. Wainwright (Ithaca: Cornell University Press, 1986), 38–81.

115 Nancey C. Murphy, *Beyond Liberalism and Fundamentalism: How Modern and Postmodern Philosophy Set the Theological Agenda*, Rockwell Lecture Series (Valley Forge, Pa.: Trinity Press International, 1996), 22–32.

116 Busch, *Karl Barth*, 153.

117 George, *Theology of the Reformers*, 81.

118 Alister E. McGrath, *A Scientific Theology*, vol. 2, *Reality* (Grand Rapids: Eerdmans, 2002), 101. Interestingly, McGrath discusses this subject in the context of reflection on the rationality of religion being like that of science and a contemporary revival of natural theology.

119 I am thinking also of the way that out of Methodism came various Holiness groups, the Nazarenes, and, one could argue, all of the Pentecostal groups.

120 While some point to Luther's experience changing his views, George Lindbeck, of what is sometimes called the Yale School of postliberal theology, says that Luther's new understanding led to his "Tower" experience. George Lindbeck, *The Nature of Doctrine: Religion and Theology in a Postliberal Age* (Philadelphia: Westminster, 1984), 39.

121 Interesting examples are Paul Tillich and Stan Grenz, both in significant ways moving beyond the modern paradigm, who still reject experience as a source for theology.

122 Augustine, *On Christian Doctrine*, in *St. Augustin's City of God and Christian Doctrine*, ed. Philip Schaff, A Select Library of the Nicene and Post-Nicene Fathers of the Christian Church 2, 1st series (Grand Rapids: Eerdmans, 1956), 2.40.60-61.

123 Paul Tillich, *Systematic Theology*, vol. 1 (Chicago: University of Chicago Press, 1951), 227.

CHAPTER 3

1   Clark H. Pinnock, *The Scripture Principle* (Vancouver: Regent College Publishing, 2002), ix.

2   B. L. Shelley, "Baptist Churches in U.S.A," in *Dictionary of Christianity in America*, ed. Daniel G. Reid (Downers Grove, Ill.: InterVarsity, 1990), 110; Bill J. Leonard, *Baptists in America* (New York: Columbia University Press, 2005), 91.

3   See Williston Walker et al., *A History of the Christian Church*, 4th ed. (New York: Charles Scribner's Sons, 1985), 419–41; John M. Todd, *Luther: A Life* (New York: Crossroad, 1982).

4   Martin Luther, "A Mighty Fortress Is Our God," Smith Creek Music, 1529, 12 September 2006, http://www.smithcreekmusic.com/Hymnology/Lutheran.Hymnody/A_Mighty_Fortress.html. This is close to the German text: *Nehmen sie den Leib, Gut, Ehr', Kind und Weib: Lass fahren dahin, Sie haben's kein'n Gewinn, Das Reich muss uns doch bleiben.*

5   Todd, *Luther*, 203.

6   Characteristically, the recent movie, *Luther*, while effectively dramatizing for a contemporary audience the significance of Luther's actions, played down Luther's role in inciting the massacres that he later lamented.

7   Or "perspicacity." See, for example, George M. Marsden, *Fundamentalism and American Culture*, 2nd ed. (Oxford: Oxford University Press, 2006), 16, 110–11.

8   This phrase is from Paul Ricoeur, *The Conflict of Interpretations*, ed. Don Ihde, Northwestern University Studies in Phenomenology and Existential Philosophy. (Evanston, Ill.: Northwestern University Press, 1974), where he applies it to the problem of conflicting interpretations in general, not just with respect to Scripture.

9   See Ian G. Barbour, *Religion and Science: Historical and Contemporary Issues*, rev. ed. (San Francisco: HarperSanFrancisco, 1997), 9–17; Phil Dowe, *Galileo, Darwin, and Hawking: The Interplay of Science, Reason, and Religion* (Grand Rapids: Eerdmans, 2005), chap. 1; Dava Sobel, *Galileo's Daughter: A Historical Memoir of Science, Faith, and Love* (New York: Penguin, 2000).

10   Sobel, *Galileo's Daughter*, 225.

11   Cesare Cardinal Baronio. Sobel, *Galileo's Daughter*, 65.

12   For broader consideration of the role of paradigms in theology, see Hans Küng and David Tracy, eds., *Paradigm Change in Theology: A*

Symposium for the Future, trans. Margaret Köhl (New York: Crossroad, 1989); Hans Küng, *Christianity: Essence, History, and Future*, trans. John Bowden (New York: Continuum, 1998).

13   Robert M. Grant and David Tracy, *A Short History of the Interpretation of the Bible*, 2nd ed. (Philadelphia: Fortress, 1984).

14   Cited in Grant and Tracy, *Interpretation of the Bible*, 86. Charles Scalise points out how the allegorical method continues in contemporary Baptist life, such as in W. A. Criswell, but also how appreciation for the exegetical history of the church can be positively appropriated today. Charles J. Scalise, "Patristic Biblical Interpretation and Postmodern Baptist Identity," *Review and Expositor* 101, no. 4 (2004): 615–28.

15   She notes concerning a study of Web sites for major Christian Right leaders,

> Even when the Bible is invoked on these web sites, only very infrequently is a concept of inerrancy alluded to, and even then rarely using that term. I do not think I ever have seen the word "fundamentalist" in cruising these web sites for the last year or so. The word and commitment are submerged. Rarely do we even see "literalist." On average it takes two or three and sometimes more links even to find a page that mentions the Bible or a biblical verse."

Margaret Mitchell, "How Biblical Is the Christian Right?" *Religion and Culture Web Forum* May 2006, 16 August 2006, http://marty-center.uchicago.edu/webforum/052006/commentary.shtml.

16   Mitchell, "How Biblical Is the Christian Right?" (emphasis in original).

17   Thomas Aquinas, *Summa Theologica*, 1a.1.10.

18   Martin Luther, *The Babylonian Captivity of the Church*, Works of Martin Luther, vol. 2 (Grand Rapids: Baker Book House, 1982), 189f.

19   For example, the aforementioned Westminster Confession of Faith, chap. 1, par. V.

20   Pinnock, *Scripture Principle*, vii.

21   Hans W. Frei, *The Eclipse of Biblical Narrative: A Study in Eighteenth- and Nineteenth-Century Hermeneutics* (New Haven: Yale University Press, 1974).

22   As pointed out in George Marsden's major study of the development of modern fundamentalism and evangelicalism, conservative

Christians in the United States self-consciously appropriated an approach that combined a Baconian understanding of science and a Scottish Common Sense Realist understanding of truth. Marsden, *Fundamentalism and American Culture*.

23 Marsden, *Fundamentalism and American Culture*, 56.

24 Even with the rise of the evangelical movement after World War II and some questioning of Scottish Common Sense Realism, a major theologian of the movement such as Carl F. H. Henry continued to have a highly rational approach that stressed Scripture as a collection of propositions. Carl F. H. Henry, *God, Revelation, and Authority*, 6 vols. (Waco, Tex.: Word, 1976–1983), 3:457.

25 Nancey C. Murphy, *Beyond Liberalism and Fundamentalism: How Modern and Postmodern Philosophy Set the Theological Agenda*, Rockwell Lecture Series (Valley Forge, Pa.: Trinity Press International, 1996), chap. 1.

26 Cited in Marsden, *Fundamentalism and American Culture*, 115 (emphasis in original). Similar praise of reason can be found in Henry.

27 Murphy, *Beyond Liberalism and Fundamentalism*, chap. 1. I say more consistently since a mark of liberalism was an effort, perhaps too zealous, to accommodate the modern mind more than to be appropriate to the founding documents of the faith.

28 For example, see the scathing criticism by the influential John Locke, no conservative!

> Since wit and fancy find easier entertainment in the world than dry truth and real knowledge, figurative speeches and allusion in language will hardly be admitted as an imperfection or abuse of it. . . . But yet if we would speak of things as they are, we allow that all the art of rhetoric, besides order and clearness; all the artificial and figurative application of words eloquence hath invented, are for nothing else but to insinuate wrong ideas, move the passions, and thereby mislead the judgment; and so indeed are perfect cheats.

> John Locke, "An Essay Concerning Human Understanding," in *Locke, Berkeley, Hume*, ed. Robert Maynard Hutchins, Great Books of the Western World 35 (Chicago: Encyclopedia Britannica, 1952), 3.10.34.

29 See, for example, Thomas Kuhn, *The Structure of Scientific Revolution*, 2nd ed. (Chicago: University of Chicago Press, 1970), 198–204.

30   Pinnock, *Scripture Principle*, 75; Stanley J. Grenz, *Theology for the Community of God*, 2nd ed. (Grand Rapids: Eerdmans, 1994), 398f.

31   Benjamin Breckinridge Warfield, *The Inspiration and Authority of the Bible*, ed. Samuel G. Craig (Philadelphia: Presbyterian & Reformed, 1948); E. J. Young, *Thy Word Is Truth: Some Thoughts on the Biblical Doctrine of Inspiration*, The Banner of Truth Trust (Grand Rapids: Eerdmans, 1957). See Roger E. Olson, *The Story of Christian Theology: Twenty Centuries of Tradition and Reform* (Downers Grove, Ill.: InterVarsity, 1999), 556–61, for the way in which key influences of this movement such as Francis Turretin in the seventeenth century and Charles Hodge in the nineteenth veered close to a dictation theory while not wanting exactly to express it that way. "The Chicago Statement on Biblical Inerrancy" expresses this tension in a common way by saying that Scripture "is of infallible divine authority in all matters upon which it touches." Of course, what it gives with one hand, it takes back with the other by acknowledging in a later comment that Scripture should be evaluated in light of its purpose, and one should allow for "observational descriptions of nature," hyperbole, and so on, which moves the statement toward a moderate inerrancy rather than strong or full inerrancy. See for these terms, Grenz, *Theology*, 398–400. It is not without reason that some have seen the Chicago statement, probably the most definitive statement of technical inerrancy, as incoherent. A more nuanced plenary-verbal view is given by David S. Dockery, "A People of the Book and the Crisis of Biblical Authority," in *Beyond the Impasse? Scripture, Interpretation, and Theology in Baptist Life*, ed. Robison James and David S. Dockery (Nashville: Broadman, 1992), 17–39, which allows for literary forms, historical context, human elements, and development. Oddly, while he recognizes that "purpose" is important earlier (21), his definition of inerrancy omits it (32), which gives rise to the problem of claiming more for Scripture than it claims for itself. In the same book, one might compare Molly Marshall's treatment, which is a high view of Scripture but sees the problems of inerrancy, especially as a restrictive political tool in the Baptist context. Molly T. Marshall, "Setting Our Feet in a Large Room," in James and Dockery, *Beyond the Impasse?* 169–94.

32   David H. Kelsey, *Proving Doctrine: The Uses of Scripture in Modern Theology*, 2nd ed. (Harrisburg, Pa.: Trinity Press International, 1999).

33   George Lindbeck, *The Nature of Doctrine: Religion and Theology in a Postliberal Age* (Philadelphia: Westminster, 1984), 16.

34 Lindbeck, *Nature of Doctrine*, chap. 2.

35 Hans W. Frei, "The 'Literal Reading' of Biblical Narrative in the Christian Tradition: Does It Stretch or Will It Break?" in *The Bible and the Narrative Tradition*, ed. Frank McConnell (Oxford: Oxford University Press, 1986); Kathryn E. Tanner, "Theology and the Plain Sense," in *Scriptural Authority and Narrative Interpretation*, ed. Garrett Green, 59–78 (Philadelphia: Fortress, 1987); Charles Wood, *The Formation of Christian Understanding* (Philadelphia: Westminster, 1981), 40ff.

36 Ben Witherington III, *The Jesus Quest: The Third Search for the Jew of Nazareth*, 2nd ed. (Downers Grove, Ill.: InterVarsity, 1997), chaps. 3, 7.

37 Kevin J. Vanhoozer, *The Drama of Doctrine: A Canonical-Linguistic Approach to Christian Theology* (Louisville: Westminster John Knox, 2005), chap. 9; Kevin J. Vanhoozer, *First Theology: God, Scripture, and Hermeneutics* (Downer's Grove, Ill.: InterVarsity, 2002), chap. 1.

38 Paul Ricoeur, "Toward a Hermeneutic of the Idea of Revelation," trans. David Pellauer, in *Essays on Biblical Interpretation*, ed. Lewis S. Mudge (Philadelphia: Fortress, 1980), 73–118.

39 Vanhoozer, *Drama of Doctrine*, 285 (emphasis in original).

40 This language is drawn from speech-act theory that emphasizes, in the words of John Austin's seminal work, that we do many things with words.

41 See Dan R. Stiver, *The Philosophy of Religious Language: Sign, Symbol, and Story* (Cambridge: Blackwell, 1996), chap. 6, for an account of narrative theology as a whole and an attempt to relate three notable schools of narrative theology.

42 Alasdair C. MacIntyre, *Three Rival Versions of Moral Enquiry: Encyclopaedia, Genealogy, and Tradition*, Gifford Lectures (Notre Dame: University of Notre Dame Press, 1990).

43 For a fuller discussion of the hermeneutic circle in light of contemporary hermeneutics, see David Tracy's section in Grant and Tracy, *Interpretation of the Bible*.

44 Vanhoozer, *Drama of Doctrine*. Vanhoozer refers to several others, especially Hans Urs von Balthasar, who are drawn to the metaphor of drama, but he develops it much more fully. Vanhoozer's book on Scripture and theology is a rich work on which I have drawn. He suggests yet another metaphor, namely, that of Scripture as a kind of map, "canonical cartography," that points in the direction that we

are to follow, suggesting an aspectival realism in terms of fit between language and reality. Vanhoozer, *Drama of Doctrine*, 295ff.

45 Vanhoozer, *Drama of Doctrine*, chap. 9.

46 For example, David McCullough, *1776* (New York: Simon & Schuster, 2006); Joseph J. Ellis, *His Excellency: George Washington* (New York: Knopf, 2005).

47 Hans-Georg Gadamer, *Truth and Method*, trans. Joel Weinsheimer and Donald G. Marshall, rev. ed. (New York: Crossroad, 1991), 297 (emphasis in original).

48 Kevin J. Vanhoozer, *Is There a Meaning in This Text? The Bible, the Reader, and the Morality of Literary Knowledge* (Grand Rapids: Zondervan, 1998).

49 See, for example, two excellent collections: Nancey C. Murphy, Brad J. Kallenberg, and Mark Thiessen Nation, eds., *Virtues and Practices in the Christian Tradition: Christian Ethics after MacIntyre* (Harrisburg, Pa.: Trinity Press International, 1997); and Miroslav Volf and Dorothy C. Bass, eds., *Practicing Theology: Beliefs and Practices in Christian Life* (Grand Rapids: Eerdmans, 2002).

50 The landmark is usually Athanasius' Festal Letter in 367, which includes the current twenty-seven books. However, it includes in the Old Testament list Baruch and the Epistle of Jeremiah, a reminder that the Old Testament canon was not established in the first several centuries of the church either.

51 This is illustrated by the account of finding the Nag Hammadi documents. When the local peasants found them and took them home, their mother reputedly threw many of them into the fire to use for cooking! We have what was left.

52 See, for example, Charles J. Scalise, *Hermeneutics as Theological Prolegomena: A Canonical Approach*, Studies in American Biblical Hermeneutics, vol. 8 (Macon, Ga.: Mercer University Press, 1994); Kevin J. Vanhoozer, ed., *Dictionary for Theological Interpretation of the Bible* (Grand Rapids: Baker Academic, 2005). For an example of a new commentary series based on theological interpretation of the Bible, see Stephen E. Fowl, *Philippians*, The Two Horizons New Testament Commentary, ed. Joel Green and Max Turner (Grand Rapids: Eerdmans, 2005).

53 *Progressive revelation* is the traditional term for this kind of theological development in history. I want to touch base with that tradition but avoid some misapprehensions. I do not mean that earlier revelation

is somehow left behind or unimportant. The full story fills out the meaning in a way that an atomistic approach focusing on later texts does not. Even though Jesus dramatically shifted the meaning of *Messiah* from the Old Testament, its meaning is understood in light of its history. *Progressive* does not always mean that the later in history is somehow better. The creation accounts, the love commandments, and the proclamations of the prophets about social justice are not necessarily surpassed in the New Testament but reframed. The phrase *progressive revelation* refers to God's dynamic, incarnational history with God's people that reflects not only historical movement but also theological movement.

54 Gadamer, *Truth and Method*, 306. See also the landmark book along this line by Anthony C. Thiselton, *The Two Horizons: New Testament Hermeneutics and Philosophical Description* (Grand Rapids: Eerdmanns, 1980).

55 Mark Noll, "Evangelicals and the Study of the Bible," in *Evangelicalism and Modern America*, ed. George Marsden (Grand Rapids: Eerdmans, 1984), 118.

56 Stiver, *Philosophy of Religious Language*, chap. 6.

57 A fascinating, albeit overly negative, account of the dynamics of a print culture and the ensuing contemporary shift to a visual, film culture is Neil Postman, *Amusing Ourselves to Death: Public Discourse in the Age of Show Business* (New York: Penguin, 1986). On the importance of an oral culture, even for Paul, see Ben Witherington III, *The Paul Quest: The Renewed Search for the Jew of Tarsus* (Downers Grove, Ill.: InterVarsity, 2001), 232.

58 John Calvin, *Calvin: Institutes of the Christian Religion*, trans. Ford Lewis Battles, ed. John T. McNeill, The Library of Christian Classics 21 (Philadelphia: Westminster, 1960), 3.21.4. Calvin credits Augustine for the idea.

59 This is found in the New Hampshire Confession of Faith, which was taken up in the Baptist Faith and Message of 1925, 1963, and 2000. See William L. Lumpkin, ed., *Baptist Confessions of Faith*, 2nd ed. (Valley Forge, Pa.: Judson, 1969); G. Hugh Wamble, "The Background and Meaning of the 1963 Southern Baptists Articles of Faith on the Bible," in *The Proceedings of the Conference on Biblical Inerrancy 1987* (Nashville: Broadman, 1987), 331–54.

60 Compare Grenz, *Theology*, 398–402. He rightly emphasizes that infallibility has to do with the trustworthiness of Scripture, that it is

"not liable to deceive," and that it is cautious about theories of inspiration taking the place of scriptural authority. This seems close to the views of E. Y. Mullins, who had perhaps the greatest influence among Baptists in the twentieth century. Mullins identified both a plenary-verbal view and a "dynamical view," which related more to thoughts than to words, but thought neither was satisfactory to all of the dimensions of Scripture. E. Y. Mullins, *The Christian Religion in Its Doctrinal Expression* (Valley Forge, Pa.: Judson, 1917), 143–44.

61   Gadamer, *Truth and Method*, 274–75.

62   See Roger E. Olson, *The Mosaic of Christian Belief: Twenty Centuries of Unity and Diversity* (Downers Grove, Ill.: InterVarsity, 2002); Steven R. Harmon, "The Authority of the Community (of All the Saints): Toward a Postmodern Baptist Hermeneutic of Tradition," *Review and Expositor* 100, no. 4 (2003): 587–621; Scalise, "Patristic Biblical Interpretation."

63   Alasdair MacIntyre, "Epistemological Crises, Dramatic Narrative, and the Philosophy of Science," in *Why Narrative? Readings in Narrative Theology*, ed. Stanley Hauerwas and Gregory Jones (Grand Rapids: Eerdmans, 1989), 146.

64   Roman Catholic theology often prefers the language of natural theology and revealed theology, which relates to placing a higher premium on the knowledge available in natural theology, for example, Aquinas' assumption that one can prove the existence of God to the unaided reason (*Summa Theologica*, 1a.2.3). Calvin and Luther were not so sanguine about the value of general revelation, considering that there might be only a dim awareness of God, but it does little good. As Calvin says, "Since, therefore, men one and all perceive that there is a God and that he is their Maker, they are condemned by their own testimony because they have failed to honor him and to consecrate their lives to his will" (*Institutes of the Christian Religion*, 1.3.1).

65   Arthur Frank Holmes, *All Truth Is God's Truth* (Grand Rapids: Eerdmans, 1977).

66   Noll, "Evangelicals and the Study of the Bible," 117.

67   Tertullian, *The Prescription against Heretics*, trans. Peter Holmes, in *Latin Christianity: Its Founder, Tertullian*, ed. Alexander Roberts and James Donaldson, The Ante-Nicene Fathers 3 (Grand Rapids: Eerdmans, 1956), bk. 7. A good source for these classic passages is Alister E. McGrath, ed., *The Christian Theology Reader*, 3rd ed. (Cambridge: Blackwell, 2007).

68 Justin the Martyr, "The First Apology of Justin," in *The Apostolic Fathers with Justin Martyr and Irenaeus*, ed. Alexander Roberts and James Donaldson, The Ante-Nicene Fathers 1 (Grand Rapids: Eerdmans, 1956), chaps. 20, 23, 46. Clement of Alexandria, *The Stromata, or Miscellanies*, in *Fathers of the Second Century*, ed. James Donaldson and Alexander Roberts, The Ante-Nicene Fathers 2 (Grand Rapids: Eerdmans, 1962), 1.5.28.

69 Augustine, *On Christian Doctrine*, 2.40.60-61.

70 Clement of Alexandria, *Stromata*, 1.5.

Chapter 4

1 Blaise Pascal, *Pensées and Other Writings*, trans. Honor Levi, The World's Classics (New York: Oxford University Press, 1995), 178.

2 Paul Tillich, *Systematic Theology* (Chicago: University of Chicago Press, 1951), 1:10–12, 14.

3 For example, John Baillie, *The Idea of Revelation in Recent Thought* (New York: Columbia University Press, 1956), 27; Tillich, *Systematic Theology*, 1:12.

4 Martin Buber, *I and Thou*, trans. Ronald Gregor Smith, 2nd ed. (Edinburgh: T&T Clark, 1958).

5 "But the formula three persons has been coined, not in order to give a complete explanation by means of it, but in order that we might not be obliged to remain silent." Augustine, *The Trinity*, trans. Stephen McKenna, The Fathers of the Church, vol. 45 (Washington, D.C.: Catholic University of America Press, 1963), 5.9.10.

6 Alternatively translated as *The Joyful Wisdom*, in Friedrich Nietzsche, *The Gay Science*, trans. Walter Kaufmann (New York: Vintage Books, 1974), par. 125 (emphasis in original).

7 Bruce Benson's chapter is titled "The Prayers and Tears of Young Fritz." Bruce Ellis Benson, *Pious Nietzsche: Decadence and Dionysian Faith* (Bloomington: Indiana University Press, 2008), chap. 1. See also Hans Küng, *Does God Exist? An Answer for Today*, trans. Edward Quinn (Garden City, N.Y.: Doubleday, 1980), 353.

8 I am thinking of Buckley with the lines of John Milbank in mind, following Stanley Hauerwas. Michael J. Buckley, *At the Origins of Modern Atheism* (New Haven: Yale University Press, 1987), 27–28. Cf. John Milbank, *Theology and Social Theory: Beyond Secular Reason* (Cambridge: Blackwell, 1993), 9; Stanley Hauerwas, *With the Grain*

of the Universe: The Church's Witness and Natural Theology (Grand Rapids: Brazos, 2001), 33. Of course, there were atheists among the ancient Greek philosophers.

9   Buckley, *Origins*, 375, n. 68.

10 As argued by Antony Flew, *The Presumption of Atheism* (New York: Barnes & Noble, 1976).

11 Küng, *Does God Exist?* 299, 329–30.

12 Cf. David Boulton, *The Trouble with God: Building the Republic of Heaven* (New York: O Books, 2005).

13 Søren Kierkegaard, *Concluding Unscientific Postscript*, ed. David F. Swenson and Walter Lowrie (Princeton: Princeton University Press, 1941), 31.

14 Kierkegaard, *Concluding Unscientific Postscript*, 182. Kierkegaard says, "For if passion is eliminated, faith no longer exists, and certainty and passion do not go together" (*Concluding Unscientific Postscript*, 30).

15 For an account of Kierkegaard's influence on both Bultmann and Barth, see Eberhard Busch, *Karl Barth: His Life from Letters and Autobiographical Texts*, trans. John Bowden, 2nd ed. (Philadelphia: Fortress, 1976), 161, 173. Barth more clearly moved away from Kierkegaard as his thought developed, but not altogether.

16 For example, see the excellent volume, Stephen H. Davis, ed., *Encountering Evil: Live Options in Theodicy* (Atlanta: John Knox, 1981). Davis says, "There is little doubt that the problem of evil is the most serious intellectual difficulty for theism" (2). See also the second edition, Stephen H. Davis, ed., *Encountering Evil: Live Options in Theodicy*, 2nd ed. (Louisville: Westminster John Knox, 2001).

17 See, for example, the article by J. L. Mackie, "Evil and Omnipotence," and the article by Alvin Plantinga, "The Free Will Defense," in Michael L. Peterson et al., *Philosophy of Religion: Selected Readings*, 3rd ed. (Oxford: Oxford University Press, 2007).

18 Étienne Gilson makes this point very well. At one point, he says,

What is perhaps the key to the whole history of Christian philosophy and, in so far as modern philosophy bears the mark of Christian thought, to the history of modern philosophy itself, is precisely the fact that, from the second century A.D. on [with the encounter of the Judeo-Christian view with Greek thought], men have had to use a Greek philosophical technique in order to express ideas that had never entered the head of any Greek philosopher." (*God and Philosophy* [New Haven: Yale University Press, 1941], 43)

19   One of the most well-known stories is the "Enuma Elish," in *The Ancient Near East: An Anthology of Texts and Pictures*, ed. James B. Pritchard (Princeton: Princeton University Press, 1958), 30–39.

20   Milbank, *Theology and Social Theory*, 5.

21   Alister E. McGrath, *A Scientific Theology*, vol. 1, *Nature* (Grand Rapids: Eerdmans, 2001), 159–66. For a defense of the traditional interpretation and discussion of the issues, see John Goldingay, *Old Testament Theology*, vol. 1, *Israel's Gospel* (Downers Grove, Ill.: InterVarsity, 2003), 78.

22   Tillich, *Systematic Theology*, 10–12.

23   Tillich, *Systematic Theology*, 10.

24   Augustine, "The Confessions," trans. Edward Bouverie Pusey, in *Augustine*, ed. Robert Maynard Hutchins, Great Books of the Western World 18 (Chicago: Encyclopedia Britannica, 1952), 1.1.

25   In John Leith, ed., *Creeds of the Churches: A Reader in Christian Doctrine from the Bible to the Present*, rev. ed. (Atlanta: Anchor, 1973), 520.

26   For a probing account, see Chris Seay, *The Tao of Enron: Spiritual Lessons from a Fortune 500 Fallout* (Colorado Springs: NavPress, 2002).

27   C. S. Lewis treated this issue in an illuminating way in C. S. Lewis, *The Four Loves* (New York: Harcourt, Brace & Company, 1960).

28   Arthur C. McGill, *Suffering: A Test of Theological Method* (Philadelphia: Westminster John Knox, 1982).

29   For example, "And truly God claims, and would have us grant him, omnipotence—not the empty, idle, and almost unconscious sort that the Sophists imagine, but a watchful, effective, active sort, engaged in ceaseless activity. . . . governing heaven and earth by his providence, he so regulates all things that nothing takes place without his deliberation." John Calvin, *Calvin: Institutes of the Christian Religion*, trans. Ford Lewis Battles, ed. John T. McNeill, The Library of Christian Classics, vol. 20 (Philadelphia: Westminster, 1960), 1.16.3.

30   Augustine's view of predestination, whereby God guarantees that those whom he chooses will respond, points to God's control. Compare this statement: "It is, therefore, in the power of the wicked to sin; but that in sinning they should do this or that by that wickedness is not in their power, but in God's, who divides the darkness and regulates it; so that even what they do contrary to God's will is not fulfilled except it be God's will." Augustine, "On the Predestination of the Saints," in

Saint Augustin: Anti-Pelagian Writings, ed. Philip Schaff, A Select Library of the Nicene and Post-Nicene Fathers of the Christian Church 5 (Grand Rapids: Eerdmans, 1971), chap. 34.

31 Cited in Mike Higton, *Difficult Gospel: The Theology of Rowan Williams* (New York: Church Publishing, 2004), 39. Higton's reference to the online source in a sermon appears to be incorrect.

32 Glen H. Stassen, *Just Peacemaking: Transforming Initiatives for Justice and Peace* (Louisville: Westminster John Knox, 1992), 64–67.

33 For example, Amos 3:2; Isa 10:1-2; 42:1-4; Jer 5:25-29; Zeph 3:17-20.

34 C. S. Lewis, *The Lion, the Witch, and the Wardrobe* (New York: Collier, 1970), 180.

35 Marshall references William Willimon and Barbara Brown Taylor (Molly T. Marshall, *Joining the Dance: A Theology of the Spirit* [Valley Forge, Pa.: Judson, 2003], 65).

36 Thomas Aquinas, *Summa Theologica*, 1a.25.4.

37 One could call this the Augustine-Calvinist position and also include Aquinas and Luther. William Hasker, for example, includes all of these plus Zwingli as theological determinists. William Hasker, *The Openness of God: A Biblical Challenge to the Traditional Understanding of God* (Downers Grove, Ill.: InterVarsity, 1994), 141. It depends on how these thinkers are interpreted. All affirm individual predestination, where God guarantees the free choices of individuals for salvation. The compatibilist view of these thinkers is usually referred to as Calvinism, but since not all Reformed thinkers who affirm Calvin are "five-point Calvinists," I will refer to the latter position as "strong Calvinism." See also Michael D. Robinson, *The Storms of Providence: Navigating the Waters of Calvinism, Arminianism, and Open Theism* (Dallas: University Press of America, 2003).

38 A helpful discussion of these issues is in Robinson, *Storms of Providence*; Terrance Tiessen, *Providence and Prayer: How Does God Work in the World?* (Downer's Grove, Ill.: InterVarsity, 2000).

39 For helpful treatment, see James K. Beilby and Paul. R. Eddy, eds., *Divine Foreknowledge: Four Views* (Downers Grove, Ill.: InterVarsity, 2001); Robinson, *Storms of Providence*.

40 Open theists often see themselves in the Arminian camp because of their common affirmation of genuine, incompatibilist views of human freedom. As such, they are on firm ground, reminding us that the lines connecting theological traditions criss-cross in complex ways. Yet they themselves recognize that they are making a rather new

and distinctive transformation of what I am calling "traditional Arminianism." As we shall see later, many Baptists represent still another variation of Arminianism in that they affirm libertarian free will like Arminians but accept eternal security, which traditional Arminians generally did not, as one can see in the Arminian traditions of Methodism and groups that developed from them such as the Holiness, Nazarene, and Pentecostal movements.

41   One of the best in articulating this is Hasker, *Openness of God*, 147–50.

42   In Beilby and Eddy, *Divine Foreknowledge*, 125.

43   Tiessen, *Providence and Prayer*, chap. 13.

44   For example, Cyril of Alexandria, "We do not mean that God the Word suffered blows or the piercing of nails or other wounds in his own nature, in that the divine is impassible because it is not physical" (Second Letter to Nestorius [Letter IV, 3–5], 4.22–6.28, cited in Alister E. McGrath, ed., *The Christian Theology Reader*, 3rd ed. [Cambridge: Blackwell, 2007], 276). For a fuller discussion, see Thomas G. Weinandy, *Does God Change?* Studies in Historical Theology Series 4 (Petersham, Mass.: St. Bede's, 1985), chap. 2. See also "Leo's Tome" in McGrath, *Christian Theology Reader*, 279–80. Roger Olson discusses others, such as Tertullian, Athanasius, and Apollinarus, and generalizes, "Absolute static perfection—including apatheia, or impassibility (passionlessness)—is the nature of God according to Greek thought, and nearly all Christian theologians came to agree with this" (*The Story of Christian Theology: Twenty Centuries of Tradition and Reform* [Downers Grove, Ill.: InterVarsity, 1999], 143).

45   A good example from a contemporary Roman Catholic perspective is Weinandy, *Does God Change?*

46   James P. Boyce, *Abstract of Systematic Theology* (Escondido, Calif.: Den Dulk Christian Foundation, 1887), 74–78. In this section, Boyce also reaffirms the idea that Christ's divine nature did not suffer, only the human.

47   For example, Hasker in Beilby and Eddy, *Divine Foreknowledge*, 129.

48   Aristotle, *Metaphysics*, 12.7, 12.9.

49   This was the theme of Ronald Goetz, "The Suffering God: The Rise of a New Orthodoxy," *The Christian Century*, 16 April 1986, 385–89, mentioned in the prolegomena.

50   Process philosophy has led the way in this respect, distinguishing between the consequent nature of God compared to the primordial

nature of God. See Alfred North Whitehead, *Process and Reality*, ed. David Ray Griffin and Donald W. Sherburne, 3rd ed. (New York: Free Press, 1978), 343–51. Paul L. Gravrilyuk defends impassibility by pointing out that at times church fathers acknowledged a relational God despite their affirmation of impassibility (*The Suffering of the Impassible God: The Dialectics of Patristic Thought*, Oxford Early Christian Studies Series [Oxford: Oxford University Press, 2006]). He bases this possibility on the distinction between God's unchanging character yet change in other ways. The problem is that this is just what those who affirm passibility assume, even process theologians. The indication that this is not full enough for a suffering God is that even Gravrilyuk limits suffering to Christ on the cross—but why? If God can suffer at any time and remain God, why limit it unless one is clearly uncomfortable with the notion? The question is whether the discomfort comes genuinely from Scripture or from the heavy influence of Greco-Roman philosophy on the early church fathers. Gravrilyuk's concession, as limited as it is, would not be satisfactory to those affirming impassibility because they do not want God to be able to suffer, even in Christ, because that makes God too vulnerable, for example, see Weinandy, *Does God Change?* 66. For affirmation of the notion of a vulnerable God, see William C. Placher, *Narratives of a Vulnerable God: Christ, Theology, and Scripture* (Louisville: Westminster John Knox, 1994).

51   Aquinas, *Summa Theologica*, 1a.13.7.

52   Walter Brueggemann, *Theology of the Old Testament: Testimony, Dispute, Advocacy* (Minneapolis: Fortress, 1997), 83.

53   Burton Cooper points out that at least we can recognize that the traditional notion of a God as perfect in the Hellenistic sense, implying that God is without limits, is not so easily seen as the only possible conception of God. The Bible, he says, can be imagined "as a coal mine with many veins." When we see this, two conclusions follow: "First, we lose the sense that the Bible clearly witnesses to God as unlimited in all aspects of being. Second, the notion of divine unlimitedness appears as an historical, provisional, and partial interpretation of the scriptural witness to God's creative and redemptive power" (Burton Z. Cooper, *Why, God?* [Atlanta: John Knox, 1988], 73).

54   Stanley J. Grenz, *Rediscovering the Triune God: The Trinity in Contemporary Theology* (Minneapolis: Augsburg, 2004).

55   See David S. Cunningham, *These Three Are One: The Practice of Trinitarian*

Theology (Oxford: Blackwell, 1998); Paul S. Fiddes, *Participating in God: A Pastoral Doctrine of the Trinity* (Louisville: Westminster John Knox, 2000); Stanley J. Grenz, *The Social God and the Relational Self: A Trinitarian Theology of the Imago Dei*, The Matrix of Christian Theology, vol. 1 (Louisville: Westminster John Knox, 2001); Catherine Mowry LaCugna, *God for Us: The Trinity and Christian Life* (New York: HarperCollins, 1993); Marshall, *Joining the Dance*; Jürgen Moltmann, *The Trinity and the Kingdom: The Doctrine of God* (New York: Harper & Row, 1981).

56 See especially Fiddes, *Participating in God*, chap. 3; Moltmann, *Trinity and the Kingdom*.

57 Fiddes, *Participating in God*, 266–67.

58 Moltmann, *Trinity and the Kingdom*; Stanley J. Grenz, *Theology for the Community of God*, 2nd ed. (Grand Rapids: Eerdmans, 1994).

59 Marshall, *Joining the Dance*.

60 See LaCugna, *God for Us*, 97–101. LaCugna points out that Augustine's formulation of this principle was consistent with "the Greek understanding of the co-inherence of the persons in each other" (97). The problem is that later thinkers could so emphasize equality over the economy that the persons are "blurred" (98). Her conclusion was, "Even if Augustine himself intended nothing of the sort, his legacy to Western theology was an approach to the Trinity largely cut off from the economy of salvation" (102).

61 For a helpful, concise discussion of the origin of the idea of *perichoresis*, its relationship to its translation into Latin as *circuminsessio* and *circumincessio*, and their relationship to the similar word, to dance (*perichoreuo*), see Fiddes, *Participating in God*, 71–80.

62 For helpful background to the following narrative, besides the books on the Trinity mentioned above, see J. N. D. Kelly, *Early Christian Doctrines*, 5th ed. (New York: HarperSanFrancisco, 1978); Williston Walker et al., *A History of the Christian Church*, 4th ed. (New York: Charles Scribner's Sons, 1985); Olson, *Story of Christian Theology*.

63 Irenaeus, *Against Heresies*, in *The Apostolic Fathers with Justin Martyr and Irenaeus*, ed. Alexander Roberts and James Donaldson, The Ante-Nicene Fathers 1 (Grand Rapids: Eerdmans, 1956), 3.18.1.

64 Hippolytus, *Against the Heresy of One Noetus*, in *Fathers of the Third Century*, ed. Alexander Roberts and James Donaldson, The Ante-Nicene Fathers 5 (Grand Rapids: Eerdmans, 1951), 1.

65 Tertullian, *Against Praxeas*, 1.

66 Grenz, *Rediscovering the Triune God*, 57; LaCugna, *God for Us*, 211.

67 Irenaeus' major work was to rebut Gnosticism, *Against Heresies*.

68 Tertullian had the right formula, but his view was not appreciated until later and he did not understand it in fully orthodox terms.

69 Henry Bettenson, ed., *Documents of the Christian Church*, 2nd ed. (New York: Oxford University Press, 1963), 25.

70 Kelly, *Early Christian Doctrines*, 255–56.

71 Kelly, *Early Christian Doctrines*, 262–63.

72 Fiddes especially has emphasized that what is most important about the divine dance is not its example of democracy to *emulate* but its life in which to *participate*. Fiddes, *Participating in God*.

73 Cunningham, *These Three Are One*, 65; Fiddes, *Participating in God*, 34, 37.

74 John Macquarrie, *Principles of Christian Theology* (New York: Charles Scribner's Sons, 1966), 182–83.

75 Karl Barth, *Church Dogmatics*, vol. 1.1, *The Doctrine of the Word of God*, 295.

76 Cunningham, *These Three Are One*.

77 A traditional way of avoiding this consequence is the "doctrine of appropriations," which means "assigning an attribute (wisdom) or an activity (creation) to one of the persons without denying that the attribute or activity applies to all three" (LaCugna, *God for Us*, 100). LaCugna is more worried that emphasizing their commonality may threaten their distinctiveness in the economy of salvation history.

78 See especially Philip Jenkins, *The Next Christendom: The Coming of Global Christianity* (New York: Oxford University Press, 2002).

79 The reference to a "thick description" is to Clifford Geertz's approach to anthropology as providing a full, elaborate account of cultural practices (Clifford Geertz, *The Interpretation of Cultures: Selected Essays* [New York: Basic, 1973], 3–30). For the connection to the church, see Hans W. Frei, "An Afterword: Eberhard Busch's Biography of Karl Barth," in *Karl Barth in Review: Posthumous Works Reviewed and Assessed*, ed. H. Martin Rumscheidt (Pittsburgh: Pickwick, 1981), 111–12.

80 J. B. Phillips, *Your God is Too Small* (New York: Macmillan, 1958).

81 Aquinas, *Summa Theologica*, 1a.9, 1a.3.2.

82 Aquinas, *Summa Theologica*, 1a.1.8, 1a.2.2.

83 "Orthodoxy therefore distinguishes between God's essence and His energies, thus safeguarding both divine transcendence and divine immanence: God's essence remains unapproachable, but His energies

come down to us" (Timothy Ware, *The Orthodox Church*, rev. ed. [London: Penguin Books, 1997], 209).

84 For further explanation of the way the contemporary philosophy of metaphor is related to Aquinas' view, see Dan R. Stiver, *The Philosophy of Religious Language: Sign, Symbol, and Story* (Cambridge: Blackwell, 1996), chap. 6. For special focus on the metaphorical nature of religious language, see Paul Ricoeur, "Biblical Hermeneutics," *Semeia* 4 (1975): 27–138; Sallie McFague, *Metaphorical Theology: Models of God in Religious Language* (Philadelphia: Fortress, 1982); Sallie McFague, *Models of God: Theology for an Ecological, Nuclear Age* (Philadelphia: Fortress, 1987); Janet Martin Soskice, *Metaphor and Religious Language* (Oxford: Clarendon, 1985).

85 Stiver, *Philosophy of Religious Language*, chap. 2.

86 Paul Tillich, *Dynamics of Faith*, 42,

87 Elizabeth A. Johnson, *She Who Is: The Mystery of God in Feminist Theological Discourse* (New York: Crossroad, 1992).

88 Aquinas, *Summa Theologica*, 1a.92.1. See Johnson, *She Who Is*, 24–25. Lest we be too harsh on the church, the Jewish context in practice also saw women as property, and the Western philosophical tradition—thus the Western intellectual tradition all the way up to Kant and Hegel—has seen women as deficient men and as incapable of higher thought and ability. Aquinas was basically following Aristotle. A sobering summary in an excellent book on the subject by Nancy Tuana says, "The problems of the woman reading philosophy intensify when the talk turns to woman. She has no doubt that she is the subject of the discourse but she cannot recognize herself in what she reads. The woman reading Aristotle cannot identify with Aristotle's description of woman, for his construction of woman's nature entails that she is unable to undertake the very thing in which she is engaged— philosophy. The woman reading Hegel in order to identify the nature of the good state cannot locate herself in the text as woman, for he tells her that woman is unable to achieve awareness of the universality of the state. The woman searching for a moral philosophy in reading Kant cannot internalize what he says about woman, for to do so would mean that she would have to accept that she is precluded from moral agency and should therefore cease her investigation" (Nancy Tuana, *Woman and the History of Philosophy*, Paragon Issues in Philosophy [New York: Paragon House, 1992], 3).

89 Daphne Hampson, *Theology and Feminism*, Signposts in Theology (Oxford: Basil Blackwell, 1990), 52.

90 For example, Alvin F. Kimel Jr., "The God Who Likes His Name: Holy Trinity, Feminism, and the Language of Faith," in *Speaking the Christian God: The Holy Trinity and the Challenge of Feminism*, ed. Alvin Kimel Jr. (Grand Rapids: Eerdmans, 1992), 188–208. The whole book has articles that address this issue.

91 See Fiddes, *Participating in God*; Moltmann, *Trinity and the Kingdom*, 164; E. Frank Tupper, *A Scandalous Providence: The Jesus Story of the Compassion of God* (Macon, Ga.: Mercer University Press, 1995), 46–56. All three use the language of "fatherly mother" or "motherly father" to convey the sense in which Jesus transcends a stilted and one-sided interpretation of Jesus' address to God as "Father."

92 Tupper, *Scandalous Providence*, 56.

CHAPTER 5

1 For example, Claus Westermann says, "Once theology imperceptibly became detached from Creator-Creation, the necessary consequence is that it must gradually become an anthropology and begin to disintegrate from within and collapse around us" (*Creation*, trans. John J. Scullion [Philadelphia: Fortress, 1974], 3).

2 I have found even seminary students to be largely pessimistic about the long-term fate of the world in classes on eschatology. The incredible popularity of the Left Behind series probably also testifies to this pessimism because it suggests that the end of the world is soon.

3 Augustine is excellent on this score.

> But evils are so thoroughly overcome by good, that though they are permitted to exist, for the sake of demonstrating how the most righteous foresight of God can make a good use even of them, yet good can exist without evil, as in the true and supreme God Himself, and as in every invisible and visible celestial creature that exists above this murky atmosphere; but evil cannot exist without good, because the natures in which evil exists, in so far as they are natures, are good. And evil is removed, not by removing any nature, or part of a nature, which had been introduced by the evil, but by healing and correcting that which had been vitiated and depraved. (*The City of God*, in *St. Augustin's City of God and Christian Doctrine*, ed. Philip Schaff, A Select Library of the Nicene and Post-Nicene Fathers of the Christian Church 2 [Grand Rapids: Eerdmans, 1956], 14.11)

4 Lynn White Jr., "On the Historical Roots of Our Ecological Crisis," *Science* 155 (1967): 1203–7.

5   As Walter Brueggemann says, "It is now conventionally accepted that current ecological concerns are intimately connected to a biblical understanding of creation. While this has become a commonplace of scholarship, it is worth noting that this accent is very recent, only alive as the question has surfaced in the larger scope of society. While the claims for ecology were latent in the material, they were unnoticed in most of scholarship (*Theology of the Old Testament: Testimony, Dispute, Advocacy* [Minneapolis: Fortress, 1997], 163, n. 35).

6   See Westermann, *Creation,* 47–60, and the next chapter.

7   *Tammy Kitzmiller et al. v. Dover Area School District et al.,* 400 F. Supp. 2d 707 (M.D.Pa.2005) (U.S. District Court for the middle district of Pennsylvania, 20 December 2005). For broader treatment of the creationist background, see Edward J. Larson, *Summer for the Gods,* 2nd ed. (New York: Basic, 2006), especially the afterword.

8   The classic work on this is Thomas Kuhn, *The Structure of Scientific Revolutions,* 2nd ed. (Chicago: University of Chicago Press, 1970). Kuhn is not suggesting, however, that science does not involve a strict adjudication process.

9   See the evidence in *Kitzmiller v. Dover* and Langdon Gilkey, *Creationism on Trial: Evolution and God at Little Rock* (Minneapolis: Winston, 1985).

10   Barbara Forrest, "The Wedge at Work: How Intelligent Design Creationism Is Wedging Its Way into the Cultural and Academic Mainstream," in *Intelligent Design Creationism and Its Critics: Philosophical, Theological, and Scientific Perspectives,* ed. Robert T. Pennock (Cambridge, Mass.: MIT Press, 2001), 6.

11   For a great deal more on ID, see the expansive collection of essays from many sides and angles in Pennock, ed., *Intelligent Design Creationism.* For a similar debate about the earlier creationist cases involving public schools, see Michael Ruse, ed., *But Is It Science? The Philosophical Question in the Creation/Evolution Controversy* (Amherst, N.Y.: Prometheus, 1996). Both have articles that explore the theological, philosophical, historical, and legal questions.

12   For further study of the development of this issue in its wider complexity, dealing not only with Galileo and evolution but also the Big Bang and chaos theory, see Arthur R. Peacocke, *Creation and the World of Science: The Bampton Lectures, 1978* (Oxford: Clarendon, 1979); Ian G. Barbour, *Religion and Science: Historical and Contemporary Issues,* rev. ed. (San Francisco: HarperSanFrancisco, 1997); D. Brian Austin,

The End of Certainty and the Beginning of Faith (Macon, Ga.: Smyth & Helwys, 2000); Dowe, *Galileo, Darwin, and Hawking.*

13 Brueggemann, *Theology of the Old Testament*, 533. One should not play off such a practical concern against history as if these texts are ahistorical and atemporal. They relate very much to history and time but relate more to its practical meaning and do not anachronistically pertain to modern historical and scientific questions. See also Westermann, *Creation*, 12.

14 Ronald L. Numbers, *The Creationists: The Evolution of Scientific Creationism* (Berkeley: University of California Press, 1992), 19, 45, 58.

15 See Marsden, *Fundamentalism and American Culture*, chap. 21, for an account of this event's importance as well as other factors. See also Larson, *Summer for the Gods.*

16 Larson, *Summer for the Gods*, 270–71.

17 For background to these views, see John P. Newport, *Life's Ultimate Questions: A Contemporary Philosophy of Religion* (Dallas: Word, 1989), 139–51.

18 Cited in David N. Livingstone, *Darwin's Forgotten Defenders: The Encounter Between Evangelical Theology and Evolutionary Thought* (Grand Rapids: Eerdmans, 1987), 115. Priest and theologian John Haught indicates that the same could be said in the twenty-first century. Perhaps as it took a couple of centuries to take in the de-centering that Galileo engendered, it will take a couple of centuries to take in the similar de-centering of evolutionary theory, seeing that it is not a threat to theology at all. Haught says, "During the many years I have studied the so-called 'problem' of science and religion, I have grown increasingly convinced that a Darwinian (or, now, 'neo-Darwinian') view of nature answers to the deepest intuitions of religion" (John F. Haught, *God After Darwin: A Theology of Evolution* [Boulder, Colo.: Westview, 2000], 6). For more on the complex response of the church to Darwinism, which shows a quite mixed response, see Barbour, *Religion and Science*, chap. 3; Dowe, *Galileo, Darwin, and Hawking*, chap. 5.

19 Larson, *Summer for the Gods*, 270.

20 This relates to personal experiences that I have had. In a published example referring to the idea of Genesis 1 as providing a theological framework, which it surely does, but not a scientific theory, Henry Morris says, "The 'framework hypothesis' of Genesis, in any of its diverse forms, is nothing but neo-orthodox sophistry and inevitably leads eventually to complete apostasy. It must be unequivocally

rejected and opposed by Bible-believing Christians" (*Scientific Creationism* [San Diego: Creation-Life Publishers, 1974], 247).

21   Richard Dawkins, *The God Delusion* (Boston: Houghton Mifflin, 2006). See also Richard Dawkins, *The Blind Watchmaker: Why the Evidence of Evolution Reveals a Universe without Design* (New York: W. W. Norton, 2004); Daniel Dennett, *Darwin's Dangerous Idea: Evoluton and the Meanings of Life* (New York: Simon & Schuster, 1995). For helpful criticism of this kind of overreaching from the scientific side, see Haught, *God after Darwin*, chap. 2; Barbour, *Religion and Science*; Gilkey, *Creationism on Trial*, 135–37.

22   Gilkey, *Creationism on Trial*, 183–84. In fact, Gilkey says, "As far as I know, the natural sciences represent the only set of disciplines that are taught without substantial reference to their own history and their philosophy. And there is no discussion at all in the training of scientists of the relations of science to other permanent and significant aspects of cultural life" (184).

23   Étienne Gilson, *God and Philosophy* (New Haven: Yale University Press, 1941), 137.

24   For these distinctions, as well as perceiving that Adam and Eve in chap. 4 could be seen as literal, see Dale Moody, *The Word of Truth* (Grand Rapids: Eerdmans, 1981), 200–2.

25   For background, see Gerhard von Rad, *Old Testament Theology*, vol. 1, *The Theology of Israel's Historical Traditions*, trans. D. M. G. Stalker (New York: Harper & Row, 1962), 139–51; Westermann, *Creation*; Richard Elliott Friedman, *Who Wrote the Bible?* 2nd ed. (San Francisco: HarperSanFrancisco, 1997).

26   Brueggemann, *Theology of the Old Testament*, 153. Brueggemann says, "The mood of this rhetoric is to evidence that God is serenely and supremely in charge. There is no struggle here, no anxiety, no risk. . . . the intent and the effect of this liturgical narrative is to enact by its very utterance a well-ordered, fully reliable, generative world of Israelites who are exiles in Babylon" (153, cf. 533).

27   Stanley J. Grenz and Denise Muir Kjesbo, *Women in the Church* (Downers Grove, Ill.: InterVarsity, 1995), 164.

28   Augustine, "The Literal Meaning of Genesis: Books 1-6," trans. J. H. Taylor, in *The Literal Meaning of Genesis*, Ancient Christian Writers: The Works of the Fathers in Translation 41, ed. J. Quasten, W. Burghardt, and T. Comerford Lawler (New York: Newman, 1982), bk. 1, chap. 19.

29 For recent books that respond more personally to issues such as 9/11, the tsunami, or to personal loss, see Nicholas Wolterstorff, *Lament for a Son* (Grand Rapids: Eerdmans, 1987); David Bentley Hart, *The Doors of the Sea: Where Was God in the Tsunami?* (Grand Rapids: Eerdmans, 2005); N. T. Wright, *Evil and the Justice of God* (Downers Grove, Ill.: InterVarsity, 2006).

30 Harold S. Kushner, *When Bad Things Happen to Good People* (New York: Avon, 1981).

31 Brueggemann, *Theology of the Old Testament*, 158.

32 Alister E. McGrath, *A Scientific Theology*, 1:159–66.

33 Not all Hindu schools are monistic. I am referring, for example, to the Advaita Vedanta school.

34 Brian Hebblethwaite in his concise but insightful theodicy begins his book with the Buddha (*Evil, Suffering, and Religion* [New York: Hawthorn Books, 1976]).

35 Thomas Aquinas, *Summa Theologica*, 1a.25.4.

36 Sometimes theodicy is used in the narrow sense of giving a rather full explanation of how God and evil can coexist. This view, which arose in the Enlightenment and might be called "Enlightenment theodicy," is rejected by many contemporary Christian theologians and philosophers. Alvin Plantinga suggests that the theologian need only provide a defense, rather than a theodicy (*God, Freedom, and Evil* [Grand Rapids: Eerdmans, 1974]). The burden of proof is then on the "atheologian" to show that Christians are not within their epistemic rights to believe in God, something which is much more difficult to do nowadays, given postmodern approaches to epistemology, than heretofore. I am using theodicy in the broader sense of any account of how God and evil could coexist. See Dan R. Stiver, "The Problem of Theodicy," *Review and Expositor* 93, no. 4 (1996): 507–17.

37 Helpful historical background is found in John Hick, *Evil and the God of Love*, 2nd ed. (San Francisco: Harper & Row, 1978).

38 John Calvin, *Calvin: Institutes of the Christian Religion*, trans. Ford Lewis Battles, ed. John T. McNeill, The Library of Christian Classics, vol. 20 (Philadelphia: Westminster, 1960), 2.2.8.

39 For background on these issues, see David Basinger and Randall Basinger, eds., *Predestination and Free Will: Four Views of Divine Sovereignty and Free Will* (Downers Grove, Ill.: InterVarsity, 1986); James K. Beilby and Paul. R. Eddy, eds., *Divine Foreknowledge: Four Views* (Downers Grove, Ill.: InterVarsity, 2001); Robinson, *Storms of*

Providence; Terrance Tiessen, *Providence and Prayer: How Does God Work in the World?* (Downer's Grove, Ill.: InterVarsity, 2000).

40 In Stephen H. Davis, ed., *Encountering Evil: Live Options in Theodicy* (Atlanta: John Knox, 1981), 12–14.

41 This question is raised in the modern period perhaps most dramatically by Ivan Karamazov in relation to the suffering of innocent children in Fyodor Dostoyevsky, *The Brothers Karamazov* (New York: Modern Library, 1950), bk. 5, chap. 4. Even here, the assumption seems to be that God could have created everyone and yet guaranteed that the creation could have been better. The import of much recent thinking in theodicy questions this and poses the sharper question, what if God's choice was between a world like this and its suffering or a world with no persons at all? See Dan R. Stiver, "Still Too High a Price? Ivan's Question in the Light of Contemporary Theodicy," in *Dostoevsky's Polyphonic Talent*, ed. Joe E. Barnhart (Lanham, Md.: University Press of America, 2005), 25–39.

42 Dostoyevsky, *The Brothers Karamazov*, bk. 5, chap. 4.

43 I am here taking up a suggestion in Hebblethwaite, *Evil, Suffering, and Religion*, 5–6, 65–67.

44 Burton Z. Cooper, *Why, God?* (Atlanta: John Knox, 1988), 7-8.

45 C. S. Lewis, *A Grief Observed* (New York: Seabury, 1961), 31.

46 E. Frank Tupper, *A Scandalous Providence: The Jesus Story of the Compassion of God* (Macon, Ga.: Mercer University Press, 1995).

47 Arthur C. McGill, *Suffering: A Test of Theological Method* (Philadelphia: Westminster John Knox, 1982).

48 Augustine, *City of God*, 14.26.

49 For example, see Westermann, *Creation*, 61.

50 Augustine, *City of God*, 22.30. Augustine imagined that God could create a body that would not be consumed in the flames but would continue to burn and hurt forever (*City of God*, 21.4). Calvin later had a more covenantal view of original sin, where the "contract," so to speak, that God had with the human race was that Adam would act for everyone. This does not imply that everyone actually sinned in some mystical way *in* Adam but that Adam acted *for* everyone else.

51 This aspect of theodicy is variously called the problem of "gratuitous," "dysteleological," "surd," or "horrendous" evil.

52 Augustine, "On the Predestination of the Saints," chaps. 13–14; and "Enchiridion," in *Augustine*, ed. and trans. Albert C. Outler, The Library of Christian Classics 7 (Philadelphia: Westminster, 1955), chaps. 25–27.

53 John Calvin, *Institutes of the Christian Religion*, 3.21.1; 3.21.5.

54 Augustine, *City of God*, 22.1. For discussion of fallen angels, see the next chapter on humanity and sin.

55 The NRSV reads, "Therefore, just as sin came into the world through one man, and death came through sin, and so death spread to all because all have sinned." For example, James D. G. Dunn said in 1988, "The classic debate on the meaning of *eph ho* has more or less been settled in favor of the meaning 'for this reason that, because'" (*Romans 1–8*, Word Biblical Commentary 38a, ed. Bruce M. Metzger [Nashville: Thomas Nelson, 1988], 273).

56 Sometimes to deal with passages like 1 Timothy 2:4, it is said that Christ's atonement is *sufficient* for all but not *efficient* for all. In a way, all are provided for; nevertheless, God only intends the benefits of the atonement for the elect. In Calvin, at least, one cannot appeal to such a distinction to limit God's responsibility because Calvin insists on the sufficiency of God's will. This is what makes grace totally unmerited.

57 See, for example, John S. Feinberg, "God Ordains All Things," in Basinger and Basinger, eds., *Predestination and Free Will*, 19–43; Gise J. Van Baren, "Irresistible Grace," in *The Five Points of Calvinism*, by Herman Hanko, Homer Hoeksema, and Gise J. Van Baren, chap. 4 (Grandville, Mich: Reformed Free Publishing, 1976), accessed 30 July 2003, http://www.prca.org/fivepoints/chapter4.html; Homer C. Hoeksema, "Limited Atonement," in Hanko, *Five Points of Calvinism*, chap. 3, accessed 30 July 2003, http://www.prca.org/fivepoints/chapter3.html; Paul Helm, "The Augustinian-Calvinist View," in *Divine Foreknowledge: Four Views*, ed. James K. Beilby and Paul R. Eddy (Downers Grove, Ill.: InterVarsity, 2001), 161–89.

58 Ever since the rise of modern science in the seventeenth century, one of the challenges has been to keep up with its dizzying advances and make sure that one does not make a theological claim to truth that contradicts a clear scientific claim to truth, which would undermine the idea of one God and one ultimate truth. This was the challenge of the Galileo episode, in which we saw that the church realized that its exegesis had been mistaken at the outset in seeing that the teaching of inspired Scripture was that the earth is flat or that the earth is at the center of the universe. The age of the universe, along with the Big Bang theory itself, is so recent that theology is still coming to grips with it, akin to being in the

first generation of Galileo. In fact, it has not been until the first few years of the twenty-first century that the age of the universe has been fixed very precisely at around 13.7 billion years. Even a decade ago, it's age could be seen as fluctuating from 8–20 billion years, plus or minus a few billion years!

59 Irenaeus, *Against Heresies*, 4.39.1.

60 Dan R. Stiver, "Hick against Himself: His Theodicy versus His Replica Theory," in *Problems in the Philosophy of Religion: Critical Studies of the Work of John Hick*, ed. Harold Hewitt Jr., Library of Philosophy and Religion (London: Macmillan, 1991), 162–72.

61 For fuller discussion of the image of God, see the next chapter, on humanity and sin.

62 Emil Brunner, *Dogmatics*, vol. 2, *The Christian Doctrine of Creation and Redemption*, trans. Olive Wyon (Philadelphia: Westminster, 1952), 57.

63 C. S. Lewis, *The Problem of Pain* (New York: Collier, 1962), chap. 2.

64 See Hick's brief account in Stephen H. Davis, ed., *Encountering Evil: Live Options in Theodicy*, 2nd ed. (Louisville: Westminster John Knox, 2001), 42.

65 Stephen Hawking, *A Brief History of Time: From the Big Bang to Black Holes* (Toronto: Bantam, 1988), 175.

66 John Polkinghorne, *Science and Providence: God's Interaction with the World*, 2nd ed. (Philadelphia: Templeton Foundation, 2005), 77. Brian Hebblethwaite also makes this point: "Just as personal being requires freedom and therefore the possibility of wrong choice, so does finite free personal being require an ordered yet flexible physical environment in which to be rooted and nurtured over against and at a certain distance from the creator" (*Evil, Suffering, and Religion*, 75).

67 Lewis, *The Problem of Pain*, 79.

68 Plantinga, *God, Freedom, and Evil*.

69 As Plantinga has argued, it is more difficult than one might have thought at first to prove or demonstrate that there was no possibility at all that God and the evil and suffering of this world are not compossible. Possibility more than proof is all that is necessary; it is probably all that can be had.

70 One of the ironies of Augustine and Aquinas is that both have elements in their thought that support more of an Irenaean theodicy than the theodicies for which they are known. Few theologians, especially those as creative as both of them, are able to develop consistently all

of their thought. That is part of the reason we keep returning to them and reflecting on them.

71   This example is taken from Michio Kaku, *Parallel Worlds: A Journey through Creation, Higher Dimensions, and the Future of the Cosmos* (New York: Anchor, 2005), 242–43. He also points out that Jupiter also played a crucial role in being just large enough, but not too large, to clear out asteroids that would have made life impossible on earth.

72   Bill Bryson, *A Short History of Nearly Everything* (New York: Broadway, 2003), 249. In science, this issue is called "the anthropic principle." See John D. Barrow and Frank J. Tipler, *The Anthropic Cosmological Principle* (Oxford: Oxford University Press, 1988); Nancey C. Murphy and George F. R. Ellis, *On the Moral Nature of the Universe: Theology, Cosmology, and Ethics*, Theology and the Sciences (Minneapolis: Fortress, 1996), 51–53, 207–11.

73   The notion of meticulous and nonmeticulous providence has especially been emphasized by Michael L. Peterson, *Evil and the Christian God* (Grand Rapids: Baker Book House, 1982).

74   For sophisticated discussion of such "special" activity of God, especially in the context of chaos and complexity theory, see the articles by Arthur Peacocke, John Polkinghorne, and Nancey Murphy in Robert J. Russell, Nancey C. Murphy, and Arthur R. Peacocke, eds., *Chaos and Complexity: Scientific Perspectives on Divine Action*, 2nd ed., Scientific Perspectives on Divine Action 2 (Vatican City State: Vatican Observatory Publications, 1997). The reference to "in, with, and under" is in Peacocke's article, 140.

75   More specifically, God has been seen as exercising primary causation that allows for secondary causation at another level. In this way, freedom can exist at the level of secondary causation and is not violated by God's primary causation. This, again, may be seen as a profound explanation, at least pointing to the differing levels of activity by God and the creature. In the end, it may be seen as sleight of hand. In a discussion of this strategy, Polkinghorne says, "It is not clear to me what is gained by so apophatic [unspeakable] an account of God's action. . . . This seems to me to be a strategy of absolutely last resort. . . . I do not believe we are in so desperate a case" (Peacocke, *Creation*, 150–51).

76   Calvin, *Institutes*, 1.16.3, 1.16.5.

77   Calvin, *Institutes*, 1.18.

78   See the influence of John Piper, especially, among college students.

For example, John Piper, *The Pleasures of God: Meditations on God's Delight in Being God*, 2nd ed. (Sisters, Oreg.: Multnomah Publishers, 2000).

79 This is a point made especially in Jerry L. Walls and Joseph R. Dongell, *Why I Am Not a Calvinist* (Downers Grove, Ill.: InterVarsity, 2004), 8.

80 See Feinberg, "God Ordains All Things"; Helm, "The Augustinian-Calvinist View"; and Piper, *Pleasures of God*.

81 Calvin, *Institutes*, 1.17.10, 1.16.3.

82 Piper, *Pleasures of God*, appendix.

83 Karl Barth, *Church Dogmatics*, ed. G. W. Bromiley and T. F. Torrance, vol. 2.2, *The Doctrine of God*, trans. G. W. Bromiley et al. (Edinburgh: T&T Clark, 1957), 14–18, 94, 111, 169–71.

84 Process thought in Whitehead rejects *creatio ex nihilo* and sees God as dependent upon the world just as the world is dependent upon God.

85 Polkinghorne, *Science and Providence*, 79.

CHAPTER 6

1 John Calvin, *Calvin: Institutes of the Christian Religion*, trans. Ford Lewis Battles, ed. John T. McNeill, The Library of Christian Classics, vol. 20 (Philadelphia: Westminster, 1960), 1.1.1.

2 Blaise Pascal, *Pensées and Other Writings*, trans. Honor Levi, The World's Classics (New York: Oxford University Press, 1995), no. 102.

3 "Rose of Lima, Saint," *Britannica Online*, http://www.britannica.com/. See also "Rose of Lima" in the *New Catholic Encyclopedia* (Florence, Ky.: Gale Cengage, 2002) and Michael Walsh, *Butler's Lives of the Saints* (San Francisco: Harper & Row, 1985), 260–61.

4 Matthew 11:19.

5 Kelly Pigott gave this account at a faculty meeting, Hardin-Simmons University, August, 2006.

6 Max Weber, *The Protestant Ethic and the Spirit of Capitalism*, trans. Talcott Parsons (London: Unwin University Books, 1930), 166. This is apparently drawn from Weber's own upbringing, but Weber points out that this asceticism did not mean withdrawal from the world but industriousness in the world. See Arthur Mitzman, *The Iron Cage: A Historical Interpretation of Max Weber* (Piscataway, N.J.: Transaction, 1984), 253; Colin Campbell, *The Romantic Ethic and the Spirit of Modern Consumerism* (Oxford: Basil Blackwell, 1987), chap. 6. His account should be balanced by James Wm. McClendon Jr., *Ethics: Systematic*

Theology (Nashville: Abingdon, 1986), part 1, where he gives a much more positive view at least of Jonathan and Sarah Edwards.

7   Nietzsche says, "I beseech you, my brothers, remain faithful to the earth, and do not believe those who speak to you of otherworldly hopes! Poison-mixers are they, whether they know it or not. Despisers of life are they, decaying and poisoned themselves, of whom the earth is weary: so let them go" (*Thus Spake Zarathustra* in Friedrich Nietzsche, *The Portable Nietzsche*, ed. and trans. Walter Kaufmann, The Viking Portable Library [New York: Penguin Books, 1954], 125).

8   Fyodor Dostoyevsky, *The Brothers Karamazov* (New York: Modern Library, 1950), 197–99.

9   Martin Luther King Jr., *Where Do We Go from Here: Chaos or Community?* (New York: Harper & Row, 1967), 73.

10   For background for the following discussion, see David Cairns, *The Image of God in Man*, rev. ed., Fontana Library of Theology and Philosophy (London: Collins, 1973); Claus Westermann, *Creation*, trans. John J. Scullion (Philadelphia: Fortress, 1974), 47–60; John Hick, *Evil and the God of Love*, 2nd ed., rev (San Francisco: Harper & Row, 1985), 210–18; Stanley J. Grenz, *Theology for the Community of God*, 2nd ed. (Grand Rapids: Eerdmans, 1994), 168–82.

11   Emil Brunner, *Dogmatics*, vol. 2, *The Christian Doctrine of Creation and Redemption*, trans. Olive Wyon (Philadelphia: Westminster, 1952), 57.

12   See Grenz, *Theology*, 178. While putting weight on the eschatological side, Grenz clearly wants to safeguard the intrinsic worth of every human.

13   Karl Barth, *Church Dogmatics*, ed. G. W. Bromiley and T. F. Torrance, vol. 3.1, *The Doctrine of Creation*, trans. J. W. Edwards, O. Bussey, and Harold Knight (Edinburgh: T&T Clark, 1958), 184–86.

14   Westermann, *Creation*, 56.

15   Edmund Jacob, *Theology of the Old Testament*, trans. Arthur W. Heathcote and Philip J. Allcock (New York: Harper & Row, 1958), 167.

16   Westermann, *Creation*, 54.

17   This is similar to Joe R. Jones: "Being so created in the image of God must be firmly seen as both a *gracious endowment* and a *teleological task*" (*A Grammar of Christian Faith: Systematic Explorations in Christian Life and Doctrine* [Lanham, Md.: Rowman & Littlefield, 2002], 1:336]. I want to stress the sense in which even the "task" is "gracious": it is a gracious summons to which one responds to by grace.

18 The "beloved community" refers to Martin Luther King Jr.'s characterization of the kingdom of God that is both now and not yet. See John J. Ansbro, *Martin Luther King Jr.: The Making of a Mind* (Maryknoll, N.Y.: Orbis, 1982), 187–98.

19 Scientific and philosophical reasons for this shift, as well as theological, are given in Warren S. Brown, Nancey C. Murphy, and H. Newton Malony, eds., *Whatever Happened to the Soul? Scientific and Theological Portraits of Human Nature*, Theology and the Sciences (Minneapolis: Fortress, 1998).

20 Antonio R. Damasio, *Descartes' Error: Emotion, Reason, and the Human Brain* (New York: G. P. Putnam's Sons, 1994).

21 Maurice Merleau-Ponty, *Phenomenology of Perception*, trans. Colin Smith, International Library of Philosophy and Scientific Method (New York: Humanities Press, 1962), 454.

22 Martin Heidegger, *Being and Time*, trans. Joan Stambaugh, State University of New York Series in Contemporary Continental Philosophy (Albany: State University of New York Press, 1996), 49.

23 Heidegger, *Being and Time*, 56–58.

24 Heidegger's thought was developed further by Merleau-Ponty in *Phenomenology of Perception*. Paul Ricoeur likewise pointed out how willing and acting, as well as thinking, involve the body. In one of his studies, he closely related freedom and nature, the voluntary and the involuntary. His summary formula was: "The involuntary is *for* the will and the will is *by reason* of the involuntary" (*Freedom and Nature: The Voluntary and the Involuntary*, trans. Erazim Kohák, Northwestern University Studies in Phenomenology and Existential Philosophy [Evanston, Ill.: Northwestern University Press, 1966], 86).

25 See the concise discussion in Natalie K. Watson, *Feminist Theology* (Grand Rapids: Eerdmans, 2003), on the attempts to find a balance in feminist theology that avoids "essentialism" that overvalues the physical versus the cultural and a social constructionist view that undervalues the physical. She says, "The aim of feminist theology, however, is not a 'gender-neutral' theology, but one that is aware of the existence of such gender bias and points out the contingency of gender constructions" (26). She suggests, "Feminist theologians aim for a sacramental theology of women's bodies. Women's bodies can no longer be seen as polluting, as the objects of male desire, but as bodies that embody the body of Christ in many different ways. Such a sacramental theology of the body affirms the goodness of creation and

enables a truly incarnational theology" (38–39). Dealing with a similar issue in secular social science, Sandra Harding says, "It needs to be stressed that it is women who should be expected to be able to reveal for the first time what women's experiences are" (Sandra Harding, ed., *Feminism and Methodology* [Bloomington: Indiana University Press, 1987], 7). For a recent, nuanced perspective, see Serene Jones, "Women's Experience between a Rock and a Hard Place: Feminist, Womanist, and Mujerista Theologies in North America," in *Horizons in Feminist Theology: Identity, Tradition, and Norms*, ed. Rebecca S. Chopp and Sheila Grave Davaney (Minneapolis: Fortress, 1997), 33–53.

26 For sources based on the Meyers-Briggs Type Indicator, see Charles Keating, *Who We Are Is How We Pray: Matching Personality and Spirituality* (Mystic, Conn.: Twenty-Third Publications, 1987); David Keirsey and Marilyn Bates, *Please Understand Me: Character and Temperament Types*, 3rd ed. (Del Mar, Calif.: Prometheus Nemesis, 1978); Sandra Hirsh and Jean Kummerow, *Lifetypes* (New York: Warner, 1989).

27 James W. Fowler, *Stages of Faith* (San Francisco: HarperSanFrancisco, 1976).

28 See John A. T. Robinson, *The Body: A Study in Pauline Theology*, Studies in Biblical Theology, vol. 5 (Naperville, Ill.: Alec R. Allenson, 1957); Brown, Murphy, and Malony, *Whatever Happened to the Soul?*; Joel B. Green and Stuart L. Palmer, *In Search of the Soul: Four Views of the Mind-Body Problem* (Downers Grove, Ill.: InterVarsity, 2005). Joel Green, for instance, says, "Biblical scholars who have addresssed this question . . . are almost unanimous in their conclusion that both Old and New Testaments assume or testify to an anthropological monism" (Green and Palmer, *In Search of the Soul*, 18).

29 Gordon Fee especially makes this point in terms of eschatology. In this sense in Paul, the "flesh" (*sarx*) "has completely lost its relationship to the physical and has become strictly eschatological—and pejorative—describing existence from the perspective of those who do not know Christ, who thus live as God's enemies" (*God's Empowering Presence: The Holy Spirit in the Letters of Paul* [Peabody, Mass.: Hendrickson, 1994], 819). As such, the works of the flesh may hardly relate to the physical body at all.

30 Graham Ward, "The Logos, the Body, and the World: On the Phenomenological Border," in *Transcending Boundaries in Philosophy and Theology: Reason, Meaning, and Experience*, ed. Kevin J. Vanhoozer and Martin Warner (Burlington, Vt.: Ashgate, 2007), 125.

31 Ben Witherington III, *The Paul Quest: The Renewed Search for the Jew of Tarsus* (Downers Grove, Ill.: InterVarsity, 2001).

32 Helen Keller, *The Story of My Life, with Her Letters (1887–1901)* (New York: Grosset & Dunlap, 1905), 23–24.

33 Søren Kierkegaard, *The Sickness unto Death: A Christian Psychological Exposition for Upbuilding and Awakening*, ed. and trans. Howard V. Hong and Edna H. Hong, Kierkegaard's Writings, vol. 19 (Princeton: Princeton University Press, 1980), 13. Kierkegaard emphasized that the relation between the two, as a "third," made things even more unstable.

34 The title of one of Søren Kierkegaard's main works, deriving from the biblical language in John 11:4.

35 The language is Paul Ricoeur's in Paul Ricoeur, *Fallible Man*, trans. Charles Kelbley, rev. ed. (New York: Fordham University Press, 1986).

36 It is interesting to note German theologian Jürgen Moltmann's comments about its significance in *The Coming of God: Christian Eschatology*, trans. Margaret Kohl (Minneapolis: Fortress, 1996), 175.

37 Mark Twain, *Mark Twain's Autobiography*, vol. 2 (New York: P. F. Collier & Son, 1924), 7.

38 Wolfhart Pannenberg, *What Is Man?* trans. Duane A. Priebe (Philadelphia: Fortress, 1970), chap. 1.

39 Jean-Paul Sartre, "Existentialism Is a Humanism," in *Existentialism from Dostoevsky to Sartre*, ed. Walter Kaufmann (New York: New American Library, 1975).

40 Paul Tillich, *Systematic Theology* (Chicago: University of Chicago Press, 1963), 3:32.

41 For example, see Gerhard von Rad, *Old Testament Theology*, vol. 1, *The Theology of Israel's Historical Traditions*, trans. D. M. G. Stalker (New York: Harper & Row, 1962), 136–65.

42 See Hick, *Evil*, 201–10, for a summary of the development from the pre-Christian era to the second century after Christ.

43 One should note that the serpent in the Old Testament context is not the Satan of the New Testament. In fact, it was rather late in the Old Testament period, and perhaps not at all, before the idea of Satan as an archenemy of God is developed. It is perhaps even after the New Testament that Satan comes to be seen as a fallen angel. So the story must be read on its own terms first. Then it can certainly be read in light of the larger canon and tradition.

44 Miroslav Volf, *Exclusion and Embrace: A Theological Exploration of Identity, Otherness, and Reconciliation* (Nashville: Abingdon, 1996), 80.

45 For example, see Reinhold Niebuhr, *Christian Realism and Political Problems* (New York: Charles Scribner's Sons, 1953). This is not necessarily to endorse all of Niebuhr's theological underpinnings, which have come under heavy criticism as in Stanley Hauerwas, *With the Grain of the Universe: The Church's Witness and Natural Theology* (Grand Rapids: Brazos, 2001), chap. 5.

46 See Mary T. Malone, *Women and Christianity* (Maryknoll, N.Y.: Orbis, 2001); Elizabeth A. Johnson, *She Who is: The Mystery of God in Feminist Theological Discourse* (New York: Crossroad, 1992), 22–28.

47 Tertullian, *On the Apparel of Women*, trans. S. Thelwall, in *Fathers of the Third Century*, ed. Alexander Roberts and James Donaldson, The Ante-Nicene Fathers 4 (Grand Rapids: Eerdmans, 1956), 1.1.

48 For a fuller discussion of this position and arguments against it, see especially by evangelical "complementarians" rather than "egalitarians" Stanley J. Grenz and Denise Muir Kjesbo, *Women in the Church* (Downers Grove, Ill.: InterVarsity, 1995), 160–69. See also Paul K. Jewett, *Man as Male and Female* (Grand Rapids: Eerdmans, 1975).

49 For example, see Augustine, *The City of God*, bks. 13–14.

50 For more on this issue, see the chapter on salvation.

51 Gerhard von Rad, *Genesis*, trans. John H. Marks, rev. ed., The Old Testament Library (Philadelphia: Westminster, 1961), 111–12.

52 For an impressive argument to this effect, see James K. A. Smith, *The Fall of Interpretation: Philosophical Foundations for a Creational Hermeneutic* (Downers Grove, Ill.: InterVarsity, 2000).

53 Serene Jones points out that the value of Calvin's notion of total depravity is not that it denies basic worth but shows how deeply immersed we are in sin, which "goes all the way down." This, however, means that "the reach of grace into our lives is just as total" (Serene Jones, *Feminist Theory and Christian Theology: Cartographies of Grace* [Minneapolis: Fortress, 2000], 102–3).

54 A fascinating example is in Jones, *Feminist Theory*, chap. 5. In her Tuesday night women's group, inspired by Calvin (!), they were able to identify sin more precisely as incest, racism, sexism, addiction, and so on.

55 Kierkegaard, *Sickness unto Death*, 49–67.

56 See Valerie Saiving, "The Human Situation: A Feminist View," in *Womanspirit Rising: A Feminist Reader in Religion*, ed. Carol P. Christ and Judith Plaskow (San Francisco: Harper & Row, 1979), 25–42

(originally published in 1960). See also Daphne Hampson, *Theology and Feminism*, Signposts in Theology (Oxford: Basil Blackwell, 1990), 50–52. Cf. Jones, *Feminist Theory*, 111; and Mary Field Belenky et al., *Women's Ways of Knowing: The Development of Self, Voice, and Mind* (New York: Basic, 1986), in which chaps. 1–4 indicate a pattern in the U.S., at least at the time it was written, where many women often must overcome a feeling of not having a voice.

57   Kathryn Tanner distinguishes between "idolatrous self-esteem" and "non-idolatrous esteem" (*The Politics of God: Christian Theologies and Social Justice* [Minneapolis: Fortress, 1992], 228ff.).

58   Reinhold Niebuhr, *The Nature and Destiny of Man* (New York: Charles Scribner's Sons, 1949), 228–40. Stanley Hauerwas, in an otherwise quite critical account of Niebuhr, remarks that this account is one of "Niebuhr's most compelling descriptions of the work of sin" (*With the Grain*, 120).

59   Peter Brown, *The Body and Society: Men, Women, and Sexual Renunciation in Early Christianity* (New York: Columbia University Press, 1988), 361.

60   Brown, *Body and Society*, 354.

61   Brown, *Body and Society*, 353. Brown then goes on to point out the influence of Ambrose on Augustine's conception of the connection between intercourse and original sin.

62   John Howard Yoder, *The Politics of Jesus*, 2nd ed. (Grand Rapids: Eerdmans, 1994).

63   Walter Wink, *Engaging the Powers: Discernment and Resistance in a World of Domination* (Minneapolis: Fortress, 1992), 7.

64   Volf, *Exclusion and Embrace*, 87.

65   Jürgen Moltmann, *God for a Secular Society: The Public Relevance of Theology*, trans. Margaret Kohl (Minneapolis: Fortress, 1999), 12.

66   E. Frank Tupper, *A Scandalous Providence: The Jesus Story of the Compassion of God* (Macon, Ga.: Mercer University Press, 1995), 138.

67   Tupper, *Scandalous Providence*, 1995: 140.

68   M. Scott Peck, *People of the Lie: The Hope of Healing Human Evil* (New York: Simon & Schuster, 1983).

69   Tupper, *Scandalous Providence*, 140–45; Wink, *Engaging the Powers*, 8.

70   Paul Ricoeur, *The Symbolism of Evil*, trans. Emerson Buchanan, Religious Perspectives, vol. 17 (New York: Harper & Row, 1967), 25–46.

71   Marcus Borg, *Jesus: Uncovering the Life, Teachings, and Relevance of a*

Religious Revolutionary (San Francisco: HarperSanFrancisco, 2006), 123.

72 Paul Tillich, *Systematic Theology*, vol. 1 (Chicago: University of Chicago Press, 1951).

CHAPTER 7

1   John Dominic Crossan, *The Historical Jesus: The Life of a Mediterranean Jewish Peasant* (San Francisco: HarperSanFrancisco, 1992).

2   Richard Dawkins, *The God Delusion* (Boston: Houghton Mifflin, 2006); Sam Harris, *Letter to a Christian Nation: The End of Faith* (New York: Knopf, 2006).

3   Timothy Ware, *The Orthodox Church*, rev. ed. (London: Penguin, 1997), 226.

4   For background to the following, see J. N. D. Kelly, *Early Christian Doctrines*, 5th ed. (New York: HarperSanFrancisco, 1978); Williston Walker et al., *A History of the Christian Church*, 4th ed. (New York: Charles Scribner's Sons, 1985); Roger E. Olson, *The Story of Christian Theology: Twenty Centuries of Tradition and Reform* (Downers Grove, Ill.: InterVarsity, 1999).

5   Kelly, *Early Christian Doctrines*, 308.

6   Kelly, *Early Christian Doctrines*, 253.

7   Examples are Athanasius and Gregory of Nazianzus. Kelly, *Early Christian Doctrines*, 286, 298.

8   Actually reported by Tertullian, *Apology*, trans. S. Thelwall, in *Latin Christianity: Its Founder, Tertullian*, ed. Alexander Roberts and James Donaldson, The Ante-Nicene Fathers 3 (Grand Rapids: Eerdmans, 1957), 39.

9   Immanuel Kant, *Religion within the Limits of Reason Alone*, trans. Theodore M. Greene and Hoyt H. Hudson (New York: Harper & Brothers, 1960), 54–58.

10 Olson, *Story of Christian Theology*, 168–72.

11 A couple of good accounts are Ben Witherington III, *The Jesus Quest: The Third Search for the Jew of Nazareth*, 2nd ed. (Downers Grove, Ill.: InterVarsity, 1997); Mark Allan Powell, *Jesus as a Figure in History: How Modern Historians View the Man from Galilee* (Louisville: Westminster John Knox, 1998).

12 Albert Schweitzer, *The Quest of the Historical Jesus: A Critical Study of Its Progress from Reimarus to Wrede*, trans. W. Montgomery (New York: Macmillan, 1968), 398.

13   Alister E. McGrath, ed., *The Christian Theology Reader*, 3rd ed. (Cambridge: Blackwell, 2007), 308.

14   See Paul Ricoeur, *Time and Narrative*, vol. 1, trans. Kathleen McLaughlin and David Pellauer (Chicago: University of Chicago Press, 1984) for a critical dialogue about this movement in historiography but which sees a responsibility in historiography to pay a debt to the past. Both historiography and fiction are imaginative and mimetic, but they are not the same. See also Paul Ricoeur, *Time and Narrative*, vol. 2, trans. Kathleen McLaughlin and David Pellauer (Chicago: University of Chicago Press, 1985); Paul Ricoeur, *Time and Narrative*, vol. 3, trans. Kathleen Blamey and David Pellauer (Chicago: University of Chicago Press, 1988). For a summary, see Dan R. Stiver, *Theology after Ricoeur: New Directions in Hermeneutical Theology* (Louisville: Westminster John Knox, 2001), chap. 4.

15   Wolfhart Pannenberg, *Jesus-God and Man*, trans. Lewis L Wilkins and Duane A. Priebe, 2nd ed. (Philadelphia: Westminster, 1977).

16   See especially N. T. Wright, *The Resurrection of the Son of God*, Christian Origins and the Question of God, vol. 3 (Minneapolis: Fortress, 2003), 736–38; N. T. Wright, *Simply Christian: Why Christianity Makes Sense* (San Francisco: HarperSanFrancisco, 2006), 55–57, 113–16.

17   Robert W. Funk, Roy W. Hoover, and the Jesus Seminar, eds., *The Five Gospels: The Search for the Authentic Words of Jesus* (San Francisco: HarperSanFrancisco, 1997), 34–37.

18   For example, see N. T. Wright, *The New Testament and the People of God*, Christian Origins and the Question of God, vol. 1 (Minneapolis: Fortress, 1992), 435–43.

19   See Wright, *New Testament*, 402, 440–42.

20   Crossan is a good example here in his study of the parables. He loves to try to find the parable as Jesus might have told it, apart from its formulation through the work of the Evangelist. The impression he gives is that his scholarly reconstruction, which is always highly speculative, is what is important and what should be interpreted.

21   Marcus Borg, *Jesus: Uncovering the Life, Teachings, and Relevance of a Religious Revolutionary* (San Francisco: HarperSanFrancisco, 2006), 213–17.

22   Ben Witherington III, *The Paul Quest: The Renewed Search for the Jew of Tarsus* (Downers Grove, Ill.: InterVarsity, 2001), 31–35.

23   Borg, *Jesus*, 83.

24   Witherington III, *Jesus Quest*, chap. 7.

25   Norman Perrin, *Jesus and the Language of the Kingdom: Symbol and Metaphor in New Testament Interpretation* (Philadelphia: Fortress, 1976); Borg, *Jesus*.

26   Perrin, *Jesus*.

27   Wright, *Resurrection*.

28   John Dominic Crossan, *In Parables: The Challenge of the Historical Jesus* (New York: Harper & Row, 1973), 66.

29   Perrin, *Jesus*, 89–107; Crossan, *In Parables*, 8–10.

30   Perrin summarizes this shift very well in Perrin, *Jesus*, 127–81. See also Crossan, *In Parables*; Sallie McFague, *Speaking in Parables: A Study in Metaphor and Theology* (Philadelphia: Fortress, 1975); Paul Ricoeur, "Biblical Hermeneutics," *Semeia* 4 (1975): 27–138.

31   John Dominic Crossan, *The Dark Interval: Towards a Theology of Story* (Allen, Tex.: Argus Communications, 1975), 122–23.

32   Crossan, *In Parables*, 57–66.

33   Crossan, *Dark Interval*, 57–62.

34   Ricoeur, "Biblical Hermeneutics," 114.

35   Borg, *Jesus*, 130–36.

36   Borg makes this point in Borg, *Jesus*, 321, n. 28.

37   Crossan especially emphasizes this in *Historical Jesus*, 261–64.

38   Borg says of his students at Oregon State University, "In surveys, they regularly characterize Christians as anti-intellectual, literalistic, self-righteous, judgmental, and bigoted" (*Jesus*, 299). A woman struggling with becoming a Christian in an email conversation with Brian McLaren feared that she would change and become "closed minded and bigoted and brainwashed and everything bad" (Brian D. McLaren, *More Ready Than You Realize: Evangelism as Dance in the Postmodern Matrix* [Grand Rapids: Zondervan, 2002], 35).

39   Stanley J. Grenz, *Theology for the Community of God*, 2nd ed. (Grand Rapids: Eerdmans, 1994), 252.

40   The historical shift came especially in Jürgen Moltmann, *The Crucified God: The Cross of Christ as the Foundation and Criticism of Christian Theology*, trans. John Bowden and R. A. Wilson (Minneapolis: Fortress, 1994), chap. 5. See also Paul S. Fiddes, *The Creative Suffering of God* (Oxford: Clarendon, 1988), 135–43; E. Frank Tupper, *A Scandalous Providence: The Jesus Story of the Compassion of God* (Macon, Ga.: Mercer University Press, 1995), chap. 8.

41   This phrase first referred to the original impact of Karl Barth's work.

42 Jürgen Moltmann, *Theology of Hope: On the Grounds and the Implications of a Christian Eschatology*, trans. James W. Leitch (Minneapolis: Fortress, 1993), 153.

43 Moltmann, *Theology of Hope*, 153.

44 Moltmann, *Theology of Hope*, 246.

45 Moltmann, *Theology of Hope*, 205.

46 Wright, *Resurrection*, chap. 4.

47 For an impressive and fairly concise account of the breadth of this re-theologizing on the part of the first Christians, see Wright, *New Testament*, chaps. 13–15.

48 John Calvin, *Calvin: Institutes of the Christian Religion*, trans. Ford Lewis Battles, ed. John T. McNeill, The Library of Christian Classics, vol. 20 (Philadelphia: Westminster, 1960), 1.7.4.

49 Grenz, *Theology*, 325.

50 George M. Marsden, *Fundamentalism and American Culture*, 117.

51 Again, for helpful background, see Kelly, Walker, and Olson.

52 Cited in Walker, *History*, 170.

53 Cited in Kelly, *Early Christian Doctrines*, 333.

54 Cited in McGrath, *Christian Theology Reader*, 280.

55 Cited in Walker, *History*, 182.

56 Both Olson and Justo González express this lamentation even while affirming the value of the results. Olson, *Story of Christian Theology*, 248; Justo González, *A History of Christian Thought*, vol. 2, *From Augustine to the Eve of the Reformation*, rev. ed. (Nashville: Abingdon, 1987), 91.

57 One might think here of Dan Kimball, *They Like Jesus but Not the Church: Insights from Emerging Generations* (Grand Rapids: Zondervan, 2007), although he himself does emphasize an important place for theology.

58 A famous example is Rudolf Bultmann, "New Testament and Mythology," in *Kerygma and Myth*, ed. Hans Werner Bartsch, trans. Reginald H. Fuller (New York: Harper, 1961), 41.

59 Paul Tillich, *The Courage to Be* (New Haven: Yale University Press, 1952).

60 For example, see Gustavo Gutierrez, *A Theology of Liberation* (Maryknoll, N.Y.: Orbis, 1973).

61 See James H. Cone, *God of the Oppressed*, 2nd ed. (Maryknoll, N.Y.: Orbis, 1997); James H. Evans Jr., *We Have Been Believers* (Minneapolis: Fortress, 1992); Miguel A. De la Torre, *Reading the Bible from the Margins* (Maryknoll, N.Y.: Orbis, 2002), 121–23.

62 This language was suggested by Marnie C. Sellers, "The Deaf Christ: A Liberation Christology for the Deaf World" (master's thesis in religion, Hardin-Simmons University, 2007), 83.

63 See Rosemary Radford Ruether, *Sexism and God-Talk: Toward a Feminist Theology* (Boston: Beacon, 1983), chap. 5; Johnson, *She Who Is*, chap. 8; Natalie K. Watson, *Feminist Theology* (Grand Rapids: Eerdmans, 2003), 33–36; Kwok Pui-lan, *Postcolonial Imagination and Feminist Theology* (Louisville: Westminster John Knox, 2005), chap. 7; De la Torre, *Reading the Bible*, 123–30.

64 From C. S. Lewis, *The Lion, the Witch, and the Wardrobe* (New York: Collier, 1970), 171–72, cited in Eleanor McLaughlin, "Christology in Dialogue with Feminist Ideology—Bodies and Boundaries" in *Christology in Dialogue*, ed. Robert F. Berkey and Sarah A. Edwards (Cleveland: Pilgrim, 1993), 308. Thanks to Marnie Sellers for these references. She applies them creatively in a further way to the idea of a deaf Christ in Sellers, "Deaf Christ."

65 McLaughlin, "Christology in Dialogue."

CHAPTER 8

1 As George Beasley-Murray points out, "We should note that the parable of the Prodigal Son is indeed a parable of the kingdom. . . . If the church had grasped this insight early on, it might have avoided the one-sided view of eschatology that it has clung to through the centuries. Traditionally it has associated the coming of the kingdom of God above all with judgment, and with connotations of condemnation at that. Yet here in the parable of the Prodigal Son Jesus presents the sovereignty of God in terms of a love that delights in restoring the wayward to the fellowship of love" (G. R. Beasley-Murray, *Jesus and the Kingdom of God* [Grand Rapids: Eerdmans, 1986], 114).

2 Miroslav Volf, *Exclusion and Embrace: A Theological Exploration of Identity, Otherness, and Reconciliation* (Nashville: Abingdon, 1996).

3 In writing a fascinating book on the church, Volf happened to provide one of the first English studies of the theology of the current Pope Benedict XVI long before he became pope. He also dealt with the Orthodox views of John Zizoulas and related them to the views of the first Baptist, John Smyth, with whom he identified most closely. See Miroslav Volf, *After Our Likeness: The Church as the Image of the Trinity*, Sacra Doctrina: Christian Theology for a Postmodern Age, ed. Alan G. Padgett (Grand Rapids: Eerdmans, 1998).

4   Volf, *Exclusion and Embrace*, 9.

5   Jacques Derrida, *On Cosmopolitanism and Forgiveness*, trans. Mark Dooley and Michael Hughes, Thinking in Action (London: Routledge, 2001), 32. There is much truth in what Derrida says: "Forgiveness is not, it *should* not be, normal, normative, normalising. It *should* remain exceptional and extraordinary, in the face of the impossible: as if it interrupted the ordinary course of historical temporality." On the other hand, it is expected to be normal among Christians!

6   The five fundamentals are (1) the inerrancy of Scripture, (2) the virgin birth of Christ, (3) his substitutionary atonement, (4) his bodily resurrection, and (5) dispensational premillennialism. See Marsden, *Fundamentalism and American Culture*, 132, 180; Roger E. Olson, *The Story of Christian Theology: Twenty Centuries of Tradition and Reform* (Downers Grove, Ill.: InterVarsity, 1999), 561-69.

7   Anselm, *Cur Deus Homo?* (Why the God-man?)

8   See Gustaf Aulén, *Christus Victor*, trans. A. G. Hebert (New York: Macmillan, 1969).

9   For example, see Irenaeus, *Against Heresies*, 5.1.1.

10   Irenaeus, *Against Heresies*, 3.8.1.

11   Joel B. Green especially emphasizes this point in his "Kaleidoscopic View," in *The Nature of the Atonement*, ed. James K. Beilby and Paul R. Eddy (Downers Grove, Ill.: InterVarsity, 2006), chap. 4.

12   Augustine, cited in Alister E. McGrath, ed., *The Christian Theology Reader*, 3rd ed. (Cambridge: Blackwell, 2007), 353.

13   Justo González, *Christian Thought Revisited: Three Types of Theology* (Nashville: Abingdon, 1989), chaps. 1, 3, 9.

14   Saint Gregory Nazianzen, "Epistle 101," trans. Charles Gordon Browne and James Edward Swallow, in the "Select Letters" section of *Cyril of Jerusalem, Gregory Nazianzen*, A Select Library of the Nicene and Post-Nicene Fathers of the Christian Church 7, ed. Philip Schaff and Henry Wace (Grand Rapids: Eerdmans, 1971), 439–43.

15   See Stephen Finlan and Vladimir Kharlamov, eds., *Theosis: Deification in Christian Theology*, Princeton Theological Monograph Series (Eugene, Oreg.: Pickwick, 2006); Timothy Ware, *The Orthodox Church*, rev. ed. (London: Penguin, 1997), 231–38.

16   See Dale Moody, *The Word of Truth* (Grand Rapids: Eerdmans, 1981), 329–31; Stanley J. Grenz, *Theology for the Community of God*, 2nd ed. (Grand Rapids: Eerdmans, 1994), 346–47.

17 See Michael Kirwan, *Discovering Girard* (Cambridge, Mass.: Cowley, 2005); Graham B. Walker Jr., "Noah and the Season of Violence: Theological Reflections on Genesis 6:5–9:17 and the Work of René Girard," *Review and Expositor* 103, no. 2 (2006): 371–90.

18 René Girard, "Are the Gospels Mythical?" *First Things*, 20 April 2006, accessed 31 December 2007, http://www.firstthings.com/article. php3?id_article=3856.

19 Cited in Serene Jones and Paul Lakeland, eds., *Constructive Theology: A Contemporary Approach to Classical Themes* (Minneapolis: Fortress, 2005), 171.

20 Stephen Oates, *Let the Trumpet Sound: The Life of Martin Luther King Jr.* (New York: Harper & Row, 1982), 89–90.

21 This language is inspired by Karl Barth's extension of the image of the prodigal son, perhaps combining it with the parables of the lost sheep and lost coin—where the father does not just wait but goes into the far country in the form of his son. Barth sees this as beginning with God's election of Israel. See Karl Barth, *Church Dogmatics*, ed. G. W. Bromiley and T. F. Torrance, vol. 4.1, *The Doctrine of Reconciliation*, trans. G. W. Bromiley (Edinburgh: T&T Clark, 1956), 157–210.

22 In the contemporary scene, Paul Fiddes has attempted to bring these objective and subjective views together with an emphasis on Abelard's view. See his *Past Event and Present Salvation: The Christian Idea of Atonement* (Louisville: Westminster John Knox, 1989).

23 González, *Christian Thought Revisited*, 23–28, 121–22.

24 D. M. Baillie, *God Was in Christ: An Essay on Incarnation and Atonement* (New York: Charles Scribner's Sons, 1948), 171–79.

25 Donald B. Kraybill, "Why the Amish Forgive: Tales of Redemption at Nickel Mines," *EMUNews*, 11 October 2006, accessed 18 June 2007, http://www.emu.edu/news/index.php/1246.

26 Paul S. Fiddes, *Participating in God: A Pastoral Doctrine of the Trinity* (Louisville: Westminster John Knox, 2000), 192.

27 One cannot miss, however, Karl Barth's massive treatment (five books) of soteriology in terms of reconciliation.

28 Sometimes medieval Roman Catholicism, with its emphasis on penance and becoming worthy of salvation in this life and in purgatory, is charged with this appellation. Roger Olson, an Arminian, charges one of the heroes of revivalism, Charles Finney in the nineteenth century, with semi-Pelagianism for believing that one can orchestrate, plan, and produce revivals. See Roger E. Olson, *The Mosaic of*

Christian Belief: Twenty Centuries of Unity and Diversity (Downers Grove, Ill.: InterVarsity, 2002), 215, 274. Both of these are arguable, depending especially on how much of the human effort is seen as being based on God's grace itself, namely, on how "Arminian" is opposed to "Pelagian." Michael Robinson has a helpful discussion in *The Storms of Providence*, 71–77. What is unclear is whether this typical Catholic view is clearly a denial of a Reformed understanding of grace. Zachary Hayes argues that there were abuses before the Reformation, but the authentic Catholic view is legitimately based on justification by faith. See Zachary J. Hayes, "The Purgatorial View," in *Four Views on Hell*, ed. William Crockett, Counterpoints (Grand Rapids: Zondervan, 1996), 113–17. See also the discussion of Arminianism below.

29 For a concise discussion of prevenient grace and its Arminian background in the context of Calvinist debates, see Olson, *Story of Christian Theology*, 460–72.

30 Of course, the context is Christ trying to get those who are already believers to let him in. While strictly speaking, the passage is not about new converts, it seems that the dynamic involved should easily apply.

31 Thomas Aquinas, *Summa Theologica*, 2a2ae.2.1; 2a2ae.4.2. Aquinas thought, however, that faith as assent was completed or formed by love (2A2ae4.3). Roger Olson says of Charles Hodge, of the nineteenth century influential Princeton theology (Reformed), that Hodge's criticism of Friedrich Schleiermacher "drove him to treat Christianity primarily as assent to a system of supernaturally revealed truths virtually devoid of any ambiguity or need of correction." As Olson comments on the way this attitude moved into American Fundamentalism: "Whereas the motto of many pietists had become 'If your heart is warm, give me your hand,' fundamentalists would say, 'If your beliefs are correct, give me your hand'" (*Story of Christian Theology*, 567).

32 See the article on faith (s.vv. *pisteuo, pistis,* and so forth) by Rudolf Bultmann in *Theological Dictionary of the New Testament*, ed. Gerhard Friedrich, trans. Geoffrey W. Bromiley (Grand Rapids: Eerdmanns, 1968), 6:174–228. See also Daniel J. Treier, "Faith," in *Dictionary for Theological Interpretation of the Bible*, ed. Kevin J. Vanhoozer (Grand Rapids: Baker Academic, 2005), 226–28.

33 Grenz, *Theology*, 442.

34 See N. T. Wright, *Paul: In Fresh Perspective* (Minneapolis: Fortress, 2005), 57, 120–22, 147.

35 See Thomas Aquinas, *Summa Theologica*, 2a2ae, q. 2, art. 1. The great Lutheran theologian Melanchthon especially developed this approach. For a critique, see Donald G. Bloesch, *God, Authority*, Essentials of Evangelical Theology 1 (San Francisco: HarperSanFrancisco, 1982), 237.

36 Augustine, *The Confessions*, trans. Edward Bouverie Pusey, in *Augustine*, ed. Robert Maynard Hutchins, Great Books of the Western World 18 (Chicago: Encyclopedia Britannica, 1952), 1.1.

37 Augustine, "On the Predestination of the Saints," chap. 23; Calvin, *Institutes*, The Library of Christian Classics 21, 4.16.

38 Ben Witherington III makes this important point in *The Paul Quest: The Renewed Search for the Jew of Tarsus* (Downers Grove, Ill.: InterVarsity, 2001), 277.

39 Jürgen Moltmann, *The Church in the Power of the Spirit: A Contribution to Messianic Ecclesiology*, trans. Margret Kohl (New York: Harper & Row, 1977); Molly T. Marshall, *Joining the Dance: A Theology of the Spirit* (Valley Forge, Pa.: Judson, 2003).

40 See Allan Anderson, *An Introduction to Pentecostalism: Global Charismatic Christianity* (Cambridge: Cambridge University Press, 2004); *The Work of the Spirit: Pneumatology and Pentecostalism*, ed. Michael Welker (Grand Rapids: Eerdmans, 2006); Grenz, *Theology*, 415–22.

41 For a classic expression, see Ernest S. Williams, *Systematic Theology* (Springfield, Mo.: Gospel Publishing House, 1953), vol. 3, chap. 7.

42 I am devoting extended attention to this movement, which is usually not covered at all by traditional theologies. One reason for this attention is because it is such an influential part of the church and apparently will become even more so over the next century. Another is because, for something so pervasive, there is a great deal of ignorance on both sides, I have noticed, compared to debates over Calvinism and Arminianism, over baptism, and even over Open Theism.

43 See James Wm. McClendon Jr., *Doctrine: Systematic Theology* (Nashville: Abingdon, 1994), 431–39, for an appreciative and careful analysis of the Pentecostal phenomenon from a Baptist who, however, includes Pentecostals in his broad range of "baptists." Interestingly, he sees Pentecostalism especially in terms of a providential sign of "giving a voice to the voiceless," to those who are marginalized.

44 Gordon D. Fee, a Pentecostal exegete himself, sees this passage as referring to conversion in *God's Empowering Presence: The Holy Spirit in the Letters of Paul* (Peabody, Mass.: Hendrickson, 1994), 180–81.

45   Paul is probably referring here to water baptism, but the context remains salvation. Fee, *God's Empowering Presence*, 704–5.

46   Frank Macchia affirms the baptism in the Holy Spirit as an aspect of Pentecostal theology, but sees it as initiating the Christian life and then continuing, saying of it what we have said of salvation, *"We have been baptized in the Spirit, we are being baptized in the Spirit, and we will be baptized in the Spirit"* (*Baptized in the Spirit: A Global Pentecostal Theology* [Grand Rapids: Zondervan, 2006], 154). I prefer to identify, as Paul seems to do, the baptism of the Holy Spirit with conversion and the filling of the Holy Spirit with ongoing participation in the life of the Spirit. In the end, differences may be largely due to semantics. Williams, who affirms a later baptism in the Holy Spirit, can also refer to "one baptism, many fillings," which is similar to my terminology. See Williams, *Systematic Theology*, 40.

47   See Grenz, *Theology*, 419–22.

48   The major examples, besides the ones already mentioned are Cornelius, representing the Gentile world (chap. 10) and followers of John the Baptist, which may well have been a larger issue then that it appears now (chap. 19). Pentecostals sometimes refer to Paul, who was filled with the Holy Spirit (Acts 9:17), as a fifth example in Acts of what they see as a pattern where everyone receives the Holy Spirit. It is implied that Paul spoke in tongues based on 1 Cor. 14:18. For example, see Williams, *Systematic Theology*, 48–49. Of course, it does not mention tongues in the case of the Samaritans or of Paul in Acts, although it may be implied. In the case of Paul, they apparently would be tied to conversion.

49   So says Fee, *God's Empowering Presence*, 235. The phraseology of "a private prayer language," referring to speaking in tongues in one's private prayer has become popular in recent years, especially among charismatics who do not push for public tongue speaking in worship. It became prominent in Southern Baptist life when their foreign mission board forbade appointing any new missionary who had a private prayer language—even though the head of the mission board did. Then there was a flap within the board of the largest Southern Baptist seminary, who moved to expel a member who had a private prayer language. The member was one of the few African-Americans on the boards, and they ended up not expelling him at that time.

50   Fee, *God's Empowering Presence*, 218.

51 Gerald Hawthorne indicates that Paul is likely responding to Jewish and possibly Gnostics who claimed to be able to reach perfection. See Gerald F. Hawthorne, *Philippians*, Word Biblical Commentary, ed. Bruce M. Metzger, vol. 43 (Nashville: Thomas Nelson, 1983), 150–51. Paul may be responding to a misinterpretation of his teaching about grace (155). In any case, he is probably using "a touch of reproachful, though loving, almost whimsical, irony" (156).

52 Plato, *Apology*, in *The Dialogues of Plato*, trans. Benjamin Jowett, Great Books of the Western World 7 (Chicago: Encyclopedia Britannica, 1952), 200–42.

53 On the complexities of this issue in Wesley himself, see Olson, *Story of Christian Theology*, 513–16. For Wesley and the later tradition, see Kenneth Cracknell and Susan J. White, *An Introduction to World Methodism* (Cambridge: Cambridge University Press, 2005), chap. 7.

54 See William L. Hendricks, *The Letters of John* (Nashville: Broadman, 1970), 83; Edward A. McDowell, "1-2-3 John," in *The Broadman Bible Commentary* (Nashville: Broadman, 1972), 210; Stephen S. Smalley, *1, 2, 3 John*, ed. David A. Hubbard and Glenn W. Barker, Word Biblical Commentary 51 (Waco, Tex.: Word, 1984), 158–65. Smalley gives a full treatment of alternatives and places the difference more in terms of the different situations. In chap. 1, John is addressing gnostics. In chap. 3, he is addressing "orthodox adherents of John's congregation" (165).

55 These words are often thought to be addressed against "pre-Gnostics" who thought that they were above sin. See McDowell, "1-2-3 John," 198.

56 Robert J. Trotter, "The Mystery of Mastery," *Psychology Today* (July 1986), 38.

57 Michael Polanyi, *Personal Knowledge: Towards a Post-Critical Philosophy*, 2nd ed. (Chicago: University of Chicago Press, 1962), 59, 195.

58 For the emphasis on practices and training throughout, see Dallas Willard, *The Divine Conspiracy: Rediscovering Our Hidden Life in God* (San Francisco: HarperSanFrancisco, 1998). For the contrast between trying and training, see Dallas Willard, *How Does the Disciple Live?* 2007, accessed 26 December 2007, http://www.dwillard.org/articles/artview.asp?artID=103. Thanks to Matt McGowan for pointing me to this contrast in Willard.

59   See Dallas M. Roark, *Dietrich Bonhoeffer*, Makers of the Modern Theological Mind (Waco, Tex.: Word, 1972). I give an account of the incarnational way that Bonhoeffer developed his acuity in Dan R. Stiver, "Felicity and Fusion: Speech Act Theory and Hermeneutical Philosophy," in *Transcending Boundaries in Philosophy and Theology: Reason, Meaning, and Experience*, ed. Kevin J. Vanhoozer and Martin Warner (Burlington, Vt.: Ashgate, 2007).

60   Martin Luther King Jr., *Why We Can't Wait* (New York: Harper & Row, 1963).

61   See Ruth Haley Barton, *Sacred Rhythms: Arranging Our Lives for Spiritual Transformation* (Downers Grove, Ill.: InterVarsity, 2006), chap. 3. I have been greatly aided in understanding *lectio divina* by participating in a retreat led by Barton and also by supervising D.Min. research by Josh Stowe on teaching *lectio divina* to a rural west Texas Baptist church.

62   Kevin J. Vanhoozer, *The Drama of Doctrine: A Canonical-Linguistic Approach to Christian Theology* (Louisville: Westminster John Knox, 2005).

63   Augustine, *Homilies on the First Epistle of John*, in *St. Augustin: Homilies on the Gospel of John, Homilies on the First Epistle of John, Soliloquies*, ed. Philip Schaff, A Select Library of the Nicene and Post-Nicene Fathers of the Christian Church 7, 1st series (Grand Rapids, Eerdmans, 1956), chap. 8.

64   McClendon, *Doctrine*, 144. McClendon is connecting discernment with Wesley's idea of sanctification, where some would have better judgment. For related work on the nature of theological reasoning that places great emphasis on discernment as an aspect of the rationality of Christianity, see Nancey C. Murphy, *Theology in the Age of Scientific Reasoning*, Cornell Studies in the Philosophy of Religion (Ithaca: Cornell University Press, 1990), chap. 5. She especially mentions Ignatius of Loyola, Jonathan Edwards, the Anabaptists, the Quakers, and the contemporary Charismatic renewal.

65   Augustine, *Confessions*, 8.29. See also Nicholas Wolterstorff, *Divine Discourse: Philosophical Reflections on the Claim That God Speaks* (Cambridge: Cambridge University Press, 1995), chap. 1. Wolterstorff makes much of this incident as a paradigm of divine discourse.

66   This was the analogy of Phil Christopher, pastor of First Baptist Church, Abilene, Texas, in the Sunday morning sermon, 13 May 2007.

67 Vanhoozer, *Drama of Doctrine*, 339–44.

68 These thoughts, too, were inspired by the sermon of Phil Christopher, noted above.

69 Fiddes, *Participating in God*, 192.

70 A strong trend in recent years is toward offering forgiveness without regard to repentance on the part of the offender. See L. Gregory Jones, *Embodying Forgiveness: A Theological Analysis* (Grand Rapids: Eerdmans, 1995); Paul Ricoeur, *Memory, History, Forgetting*, trans. Kathleen Blamey and David Pellauer (Chicago: University of Chicago Press, 2004), 412–506. This follows Jesus' example on the cross: "Father, forgive them for they know not what they do" (Luke 23:24) and has much to commend it. The problem is that it seems not to hold the offender accountable and can lead toward abuses. Those who advocate this approach usually make a strong distinction between forgiveness and punishment, calling for the latter even if one offers the former. See Jones, *Embodying Forgiveness*, 269–70, n. 46. The norm or prototypical case, however, is repentance followed by forgiveness, which leads someone like Richard Swinburne to insist that this must always be the case. See Richard Swinburne, *Responsibility and Atonement* (New York: Clarendon, 1989). Forgiveness without repentance can lead to injustice: forgiveness with repentance allows for the full meaning of forgiveness to include waiving many of the consequences. One of the passages where Jesus says that one should forgive in an unlimited way, seventy times seven, is paired with repentance (Luke 17:3-4). The quintessential case of forgiveness, its role in salvation, involves repentance. Much can be said for this being the typical pattern. Perhaps it is helpful to distinguish between typical and atypical cases. The tendency among theologians is to collapse all cases into one when cases differ. The philosopher Ludwig Wittgenstein saw this as a common "essentialist fallacy." We do not realize that commonalities are sometimes more a matter of "family resemblance" than of everyone having the same features. See Ludwig Wittgenstein, *Philosophical Investigations*, trans. G. E. M. Anscombe, 3rd ed. (New York: Macmillan, 1958), par. 124. One can recognize that the norm is love, followed by repentance, followed by forgiveness—and also recognize unusual situations. Situations where actual reconciliation is not possible are different. One can think of Jesus' dying on the cross, when he was not going to have a chance, humanly, to be reconciled with his captors. Sometimes children in later years

forgive parents who have died. One might choose to forgive someone whom one will likely never meet again and someone who will likely never hurt one again. The need for great spiritual wisdom is again apparent.

71 Fiddes, *Participating in God*, 198.

72 Jones, *Embodying Forgiveness*, 12.

CHAPTER 9

1 The Fall 2003 issue of the *Review and Expositor* was devoted to the question of whether Baptists, who arose and multiplied in the context of modernity, could survive postmodernity.

2 James Wm. McClendon Jr., *Ethics: Systematic Theology* (Nashville: Abingdon Press, 1986); James Wm. McClendon Jr., *Doctrine: Systematic Theology* (Nashville: Abingdon Press, 1994).

3 See H. Leon McBeth, *The Baptist Heritage: Four Centuries of Baptist Witness* (Nashville: B&H Publishing, 1987), 447–61.

4 McBeth, *Baptist Heritage*, 124–36.

5 See McBeth, *Baptist Heritage*, 21–39; Bill J. Leonard, *Baptist Ways: A History* (Valley Forge, Pa.: Judson, 2003), 23–27.

6 Cited in McBeth, *Baptist Heritage*, 34.

7 Thomas Helwys, *A Short Declaration of the Mystery of Iniquity* (Macon, Ga.: Mercer University Press, 1998); Leonard, *Baptist Ways*, 26.

8 For the significance of this point in both Helwys and Murton, see William H. Brackney, *The Baptists* (Westport, Conn.: Praeger, 1994), 5.

9 See Brackney, *Baptists*, 97-100.

10 Langdon Gilkey, *Creationism on Trial: Evolution and God at Little Rock* (Minneapolis: Winston, 1985), 11.

11 Barry A. Harvey, *Another City* (Harrisburg, Pa.: Trinity Press International, 1999).

12 Georges Florovsky, cited in Harvey, *Another City*, 22.

13 Harvey, *Another City*, 137.

14 Paul Tillich, *Systematic Theology* (Chicago: University of Chicago Press, 1951), 1:83–86.

15 Cf. Augustine, *City of God*, 22.30.

16 See Hans Küng, *The Church*, trans. Edward Quinn (Garden City, N.Y.: Image, 1976), 403–11.

17 Alan Cooperman, "Evangelical Leader Returns to Catholicism," *washingtonpost.com* 12 May 2007, accessed 12 May 2007, http://

www.washingtonpost.com/wp-dyn/content/article/2007/05/11/AR2007051101929. html?nav=hcmodule.

18 Findley Edge, a pioneer in Christian education, used to distinguish between seeing the church as a hotel or as a hospital. This recollection is based on a sermon by Findley Edge at Saint Matthews Baptist Church in Louisville, Kentucky.

19 An impressive example of this in the Roman Catholic Church is Hans Küng, who was a major young theologian behind Vatican II's reforms but whose questioning of the infallibility of the pope later led to removal of his teaching license in a move spearheaded by the current Pope Benedict XVI. Küng has refused, however, to leave the Catholic Church and has continued to argue for reform, in the process becoming a strong voice far beyond Catholicism. See especially his *My Struggle for Freedom: Memoirs*, trans. John Bowden (Grand Rapids: Eerdmans, 2003).

20 Miroslav Volf points out how the current Pope Benedict XVI and the prominent Eastern Orthodox theologian John Zizioulas both emphasize the centrality and sufficiency of the local church in Volf's *Exclusion and Embrace: A Theological Exploration of Identity, Otherness, and Reconciliation* (Nashville: Abingdon, 1996), 43, 103. In going over the theology of the Pope and Zizioulas, my Baptist students thought that they sounded just like them in their emphasis on the local church—at first.

21 Both Irenaeus and Tertullian, in dealing with what they perceived to be gnostic heresies, turned to apostolic teaching and succession to protect the church. See Alister E. McGrath, ed., *The Christian Theology Reader*, 3rd ed. (Cambridge: Blackwell, 2007), 79, 83.

22 Cited in McGrath, *Christian Theology Reader*, 90. Ironically, Vincent was concerned about Augustine's teaching of double predestination as not fitting.

23 See, for example, Eddie Gibbs, *ChurchNext: Quantum Changes in How We Do Ministry* (Downers Grove, Ill.: InterVarsity, 2000); Reggie McNeal, *The Present Future: Six Tough Questions for the Church* (San Francisco: Jossey-Bass, 2003); Milfred Minatrea, *Shaped by God's Heart: The Passion and Practices of Missional Churches* (San Francisco: Jossey-Bass, 2004). Jürgen Moltmann wrote in 1977 (originally in German in 1975), "The mission of Christ creates its own church. Mission does not come from the church; it is from mission and in the light of mission that the church has to be understood" (*The Church*

in the Power of the Spirit: A Contribution to Messianic Ecclesiology, trans. Margaret Kohl [New York: Harper & Row, 1977], 10).

24   Craig Van Gelder, "From Corporate Church to Missional Church: The Challenge Facing Congregations Today," Review and Expositor 101 (2004): 437.

25   Moltmann, The Church in the Power of the Spirit.

26   Findley Edge, The Greening of the Church (Waco, Tex.: Word, 1972); Elton Trueblood, The Incendiary Fellowship (New York: Harper & Row, 1967).

27   Jimmy Long, Emerging Hope: A Strategy for Reaching Postmodern Generations (Downers Grove, Ill.: InterVarsity, 2004), 12.

28   Ed Stetzer and David Putman, Breaking the Missional Code: Your Church Can Become a Missionary in Your Community (Nashville: B & H Publishing, 2006), 31–33.

29   Dan Kimball, The Emerging Church (Grand Rapids: Zondervan, 2003), 91.

30   Darrell Guder, ed., The Missional Church: A Vision for the Sending of the Church in North America (Grand Rapids: Eerdmans, 1998).

31   Gibbs, ChurchNext, 56.

32   Dallas Willard similarly laments the gap between "the Gospel on the right" that sees "atonement as the whole story" and the "Gospel on the left" that sees "the Gospel as entirely social" (Dallas Willard, The Divine Conspiracy: Rediscovering Our Hidden Life in God [San Francisco: HarperSanFrancisco, 1998], 42–54).

33   Robert P. Sellers, "A Baptist View of Missions for Postmodernity," Review and Expositor 100 (2003): 662–67. This article is an excellent representation of the shift from a modern to a postmodern paradigm in missions. See also Robert P. Sellers, "Is Mission Possible in a Postmodern World?" Review and Expositor 101 (2004): 389–424.

34   For example, see Brian D. McLaren, More Ready Than You Realize: Evangelism as Dance in the Postmodern Matrix (Grand Rapids: Zondervan, 2002). My colleague Bill Tillman has used Thomas Cahill, How the Irish Saved Civilization (New York: Anchor, 1996) in evangelism courses to emphasize a holistic way of evangelism. This does not mean, of course, using friendship as an ulterior motive to reach someone, but then dropping them if little interest is shown.

35   E. Glenn Hinson, Spiritual Preparation for Christian Leadership (Nashville: Upper Room, 1999), 67.

36   Dan Kimball observes that among younger Christians, in contrast to those who like Seeker churches, there is a desire for the mystery

and the tradition of liturgy, architecture, and holistic worship. See Kimball, *Emerging Church*, chaps. 2, 12.

37 We might note here again Roger Olson's criticism, which is a bit harsh but a salutary reminder, of the revivalism of Charles Finney who thought that he could plan, program, and deliver revivals in Roger E. Olson, *The Mosaic of Christian Belief: Twenty Centuries of Unity and Diversity* (Downers Grove, Ill.: InterVarsity, 2002), 215, 274.

38 While there is much to admire about the Amish, it is apparent that they have baptized an entire culture and style of the early 1700s and devoted themselves to changing it as little as possible. See Donald B. Kraybill, *The Riddle of Amish Culture*, rev. ed., Center Books in Anabaptist Studies (Baltimore: Johns Hopkins University Press, 2001), chaps. 1–3.

39 Søren Kierkegaard, *Purity of Heart Is to Will One Thing: Spiritual Preparation for the Office of Confession*, trans. Douglas V. Steere (New York: Harper Torchbooks, 1956), 180–81.

40 For example, our church, a downtown First Baptist church where the population has moved to the outskirts, has spent several years figuring out whether to go from one service on Sunday morning to two (one), what kind of music (blended), how to respond to a denominational split (go with the smaller, split-off group), who to do missions with after decades of working with one group (work with multiple groups), and how to reach postmodern young adults (have no answer yet). Virtually every church I know of feels like they are going through major transitions. This sense of change is captured in the subtitle of Lyle Schaller's book, *The New Reformation: Tomorrow Arrived Yesterday* (Nashville: Abingdon, 1995).

41 G. Hugh Wamble, *The Shape of Faith* (Nashville: Broadman, 1962).

42 Wamble, *Shape of Faith*, chap. 7.

43 Wamble, *Shape of Faith*, 75.

44 Robert D. Putnam, *Bowling Alone: The Collapse and Revival of American Community*, rev. ed. (New York: Simon & Schuster, 2001); Robert E. Webber, *The Younger Evangelicals: Facing the Challenges of the New World* (Grand Rapids: Baker, 2002), chap. 7; Robert Wuthnow, *Sharing the Journey: Support Groups and America's New Quest for Community* (New York: Free Press, 1996); Robert Wuthnow, ed., *I Come Away Stronger: How Small Groups Are Shaping American Religion* (Grand Rapids: Eerdmans, 2001); Robert Wuthnow, *Loose Connections: Joining Together in America's Fragmented Communities* (Cambridge, Mass.: Harvard University Press, 2002).

45 Gushee nuances the issue carefully but concludes with an emphasis on the formative power of the church and its families. See David P. Gushee, *The Righteous Gentiles of the Holocaust: A Christian Interpretation* (Minneapolis: Fortress, 1994).

46 Donald B. Kraybill, "Why the Amish Forgive: Tales of Redemption at Nickel Mines," in *EMUNews*, 11 October 2006, accessed 18 June 2007, http://www.emu.edu/news/index.php/1246.

47 David S. Cunningham, *These Three Are One: The Practice of Trinitarian Theology* (Oxford: Blackwell, 1998), 140.

48 N. T. Wright emphasizes this: "We know far less about the history of the church from AD 30-135 than we do about second-temple Judaism. This stark fact is not, I think, faced as often as it should be. There is no equivalent of Josephus for the early church" (*The New Testament and the People of God*, Christian Origins and the Question of God 1 [Minneapolis: Fortress, 1992], 341).

49 See Williston Walker et al., *A History of the Christian Church*, 4th ed. (New York: Charles Scribner's Sons, 1985), chap. 13; G. Hugh Wamble, "Historic Practices Regarding Children," in *Children and Conversion*, ed. Clifford Ingle (Nashville: Broadman, 1970), 71–83.

50 "Catholic Church Buries Limbo after Centuries," *ReligionNewsBlog*, 20 April 2007, accessed 26 December 2007, http://www.religionnews-blog.com/18025/limbo.

51 Calvin, *Institutes*, The Library of Christian Classics 21, 4.16.

52 G. Temp Sparkman, *The Salvation and Nurture of the Child of God* (Valley Forge, Pa.: Judson, 1983), 22.

53 Several good books that early explored these issues among Baptists as they were being manifested in the late twentieth century are Clifford Ingle, ed., *Children and Conversion* (Nashville: Broadman, 1970); William L. Hendricks, *A Theology for Children* (Nashville: Broadman, 1980); Sparkman, *Salvation and Nurture*.

54 Glen H. Stassen, "Anabaptist Influence in the Origin of the Particular Baptists," *The Mennonite Quarterly Review* 36 (1962): 322–48.

55 My mother was a good example of this: baptized into a Christian church by immersion as a believer, she had to be rebaptized in my home Baptist church, something which never did sit well with her.

56 Walker, *History*, chap. 14.

57 See Roger E. Olson, *The Story of Christian Theology: Twenty Centuries of Tradition and Reform* (Downers Grove, Ill.: InterVarsity, 1999), 394–96, 404–8, 412–13; Walker, *History*, 445–46.

58 A notorious example is John Wesley, after a broken relationship, refusing to serve Communion to the woman and the man whom she had married. The bitter aftermath led to his hasty return to England from Georgia. See Kenneth Cracknell and Susan J. White, *An Introduction to World Methodism* (Cambridge: Cambridge University Press, 2005), 11.

59 Cyprian, "The Epistles of Cyprian," in *Fathers of the Third Century*, The Ante-Nicene Fathers 5, ed. Alexander Roberts and James Donaldson (Grand Rapids: Eerdmans, 1951), par. 6.

60 Cyprian, "Epistles," 39.5. Oxford ed., 43.5.

61 See Markus Barth, *Ephesians: Translation and Commentary on Chapters 4-6*, Anchor Bible, vol. 34a (Garden City, N.Y.: Doubleday, 1974), 478–84.

62 "Violated Trust: Special Report," *Baptist Standard*, 11 June 2007, 8–13.

63 As in the words of Richard J. Foster, *Money, Sex, and Power*, rev. ed. (London: Hodder & Stoughton Religious, 1999).

64 In the words of Markus Barth, "In summary, the task of the special ministers mentioned in Eph. 4:11 is . . . not above but below the great number of saints who are not adorned by resounding titles" (*Ephesians*, 481).

65 McClendon, *Doctrine*, 369.

66 Markus Barth even suggests that baptism earlier played the role of ordination (or rather, ordination took its cue from baptism), which meant that all were called to ministry. See Barth, *Ephesians*, 481–82. For a similar view, see McClendon, *Doctrine*, 369.

67 For wider discussion, see Stanley J. Grenz and Denise Muir Kjesbo, *Women in the Church* (Downers Grove, Ill.: InterVarsity, 1995), chaps. 6–7; James R. Beck and Craig L. Blomberg, eds., *Two Views on Women in Ministry*, Counterpoints, ed. Stanley N. Gundry (Grand Rapids: Zondervan, 2001). See also the Winter 1986 issue of the *Review and Expositor*, vol. 83, no. 1, on women in ministry, which deals with various facets of this issue.

CHAPTER 10

1 Robert G. Clouse, Robert N. Hosack, and Richard Pierard, *The New Millenium Manual: A Once and Future Guide* (Grand Rapids: Baker, 1999), 116; Richard Kyle, *The Last Days Are Here Again* (Grand Rapids: Baker, 1998), 90.

2   "Millerites," *Ohio History Central: An Online Encyclopedia of Ohio History*, 2005, accessed 17 January 2007, http://www.ohiohistorycentral.org/entry.php?rec=607.

3   Clouse, Hosack, and Pierard, *New Millennium Manual*, 116–17.

4   This account is based largely on the account by Stephen Oates, *Let the Trumpet Sound: The Life of Martin Luther King Jr.* (New York: Harper & Row, 1982), 470–74.

5   Karl Marx, *Critique of Hegel's "Philosophy of Right,"* trans. Annette Jolin and Joseph O'Malley, ed. Joseph O'Malley (Cambridge: Cambridge University Press, 1970), introduction, 131.

6   See John J. Ansbro, *Martin Luther King Jr.: The Making of a Mind* (Maryknoll, N.Y.: Orbis, 1982), 187–98. The section is titled "The Beloved Community: The Ultimate Norm and Goal."

7   To refer to the title of Stanley Hauerwas, *The Peaceable Kingdom*, 2nd rev. ed. (London: SCM Press, 2003).

8   The former is quoted in Claborne Carson, ed., *The Autobiography of Martin Luther King Jr.* (New York: Warner, 1998), chap. 18. The latter refers to Martin Luther King Jr., *Why We Can't Wait* (New York: Harper & Row, 1963).

9   Drawn from the striking title of Stanley Hauerwas' Gifford Lectures, *With the Grain of the Universe: The Church's Witness and Natural Theology* (Grand Rapids: Brazos, 2001).

10   See Wolfhart Pannenberg, *Jesus–God and Man*, trans. Lewis L Wilkins and Duane A. Priebe, 2nd ed. (Philadelphia: Westminster, 1977); Wolfhart Pannenberg, *Theology and the Kingdom of God*, ed. Richard John Neuhaus (Philadelphia: Westminster, 1969); Jürgen Moltmann, *Theology of Hope: On the Grounds and the Implications of a Christian Eschatology*, trans. James W. Leitch (Minneapolis: Fortress, 1993); Jürgen Moltmann, *The Coming of God: Christian Eschatology*, trans. Margaret Kohl (Minneapolis: Fortress, 1996).

11   Pannenberg, *Jesus–God and Man*, 108, 157.

12   Dale Moody, *The Hope of Glory* (Grand Rapids: Eerdmans, 1964).

13   Dale Moody, *The Word of Truth* (Grand Rapids: Eerdmans, 1981). He has been followed in this pattern by two others in the free church tradition, James McClendon and Thomas Finger. See James Wm. McClendon Jr., *Doctrine: Systematic Theology* (Nashville: Abingdon, 1994). Thomas N. Finger, *Christian Theology: An Eschatological Approach* (Scottdale, Pa.: Herald, 1989).

14   Moltmann, *Coming of God*, 25–26. The spirit of this attitude is expressed well by Leonard Sweet, who emphasizes that the risen

Christ is not just behind us, pushing us, but is ahead of us, pulling us. When we quail before the challenges of our time and seek the safe harbor of the past, we should instead set sail for the open seas, realizing that Jesus is already there, pulling us toward and greeting us from the future. Based on an address by Leonard Sweet, Hardin-Simmons University, 30 January 2007.

15 "Ted Williams Frozen in Two Pieces," *CBS News*, 12 August 2003, accessed 6 April 2007, http://www.cbsnews.com/stories/2002/12/20/national/main533849.shtml.

16 For these fantastic speculations by a reputable and prominent physicist, see Michio Kaku, *Hyperspace: A Scientific Odyssey through Parallel Universes, Time Warps, and the Tenth Dimension* (New York: Anchor, 1994), chap. 14; Michio Kaku, *Parallel Worlds: A Journey through Creation, Higher Dimensions, and the Future of the Cosmos* (New York: Anchor, 2005), chap. 11. Cf. the earlier Freeman Dyson, *Disturbing the Universe* (New York: Basic, 1979), chaps. 11, 18.

17 Ludwig Wittgenstein, *Lectures and Conversations on Aesthetics, Psychology, and Religious Belief*, ed. Cyril Barrett (Berkeley: University of California Press, 1966), 55. Wittgenstein says of the way the different paradigms do not allow one to argue in the same context: "I think differently, in a different way. I say different things to myself. I have different pictures."

18 Williston Walker et al., *A History of the Christian Church*, 4th ed. (New York: Charles Scribner's Sons, 1985), 459.

19 Moltmann, *Coming of God*, 153.

20 Moltmann, *Coming of God*, 43.

21 To be precise, the Suffering Servant passages are from the sixth-century prophet usually known as Second Isaiah, occurring in Isaiah 42–53. For the Son of Man, see Daniel 7:13.

22 See N. T. Wright, *The New Testament and the People of God*, Christian Origins and the Question of God 1 (Minneapolis: Fortress, 1992), 307–20.

23 Two examples are the process philosophy of Alfred North Whitehead and the philosophy of D. Z. Phillips. See Alfred North Whitehead, *Process and Reality*, ed. David Ray Griffin and Donald W. Sherburne, 3rd ed. (New York: Free Press, 1978), 351; John B. Cobb Jr. and David Ray Griffin, *Process Theology: An Introductory Exposition* (Philadelphia: Westminster, 1976), 123–24; D. Z. Phillips, *Death and Immortality* (London: Macmillan, 1970), chaps. 2–3.

24 For extensive treatment, see N. T. Wright, *The Resurrection of the Son of God*, Christian Origins and the Question of God, vol. 3 (Minneapolis: Fortress, 2003), chaps. 3–4.

25 Wright, *Resurrection*, 88–89.

26 See Wright, *Resurrection*, 192. Wright cites Antigonus, one of the first great rabbis, and his disciples.

27 N. T. Wright makes this point in a thorough way in *Resurrection*. He especially stresses the continuity in the transposition of the Hebrew hopes for the nation in this world to the New Testament eschatological hope.

28 Thomas Aquinas, *Summa Theologica*, 3a.92.

29 This appears related to the Catholic emphasis on righteousness as not imputed in a forensic way but as perfected, albeit by grace. C. S. Lewis interestingly attested to purgatory. He said, "Enter into joy. If there is no objection, I'd *rather* be clean first" [*Letters to Malcolm: Chiefly on Prayer* (New York: Harcourt, Brace, & World, 1964], 140).

30 For background, see David E. Garland, *1 Corinthians*, Baker Exegetical Commentary on the New Testament (Grand Rapids: Baker Academic, 2003), 725–38.

31 On the other hand, N. T. Wright does cite evidence that in the first century there was an idea of some kind of existence, only vaguely affirmed, between death and the final resurrection. Paul could have been acknowledging, grudgingly, that he would have to exist "naked" for awhile. On the other hand, the reluctant way in which Paul even brings up the distasteful notion of being naked or disembodied, suggests that he had moved to affirm a resurrection body at death. It would not be the first time that Paul was groundbreaking in theology! See Wright, *Resurrection*.

32 John Hick, *Death and Eternal Life*, rev. ed. (Louisville: Westminster John Knox, 1994), 278–88. Hick does not at this time use the language of hardware and software but of "pattern."

33 Oscar Cullmann, *Immortality of the Soul; or, Resurrection of the Dead? The Witness of the New Testament* (New York: Macmillan, 1958).

34 For a helpful discussion of the various views and literature, see Ralph P. Martin, *2 Corinthians*, ed. Bruce M. Metzger, Word Biblical Commentary 40 (Nashville: Thomas Nelson, 1986), 95–116. Martin presents well the arguments for the view that Paul thought of an immediate resurrection body but himself argues for a disembodied state. He concedes, however, that on his reading Paul desired to avoid the intermediate state, even possibly abhorring it (105). While

it is conceivable that Paul could entertain "two minds about death," (101) it is difficult to imagine holding abhorrence together with his intense desire to be in the intermediate state.

35   Cf. Jones, *A Grammar of Christian Faith*, 2:734.

36   Donald G. Bloesch, *The Last Things: Resurrection, Judgment, Glory*, Christian Foundations (Downers Grove, Ill.: IVP Academic, 2004), 139. Bloesch says succinctly, "Paradise is a kind of interim heaven, just as hades is a kind of interim hell. These are fluid concepts where the meaning is not always fixed. Paradise will eventually merge into heaven, and hades into hell." (138). Of course, Bloesch, with his strong view of sovereignty, suggests that in the end, all might be saved: "It is my contention that a change of heart can still happen on the other side of death" (146) based on the meaning of Christ's descent into hell. He says that he has a "reverent agnosticism" (239) on this matter but hopes, like Karl Barth, Herman Bavinck, and G. C. Berkouwer, that God will reach all, even beyond the grave. He bases this on the fact of "the good news that Christ has come to save the lost and that his grace is irresistible and invincible" (148).

37   Moltmann, *Coming of God*, 104.

38   As we will see below, not all in the Roman Catholic Church thought of the afterlife for people as timeless in the way that God was timeless. For example, Augustine seemed to imagine action of a sort, even if it is but praise. See *City of God*, 22.30.

39   Dan R. Stiver, "Hick against Himself: His Theodicy versus His Replica Theory," in *Problems in the Philosophy of Religion: Critical Studies of the Work of John Hick*, ed. Harold Hewitt Jr., Library of Philosophy and Religion (London: Macmillan, 1991), 162–72.

40   Stanley J. Grenz, *Theology for the Community of God*, 2nd ed. (Grand Rapids: Eerdmans, 1994), 596–98. Grenz adds, "The unrighteous are kept by God unto judgment and eternal death. The righteous are kept with God unto resurrection and eternal life, surrounded by God's love and blissfully resting" (597).

41   Moltmann, *Coming of God*, 100–5.

42   Augustine, *City of God*, 20.22. Thomas Aquinas, *Summa Theologica*, 3a. 94.1, 3a.94.1.3.

43   As John Calvin says in a peremptory way, "Since it clearly appears that he is there concerned with classes of men, not men as individuals, away with further discussion!" Calvin, *Institutes*, The Library of Christian Classics 21, 3.24.16.

44   Clark Pinnock makes this point succinctly: "God may wish to save everybody, but what if someone does not want to be saved? What then? Will God predetermine such a person to love him? That does not make a lot of sense. How can God predestine the free response of love? This is something even God cannot do. All we can say is this: God does not cease to work for the salvation of the world but has to accept the outcome. Hell is proof of how seriously God takes human freedom" ("The Conditional View," in *Four Views on Hell*, ed. William Crockett, Counterpoints [Grand Rapids: Zondervan, 1996], 142).

45   Bernard Ramm, *The Evangelical Heritage* (Waco, Tex.: Word, 1973), 136–37.

46   Bloesch, *Last Things*, 236.

47   Examples would be Karl Barth, Donald Bloesch, Jürgen Moltmann, and John Hick. The former two hedge their bets more than the latter two, but the logic of their positions is strongly universalist. For a wide discussion of various alternatives to an evangelical proposal of universalism, see Robin A. Parry and Christopher H. Partridge, eds., *Universal Salvation? The Current Debate* (Grand Rapids: Eerdmans, 2003).

48   Clark Pinnock underscores this implication: "To be a universalist one really has to work with a predestinarian theology. How would it even be possible for God to save everyone if not by forcing some to be saved who do not want that? . . . One might posit that a Christian who is predestinarian ought to be a universalist in principle. A good God who could save everyone surely would save everyone" ("Conditional View," 128).

49   For discussion of several options, see Okholm and Phillips, eds., *Four Views on Salvation in a Pluralistic World*, ed. Stanley N. Gundry, Counterpoints (Grand Rapids: Zondervan, 1996).

50   Alister E. McGrath, "A Particularist View: A Post-Enlightenment Approach," in Okholm and Phillips, eds., *Four Views on Salvation*, 178.

51   Even many in the church who affirm predestination can enthusiastically commend evangelism, even when they know that the results are guaranteed. In this light, others who do not affirm predestinationa should easily be able to do so.

52   Augustine, *City of God*, 21.1-4.

53   Actually, these two contrary terms are often related in metaphorical ways in the intertestamental literature. For a helpful discussion, see

William V. Crockett, "The Metaphorical View," in *Four Views on Hell*, ed. William Crockett, Counterpoints (Grand Rapids: Zondervan, 1996), 59.

54 Moody did not favor the term *annihilation*, however, preferring the more biblical term *perishing* (Rom 2:12; John 3:16). He also thought that "notorious sinners" would not be destroyed but would be "tormented day and night forever and ever" (Rev 20:10). See Moody, *The Word of Truth*, 513–15.

55 Pinnock, "Conditional View."

56 For background on millennialism, see G. Eldon Ladd, *The Meaning of the Millennium: Four Views* (Downers Grove, Ill.: InterVarsity, 1977); Stanley J. Grenz, *The Millennial Maze: Sorting Out Evangelical Options* (Downers Grove, Ill.: InterVarsity, 1992); Kyle, *Last Days*; Clouse, Hosack, and Pierard, *New Millennium Manual*.

57 I am referring here to Dale Moody and Wayne Ward.

58 Revelation 22:20, "Lord, come quickly," is the translation of the early Christian Aramaic confession, *Maranatha*. See Morris Ashcraft, "Revelation," in *The Broadman Bible Commentary*, ed. Clifton Allen, vol. 12, *General Articles, Hebrews–Revelation* (Nashville: Broadman, 1972), 361.

59 Moltmann, *Coming of God*, 178–84. Moltmann also argues that modernist teleological hope for history as in Kant, Hegel, and Marx is rooted in millenarianism (chiliasm) (184–92). He says, "For Fichte, Schelling, and Hegel, these transferences from theological millenarianism into universal-history systems are already so much a matter of course that they no longer mention these roots at all" (189). Joachim of Fiore (ca. 1135–1202)—whose idea of three ages (of the Father, the Son, and the Spirit) influenced greatly later millennarian speculation as well as philosophers like Hegel and Marx—should also be mentioned. His idea that the new age of the Spirit had dawned or was about to dawn aroused hopes religious and secular. See Kyle, *Last Days*, 47–49.

60 For instance, Ray Summers says, "If verses 4, 5, and 6 of Revelation 20 had been omitted, no one would ever have dreamed of a literal thousand years of Christ's reign upon the earth." He is a bit sanguine about the Christian imagination, but his point is well made. See Ray Summers, *Worthy is the Lamb: An Interpretation of Revelation* (Nashville: Broadman, 1951), 203.

61 For a discussion, see Grenz, *Millennial Maze*, 163–65.

62   Augustus Strong, *Outlines of Systematic Theology* (Philadelphia: Griffith & Rowland, 1908), 263.

63   See James Spivey, "Benajah Harvey Carroll," in *Baptist Theologians*, ed. Timothy George and David S. Dockery (Nashville: Broadman, 1990), 319–20.

64   For background, see also Timothy P. Weber, *Living in the Shadow of the Second Coming: American Premillennialism, 1875–1982*, 2nd ed. (Chicago: University of Chicago Press, 1987). On this issue, see 21–22.

65   See Weber, chap. 5, and Marsden, 143–49. Both point out that their reticence about war was also driven by pacifism and that they were not endorsing being unpatriotic. Things dramatically changed after 1918, however, when extreme support for the United States became mandatory.

66   A good discussion is in Marsden, 247–50, in a section entitled "The Premillennial Paradox."

67   See especially the section on exegetical issues for dispensationism in Ben Witherington III, *The Problem with Evangelical Theology: Testing the Exegetical Foundations of Calvinism, Dispensationalism, and Wesleyanism* (Waco, Tex.: Baylor University Press, 2005).

68   Moltmann, *Coming of God*, 192. Moltmann here distinguishes between "historical millennialism," which "is exposed to acts of messianic violence and the disappointments of history," and "eschatological millennarianism," which is positive. Moltmann, however, imagines an actual millennial period on earth between the Parousia and the final eschaton as in historical premillennialism (201–2).

69   N. T. Wright points out the misunderstanding of apocalyptic as meaning the end of the world altogether. In the first century, he says, "The 'kingdom of god' has nothing to do with the world itself coming to an end. That makes no sense either of the basic Jewish worldview or of the texts in which the Jewish hope is expressed. It was after all the Stoics, not the first-century Jews, who characteristically believed the world would be dissolved in fire." See Wright, *New Testament*, 285. Wright continues, "What, then, did they believe was going to happen? They believed that *the present world order* would come to an end. . . . Jews simply did not believe that the space-time order was shortly to disappear" (333).

70   See especially Colleen McDannell and Bernhard Lang, *Heaven: A History* (New Haven: Yale University Press, 1988). Also see Jerry L. Walls, *Heaven: The Logic of Eternal Joy* (Oxford: Oxford University

Press, 2002), 7; Alister E. McGrath, A Brief History of Heaven (Oxford: Blackwell, 2003). An example on the one side is Aquinas, whose focus was a kind of intellectual vision of God who did not see any particular need for fellowship with others. See McDannell and Lang, Heaven, 88–92. On the other side were the millennial visions of Irenaeus that imagined abundant delicacies and wine with fruitful bearing and raising of children (52–53). Luther and Calvin had a greater sense of fellowship but also tended to see heaven as timeless, making it difficult to imagine activity, which involves before and after (146–65).

71 McDannell and Lang, Heaven, 54–68.

72 Bloesch argues that there is work to be done both in paradise and in heaven. Bloesch, Last Things, 142, 231–32.

73 See Walls, Heaven, 7–8.

74 Karl Barth, Church Dogmatics, ed. G. W. Bromiley and T. F. Torrance, vol. 3.4, The Doctrine of Creation, trans. A. T. Mackay et al. (Greenwood, S.C.: Attic, 1961), 507.

75 Moltmann, Coming of God, 294.

76 Christoforos Stavropoulos, "Partakers of Divine Nature," in Eastern Orthodox Theology: A Contemporary Reader, ed. Daniel B. Clendenin, 2nd ed. (Grand Rapids: Baker Book House, 2003), 183–92.

BIBLIOGRAPHY

Anderson, Allan. *An Introduction to Pentecostalism: Global Charismatic Christianity.* Cambridge: Cambridge University Press, 2004.

Ansbro, John J. *Martin Luther King Jr.: The Making of a Mind.* Maryknoll, N.Y.: Orbis, 1982.

Anselm. *Cur Deus Homo.* Chicago: Open Court, 1962.

Aristotle. *Metaphysics.* Edited by Robert Maynard Hutchins. Translated by W. Rhys Roberts. Pages 499–626 in *The Works of Aristotle,* bk. 1. Great Books of the Western World 8. Chicago: Encyclopedia Britannica, 1952.

———. *Nichomachean Ethics.* Edited by Robert Maynard Hutchins. Translated by W. D. Ross. Pages 339–436 in *The Works of Aristotle,* bk. 2. Great Books of the Western World 9. Chicago: Encyclopedia Britannica, 1952.

Ashcraft, Morris. "Revelation." In *The Broadman Bible Commentary,* edited by Clifton Allen. Vol. 12, *General Articles, Hebrews–Revelation,* 240–361. Nashville: Broadman, 1972.

Augustine. *The City of God.* In *St. Augustin's City of God and Christian Doctrine,* edited by Philip Schaff, 1–511. A Select Library of the Nicene and Post-Nicene Fathers of the Christian Church 2. Grand Rapids: Eerdmans, 1956.

———. *The Confessions*. Translated by Edward Bouverie Pusey. In *Augustine*, edited by Robert Maynard Hutchins, 1–125. Great Books of the Western World 18. Chicago: Encyclopedia Britannica, 1952.

———. *On Christian Doctrine*. In *St. Augustin's City of God and Christian Doctrine*, edited by Philip Schaff, 519–97. A Select Library of the Nicene and Post-Nicene Fathers of the Christian Church 2. 1st series. Grand Rapids: Eerdmans, 1956.

———. "Enchiridion." In *Augustine*, edited and translated by Albert C. Outler, 337–412. The Library of Christian Classics 7. Philadelphia: Westminster, 1955.

———. *Homilies on the First Epistle of John*. In *St. Augustin: Homilies on the Gospel of John, Homilies on the First Epistle of John, Soliloquies*, edited by Philip Schaff, 459–529. A Select Library of the Nicene and Post-Nicene Fathers of the Christian Church 7. 1st series. Grand Rapids: Eerdmans, 1956.

———. "On the Predestination of the Saints." In *Saint Augustin: Anti-Pelagian Writings*, edited by Philip Schaff, 493–519. A Select Library of the Nicene and Post-Nicene Fathers of the Christian Church 5. Grand Rapids: Eerdmans, 1971.

———. *The Trinity*. Translated by Stephen McKenna. The Fathers of the Church 45. Washington, D.C.: Catholic University of America Press, 1963.

Aulén, Gustaf. *Christus Victor*. Translated by A. G. Hebert. New York: Macmillan, 1969.

Austin, D. Brian. *The End of Certainty and the Beginning of Faith*. Macon, Ga.: Smyth & Helwys, 2000.

Austin, John L. *How to Do Things with Words*. Edited by J. O. Urmson and Marina Sbisà. 2nd ed. Cambridge, Mass.: Harvard University Press, 1975.

Baillie, D. M. *God Was in Christ: An Essay on Incarnation and Atonement*. New York: Charles Scribner's Sons, 1948.

— — —. "The Literal Meaning of Genesis: Books 1–6." Translated by J. H. Taylor. In *The Literal Meaning of Genesis*. Ancient Christian Writers: The Works of the Fathers in Translation 41, edited by J. Quasten, W. Burghardt, and T. Comerfield Lawler, 17–207. New York: Newman, 1982.

Baillie, John. *The Idea of Revelation in Recent Thought*. New York: Columbia University Press, 1956.

Bain, Ken. *What the Best College Teachers Do*. Cambridge, Mass.: Harvard University Press, 2004.

Balmer, Randall. *Thy Kingdom Come: How the Religious Right Distorts the Faith and Threatens America: An Evangelical's Lament*. New York: Basic, 2006.

Barbour, Ian G. *Religion and Science: Historical and Contemporary Issues*. Rev. ed. San Francisco: HarperSanFrancisco, 1997.

Baren, Gise J. Van. "Irresistible Grace." Chap. 4 in *The Five Points of Calvinism*, by Herman Hanko, Homer Hoeksema, and Gise J. Van Baren. Grandville, Mich.: Reformed Free Publishing, 1976. Accessed 30 July 2003. http://www.prca.org/fivepoints/chapter4.html.

Barrow, John D., and Frank J. Tipler. *The Anthropic Cosmological Principle*. Oxford: Oxford University Press, 1988.

Barth, Karl. *Church Dogmatics*. Edited by G. W. Bromiley and T. F. Torrance. Vol 3.1, *The Doctrine of Creation*, translated by J. W. Edwards, O. Bussey, and Harold Knight. Edinburgh: T&T Clark, 1958.

— — —. *Church Dogmatics*. Edited by G. W. Bromiley and T. F. Torrance. Vol. 3.4, *The Doctrine of Creation*, translated by A. T. Mackay et al. Greenwood, S.C.: Attic, 1961.

— — —. *Church Dogmatics*. Edited by G. W. Bromiley and T. F. Torrance. Vol. 2.2, *The Doctrine of God*, translated by G. W. Bromiley, J. C. Campbell, Iain Wilson, J. Strathearn, Harold Knight, and R. A. Stewart. Edinburgh: T&T Clark, 1957.

— — —. *Church Dogmatics*. Edited by G. W. Bromiley and T. F. Torrance. Vol. 4.1, *The Doctrine of Reconciliation*, translated by G. W. Bromiley. Edinburgh: T&T Clark, 1956.

———. *Church Dogmatics.* Edited by G. W. Bromiley and T. F. Torrance. Vol. 1.1, *The Doctrine of the Word of God,* translated by J. W. Edwards, O. Bussey, and Harold Knight. Greenwood, S.C.: Attic, 1975.

Barth, Markus. *Ephesians: Translation and Commentary on Chapters 4–6.* Anchor Bible 34a. Garden City, N.Y.: Doubleday, 1974.

Barton, Ruth Haley. *Sacred Rhythms: Arranging Our Lives for Spiritual Transformation.* Downers Grove, Ill.: InterVarsity, 2006.

Basinger, David, and Randall Basinger, eds. *Predestination and Free Will.* Downers Grove, Ill.: InterVarsity, 1986.

Beasley-Murray, G. R. *Jesus and the Kingdom of God.* Grand Rapids: Eerdmans, 1986.

Beck, James R., and Craig L. Blomberg, eds. *Two Views on Women in Ministry.* Counterpoints, edited by Stanley N. Gundry. Grand Rapids: Zondervan, 2001.

Beilby, James K., and Paul. R. Eddy, eds. *Divine Foreknowledge: Four Views.* Downers Grove, Ill.: InterVarsity, 2001.

Belenky, Mary Field, et al. *Women's Ways of Knowing: The Development of Self, Voice, and Mind.* New York: Basic, 1986.

Benson, Bruce Ellis. *Pious Nietzsche: Decadence and Dionysian Faith.* Bloomington: Indiana University Press, 2008.

Bettenson, Henry, ed. *Documents of the Christian Church.* 2nd ed. New York: Oxford University Press, 1963.

Bloesch, Donald G. *God, Authority.* Essentials of Evangelical Theology 1. San Francisco: HarperSanFrancisco, 1982.

———. *The Last Things: Resurrection, Judgment, Glory.* Christian Foundations. Downers Grove, Ill.: IVP Academic, 2004.

Bloom, Harold. *The American Religion: The Emergence of the Post-Christian Nation.* New York: Simon & Schuster, 1992.

Bonhoeffer, Dietrich. *Life Together: A Discussion of Christian Fellowship.* Translated by John W. Doberstein. Rev. ed. New York: HarperCollins, 1992.

Borg, Marcus. *Jesus: Uncovering the Life, Teachings, and Relevance of a Religious Revolutionary.* San Francisco: HarperSanFrancisco, 2006.

Boulton, David. *The Trouble with God: Building the Republic of Heaven.* New York: O Books, 2005.

Boyce, James P. *Abstract of Systematic Theology.* Escondido, Calif.: Den Dulk Christian Foundation, 1887.

Brackney, William H. *The Baptists.* Westport, Conn.: Praeger, 1994.

Brown, Peter. *The Body and Society: Men, Women, and Sexual Renunciation in Early Christianity.* New York: Columbia University Press, 1988.

Brown, Warren S., Nancey C. Murphy, and H. Newton Malony, eds. *Whatever Happened to the Soul? Scientific and Theological Portraits of Human Nature.* Theology and the Sciences. Minneapolis: Fortress, 1998.

Brueggemann, Walter. *Theology of the Old Testament: Testimony, Dispute, Advocacy.* Minneapolis: Fortress, 1997.

Brunner, Emil. *Dogmatics.* Vol. 2, *The Christian Doctrine of Creation and Redemption.* Translated by Olive Wyon. Philadelphia: Westminster, 1952.

Bryson, Bill. *A Short History of Nearly Everything.* New York: Broadway, 2003.

Buber, Martin. *I and Thou.* Translated by Ronald Gregor Smith. 2nd ed. Edinburgh: T&T Clark, 1958.

Buckley, Michael J. *At the Origins of Modern Atheism.* New Haven: Yale University Press, 1987.

Bultmann, Rudolf. "New Testament and Mythology." In *Kerygma and Myth,* edited by Hans Werner Bartsch, translated by Reginald H. Fuller, 1–44. New York: Harper, 1961.

———. "*pisteuo, pistis,* etc." In *Theological Dictionary of the New Testament,* edited by Gerhard Friedrich, translated by Geoffrey W. Bromiley, 6:174–228. Grand Rapids: Eerdmanns, 1968.

Busch, Eberhard. *Karl Barth: His Life from Letters and Autobiographical Texts.* Translated by John Bowden. 2nd ed. Philadelphia: Fortress, 1976.

Cahill, Thomas. *How the Irish Saved Civilization.* New York: Anchor, 1996.

Cairns, David. *The Image of God in Man.* Rev. ed. Fontana Library of Theology and Philosophy. London: Collins, 1973.

Calvin, John. *Calvin: Institutes of the Christian Religion.* Translated by Ford Lewis Battles. Edited by John T. McNeill. The Library of Christian Classics 20. Philadelphia: Westminster, 1960.

———. *Calvin: Institutes of the Christian Religion.* Translated by Ford Lewis Battles. Edited by John T. McNeill. The Library of Christian Classics 21. Philadelphia: Westminster, 1960.

Campbell, Colin. *The Romantic Ethic and the Spirit of Modern Consumerism.* Oxford: Basil Blackwell, 1987.

Campbell, Ted A., and Michael T. Burns. *Wesleyan Essentials in a Multicultural Society.* Edited by Robert Mulholland. Nashville: Abingdon, 2004.

Carson, Claborne, ed. *The Autobiography of Martin Luther King Jr.* New York: Warner, 1998.

"Catholic Church Buries Limbo after Centuries." *ReligionNewsBlog.* 20 April 2007. Accessed 26 December 2007. http://www.religionnewsblog.com/18025/limbo.

Clement of Alexandria. *The Stromata, or Miscellanies.* In *Fathers of the Second Century,* edited by James Donaldson and Alexander Roberts, 299–568. The Ante-Nicene Fathers 2. Grand Rapids: Eerdmans, 1962.

Clouse, Robert G., Robert N. Hosack, and Richard Pierard. *The New Millenium Manual: A Once and Future Guide.* Grand Rapids: Baker, 1999.

Cobb, John B. Jr., and David Ray Griffin. *Process Theology: An Introductory Exposition.* Philadelphia: Westminster, 1976.

Cone, James H. *God of the Oppressed.* 2nd ed. Maryknoll, N.Y.: Orbis, 1997.

Cooper, Burton Z. *Why, God?* Atlanta: John Knox, 1988.

Cooperman, Alan. "Evangelical Leader Returns to Catholicism." *washingtonpost.com*. 12 May 2007. Accessed 12 May 2007. http://www.washingtonpost.com/wp-dyn/content/article/2007/05/11/AR2007051101929.html?nav=hcmodule.

Cracknell, Kenneth, and Susan J. White. *An Introduction to World Methodism*. Cambridge: Cambridge University Press, 2005.

Crockett, William V. "The Metaphorical View." In *Four Views on Hell*, edited by William Crockett, 43–76. Counterpoints. Grand Rapids: Zondervan, 1996.

Crossan, John Dominic. *The Dark Interval: Towards a Theology of Story*. Allen, Tex.: Argus Communications, 1975.

―――. *The Historical Jesus: The Life of a Mediterranean Jewish Peasant*. San Francisco: HarperSanFrancisco, 1992.

―――. *In Parables: The Challenge of the Historical Jesus*. New York: Harper & Row, 1973.

Cullmann, Oscar. *Immortality of the Soul; or, Resurrection of the Dead? The Witness of the New Testament*. New York: Macmillan, 1958.

Cunningham, David S. *These Three Are One: The Practice of Trinitarian Theology*. Oxford: Blackwell, 1998.

Cunningham, Richard B. "A Case for Christian Philosophy." *Review and Expositor* 82 (1985): 493–506.

Cyprian. "The Epistles of Cyprian." In *Fathers of the Third Century*, 275–420. The Ante-Nicene Fathers 5, edited by Alexander Roberts and James Donaldson. Grand Rapids: Eerdmans, 1951. 1951 American edition edited by Roberts, Donaldson, and A. Cleveland Coxe.

Dalhouse, Mark Taylor. "Jones, Robert Reynolds Jr." In *Notable Americans Who Died between 1997 and 1999. The Scribner Encyclopedia of American Lives*. Edited by Kenneth T. Jackson, Karen Markoe, and Arnie Markoe. New York: Simon & Schuster, 2004.

Damasio, Antonio R. *Descartes' Error: Emotion, Reason, and the Human Brain*. New York: G. P. Putnam's Sons, 1994.

Davis, Stephen H., ed. *Encountering Evil: Live Options in Theodicy*. Atlanta: John Knox, 1981.

———. Encountering Evil: Live Options in Theodicy. 2nd ed. Louisville: Westminster John Knox, 2001.

Dawkins, Richard. The Blind Watchmaker: Why the Evidence of Evolution Reveals a Universe without Design. New York: W. W. Norton, 2004.

———. The God Delusion. Boston: Houghton Mifflin, 2006.

De la Torre, Miguel A. Reading the Bible from the Margins. Maryknoll, N.Y.: Orbis, 2002.

Dennett, Daniel. Darwin's Dangerous Idea: Evolution and the Meanings of Life. New York: Simon & Schuster, 1995.

Derrida, Jacques. On Cosmopolitanism and Forgiveness. Translated by Mark Dooley and Michael Hughes. Thinking in Action. London: Routledge, 2001.

Descartes, René. "Discourse on the Method of Rightly Conducting the Reason." In Descartes, Spinoza, edited by Robert Maynard Hutchins, 41–67. Great Books of the Western World 31. Chicago: Encyclopedia Britannica, 1952.

Dickens, Charles. Hard Times. 2nd ed. New York: The New American Library, 1980.

Dockery, David S. "A People of the Book and the Crisis of Biblical Authority." In Beyond the Impasse? Scripture, Interpretation, and Theology in Baptist Life, edited by Robison James and David S. Dockery, 17–39. Nashville: Broadman, 1992.

Dostoyevsky, Fyodor. The Brothers Karamazov. New York: Modern Library, 1950.

Dowe, Phil. Galileo, Darwin, and Hawking: The Interplay of Science, Reason, and Religion. Grand Rapids: Eerdmans, 2005.

Dunn, James D. G. Romans 1–8. Word Biblical Commentary 38a, edited by Bruce M. Metzger. Nashville: Thomas Nelson, 1988.

Dunne, Joseph. Back to the Rough Ground: "Phronesis" and "Techne" in Modern Philosophy and in Aristotle. Notre Dame: University of Notre Dame Press, 1993.

Dyson, Freeman. Disturbing the Universe. New York: Basic, 1979.

Edge, Findley. The Greening of the Church. Waco, Tex.: Word, 1972.

Ellis, Joseph J. *His Excellency: George Washington.* New York: Knopf, 2005.

"Enuma Elish." In *The Ancient Near East: An Anthology of Texts and Pictures*, edited by James B. Pritchard, 30–39. Princeton: Princeton University Press, 1958.

Evans, James H. Jr. *We Have Been Believers.* Minneapolis: Fortress, 1992.

Fee, Gordon D. *God's Empowering Presence: The Holy Spirit in the Letters of Paul.* Peabody, Mass.: Hendrickson, 1994.

Feinberg, John S. "God Ordains All Things." In *Predestination and Free Will: Four Views of Divine Sovereignty and Human Freedom*, edited by David Basinger and Randall Basinger, 19–43. Downers Grove, Ill.: InterVarsity, 1986.

Fiddes, Paul S. *The Creative Suffering of God.* Oxford: Clarendon, 1988.

———. *Participating in God: A Pastoral Doctrine of the Trinity.* Louisville: Westminster John Knox, 2000.

———. *Past Event and Present Salvation: The Christian Idea of Atonement.* Louisville: Westminster John Knox, 1989.

Finger, Thomas N. *Christian Theology: An Eschatological Approach.* 2 vols. Scottdale, Pa.: Herald, 1989.

Finlan, Stephen, and Vladimir Kharlamov, eds. *Theosis: Deification in Christian Theology.* Princeton Theological Monograph Series. Eugene, Oreg.: Pickwick, 2006.

Flew, Antony. *The Presumption of Atheism.* New York: Barnes & Noble, 1976.

Forrest, Barbara. "The Wedge at Work: How Intelligent Design Creationism Is Wedging Its Way into the Cultural and Academic Mainstream." In *Intelligent Design Creationism and Its Critics: Philosophical, Theological, and Scientific Perspectives*, edited by Robert T. Pennock, 5–53. Cambridge: MIT Press, 2001.

Foster, Richard J. *Money, Sex, and Power.* Rev. ed. London: Hodder & Stoughton Religious, 1999.

Fowl, Stephen E. *Philippians.* The Two Horizons New Testament

Commentary, edited by Joel Green and Max Turner. Grand Rapids: Eerdmans, 2005.

Fowler, James W. *Stages of Faith*. San Francisco: HarperSanFrancisco, 1976.

Frei, Hans W. "The 'Literal Reading' of Biblical Narrative in the Christian Tradition: Does It Stretch or Will It Break?" In *The Bible and the Narrative Tradition*, edited by Frank McConnell. Oxford: Oxford University Press, 1986.

———. "An Afterword: Eberhard Busch's Biography of Karl Barth." In *Karl Barth in Review: Posthumous Works Reviewed and Assessed*, edited by H. Martin Rumscheidt. Pittsburgh: Pickwick, 1981.

———. *The Eclipse of Biblical Narrative: A Study in Eighteenth- and Nineteenth-Century Hermeneutics*. New Haven: Yale University Press, 1974.

Friedman, Richard Elliott. *Who Wrote the Bible?* 2nd ed. San Francisco: HarperSanFrancisco, 1997.

Friedman, Thomas L. *The World Is Flat: A Brief History of the Twenty-First Century*. 2nd ed. New York: Farrar, Straus, & Giroux, 2006.

Funk, Robert W., Roy W. Hoover, and the Jesus Seminar, eds. *The Five Gospels: The Search for the Authentic Words of Jesus*. San Francisco: HarperSanFrancisco, 1997.

Gadamer, Hans-Georg. *Truth and Method*. Translated by Joel Weinsheimer and Donald G. Marshall. Rev. ed. New York: Crossroad, 1991.

———. "The Universality of the Hermeneutical Problem." In *Philosophical Hermeneutics*, edited by David E. Linge, 3–17. Berkeley: University of California Press, 1976.

Garland, David E. *1 Corinthians*. Baker Exegetical Commentary on the New Testament. Grand Rapids: Baker Academic, 2003.

Geertz, Clifford. *The Interpretation of Cultures: Selected Essays*. New York: Basic, 1973.

Gelder, Craig Van. "From Corporate Church to Missional Church: The Challenge Facing Congregations Today." *Review and Expositor* 101 (2004): 425–50.

George, Timothy. *Theology of the Reformers*. Nashville: Broadman, 1988.

Gibbs, Eddie. *ChurchNext: Quantum Changes in How We Do Ministry*. Downers Grove, Ill.: InterVarsity, 2000.

Gilkey, Langdon. *Creationism on Trial: Evolution and God at Little Rock*. Minneapolis: Winston, 1985.

Gilson, Étienne. *God and Philosophy*. New Haven: Yale University Press, 1941.

Girard, René. "Are the Gospels Mythical?" *First Things*. 20 April 1996. Accessed 31 December 2007. http://www.firstthings.com/article.php3?id_article=3856.

Goetz, Ronald. "The Suffering God: The Rise of a New Orthodoxy." *The Christian Century* 103, no. 13 (16 April 1986): 385–89.

Goldingay, John. *Old Testament Theology*. Vol. 1, *Israel's Gospel*. Downers Grove, Ill.: InterVarsity, 2003.

González, Justo. *Christian Thought Revisited: Three Types of Theology*. Nashville: Abingdon, 1989.

———. *A History of Christian Thought*. Vol. 2, *From Augustine to the Eve of the Reformation*. Rev. ed. Nashville: Abingdon, 1987.

Grant, Robert M., and David Tracy. *A Short History of the Interpretation of the Bible*. 2nd ed. Philadelphia: Fortress, 1984.

Gravrilyuk, Paul L. *The Suffering of the Impassible God: The Dialectics of Patristic Thought*. Oxford Early Christian Studies Series. Oxford: Oxford University Press, 2006.

Green, Joel B. "Kaleidoscopic View." In *The Nature of the Atonement*, edited by James K. Beilby and Paul. R. Eddy, 157–85. Downers Grove, Ill.: InterVarsity, 2006.

———. "Scripture in the Church." In *The Wesleyan Tradition*, edited by Paul W. Chilcote, 38–51. Nashville: Abingdon, 2002.

Green, Joel B., and Stuart L. Palmer. *In Search of the Soul: Four Views of the Mind-Body Problem*. Downers Grove, Ill.: InterVarsity, 2005.

Grenz, Stanley J. *The Millennial Maze: Sorting Out Evangelical Options*. Downers Grove, Ill.: InterVarsity, 1992.

———. *Rediscovering the Triune God: The Trinity in Contemporary Theology.* Minneapolis: Augsburg, 2004.

———. *The Social God and the Relational Self: A Trinitarian Theology of the Imago Dei.* The Matrix of Christian Theology 1. Louisville: Westminster John Knox, 2001.

———. *Theology for the Community of God.* 2nd ed. Grand Rapids: Eerdmans, 1994.

Grenz, Stanley J., and John R. Franke. *Beyond Foundationalism: Shaping Theology in a Postmodern Context.* Louisville: Westminster John Knox, 2001.

Grenz, Stanley J., and Denise Muir Kjesbo. *Women in the Church.* Downers Grove, Ill.: InterVarsity, 1995.

Grenz, Stanley J., and Roger E. Olson. *Who Needs Theology? An Invitation to the Study of God.* Downers Grove, Ill.: InterVarsity, 1996.

Grey, Mary. "Feminist Theology: A Critical Theology of Liberation." In *The Cambridge Companion to Liberation Theology,* edited by Christopher Rowland. Cambridge: Cambridge University Press, 1999.

Griffin, David Ray. *God and Religion in the Postmodern World: Essays in Postmodern Theology.* State University of New York Series in Constructive Postmodern Thought. Albany: State University of New York Press, 1989.

Guder, Darrell, ed. *The Missional Church: A Vision for the Sending of the Church in North America.* Grand Rapids: Eerdmans, 1998.

Gushee, David P. *The Righteous Gentiles of the Holocaust: A Christian Interpretation.* Minneapolis: Fortress, 1994.

Guthrie, Shirley C. *Christian Doctrine.* 2nd ed. Louisville: Westminster John Knox, 1994.

Gutierrez, Gustavo. *A Theology of Liberation.* Maryknoll, N.Y.: Orbis, 1973.

Hampson, Daphne. *Theology and Feminism.* Signposts in Theology. Oxford: Basil Blackwell, 1990.

Hanko, Herman, Homer Hoeksema, and Gise J. Van Baren. *The Five*

Points of Calvinism. Grandville, Mich.: Reformed Free Publishing, 1976.

Harding, Sandra, ed. *Feminism and Methodology.* Bloomington: Indiana University Press, 1987.

Harmon, Steven R. "The Authority of the Community (of All the Saints): Toward a Postmodern Baptist Hermeneutic of Tradition." *Review and Expositor* 100, no. 4 (2003): 587–621.

Harris, Sam. *Letter to a Christian Nation: The End of Faith.* New York: Knopf, 2006.

Hart, David Bentley. *The Doors of the Sea: Where Was God in the Tsunami?* Grand Rapids: Eerdmans, 2005.

Harvey, Barry A. *Another City.* Harrisburg, Pa.: Trinity Press International, 1999.

Hasker, William. *The Openness of God: A Biblical Challenge to the Traditional Understanding of God.* Downers Grove, Ill.: InterVarsity, 1994.

Hauerwas, Stanley. *The Peaceable Kingdom.* 2nd rev. ed. London: SCM Press, 2003.

———. *With the Grain of the Universe: The Church's Witness and Natural Theology.* Grand Rapids: Brazos, 2001.

Haught, John F. *God after Darwin: A Theology of Evolution.* Boulder, Colo.: Westview, 2000.

Hawking, Stephen. *A Brief History of Time: From the Big Bang to Black Holes.* Toronto: Bantam, 1988.

Hawthorne, Gerald F. *Philippians.* Word Biblical Commentary 43, edited by Bruce M. Metzger. Nashville: Thomas Nelson, 1983.

Hayes, Zachary J. "The Purgatorial View." In *Four Views on Hell,* edited by William Crockett, 91–121. Counterpoints. Grand Rapids: Zondervan, 1996.

Hebblethwaite, Brian. *Evil, Suffering, and Religion.* New York: Hawthorn, 1976.

Heidegger, Martin. *Being and Time.* Translated by Joan Stambaugh. State University of New York Series in Contemporary Continental Philosophy. Albany: State University of New York Press, 1996.

Hekman, Susan J. *Gender and Knowledge: Elements of a Postmodern Feminism.* Northeastern Series in Feminist Theory. Boston: Northeastern University Press, 1990.

Helm, Paul. "The Augustinian-Calvinist View." In *Divine Foreknowledge: Four Views,* edited by James K. Beilby and Paul R. Eddy, 161–89. Downers Grove, Ill.: InterVarsity, 2001.

Helwys, Thomas. *A Short Declaration of the Mystery of Iniquity.* Macon, Ga.: Mercer University Press, 1998.

Hendricks, William L. *The Letters of John.* Nashville: Broadman, 1970.

———. *A Theology for Children.* Nashville: Broadman, 1980.

Henry, Carl F. H. *God, Revelation, and Authority.* 6 vols. Waco, Tex.: Word, 1976–1983.

Herzog, Frederick. "The End of Systematic Thinking." In *Theology from the Belly of the Whale,* edited by Joerg Rieger. Harrisburg, Pa.: Trinity Press International, 1999.

Hick, John. *Death and Eternal Life.* Rev. ed. Louisville: Westminster John Knox, 1994.

———. *Evil and the God of Love.* 2nd ed. San Francisco: Harper & Row, 1978.

———. *Evil and the God of Love.* 2nd ed., rev. San Francisco: Harper & Row, 1985.

Higton, Mike. *Difficult Gospel: The Theology of Rowan Williams.* New York: Church Publishing, 2004.

Hinson, E. Glenn. *Spiritual Preparation for Christian Leadership.* Nashville: Upper Room, 1999.

Hippolytus. *Against the Heresy of One Noetus.* In *Fathers of the Third Century,* edited by Alexander Roberts and James Donaldson, 223–31. The Ante-Nicene Fathers 5. Grand Rapids: Eerdmans, 1951.

Hirsh, Sandra, and Jean Kummerow. *Lifetypes.* New York: Warner, 1989.

Hoeksema, Homer C. "Limited Atonement." Chap. 3 in *The Five Points of Calvinism,* by Herman Hanko, Homer C. Hoeksema, and Gise

J. Van Baren. Grandville, Mich.: Reformed Free Publishing, 1976. Accessed 30 July 2003. http://www.prca.org/fivepoints/chapter3.html.

Holmes, Arthur Frank. *All Truth is God's Truth*. Grand Rapids: Eerdmans, 1977.

Ingle, Clifford, ed. *Children and Conversion*. Nashville: Broadman, 1970.

Irenaeus. *Against Heresies*. In *The Apostolic Fathers with Justin Martyr and Irenaeus*, edited by Alexander Roberts and James Donaldson, 309–567. The Ante-Nicene Fathers 1. Grand Rapids: Eerdmans, 1956.

Jacob, Edmund. *Theology of the Old Testament*. Translated by Arthur W. Heathcote and Philip J. Allcock. New York: Harper & Row, 1958.

Jenkins, Philip. *The New Faces of Christianity: Believing the Bible in the Global South*. Oxford: Oxford University Press, 2006.

———. *The Next Christendom: The Coming of Global Christianity*. New York: Oxford University Press, 2002.

Jewett, Paul K. *Man as Male and Female*. Grand Rapids: Eerdmans, 1975.

Johnson, Elizabeth A. *She Who Is: The Mystery of God in Feminist Theological Discourse*. New York: Crossroad, 1992.

Johnson, Mark. *Moral Imagination: Implications of Cognitive Science for Ethics*. Chicago: University of Chicago Press, 1993.

Jones, Joe R. *A Grammar of Christian Faith: Systematic Explorations in Christian Life and Doctrine*. Vols. 1–2. Lanham, Md.: Rowman & Littlefield, 2002.

Jones, L. Gregory. *Embodying Forgiveness: A Theological Analysis*. Grand Rapids: Eerdmans, 1995.

Jones, Serene. *Feminist Theory and Christian Theology: Cartographies of Grace*. Minneapolis: Fortress, 2000.

———. "Women's Experience between a Rock and a Hard Place: Feminist, Womanist, and Mujerista Theologies in North

America." In *Horizons in Feminist Theology: Identity, Tradition, and Norms*, edited by Rebecca S. Chopp and Sheila Grave Davaney, 33–53. Minneapolis: Fortress, 1997.

Jones, Serene, and Paul Lakeland, eds. *Constructive Theology: A Contemporary Approach to Classical Themes*. Minneapolis: Fortress, 2005.

Justin the Martyr. "The First Apology of Justin." In *The Apostolic Fathers with Justin Martyr and Irenaeus*, edited by Alexander Roberts and James Donaldson, 163–87. The Ante-Nicene Fathers 1. Grand Rapids: Eerdmans, 1956.

Kaku, Michio. *Hyperspace: A Scientific Odyssey through Parallel Universes, Time Warps, and the Tenth Dimension*. New York: Anchor, 1994.

———. *Parallel Worlds: A Journey through Creation, Higher Dimensions, and the Future of the Cosmos*. New York: Anchor, 2005.

Kant, Immanuel. *Religion within the Limits of Reason Alone*. Translated by Theodore M. Greene and Hoyt H. Hudson. New York: Harper & Brothers, 1960.

Keating, Charles. *Who We Are Is How We Pray: Matching Personality and Spirituality*. Mystic, Conn.: Twenty-Third Publications, 1987.

Keirsey, David, and Marilyn Bates. *Please Understand Me: Character and Temperament Types*. 3rd ed. Del Mar, Calif.: Prometheus Nemesis, 1978.

Keller, Helen. *The Story of My Life, with Her Letters (1887–1901)*. New York: Grosset & Dunlap, 1905.

Kelly, J. N. D. *Early Christian Doctrines*. 5th ed. New York: HarperSanFrancisco, 1978.

Kelsey, David H. *Proving Doctrine: The Uses of Scripture in Modern Theology*. 2nd ed. Harrisburg, Pa.: Trinity Press International, 1999.

Kierkegaard, Søren. *Concluding Unscientific Postscript*. Edited by David F. Swenson and Walter Lowrie. Princeton: Princeton University Press, 1941.

———. *Purity of Heart Is to Will One Thing: Spiritual Preparation for the Office of Confession*. Translated by Douglas V. Steere. New York: Harper Torchbooks, 1956.

———. *The Sickness unto Death: A Christian Psychological Exposition for Upbuilding and Awakening.* Edited and translated by Howard V. Hong and Edna H. Hong. Kierkegaard's Writings 19. Princeton: Princeton University Press, 1980.

Kimball, Dan. *The Emerging Church.* Grand Rapids: Zondervan, 2003.

———. *They Like Jesus but Not the Church: Insights from Emerging Generations.* Grand Rapids: Zondervan, 2007.

Kimel, Alvin F., Jr. "The God Who Likes His Name: Holy Trinity, Feminism, and the Language of Faith." In *Speaking the Christian God: The Holy Trinity and the Challenge of Feminism,* edited by Alvin F. Kimel Jr., 188–208. Grand Rapids: Eerdmans, 1992.

King, Martin Luther, Jr. *Where Do We Go from Here: Chaos or Community?* New York: Harper & Row, 1967.

———. *Why We Can't Wait.* New York: Harper & Row, 1963.

Kirwan, Michael. *Discovering Girard.* Cambridge, Mass.: Cowley, 2005.

Kraybill, Donald B. *The Riddle of Amish Culture.* Rev. ed. Center Books in Anabaptist Studies. Baltimore: Johns Hopkins University Press, 2001.

———. "Why the Amish Forgive: Tales of Redemption at Nickel Mines." In *EMUNews.* 11 October 2006. Accessed 18 June 2007. http://www.emu.edu/news/index.php/1246.

Kuhn, Thomas. *The Structure of Scientific Revolutions.* 2nd ed. Chicago: University of Chicago Press, 1970.

Küng, Hans. *Christianity: Essence, History, and Future.* Translated by John Bowden. New York: Continuum, 1998.

———. *The Church.* Garden City, N.Y.: Image, 1976.

———. *Does God Exist? An Answer for Today.* Translated by Edward Quinn. Garden City, N.Y.: Doubleday, 1980.

———. *My Struggle for Freedom: Memoirs.* Translated by John Bowden. Grand Rapids: Eerdmans, 2003.

Küng, Hans, and David Tracy, eds. *Paradigm Change in Theology: A*

Symposium for the Future. Translated by Margaret Köhl. New York: Crossroad, 1989.

Kushner, Harold S. *When Bad Things Happen to Good People*. New York: Avon, 1981.

Kyle, Richard. *The Last Days Are Here Again*. Grand Rapids: Baker, 1998.

LaCugna, Catherine Mowry. *God for Us: The Trinity and Christian Life*. New York: HarperCollins, 1993.

Ladd, G. Eldon. *The Meaning of the Millennium: Four Views*. Downers Grove, Ill.: InterVarsity, 1977.

Lakoff, George, and Mark Johnson. *Philosophy in the Flesh: The Embodied Mind and Its Challenge to Western Thought*. New York: Basic, 1999.

Larson, Edward J. *Summer for the Gods*. 2nd ed. New York: Basic Books, 2006.

Lavine, T. Z. *From Socrates to Sartre: The Philosophic Quest*. Toronto: Bantam, 1984.

Leith, John, ed. *Creeds of the Churches: A Reader in Christian Doctrine from the Bible to the Present*. Rev. ed. Atlanta, Ga.: Anchor, 1973.

Leonard, Bill J. *Baptist Ways: A History*. Valley Forge, Pa.: Judson, 2003.

———. *Baptists in America*. New York: Columbia University Press, 2005.

Lewis, C. S. *The Four Loves*. New York: Harcourt, Brace & Company, 1960.

———. *A Grief Observed*. New York: Seabury, 1961.

———. *Letters to Malcolm: Chiefly on Prayer*. New York: Harcourt, Brace & World, 1964.

———. *The Lion, the Witch, and the Wardrobe*. New York: Collier, 1970.

———. *Mere Christianity*. New York: Macmillan, 1981.

———. *The Problem of Pain*. New York: Collier, 1962.

Lindbeck, George. *The Nature of Doctrine: Religion and Theology in a Postliberal Age*. Philadelphia: Westminster, 1984.

Livingstone, David N. *Darwin's Forgotten Defenders: The Encounter between Evangelical Theology and Evolutionary Thought*. Grand Rapids: Eerdmans, 1987.

Locke, John. "An Essay Concerning Human Understanding." In *Locke, Berkeley, Hume*, edited by Robert Maynard Hutchins, 85–395. Great Books of the Western World 35. Chicago: Encyclopedia Britannica, 1952.

Long, Jimmy. *Emerging Hope: A Strategy for Reaching Postmodern Generations*. Downers Grove, Ill.: InterVarsity, 2004.

Lumpkin, William L., ed. *Baptist Confessions of Faith*. 2nd ed. Valley Forge, Pa.: Judson, 1969.

Luther, Martin. *The Babylonian Captivity of the Church*. Works of Martin Luther 2. Grand Rapids: Baker Book House, 1982.

———. "A Mighty Fortress is Our God." In *Smith Creek Music*. 1529. Accessed 12 September 2006. http://www.smithcreekmusic.com/ Hymnology/Lutheran.Hymnody/ A_Mighty_Fortress.html.

Macchia, Frank. *Baptized in the Spirit: A Global Pentecostal Theology*. Grand Rapids: Zondervan, 2006.

MacIntyre, Alasdair C. "Epistemological Crises, Dramatic Narrative, and the Philosophy of Science." In *Why Narrative? Readings in Narrative Theology*, edited by Stanley Hauerwas and Gregory Jones, 138–57. Grand Rapids: Eerdmans, 1989.

———. *Three Rival Versions of Moral Enquiry: Encyclopaedia, Genealogy, and Tradition*. Gifford Lectures. Notre Dame: University of Notre Dame Press, 1990.

———. *Whose Justice? Which Rationality?* Notre Dame: University of Notre Dame Press, 1988.

Mackie, J. L. "Evil and Omnipotence." In *Philosophy of Religion: Selected Readings*, edited by Michael L. Peterson et al. Oxford: Oxford University Press, 2007.

Macquarrie, John. *Principles of Christian Theology*. New York: Charles Scribner's Sons, 1966.

Malone, Mary T. *Women and Christianity*. Maryknoll, N.Y.: Orbis, 2001.

Marsden, George M. *Fundamentalism and American Culture.* 2nd ed. Oxford: Oxford University Press, 2006.

Marshall, Molly T. *Joining the Dance: A Theology of the Spirit.* Valley Forge, Pa.: Judson, 2003.

———. "Setting Our Feet in a Large Room." In *Beyond the Impasse? Scripture, Interpretation, and Theology in Baptist Life,* edited by Robison James and David S. Dockery, 169–94. Nashville: Broadman, 1992.

Martin, Ralph P. *2 Corinthians.* Edited by Bruce M. Metzger. Word Biblical Commentary 40. Nashville: Thomas Nelson, 1986.

Marx, Karl. *Critique of Hegel's "Philosophy of Right."* Translated by Annette Jolin and Joseph O'Malley. Edited by Joseph O'Malley. Cambridge: Cambridge University Press, 1970.

McBeth, H. Leon. *The Baptist Heritage: Four Centuries of Baptist Witness.* Nashville: B&H Publishing, 1987.

McClendon, James Wm. Jr. *Doctrine: Systematic Theology.* Nashville: Abingdon, 1994.

———. *Ethics: Systematic Theology.* Nashville: Abingdon, 1986.

McCullough, David. *1776.* New York: Simon & Schuster, 2006.

McDannell, Colleen, and Bernhard Lang. *Heaven: A History.* New Haven: Yale University Press, 1988.

McDowell, Edward A. "1-2-3 John." In *The Broadman Bible Commentary,* 188–231. Nashville: Broadman, 1972.

McFague, Sallie. *The Body of God: An Ecological Theology.* Minneapolis: Fortress, 1993.

———. *Metaphorical Theology: Models of God in Religious Language.* Philadelphia: Fortress, 1982.

———. *Models of God: Theology for an Ecological, Nuclear Age.* Philadelphia: Fortress, 1987.

———. *Speaking in Parables: A Study in Metaphor and Theology.* Philadelphia: Fortress, 1975.

McGill, Arthur C. *Suffering: A Test of Theological Method.* Philadelphia: Westminster John Knox, 1982.

McGrath, Alister E. *A Brief History of Heaven*. Oxford: Blackwell, 2003.

— — —. *A Scientific Theology*. Vol. 1, *Nature*. Grand Rapids: Eerdmans, 2001.

— — —. "A Particularist View: A Post-Enlightenment Approach." In *Four Views on Salvation in a Pluralistic World*, edited by Dennis L. Okholm and Timothy R. Phillips. Counterpoints. Grand Rapids: Zondervan, 1996.

— — —. *A Scientific Theology*. Vol. 2, *Reality*. Grand Rapids: Eerdmans, 2002.

— — —. *A Scientific Theology*. Vol. 3.1, *Theory*. Grand Rapids: Eerdmans, 2005.

McGrath, Alister E., ed. *The Christian Theology Reader*. 2nd ed. Cambridge: Blackwell, 2001.

— — —. *The Christian Theology Reader*. 3rd ed. Cambridge: Blackwell, 2007.

McLaren, Brian D. *More Ready Than You Realize: Evangelism as Dance in the Postmodern Matrix*. Grand Rapids: Zondervan, 2002.

— — —. *A New Kind of Christian: A Tale of Two Friends on a Spiritual Journey*. San Francisco: Jossey-Bass, 2001.

McLaughlin, Eleanor. "Christology in Dialogue with Feminist Ideology—Bodies and Boundaries." In *Christology in Dialogue*, edited by Robert F. Berkey and Sarah A. Edwards. Cleveland: Pilgrim, 1993.

McNeal, Reggie. *The Present Future: Six Tough Questions for the Church*. San Francisco: Jossey-Bass, 2003.

Merleau-Ponty, Maurice. *Phenomenology of Perception*. Translated by Colin Smith. International Library of Philosophy and Scientific Method. New York: Humanities Press, 1962.

Migliore, Daniel L. *Faith Seeking Understanding: An Introduction to Christian Theology*. 2nd ed. Grand Rapids: Eerdmans, 2004.

Milbank, John. *Theology and Social Theory: Beyond Secular Reason*. Cambridge: Blackwell, 1993.

"Millerites." In *Ohio History Central: An Online Encyclopedia of Ohio History.* 2005. Accessed 17 January 2007. http://www.ohiohisto-rycentral.org/entry.php?rec=607.

Minatrea, Milfred. *Shaped by God's Heart: The Passion and Practices of Missional Churches.* San Francisco: Jossey-Bass, 2004.

Mitchell, Margaret. "How Biblical Is the Christian Right?" *Religion and Culture Web Forum* May 2006. Accessed 16 August 2006. http://marty-center.uchicago.edu/webforum/052006/commen-tary.shtml.

Mitzman, Arthur. *The Iron Cage: A Historical Interpretation of Max Weber.* Piscataway, N.J.: Transaction, 1984.

Moltmann, Jürgen. *The Church in the Power of the Spirit: A Contribution to Messianic Ecclesiology.* Translated by Margret Kohl. New York: Harper & Row, 1977.

———. *The Coming of God: Christian Eschatology.* Translated by Margaret Kohl. Minneapolis: Fortress, 1996.

———. *The Crucified God: The Cross of Christ as the Foundation and Criticism of Christian Theology.* Translated by John Bowden and R. A. Wilson. Minneapolis: Fortress, 1994.

———. *God for a Secular Society: The Public Relevance of Theology.* Translated by Margaret Kohl. Minneapolis: Fortress, 1999.

———. *God in Creation.* Minneapolis: Fortress, 1993.

———. *Theology of Hope: On the Grounds and the Implications of a Christian Eschatology.* Translated by James W. Leitch. Minneapolis: Fortress, 1993.

———. *The Trinity and the Kingdom: The Doctrine of God.* New York: Harper & Row, 1981.

———. *The Way of Jesus Christ: Christology in Messianic Dimensions.* Minneapolis: Fortress, 1993.

Moody, Dale. *The Hope of Glory.* Grand Rapids: Eerdmans, 1964.

———. *The Word of Truth.* Grand Rapids: Eerdmans, 1981.

Morris, Henry. *Scientific Creationism.* San Diego: Creation-Life Publishers, 1974.

Mullins, E. Y. *The Christian Religion in Its Doctrinal Expression.* Valley Forge, Pa.: Judson, 1917.

Murphy, Nancey C. *Beyond Liberalism and Fundamentalism: How Modern and Postmodern Philosophy Set the Theological Agenda.* Rockwell Lecture Series. Valley Forge, Pa.: Trinity Press International, 1996.

— — —. *Theology in the Age of Scientific Reasoning.* Cornell Studies in the Philosophy of Religion. Ithaca: Cornell University Press, 1990.

Murphy, Nancey C., and George F. R. Ellis. *On the Moral Nature of the Universe: Theology, Cosmology, and Ethics.* Theology and the Sciences. Minneapolis: Fortress, 1996.

Murphy, Nancey C., Brad J. Kallenberg, and Mark Thiessen Nation, eds. *Virtues and Practices in the Christian Tradition: Christian Ethics after MacIntyre.* Harrisburg, Pa.: Trinity Press International, 1997.

Murphy, Nancey C., and James Wm. McClendon Jr. "Distinguishing Modern and Postmodern Theologies." *Modern Theology* 5 (1989): 191–214.

Nazianzen, Saint Gregory. "Select Letters." Translated by Charles Gordon Browne and James Edward Swallow. In *Cyril of Jerusalem, Gregory Nazianzen*, 435–82. A Select Library of the Nicene and Post-Nicene Fathers of the Christian Church 7, edited by Philip Schaff and Henry Wace. Grand Rapids: Eerdmans, 1971.

Newport, John P. *Life's Ultimate Questions: A Contemporary Philosophy of Religion.* Dallas: Word, 1989.

Niebuhr, Reinhold. *Christian Realism and Political Problems.* New York: Charles Scribner's Sons, 1953.

— — —. *The Nature and Destiny of Man.* New York: Charles Scribner's Sons, 1949.

Nietzsche, Friedrich. *The Gay Science.* Translated by Walter Kaufmann. New York: Vintage, 1974.

— — —. *The Portable Nietzsche.* Edited and translated by Walter Kaufmann, The Viking Portable Library. New York: Penguin Books, 1954.

Noll, Mark. "Evangelicals and the Study of the Bible." In *Evangelicalism and Modern America*, edited by George Marsden, 103–21. Grand Rapids: Eerdmans, 1984.

Numbers, Ronald L. *The Creationists: The Evolution of Scientific Creationism*. Berkeley: University of California Press, 1992.

Oates, Stephen. *Let the Trumpet Sound: The Life of Martin Luther King Jr.* New York: Harper & Row, 1982.

Okholm, Dennis L., and Timothy R. Phillips, eds. *Four Views on Salvation in a Pluralistic World*. Edited by Stanley N. Gundry. Counterpoints. Grand Rapids: Zondervan, 1996.

Olson, Roger E. *The Mosaic of Christian Belief: Twenty Centuries of Unity and Diversity*. Downers Grove, Ill.: InterVarsity, 2002.

———. *The Story of Christian Theology: Twenty Centuries of Tradition and Reform*. Downers Grove, Ill.: InterVarsity, 1999.

Pannenberg, Wolfhart. *Jesus–God and Man*. Translated by Lewis L Wilkins and Duane A. Priebe. 2nd ed. Philadelphia: Westminster, 1977.

———. *Theology and the Kingdom of God*. Edited by Richard John Neuhaus. Philadelphia: Westminster, 1969.

———. *What Is Man?* Translated by Duane A. Priebe. Philadelphia: Fortress, 1970.

Parry, Robin A., and Christopher H. Partridge, eds. *Universal Salvation? The Current Debate*. Grand Rapids: Eerdmans, 2003.

Pascal, Blaise. *Pensées and Other Writings*. Translated by Honor Levi. The World's Classics. New York: Oxford University Press, 1995.

Peacocke, Arthur R. *Creation and the World of Science: The Bampton Lectures, 1978*. Oxford: Clarendon, 1979.

Peck, M. Scott. *People of the Lie: The Hope of Healing Human Evil*. New York: Simon & Schuster, 1983.

Pennock, Robert T., ed. *Intelligent Design Creationism and Its Critics: Philosophical, Theological, and Scientific Perspectives*. Cambridge, Mass.: MIT Press, 2001.

Perrin, Norman. *Jesus and the Language of the Kingdom: Symbol and Metaphor in New Testament Interpretation*. Philadelphia: Fortress, 1976.

Peters, Ted. *God–The World's Future: Systematic Theology for a New Era.* 2nd ed. Minneapolis: Fortress, 2000.

Peterson, Michael L. *Evil and the Christian God.* Grand Rapids: Baker Book House, 1982.

Peterson, Michael L., William Hasker, Bruce Reichenbach, and David Basinger, eds. *Philosophy of Religion: Selected Readings.* 3rd ed. Oxford: Oxford University Press, 2007.

Phillips, D. Z. *Death and Immortality.* London: Macmillan, 1970.

Phillips, J. B. *Your God Is Too Small.* New York: Macmillan, 1958.

Pinnock, Clark H. "The Conditional View." In *Four Views on Hell,* edited by William Crockett, 135–70. Counterpoints. Grand Rapids: Zondervan, 1996.

———. *The Scripture Principle.* Vancouver: Regent College Publishing, 2002.

Piper, John. *The Pleasures of God: Meditations on God's Delight in Being God.* 2nd ed. Sisters, Oreg.: Multnomah, 2000.

Placher, William C. *Narratives of a Vulnerable God: Christ, Theology, and Scripture.* Louisville: Westminster John Knox, 1994.

———. *Unapologetic Theology: A Christian Voice in a Pluralistic Conversation.* Louisille: Westminster John Knox, 1989.

Plantinga, Alvin C. *God, Freedom, and Evil.* Grand Rapids: Eerdmans, 1974.

———. "The Free Will Defense." In *Philosophy of Religion: Selected Readings,* edited by Michael L. Peterson et al. 3rd ed. Oxford: Oxford University Press, 2007.

———. "Reason and Belief in God." In *Faith and Rationality: Reason and Belief in God.* Edited by Alvin Plantinga and Nicholas Wolterstorff. Notre Dame: University of Notre Dame Press, 1983.

Plato. *The Republic.* Translated by Benjamin Jowett. Great Books of the Western World 7, edited by Robert Maynard Hutchins, 295–441. Chicago: Encyclopedia Britannica, 1952.

———. *Theaetetus.* Translated by Benjamin Jowett. Great Books of the Western World 7, edited by Robert Maynard Hutchins, 512–550. Chicago: Encyclopedia Britannica, 1952.

Poe, Harry Lee. "The Gospel in a Postmodern Culture." *Review and Expositor* 101 (2004): 497–510.

Polanyi, Michael. *Personal Knowledge: Towards a Post-Critical Philosophy.* 2nd ed. Chicago: University of Chicago Press, 1962.

———. *The Tacit Dimension.* Gloucester, Mass.: Peter Smith, 1983.

Polkinghorne, John. *Science and Providence: God's Interaction with the World.* 2nd ed. Philadelphia: Templeton Foundation, 2005.

Postman, Neil. *Amusing Ourselves to Death: Public Discourse in the Age of Show Business.* New York: Penguin, 1986.

Powell, Mark Allan. *Jesus as a Figure in History: How Modern Historians View the Man from Galilee.* Louisville: Westminster John Knox, 1998.

Pui-lan, Kwok. *Postcolonial Imagination and Feminist Theology.* Louisville: Westminster John Knox, 2005.

Putnam, Robert D. *Bowling Alone: The Collapse and Revival of American Community.* Rev. ed. New York: Simon & Schuster, 2001.

Rad, Gerhard von. *Genesis.* Translated by John H. Marks. Rev. ed. The Old Testament Library. Philadelphia: Westminster, 1961.

———. *Old Testament Theology.* Vol. 1, *The Theology of Israel's Historical Traditions,* translated by D. M. G. Stalker. New York: Harper & Row, 1962.

Ramm, Bernard. *The Evangelical Heritage.* Waco, Tex.: Word, 1973.

Randall, Lisa. *Warped Passages: Unraveling the Mysteries of the Universe's Hidden Dimensions.* San Francisco: HarperCollins, 2005.

Ricoeur, Paul. "Biblical Hermeneutics." *Semeia* 4 (1975): 27–138.

———. *The Conflict of Interpretations.* Edited by Don Ihde. Northwestern University Studies in Phenomenology and Existential Philosophy. Evanston, Ill. : Northwestern University Press, 1974.

———. *Fallible Man.* Translated by Charles Kelbley. Rev. ed. New York: Fordham University Press, 1986.

———. *Freedom and Nature: The Voluntary and the Involuntary.*

Translated by Erazim Kohák. Northwestern University Studies in Phenomenology and Existential Philosophy. Evanston, Ill.: Northwestern University Press, 1966.

———. *Interpretation Theory: Discourse and the Surplus of Meaning.* Fort Worth: Texas Christian University Press, 1976.

———. *Memory, History, Forgetting.* Translated by Kathleen Blamey and David Pellauer. Chicago: University of Chicago Press, 2004.

———. "Metaphor and the Central Problem of Hermeneutics." In *Hermeneutics and the Human Sciences: Essays on Language, Action, and Interpretation,* edited by John B. Thompson. Cambridge: Cambridge University Press, 1981.

———. *Political and Social Essays.* Athens: Ohio University Press, 1974.

———. "The Model of the Text: Meaningful Action Considered as a Text." In *Hermeneutics and the Human Sciences: Essays on Language, Action, and Interpretation,* edited by John B. Thompson, 131–44. Cambridge: Cambridge University Press, 1981.

———. *The Symbolism of Evil.* Translated by Emerson Buchanan. Religious Perspectives 17. New York: Harper & Row, 1967.

———. *Time and Narrative.* Vol. 1, translated by Kathleen McLaughlin and David Pellauer. Chicago: University of Chicago Press, 1984.

———. *Time and Narrative.* Vol. 2, translated by Kathleen McLaughlin and David Pellauer. Chicago: University of Chicago Press, 1985.

———. *Time and Narrative.* Vol. 3, translated by Kathleen Blamey and David Pellauer. Chicago: University of Chicago Press, 1988.

———. "Toward a Hermeneutic of the Idea of Revelation." Translated by David Pellauer. In *Essays on Biblical Interpretation,* edited by Lewis S. Mudge, 73–118. Philadelphia: Fortress, 1980.

Roark, Dallas M. *Dietrich Bonhoeffer.* Makers of the Modern Theological Mind. Waco, Tex.: Word, 1972.

Robinson, John A. T. *The Body: A Study in Pauline Theology.* Studies in Biblical Theology 5. Naperville, Ill.: Alec R. Allenson, 1957.

Robinson, Michael D. *The Storms of Providence: Navigating the Waters of Calvinism, Arminianism, and Open Theism.* Dallas: University Press of America, 2003.

"Rose of Lima." *New Catholic Encyclopedia.* Florence, Ky.: Gale Cengage, 2002.

Ruether, Rosemary Radford. *Sexism and God-Talk: Toward a Feminist Theology.* Boston: Beacon, 1983.

Ruse, Michael, ed. *But Is It Science? The Philosophical Question in the Creation/Evolution Controversy.* Amherst, N.Y.: Prometheus, 1996.

Russell, Robert J., Nancey C. Murphy, and Arthur R. Peacocke, eds. *Chaos and Complexity: Scientific Perspectives on Divine Action.* 2nd ed. Scientific Perspectives on Divine Action 2. Vatican City State: Vatican Observatory Publications, 1997.

Saiving, Valerie. "The Human Situation: A Feminist View." In *Womanspirit Rising: A Feminist Reader in Religion,* edited by Carol P. Christ and Judith Plaskow, 25–42. San Francisco: Harper & Row, 1979.

Sartre, Jean-Paul. "Existentialism Is a Humanism." In *Existentialism from Dostoevsky to Sartre,* edited by Walter Kaufmann. New York: New American Library, 1975.

Scalise, Charles J. *Hermeneutics as Theological Prolegomena: A Canonical Approach.* Studies in American Biblical Hermeneutics 8. Macon, Ga.: Mercer University Press, 1994.

———. "Patristic Biblical Interpretation and Postmodern Baptist Identity." *Review and Expositor* 101, no. 4 (2004): 615–28.

Schaller, Lyle E. *The New Reformation: Tomorrow Arrived Yesterday.* Nashville: Abingdon, 1995.

Schweitzer, Albert. *The Quest of the Historical Jesus: A Critical Study of Its Progress from Reimarus to Wrede.* Translated by W. Montgomery. New York: Macmillan, 1968.

Seay, Chris. *The Tao of Enron: Spiritual Lessons from a Fortune 500 Fallout.* Colorado Springs: NavPress, 2002.

Sellers, Marnie C. "The Deaf Christ: A Liberation Christology for the Deaf World." Master's thesis in religion. Hardin-Simmons University, 2007.

Sellers, Robert P. "A Baptist View of Missions for Postmodernity." *Review and Expositor* 100 (2003): 641–84.

————. "Is Mission Possible in a Postmodern World?" *Review and Expositor* 101 (2004): 389–424.

Shakespeare, J. H. *Baptist Congregational Pioneers.* London: Kingsgate, 1906.

Shelley, B. L. "Baptist Churches in U.S.A." In *Dictionary of Christianity in America*, edited by Daniel G. Reid, 110–13. Downers Grove, Ill.: InterVarsity, 1990.

Smalley, Stephen S. *1, 2, 3 John.* Edited by David A. Hubbard and Glenn W. Barker. Word Biblical Commentary 51. Waco, Tex.: Word, 1984.

Smith, James K. A. *The Fall of Interpretation: Philosophical Foundations for a Creational Hermeneutic.* Downers Grove, Ill.: InterVarsity, 2000.

————. "A Little Story about Metanarratives: Lyotard, Religion, and Postmodernism Revisited." In *Christianity and the Postmodern Turn*, edited by Myron B. Penner, 123–40. Grand Rapids: Brazos Press, 2005.

————. *Who's Afraid of Postmodernism? Taking Derrida, Lyotard, and Foucault to Church.* The Church and Postmodern Culture. Grand Rapids: Baker Academic, 2006.

Smith, Norman Kemp. *New Studies in the Philosophy of Descartes: Descartes as Pioneer.* London: Macmillan, 1952.

Sobel, Dava. *Galileo's Daughter: A Historical Memoir of Science, Faith, and Love.* New York: Penguin, 2000.

Soskice, Janet Martin. *Metaphor and Religious Language.* Oxford: Clarendon, 1985.

Sparkman, G. Temp. *The Salvation and Nurture of the Child of God.* Valley Forge, Pa.: Judson, 1983.

Spivey, James. "Benajah Harvey Carroll." In *Baptist Theologians*, edited by Timothy George and David S. Dockery, 307–29. Nashville: Broadman, 1990.

Stassen, Glen H. "Anabaptist Influence in the Origin of the Particular Baptists." *The Mennonite Quarterly Review* 36 (1962): 322–48.

————. *Just Peacemaking: Transforming Initiatives for Justice and Peace.*

Louisville: Westminster John Knox, 1992.

Stavropoulos, Christoforos. "Partakers of Divine Nature." In *Eastern Orthodox Theology: A Contemporary Reader*, edited by Daniel B. Clendenin, 183–92. 2nd ed. Grand Rapids: Baker Book House, 2003.

Stendahl, Krister. "Biblical Theology, Contemporary, 1." In *Interpreters Dictionary of the Bible*, 419–20. New York: Abingdon, 1962.

Stetzer, Ed, and David Putman. *Breaking the Missional Code: Your Church Can Become a Missionary in Your Community*. Nashville: B & H Publishing, 2006.

Stiver, Dan R. "Baptists: Modern or Postmodern?" *Review and Expositor* 100 (2003): 521–52.

———. "Felicity and Fusion: Speech Act Theory and Hermeneutical Philosophy." In *Transcending Boundaries in Philosophy and Theology: Reason, Meaning, and Experience*, edited by Kevin J. Vanhoozer and Martin Warner. Burlington, Vt.: Ashgate, 2007.

———. "Hick against Himself: His Theodicy versus His Replica Theory." In *Problems in the Philosophy of Religion: Critical Studies of the Work of John Hick*, edited by Harold Hewitt Jr., 162–72. Library of Philosophy and Religion. London: Macmillan, 1991.

———. "Much Ado About Athens and Jerusalem: The Implications of Postmodernism for Faith." *Review and Expositor* 91 (1994): 83–102.

———. *The Philosophy of Religious Language: Sign, Symbol, and Story*. Cambridge: Blackwell, 1996.

———. "The Problem of Theodicy." *Review and Expositor* 93, no. 4 (1996): 507–17.

———. "Still Too High a Price? Ivan's Question in the Light of Contemporary Theodicy." In *Dostoevsky's Polyphonic Talent*, edited by Joe E. Barnhart, 25–39. Lanham, Md.: University Press of America, 2005.

———. *Theology after Ricoeur: New Directions in Hermeneutical Theology*. Louisville: Westminster John Knox, 2001.

Strong, Augustus. *Outlines of Systematic Theology*. Philadelphia:

Griffith & Rowland, 1908.

Stout, Jeffrey. *The Flight from Authority: Religion, Modernity, and the Quest for Autonomy.* Notre Dame: University of Notre Dame Press, 1981.

Summers, Ray. *Worthy Is the Lamb: An Interpretation of Revelation.* Nashville: Broadman, 1951.

Swinburne, Richard. *Responsibility and Atonement.* New York: Clarendon, 1989.

"*Tammy Kitzmiller et al. v. Dover Area School District et al.*" 400 F. Supp. 2d 700 (M.D.Pa.2005) (U.S. District Court for the middle district of Pennsylvania, 20 December 2005).

Tankersley, David. "Scripture and Experience: A Postconservative Approach to Theological Methods." Master's thesis. Hardin-Simmons University, 2007.

Tanner, Kathryn E. *The Politics of God: Christian Theologies and Social Justice.* Minneapolis: Fortress, 1992.

———. "Theology and the Plain Sense." In *Scriptural Authority and Narrative Interpretation*, edited by Garrett Green, 59–78. Philadelphia: Fortress, 1987.

"Ted Williams Frozen in Two Pieces." *CBS News* 12 August 2003. Accessed 6 April 2007. http://www.cbsnews.com/stories/2002/12/20/national/main533849.shtml.

Tertullian. *Against Praxeas.* Translated by Peter Holmes. In *Latin Christianity: Its Founder, Tertullian*, edited by Alexander Roberts and James Donaldson, 597–627. The Ante-Nicene Fathers 3. Grand Rapids: Eerdmans, 1956.

———. *The Apology.* Translated by S. Thelwall. In *Latin Christianity: Its Founder, Tertullian*, edited by Alexander Roberts and James Donaldson, 17–60. The Ante-Nicene Fathers 3. Grand Rapids: Eerdmans, 1957.

———. *On the Apparel of Women.* Translated by S. Thelwall. In *Fathers of the Third Century*, edited by Alexander Roberts and James Donaldson, 14–26. The Ante-Nicene Fathers 4. Grand Rapids: Eerdmans, 1956.

———. *The Prescription Against Heretics.* Translated by Peter Holmes.

In *Latin Christianity: Its Founder, Tertullian,* edited by Alexander Roberts and James Donaldson, 243–67. The Ante-Nicene Fathers 3. Grand Rapids: Eerdmans, 1956.

Thiselton, Anthony C. *The Two Horizons: New Testament Hermeneutics and Philosophical Description.* Grand Rapids: Eerdmanns, 1980.

Thomas Aquinas. *The Summa Theologica of Saint Thomas Aquinas.* Great Books of the Western World 20–21, edited by Robert Maynard Hutchins. Chicago: Encyclopedia Britannica, 1952.

Thorsen, Donald A. D. *The Wesleyan Quadrilateral: Scripture, Tradition, Reason, and Experience as a Model of Evangelical Theology.* Grand Rapids: Zondervan, 1990.

Tiessen, Terrance. *Providence and Prayer: How Does God Work in the World?* Downer's Grove, Ill.: InterVarsity, 2000.

Tillich, Paul. *The Courage to Be.* New Haven: Yale University Press, 1952.

———. *Systematic Theology.* Vols. 1–3. Chicago: University of Chicago Press, 1951, 1957, 1963.

Todd, John M. *Luther: A Life.* New York: Crossroad, 1982.

Treier, Daniel J. "Faith." In *Dictionary for Theological Interpretation of the Bible,* edited by Kevin J. Vanhoozer, 226–28. Grand Rapids: Baker Academic, 2005.

Trotter, Robert J. "The Mystery of Mastery." *Psychology Today* (July 1986): 32–38.

Trueblood, Elton. *The Incendiary Fellowship.* New York: Harper & Row, 1967.

Tuana, Nancy. *Woman and the History of Philosophy.* Paragon Issues in Philosophy. New York: Paragon House, 1992.

Tupper, E. Frank. *A Scandalous Providence: The Jesus Story of the Compassion of God.* Macon, Ga.: Mercer University Press, 1995.

Twain, Mark. *Mark Twain's Autobiography.* Vol. 2. New York: P. F. Collier & Son, 1924.

Vanhoozer, Kevin J. *The Drama of Doctrine: A Canonical-Linguistic Approach to Christian Theology.* Louisville: Westminster John

Knox, 2005.

———. *First Theology: God, Scripture, and Hermeneutics.* Downer's Grove, Ill.: InterVarsity, 2002.

———. *Is There a Meaning in This Text? The Bible, the Reader, and the Morality of Literary Knowledge.* Grand Rapids: Zondervan, 1998.

Vanhoozer, Kevin J., ed. *The Cambridge Companion to Postmodern Theology.* Cambridge: Cambridge University Press, 2003.

———. *Dictionary for Theological Interpretation of the Bible.* Grand Rapids: Baker Academic, 2005.

"Violated Trust: Special Report." *Baptist Standard.* 11 June 2007.

Volf, Miroslav. *After Our Likeness: The Church as the Image of the Trinity.* Sacra Doctrina: Christian Theology for a Postmodern Age, edited by Alan G. Padgett. Grand Rapids: Eerdmans, 1998.

———. *Exclusion and Embrace: A Theological Exploration of Identity, Otherness, and Reconciliation.* Nashville: Abingdon, 1996.

Volf, Miroslav, and Dorothy C. Bass, eds. *Practicing Theology: Beliefs and Practices in Christian Life.* Grand Rapids: Eerdmans, 2002.

Vrooman, Jack R. *René Descartes: A Biography.* New York: G. P. Putnam's Sons, 1970.

Walker, Graham B., Jr. "Noah and the Season of Violence: Theological Reflections on Genesis 6:5–9:17 and the Work of René Girard." *Review and Expositor* 103 no. 2 (2006): 371–90.

Walker, Williston, et al. *A History of the Christian Church.* 4th ed. New York: Charles Scribner's Sons, 1985.

Walls, Jerry L. *Heaven: The Logic of Eternal Joy.* Oxford: Oxford University Press, 2002.

Walls, Jerry L., and Joseph R. Dongell. *Why I Am Not a Calvinist.* Downers Grove, Ill.: InterVarsity, 2004.

Walsh, Michael. *Butler's Lives of the Saints.* San Francisco: Harper & Row, 1985.

Wamble, G. Hugh. "The Background and Meaning of the 1963

Southern Baptists Articles of Faith on the Bible." In *The Proceedings of the Conference on Biblical Inerrancy 1987*, 331–54. Nashville: Broadman, 1987.

———. "Historic Practices Regarding Children." In *Children and Conversion*, edited by Clifford Ingle, 71–83. Nashville: Broadman, 1970.

———. *The Shape of Faith*. Nashville: Broadman, 1962.

Ward, Graham. "The Logos, the Body, and the World: On the Phenomenological Border." In *Transcending Boundaries in Philosophy and Theology: Reason, Meaning, and Experience*, edited by Kevin J. Vanhoozer and Martin Warner. Burlington, Vt.: Ashgate, 2007.

———. "Postmodern Theology." In *The Modern Theologians: An Introduction to Christian Theology in the Twentieth Century*, edited by David F. Ford. 2nd ed. Malden, Mass.: Blackwell, 1997.

Ware, Timothy. *The Orthodox Church*. Rev. ed. London: Penguin, 1997.

Warfield, Benjamin Breckinridge. *The Inspiration and Authority of the Bible*. Edited by Samuel G. Craig. Philadelphia: Presbyterian & Reformed, 1948.

Watson, Natalie K. *Feminist Theology*. Grand Rapids: Eerdmans, 2003.

Webber, Robert E. *The Younger Evangelicals: Facing the Challenges of the New World*. Grand Rapids: Baker, 2002.

Weber, Max. *The Protestant Ethic and the Spirit of Capitalism*. Translated by Talcott Parsons. London: Unwin University Books, 1930.

Weber, Timothy P. *Living in the Shadow of the Second Coming: American Premillennialism, 1875–1982*. 2nd ed. Chicago: University of Chicago Press, 1987.

Weinandy, Thomas G. *Does God Change?* Studies in Historical Theology Series 4. Petersham, Mass.: St. Bede's, 1985.

Welker, Michael, ed. *The Work of the Spirit: Pneumatology and Pentecostalism*. Grand Rapids: Eerdmans, 2001.

Westermann, Claus. *Creation*. Translated by John J. Scullion. Philadelphia: Fortress, 1974.

White, Lynn Jr. "On the Historical Roots of Our Ecological Crisis."

Science 155 (1967): 1203–7.

Whitehead, Alfred North. *Process and Reality*. Edited by David Ray Griffin and Donald W. Sherburne. 3rd ed. New York: Free Press, 1978.

Willard, Dallas. *The Divine Conspiracy: Rediscovering Our Hidden Life in God*. San Francisco: HarperSanFrancisco, 1998.

———. *How Does the Disciple Live?* 2007. Accessed 26 December 2007. http://www.dwillard.org/articles/artview.asp?artID=103.

Williams, Ernest S. *Systematic Theology*. 3 vols. Springfield, Mo.: Gospel Publishing House, 1953.

Wink, Walter. *Engaging the Powers: Discernment and Resistance in a World of Domination*. Minneapolis: Fortress, 1992.

Witherington III, Ben. *The Jesus Quest: The Third Search for the Jew of Nazareth*. 2d ed. Downers Grove, Ill.: InterVarsity, 1997.

———. *The Paul Quest: The Renewed Search for the Jew of Tarsus*. Downers Grove, Ill.: InterVarsity, 2001.

———. *The Problem with Evangelical Theology: Testing the Exegetical Foundations of Calvinism, Dispensationalism, and Wesleyanism*. Waco, Tex.: Baylor University Press, 2005.

Wittgenstein, Ludwig. *Culture and Value*. Edited by G. H. von Wright. Translated by Peter Winch. Chicago: University of Chicago Press, 1980.

———. *Lectures and Conversations on Aesthetics, Psychology, and Religious Belief*. Edited by Cyril Barrett. Berkeley: University of California Press, 1966.

———. *On Certainty*. Edited by G. E. M. Anscombe and G. H. von Wright. Translated by Denis Paul and G. E. M. Anscombe. New York: Harper Torchbooks, 1969.

———. *Philosophical Investigations*. Translated by G. E. M. Anscombe. 3rd ed. New York: Macmillan, 1958.

———. *Zettel*. Edited by G. E. M. Anscombe and G. H. von Wright. Translated by G. E. M. Anscombe. Berkeley: University of California Press, 1967.

Wolterstorff, Nicholas. *Divine Discourse: Philosophical Reflections on the Claim*

That God Speaks. Cambridge: Cambridge University Press, 1995.

———. *Lament for a Son*. Grand Rapids: Eerdmans, 1987.

———. "The Migration of the Theistic Arguments: From Natural Theology to Evidentialist Apologetics." In *Rationality, Religious Belief, and Moral Commitment: New Essays in the Philosophy of Religion*, edited by Robert Audi and William J. Wainwright, 38–81. Ithaca: Cornell University Press, 1986.

Wood, Charles. *The Formation of Christian Understanding*. Philadelphia: Westminster, 1981.

Wright, N. T. *Evil and the Justice of God*. Downers Grove, Ill.: InterVarsity, 2006.

———. *The New Testament and the People of God*. Christian Origins and the Question of God 1. Minneapolis: Fortress, 1992.

———. *Paul in Fresh Perspective*. Minneapolis: Fortress, 2005.

———. *The Resurrection of the Son of God*. Christian Origins and the Question of God 3. Minneapolis: Fortress, 2003.

———. *Simply Christian: Why Christianity Makes Sense*. San Francisco: HarperSanFrancisco, 2006.

Wuthnow, Robert. *Loose Connections: Joining Together in America's Fragmented Communities*. Cambridge, Mass.: Harvard University Press, 2002.

———. *Sharing the Journey: Support Groups and America's New Quest for Community*. New York: Free Press, 1996.

Wuthnow, Robert, ed. *I Come Away Stronger: How Small Groups Are Shaping American Religion*. Grand Rapids: Eerdmans, 2001.

Yoder, John Howard. *The Politics of Jesus*. 2nd ed. Grand Rapids: Eerdmans, 1994.

Young, E. J. *Thy Word Is Truth: Some Thoughts on the Biblical Doctrine of Inspiration*. The Banner of Truth Trust. Grand Rapids: Eerdmans, 1957.

Scripture Index

Genesis

1–11	226, 235
1	114–17, 163–70, 175, 176, 178–81, 187, 211, 219, 465
1:1-2	175
1:26-27	158, 211
1:28	167
1:31	115
2	66, 178–81, 187, 189, 222, 226, 465, 474
3–11	187, 226
3	179, 215, 226–32, 248
3:12	226
3:16	229
3:22-24	197
3:24	474
4	231
4:17	178
4:24	232
6–11	121
6	66, 232
6:4	232
6:5	99, 121
6:5-8	232
6:6	117, 233
6:11	121, 232
6:13	232
9	214
9:21-22	233
12	99, 226, 234
32:22-32	186

Exodus

10:1	92
14:1-12	338
20:3	118
20:7	118
33:23	195

Leviticus

9:18	92

Deuteronomy

6:5	92
32:5	235

Judges

20:2	373

Ruth 86, 102

1 Samuel 84

2:26	280

2 Samuel 84

Esther 86, 95, 101

Job

3:3	186
3:3-4	187
3:11	443
3:13-19	443
14:11-14	443
14:14	473
38:1	107

Psalms

8	211–12
8:3-4	168
8:5	169
22:14	287
22:18	287
22:28	287
88	442–43
119:105	351
137:9	92–93
139:8	123

Ecclesiastes 86

Isaiah

2:1-4	439, 445
2:4	273
6	100
11:6-9	439
40:31	362
42–53	549n21
43:18-19	292
55:6-8	332

Jeremiah

7:22	84
20:14	186
31:29-30	83

Ezekiel

18:2-3	83
18:23	454
38:2	439
38:14-15	439

Daniel 101

7:13	549n21
9:27	439

Hosea

3	316

Amos

5:21-24	84
7:7-9	244
9:7	99

Joel

2:28	154

Jonah 102

Micah

4:1-4	445

Matthew	80, 83, 84
3:13	409
4:1-11	283
4:5-7	437
4:19	394
5-7	83, 92
5:4	273
5:10	468
5:13	374
5:21-26	323
5:32	332
5:44	95, 363
5:45	199
6:9-10	355
6:10	358
6:12	313
6:15	313
7:14	360
7:21	273
7:28	282
8:12	460
9:17	272
10:16	358
10:24	196
10:29	353
10:37	119
11:19	278, 279
11:28-30	345
12:22-32	247
12:24	196
13:49-50	460
13:51	58
16:13	282
16:17-18	283
16:18	418
16:22	283
16:23	283
16:25	377
18:6	176
18:12-14	311
19:30	273
20:16	241
20:25-28	423
20:28	316
21:33-41	168, 215
22:13	460
24	470
24:6	468
24:9-21	468
24:22	468
24:32	467
24:33	273
24:34	467
24:36	472
24:37-41	470
24:45-61	168, 215
25:14-29	168, 215, 237
25	349
25:30	460
25:35	176
25:40	273
26:39	188
27:46	287
28:18	301
28:19	409
28:19-20	336
Mark	80, 83, 84, 88
1:4	326
1:15	326
1:12	283
1:14	273
1:15	272
1:35	282
2:27	279
3:1-6	279–80
8:27	282
8:29	140, 254
9:48	460
13:14	439
15:34	287

Luke   80, 83, 84
1:1-4   83
1:52   280
2:46-47   280
3:16   342
4:1-13   283
6:20   37
6:21   273
7:50   326
9:5   360
9:18   282
9:51   283
10:27   118
11:1   282
11:4   278
11:14-23   244
14:26   359
14:31-33   438
15   235
15:3-7   99
15:4   353
15:11-32   309–11
17:7-10   338
18   136
18:20   399
19:10   399
23:43   450

John   80, 88
1:9   101, 300, 457
1:14   7, 9, 219
1:30   60
3:3   332, 479
3:8   100, 292
3:36   273
6:67   283
10:10   477
13:35   406
14–16   302
14:3   273
14:6   273, 300
14:14   355

15:5   338
15:7   74, 355
15:13   319
15:15   479
16:7   154
16:8   123, 154, 328
17   318
17:15-18   239
17:21   478
17:22-23   479
17:23   355
20:31   94
21:25   82

Acts
1:5   342
1:7-8   472
1:8   342, 394, 397
1:17   154
2   341
2:4   342
2:6   343
2:18   342
2:38   342
6   93, 423
8:1   362
8:15-16   342
8:18-19   342
9:2   307, 365
13   93
15   405
16:6   359–60
17:28   99, 105
17:55   301

Romans
1   236
1–2   93, 99
1:8   328
1:20   99
2:6   337
2:13   337

2:25-29	457
2:29	99, 301
3	236
3:23	99, 229, 233
4	457
4:9	459
4:9-12	457
5:1	333
5:8	479
5:12	191, 231
6:1-11	317
6:2	459
6:4	326, 341
7:4	374
7:7	235
7:13-24	338
8	402
8:1-11	333, 339
8:4	249
8:9	302, 339
8:21-22	472
8:22	199, 302
8:26	354
8:37	356
12:15	402, 404
13	242, 359
13:14	357
14	93

1 Corinthians

1:2	385
1:25	272, 289
3:1	344
8	93, 384
11:1	284
11:24-36	413
12	379
12:13	341
12:27	374
12:30	343
12:31	343, 344

13	344
13:1-3	344
13:12	96, 101, 358
14:17	343
14:27	343
15	6, 448, 449, 450, 451, 473, 474
15:20	273
15:37-38	449
15:44	169, 448–49
15:52	449
15:55	446

2 Corinthians

1:8	450
4:7	85
5	449, 450, 451, 453
5:17	333
5:18	393
5:19	289, 324
5:21	319
6:17	101
12:9	74
15:6	292

Galatians

2:11-21	405
2:20	302, 339
3–4	457
3:20	317
5:16	333
5:22-23	337
6:1-2	404

Ephesians

2:8	326
3:20	355, 472
4–5	379
4:3	154
4:4-5	341
4:11-12	424
4:12	374, 420

5:18	341
5:27	261
6:4	161
6:11	183

Philippians

1:7	300
1:12	384
1:23	450
2:1-11	261–62
2:1	374
2:12	326, 337
2:13	337, 362
3:12	345–46
3:14-16	346
3:14	347
3:15	96
4:7	356
4:11	187
4:12-13	438

Colossians

1:17	300
2:12	341
3:1-3	479
3:2	249, 347
3:3	347
3:15	354, 357, 358

1 Thessalonians

1:8	328
4	452
4:11	437
4:13-18	449–50, 462
5:16-17	356
5:19-21	422
5:21	51

2 Thessalonians

3:10	437

1 Timothy

1:15	362
2	93, 417
2:4	192
4:4	244

2 Timothy

1:7	237
2:3	453, 454
2:15	425
3:16	406
3:16-17	75, 94

Philemon 86, 95

Hebrews 80, 81, 88

1:1	86
2:10	281
2:17-18	281
4:9	373
4:15	284
4:16	281
5:8	281
5:10	457
5:13-14	344
5:14	348, 358
11:26	373
11:39-40	301, 459
12:6	387

James 68, 81

1:14	249
2	405
2:18	337

1 Peter 81

1:5	326
2:9	469
3:19	300
4:6	300, 458

2 Peter — 81, 86
2:17 — 460
3:9 — 125, 454
3:10 — 473
3:15-16 — 83

1 John
1 — 404
1:8 — 346-47
1:9 — 346
2:16 — 226
3:9 — 346–47
4:8 — 120, 311
4:18 — 249
4:19 — 306, 373, 479

Jude — 86
13 — 460

Revelation — 86
3:20 — 328
13 — 359
13:5-6 — 242
19–20 — 464–65
20 — 145
20–22 — 439
20:4 — 462
20:4-6 — 470
20:8 — 439
20:15 — 460
21–22 — 135
21:1-5 — 170, 474–75
21:3 — 278
21:4 — 472
21:10 — 445
21:24-25 — 446
22:1-5 — 474
22:1-2 — 476
22:20 — 461, 553n58

Index of Names

Abelard, 314, 322, 323

Abraham, 68, 86, 99, 105, 121, 226, 233, 235, 445, 457, 459

Aetius, 148

Ansbro, John J., 524n18, 548n6

Anselm, 314, 317, 318, 319, 322

Apollinaris, 149–50, 256–57

Aquinas, Thomas; see Thomas Aquinas

Aristotle, 23–24, 25, 30, 33, 64–65, 95, 131, 133, 134, 157, 158, 296, 414, 448, 450, 488n37, 489n42, 512n88

Arius, 145–49

Arminius, Jacob, 126–27, 327

Ashcraft, Morris, 553n58

Athanasius, 147–50, 262, 296, 501n50, 508n44, 529n7

Augustine, 15, 21, 22, 56, 102, 107, 110, 119, 121, 124, 138, 142, 143, 149, 180, 185, 189, 190, 191, 193, 194, 195, 197, 203, 215, 230, 239, 311, 317, 320, 327, 329, 333, 357, 373, 399, 410, 459, 475, 481, 502n58, 504n5, 506n30, 507n37, 510n60, 513n3, 518n50, 519n54, 520n70, 527n49, 528n61, 543n22, 551n38

Aulén, Gustav, 314, 319

Austin, John, 29–30, 500n40

Baillie, D. M., 323–24, 504n3

Bain, Ken, 491n68

Ballmer, Randall, 36

Balthasar, Hans Urs von, 500n44

Barbour, Ian, 496n9, 514n12, 515n18, 516n21

Barth, Karl, 3, 20, 44, 53, 111, 119, 205, 214, 477, 505n15, 531n41, 535n21, 535n27, 551n36, 552n47

Basil of Caesarea, 150
Bavinck, Herman, 551n36
Beasley-Murray, George, 533n1
Bellah, Robert, 16
Berkouwer, G. C., 553n36
Bloesch, Donald, 451, 454, 458, 537n35, 551n36, 552n47, 555n72
Bloom, Harold, 19
Bohr, Niels, 25
Bonhoeffer, Dietrich, 349, 483n3, 540n59
Borg, Marcus, 250, 278, 531n25, 531n36, 531n38
Boyce, James P., 133, 508n46
Bradford, William, 368, 371
Brewster, William, 368, 371
Brown, Peter, 239, 528n61
Brueggemann, Walter, 31–32, 135, 173, 179, 513–14n5, 515n13, 516n26
Brunner, Emil, 194, 214
Bryan, William Jennings, 175
Buber, Martin, 107
Buckley, Michael, 109, 504n8
Bultmann, Rudolf, 111, 264, 269, 505n15, 532n58, 536n32
Bush, George, 39, 170

Calvin, John, 67, 68, 92, 101, 103, 121, 124, 184, 190, 202, 203, 204, 205, 207, 208, 235, 293, 325, 367, 381, 410, 414, 464, 502n58, 503n64, 506n29, 507n37, 518n50, 519n56, 527n53, 527n54, 551n43, 555n70
Campbell, Alexander, 367
Carroll, B. H., 465

Chaucer, 83
Chrysostom, John, 256
Clement of Alexandria, 102, 323, 504n68
Clouse, Robert G., 547n1, 548n3, 553n56
Cobb, John B., Jr., 549n23
Columbus, Christopher, 14
Cone, James, 255, 532n61
Constans, 147–48
Constantine, 145–47, 464, 465
Cooper, Burton, 188, 509n53
Craig, William Lane, 129, 130
Criswell, W. A., 497n14
Crockett, William V., 552–53n53
Crossan, John, 530n20, 531n30, 531n37
Cullmann, Oscar, 451
Cunningham, David, 407, 509n55, 511n73
Cunningham, Richard B., 489n46
Cyprian, 419
Cyril of Alexandria, 257–59, 296–97, 508n44

Damasio, Antonio R., 486n16, 524n20
Darby, John Nelson, 466
Davis, Stephen, 505n16
Dawkins, Richard, 21, 22, 177, 516n21
Derrida, Jacques, 313, 324, 534n5
Descartes, René, 13–23, 45, 51, 55, 63, 110, 165, 216, 486n7, 486n12
Dickens, Charles, 491n67
Diodorus, 256
Dockery, David S., 499n31
Dongell, Joseph R., 522n79

Dostoyevsky, Fyodor, 186, 210, 475, 518n41
Dunn, James D. G., 519n55
Dunne, Joseph, 488n35, 488n37
Dyson, Freeman, 549n16

Edge, Findley, 392, 424, 543n18
Edwards, Jonathan, 465, 523n6, 540n64
Eusebius of Caesarea, 146
Eutyches, 297–99

Falwell, Jerry, 7, 36
Farley, Edward, 20
Fee, Gordon, 344, 525n29, 537n44, 538n45, 538n49
Feinberg, John, 519n57
Fichte, Johann Gottlob, 553n59
Fiddes, Paul, 324, 361, 364, 509n55, 510n56, 510n61, 511n72, 511n73, 513n91, 531n40, 535n22
Finger, Thomas, 41, 493n92, 548n13
Fowl, Stephen, 501n52
Fowler, James, 218
Frei, Hans, 69, 71, 85, 511n79
Freud, Sigmund, 110, 114, 469
Friedman, Thomas, 39

Gadamer, Hans-Georg, 23–24, 26, 33, 47–51, 76, 87, 95, 98, 488n36, 491n63, 491n65
Galileo, 14, 45–46, 63–65, 93, 116, 170, 172, 173, 174, 177, 193, 216, 514n12, 515n18, 519–20n58
Garland, David E., 550n30
Geertz, Clifford, 511n79

George, Timothy, 54
Gibbs, Eddie, 394, 543n23
Gilkey, Langdon, 371, 514n9, 516n21, 516n22
Gilson, Étienne, 177, 505n18
Girard, René, 321
Goethe, 34
Goetz, Ronald, 493n96, 508n49
Goldingay, John, 506n21
González, Justo, 317, 323
Graham, Billy, 7, 31, 39, 335
Gravrilyuk, Paul, 509n50
Green, Joel, 525n28, 534n11
Gregory of Nazianzus, 150, 317, 529n7
Gregory of Nyssa, 150
Grenz, Stanley, 45, 138, 285, 294, 453, 483n2, 485n13, 495n112, 495n113, 495n121, 499n30, 499n31, 502n60, 510n55, 510n58, 523n10, 523n12, 527n48, 534n16, 537n40, 538n47, 547n67, 551n40, 553n56, 553n61
Grey, Mary, 485n3
Griffin, David Ray, 22, 549n23
Guder, Darrell, 393
Gushee, David, 407, 546n45

Hampson, Daphne, 158, 528n56
Harnock, Adolf, 263
Hart, David, 517n29
Harvey, Barry, 373, 374
Hasker, William, 507n37, 508n41, 508n47
Haught, John, 515n18, 516n21
Hebblethwaite, Brian, 520n66
Hegel, G. W. H., 68, 116, 182, 223, 432, 512n88, 553n59

Heidegger, Martin, 18, 218, 220, 524n24
Hekman, Susan, 24
Helwys, Thomas, 3–4, 7, 223, 367–72, 542n7
Henry, Carl F. H., 31, 490n24, 490n26
Herzog, Frederick, 35, 37
Hick, John, 194, 195, 451, 452, 517n37, 520n60, 520n64, 523n10, 526n42, 550n32, 552n47
Hitler, Adolf, 119
Holmes, Arthur, 101, 300
Hosack, Robert N., 547n1, 548n3, 553n56
Hume, David, 110, 491n67
Hus, John, 62

Ignatius of Antioch, 81
Irenaeus, 142, 189, 194, 197, 213, 214, 315, 316, 317, 511n67, 534n9, 543n21, 555n70

James I, King, 3–4, 368
Jefferson, Thomas, 53
Jenkins, Philip, 38, 39, 250, 485n4, 492n82, 511n78
Jeremias, Joachim, 264
Joachim of Fiore, 553n59
John the Baptist, 60, 271, 326, 341, 367, 409, 538n48
Johnson, Elizabeth, 157–58, 512n88, 527n46, 533n63
Johnson, Luke Timothy, 269
Johnson, Mark, 32
Jones, Bob, 7
Jones, Joe, 523n17, 551n35
Jones, Serene, 484n1

Julian, 149
Julius, Bishop, 148
Justin the Martyr, 81, 102, 142

Kaku, Michio, 489n41, 521n71, 549n16
Kant, Immanuel, 68, 262, 432, 512n88, 553n59
Käsemann, Ernst, 264
Keller, Helen, 221
Kelly, J. N. D., 257–58, 510n62, 529n4, 529n7, 532n51
Kelsey, David, 71, 72
Kennedy, John F., 130
Kennedy, Robert, 130
Kierkegaard, Søren, 110, 111, 113, 222, 236, 259, 401, 505n14, 505n15, 526n33, 526n34
Kimball, Dan, 393, 532n57, 544–45n36
King Jr., Martin Luther, 213, 322, 349, 373, 429–31, 437, 524n18
Kraybill, Donald, 323–24
Kuhn, Thomas, 70, 485n1, 485n2, 487n28, 498n29, 514n8
Küng, Hans, 110, 485n2, 496n12, 504n7, 542n16, 543n19
Kushner, Harold, 182
Kyle, Richard, 547n1, 553n56, 553n59

LaCugna, Catherine, 510n55, 510n60, 511n77
Ladd, G. Eldon, 553n56
Lakeland, Paul, 485n1
Lakoff, George, 32
Lang, Bernard, 554–55n70, 555n71
Larkin, Clarence, 466

Larson, Edward, 514n7, 515n15
Lavine, T. Z., 486n13
Leo I, Pope, 297
Leonard, Bill, 492n87, 496n3, 542n5, 542n7
Lewis, C. S., 12, 31, 123, 124, 188, 195, 196, 306, 458, 459, 460, 506n27, 533n64, 550n29
Lincoln, Abraham, 223, 429
Lindbeck, George, 71, 72, 495n120
Lindsey, Hal, 467, 470
Locke, John, 14, 53, 94, 491n67, 498n28
Long, Jimmy, 392
Luther, Martin, 2, 23, 34, 51, 52, 62–63, 65, 67, 68, 107, 204, 210, 223, 302, 311, 325, 329, 351, 367, 381, 414, 415, 452, 464, 498n120, 496n4, 496n6, 503n64, 507n37, 555n70

Macchia, Frank, 538n46
MacIntyre, Alasdair, 26, 73, 98, 489, 501n49
Madison, James, 223, 371
Marcion, 81, 166, 198, 389
Marsden, George, 69, 496n7, 497–98n22, 515n15, 534n6, 554n65, 554n66
Marshall, Molly, 124, 499n31, 507n35, 510n55, 537n39
Martin, Ralph P., 550–51n34
Marx, Karl, 110, 114, 430, 431, 437, 439, 553n59
McDannell, Colleen, 554–55n70, 555n71
McFague, Sally, 493n98, 512n84, 531n30
McLaren, Brian, 488n33, 531n38, 544n34

McLaughlin, Eleanor, 306, 533n64
McClendon, Wm. James, 41, 357, 367, 424, 486n15, 493n92, 522–23n6, 537n43, 540n64, 547n66, 548n13
McGill, Arthur, 121
McGrath, Alister, 54, 456, 495n113, 495n118, 503n67, 555n70
Meacham, Jon, 490n60
Merleau–Ponty, Maurice, 217–18, 524n24
Milbank, John, 116, 504n8
Miller, William, 428–29, 430, 432, 437, 439, 466, 467, 470
Mitchell, Margaret, 67, 497n16
Molina, Luis de, 129–30
Moltmann, Jürgen, 41, 392, 493n96, 493n98, 494n108, 526n36, 543n23, 552n47, 553n59, 554n68,
Moody, Dale, 41, 319, 335, 433, 460, 516n24, 534n16, 553n54, 553n57
Moses, 66, 86, 195, 236, 429, 457
Mother Teresa, 437
Mullins, E. Y., 503n60
Murphy, Nancey, 69, 70, 486n14, 486n15, 498n27, 501n49, 521n72, 521n74, 524n19, 525n28, 540n64
Murton, John, 370–71, 542n8

Nero, 242
Nestorius, 256–61, 297
Newman, Carey, 485n14
Newport, John, 515n17
Newton, Isaac, 14
Niebuhr, Reinhold, 228 238, 358, 360, 527n45, 528n58

Nietzsche, Friedrich, 108–14, 210, 504n6, 523n7

Noetus, 143

Noll, Mark, 87, 101

Oates, Stephen, 535n20, 548n4

Olson, Roger, 8, 9, 52, 483–84n2, 484–85n13, 499n31, 503n62, 508n44, 510n62, 529n4, 532n51, 532n56, 534n6, 535–56n28, 536n29, 536n31, 539n53, 545n37, 546n57

Origen, 68, 145, 146, 148, 248, 323

Osman, Agnes, 339

Outler, Albert, 494n110,

Pannenberg, Wolfhart, 41, 224, 265, 432, 433, 548n10

Parham, Charles, 339

Pascal, 105, 106, 107, 208

Paul of Samosota, 141, 256

Peacocke, Arthur, 514n12

Peck, M. Scott, 249

Pelagius, 327

Perrin, Norman, 490n49

Peter, the Apostle, 69, 74, 154, 283, 342, 367, 388, 394, 416, 417, 418

Peterson, Michael, 521n73

Phillips, D. Z., 549n23

Phillips, J. B., 154

Philo, 270

Pierard, Richard, 547n1, 548n3, 553n56

Pigott, Kelly, 208–11

Pinnock, Clark, 60, 69, 70, 552n44, 552n48

Piper, John, 205, 521–22n78, 522n80

Placher, William C., 491n75, 509n50

Plantinga, Alvin, 197, 487n21, 505n17, 517n36, 520n69

Plato, 2, 15, 17, 19–21, 23, 30, 33, 102, 106, 116, 117, 131, 144, 155, 164, 181, 216, 269, 284, 296, 300, 354, 400, 429, 434, 446, 447, 448

Poe, Harry, 40

Polanyi, Michael, 25, 34, 348, 489n42

Polkinghorne, 196, 205, 521n74, 521n75

Polycarp, 142

Postman, Neil, 502n57

Praxeas, 143

Rahner, Karl, 143, 151, 452

Ramm, Bernard, 454

Randall, Lisa, 489n41

Richard of St. Victor, 138

Rich, Adrienne, 485n3

Ricoeur, Paul, 23, 33, 47–51, 72, 73, 74, 75, 107, 220, 250, 277, 490n50, 491n75, 493n99, 496n8, 512n84, 524n24, 526n34, 530n14, 531n30, 541n70

Robinson, John, 484n9

Robinson, Michael, 507n37, 507n38, 536n28

Rose of Lima, 208–11, 239

Roth, John, 185

Sabellius, 143

Sartre, Jean-Paul, 224

Scalise, Charles, 497n14, 501n52, 503n62

Schelling, Friedrich Wilhelm Joseph, 553n59

Schleiermacher, Friedrich, 44, 194, 536n31

Schweitzer, Albert, 263–64
Scofield, C. I., 466
Seay, Chris, 506n26
Sellers, Marnie, 533n62, 533n64
Sellers, Rob, 395, 544n33
Seymour, William J., 339
Shakespeare, J. H., 484n9
Shakespeare, William, 24
Smith, James K. A., 22, 24–25, 527n52
Smith, Norman Kemp, 486n12
Smyth, John, 368–70, 533n3
Socrates, 20, 102, 132, 288, 346, 451, 479
Sparkman, G. Temp, 411, 546n58
Spinoza, Baruch, 116, 117, 182
Spivey, James, 554n63
Stassen, Glen H., 412
Stavropoulos, Christoforos, 555n76
Stendahl, Krister, 490n63
Stiver, Dan R., 486n6, 487n30, 490n48, 490n58, 493n99, 500n41, 512n84, 517n36, 518n41, 520n60, 530n14, 540n59, 551n39
Stout, Jeffrey, 25–26
Strong, A. H., 465
Sullivan, Annie, 221
Summers, Ray, 553n60
Sweet, Leonard, 548–49n14

Tatian, 81
Tertullian, 21, 101, 142, 143, 152, 228, 297, 508n44, 511n68, 529n8, 543n21
Theodore of Mopsuestia, 256–57
Theodotus the Tanner, 141
Thiselton, Anthony, 502n54

Thomas Aquinas, 4, 21, 25, 30, 42, 67, 106, 110, 124, 132, 134, 154, 155, 156, 157, 158, 184, 185, 194, 202, 328, 414, 448, 487n25, 503n64, 507n37, 512n84, 512n88, 520n70, 536n31, 537n35, 555n70
Thorsen, Thomas, 494n110
Tiessen, Terrence, 130, 131, 507n38, 518n39
Tillich, Paul, 29, 57, 105, 118, 156, 225, 251, 303, 307, 375, 495n121, 504n3
Toland, John, 21
Toulmin, Stephen, 16, 486n7, 486n11
Tracy, David, 500n43
Trueblood, Elton, 392
Tuana, Nancy,
Tupper, E. Frank, 161, 188, 246, 247, 513n91, 528n69, 531n40
Twain, Mark, 75, 224
Tyrrell, George, 263

Urban VIII, Pope, 63–64

Valentinus, 81
Vanhoozer, Kevin, 35, 72, 73, 74, 75, 78, 351, 359, 407, 488n35, 493n98, 501n52
Volf, Miroslav, 227, 242, 312–13, 361, 501n49, 533n3, 543n20
Voltaire, 109
Vrooman, Jack R., 486n7

Walls, Jerry L., 522n79, 554–55n70, 555n73
Wamble, G. Hugh, 404, 484n8, 502n59, 546n49
Ward, Graham, 219, 487n30

Ward, Wayne, 553n57

Ware, Timothy, 511n83

Warfield, B. B., 70, 175

Washington, George, 75

Watson, Natalie, 524n25, 533n63

Weber, Max, 210, 522n6

Weber, Timothy P., 554n64, 554n65

Weinandy, Thomas, 508n45, 509n50

Wesley, John, 52, 55, 56, 58, 311, 329, 346, 347, 367, 494n110, 539n53, 540n64, 547n58

Westermann, Claus, 214, 215, 513n1, 514n6, 515n13, 5116n25, 518n49, 523n10

White, Ellen, 429, 466

White, Lynn, 167, 173

Whitehead, Alfred North, 508n50, 522n84, 549n23,

Wiesel, Elie, 321

Willard, Dallas, 348, 539n58, 544n32

William of Ockham, 203–4

Williams, Ernest, 537n41, 538n46, 538n48,

Williams, Roger, 368

Williams, Rowan, 122–23, 507n31

Williams, Ted, 435

Wink, Walter, 241–42, 528n69

Witherington III, Ben, 269, 490n49, 502n57, 529n11, 537n38, 554n67

Wittgenstein, Ludwig, 19, 30, 34, 71, 437, 491n71, 541n70, 549n17

Wright, N. T., 265, 269, 443, 517n29, 530n16, 530n18, 530n19, 532n47, 536n34, 546n48, 549n22, 550n24, 550n26, 550n27, 550n31, 554n69

Wycliffe, John, 62

Yoder, John Howard, 241

Zwingli, Ullrich, 414, 415, 507n37

Index of Subjects

Abba, 156, 159, 160, 180, 271, 277–78, 285

Adam, 142, 178, 179, 189, 190, 191, 194, 196, 201, 203, 207, 213, 214, 222, 224, 226, 227, 228, 229, 230, 231, 233, 236, 242, 284, 285, 318, 334, 456, 474, 516n24, 518n50

Alexandrian school, 65–66

analogy, 30, 31, 32, 106, 134, 154, 156, 157, 490n58, 512n84

Antioch school, 66–68

apocalyptic, 73, 166, 439–41, 468, 471, 554n69

Arminianism, 10, 112, 128, 129, 327–28, 335, 453–56, 507–50n40, 535–36n28

ascension, 301–2, 342

Augustinian free-will defense, 184–93, 198–99, 520n70

baptism, 409–13

baptism, believer's, 3, 9, 10, 11, 190, 333, 334, 369, 371, 383, 390, 404, 409–13, 417, 484n7, 545n55

Baptists, 3, 6, 7, 19, 60, 61, 97, 119, 202, 244, 245, 307, 332, 336, 366–74, 378, 381, 386, 391, 404, 409–13, 416, 417, 420–23, 465–66, 487n7, 488n30, 492n87, 508n40, 533n3, 542n1, 543n20, 544n33

Believers' churches; *see* free church

Bible; *see* Scripture

Bible study, 350–53

Calvinism, strong, five-point, 10, 112, 121–29, 131, 184–85, 190, 191–93, 199, 201–206, 327, 390, 410, 453–56, 506n29, 507n37, 519n56, 551n43

Common Sense philosophy, 69,
497–98n22, 498n24
compatibilism, 126, 185, 191–92,
201–6, 327
contextuality, 35–38, 64–65, 88,
90–91, 401
creation science, 174–76, 514n11,
515n20

discernment, 356–61
divinization, 147, 258, 315, 317–18,
478
doctrines, 9
dogmas, 9

Eastern Orthodox church; see
Orthodox Church
election; see predestination
emergent church, 299, 367, 372,
393, 405, 544–45n36
experience, 17–20
eternal security, 5, 508n40
evangelism, 33, 36, 39, 111, 307,
350, 390, 393–98, 459, 544n34,
545n37, 552n51
Eve, 178, 179, 189, 190, 194, 201,
207, 222, 226, 227, 228, 229,
230, 231, 233, 234, 236, 242,
284, 285, 318, 474

falling from grace, 5, 325
fellowship, 144, 176, 179, 279,
374–75, 382, 388, 391, 392,
403–6, 408, 414, 415, 458, 480,
555n70
feminist theology, 1, 12, 36, 43–44,
54, 78, 157–61, 278, 306–306,
321, 417–18, 423, 426, 512n88,
513n91, 524–25n25, 527n48,
533n64, 547n67

fideism, 21, 24, 54–55
forgiveness, 309–13, 323–24,
331–32, 361–64, 408, 534n5,
541n70
foundationalism, 20, 55, 70, 71,
487n21
free church, 3, 11, 190, 191, 334,
350, 352, 353, 356, 366–74,
384, 388, 392, 410, 411, 418,
420–26, 456, 484n7
freedom of religion, 240–41, 367,
370–71, 418
free-will defense; see Augustinian
free-will defense, Irenaean
free-will defense, libertarian
free-will

general revelation, 59, 61, 98–103,
503n64
globalization, 38–39
Gnosticism, 19, 26, 87–88, 143–44,
164, 165, 170, 182, 284, 294,
295, 351, 511n67, 539n54,
539n55, 543n21

heaven, 8, 9, 40, 41, 46, 64, 65, 80,
82, 115, 121, 164, 168, 169,
170, 180, 191, 211, 212, 214,
222, 243, 247, 273, 283, 301,
344, 351, 355, 358, 373, 385,
389, 394, 394, 410, 411, 414,
427, 428, 429, 433, 435, 438,
439, 442, 443, 445, 448, 449,
451, 453–465, 472, 473, 474,
475, 476, 551n36, 555n70
hell, 9, 40, 41, 190, 203, 204, 230,
246, 247, 300, 301, 340, 427,
442–61, 453, 551n36, 552n44,
552–53n53, 553n54
hermeneutical arc, 47, 48, 50, 74,
75, 107

hermeneutics, 24, 62–98, 493n99

Holy Spirit, 76, 123, 153–54, 392, 398, 411

incarnational theology, 7–8, 10, 26, 33, 65, 79–103, 260, 267–68, 286, 299, 300, 348, 349–50, 351, 353, 375, 380, 381, 383, 388, 396, 399, 404, 425, 448, 449, 473, 540n59

incompatibilism; *see* libertarian free will

inerrancy, 64, 69–71, 75, 94, 175, 499n31, 534n6

infallibility, 68, 94, 502–503n60

inspiration of Scripture, 65–79

Intelligent Design, 170–78, 514n11

Irenaean free-will defense, 193–201, 520n70

Kingdom of God, 170, 223, 228, 233, 235, 248, 271–74, 278, 279, 291, 292, 302, 330, 347, 355, 358, 359, 385, 386, 392, 431, 437, 463, 465, 466, 471, 472, 493, 524n18, 533n1, 554n69

knowledge, 20–26

language, 26–32

liberation theology, 7, 12, 35, 36, 37–41, 42, 54, 303–6, 316–17, 393

libertarian free will, 112, 126, 184, 192, 355, 520n66

liberty of conscience, 3, 370–71

meticulous providence, 199, 201–206, 521n73

middle knowledge; *see* Molinism

millennialism, 9, 41, 145, 164, 390, 427, 461–72, 534n6, 553n56, 553n59, 553n60, 554n65, 554n68

miracle, 21. 200, 209 234, 265, 282, 283, 295, 308, 343, 429

mission, 4, 98, 100, 193, 218, 286, 302, 303, 366, 374, 384, 390, 391, 392–98, 404, 408, 409, 421, 459, 538n49, 543n23, 544n33, 545n40

modernity, 12–40, 55, 57, 69–70, 106, 116, 138, 263, 275, 328, 350, 374, 376, 432, 544n33

Molinism, 129–30

mysticism, 30–31

New Age religion, 19, 39

Nicene Creed, 6

nonmeticulous providence, 199–201, 360, 521n73

Open Theism, 127–28, 507n40, 537n42

Orthodox Church, 9, 11, 44, 57, 137–40, 142, 150, 155, 194, 202, 255, 258, 298, 315, 318, 336, 370, 378, 380–81, 388, 408, 415, 416, 417, 419, 478, 533n3, 543n20

parables, 28–29, 271, 274–77

Paul, the Apostle, 74, 76, 80, 81, 83, 86, 88, 93, 96, 99, 100, 101, 107, 119, 122, 140, 142, 153, 169, 204, 219, 220, 229, 230, 231, 233, 234, 235, 237, 240, 241, 242, 248, 250, 260, 270, 272, 273, 274, 282, 284, 289, 292, 293, 300, 301, 302, 311, 318, 320, 323, 326, 329, 330,

332, 333, 337, 338, 339, 340, 341, 342, 343, 344, 345, 346, 347, 348, 356, 360, 362, 374, 378, 379, 382, 384, 385, 387, 405, 413, 415, 417, 419, 422, 426, 428, 437, 438, 446, 449, 450, 451, 453, 456, 457, 459, 461, 473, 474, 479, 490n49, 538n45, 538n46, 538n48, 539n51, 550n31, 550–51n34

Pelagianism, 259, 327, 329, 535–36n28

Pentecostals, 11–12, 56, 97, 339–44, 354, 420, 495n119, 508n40, 537n42, 537n43, 537n44, 538n46, 538n48, 538n49

perspicuity of Scripture, 63, 496n7

phronesis, 23–24, 50, 95, 107, 113, 328–29, 338, 359, 438, 488n35, 488–89n37, 489n42

Pilgrims, 6, 371

postmodernity, 12, 18–40, 47, 55, 74, 111, 113, 139, 263, 275, 366, 544n33

practice, 32–35, 74–79, 344–64, 391–415

prayer, 34, 51, 56, 74, 92, 107, 282–82, 285, 353–56, 401–402

preaching, 3, 29, 407

predestination, 10, 121, 190, 191–92, 202, 327, 453–56, 543n22, 552n48, 552n51

prevenient grace, 328, 536n29

priesthood of all believers, 3, 352, 366, 370, 371, 392, 400, 420, 421, 547n64, 547n66

progressive revelation, 53, 91, 92, 501, 502

purgatory, 448, 535n28, 550n29

Quadrilateral, Wesleyan; *see* Wesleyan Quadrilateral

Radical Reformation, 25, 347, 387, 373–74, 378, 391

Reformation, 4, 11, 23, 47, 52, 59, 60, 61, 79, 97, 145, 254, 314, 326, 328, 329, 331, 333, 368, 369, 378, 380, 381, 387, 391, 393, 411, 414, 420, 438, 464, 536n28

religious liberty, 3, 404

Roman Catholic Church, 9, 45, 47, 52, 57, 60, 62–63, 201–202, 254, 263, 298, 339, 350, 365, 367, 370, 377, 378, 380–81, 386, 388–89, 391, 408, 410, 414, 415, 416, 417, 418, 422, 503n64, 535–36n28, 543n19, 543n20, 551n38

rule of faith, 66, 274

science, 4, 7, 21–22, 24, 25, 45–46, 57, 61, 63–65, 69, 70, 93–94, 116, 156, 166, 170–78, 180, 193, 485n1, 487n25, 487n28, 519–20n58

Scripture, 28–30, 33, 35, 46, 52, 55, 56, 59–98

separation of church and state; *see* freedom of religion

special revelation, 59–98

theodicy, 112, 117, 120, 130, 181–206, 517n34, 517n36, 518n41, 519n51, 520n69

theosis; see divinization

tradition, 25–26, 53, 54–55, 57, 97–98, 352

Trinity, 44–45, 137–61, 365, 372, 403, 510n60, 510n61, 511n72, 511n77

two-thirds world, 7, 12, 41, 90, 492n82

via negativa, 106, 155, 156

Wesleyan Quadrilateral, 52–58, 494n110

worship, 20, 34, 51, 83, 84, 120, 140, 154, 244, 261, 269, 280, 300, 343, 352, 375, 382, 385, 388, 391, 398–403, 404, 406, 408, 409, 411, 413, 448, 452, 474, 475, 492n82, 494n105, 538n49, 549n36

CPSIA information can be obtained
at www.ICGtesting.com
Printed in the USA
LVHW091935221220
674910LV00004B/90

9 781481 314756